Frommer's
Costa Rica 2015

by Eliot Greenspan

FrommerMedia LLC

Published by:
Frommer Media LLC

ISBN 978-1-62887-142-5 (paper), 978-1-62887-143-2 (e-book)

Editorial Director: Pauline Frommer
Editor: Melinda Quintero
Production Editor: Heather Wilcox
Cartographer: Roberta Stockwell
Cover Design: Howard Grossman
For information on our other products or services, see www.frommers.com.
Frommer Media LLC also publishes its books in a variety of electronic formats. Some content that appears in print may not be available in electronic formats.

Manufactured in China

FROMMER'S STAR RATINGS, ICONS & ABBREVIATIONS

Every hotel, restaurant, and attraction listing in this guide has been ranked for quality, value, service, amenities, and special features using a star-rating system. In country, state, and regional guides, we also rate towns and regions to help you narrow down your choices and budget your time accordingly. Hotels and restaurants are rated on a scale of one (recommended) to three stars (exceptional). Attractions, shopping, nightlife, towns, and regions are rated according to the following scale: one star (recommended), two stars (highly recommended), and three stars (must-see).

HOW TO CONTACT US

In researching this book, we discovered many wonderful places—hotels, restaurants, shops, and more. We're sure you'll find others. Please tell us about them, so we can share the information with your fellow travelers in upcoming editions. If you were disappointed with a recommendation, we'd love to know that, too. Please write to Support@FrommerMedia.com

AN IMPORTANT NOTE

The world is a dynamic place. Hotels change ownership, restaurants hike their prices, museums alter their opening hours, and busses and trains change their routings. And all of this can occur in the several months after our authors have visited, inspected, and written about, these hotels, restaurants, museums and transportation services. Though we have made valiant efforts to keep all our information fresh and up-to-date, some few changes can inevitably occur in the periods before a revised edition of this guidebook is published. So please bear with us if a tiny number of the details in this book have changed. Please also note that we have no responsibility or liability for any inaccuracy or errors or omissions, or for inconvenience, loss, damage, or expenses suffered by anyone as a result of assertions in this guide.

CONTENTS

LIST OF MAPS v

1 THE BEST OF COSTA RICA 1

2 COSTA RICA IN CONTEXT 18

3 SUGGESTED COSTA RICA ITINERARIES 41

Costa Rica Regions in Brief 42

Costa Rica Highlights 46

The Best Undiscovered Costa Rica 50

The Best Costa Rica Adventures 54

Costa Rica for Families 56

The Best of San José & the Central Valley 58

4 COSTA RICA'S NATURAL WORLD 63

The Lay of the Land 64

Costa Rica's Top National Parks & Bioreserves 67

Health, Safety & Etiquette in the Wild 71

Responsible Tourism 73

Costa Rican Wildlife 75

Fauna 75

Flora 87

5 THE BEST SPECIAL-INTEREST TRIPS 90

Organized Adventure Trips 91

Activities A to Z 94

Study & Volunteer Programs 106

Medical & Dental Tourism 108

6 SAN JOSÉ 109

The Best San José Experiences 110

Orientation 111

Getting Around 116

Fast Facts: San José 118

Exploring San José 120

Where to Stay 128

Where to Dine 133

Shopping 138

Entertainment & Nightlife 143

Day Trips from San José 149

7 THE CENTRAL VALLEY 154

The Best Central Valley Experiences 155

Escazú & Santa Ana 156

Alajuela, Poás & the Airport Area 164

Heredia 170

Grecia, Sarchí & Zarcero 174

Cartago 178

The Orosi Valley 183

Turrialba 186

8 GUANACASTE 189

The Best Guanacaste Experiences 191

Liberia 191

Rincón de la Vieja National Park 199

La Cruz & Bahía Salinas 204

Playa Hermosa, Playa Panamá & Papagayo 208

Playa del Coco & Playa Ocotal 217

Playas Conchal & Brasilito 225

Playas Flamingo & Potrero 230

Playa Grande 235

Playa Tamarindo & Playa Langosta 237

Playa Junquillal 250

9 PUNTARENAS & THE NICOYA PENINSULA 253

The Best Puntarenas & the Nicoya Peninsula Travel Experiences 254

Puntarenas 255

Playa Tambor 261

Playa Montezuma 265

Malpaís & Santa Teresa 273

Playa Sámara 279

Playa Nosara 287

10 THE NORTHERN ZONE 294

The Best Northern Zone Travel Experiences 295

Arenal Volcano & La Fortuna 296

Along the Shores of Lake Arenal 317

Monteverde 323

Puerto Viejo de Sarapiquí 341

11 THE CENTRAL PACIFIC COAST 348

The Best Central Pacific Travel Experiences 349

Playa Herradura 350

Playa de Jacó 358

Manuel Antonio National Park 369

Dominical 387

San Isidro de El General: A Base for Exploring Chirripó National Park 398

12 THE SOUTHERN ZONE 406

The Best Southern Zone Travel Experiences 407

Drake Bay 408

Puerto Jiménez: Gateway to Corcovado National Park 418

Golfito: Gateway to the Golfo Dulce 431

Playa Zancudo 438

Playa Pavones: A Surfer's Mecca 442

13 THE CARIBBEAN COAST 446

The Best Caribbean Coast Travel Experiences 448

Barra del Colorado 448

Tortuguero National Park 452

Limón: Gateway to Tortuguero National Park & Southern Coastal Beaches 461

Cahuita 466

Puerto Viejo 475

Playas Cocles, Chiquita, Manzanillo & South of Puerto Viejo 486

14 PLANNING YOUR TRIP TO COSTA RICA 495

Getting There 496

Getting Around 499

Tips on Where to Stay 502

Staying Healthy 504

Fast Facts: Costa Rica 507

15 SPANISH TERMS & PHRASES 516

Basic Words & Phrases 516

Some Typical Tico Words & Phrases 519

Menu Terms 520

Other Useful Terms 522

INDEX 524

LIST OF MAPS

Costa Rica Regions in Brief   43

Costa Rica Highlights   49

The Best Undiscovered Costa Rica   51

The Best Costa Rica Adventures   55

Costa Rica for Families   57

San José & the Central Valley in 4
    Days   59

San José   122

The Central Valley   157

The Western Central Valley   159

Cartago, Orosi & Irazú   179

Guanacaste   192

Santa Rosa National Park   206

Playa Hermosa   210

Papagayo Peninsula   211

Playa del Coco & Playa Ocotal   219

Playas Flamingo, Brasilito &
    Conchal   227

Tamarindo   239

Around Tamarindo   241

The Nicoya Peninsula   257

Montezuma   271

Malpaís & Santa Teresa   274

The Northern Zone   297

Arenal National Park/La Fortuna   299

Along the Shores of Lake Arenal   319

Monteverde   325

The Central Pacific Coast   351

Playas Herradura & Hermosa   353

Playa de Jacó   363

Manuel Antonio & Quepos   381

The Southern Zone   409

Drake Bay   411

Puerto Jiménez   419

Corcovado National Park   425

Golfito & the Golfo Dulce   433

Playa Zancudo & Pavones   439

The Caribbean Coast   449

Tortuguero   453

Cahuita   467

Puerto Viejo   477

ABOUT THE AUTHOR

Eliot Greenspan is a poet, journalist, musician, and travel writer who took his backpack and typewriter the length of Mesoamerica before settling in Costa Rica in 1992. Since then, he has worked steadily as a travel writer, food critic, freelance journalist, translator, and personal travel planner, while continuing his travels in the region. In addition to this book, he has authored "Frommer's Belize," "Frommer's Cuba," "Frommer's Ecuador," "Frommer's Guatemala," "Costa Rica For Dummies," and "Costa Rica Day by Day."

DEDICATION

I'd like to dedicate this edition, with love, appreciation and gratitude, to Warren Greenspan, November 26, 1932–January 11, 2011.

—Eliot Greenspan

ACKNOWLEDGMENTS

I say this every year, but I continue to be eternally grateful to Anne Becher and Joe Richey, who were instrumental in getting me this gig—muchas gracias. I'd also like to thank my parents, Marilyn and Warren Greenspan, who showed unwavering love, support, and encouragement (well, one out of three ain't bad) when I chose words and world-wandering over becoming a lawyer or a doctor. Jody and Ted Ejnes (my sister and brother-in-law) deserve a mention; they risked life and limb—literally—leading to two important tips that may help you save yours. (I now believe Ted, and he may have actually almost stepped on a crocodile.) Both Giovana Longhi Garita and Maria Jose Longhi Garita did extensive and meticulous fact checking—my hat's off to their OCD family genes. Finally, all my love to Maria Jose, Fabrizio and Patitas, who continue to accompany me on this journey.

—Eliot Greenspan

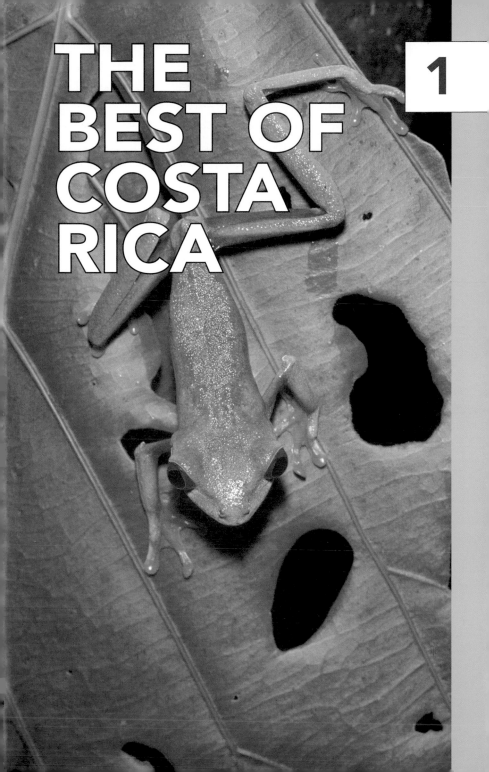

THE
BEST OF
COSTA
RICA

Costa Rica is one of the hottest vacation and adventure-travel destinations in Latin America, and for good reason. The country is a place rich in natural wonders and biodiversity, where you can still find yourself far from the maddening crowds. Costa Rica boasts a wealth of unsullied beaches for sun-bathing and surfing, jungle rivers for rafting and kayaking, and spectacular cloud forests and rainforests with ample opportunities for bird-watching, wildlife viewing, and hiking. In addition to the country's trademark eco- and adventure-tourism offerings, you will also find luxury resorts and golf courses, plush spas, and some truly spectacular boutique hotels and lodges.

Having lived in Costa Rica for more than 21 years, I continue to explore and discover new spots, adventures, restaurants, and lodgings—and my "best of" experiences keep on coming. In this chapter, I select the very best of what this unique country has to offer. This chapter is meant to give you an overview of the highlights so that you can start planning your own adventure.

COSTA RICA'S best AUTHENTIC EXPERIENCES

o **Taking a Night Tour in a Tropical Forest:** Most Neotropical forest dwellers are nocturnal, so nighttime tours are offered at most rainforest and cloud forest destinations throughout the country. Some of the better spots for night tours are **Monteverde** (p. 330), **Tortuguero** (p. 456), and **Drake Bay** (p. 415).

A male Resplendent Quetzal in flight. PREVIOUS PAGE: A red-eyed tree frog in Tortuguero.

Black Howler Monkey.

o **Soaking in a Volcanic Hot Spring:** Costa Rica's volcanoes have blessed the country with a host of natural hot spring spots. From the opulent grandeur of **Tabacón Grand Spa Thermal Resort** (p. 311) to the more humble options around **Rincón de la Vieja** (p. 201), all offer mineral-rich, naturally heated waters to soothe what ails you.

o **Spotting a Resplendent Quetzal:** The iridescent colors and long, flowing tail feathers of this aptly named bird are breathtaking. Revered by ancient Mesoamerican peoples throughout the region, this extremely endangered species can still be regularly sighted in the **Monteverde Cloud Forest Biological Reserve** (p. 328).

o **Meeting Monkeys:** Costa Rica's rain- and cloud forests are home to four species of New World Monkeys—howler, capuchin, squirrel, and spider. I can't guarantee you'll see one or more, but your odds are good if you visit the trails and reserves around **Monteverde** (p. 328), **Tortuguero** (p. 456), **Manuel Antonio** (p. 369), or the **Osa Peninsula** (p. 423).

Poás Volcano National Park.

3

o **Zipping through the Treetops:** You'll find zip-line canopy tours all over Costa Rica. In most cases, after a bit of a hike, you strap on a harness and zip from treetop to treetop while dangling from a cable. Chapter 5, "The Best Special-Interest Trips & Tours," and the various destination chapters list canopy-tour operators all over the country.

o **Pouring on the Salsa Lizano:** Whether you're eating at a soda or having breakfast at the Four Seasons, be sure to try some Salsa Lizano, a tangy, tamarind-based sauce that's used on everything from salad to rice and beans to grilled meats and poultry.

o **Playing in a Pickup Football (Soccer) Game:** You'll find informal, friendly *fútbol* matches all across the country. You can head to

Zip-lining through the jungle.

La Sabana Park (p. 125) and find one just about any weekend or afternoon. But I prefer to jump into a game on the beach, with some simple sticks stuck in the sand as goal posts.

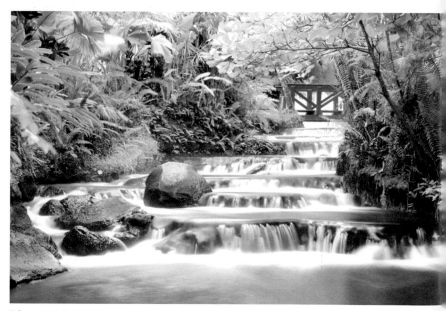

Tabacón Hot Springs.

o **Touring a Coffee Plantation:** World renowned and highly coveted, you can enjoy freshly brewed Costa Rican coffee at the source all across the country. Go deeper and learn how the bean is grown and processed. Coffee tours are offered around the Central Valley and outside Monteverde. See chapters 7 and 10.

o **Eating at a Soda:** The Costa Rican equivalent of a diner, *sodas* are simple, family-run restaurants serving local standards. You'll find them in every town and city in the country. Order a *casado,* a

Monteverde Cloud Forest Biological Reserve.

bowl of *olla de carne,* or a plate of *gallo pinto.* **Soda Tapia** (p. 136) in San José, **Soda Carolina** (p. 430) in Puerto Jiménez, and **Soda Tamara** (p. 485) are a few classics you'll come across as you travel the country, but you'll find one or more in every town and city in Costa Rica.

COSTA RICA'S best PLACES TO SEE WILDLIFE

o **Santa Rosa National Park** (northeast of Liberia, in Guanacaste): One of the largest and last remaining stands of tropical dry forest in Costa Rica, Santa Rosa National Park is a great place for all sorts of wildlife viewing. The sparse foliage, especially during the dry season, makes observation that much easier for novice naturalists. See p. 205.

Manuel Antonio National Park.

Corcovado National Park.

o **Monteverde Cloud Forest Biological Reserve** (in the mountains northwest of San José): There's something both eerie and majestic about walking around in the early-morning mist surrounded by bird calls, animal rustlings, and towering trees hung heavy in broad bromeliads, flowering orchids, and hanging moss and vines. The reserve has a well-maintained network of trails, and the community is truly involved in conservation. See p. 328.

o **The Río Sarapiquí Region** (north of San José btw. Guanacaste in the west and the Caribbean coast in the east): Protected tropical forests climb from the Caribbean coastal lowlands up into the central mountains, affording you a glimpse of a plethora of life zones and ecosystems. **Braulio Carrillo National Park** borders several private reserves, and here you'll find a variety of ecolodges, to suit any budget. See "Puerto Viejo de Sarapiquí," in chapter 10.

o **Manuel Antonio** (near Quepos on the central Pacific Coast): The reason this place is so popular and renowned? Monkeys! The national park here is full of them, even the endangered squirrel monkeys. White-faced capuchin monkeys are quite common here, and have been known to rifle through backpacks in search of a snack. See "Manuel Antonio National Park," in chapter 11.

o **Osa Peninsula** (in southern Costa Rica): This is Costa Rica's most remote and biologically rich region. **Corcovado National Park,** the largest remaining patch of virgin lowland tropical rainforest in Central America, takes up much of the Osa Peninsula. Jaguars, crocodiles, and scarlet macaws all call this place home. Whether you stay in a luxury nature lodge in **Drake Bay** or outside of **Puerto Jiménez,** or camp in the park itself, you will be surrounded by some of the most lush and most intense jungle this country has to offer. See chapter 12.

o **Tortuguero Village & Jungle Canals** (on the Caribbean coast, north of Limón): Tortuguero has been called Costa Rica's Venice, but it actually has more in common with the South American Amazon. As you explore the narrow canals here, you'll see a wide variety of herons and other water birds, three types of monkeys, three-toed sloths, and caimans. If you come between June and October, you could be treated to the awe-inspiring spectacle of a green turtle nesting—the small stretch of Tortuguero beach is the last remaining major nesting site of this endangered animal. See "Exploring Tortuguero National Park," in chapter 13.

COSTA RICA'S best ECOLODGES & WILDERNESS RESORTS

Ecolodge options in Costa Rica range from tent camps with no electricity or hot water, and communal, buffet-style meals to some of the most luxurious accommodations in the country. See "Responsible Tourism" on p. 73 for more info on sustainable travel to Costa Rica.

- **Arenal Observatory Lodge** (near La Fortuna): Originally a research facility, this lodge now features comfy rooms with impressive views of Arenal Volcano. Excellent trails lead to nearby lava flows and a nice waterfall. Toucans frequent the trees near the lodge, and howler monkeys provide the wake-up calls. See p. 312.

- **Monteverde Lodge & Gardens** (Monteverde): One of the original ecolodges in Monteverde, this place has only improved over the years, with great guides, updated rooms, and lush gardens. The operation is run by the very dependable and experienced Costa Rica Expeditions. See p. 336.

- **La Paloma Lodge** (Drake Bay): If your idea of the perfect nature lodge is one where your front porch provides prime-time viewing of flora and fauna, this place is for you. If you decide to leave the comfort of your porch, the Osa Peninsula's lowland rainforests are just outside your door. See p. 417.

- **Bosque del Cabo Rainforest Lodge** (Osa Peninsula): Large, unique, and cozy private cabins perched on the edge of a cliff overlooking the Pacific Ocean and surrounded by lush rainforest make this one of my favorite spots in the country. See p. 429.

- **Playa Nicuesa Rainforest Lodge** (Golfo Dulce): This lodge is by far the best option on the Golfo Dulce. Set in deep forest, the individual bungalows here are a perfect blend of rusticity and luxury, and the guides, service, and surrounding wildlife are all superb. See p. 437.

- **Tortuga Lodge** (Tortuguero): This is another of the excellent ecolodges run by Costa Rica Expeditions, and features a beautiful riverfront restaurant and swimming pool. The canals of Tortuguero snake through its maze of lowland primary rainforest. The beaches here are major sea-turtle nesting sites. See p. 459.

- **Selva Bananito Lodge** (in the Talamanca Mountains south of Limón): This is one of the few lodges providing direct access to the southern Caribbean lowland rainforests. You can hike along a riverbed, ride horses through the rainforest, climb 30m (100 ft.) up a ceiba tree, or rappel down a jungle waterfall here. See p. 464.

COSTA RICA'S best HOTELS

o **Hotel Grano de Oro** (San José): San José boasts dozens of old homes that have been converted into hotels, but few offer the luxurious accommodations or professional service found at the Grano de Oro. All the guest rooms have attractive hardwood furniture, including old-fashioned wardrobes in some rooms. When it's time to relax, you can soak in a hot tub or have a drink in the rooftop lounge while taking in San José's commanding view. See p. 131.

o **Finca Rosa Blanca Coffee Plantation & Inn** (Heredia): If the cookie-cutter rooms of international resorts leave you cold, perhaps this unusual inn will be more your style. Square corners seem to have been prohibited here in favor of turrets and curving walls of glass, arched windows, and semicircular built-in couches. It's set into the lush hillside just 20 minutes from San José. See p. 173.

o **Hotel Capitán Suizo** (Tamarindo): With a perfect beachfront setting, spacious, rooms, lush gardens and grounds, and a wonderful pool, this is easily the best option in Tamarindo, and one of the best along the whole Gold Coast. See p. 244.

o **Amor de Mar** (Montezuma): Clean, spacious, and comfortable rooms set on a sloping lawn that leads down to a rocky coastline, with a natural pool carved into the rocks, all add up to my idea of a tropical paradise. See p. 270.

o **Florblanca Resort** (Playa Santa Teresa): The individual villas at this intimate resort are some of the largest and most luxurious in the country. The service and food are outstanding, and the location is breathtaking, spread over a lushly planted hillside, steps away from Playa Santa Teresa. See p. 276.

Tamarindo's resorts seen from above.

Sunset on Santa Teresa beach.

o **Hidden Canopy Treehouses** (Monteverde): The individual cabins here are set on high stilts and nestled into the surrounding cloud forest canopy. All abound in brightly varnished local hardwoods. The refined, yet convivial vibe is especially palpable in the afternoon over tea or cocktails, when guests enjoy the main lodge's sunset view. See p. 336.

o **Arco Iris Lodge** (Monteverde): This small lodge is set on an expansive piece of property, but within easy walking distance of everything in Santa Elena. And it's the best deal in the Monteverde area to boot. The owners are extremely knowledgeable and helpful. See p. 337.

o **Arenas del Mar** (Manuel Antonio): With large and ample rooms, excellent service and amenities, a beautiful little spa, and the best beach access and location in Manuel Antonio, this hotel has a lot to offer. See p. 380.

o **Playa Negra Guesthouse** (Cahuita): Located just across a dirt road from a long desolate section of Playa Negra, the individual Caribbean-style bungalows here are cozy and beautifully done. The grounds are lushly planted, and the whole operation has a refined ambience. See p. 473.

o **Cariblue Bungalows** (Playa Cocles): Try to get one of the private wooden bungalows here. If you do, you might be so happy and comfortable that you won't want to leave. Just 90m (300 ft.) or so away, however, are the warm waves of the Caribbean Sea. See p. 492.

COSTA RICA'S best RESTAURANTS

o **Grano de Oro Restaurant** (San José): This elegant boutique hotel has an equally fine restaurant serving contemporary dishes and decadent desserts based on fresh local ingredients. The open-air seating in the lushly planted central courtyard is delightful, especially for lunch. See p. 136.

o **Abbocato** (Playa Panamá): The dynamic husband-wife team here serves up two unique nightly tasting menus executed with skill and creativity. This is "author cuisine" as it should be, adventurous and personal, appealing to a refined palate. See p. 216.

o **Ginger** (Playa Hermosa): Serving an eclectic mix of traditional and Pan Asian–influenced tapas, this sophisticated little joint is taking this part of Guanacaste by storm. A list of creative cocktails complements the inventive dishes. See p. 216.

o **Papaya** (Brasilito): Housed in a simple, unassuming roadside hotel, this lively little spot serves up a creative and tasty mix of dishes based on the region's freshest fish and seafood and other local

A pineapple plantation.

ingredients. Asian and Latin American influences serve as the inspiration for the fusion fare served here. See p. 230.

o **Pangas Beach Club** (Tamarindo): This relaxed, casually elegant restaurant serves up fresh seafood and grilled meats in creative, contemporary preparations. Executive chef Jean-Luc Taulere had a long, successful run over in Playa Flamingo, before moving here. See p. 247.

o **Lola's** (Playa Avellanas): With a perfect setting on the sand and excellent hearty fare, Lola's gets my vote for the best casual beachfront restaurant in the country. The ocean-loving namesake mascot—a pet pig—just adds to the restaurant's quirky charm. See p. 250.

o **Playa de los Artistas** (Montezuma): This place has the perfect blend of refined cuisine and beachside funkiness. There are only a few tables, so get here early. Fresh, grilled seafood is served in oversized ceramic bowls and on large wooden slabs lined with banana leaves. See p. 272.

o **Brisas del Mar** (Malpaís): With world-class sunset views and open-air seating on a broad wooden deck, this place serves up a regularly changing menu of freshly caught local seafood and fine meat and poultry. The fusion creations showcase world cuisine influences, ranging from Asia to Latin America to classic Continental Europe. See p. 279.

o **Café Caburé** (Monteverde): In addition to the wonderful food served here, these folks have a delicious, wide ranging and very tempting selection of homemade chocolate treats. I love the casual open-air seating, friendly attention, and broad and always tasty menu. See p. 338.

o **Trio** (Monteverde): Set right in the tiny village of Santa Elena, this open-air bistro–style place has creative, contemporary cuisine and cocktails. I like the slight twists on simple items such as burgers, salads, and wraps. The owner and chef here also has the nearby sister restaurant, **Sofia** (p. 338), which is a slightly fancier and more formal Nuevo Latino venue. See p. 339.

- **Graffiti Resto Café & Wine Bar** (Playa de Jacó): From the small sushi bar in one corner to the graffiti-painted walls, this place is full of whimsy and surprise. The nightly chalkboard specials are always worth checking out, but so are the longstanding regular menu staples. See p. 365.

- **Milagro** (Manuel Antonio): A casually elegant little place, Milagro has made a name for itself in the Manuel Antonio area. A humble coffee shop, breakfast joint, and lunch stop, things get kicked up a notch at night with a creative Nuevo Latino menu that takes full advantage of the freshest local ingredients available. See p. 385.

- **La Pecora Nera** (Puerto Viejo): I'm not sure that a tiny surfer town on the remote Caribbean coast deserves such fine Italian food, but it's got it. Your best bet here is to allow yourself to be taken on a culinary roller-coaster ride with a mixed feast of the chef's nightly specials and suggestions. See p. 493.

COSTA RICA'S best FAMILY DESTINATIONS

- **La Paz Waterfall Gardens** (near Varablanca and the Poás Volcano): This multifaceted attraction features paths and suspended walkways set alongside a series of impressive jungle waterfalls. Kids will love the variety and vibrancy of the various offerings, from the hummingbird, wild cat, and reptile exhibits to the impressive power of the waterfalls. See p. 166.

- **Playa Hermosa:** The protected waters of this Pacific beach make it a family favorite. Just because its waters are calm, however, doesn't mean it's boring. I recommend staying at the beachfront **Hotel Playa Hermosa Bosque del Mar** (p. 215) and checking in at **Aqua Sport** (p. 213), where you can rent sea kayaks, sailboards, paddleboats, beach umbrellas, and bicycles.

- **Playa Tamarindo:** This surf town has a bit of something for everyone. It's a great spot for kids to learn how to surf or boogie-board, and a host of tours and activities to please the entire family are available. **Hotel Capitán Suizo** (p. 244) has an excellent location on a calm section of beach, spacious rooms, and a great pool for kids and adults alike. See "Playa Tamarindo & Playa Langosta," in chapter 8.

LEFT: **A butterfly exhibit at La Paz Waterfall Gardens.** RIGHT: **A hummingbird at the Monteverde Hummingbird Gallery.**

o **Monteverde:** This area not only has the country's most famous cloud forest, but also offers up a wide variety of attractions and activities. After hiking through the reserve, you should be able to keep everyone happy and occupied riding horses; squirming at the serpentarium; or visiting the Monteverde Butterfly Garden, Frog Pond, Bat Jungle, and Orchid Garden. See "Monteverde," in chapter 10.

o **Playa de Jacó:** Jacó's streets are lined with souvenir shops, ice-cream stands, and inexpensive eateries. Activity options range from surf lessons and bungee jumping to a small-boat cruise among the crocodiles on the Tárcoles River. **Club del Mar Condominiums & Resort** (p. 362) is accommodating to families with small children. See "Playa Herradura & Playa de Jacó," in chapter 11.

o **Manuel Antonio:** This national park has a bit of everything: miles of gorgeous beaches, tons of wildlife (with almost guaranteed monkey sightings), and plenty of active-tour options. Of the loads of lodging options, **Hotel Sí Como No** (p. 380), with its large suites, two pools, water slide, and nightly movies, is probably your best bet. See "Manuel Antonio National Park," in chapter 11.

COSTA RICA'S best BEACHES

With more than 1,200km (750 miles) of shoreline on its Pacific and Caribbean coasts, Costa Rica offers beachgoers an embarrassment of riches.

o **Santa Rosa National Park:** You'll have to four-wheel-drive or hike 13km (8 miles) from the central ranger station to reach these remote beaches, but you'll probably have the place almost to yourself. In fact, the only time it gets crowded is in October, when thousands of olive ridley sea turtles nest in one of their yearly *arribadas* (arrivals). See p. 205.

Punta Uva.

Surfers on Malpaís beach.　　　A surf class in Santa Teresa.

- **Playa Nacascolo:** With silky, soft white sand, this is the best stretch of beach on the Papagayo Peninsula. The waters here are protected from ocean swells and are great for swimming. See "Playa Hermosa, Playa Panamá & Papagayo," in chapter 8.

- **Playa Avellanas:** Just south of Tamarindo, this white-sand beach has long been a favorite haunt for surfers, locals, and those in the know. Playa Avellanas stretches on for miles, backed largely by protected mangrove forests. This beach is home to **Lola's** (p. 250), perhaps my favorite beachfront restaurant in the country. See p. 248.

- **The Beaches around Playa Sámara:** Playa Sámara is nice enough, but venturing just slightly farther afield, you'll find two of the prettiest beaches along the entire Pacific Coast. **Playa Carrillo** is a long crescent of palm-backed white sand located just south of Sámara, while **Playa Barrigona** is a hidden gem tucked down a rugged dirt road to the north. See "Playa Sámara," in chapter 9.

- **Playa Montezuma:** This tiny beach town at the southern tip of the Nicoya Peninsula has weathered fame and infamy but retains a funky sense of individuality, with plenty of isolated spots to plop down your towel or mat. Nearby, you'll find two beautiful waterfalls, as well as the **Cabo Blanco** and **Curú** wildlife preserves. See "Playa Montezuma," in chapter 9.

- **Malpaís & Santa Teresa:** With just a smattering of luxury lodges, surf camps, and assorted hotels and cabinas, this is the place to come if you're looking for miles of deserted beaches and great surf. See "Malpaís & Santa Teresa," in chapter 9.

- **Manuel Antonio:** Manuel Antonio National Park was the first beach destination to become popular in Costa Rica, and its beaches are still idyllic. The views from the hills approaching the park are enchanting. This is also one of

Tortuga Lodge.

the few remaining habitats for the endangered squirrel monkey. See "Manuel Antonio National Park," in chapter 11.

o **Punta Uva & Manzanillo:** These beaches deliver true Caribbean splendor, with turquoise waters, coral reefs, and palm-lined stretches of nearly deserted white-sand beach. Tall coconut palms line the shore, providing shady respite, and the water is usually quite calm and good for swimming. See "Cahuita, Puerto Viejo & the Beaches of Costa Rica's Southern Caribbean Coast," in chapter 13.

COSTA RICA'S best ADVENTURE SPORT EXPERIENCES

o **Mountain Biking the Back Roads of Costa Rica:** The lack of infrastructure and paved roads here that most folks bemoan is a huge boon for mountain bikers. The country has endless back roads and trails to explore. The area around La Fortuna and Lake Arenal is my favorite destination for mountain biking. The views are stunning, and the terrain is widely varied. See p. 95.

o **Rafting the Pacuare River** (near Turrialba): Arguably the best and most beautiful river for rafting in Costa Rica, the Pacuare winds through primary and secondary forests and features one stunning section that passes through a gorgeous steep gorge. For a real treat, take the 2-day Pacuare River trip, which includes an overnight at a lodge or tent camp on the side of the river. See p. 104.

o **Surfing & Four-Wheeling Guanacaste Province:** From Witch's Rock at Playa Naranjo near the Nicaraguan border to Playa Nosara, more than 100km (60 miles) away, you'll find scores of world-class surf spots. In addition to the two mentioned, try a session at Playa Grande, Punta Langosta, and playas Negra, Avellanas, and Junquillal. Or find your own secret spot. See chapter 8.

o **Trying the Adventure Sport of Canyoning:** While every canyoning tour is unique, it usually involves hiking along and through the rivers and creeks of a steep mountain canyon, with periodic breaks to rappel down the face of a waterfall, jump off a rock into a jungle pool, or float down a small rapid. See chapters 8, 10, and 11.

o **Battling a Billfish off the Pacific Coast:** Billfish are plentiful all along Costa Rica's Pacific Coast, and boats operate from Playa del Coco down to the Golfo Dulce. Costa Rican anglers hold world records for both blue marlin and Pacific sailfish. Go to Quepos (just outside Manuel Antonio) for the best après-fish scene, or head down the Osa Peninsula or Golfo Dulce if you want some isolation. See chapter 8, 9, 11 and chapter 12.

o **Windsurfing or Kitesurfing on Lake Arenal:** With steady gale-force winds (at certain times of the year) and stunning scenery, the northern end of Lake Arenal has become a major international windsurfing and kitesurfing hot spot. See chapter 10.

o **Diving off the Shores of Isla del Coco** (off the Pacific Coast): Legendary among treasure seekers, pirate buffs, and scuba divers, this small island is surrounded by clear Pacific waters, and its reefs are teeming with life (divers regularly encounter large schools of hammerhead sharks, curious manta rays, and docile whale sharks). See p. 259.

o **Hiking Mount Chirripó** (near San Isidro de El General on the central Pacific Coast): The highest peak in Costa Rica, hiking to Mount Chirripó's 3,724m (12,215-ft.) summit takes you through a number of distinct bioregions,

A canyoning tour.   Windsurfing on Lake Arenal.

ranging from lowland pastures and a cloud forest to a high-altitude páramo, a tundralike landscape with stunted trees and morning frosts. See "San Isidro de El General: A Base for Exploring Chirripó National Park," in chapter 11.

COSTA RICA'S best DAY HIKES & NATURE WALKS

- **Lankester Gardens:** If you want a really pleasant but not overly challenging day hike, consider a walk among the hundreds of distinct species of flora on display here. The trails meander from areas of well-tended open garden to shady natural forest, and their orchid collection is stellar. See p. 182.
- **Rincón de la Vieja National Park:** This park has trails through a variety of ecosystems. My favorite hike is down to the Blue Lake and Cangrejo Falls. You can also hike up to two craters and a crater lake here, while the Las Pailas loop is ideal for those seeking a less strenuous hike. See p. 199.
- **Arenal National Park:** Arenal National Park has several excellent trails that visit a variety of ecosystems, including rainforest, secondary forest, savanna, and, my favorite, old lava flows. Most of them are on the relatively flat flanks of the volcano, so there's not too much climbing involved. See "Arenal Volcano & La Fortuna," in chapter 10.
- **Monteverde Cloud Forest Biological Reserve:** Take a guided tour in the morning to familiarize yourself with the cloud forest, and then spend the afternoon (your entrance ticket is good for the entire day) exploring the reserve on your own. Off the main thoroughfares, Monteverde reveals its rich mysteries with stunning regularity. See p. 328.
- **La Selva Biological Station:** La Selva has an extensive and well-marked network of trails. You'll have to reserve in advance and take the guided tour if you aren't a guest at the lodge. But the hikes are led by very informed naturalists, so you might not mind the company. See p. 345.
- **Corcovado National Park:** The park has a well-designed network of trails, ranger stations, and camping facilities. Most of the lodges in Drake Bay and Puerto Jiménez offer day hikes through the park, but if you really want to experience it, you should hike in and stay at one or more of the campgrounds. See "Puerto Jiménez: Gateway to Corcovado National Park," in chapter 12.
- **Cahuita National Park:** Fronted by the Caribbean and a picture-perfect white-sand beach, the trails here are flat, well-maintained paths through thick lowland forest. Most of the way they parallel the beach, so you can hike out on the trail and back along the beach, or vice versa. White-faced and howler monkeys are common, as are brightly colored land crabs. See p. 469.

COSTA RICA'S best BIRD-WATCHING

- **Spotting Hundreds of Marsh & Stream Birds along the Río Tempisque Basin:** This area is an important breeding ground for gallinules, jacanas, and limpkins, and is a common habitat for numerous heron and kingfisher species. Options here include visits to **Palo Verde National Park** (p. 196), **El Viejo Wetlands** (p. 229), and **Rancho Humo** (p. 283).

○ **Looking for 300-Plus Species of Birds in La Selva Biological Station:** With an excellent trail system through a variety of habitats, from dense primary rainforest to open pasturelands and cacao plantations, this is one of the finest places for bird-watching in Costa Rica. With such a variety of habitats, the number of species spotted runs to well over 300. See p. 345.

○ **Sizing up a Jabiru Stork at Caño Negro National Wildlife Refuge:** Caño Negro Lake and the Río Frío that feeds it are incredibly rich in wildlife and a major nesting and gathering site for aquatic bird species. These massive birds are getting less common in Costa Rica, but this is still one of the best places to spot one. See p. 307.

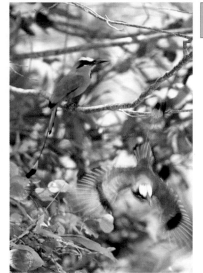

Blue-crowned motmots.

○ **Catching a Scarlet Macaw in Flight over Carara National Park:** Macaws are noisy and colorful birds that spend their days in the park but choose to roost in the evenings near the coast. They arrive like clockwork every morning and then head for the coastal mangroves around dusk. These daily migrations give birders a great chance to see these magnificent birds in flight. See p. 355.

○ **Looking for a Resplendent Quetzal in the Cerro de la Muerte:** Serious bird-watchers won't want to leave Costa Rica without crossing this bird off their lists, and neophytes might be hooked for life after seeing one of these iridescent green wonders fly overhead. See "Where to See Quetzals in the Wild: Cerro de la Muerte & San Gerardo de Dota" in chapter 11.

○ **Spotting Hundreds of Species at Wilson Botanical Gardens:** With more than 7,000 species of tropical plants and flowers, the trails of this gorgeous research facility are fabulous for bird-watching. Hummingbirds and tanagers are particularly plentiful, but the bounty doesn't end there—more than 360 different species of birds have been recorded here. See "Golfito: Gateway to the Golfo Dulce," in chapter 12.

○ **Taking Advantage of the Caribbean's Best Birding at Aviarios Sloth Sanctuary of Costa Rica:** If it flies along this coast, chances are good that you'll spot it here; more than 330 species of birds have been spotted so far. In the afternoon, large flocks of several heron species nest here, including white, cattle, and boat-billed herons. See p. 471.

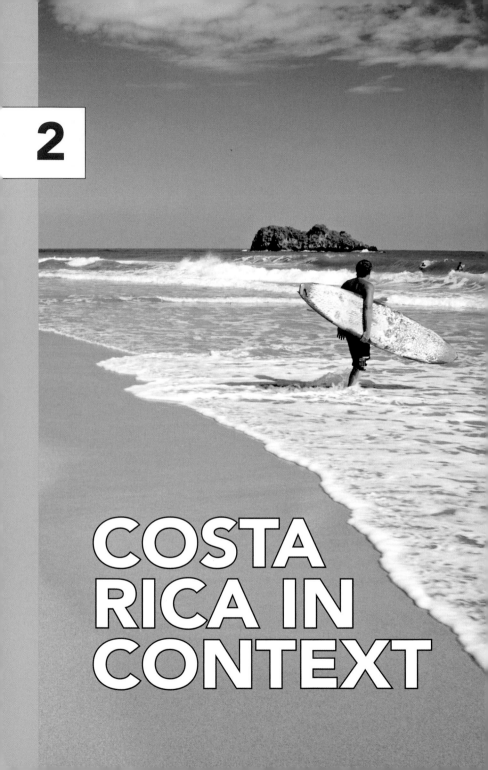

2

COSTA RICA IN CONTEXT

*P**ura Vida!* (Pure Life!) is Costa Rica's unofficial national slogan, and in many ways it defines the country. You'll hear it exclaimed, proclaimed, and simply stated by Ticos from all walks of life, from children to octogenarians. It can be used as a cheer after your favorite soccer team scores a goal, or as a descriptive response when someone asks you, "¿Como estas?" ("How are you?"). It is symbolic of the easygoing nature of this country's people, politics, and personality.

Costa Rica itself is a mostly rural country with vast areas of protected tropical forests. It is one of the biologically richest places on earth, with a wealth of flora and fauna that attracts and captivates biologists, photographers, ecotourists, and casual visitors alike.

Often called the "Switzerland of Central America," Costa Rica is, and historically has been, a sea of tranquillity in a region that has been troubled by turmoil for centuries. For more than 100 years, it has enjoyed a stable democracy and a relatively high standard of living for Latin America. The literacy rate is high, as are medical standards and facilities. Perhaps most significant, at least for proud and peace-loving Costa Ricans, is that this country does not have an army.

COSTA RICA TODAY

Costa Rica has a population of around five million, more than half of whom live in the Central Valley and are considered as urban. Some 94% of the population is of Spanish or otherwise European descent, and it is not at all unusual to see fair-skinned and blond Costa Ricans. This is largely because the indigenous population in place when the first Spaniards arrived was small and thereafter was quickly reduced to even more of a minority by wars and disease. Some indigenous populations still remain, primarily on reservations around the country; the principal tribes include the Bribri, Cabécar, Boruca, and Guayamí. In addition, on the Caribbean coast and in the big cities is a substantial population of English-speaking black Creoles who came over from the Antilles to work on building the railroad and on the banana plantations. Racial tension isn't palpable, but it exists, perhaps more out of standard ignorance and fear rather than an organized or articulated prejudice.

In general, Costa Ricans are a friendly and outgoing people. While interacting with visitors, Ticos are very open and helpful. Time has relative meaning to Ticos. Although most tour companies and other establishments operate efficiently, don't expect punctuality, in general.

In a region historically plagued by internal strife and civil wars, Costa Ricans are proud of their peaceful history, political stability, and relatively high level of development. However, this can also translate into arrogance and prejudice toward immigrants from neighboring countries, particularly Nicaraguans, who make up a large percentage of the workforce on the banana and coffee plantations.

PREVIOUS PAGE: **A surfer at Playa Cocles on the Caribbean Coast.**

Where There Is a Tico, There Is Freedom

In 1989, on a visit to Costa Rica, Uruguayan President Julio María Sanguinetti famously declared: *"Donde hay un costarricense, esté donde esté, hay libertad,"* which is roughly translated in the title above.

Personally, I get a kick out of the version co-opted by a local condiment company in its advertising campaign, which states, "Where there is a Tico, there is Salsa Lizano." I find it to be equally true.

Roman Catholicism is the official religion of Costa Rica, although freedom to practice any religion is guaranteed by the country's constitution. More than 75% of the population identifies itself as Roman Catholic, while another 14% are part of a number of evangelical Christian congregations. There is a small but visible Jewish community as well. By and large, a large section of Ticos are religiously observant, if not fervent, though it seems that just as many lead quite secular lives.

Costa Rica is the most politically stable nation in Central America, and it has the largest middle class. Even the smallest towns have electricity, the water is mostly safe to drink, and the phone system is relatively good and very widespread. Still, the gap between rich and poor is wide, and there are glaring infrastructure needs. The roads, hospitals, and school systems have been in a slow but steady state of decay for decades, with no immediate signs that these matters will improve anytime soon.

Tourism is the nation's true principal source of income, surpassing cattle ranching, textiles, and exports of coffee, pineapples, bananas, and Intel microchips. More than two million tourists visit Costa Rica each year, and over half the working population is employed in the tourism and service industries. Ticos whose fathers and grandfathers were farmers and ranchers find themselves hotel owners, tour guides, and waiters. Although most have adapted gracefully and regard the industry as a source of new jobs and opportunities for economic advancement, restaurant and hotel staff can seem gruff and uninterested at times, especially in rural areas. And, unfortunately, an increase in the number of visitors has led to an increase in crime, prostitution, and drug trafficking. Common sense and street savvy are required in San José and in many of the more popular tourist destinations.

The global economic crisis definitely hit Costa Rica. Tourism took a noticeable hit, especially in 2009 to 2010. But it has bounced back nicely. More importantly, perhaps, since credit has historically been so

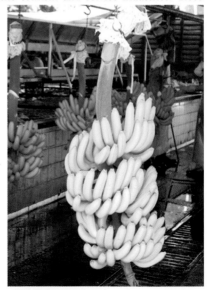

Processing bananas at one of Costa Rica's many banana plantations.

tight, there was never a major mortgage or banking crisis in the country. Today, Costa Rica continues to be a beautiful and diminutive Central American nation struggling to meet the economic and development needs of its population. It seems to be moving in the right direction, even though that movement is maddeningly slow most of the time.

THE MAKING OF COSTA RICA

Early History

Little is known of Costa Rica's history before its colonization by Spanish settlers. The pre-Columbian Indians who made their home in this region of Central America never developed the large cities or advanced culture that flowered farther north in what would become Guatemala, Belize, and Mexico. However, ancient artifacts indicating a strong sense of aesthetics have been unearthed from scattered excavations around the country. Beautiful gold and jade jewelry, intricately carved grinding stones, and artistically painted terra-cotta objects point to a small but highly skilled population.

Spain Settles Costa Rica

In 1502, on his fourth and last voyage to the New World, Christopher Columbus anchored just offshore from present-day Limón. Whether he actually gave the country its name—"the rich coast"—is open to debate, but the Spaniards never did find much gold or minerals to exploit here.

Juan Santamaría Memorial Park in Alajuela.

Cartago's Basilica.

The earliest Spanish settlers found that, unlike settlements to the north, the native population of Costa Rica was unwilling to submit to slavery. Despite their small numbers, scattered villages, and tribal differences, they fought back against the Spanish until they were overcome by superior firepower and European diseases. When the fighting ended, the European settlers in Costa Rica found that very few Indians were left to force into servitude. The settlers were thus forced to till their own lands, a situation unheard of in other parts of Central America. Few pioneers headed this way because they could settle in Guatemala, with its large native workforce. Costa Rica was nearly forgotten, as the Spanish crown looked elsewhere for riches to plunder and souls to convert.

It didn't take long for Costa Rica's few Spanish settlers to head for the hills, where they found rich volcanic soil and a climate that was less oppressive than in the lowlands. **Cartago,** the colony's first capital, was founded in 1563, but it was not until the 1700s that additional cities were established in this agriculturally

The Little Drummer Boy

Costa Rica's national hero is Juan Santamaría. The legend goes that young Juan enlisted as a drummer boy in the campaign against William Walker (p. 23). On April 11, 1865, when Costa Rican troops had a band of Walker's men cornered in a downtown hostel in Rivas, Nicaragua, Santamaría volunteered for a nearly certain suicide mission to set the building on fire. Although he was mortally wounded, Santamaría was successful in torching the building and driving Walker's men out, where they were swiftly routed. Today, April 11 is a national holiday.

Presidential Welcome

President John F. Kennedy visited Costa Rica in March 1963. Upon his arrival, the Irazú Volcano woke up and erupted, after more than 2 decades of dormancy. Soot and ash reached as far as San José, where the soon-to-be-assassinated leader addressed students and political figures.

rich region. In the late 18th century, the first coffee plants were introduced, and because these plants thrived in the highlands, Costa Rica began to develop its first cash crop. Unfortunately, it was a long and difficult journey transporting the coffee to the Caribbean coast and then onward to Europe, where the demand for coffee was growing.

From Independence to the Present Day

In 1821, Spain granted independence to its colonies in Central America. Costa Rica joined with its neighbors to form the Central American Federation; but in 1838, it withdrew to form a new nation and pursue its own interests. By the mid-1800s, coffee was the country's main export. Free land was given to anyone willing to plant coffee on it, and plantation owners soon grew wealthy and powerful, creating Costa Rica's first elite class. Coffee plantation owners were powerful enough to elect their own representatives to the presidency.

This was a stormy period in Costa Rican history. In 1856, the country was invaded by **William Walker,** a soldier of fortune from Tennessee who, with the backing of U.S. President James Buchanan, was attempting to fulfill his grandiose dreams of presiding over a slave state in Central America (before his invasion of Costa Rica, he had invaded Nicaragua and Baja, California). The people of Costa Rica, led by their own president, Juan Rafael Mora, marched against Walker and chased him back to Nicaragua. Walker eventually surrendered to a U.S. warship in 1857, but, in 1860, he attacked Honduras, claiming to be the president of that country. The Hondurans, who had had enough of Walker's shenanigans, promptly executed him.

The Last Costa Rican Warrior

"Military victories, by themselves, are not worth much. It's what is built from them that matters."

—José "Pepe" Figueres

Until 1890, coffee growers had to transport their coffee either by oxcart to the Pacific port of Puntarenas or by boat down the Río Sarapiquí to the Caribbean. In the 1870s, a progressive president proposed a railway from San José to the Caribbean coast to facilitate the transport of coffee to European markets. It took nearly 20 years for this plan to reach fruition, and more than 4,000 workers lost their lives constructing the railway, which passed through dense jungles and rugged mountains on its journey from the Central Valley to the coast. Partway through the project, as funds were dwindling, the second chief engineer, Minor Keith, proposed an idea that not only enhanced his fortunes, but also changed the course of Central American history. Banana plantations would be developed along the railway right of way (land on either side of the tracks). The export of this crop would help to finance the railway, and, in exchange, Keith would get a 99-year lease on 1,976,000 hectares (800,000 acres) of land with a 20-year tax deferment. The Costa Rican government gave its consent, and in 1878 the first bananas were shipped from the country. In 1899, Keith and a partner formed the **United Fruit Company,** a business that eventually became the largest landholder in Central America and caused political disputes and wars throughout the region.

In 1889, Costa Rica held what is considered the first free election in Central American history. The opposition candidate won the election, and the control of the government passed from the hands of one political party to those of another without bloodshed or hostilities. Thus, Costa Rica established itself as the region's only true democracy. In 1948, this democratic process was challenged by **Rafael Angel Calderón,** who had served as the country's president from 1940 to 1944. After losing by a narrow margin, Calderón, who had the backing of the communist labor unions and the Catholic Church, refused to concede the country's leadership to the rightfully elected president, **Otillio Ulate,** and a civil war ensued. Calderón was eventually defeated by José "Pepe" Figueres. In the wake of this crisis, a new constitution was drafted; among other changes, it abolished Costa Rica's army so that such a revolution could never happen again.

In 1994, history seemed to repeat itself—peacefully this time—when **José María Figueres** took the reins of government from the son of his father's adversary, Rafael Angel Calderón. In 2001, Otton Solís and his new Citizen's Action Party (PAC) forced the presidential elections into a second round, opening a

The Peace President

"Peace is the most honorable form of exhaustion, and the most exhausting form of honor."

—Oscar Arias

Pre-Colombian foundations at Guayabo National Monument.

crack in a two-party system that had become seemingly entrenched for good. Although Solís himself finished third and didn't make it to the run-off, his upstart Citizen's Action Party won quite a few deputy slots.

The battered traditional two-party system was further threatened in 2004, when major corruption scandals became public. Two former presidents were arrested (Miguel Angel Rodríguez and Rafael Angel Calderón), and another (José María Figueres) fled to Switzerland. All were implicated, as well as a long list of high-level government employees and deputies, in various financial scandals or bribery cases. Both Calderón and Rodríguez were convicted and sentenced to jail time, while charges have been dropped against Figueres.

In 2010, Costa Rica elected its first female president, **Laura Chinchilla,** who was a vice-president in the

Wood artwork at Original Grand Gallery in La Fortuna.

outgoing Arias administration. While on April 6, 2014, former University professor Luis Guillermo Solis of the opposition Citizen's Action Party won a run-off presidential election by a landslide over longtime San José mayor Johnny Araya.

ART & ARCHITECTURE

It's a small and provincial country, so you'll find Costa Rica's culture somewhat limited in size and scope. That said, the culture does have vibrant current scenes in all the major arts—music, literature, architecture, dance, and even film.

Art

Unlike Guatemala, Mexico, or even Nicaragua, Costa Rica does not have a strong tradition of local or indigenous arts and crafts. The strong suit of Costa Rican art is European and Western influenced, ranging from neoclassical to modern in style.

Early painters to look out for include **Max Jimenez, Francisco Amighetti, Manuel de la Cruz,** and **Teodorico Quiros.** Deceased and living legends of the art world include **Rafa Fernández, Lola Fernández,** and **Cesar Valverde.** Contemporary artists making waves and names for themselves include

Colonial-Era Remnant or Crime Deterrent?

Most Costa Rican homes feature steel or iron grating over the doors and windows. I've heard more than one tour guide say this can be traced back to colonial-era architecture and design. However, I'm fairly convinced it is a relatively modern adaptation to the local crime scene.

Fernando Carballo, Rodolfo Stanley, Lionel Gonzalez, Manuel Zumbado, and **Karla Solano.**

Sculpture is perhaps one of the strongest aspects of the Costa Rican art scene, with the large bronze works of **Francisco "Paco" Zuñiga** among the best of the genre. Meanwhile, the artists **José Sancho, Edgar Zuñiga,** and **Jiménez Deredia** are all producing internationally acclaimed pieces, many of monumental proportions. You can see examples by all these sculptors around the country, as well as at San José's downtown **Museo de Arte Costarricense ★★** (p. 123). I also enjoy the whimsical works of **Leda Astorga,** who sculpts and then paints a pantheon of plump and voluptuous figures in interesting, and at times, compromising, poses.

You'll find several excellent museums and galleries in San José (p. 120), as well as in some of the country's larger and more popular tourist destinations.

Architecture

Costa Rica lacks the large-scale pre-Columbian ceremonial ruins found throughout much of the rest of Mesoamerica. The only notable early archaeological site is **Guayabo** (p. 187). However, only the foundations of a few dwellings, a handful of carved petroglyphs, and some road and water infrastructure are still visible here.

Similarly, Costa Rica lacks the large and well-preserved colonial-era cities found throughout much of the rest of Latin America. The original capital of **Cartago** (p. 178) has some old ruins and a few colonial-era buildings, as well as the country's grandest church, the **Basílica de Nuestra Señora de los Angeles**

The Basílica de Nuestra Señora de los Angeles in Cartago.

(**Basilica of Our Lady of the Angels**) ★ (p. 180), which was built in honor of the country's patron saint, La Negrita, or the Virgin of Guadalupe.

In downtown San José, Barrio Amón and Barrio Otoya are two side-by-side upscale neighborhoods replete with a stately mix of architectural stylings, with everything from colonial-era residential mansions, to Art Deco apartment buildings, and modern high-rise skyscrapers. One of the standout buildings here is the **Metal School (Escuela Metalica),** which dates to the 1880s, and was shipped over piece-by-piece from France, and erected in place.

On much of the Caribbean coast, you will find mostly wooden houses, built on raised stilts to rise above the wet ground and occasional flooding. Some of these houses feature ornate gingerbread trim. Much of the rest of the country's architecture is pretty plain. Most residential houses are simple concrete-block affairs, with zinc roofs.

A few modern architects are creating names for themselves. **Ronald Zurcher,** who designed the **Four Seasons Resort** (p. 213) and several other large hotel projects, is one of the shining lights of contemporary Costa Rican architecture.

COSTA RICA IN POPULAR CULTURE

Books

Though Costa Rica's literary output is sparsely translated and little known outside of Costa Rica, there are some notable authors to look out for, especially if you can read in Spanish.

Some of the books mentioned below might be difficult to track down in U.S. bookstores, but you'll find them all in abundance in Costa Rica. A good place to check for many of these titles is at a well-stocked gift shop, or any branch of **Libreria Internacional** (📞 800/542-7374; www.libreriainternacional. com), which has storefronts at most major modern malls, and several other stand-alone locations around the country.

GENERAL INTEREST For a straightforward, albeit somewhat dry, historical overview, there's **"The History of Costa Rica,"** by **Ivan Molina** and **Steven Palmer.** For a more readable look into Costa Rican society, pick up **"The Ticos: Culture and Social Change"** by **Richard, Karen,** and **Mavis Biesanz,** an examination of the country's politics and culture, by the authors of the out-of-print "The Costa Ricans." Another work worth checking out is **"The Costa Rica Reader: History, Culture, Politics,"** a broad selection of stories, essays, and excerpts edited by Steven Palmer and Ivan Molina, the authors of the history book mentioned above.

To learn more about the life and culture of Costa Rica's Talamanca coast, an area populated by Afro-Caribbean people whose forebears emigrated from Caribbean islands in the early 19th century, look for **"What Happen: A Folk-History of Costa Rica's Talamanca Coast"** by **Paula Palmer.** This book is a collection of oral histories taken from a wide range of local characters.

FICTION & POETRY "Costa Rica: A Traveler's Literary Companion," edited by **Barbara Ras** and with a foreword by **Oscar Arias Sánchez,** is a collection of short stories by Costa Rican writers, organized by region of the country. If you're lucky, you might find a copy of **"Stories of Tatamundo,"** by **Fabian Dobles,** or **"Lo Peor/The Worst,"** by **Fernando Contreras.**

Young adults will enjoy **Kristin Joy Pratt**'s **"A Walk in the Rainforest,"** while younger children will like the beautifully illustrated **"The Forest in the Clouds,"** by **Sneed Collard** and **Michael Rothman,** and **"The Umbrella."** **Pachanga Kids** (www.pachangakids.com) has published several illustrated bilingual children's books with delightful illustrations by **Ruth Angulo,** including **"Mar Azucarada/Sugar Sea"** by **Roberto Boccanera** and **"El Coyote y la Luciernaga/The Coyote and the Firefly"** by **Yazmin Ross,** which (full disclosure) I translated, and which includes a musical CD that also features your humble author's singing. Another bilingual children's book worth checking out is **"Zari & Marinita: Adventures in a Costa Rican Rainforest."**

One of the most important pieces in the Costa Rican canon, **Carlos Luis Fallas**'s 1941 tome **"Mamita Yunai"** is a stark look at the impact of the large banana giant United Fruit on the country. More recently, **Fernando Contreras** takes up where his predecessor left off in **"Unico Mirando al Mar,"** which describes the conditions of the poor, predominantly children, who scavenge Costa Rica's garbage dumps.

In the field of poetry, Eunice Odio, Juaquín Gutiérrez, and Jorge Debravo are early poets who set the gold standard. Their more modern successors include Alfonso Chase, Virginia Grutter, Laureano Alban, Ana Istaru, and Luis Chavez.

NATURAL HISTORY I think that everyone coming to Costa Rica should read **"Tropical Nature"** by **Adrian Forsyth** and **Ken Miyata.** My all-time favorite book on tropical biology, this is a wonderfully written and lively collection of tales and adventures by two Neotropical biologists who spent quite some time in the forests of Costa Rica.

Mario A. Boza's beautiful **"Costa Rica National Parks"** has been reissued in an elegant coffee-table edition. Other worthwhile coffee-table books include **"Rainforests: Costa Rica and Beyond"** by **Adrian Forsyth,** with photographs by **Michael** and **Patricia Fogden, "Costa Rica: A Journey Through Nature"** by **Adrian Hepworth,** and **"Osa: Where the Rainforest Meets the Sea"** by **Roy Toft** (photographer) and **Trond Larsen** (author).

For an introduction to a wide range of Costa Rican fauna, there's **"The Wildlife of Costa Rica: A Field Guide"** by **Fiona Reid, Jim Zook, Twan Leenders,** and **Robert Dean,** or **"Costa Rica: Traveller's Wildlife Guides"** by **Les Beletsky.** Both pack a lot of useful information into a concise package and make great field guides for amateur naturalists and inquisitive tourists.

"A Guide to the Birds of Costa Rica," by **F. Gary Stiles** and **Alexander Skutch,** is an invaluable guide to identifying the many birds you'll see during your stay. Most guides and nature lodges have a copy of this book on hand. This classic faces competition from the more recent **"Birds of Costa Rica,"** by **Richard Garrigues** and **Robert Dean.** Bird-watchers might want a copy of **"A Bird-Finding Guide to Costa Rica"** by **Barrett Lawson,** which details each country's bird-watching bounty by site and region.

Other interesting natural-history books that will give you a look at the plants and animals of Costa Rica include **"Costa Rica Natural History,"** by **Daniel Janzen; "A Guide to Tropical Plants of Costa Rica,"** by **Willow Zuchowsky; "The Natural History of Costa Rican Mammals,"** by **Mark Wainwright; "A Guide to the Amphibians and Reptiles of Costa Rica,"** by **Twan Leenders;** and the classic **"A Neotropical Companion,"** by **John C. Kricher,** reissued in an expanded edition with color photos.

For a fairly complete list of field guides, check out **www.zonatropical.net.**

Film

Costa Rica has a budding and promising young film industry. Local feature films like **"Tropix," "Caribe,"** and **"Gestación (Gestation)"** are all out on subtitled DVD. **"El Camino (The Path)"** by Costa Rican filmmaker **Ishtar Yasin Gutiérrez** was screened at the Berlin Film Festival, while **Paz Fabrega**'s **"Agua Fría de Mar (Cold Sea)"** is a touching story set on a remote Costa Rican beach that has picked up a few prizes at international festivals. Released in 2010, **Hilda Hidalgo**'s **"Del Amor y Otros Demonios (Of Love and Other Demons)"** is a compelling treatment of Gabriel García Márquez's novel of the same name.

If you want to see Costa Rica used simply as a backdrop, the major motion picture productions of **"1492,"** by **Ridley Scott** and starring Gerard Depardieu and Sigourney Weaver; **"Congo,"** featuring Laura Linney and Ernie Hudson; and **"The Blue Butterfly,"** with William Hurt, all feature sets and scenery from around the country. Serving as more than a mere visual backdrop, Costa Rica appears prominently in the seminal surfer flick **"Endless Summer II."**

The small **Costa Rican Film and Video festival** (www.centrodecine. go.cr) is each November in San José.

Music

Several musical traditions and styles meet and mingle in Costa Rica. The northern Guanacaste region is a hotbed of folk music that is strongly influenced by the *marimba* (wooden xylophone) traditions of Guatemala and Nicaragua, while also featuring guitars, maracas, and the occasional harp. On the Caribbean coast, you can hear traditional calypso sung by descendants of the original black workers brought over to build the railroads and tend the banana plantations. Roving bands play a mix of guitar, banjo, washtub bass, and percussion in the bars and restaurants of Cahuita and Puerto Viejo.

Costa Rica also has a healthy contemporary music scene. The jazz-fusion trio **Editus** has won two Grammy awards for its work with Panamanian salsa

Costa Rican musicians playing folk music.

TICO etiquette & CUSTOMS

In general, Costa Ricans are easygoing, friendly, and informal. That said, Ticos tend to be conservative and try to treat everyone very respectfully. Moreover, in conversation, Ticos are relatively formal. When addressing someone, they use the formal *usted* in most instances, reserving the familiar *vos* for close friends, family, and children or teenagers.

Upon greeting or saying goodbye, both sexes shake hands, although across genders, a light kiss on one cheek is common.

Proud of their neutrality and lack of armed forces, everyday Costa Ricans are uncomfortable with confrontation. What may seem like playful banter or justified outrage to a foreign tourist may be taken very badly by a Tico.

In some cases, especially in the service industry, a Tico may tell you what he or she thinks you want to hear, just to avoid a confrontation—even if he or she knows there's little chance of follow-through or ultimate customer satisfaction. I've also had, on more than one occasion, Ticos give me wrong directions, instead of telling me they didn't know the way.

The two words mentioned at the start of this chapter—*pura vida*—will go a long way to endearing you to most Ticos. In conversation, *pura vida* is used as a greeting, exclamation, adjective, and general space filler. Feel free to sprinkle a *pura vida* or two into your conversations with locals. I'm sure it will be well received. For more tips on talking like a Tico, see "Some Typical Tico Words & Phrases" on p. 519.

Tico men dress conservatively. It is very rare to see Costa Rican men wear short pants except at the beach. In most towns and cities, while accepted, tourists will stand out when wearing short pants, sandals, and other typical beach, golf, or vacation wear. Costa Rican women, on the other hand, especially young women, do tend to show some skin in everyday, and even business, situations. Still, be respectful in your dress, especially if you plan on visiting churches, small towns, or local families.

Women, no matter how they dress, may find themselves on the receiving end of whistles, honks, hoots, hisses, and catcalls. For more information on this manifestation of Costa Rican machismo, see "Women Travelers," on p. 515.

Punctuality is not a Costa Rican strong suit. Ticos often show up anywhere from 15 minutes to an hour or more late to meetings and appointments—this is known as *la hora tica*, or "Tico time." That said, buses and local airlines, tour operators, movie theaters, and most businesses do tend to run on a relatively timely schedule.

---

giant (and movie star) **Rubén Blades. Malpaís,** the closest thing Costa Rica had to a super-group, suffered the sudden and tragic loss of its lead singer, but still has several excellent albums out.

You should also seek out **Cantoamérica,** which plays upbeat dance music ranging from salsa to calypso to merengue. Jazz pianist, and acting Minister of Culture, **Manuel Obregón** (also a member of Malpaís) has several excellent solo albums out, including **"Simbiosis,"** on which he improvises along with the sounds of Costa Rica's wildlife, waterfalls, and weather; as well as his work with the **"Papaya Orchestra,"** a collaboration and gathering of musicians from around Central America.

Local label **Papaya Music ★★★** (www.papayamusic.com) has done an excellent job promoting and producing albums by Costa Rican musicians in a range of styles and genres. Their offerings range from the Guanacasteca folk songs of **Max Goldemberg,** to the boleros of **Ray Tico,** to the original calypso of **Walter "Gavitt" Ferguson.** You can find their CDs at gift shops and record stores around the country, as well as at airport souvenir stores.

Classical music lovers will want to head to San José, which has a symphony orchestra, youth symphony, opera company, and choir. The local symphony sometimes features the works of local composers like **Benjamin Guitiérrez** and **Eddie Mora.** On occasion, small-scale music festivals will bring classical offerings to some of the beach and inland tourist destinations around the country.

Bars and discos around the country spin salsa, merengue, and cumbia, as well as more modern grooves that include house, electronic, trip-hop, and reggaeton.

EATING & DRINKING

Costa Rican food is not especially memorable, although some of the exotic fruits and vegetables served up here certainly are. Moreover, creative chefs using fresh local ingredients have livened up the dining scene in San José and at most of the major tourist destinations. A few are even serving up creative takes on traditional Costa Rican classics.

Outside of the capital and the major tourist destinations, your options get very limited very fast. In fact, many destinations are so remote that you have no choice but to eat in the hotel's restaurant. At remote jungle lodges, the food is usually served buffet- or family-style and can range from bland to inspired, depending on who's doing the cooking, and turnover is high.

If you see a restaurant billing itself as a *mirador,* it means it has a view. If you are driving around the country, don't miss an opportunity to dine with a view at some little roadside restaurant. The food might not be all that great, but the view and scenery will be.

At even the more expensive restaurants, it's hard to spend more than $50 per person unless you really splurge on drinks. It gets even cheaper outside the city and high-end hotels. However, if you really want to save money, Costa Rican, or *típico,* food is always the cheapest nourishment available. It's primarily served in *sodas,* Costa Rica's equivalent of diners. At a *soda,* you'll have lots of choices: rice and beans with steak, rice and beans with fish, rice and beans with chicken, or, for vegetarians, rice and beans. You get the picture.

I have separated restaurant listings throughout this book into three price categories, based on the average cost of a meal per person, including tax and service charge: **Expensive,** more than $30 (C16,500); **Moderate,** $15 to $30 (C8,250–C16,500); and **Inexpensive,** less than $15 (C8,250). (Note, however, that individual items in the listings—entrees, for instance—do not include the sales or service taxes.) Keep in mind that an additional 13% sales tax applies, as

A typical *casado.*

well as a 10% service charge. Ticos rarely tip, but that doesn't mean that you shouldn't. If the service was particularly good and attentive, you should probably leave a little extra.

Meals & Dining Customs

Rice and beans are the bases of Costa Rican meals—all three of them. At breakfast, they're called *gallo pinto* and come with everything from eggs to steak to seafood. At lunch or dinner, rice and beans are an integral part of a *casado* (which translates as "married" and is the name for the local version of a blue-plate special). A *casado* usually consists of cabbage-and-tomato salad, fried plantains (a starchy,

A waiter at a *soda* in Puerto Viejo.

banana-like fruit), and a chicken, fish, or meat dish of some sort. On the Caribbean coast, rice and beans are called "rice 'n' beans," and are cooked in coconut milk.

Dining hours in Costa Rica are flexible but generally follow North American customs. Some downtown restaurants in San José are open 24 hours; however, expensive restaurants tend to be open for lunch between 11am and 3pm and for dinner between 6 and 11pm.

APPETIZERS Known as *bocas* in Costa Rica, appetizers are served with drinks in most bars. Often the *bocas* are free, but even if they aren't, they're very inexpensive. Popular *bocas* include *gallos* (tortillas piled with meat, chicken, cheese, or beans), *ceviche* (a marinated seafood salad), tamales (stuffed cornmeal patties wrapped and steamed inside banana leaves), *patacones* (fried green plantain chips), and fried yuca.

SANDWICHES & SNACKS Ticos love to snack, and a large variety of tasty little sandwiches and snacks are available on the street, at snack bars, and in *sodas.* *Arreglados* are little meat-filled sandwiches, as are *tortas,* which are served on little rolls with a bit of salad tucked into them. Tacos, tamales, *gallos* (see above), and *empanadas* (turnovers) also are quite common.

MEAT Costa Rica is beef country, having converted much of its rainforest land to pastures for raising beef cattle. Consequently, beef is cheap and plentiful, although it might be a bit tougher—and cut and served thinner—than it is back home. One typical local dish is called *olla de carne,* a bowl of beef broth with large chunks of meat, local tubers, and corn. Spit-roasted chicken is also very popular here and is surprisingly tender; I much prefer it to most steaks I find on menus around the country. Lamb is very sparsely used in Costa Rican cooking, although finer restaurants often have a lamb dish or two on the menu, usually imported from New Zealand.

SEAFOOD Costa Rica has two coasts, and, as you'd expect, plenty of seafood is available everywhere in the country. *Corvina* (sea bass) is the most commonly served fish and is prepared innumerable ways, including as *ceviche.* (**Be careful:** In many cheaper restaurants, particularly in San José, shark meat is often sold as *corvina.*) You should also come across *pargo* (red snapper), *dorado* (mahimahi), and tuna on some menus, especially along the coasts. Although Costa Rica is a

Coconut, Straight Up

Throughout Costa Rica (particularly on the coastal road btw. Limón and Cahuita), keep your eye out for roadside stands selling fresh, green coconuts, or *pipas* in Spanish. Green coconuts have very little meat, but are filled with copious amounts of a slightly sweet, clear liquid that is amazingly refreshing.

According to local legend, this liquid is pure enough to be used as plasma in an emergency situation. Armed with a machete, the *pipa* seller will cut out the top and stick in a straw. In the best of cases, the *pipa* will have been cooled over ice. The entire thing should cost around C500.

major exporter of shrimp and lobster, both are relatively expensive and in short supply here.

VEGETABLES On the whole, you'll find vegetables surprisingly lacking in the meals you're served in Costa Rica—usually nothing more than a little pile of shredded cabbage topped with a slice or two of tomato. For a much more satisfying and filling salad, order *palmito* (hearts of palm salad). The heart (actually the stalk or trunk of these small palms) is first boiled and then chopped into circular pieces and served with other fresh vegetables, with salad dressing on top. If you want something more than this, you'll have to order a side dish such as *picadillo*, a stew or purée of vegetables with a bit of meat in it.

Though they are giant relatives of bananas and are technically considered a fruit, *plátanos* (plantains) are really more like vegetables and require cooking before they can be eaten. Green plantains have a very starchy flavor and consistency, but they become as sweet as candy as they ripen. Fried *plátanos* are one of my favorite dishes. Yuca (manioc root or cassava in English) is another starchy staple root vegetable in Costa Rica.

One more vegetable worth mentioning is the *pejibaye*, a form of palm fruit that looks like a miniature orange coconut. Boiled *pejibayes* are frequently sold from carts on the streets of San José. When cut in half, a *pejibaye* reveals a large seed surrounded by soft, fibrous flesh. You can eat it plain, but it's usually topped with a dollop of mayonnaise.

paya, star fruit, and passion fruit.

FRUITS Costa Rica has a wealth of delicious tropical fruits. The most common are mangoes (the season begins in May), papayas, pineapples, melons, and bananas. Other fruits include *marañón*, which is the fruit of the cashew tree and has orange or yellow glossy skin; *granadilla* or *maracuyá* (passion fruit); *mamón chino*, which Asian travelers will immediately recognize as rambutan; and *carambola* (star fruit).

DESSERTS *Queque seco*, literally "dry cake," is the same as pound cake. *Tres leches* cake, on the other hand, is so moist that you almost need to eat it with a spoon. Flan is a typical custard dessert. It often comes as either *flan de caramelo* (caramel) or *flan de coco* (coconut). Numerous other sweets are available, many of which are made with condensed milk and raw sugar. *Cajetas* are popular hand-made candies, made from sugar and various mixes of evaporated, condensed, and powdered milk. They are sold in differing-size bits and chunks at most *pulperías* (general stores) and streetside food stands.

Beverages

Frescos, refrescos, and *jugos naturales* are my favorite drinks in Costa Rica. They are usually made with fresh fruit and milk or water. Among the more common fruits used are mangoes, papayas, blackberries, and pineapples. You'll also come across *maracuyá* (passion fruit) and *carambola* (star fruit). Some of the more unusual frescos are *horchata* (made with rice flour and a lot of cinnamon) and *chan* (made with the seed of a plant found mostly in Guanacaste—definitely an acquired taste). The former is wonderful; the latter requires an open mind (it's reputed to be good for the digestive system). Order *un fresco con leche sin hielo* (a *fresco* with milk but without ice) if you're avoiding untreated water.

If you're a coffee drinker, you might be disappointed here. Most of the best coffee has traditionally been targeted for export, and Ticos tend to prefer theirs weak and sugary. Better hotels and restaurants are starting to cater to gringo and European tastes and are serving up superior blends. If you want black coffee, ask for *café negro;* if you want it with milk, order *café con leche.*

A San José street scene.

Stop! Be Careful of What You Buy!

International laws prohibit trade in endangered wildlife, so don't buy any plants or animals, even if they're readily for sale. Do not buy any kind of sea-turtle products (including jewelry); wild birds; lizards, snakes, or cat skins; corals; or orchids (except those grown commercially). No matter how unique, beautiful, insignificant, or inexpensive it might seem, your purchase will directly contribute to the further hunting of these species.

In addition, be careful when buying wood products. Costa Rica's rainforest hardwoods are a finite and rapidly disappearing resource. Try to buy sustainably harvested woods, if at all possible.

For something different for your morning beverage, ask for *agua dulce,* a warm drink made from melted sugar cane and served either with milk or lemon, or straight.

WATER Although water in most of Costa Rica is safe to drink, bottled water is readily available and is a good option if you're worried about an upset stomach. *Agua mineral,* or simply soda, is sparkling water in Costa Rica. If you like your water without bubbles, request *aqua mineral sin gas,* or *agua en botella.*

BEER, WINE & LIQUOR The German presence in Costa Rica over the years has produced several fine beers, which are fairly inexpensive. Most Costa Rican beers are light pilsners. The most popular brands are Bavaria, Imperial, and Pilsen. I personally can't tell much of a difference between any of them. Licensed local versions of Heineken and Rock Ice are also available.

You can find imported wines at reasonable prices in the better restaurants throughout the country. You can usually save money by ordering a Chilean or Argentine wine over a Californian or European one.

Costa Rica distills a wide variety of liquors, and you'll save money by ordering these over imported brands. The national liquor is *guaro,* a crude cane liquor that's often combined with a soft drink or tonic. When drinking it straight, it's customary to follow a shot with a bite into a fresh lime covered in salt. If you want to try *guaro,* stick to the Cacique brand.

Several brands and styles of coffee-based liqueurs are also produced in Costa Rica. **Café Rica** is similar to Kahlúa, and you can find several types of coffee cream liqueurs. The folks at **Café Britt** produce their own line of coffee liqueurs which are quite good and available in most supermarkets, liquor stores, and tourist shops.

Costa Ricans also drink a lot of rum. The premier Costa Rican rum is **Centenario.**

TIPS ON SHOPPING IN COSTA RICA

Costa Rica is not known for shopping. Most of what you'll find for sale is pretty run-of-the-mill mass-produced souvenir fare. So scant are its handicraft offerings that most tourist shops sell Guatemalan clothing, Panamanian appliquéd textiles,

El Salvadoran painted wood souvenirs, and Nicaraguan rocking chairs. Still, Costa Rica does have a few locally produced arts and handicrafts to look out for, and a couple of towns and villages with well-deserved reputations for their unique works.

Perhaps the most famous of all towns for shopping is **Sarchí ★** (p. 175), a Central Valley town filled with handicraft shops. Sarchí is best known as the citadel of the colorfully painted Costa Rican **oxcart,** reproductions of which are manufactured in various scaled-down sizes. These make excellent gifts. (Larger oxcarts can be easily disassembled and shipped to your home.) A lot of furniture is also made in Sarchí.

Up in Guanacaste, the small town of **Guaitíl** (p. 248) is famous for its pottery. A host of small workshops, studios, and storefronts ring the town's central park (which is actually a soccer field). Many of the low-fired ceramic wares here carry ancient local indigenous motifs, while others get quirky modern treatments. You can find examples of this low-fired simple ceramic work in many gift shops around the country, and even at roadside stands all across Guanacaste.

You might also run across **carved masks ★★★** made by the indigenous **Boruca** people of southern Costa Rica. The small Boruca villages where these masks are carved are off the beaten path, but you will find them for sale at some of the better gift shops around the country. These full-size wood masks come in a variety of styles, both painted and unpainted, and run anywhere from $20 to $150, depending on the quality of workmanship. *Tip:* Don't be fooled. You'll see scores of mass-produced wooden masks at souvenir and gift shops around Costa Rica. Many are imported from Mexico, Guatemala, and Indonesia. Real Boruca masks are unique indigenous art works, and the better ones are signed by their carvers.

In addition to the masks, quite a bit of Costa Rican woodwork is for sale, but it's mainly mass-produced wooden bowls, napkin holders, placemats, and the like. A couple of notable exceptions include the work of **Barry Biesanz ★★** (p. 141), whose excellent hardwood creations are sold at better gift shops around the country, and the unique, large-scale sculptures created and sold at the **Original Grand Gallery** (p. 314), in La Fortuna.

Coffee remains my favorite gift item. It's a great deal, it's readily available, and Costa Rican coffee is some of the best in the world. See the "Joe to Go" box on p. 140 for tips on buying **coffee** in Costa Rica.

A few other items worth keeping an eye out for include reproductions of **pre-Columbian gold jewelry** and **carved-stone figurines.** The former are available as either solid gold, silver, or gold-plated. The latter, although interesting, can be extremely heavy.

Across the country you'll find hammocks for sale. I personally find the Costa Rican **hammocks** a little crude and unstable. The same vendors usually have single-person hanging chairs, which are strung similarly to the full-size hammocks and are a better bet.

It's especially hard to capture the subtle shades and colors of the rainforests and cloud forests, and many a traveler has gone home thinking that his or her digital camera contained the full beauty of the jungle, only to see dozens of bright-green and random blurs when viewing the photos on a larger screen. To avoid this heartache, you might want to pick up a good **coffee-table book** or at least some **postcards** of the sights you want to remember forever and send them to yourself. For recommendations of coffee-table books, see "Costa Rica in Popular Culture," above.

Contemporary and **classic Costa Rican art** is another great option, both for discerning collectors and those looking for a unique reminder of their time in the country. San José has the greatest number of galleries and shops, but you will find good, well-stocked galleries in some of the more booming tourist destinations, including Liberia, Manuel Antonio, Jacó, and Monteverde. Throughout the book, I list my favorite galleries, and you can check out "Art & Architecture," above, for a list of some of the country's more prominent artists.

Finally, one item that you'll see at gift shops around the country is **Cuban cigars.** Although these are illegal to bring into the United States, they are perfectly legal and readily available in Costa Rica.

WHEN TO GO

Costa Rica's high season for tourism runs from late November to late April, which coincides almost perfectly with the chill of winter in the United States, Canada, and Great Britain, and includes Christmas, New Year's, Easter, and most school spring breaks. The high season is also the dry season. If you want some unadulterated time on a tropical beach and a little less rain during your rainforest experience, this is the time to come. During this period (and especially around the Christmas holiday), the tourism industry operates at full tilt—prices are higher, attractions are more crowded, and reservations need to be made in advance.

Local tourism operators often call the tropical rainy season (May through mid-Nov) the "green season." The adjective is appropriate. At this time of year, even brown and barren Guanacaste province becomes lush and verdant. I personally love traveling around Costa Rica during the rainy season (but then again, I'm not trying to flee cold snaps in Canada). It's easy to find or at least negotiate reduced rates, there are far fewer fellow travelers, and the rain is often limited to a few hours each afternoon (although you can occasionally get socked in for a week at a time). *A drawback:* Some of the country's rugged roads become downright impassable without four-wheel-drive during the rainy season.

Weather

Costa Rica is a tropical country and has distinct wet and dry seasons. However, some regions are rainy all year, and others are very dry and sunny for most of the year. Temperatures vary primarily with elevations, not with seasons: On the coasts, it's hot all year; in the mountains, it can be cool at night any time of year. Frost is common at the highest elevations (3,000–3,600m/9,840–11,808 ft.).

Average Daytime High Temperatures & Rainfall in San José

	JAN	FEB	MAR	APR	MAY	JUNE	JULY	AUG	SEPT	OCT	NOV	DEC
TEMP (°F)	75	76	79	79	80	79	77	78	79	77	77	75
TEMP (°C)	24	24	26	26	27	26	25	26	26	25	25	24
DAYS OF RAIN	1.3	1.5	2.2	4.2	11.5	14.5	13.7	14.5	18.1	17.9	8.6	2.3

Generally, the **rainy season** (or "green season") is from May to mid-November. Costa Ricans call this wet time of year their winter. The **dry season,** considered summer by Costa Ricans, is from mid-November to April. In Guanacaste, the dry northwestern province, the dry season lasts several weeks longer than in other places. Even in the rainy season, days often start sunny, with rain falling in the afternoon and evening. On the Caribbean coast, especially south of Limón, you can count on rain year-round, although this area gets less rain in September and October than the rest of the country.

In general, the best time of year to visit weatherwise is in December and January, when everything is still green from the rains, but the sky is clear.

Holidays

Because Costa Rica is a Roman Catholic country, most of its holidays are church-related. The biggies are Christmas, New Year's, and Easter, which are all celebrated for several days. Keep in mind that Holy Week (Easter week) is the biggest holiday time in Costa Rica, and many families head for the beach. (This is the last holiday before school starts.) Also, there is no public transportation on Holy Thursday or Good Friday. Government offices and banks are closed on official holidays, transportation services are reduced, and stores and markets might also close.

Official holidays in Costa Rica include **January 1** (New Year's Day), **March 19** (St. Joseph's Day), Thursday and Friday of Holy Week, **April 11** (Juan Santamaría's Day), **May 1** (Labor Day), **June 29** (St. Peter and St. Paul Day), **July 25** (annexation of the province of Guanacaste), **August 2** (Virgin of Los Angeles's Day), **August 15** (Mother's Day), **September 15** (Independence Day), **October 12** (Discovery of America/Día de la Raza), **December 8** (Immaculate Conception of the Virgin Mary), **December 24** and **25** (Christmas), and **December 31** (New Year's Eve).

Calendar of Events

Some of the events listed here might be considered more of a *happening* than an event—there's not, for instance, a Virgin of Los Angeles PR Committee that readily dispenses information. If you don't see a contact number listed, your best bet is to call the **Costa Rican Tourist Board (ICT)** at ✆ **866/COSTA RICA** in the U.S. and Canada, or 2223-1733 in Costa Rica, or visit **www.visitcostarica.com.**

JANUARY

Copa del Café (Coffee Cup), San José. Matches for this international event on the junior tennis tour are held at the Costa Rica Country Club (www.copacafe. com; ✆ **2228-9333**). First week in January.

Fiestas of Palmares, Palmares. Perhaps the largest and best organized of the traditional *fiestas*, it includes bullfights, a horseback parade *(tope)*, and many concerts, carnival rides, and food booths

(www.fiestaspalmares.com). First 2 weeks in January.

Fiestas of Santa Cruz, Santa Cruz, Guanacaste. This religious celebration honors the Black Christ of Esquipulas (a famous Guatemalan statue), featuring folk dancing, marimba music, and bullfights. Mid-January.

Fiesta of the Diablitos, Rey Curré village near San Isidro de El General. Boruca Indians wearing wooden devil and bull masks perform dances representative of the Spanish conquest of Central America; there are fireworks displays and an Indian handicrafts market. Late January.

MARCH

Día del Boyero (Oxcart Drivers' Day), San Antonio de Escazú. Colorfully painted oxcarts parade through this suburb of San José, and local priests bless the oxen. Second Sunday in March.

National Orchid Show, San José. Orchid growers throughout the world gather to show their wares, trade tales and secrets, and admire the hundreds of species on display. Contact the Costa Rican Tourist Board for the current year location and dates. Mid-March.

APRIL

Holy Week. Religious processions are held in cities and towns throughout the country. Week before Easter.

Juan Santamaría Day, Alajuela. Costa Rica's national hero is honored with parades, concerts, and dances. April 11.

MAY

Carrera de San Juan. The country's biggest marathon runs through the mountains, from the outskirts of Cartago to the outskirts of San José. May 17.

JULY

Fiesta of the Virgin of the Sea, Puntarenas. A regatta of colorfully decorated boats carrying a statue of Puntarenas's patron saint marks this festival. A similar event is held at Playa de Coco. Saturday closest to July 16.

Annexation of Guanacaste Day, Liberia. Tico-style bullfights, folk dancing, horseback parades, rodeos, concerts, and other events celebrate the day when this region became part of Costa Rica. July 25.

AUGUST

Fiesta of the Virgin of Los Angeles, Cartago. This is the annual pilgrimage day of the patron saint of Costa Rica. Many people walk from San José 24km (15 miles) to the basilica in Cartago. August 2.

Día de San Ramón, San Ramón. More than two dozen statues of saints from various towns are brought to San Ramón, where they are paraded through the streets. August 31.

SEPTEMBER

Costa Rica's Independence Day, celebrated all over the country. One of the most distinctive aspects of this festival is the nighttime marching band parades of children in their school uniforms, who play the national anthem on steel xylophones. September 15.

International Beach Clean-Up Day. This is a good excuse to chip in and help clean up the beleaguered shoreline of your favorite beach. Third Saturday in September.

OCTOBER

Fiesta del Maíz, Upala. At this celebration of corn, local beauty queens wear outfits made from corn plants. October 12.

Limón Carnival/Día de la Raza, Limón. A smaller version of Mardi Gras, complete with floats and dancing in the streets, commemorates Columbus's discovery of Costa Rica. Week of October 12.

NOVEMBER

All Souls' Day/Día de los Muertos, celebrated countrywide. Although it is not as elaborate or ritualized as in Mexico, most Costa Ricans take some time this day to remember the dead with flowers and trips to cemeteries. November 2.

DECEMBER

Fiesta de los Negritos, Boruca. Boruca Indians celebrate the feast day of their patron saint, the Virgin of the Immaculate Conception, with costumed dances and traditional music. December 8.

Día de la Pólvora, San Antonio de Belén and Jesús María de San Mateo. Fireworks honor Our Lady of the Immaculate Conception. December 8.

Las Posadas. Countrywide, children and carolers go door-to-door seeking lodging in a reenactment of Joseph and

Mary's search for a place to stay. Begins December 15.

El Tope and Carnival, San José. The streets of downtown belong to horses and their riders in a proud recognition of the country's important agricultural heritage. The next day, those same streets are taken over by carnival floats, marching bands, and street dancers. December 26 and 27.

Festejos Populares, San José. Bullfights and a pretty respectable bunch of carnival rides, games of chance, and fast-food stands are set up at the fairgrounds in Zapote (www.festejospopulares.com). Last week of December.

3

SUGGESTED COSTA RICA ITINERARIES

Costa Rica is a compact yet varied destination with numerous natural attractions and a broad selection of exciting sights, scenery, adventure activities, and ecosystems. On a trip to Costa Rica, you can visit rainforests, cloud forests, and active volcanoes, and walk along miles of beautiful beaches on both the Pacific and Caribbean coasts. Adventure hounds will have their fill choosing from an exciting array of activities, and those looking for some rest and relaxation can grab a chaise lounge and a good book. Costa Rica's relatively small size makes visiting several destinations during a single vacation both easy and enjoyable.

The fastest and easiest way to get around the country is by small commuter aircraft. Most major destinations are serviced by regular commuter or charter airline companies. However, this does imply using San José or Liberia as periodic transfer hubs. If your connections don't line up, you may end up having to tack on nights in either of these cities in the middle of your trip. Luckily, sufficient flights and internal connections make this an infrequent inconvenience.

Getting around Costa Rica by car is another excellent option. Most major destinations are between 2 and 5 hours from San José by car, and many can be linked together in a well-planned and convenient loop. For example, one popular loop links Arenal Volcano, Monteverde, and Manuel Antonio. However, be forewarned that the roads here are often in terrible shape, many major roads and intersections are unmarked, and Tico drivers can be reckless and rude. See "By Car" under "Getting Around," in chapter 14 for more information on driving in Costa Rica.

The itineraries in this chapter are specific blueprints for fabulous vacations, and you can follow them to the letter. You might also decide to use one or more of them as an outline and then fill in some blanks with other destinations, activities, and attractions that strike your fancy from the rest of this book.

COSTA RICA REGIONS IN BRIEF

Costa Rica rightfully should be called "Costas Ricas" because it has two coasts: one on the Pacific Ocean and one on the Caribbean Sea. These two coasts are as different from each other as are the Atlantic and Pacific coasts of North America.

Costa Rica's **Pacific coast** is the most extensive, and is characterized by a rugged (although mostly accessible) coastline where forested mountains often meet the sea. It can be divided into four distinct regions—Guanacaste, the Nicoya Peninsula, the Central Coast, and the Southern Coast. There are some spectacular stretches of coastline, and most of the country's top beaches are here. This coast varies from the dry, sunny climate of the northwest to the hot, humid rainforests of the south.

PREVIOUS PAGE: **A tourist gliding on a canopy tour.**

The **Caribbean coast** can be divided into two roughly equal stretches. The remote northeast coastline is a vast flat plain laced with rivers and covered with rainforest; it is accessible only by boat or small plane. Farther south, along the stretch of coast accessible by car, are uncrowded beaches and even a bit of coral reef.

Bordered by Nicaragua in the north and Panama in the southeast, Costa Rica is only slightly larger than Vermont and New Hampshire combined. Much of the country is mountainous, with three major ranges running northwest to southeast. Among these mountains are several volcanic peaks, some of which are still active. Between the mountain ranges are fertile valleys, the largest and most populated of which is the Central Valley. With the exception of the dry Guanacaste region, much of Costa Rica's coastal area is hot and humid and covered with dense rainforests.

See the map above for a visual of the regions detailed below.

SAN JOSÉ San José is Costa Rica's capital and its primary business, cultural, and social center—it sits fairly close to the country's geographical center, in the heart of its Central Valley (see below). It's a sprawling, urban area, with a population of around one million. Its streets are narrow, in poor repair, poorly marked and often chock-full with traffic. However, a few notable parks, like the Parque La Sabana and Parque del Este, do serve to lessen the urban blight. San José is home to the country's greatest collection of museums, fine restaurants and stores, galleries, and shopping centers.

THE CENTRAL VALLEY The Central Valley is surrounded by rolling green hills and mountains that rise to heights between 900 and 1,200m (2,952–3,936 ft.) above sea level. The climate here is mild and springlike year-round. It's Costa Rica's primary agricultural region, with coffee farms making up the majority of landholdings. The rich volcanic soil of this region makes it ideal for farming. The country's earliest settlements were in this area, and today the Central Valley (which includes San José) is densely populated, crisscrossed by decent roads, and dotted with small towns. Surrounding the Central Valley are high mountains, among which are four volcanic peaks. Two of these, **Poás** and **Irazú,** are still active and have caused extensive damage during cycles of activity in the past 2 centuries. Many of the mountainous regions to the north and to the south of the capital of San José have been declared national parks (Tapantí, Juan Castro, and Braulio Carrillo) to protect their virgin rainforests against logging.

GUANACASTE The northwestern corner of the country near the Nicaraguan border is the site of many of Costa Rica's sunniest and most popular **beaches,** including **Playa del Coco, Playa Hermosa, Playa Flamingo, Playa Conchal, Tamarindo,** and the **Papagayo Peninsula.** Scores of beach destinations, towns, and resorts are along this long string of coastline. Because many foreigners have chosen to build beach houses and retirement homes here, Guanacaste has experienced considerable development over the years. You won't find a glut of Cancún-style high-rise hotels, but condos, luxury resorts, and golf courses have sprung up along the coastline here. Still, you won't be towel-to-towel with thousands of strangers. On the contrary, you can still find long stretches of deserted sands. However, more and more travelers are using Liberia as their gateway to Costa Rica, bypassing San José and the central and southern parts of the country entirely.

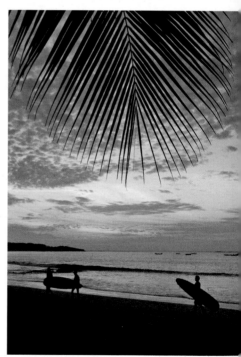
Tamarindo at sunset.

With about 165cm (65 in.) of rain a year, this region is by far the driest in the country and has been likened to west Texas. Guanacaste province is named after the shady trees that still shelter the herds of cattle roaming the dusty savanna here. In addition to cattle ranches, Guanacaste has semiactive volcanoes, several lakes, and one of the last remnants of tropical dry forest left in Central America. (Dry forest once stretched all the way from Costa Rica up to the Mexican state of Chiapas.)

PUNTARENAS & THE NICOYA PENINSULA Just south of Guanacaste lies the Nicoya Peninsula. Similar to Guanacaste in many ways, the Nicoya Peninsula is nonetheless somewhat more inaccessible, and thus much less developed and crowded. However, this is already starting to change. The neighboring beaches of **Malpaís** and **Santa Teresa** are perhaps the fastest growing hot spots anywhere along the Costa Rican coast.

As you head south from Guanacaste, the region is similar in terms of geography, climate, and ecosystems, but begins to get more humid and moist. The forests are taller and lusher than those found in Guanacaste. The Nicoya Peninsula itself juts out to form the Golfo de Nicoya (Nicoya Gulf), a large, protected body of water. **Puntarenas,** a small fishing city, is

Corcovado National Park in the Southern Zone.

the main port found inside this gulf, and one of the main commercial ports in all of Costa Rica. Puntarenas is also the departure point for the regular ferries that connect the Nicoya Peninsula to San José and most of mainland Costa Rica.

THE NORTHERN ZONE This inland region lies to the north of San José and includes rainforests, cloud forests, hot springs, the country's two most active volcanoes (**Arenal** and **Rincón de la Vieja**), **Braulio Carrillo National Park,** and numerous remote lodges. Because this is one of the few regions of Costa Rica without any beaches, it primarily attracts people interested in nature and active sports. **Lake Arenal** has some of the best windsurfing and kitesurfing in the world, as well as several good mountain-biking trails along its shores. The **Monteverde Cloud Forest,** perhaps Costa Rica's most internationally recognized attraction, is another top draw in this region.

THE CENTRAL PACIFIC COAST Because it's the most easily accessible coastline in Costa Rica, the central Pacific coast has a vast variety of beach resorts and hotels. **Playa de Jacó,** a beach just an hour or so drive from San José, attracts many sunbirds, charter groups, and a mad rush of Tico tourists every weekend. It is also very popular with young surfers, and has a distinct party vibe. **Manuel Antonio,** one of the most emblematic destinations in Costa Rica, is built up around a popular coastal national park, and caters to people looking to blend beach time and fabulous panoramic views with some wildlife viewing and active adventures. This region is also home to the highest peak in Costa Rica—**Mount Chirripó**—a beautiful summit, where frost is common.

THE SOUTHERN ZONE This hot, humid region is one of Costa Rica's most remote and undeveloped. It is characterized by dense rainforests, large national parks and protected areas, and rugged coastlines. Much of the area is uninhabited and protected in **Corcovado, Piedras Blancas,** and **La Amistad** national parks. A number of wonderful nature lodges are spread around the shores of the **Golfo Dulce** and along the **Osa Peninsula.** There's a lot of solitude to be found here, due in no small part to the fact that it's hard to get here and hard to get around. But if you like your ecotourism authentic and challenging, you'll find the southern zone to your liking.

THE CARIBBEAN COAST Most of the Caribbean coast is a wide, steamy lowland laced with rivers and blanketed with rainforests and banana plantations. The culture here is predominantly Afro-Caribbean, with many residents speaking an English or Caribbean patois. The northern section of this coast is accessible only by boat or small plane and is the site of **Tortuguero National Park,** which is known for its nesting sea turtles and riverboat trips. The towns of **Cahuita, Puerto Viejo,** and **Manzanillo,** on the southern half of the Caribbean coast, are increasingly popular destinations. The beautiful beaches and coastline here, as yet, have few large hotels. This area can be rainy, especially between December and April.

COSTA RICA HIGHLIGHTS

The timing is tight, but this itinerary packs a lot into a typical weeklong vacation. This route takes you to a trifecta of Costa Rica's primary tourist attractions: Arenal Volcano, Monteverde, and Manuel Antonio. You can explore and enjoy tropical nature, take in some beach time, and experience a few high-adrenaline adventures.

DAY 1: Arrive & Settle into San José

Arrive and get settled in **San José.** If your flight gets in early enough and you have time, head downtown and tour the **Museos del Banco Central de Costa Rica (Gold Museum)** ★★ (p. 121) and the nearby **Museo de Jade Marco Fidel Tristán (Jade Museum)** ★ (p. 122).

☕ Fresh Fruit

As you walk around town, stop at one of the roadside stands or kiosks selling small bags of precut and prepared fruit. Depending on the season, you might find mango, pineapple, or papaya on offer. If you're lucky, they'll have *mamon chino*, an odd-looking golf ball–size fruit you might also know as rambutan or litchi nut.

Head over to the **Teatro Nacional** (**National Theater;** p. 144). If anything is playing that night, buy tickets for the show. For an elegant and delicious dinner, I recommend **Grano de Oro Restaurant** ★★★ (p. 136), a refined restaurant with seating in and around an open-air central courtyard in a beautiful downtown hotel.

Streets of San José.

DAY 2: Hot Stuff ★★

Rent a car and head to the Arenal National Park and the **Arenal Volcano** ★★ area. Hike the **Sendero Coladas (Lava Flow Trail) ★★**, which will take you onto and over a cooled-off lava flow. Spend the evening at the **Tabacón Grand Spa Thermal Resort ★★★** (p. 311), working out the kinks from the road and hike. (The volcano may be technically dormant right now, but the natural hot springs are still working just fine.) I recommend reserving a massage or spa treatment in advance.

DAY 3: Adventures Around Arenal, Ending in Monteverde ★★

Spend the morning doing something adventurous around Arenal National Park. Your options range from white-water rafting to mountain biking to horseback riding and then hiking to the Río Fortuna Waterfall. My favorite is the **canyoning** adventure offered by **Desafío Expeditions ★★** (p. 304). Allow at least 4 hours of daylight to drive around **Lake Arenal** to **Monteverde.** Stop for a break at the **Lucky Bug Gallery ★★** (p. 319), along the road between Tabacón and Nuevo Arenal, and an excellent place to shop for gifts, artwork, and souvenirs. Once you get to Monteverde, settle into your hotel and head for a drink and dinner at **Trio ★★★** (p. 339).

DAY 4: Monteverde Cloud Forest Biological Reserve ★★★

Wake up early and take a guided tour of the **Monteverde Cloud Forest Biological Reserve ★★★** (p. 328). Spend the afternoon visiting several of the area's attractions, which might include any combination of the following: the **Butterfly Garden ★** (p. 333), **Orchid Garden ★★** (p. 334), **Monteverde Serpentarium ★** (p. 333), **Frog Pond of Monteverde** (p. 333), and the **Bat Jungle ★★★** (p. 333).

DAY 5: From the Treetops to the Coast ★★★

Use the morning to take one of the **zip-line canopy tours** here. I recommend **Selvatura Park ★★** (p. 331), which has a wonderful canopy tour, as well as other interesting exhibits. Be sure to schedule the tour early enough so that you can hit the road by noon for your drive to **Manuel Antonio National Park.** Settle into your hotel and head for a **sunset drink** at

A canopy tour at Selvatura.

Río Fortuna Waterfall.

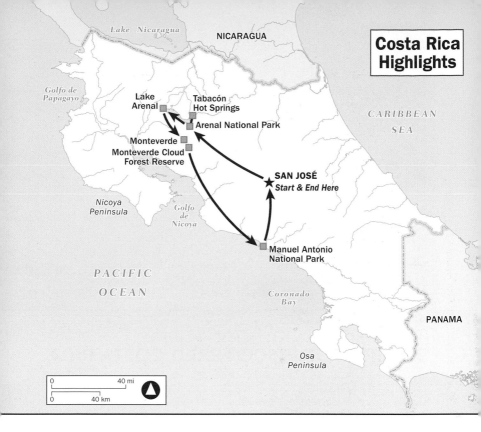

NICARAGUA

Lake Nicaragua

Golfo de Papagayo

Lake Arenal

Tabacón Hot Springs

Arenal National Park

CARIBBEAN SEA

Monteverde
Monteverde Cloud Forest Reserve

SAN JOSÉ
Start & End Here

Nicoya Peninsula

Golfo de Nicoya

Manuel Antonio National Park

PACIFIC OCEAN

Coronado Bay

PANAMA

Osa Peninsula

0   40 mi
0   40 km

Agua Azul ★★ (p. 385), which offers up spectacular views over the rainforest to the sea. You can drop your car off at any point now and just rely on taxis and tours.

DAY 6: Manuel Antonio ★★

In the morning, take a boat tour of the **Damas Island estuary** (p. 375), and then reward yourself for all the hard touring so far with an afternoon lazing on one of the beautiful beaches inside **Manuel Antonio National Park ★★** (p. 369). If you just can't lie still, be sure to hike the loop trail through the rainforest here and around **Cathedral Point ★★**. Make reservations at **Milagro ★★★** (p. 385) for an intimate and relaxed final dinner in Costa Rica.

DAY 7: Saying Adiós

Fly back to **San José** in time to connect with your departing flight home. If you have extra time in the morning, feel free to head back into Manuel Antonio National Park, do some souvenir shopping, or simply relax by your hotel pool. You've earned it.

Tabacón Grand Spa Thermal Resort.

THE BEST UNDISCOVERED COSTA RICA

Despite Costa Rica's popularity and booming tourism industry, plenty of places are still off the beaten track. And believe me, you'll be richly rewarded for venturing down the road less traveled. Start your trip off with a rental car, which you can turn in after Montezuma. After that, you'll want to fly to Golfito and then arrange for a boat ride to Playa Zancudo.

DAY 1: Rincón de la Vieja National Park

Not nearly as popular as the Arenal Volcano, the **Rincón de la Vieja volcano,** along with its namesake **national park ★★** (p. 199), is an underexplored gem. The park features challenging and rewarding hikes, sulfur hot springs, volcanic mud deposits, and stunning jungle waterfalls. My favorite hike here is a vigorous 2-hour trek to **Blue Lake and La Cangrejo Waterfall ★★** (p. 200), which leads to a beautiful forest waterfall emptying into a postcard-perfect turquoise lake. This is a great spot for a picnic lunch and a cool dip. If you have time and energy afterward, finish up with the relatively short and gentle **Las Pailas Loop ★**, which showcases the volcanic fumaroles and mud pots here.

DAY 2: Horses, High Wires & Hot Springs

You did plenty of hiking yesterday, so start this day off with a horseback ride and some zip-line gliding, and finish up with a relaxing soak in some mineral hot springs. **Hacienda Guachipelín ★★** (p. 204) offers a range of adventure activities, including horseback riding, river tubing, two zip-line canopy tours, and a waterfall rappel canyoning tour (see p. 201 for more about

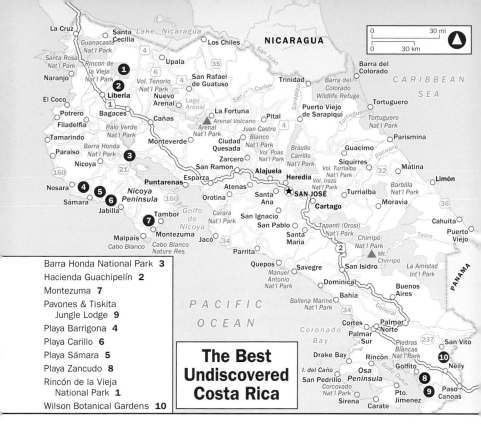

Barra Honda National Park **3**

Hacienda Guachipelín **2**

Montezuma **7**

Pavones & Tiskita
Jungle Lodge **9**

Playa Barrigona **4**

Playa Carillo **6**

Playa Sámara **5**

Playa Zancudo **8**

Rincón de la Vieja
National Park **1**

Wilson Botanical Gardens **10**

**The Best
Undiscovered
Costa Rica**

canyoning), in addition to a gorgeous set of natural hot mineral springs set along the side of a jungle river.

DAY 3: Going Deep Down Under

Sitting on top of a massive cave system, **Barra Honda National Park ★** (p. 283) is Costa Rica's top spot for spelunking. On a typical tour here, you'll descend into the depths of the **Terciopelo Cave** and visit the waterfalls and pools of **La Cascada.** After your visit here, drive to nearby **Playa Sámara,** about an hour away.

☕ Gusto Beach

With tables set in the sand, and palm trees lit with rope lighting, **Gusto Beach ★★** serves up excellent Italian fare, as well as fresh grilled fish and meats. See p. 286.

DAY 4: Beautiful Beaches

The Nicoya Peninsula has many of the same charms and nearly as many miles of beach as Guanacaste, but far fewer crowds. Although the beach at **Playa Sámara** is nice enough, I recommend heading to neighboring gems **Playa Barrigona ★★** (p. 282) and **Playa Carrillo ★★** (p. 282). While in the area, be sure to sign up for an ultralight flight with the folks at the **Flying Crocodile** (p. 283).

DAYS 5 & 6: Montezuma

Montezuma is a great place to mix more beach time with wildlife sightings and visits to some wonderful waterfalls. While you can certainly hike to the foot of the **Montezuma Waterfall** ★★ (p. 267), I prefer visiting it as part of the **Waterfall Canopy Tour** ★ (p. 268). I recommend taking a horseback tour to **El Chorro Falls** ★ (p. 267). If you time it right, you can ride home along the beach as the sun sets.

While in Montezuma, visit the **Cabo Blanco Absolute Nature Reserve** ★★ (p. 268), the country's first officially protected area. The main trail inside this park, **Sendero Sueco,** leads to the gorgeous and almost always deserted beach **Playa Balsita.** A trip to Cabo Blanco Nature Reserve can easily be combined with a **kayaking and snorkel tour** to the little cemetery island located just off the village of **Cabuya.**

☕ Playa de los Artistas

Fresh grilled fish and other Mediterranean fare are the specialty at **Playa de los Artistas ★★★**. If you're limber, slide onto a tatami mat set around one of the low tables closest to the water. See p. 272.

Sunset in Coco Beach, Guanacaste.

DAYS 7, 8 & 9: Playa Zancudo

You'll want to finish off this itinerary at one of Costa Rica's most remote and undiscovered beach towns. Playa Zancudo is a sleepy little town on a narrow strip of land set between the Golfo Dulce and a saltwater mangrove lagoon. While here, you can go **sportfishing** (p. 441), head over to nearby **Pavones** (p. 442) for a surf session, or take an organized tour with **Zancudo Boat Tours** (p. 441).

One of the better day trips heads southward to **Tiskita Jungle Lodge ★★** (p. 445), which has a wonderful network of trails through the rainforests

TOP: **It's no mystery how the Blue Lake in Rincón de la Vieja National Park got its name.** BOTTOM: **A horseback ride on the beach in Montezuma.**

and fruit orchards of its private reserve. Any wannabe botanist will also want to allot enough time for a visit to the **Wilson Botanical Gardens ★★★** (p. 434), the most impressive botanical gardens in the entire country.

☕ Sol y Mar ★★

Sol y Mar is a quintessential beach bar. Stop by for a drink, meal, or friendly game of horseshoes. See p. 442.

THE BEST COSTA RICA ADVENTURES

Costa Rica is a major adventure-tourism destination. The following basic itinerary packs a lot of adventure into a single week; if you want to do some surfing, mountain biking, or kayaking, just schedule some more time in. If you're into windsurfing or kiteboarding, you'll definitely want to visit Lake Arenal between December and March.

DAY 1: Starting in San José

Arrive and get settled in **San José.** If your flight gets in early enough and you have time, head downtown and tour the **Museos del Banco Central de Costa Rica** ★★ (p. 121) and the **Teatro Nacional** (p. 144). Take a break for an afternoon coffee at **Alma de Café** ★ (p. 135). For a delicious dinner with a spectacular view, head to **Cantina La Cava** ★ (p. 163), which is in the hills above Escazú.

DAYS 2 & 3: Get Wet & Wild

Take a 2-day white-water rafting expedition on the **Pacuare River** with **Ríos Tropicales** ★★ (p. 152). You'll spend the night at their lovely lodge on the river's edge. When you finish running the Pacuare, they will transport you (as part of the trip package) to **La Fortuna** ★★. Settle into your hotel and head to the **Tabacón Grand Spa Thermal Resort** ★★★ (p. 311) to have a soothing soak and to watch the volcano.

Santa Elena Cloud Forest.

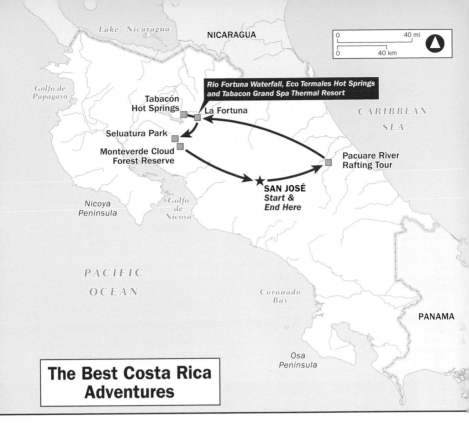

Rio Fortuna Waterfall, Eco Termales Hot Springs
and Tabacon Grand Spa Thermal Resort

NICARAGUA

Lake Nicaragua

Golfo de
Papagayo

Tabacón
Hot Springs   La Fortuna

Seluatura Park

Monteverde Cloud
Forest Reserve   Pacuare River
                                        Rafting Tour

★
SAN JOSÉ
Start &
End Here

Nicoya
Peninsula

Golfo
de
Nicoya

CARIBBEAN
SEA

PACIFIC
OCEAN   Coronado
                     Bay

PANAMA

Osa
Peninsula

The Best Costa Rica Adventures

DAY 4: Waterfalls Two Ways

Go canyoning with **Desafío Expeditions ★★** (p. 304) in the morning, and then hop on a horse or a mountain bike in the afternoon and be sure to stop at the **Río Fortuna Waterfall ★** (p. 305). Take the short hike down to the base of the falls and take a dip in one of the pools there. In the evening, check out the hot springs at **Eco Termales ★★** (p. 309).

DAY 5: Getting There Is Part of the Fun & Adventure

Arrange a **taxi-to-boat-to-horse** transfer over to **Monteverde** with **Desafío Expeditions ★★** (p. 326). Settle in quickly at your hotel and take a zip-line **canopy tour** in the afternoon. I recommend **Selvatura Park ★★**, which is located near the **Santa Elena Cloud Forest Reserve**. Finally, if you've got the energy, take a **night tour** through either the Santa Elena or Monteverde Cloud Forest Reserve.

DAY 6: Monteverde Cloud Forest Biological Reserve ★★★

Wake up early and head back to take a daytime guided tour of the **Monteverde Cloud Forest Biological Reserve ★★★**. Be sure to bring a packed lunch. After the guided tour, spend the next few hours continuing to explore the trails through the cloud forest here. See if you can spot a **quetzal** (p. 328) on your own. Then transfer back to San José.

DAY 7: Squeeze in a Soccer Game before Splitting

Unfortunately, you'll most likely be on an early flight home from **San José.** If you have a few hours to kill, head for a **hike** or **jog** around Parque La Sabana or, better yet, try to join a **pickup soccer game** (p. 125) here.

COSTA RICA FOR FAMILIES

Costa Rica is a terrific destination for families. If you're traveling with very small children, you might want to stick close to the beaches, or consider a large resort with a children's program and babysitting services. But for slightly older kids and teens, particularly those with an adventurous streak, Costa Rica is a lot of fun. Youngsters and teens, especially those with strong adventurous and inquisitive traits, will do great here. The biggest challenges to families traveling with children are travel distances and the logistical trials of moving around within the country, which is why I recommend flying in and out of Liberia and basing yourself in Guanacaste.

DAY 1: Arrive in Guanacaste

Fly directly into **Liberia.** From here it's a drive of 30 to 45 minutes to any of the area's many beach resorts, especially around the **Papagayo**

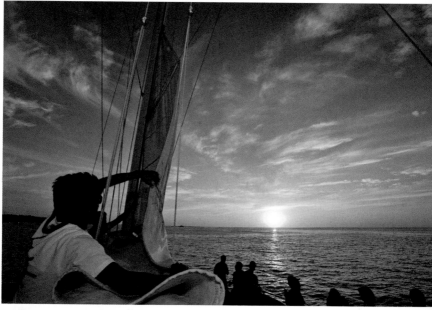

A sailboat cruise on the Pacific Ocean.

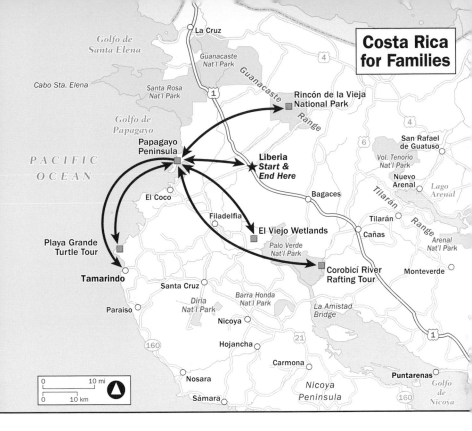

Costa Rica
for Families

Peninsula. I recommend either the **Four Seasons Resort ★★★** (p. 213) or the **Hilton Papagayo Resort ★** (p. 214). Both have excellent children's programs and tons of activity and tour options. Alternatively, **Hotel Playa Hermosa Bosque del Mar ★★★** (p. 215) is a lovely beachfront boutique hotel on a quiet and calm section of Playa Hermosa.

DAY 2: Get Your Bearings & Enjoy Your Resort

Get to know and enjoy the facilities and activities offered up at your hotel or resort. Spend time on the beach or at the pool. Build some sand castles, or get involved in a pickup game of beach volleyball or soccer. In the afternoon, go on a **sail and snorkel cruise.** If you choose a large resort, check out the **children's program** and any scheduled **activities** or **tours** that particularly appeal to anyone in the family. Feel free to adapt the following days' suggestions accordingly.

DAY 3: Rafting on the Corobicí River

The whole family will enjoy a **rafting tour** on the gentle Corobicí River. **Rios Tropicales ★★** (p. 196) offers leisurely trips that are appropriate for all ages, except infants. In addition to the slow float and occasional mellow rapids, there'll be plenty of opportunities to watch birds and other wildlife along the way. If you're here between late September and late February, book a **turtle tour** (p. 235) at nearby **Playa Grande** for the evening. The whole family will be awe-struck by the amazing spectacle of a giant leatherback turtle digging a nest and laying its eggs.

DAY 4: El Viejo Wetlands ★★

Located about an hour or so drive from the Guancaste beaches, **El Viejo Wildlife Refuge & Wetlands** ★★ (p. 229) is a fabulous day-trip destination. Set on a massive old farmstead bordering Palo Verde National Park, this private reserve offers up some of Guanacaste's best wildlife viewing, with boat trips on the Tempisque river and safari-style open Jeep tours through surrounding wetlands, as well as a host of other cultural and adventure tour options. Lunch is served in a beautiful farm building, more than a century old.

DAY 5: Hacienda Guachipelín ★

It's time to head for the hills, which are mostly volcanoes in this neck of the woods. Book a full-day Adventure Pass outing to **Hacienda Guachipelín** (p. 204), near **Rincón de la Vieja National Park.** Older and more adventurous children can go river tubing, do a **horseback ride,** or take one of the zip-line **canopy tours.** Younger children should get a kick out of visiting the working farm and cattle ranch, butterfly garden, and serpentarium here.

DAY 6: Learn to Surf

Head to **Tamarindo** ★ (p. 237) and arrange for the whole family to take **surf** or **boogie-board lessons.** Hopefully you will have already booked a class with **Kelly's Surf Shop** ★ (p. 244) or **Witch's Rock Surf Camp** ★ (p. 244). Be sure to rent your boards for a full day, so that you can practice after the lesson is over.

DAY 7: Leaving Liberia

Use any spare time you have before your flight out of **Liberia** to buy last-minute souvenirs and gifts, or just laze on the beach or by the pool. Your best bet for gift shopping is probably **La Gran Nicoya** (p. 198). If you want a piece of fine art or a local print, head to **Hidden Garden Art Gallery** ★★ (p. 199). Both stores are conveniently located on the way to the airport.

THE BEST OF SAN JOSÉ & THE CENTRAL VALLEY

While most tourists seek to almost immediately get out of San José for greener pastures, Costa Rica's vibrant capital and the surrounding Central Valley offer plenty to see and do. If you have even more days, take a white-water rafting trip on the Pacuare River, tour a coffee farm, or head out to Turrialba for a canyoning adventure and visit to the Guayabo National Monument, Costa Rica's largest and best excavated archaeological site.

DAY 1: Getting to Know the City

Start your day on the **Plaza de la Cultura.** Visit the **Museos del Banco Central de Costa Rica** ★★ (p. 121), and see if you can get tickets for a

San José & the Central Valley in 4 Days

| 0 | 5 mi |
| 0 | 5 km |

THE CENTRAL VALLEY

Volcán Poás Nat'l Park
Volcán Poás
Poasito
Vara Blanca
Braulio Carrillo Nat'l Park
Volcán Barva
Central Range
Volcán Turrialba Nat'l Park
Volcán Turrialba
San Pedro de Poás
Grecia
Volcán Irazú Nat'l Park
Volcán Irazú
Sta. Bárbara
Barva
Alajuela
Heredia
Pan-American Highway
La Garita
San Antonio de Belén
Santo Domingo
Guadalupe
Santa Ana
SAN JOSÉ
San Pedro
Escazú
Curridabat
Pacayas
Alajuelita
Desamparados
Tres Ríos
Cartago
Aserrí
Paraíso

NICARAGUA
CARIBBEAN SEA
SAN JOSÉ
The Central Valley
PACIFIC OCEAN
PANAMA

SAN JOSÉ

| 0 | 1/4 mi |
| 0 | 0.25 km |

COCA-COLA
PASO DE LA VACA
EL PUEBLO
Río Torres
MEXICO
CARMEN
AMÓN
Paseo Colón
PARQUE LA SABANA
Parque Morazán
Parque Central
MERCED
SANTA LUCIA

Av. 7, Av. 5, Av. 3, Av. 1, Av. 13, Av. 11, Av. 7, Av. 5, Av. 3, Av. 1, Av. Central, Av. 2, Av. 4, Av. 6, Av. 8, Av. 10, Av. 11, Av. 9, Av. 7, Av. 1, Av. Central, Av. 2, Av. 8, Av. 12

Calle 42, Calle 40, Calle 38, Calle 36, Calle 34, Calle 32, Calle 30, Calle 28, Calle 26, Calle 24, Calle 22, Calle 20, Calle 18, Calle 16, Calle 14, Calle 12, Calle 10, Calle 8, Calle 6, Calle 4, Calle Central, Calle 3, Calle 5, Calle 1, Calle 2, Calle 7, Calle 9, Calle 11, Calle 13, Calle 15, Calle 17

Day 1

1 Plaza de la Cultura
2 Museos del Banco Central de Costa Rica
3 Museo Nacional de Costa Rica
4 Restaurante Nuestra Tierra 🍵
5 Museo de Jade
6 Plaza de la Democracia
7 Café Mundo 🍵
8 Teatro Nacional

Day 2

9 Poás Volcano
10 La Paz Waterfall Gardens
11 INBio Park

Day 3

12 Irazú volcano
13 Las Ruinas & Basílica de Nuestra Señora de los Angeles
14 Ujarrás
15 La Casa del Soñador

16 La Casona del Cafetal 🍵
17 Museo de Arte Religioso
18 Jardín Botánico Lankester

Day 4

19 Museo de Arte Costarricense
20 Parque La Sabana
21 Mercado Central
22 Grano de Oro Restaurant 🍵
23 Vértigo
24 Castro's

"Take a Break" 🍵

59

View into the main crater of the Poás Volcano.

performance that night at the **Teatro Nacional** (p. 144). From the Plaza de la Cultura, stroll up Avenida Central to the **Museo Nacional de Costa Rica (National Museum)** ★★ (p. 121).

☕ Restaurante Nuestra Tierra

It's a bit of a tourist trap, sure, but this Costa Rican-themed restaurant is very, very conveniently located, and does serve up dependable local cuisine. Order a casado for lunch. It will come served on a banana leaf spread over a large platter, by a waiter or waitress in traditional rural garb from a bygone era. See p. 134.

After lunch, head over to the nearby **Museo de Jade Marco Fidel Tristán (Jade Museum)** ★★ (p. 122). As soon as you're finished taking in all this culture, some shopping at the open-air stalls at the **Plaza de la Democracia** (p. 138) is in order.

☕ Café Mundo ★

Try dinner at the trendy local hangout **Café Mundo,** at Calle 15 and Avenida 9, 3 blocks east and 1 block north of the INS building. See p. 135.

After dinner, head to the **Teatro Nacional** for the night's performance.

DAY 2: Alajuela, Heredia & Environs

Get an early start for the **Poás Volcano ★★** (p. 166), before the clouds sock the main crater in. After visiting the volcano, head to **La Paz Waterfall Gardens ★★** (p. 166). Take a walk on the waterfall trail, and also enjoy the immense butterfly garden and lively hummingbird garden. This is a good place to have lunch. On your way back to San José, you'll be making a loop through the hills of **Heredia,** with a stop at **INBio Park ★★** (p. 172). In addition to being a fascinating natural-history museum, INBio Park also has a wonderful collection of intriguing animal sculptures by Costa Rican artist José Sancho.

DAY 3: Cartago & the Orosi Valley

Start your day off taking in the scenery from 3,378m (11,080 ft.), at the top of the **Irazú volcano ★★** (p. 181). After admiring the view and hiking the crater trail, head down into the country's first capital city, visiting **Las Ruinas ★** (p. 180) and the **Basílica de Nuestra Señora de los Angeles ★★★** (p. 180), on your way out to the Orosi valley. As you drive the loop road around Lake Cachí, stop in **Ujarrás** (p. 183) to see the ruins of Costa Rica's oldest church, and to check out the sculpture offerings at **La Casa del Soñador** (p. 183).

☕ La Casona del Cafetal

Set on expansive grounds overlooking Lake Cachí, this place serves good, traditional Costa Rican fare. If the weather's nice, grab an outdoor patio table with a view. See p. 184.

The Museo Nacional de Costa Rica.

After lunch, be sure to visit the **Museo de Arte Religioso** ★ (p. 184) in the town of **Orosi** (p. 183) itself. On your way home, stop at **Jardín Botánico Lankester** ★★ (p. 182), one of the top botanical gardens in the country.

DAY 4: More City Sights & Shopping

Spend this day further exploring the capital. Start by heading out on Paseo Colón to the **Museo de Arte Costarricense (Costa Rican Art Museum)** ★★ (p. 123). Be sure to spend some time in their wonderful open-air sculpture garden. After visiting the museum, take a stroll around the beautiful and expansive downtown **Parque La Sabana** (p. 125). Intrepid travelers can also do some shopping at the **Mercado Central** ★ (p. 143).

Grano de Oro Restaurant

For your final dinner, splurge a bit and head to the elegant **Grano de Oro Restaurant** ★★★, located inside the boutique hotel of the same name. See p. 136.

After dinner take a late-night turn on the dance floor at **Castro's** ★ (p. 145) or **Vértigo** ★★ (p. 145).

4

COSTA RICA'S NATURAL WORLD

C osta Rica occupies a central spot in the isthmus that joins North and South America. For millennia, this land bridge served as a migratory thoroughfare and mating ground for species native to the once-separate continents. It was also where the Mesoamerican and Andean pre-Columbian indigenous cultures met.

In any one spot in Costa Rica, temperatures remain relatively constant year-round. However, they vary dramatically according to altitude, from tropically hot and steamy along the coasts to below freezing at the highest elevations. These variations in altitude, temperature, and precipitation give rise to a wide range of ecosystems and habitats, which are described in "Costa Rica's Ecosystems," below.

For its part, the wide variety of ecosystems and habitats has blessed the country with a unique biological bounty. More than 10,000 identified species of plants, 880 species of birds, 9,000 species of butterflies and moths, and 500 species of mammals, reptiles, and amphibians are found here. For detailed information on some of the more common or evocative representatives of Costa Rica's flora and fauna, see "Costa Rican Wildlife," p. 75.

Thankfully, for both visitors and the local flora and fauna alike, nearly one-quarter of Costa Rica's entire landmass is protected either as part of a national park or private nature reserve. This chapter includes a rundown and description of the most important national parks and bioreserves in the country. For information on sustainable issues in Costa Rica, see "Responsible Tourism," p. 73.

THE LAY OF THE LAND
Costa Rica's Ecosystems
RAINFORESTS

Costa Rica's **rainforests** are classic tropical jungles. Some receive more than 508cm (200 in.) of rainfall per year, and their climate is typically hot and humid, especially in the lowland rainforests. Trees grow tall and fast, fighting for sunlight in the upper reaches. In fact, life and foliage on the forest floor are surprisingly sparse. The action is typically 30m (98 ft.) up, in the canopy, where long vines stream down, lianas climb up, and bromeliads grow on the branches and trunks of towering hardwood trees.

Some of the more indicative rainforest tree species include the parasitic strangler fig and the towering ceiba, which can reach some 60m (196 ft.). Mammal species that call the Costa Rican rainforests home include the jaguar, three-toed sloth, all four native monkey species, and Baird's Tapir, while some of the more prominent birds you might spot are the Harpy eagle, Scarlet Macaw, and the Chesnut-mandibled toucan.

PREVIOUS PAGE: **Resplendent Quetzal.**

You can find these lowland rainforests along the southern Pacific coast and Osa Peninsula, as well as along the Caribbean coast. **Corcovado, Cahuita,** and **Manuel Antonio** national parks, as well as the **Gandoca–Manzanillo Wildlife Refuge,** are fine examples of lowland rainforests. Examples of mid-elevation rainforests include the **Braulio Carillo National Park** and the forests around **La Selva** and the **Puerto Viejo de Sarapiquí** region, and those around the **Arenal Volcano** and **Lake Arenal** area.

TROPICAL DRY FORESTS

In a few protected areas of Guanacaste (chapter 8), you will still find examples of the otherwise vanishing **tropical dry forest.** During the long and pronounced dry season (late Nov to late Apr), no rain relieves the unabated heat. In an effort to conserve much-needed water, the trees drop their leaves but bloom in a riot of color: Purple jacaranda, scarlet *poró,* and brilliant orange flame-of-the-forest are just a few examples. Then during the rainy season, this deciduous forest is transformed into a lush and verdant landscape.

Other common dry forest trees include the Guanacaste, with its broad, shade canopy, and distinctive pochote, whose trunk is covered with thick, broad thorns.

Because the foliage is less dense than that found in cloud forests and rainforests, dry forests are excellent places to view a variety of wildlife. Howler monkeys are commonly seen in the trees, and coatimundi, puma, and coyote roam the ground. Costa Rica's remaining dry forests are most prominently found in **Santa Rosa, Guanacaste, Rincón de la Vieja,** and **Palo Verde** national parks.

CLOUD FORESTS

At higher altitudes, you'll find Costa Rica's famed **cloud forests.** Here the steady flow of moist air meets the mountains and creates a nearly constant mist. Epiphytes—resourceful plants that live cooperatively on the branches and trunks of other trees—grow abundantly in the cloud forests, where they must extract moisture and nutrients from the air. Because cloud forests are found in generally steep, mountainous terrain, the canopy here is lower and less uniform than in lowland rainforests, providing better chances for viewing elusive fauna.

The remarkable **Resplendent Quetzal** is perhaps the most famous and sought-after denizen of Costa Rica's cloud forests, but you'll also find a broad and immense variety of flora and fauna, including a dozen or more hummingbird species, wild cats, monkeys, reptiles, and amphibians. **Orchids,** many of them epiphytic, thrive in cloud forests, as do mosses, ferns, and a host of other plants, many of which are cultivated and sold as

A Guaria Morada, Costa Rica's national flower.

common household plants throughout the rest of the world.

Costa Rica's most spectacular cloud forest is the **Monteverde Cloud Forest Biological Reserve** (p. 328), but you can also explore Monteverde's neighbor, the **Santa Elena Cloud Forest Reserve** (p. 330), or, much closer to San José, the **Los Angeles Cloud Forest Reserve** (p. 97).

MANGROVES & WETLANDS

Along the coasts, primarily where river mouths meet the ocean, you will find extensive **mangrove forests, wetlands,** and **swamps.** Mangroves, in particular, are an immensely important ecological

Hotlips flowers can be spotted throughout the country's forests.

phenomenon. Around the intricate tangle of mangrove roots exists one of the most diverse and rich ecosystems on the planet. All sorts of fish and crustaceans live in the brackish tidal waters. Many larger salt water and open-ocean fish species begin life in the nutrient rich, and relatively safe and protected environment of a mangrove swamp.

Mangrove swamps and wetlands are havens for and home to scores of water birds: **cormorants, magnificent frigate birds, pelicans, kingfishers, egrets, ibises,** and **herons.** The larger birds tend to nest up high in the canopy, while the smaller ones nestle in the underbrush. And in the waters, **caimans** and **crocodiles** cruise the maze of rivers and unmarked canals.

Mangrove forests, swamps, and wetlands exist all along both of Costa Rica's coasts. Some of the prime areas that can be explored by tourists include the areas around the **Sierpe river mouth** and **Diquis delta** near **Drake Bay** (p. 408), the **Golfo Dulce** (p. 431) in the southern zone, **Palo Verde National Park** and the **Tempisque river** basin in Guanacaste (chapter 8), and the **Gandoca– Manzanillo Wildlife Refuge** on the Caribbean coast (chapter 13).

PÁRAMO

At the highest reaches, the cloud forests give way to **elfin forests** and **páramos.** More commonly associated with the South American Andes, a páramo is characterized by a variety of tundralike shrubs and grasses, with a scattering of twisted, windblown trees. Reptiles, rodents, and raptors are the most common residents here, and since the vegetation is so sparse, they're often easier to spot. **Mount Chirripó, Chirripó National Park** (p. 400), and the **Cerro de la Muerte** (**Mountain of Death;** p. 404) are the principal areas of páramo in Costa Rica.

VOLCANOES

Costa Rica is a land of high volcanic and seismic activity. The country has three major **volcanic mountain ranges,** and many of the volcanoes are still active, allowing visitors to experience the awe-inspiring sight of steaming **fumaroles,** sky-lighting **eruptions,** and intense **lava flows** during their stay. In ecological terms, cooled-off lava flows are fascinating laboratories, where you can watch pioneering lichen and mosses eventually give way to plants and shrubs, and eventually trees and forests.

The top spot to see volcanic activity is, hands-down, the **Arenal Volcano** (chapter 10). Another reliable place to see steady volcanic activity, in the form of mud pots, fumaroles, and hot springs, is in the **Rincón de la Vieja National Park** (p. 200). Closer to San José, the **Poás** (p. 166) and **Irazú volcanoes** (p. 181) are both currently active, although relatively quiet.

COSTA RICA'S TOP NATIONAL PARKS & BIORESERVES

Costa Rica has 34 national parks and reserves, protecting more than 12% of the country. Scores of other private reserves bring the total protected area up to some 23% of the national territory. Official state-protected parks range in size from the 212-hectare (524-acre) Guayabo National Monument to the 189,696-hectare (468,549-acre) La Amistad National Park. Many of these national parks are undeveloped tropical forests, with few services or facilities available for visitors. Others, however, offer easier access to their wealth of natural wonders.

Most of the national parks charge a $10 per-person per-day fee for any foreigner, although Chirripó National Park costs $15 per day. Costa Ricans and foreign residents continue to pay just $1. At parks where camping is allowed, an additional charge of around $2 per person per day usually applies.

This section is not a complete listing of all of Costa Rica's national parks and protected areas, but rather a selective list of those parks that are of greatest interest and accessibility. They're popular, and they're also among the best. You'll find detailed information about food and lodging options near some of the individual parks in the regional chapters that follow. As you'll see from the descriptions, Costa Rica's national parks vary greatly in terms of attractions, facilities, and accessibility.

If you're looking for a camping adventure or an extended stay in one of the national parks, I recommend **Santa Rosa, Rincón de la Vieja, Chirripó,** or **Corcovado.** Any of the others are better suited for day trips or guided hikes, or in combination with your travels around the country.

For more information, call the national parks information line at ✆ **1192,** or the main office at ✆ **2283-8004.** You can also stop by the **National Parks Foundation office** (✆ **2257-2239**) in San José, located between Calle 23 and Avenida 15. Both offices are open Monday through Friday from 8am to 5pm.

The Central Valley

GUAYABO NATIONAL MONUMENT   This is the country's only significant pre-Columbian archaeological site. It's believed that Guayabo supported a population of about 10,000 people some 3,000 years ago. The park is set in a forested area rich in flora and fauna, although the ruins are quite small and limited when compared to sites in Mexico, Guatemala, and South America. **Location:** 19km (12 miles) northeast of Turrialba, which is 53km (33 miles) east of San José. See p. 187.

IRAZÚ VOLCANO NATIONAL PARK ★   Irazú Volcano is the highest (3,378m/11,080 ft.) of Costa Rica's four active volcanoes and a popular day trip from San José. A paved road leads right up to the crater, and the lookout also has

A petroglyph at Guayabo National Monument.

a view of both the Pacific and the Caribbean on a clear day. The volcano last erupted in 1963 on the same day U.S. President John F. Kennedy visited the country. The park has picnic tables, restrooms, an information center, and a parking area. **Location:** 55km (34 miles) east of San José. See p. 181.

POÁS VOLCANO NATIONAL PARK ★★   Poás is the other active volcano close to San José. The main crater is more than 1.6km (1 mile) wide, and it is constantly active with fumaroles and hot geysers. I slightly prefer Poás to Irazú because Poás is surrounded by dense cloud forests and has some nice gentle trails to hike. Although the area around the volcano is lush, much of the growth is stunted due to the gases and acid rain. On January 8, 2009, a 6.1 magnitude earthquake struck Costa Rica, with its epicenter very close to Poás. The park was closed for several days, and an uptick in volcanic activity was noted. The park still sometimes closes when the gases get too feisty. The park has picnic tables, restrooms, and an information center. **Location:** 37km (23 miles) northwest of San José. See p. 166.

Guanacaste & the Nicoya Peninsula

PALO VERDE NATIONAL PARK   A must for bird-watchers, Palo Verde National Park is one of Costa Rica's best-kept secrets. This part of the Tempisque River lowlands supports a population of more than 50,000 waterfowl and forest bird species. Various ecosystems here include mangroves, savanna brush lands, and evergreen forests. The park has camping facilities, an information center, and some nice accommodations at the Organization for Tropical Studies (OTS) research station here. **Location:** 200km (124 miles) northwest of San José. Be warned that the park entrance is 28km (17 miles) off the highway down a very rugged dirt road; it's another 9km (5½ miles) to the OTS station and campsites. For more information, call the OTS (© **2524-0607;** www.threepaths.co.cr). See chapter 8.

RINCÓN DE LA VIEJA NATIONAL PARK ★★ This large tract of parkland experiences high volcanic activity, with numerous fumaroles and geysers, as well as hot springs, cold pools, and mud pots. You'll find excellent hikes to the upper craters and to several waterfalls. You should hire a guide for any hot-spring or mud-bath expeditions; inexperienced visitors have been burned. Camping is permitted at two sites, each with an information center, a picnic area, and restrooms. **Location:** 266km (165 miles) northwest of San José. See p. 200.

SANTA ROSA NATIONAL PARK ★ Occupying a large section of Costa Rica's northwestern Guanacaste province, Santa Rosa has the country's largest area of tropical dry forest, important turtle-nesting sites, and the historically significant La Casona monument. The beaches are pristine and have basic camping facilities, and the waves make them quite popular with surfers. An information center, a picnic area, and restrooms are at the main campsite and entrance. Additional campsites are located on pristine and undeveloped beaches here. **Location:** 258km (160 miles) northwest of San José. For more information, you can call the park office at ✆ **2666-5051.** See p. 205.

The Nicoya Peninsula

BARRA HONDA NATIONAL PARK Costa Rica's only underground national park, Barra Honda features a series of limestone caves that were once part of a coral reef some 60 million years ago. Today the caves are home to millions of bats and impressive stalactite and stalagmite formations. Only Terciopelo Cave is open to the public. A camping area, restrooms, and an information center are here, as well as trails through the surrounding tropical dry forest. **Location:** 335km (208 miles) northwest of San José. See p. 283.

The Northern Zone

ARENAL NATIONAL PARK ★★ This park, created to protect the ecosystem that surrounds Arenal Volcano, has a couple of good trails, and a prominent lookout point that is extremely close to the volcano. The main trail here will take you through a mix of transitional forest, rainforest, and open savanna, before an invigorating scramble over a massive rock field formed by a cooled-off lava flow. **Location:** 129km (80 miles) northwest of San José. See p. 302.

CAÑO NEGRO NATIONAL WILDLIFE REFUGE ★ A lowland swamp and drainage basin for several northern rivers, Caño Negro is excellent for bird-watching. A few basic cabinas and lodges are in this area, but the most popular way to visit is on a combined van and boat trip from the La Fortuna/Arenal area. **Location:** 20km (12 miles) south of Los Chiles, near the Nicaraguan border. See "Arenal Volcano & La Fortuna," in chapter 10.

MONTEVERDE CLOUD FOREST BIOLOGICAL RESERVE ★★★ This private reserve might be the most famous patch of forest in Costa Rica. It covers some 10,520 hectares (26,000 acres) of primary forest, mostly mid-elevation cloud forest, with a rich variety of flora and fauna. Epiphytes thrive in the cool, misty climate. The most famous resident is the spectacular Resplendent Quetzal. The park has a well-maintained trail system, as well as some of the best-trained and experienced guides in the country. Nearby you can visit both the Santa Elena and Sendero Tranquilo reserves. **Location:** 167km (104 miles) northwest of San José. See p. 328.

Central Pacific Coast

CARARA NATIONAL PARK ★★ Located just off the highway near the Pacific coast, on the road to Jacó, this is one of the best places in Costa Rica to see scarlet macaws. Several trails run through the park, including one that is wheelchair accessible. The park is comprised of various ecosystems, ranging from rainforests to transitional forests to mangroves. **Location:** 102km (63 miles) west of San José. See p. 355.

CHIRRIPÓ NATIONAL PARK ★★ Home to Costa Rica's tallest peak, 3,761m (12,336-ft.) Mount Chirripó, Chirripó National Park is a hike, but on a clear day you can see both the Pacific Ocean and the Caribbean Sea from its summit. A number of interesting climbing trails are here, and camping is allowed. **Location:** 151km (94 miles) southeast of San José. See p. 400.

MANUEL ANTONIO NATIONAL PARK ★★ Though relatively small, Manuel Antonio is the most popular national park and supports the largest number of hotels and resorts. This lowland rainforest is home to a healthy monkey population, including the endangered squirrel monkey. The park is best known for its splendid beaches. **Location:** 129km (80 miles) south of San José. See p. 373.

The Southern Zone

CORCOVADO NATIONAL PARK ★★★ The largest single block of virgin lowland rainforest in Central America, Corcovado National Park receives more than 508cm (200 in.) of rain per year. It's increasingly popular but still very remote. (It has no roads; only dirt tracks lead into it.) Scarlet macaws live here, as do

Monteverde Cloud Forest Biological Reserve.

A boat tour leaving Tortuguero village.

countless other Neotropical species, including two of the country's largest cats, the puma and the endangered jaguar. Camping facilities and trails are throughout the park. **Location:** 335km (208 miles) south of San José, on the Osa Peninsula. See p. 423.

The Caribbean Coast

CAHUITA NATIONAL PARK ★★   A combination land and marine park, Cahuita National Park protects one of the few remaining living coral reefs in the country. The topography here is lush lowland tropical rainforest. Monkeys and numerous bird species are common. **Location:** On the Caribbean coast, 42km (26 miles) south of Limón. See p. 469.

TORTUGUERO NATIONAL PARK ★★   Tortuguero National Park has been called the Venice of Costa Rica due to its maze of jungle canals that meander through a dense lowland rainforest. Small boats, launches, and canoes carry visitors through these waterways, where caimans, manatees, and numerous bird and mammal species are common. The extremely endangered great green macaw lives here. Green sea turtles nest on the beaches here every year between June and October. The park has a small but helpful information office and some well-marked trails. **Location:** 258km (160 miles) northeast of San José. See p. 456.

HEALTH, SAFETY & ETIQUETTE IN THE WILD

Much of what is discussed here is common sense. For more detailed information, see "Staying Healthy," in chapter 14. Although most tours and activities are safe, risks are involved in any adventure activity. Know and respect your own physical limits before undertaking any strenuous activity. Be prepared for extremes in temperature and rainfall and for wide fluctuations in weather. A sunny morning hike can quickly become a cold and wet ordeal, so it's usually a good idea to carry along some form of rain gear when hiking in the rainforest, or to have a dry change of clothing waiting at the end of the trail. Be sure to bring along plenty of sunscreen when you're not going to be covered by the forest canopy.

If you do any backcountry packing or camping, remember that it really *is* a jungle out there. Don't go poking under rocks or fallen branches. Snakebites are very rare, but don't do anything to increase the odds. If you encounter a snake, stay calm, don't make any sudden movements, and *do not* try to touch the snake. Also avoid swimming in major rivers unless a guide or local operator can vouch for their safety. Although white-water sections and stretches in mountainous areas are generally safe, most mangrove canals and river mouths in Costa Rica support healthy crocodile and caiman populations.

Bugs and bug bites will probably be your greatest health concern in the Costa Rican wilderness, and even they aren't as big of a problem as you might expect. Mostly, bugs are an inconvenience, although mosquitoes can carry malaria or dengue (see "Staying Healthy," in chapter 14, for more information). A strong repellent and proper clothing minimize both the danger and the inconvenience; you might also want to bring along some cortisone or Benadryl cream to soothe itching. **And remember:** Whenever you enter and enjoy nature, you should tread lightly and try not to disturb the natural environment. The popular slogan well known to most campers certainly applies here: "Leave nothing but footprints; take nothing but memories." If you must take home a souvenir, take photos. Do not cut or uproot plants or flowers. Pack out everything you pack in, and *please* do not litter.

Searching for Wildlife

Animals in the forests are predominantly nocturnal. When they are active in the daytime, they are usually elusive and on the watch for predators. Birds are easier to spot in clearings or secondary forests than they are in primary forests. Unless you have lots of experience in the Tropics, your best hope for enjoying a walk through the jungle lies in employing a trained and knowledgeable guide. (By the way, if it's been raining a lot and the trails are muddy, a good pair of rubber boots comes in handy. These are usually provided by the lodges or at the sites, where necessary.)

Here are a few helpful hints:

- **Listen.** Pay attention to rustling in the leaves; whether it's monkeys up above or *pizotes* on the ground, you're most likely to hear an animal before seeing one.

- **Keep quiet.** Noise will scare off animals and prevent you from hearing their movements and calls.

- **Don't try too hard.** Soften your focus and allow your peripheral vision to take over. This way you can catch glimpses of motion and then focus in on the prey.

- **Bring binoculars.** It's also a good idea to practice a little first to get the hang of them. It would be a shame to be fiddling around and staring into space while everyone else in your group oohs and aahs over a quetzal.

- **Dress appropriately.** You'll have a hard time focusing your binoculars if you're busy swatting mosquitoes. Light, long pants and long-sleeved shirts are your best bet. Comfortable hiking boots are a real boon, except where heavy rubber boots are necessary. Avoid loud colors; the better you blend in with your surroundings, the better your chances are of spotting wildlife.

○ **Be patient.** The jungle isn't on a schedule. However, your best shots at seeing forest fauna are in the very early morning and late afternoon hours.

○ **Read up.** Familiarize yourself with what you're most likely to see. Most nature lodges and hotels have a copy of a few wildlife field guides, although it's always best to have your own. A good all-around book to use is Carrol Henderson's "The Field Guide to the Wildlife of Costa Rica."

RESPONSIBLE TOURISM

Costa Rica is one of the planet's prime ecotourism destinations. Many of the hotels, isolated nature lodges, and tour operators around the country are pioneers and dedicated professionals in the sustainable tourism field. Many other hotels, lodges, and tour operators are honestly and earnestly jumping on the bandwagon and improving their practices, while still others are simply "green-washing," using the terms "eco," "green," and "sustainable" in their promo materials, but doing little real good in their daily operations.

In 2014, Costa Rica was ranked 54th globally in the Environmental Performance Index (EPI; http://epi.yale.edu). This was a huge drop from just 2 years earlier when they were ranked fifth. Despite its reputation, the substantial amount of good work being done, and ongoing advances being made in the field, Costa Rica is by no means an ecological paradise free from environmental and social threats. Untreated sewage is dumped into rivers, bays, oceans, and watersheds at an alarming rate. Child labor and sexual exploitation are rampant, and certain sectors of the tourism trade only make these matters worse.

Over the last decade or so, Costa Rica has taken great strides toward protecting its rich biodiversity, however. Thirty years ago, it was difficult to find a protected area anywhere, but now more than 11% of the country is protected within the national park system. Another 10 to 15% of the land enjoys moderately effective preservation as part of private and public reserves, Indian reserves, and wildlife refuges and corridors. Still, Costa Rica's precious tropical hardwoods continue to be harvested at an alarming rate, often illegally, while other primary forests are clear-cut for short-term agricultural gain. Many experts predict that Costa Rica's unprotected forests could be gone within the early part of this century.

Recycling is beginning to gather momentum in Costa Rica. More and more you will see separate bins for plastics, glass, and paper on town and city streets, at national parks, and at the country's more sustainable hotels and restaurants. Your hotel will be your best bet for finding a place to deposit recyclable waste, especially if you choose a hotel that has instituted sustainable practices.

While you can find hotels and tour operators using comprehensive sustainable practices all across Costa Rica—even in the San José metropolitan area—a few prime destinations are particular hot spots for sustainable tourism practices. Of note are the remote and wild Osa Peninsula and Golfo Dulce area of southern Costa Rica, the rural northern zone that includes both Monteverde and the Arenal Volcano and Lake Arenal attractions, and the underdeveloped Caribbean coast, with the rainforest canals of Tortuguero, Cahuita National Park, and the Manzanillo-Gandoca Wildlife Refuge.

In addition to focusing on wildlife viewing and adventure activities in the wild, ecolodges in these areas tend to be smaller, often lacking televisions, air-conditioning, and other typical luxury amenities. The more remote lodges usually depend largely or entirely on small solar and hydro plants for their power consumption. That said, some of these hotels and lodges provide levels of comfort and service that are quite luxurious.

In Costa Rica, the government-run tourism institute (ICT) provides a sustainability rating of a host of hotels and tour agencies under its **Certificate of Sustainable Tourism Program (CST).** You can look up the ratings at the website www.turismo-sostenible.co.cr.

Bear in mind that this program is relatively new and the list is far from comprehensive. Many hotels and tour operators in the country haven't completed the extensive review and rating process. Moreover, die-hard ecologists find some of these listings and the criteria used somewhat suspect. Still, this list and rating system is a good start, and is improving and evolving constantly.

A parallel program, **"The Blue Flag,"** is used to rate specific beaches and communities in terms of their environmental condition and practices. The Blue Flags are reviewed and handed out annually. Current listings of Blue Flag–approved beaches and communities can be found at www.visitcostarica.com.

See individual chapters for recommendations on the hotels and lodges that I consider leaders in sustainable tourism practices in Costa Rica. As I mentioned earlier, more and more hotels are continuing to adopt sustainable and ethical tourism practices. Please supplement my recommendations with your own online research, and sites such as the CST's, mentioned above.

While sustainable tourism options are widespread in Costa Rica, organic and sustainably grown fruits and vegetables (as well as coffee) are just beginning to become available. Very few restaurants feature organic produce, although that is starting to change.

If you're not booking your hotel, tours, and transportation by yourself, you might want to consider using a tour agency that has earned high marks in this area. In Costa Rica, **Horizontes** ★★, Calle 32 between avenidas 3 and 5 (✆ 888/786-8748 in the U.S. and Canada, or 2222-2022 in Costa Rica; www.horizontes.com), has garnered particularly high marks from several rating agencies and organizations. Other exemplary operators include **Costa Rica Expeditions** ★★ (✆ 2257-0766; www.costaricaexpeditions.com), **Costa Rica Sun Tours** ★ (✆ 866/271-6263 in the U.S. and Canada, or 2296-7757 in Costa Rica; www.crsuntours.com), and **Swiss Travel Service** (✆ 2282-4898; www.swisstravelcr.com).

In addition, those looking for a taste of what many consider "the real" Costa Rica should consider booking through **ACTUAR** ★★ (✆ 866/393-5889 in the U.S., or 2248-9470 in Costa Rica; www.actuarcostarica.com). This organization groups together a network of small, rural lodges and tour operators. In many cases, accommodations are quite rustic. Bunk beds and thin foam mattresses are common. However, all the hotels, lodges, and tour operators are small-scale and local. In many cases, they are family operations. If you want a true taste of typical, rural Costa Rica, traveling with ACTUAR is a great way to go.

Finally, another great way to make your tourism experience more sustainable is to volunteer. For specific information on volunteer options in Costa Rica, see "Study & Volunteer Programs," in chapter 4, "The Best Special-Interest Trips."

Beyond the country's hotels, tour operators, and volunteer options, it's worth noting here that the local commuter airline **Nature Air** (✆ 800/235-9272 in the U.S. and Canada, or 2299-6000; www.natureair.com) has been a pioneer in the field. In 2004, Nature Air became the first certified carbon-neutral airline on the planet, and it continues to supplement its own sustainable practices with contributions to reforestation and conservation programs.

COSTA RICAN WILDLIFE

For such a small country, Costa Rica is incredibly rich in biodiversity. With just .03% of the earth's landmass, the country is home to some 5% of its biodiversity. Whether you come to Costa Rica to check 100 or more species off your lifetime list, or just to check out of the rat race for a week or so, you'll be surrounded by a rich and varied collection of flora and fauna.

In many instances, the prime viewing recommendations should be understood within the reality of actual wildlife viewing. Most casual visitors and even many dedicated naturalists will never see a wild cat or kinkajou. However, anyone working with a good guide should be able to see a broad selection of Costa Rica's impressive flora and fauna. The information below is meant to be a selective introduction to some of what you might see.

Scores of good field guides are available; two of the best general guides are **"The Field Guide to the Wildlife of Costa Rica,"** by Carrol Henderson, and **"Costa Rica: Traveller's Wildlife Guides,"** by Les Beletsky. Bird-watchers will want to pick up one or both of the following two books: **"A Guide to the Birds of Costa Rica,"** by F. Gary Stiles and Alexander Skutch, and **"Birds of Costa Rica,"** by Richard Garrigues and Robert Dean. Other specialized guides to mammals, reptiles, insects, flora, and more are also available. Zona Tropical (www.zonatropical.net) is a Costa Rican-based publishing house that specializes in field guides and wildlife books.

See also "Bugs, Bites & Other Wildlife Concerns" in chapter 14.

FAUNA
Mammals

Costa Rica has nearly 250 species of mammals. Roughly half of these are bats. While it is very unlikely that you will spot a wildcat, you have good odds of catching a glimpse of a monkey, coatimundi, peccary, or sloth, and any number of bats.

Jaguar.

Jaguar (Panthera onca) This cat measures from 1 to 1.8m (3½–6 ft.) plus tail and is distinguished by its tan/yellowish fur with black spots. Often called simply *tigre* (tiger) in Costa Rica. Jaguars are classified as nocturnal, although some say it would be more accurate to describe them as crepuscular, most active in the periods around dawn and dusk. **Prime Viewing:** Major tracts of primary and secondary forest in Costa Rica, as well as some open savannas; the greatest concentration is in

Ocelot.

Corcovado National Park (p. 423) on the Osa Peninsula. However, jaguars are endangered and extremely hard to see in the wild.

Ocelot (Leopardus pardalis) Known as *manigordo,* or "fat paws," in Costa Rica, the tail of this small cat is longer than its rear leg, which makes for easy identification. Ocelots are mostly nocturnal, and they sleep in trees. **Prime Viewing:** Forests in all regions of Costa Rica, with the greatest concentration found on the Osa Peninsula.

Baird's Tapir (Tapirus bairdii) Known as the *danta* or *macho de monte,* Baird's Tapir is the largest land mammal in Costa Rica. An endangered species, tapirs are active both day and night, foraging along riverbanks, streams, and forest clearings. **Prime Viewing:** Tapirs can be found in wet forested areas, particularly on the Caribbean and south Pacific slopes.

Three-Toed Sloth (Bradypus variegates) The larger and more commonly sighted of Costa Rica's two sloth species, the three-toed sloth has long, coarse, brown-to-gray fur and a distinctive eye-band. Each foreleg has three long, sharp claws. Except for brief periods to defecate, these slow-moving creatures are entirely arboreal. **Prime Viewing:** Low- and middle-elevation forests in most of Costa Rica. While sloths can be found in a wide variety of trees, they are most commonly spotted in the relatively sparsely leaved Cecropia (see later in this chapter).

Mantled Howler Monkey (Alouatta palliate) Known locally as *mono congo,* the highly social mantled howler monkey grows to 56cm (22 in.) in size and often travels in groups of 10 to 30. The loud roar of the male can be heard as far as 1.6km (1 mile) away. **Prime Viewing:** Wet and dry forests across Costa Rica. Almost entirely arboreal, they tend to favor the higher reaches of the canopy.

Three-Toed Sloth.

Mantled Howler Monkey.

Red-Backed Squirrel Monkey.

Central American Spider Monkey.

Red-Backed Squirrel Monkey (Saimiri oerstedii)   The smallest and friskiest of Costa Rica's monkeys, the red-backed squirrel monkey, or *mono tití*, is also its most endangered. Active in the daytime, these monkeys travel in small to midsize groups. Squirrel monkeys do not have a prehensile (grasping) tail. **Prime Viewing:** Manuel Antonio National Park and Corcovado National Park.

Central American Spider Monkey (Ateles geoffroyi)   Known as both *mono araña* and *mono colorado* in Costa Rica, the spider monkey is one of the more acrobatic monkey species. A large monkey (64cm/25 in.) with brown or silvery fur, it has long thin limbs and a long prehensile tail. It is active both day and night, and travels in small to midsize bands or family groups. **Prime Viewing:** Wet and dry forests across Costa Rica.

Coatimundi (Nasua narica)   Known as *pizote* in Costa Rica, the raccoonlike coatimundi can adapt to habitat disturbances and is often spotted near hotels and nature lodges. Active both day and night, they are social animals, often found in groups of 10 to 20. Coatimundi are equally comfortable on the ground and in trees. **Prime Viewing:** Found in a variety of habitats across Costa Rica, from dry scrub to dense forests, on the mainland as well as the coastal islands.

Paca (Agouti paca)   The paca, known as *tepezquintle* in Costa Rica, is a nocturnal rodent that feeds on fallen fruit, leaves, and tubers it digs from the ground. It features dark brown to black fur on its back, usually with three to five rows of white spots. Its belly fur tends to be lighter in color. However, since this species is nocturnal, you're more likely to see its cousin, the diurnal agouti or *guatusa*, which in addition to being smaller, is of a lighter brown coloring, with no spots. **Prime Viewing:** Most often found near water throughout many habitats of Costa Rica, from river valleys to swamps to dense tropical forest.

Tayra (Eira Barbara)   Known as *tolumuco* or *gato de monte* in Costa Rica, this midsize rodent is in the weasel family. Tayras run from dark brown to black, with a brown to tan head and neck. Long and low to the ground, they have a long, bushy tail. **Prime Viewing:** Tayras are found across the country, in forests as well as plain areas, and in trees, as well as on the ground.

Collared Peccary (Tayassu tajacu)   Called *saíno* or *chancho de monte* in Costa Rica, the collared peccary is a black or brown piglike animal that travels in groups and has a strong musk odor. **Prime Viewing:** Low- and middle-elevation forests in most of Costa Rica.

Northern Tamandua (Tamandua Mexicana)   Also known as the collared anteater (*oso hormiguero* in Spanish), the Northern Tamandua grows up to 77cm (30 in.) long, not counting its thick tail, which can be as long as its body. It is active diurnally and nocturnally. **Prime Viewing:** Low- and middle-elevation forests in most of Costa Rica.

White-Faced Monkey (Cibus capucinus)   Known as both *mono cariblanca* and *mono capuchin* in Costa Rica, the white-faced or capuchin monkey is a midsize species (46cm/18 in.) with distinct white fur around its face, head, and forearms. It can be found in forests all around the country and often travels in large troops or family groups. **Prime Viewing:** Wet and dry forests across Costa Rica.

Birds

Costa Rica has more than 880 identified species of resident and migrant birds. The variety of habitats and compact nature of the country make it a major bird-watching destination.

Jabiru Stork (Jabiru mycteria) One of the largest birds in the world, this stork stands 1.5m (5 ft.) tall and has a wingspan of 2.4m (8 ft.) and a 30cm-long (1-ft.) bill. An endangered species, the jabiru is very rare, with only a dozen or so nesting pairs in Costa Rica. **Prime Viewing:** The wetlands of Palo Verde National Park and Caño Negro Wildlife Reserve are the best places to try to spot the jabiru stork. The birds arrive in Costa Rica from Mexico in November and fly north with the rains in May or June.

Keel-Billed Toucan (Ramphastos sulfuratus) The rainbow-colored canoe-shape bill and brightly colored feathers make the keel-billed toucan a favorite of bird-watching tours. The toucan can grow to about 51cm (20 in.) in length. Aside from its bill coloration, it is similar in shape and coloring to the chestnut-mandibled toucan. Costa Rica also is home to several smaller toucanet and aracari species. **Prime Viewing:** Lowland forests on the Caribbean and north Pacific slopes, up to 1,200m (4,000 ft.).

Scarlet Macaw (Ara macao) Known as *guacamaya* or *lapa* in Costa Rica, the scarlet macaw is a long-tailed member of the parrot family. It can reach 89cm (35 in.) in length, including its long pointed tail. The bird is endangered over most of its range, mainly because it is coveted as a pet. Its loud squawk and rainbow-colored feathers are quite distinctive. **Prime Viewing:** Carara National Park, Corcovado National Park, and Piedras Blancas National Park.

Resplendent Quetzal (Pharomchrus mocinno) Arguably the most spectacular bird in Central America, the Resplendent Quetzal, of the trogon family, can grow to 37cm (15 in.). The males are distinctive, with bright red chests, iridescent blue-green coats, yellow bills, and tail feathers that can reach another 76cm (30 in.) in length. The females lack the long tail feathers and have a duller beak and less pronounced red chest. **Prime Viewing:** High-elevation wet and cloud forests, particularly in the Monteverde Cloud Forest Biological Reserve and along the Cerro de la Muerte.

Jabiru Stork.

Keel-Billed Toucan.

Scarlet Macaw.

Magnificent Frigate Bird (Fregata magnificens) The magnificent frigate bird is a naturally agile flier, and it swoops (unlike other seabirds, it doesn't dive or swim) to pluck food from the water's surface—or more commonly, it steals catch from the mouths of other birds. **Prime Viewing:** Often seen soaring high overhead, along the shores and coastal islands of both coasts.

Montezuma's Oropendola (Psarocolius Montezuma) Montezuma's oropendola has a black head, brown body, a yellow-edged tail, a large black bill with an orange tip, and a blue patch under the eye. These birds build long, teardrop-shaped hanging nests, often found in large groups. They have several distinct loud calls, including one that they make while briefly hanging upside down. **Prime Viewing:** Low and middle elevations along the Caribbean slope, and some sections of eastern Guanacaste.

Scarlet Rumped Tanager (Ramphocelus costaricensis) With a striking scarlet red patch on its backside, this is one of the most commonly sighted tanagers in Costa Rica. It is known locally as *sargento* or *sangre de toro*. For true ornithologists, a reclassification has divided the Costa Rican scarlet rumped tanagers into two distinct species, Passerini's Tanager, which is found on the Caribbean slope and lowlands, and Cherrie's Tanager, which is found along the Pacific slope and lowlands. **Prime Viewing:** Throughout the country, in lowland and mid-elevation areas.

Osprey (Pandion haliatus) This large (.6m/2-ft.-tall, with a 1.8m/6-ft. wingspan) brownish bird with a white head is also known as *gavilan pescador*, or "fishing eagle." In flight, the osprey's wings "bend" backward. **Prime Viewing:** Found in lowland coastal areas and wetlands throughout Costa Rica; seen flying or perched in trees near water. A small population is resident year-round, although most are winter migrants, arriving September to October and departing April to May.

Violet Sabrewing (Campylopterus hemileucurus) The largest hummingbird found in Costa Rica, the violet sabrewing shines a deep purple when the sun strikes it right. Its

Resplendent Quetzal.

Magnificent Frigate Bird.

Montezuma's Oropendola.

beak is long, thick, and gently curving. **Prime Viewing:** Mid- and higher-elevation cloud forests and rainforests countrywide.

Roseate Spoonbill (Ajaia ajaja) The roseate spoonbill is a large water bird, pink or light red in color and with a large spoon-shaped bill. Also known as *garza rosada* (pink heron). The species almost became extinct in the United States because its pink wing feathers were used to make fans. **Prime Viewing:** Found in low-lying freshwater and saltwater wetlands nationwide, although rare along the Caribbean coast and plains. Common on the Pacific coast, north-central lowlands, and in the Golfo de Nicoya and Golfo Dulce areas.

Scarlet Rumped Tanager.

Cattle Egret (Bubulcus ibis) The cattle egret is a snow-white bird, with a yellow bill and irises, and black legs. It changes color for the breeding season: A yellowish buff color appears on the head, chest, and back, and a reddish hue emerges on the bill and legs. **Prime Viewing:** Found near cattle, or following tractors, throughout Costa Rica.

Osprey.

Boat-Billed Heron (Cochlearius cochlearius) The midsize boat-billed heron (about 51cm/20 in.) has a large black head, a large broad bill, and a rusty brown color. **Prime Viewing:** Throughout the country, near marshes, swamps, rivers, and mangroves.

Laughing Falcon (Herpetotheres cachinnans) The laughing falcon is also known as the *guaco* in Costa Rica. It gets its name from its loud, piercing call.

Violet Sabrewing.

This largish (56cm/22-in.) bird of prey's wingspan reaches an impressive 94cm (37 in.). It specializes in eating both venomous and nonvenomous snakes but will also hunt lizards and small rodents. **Prime Viewing:** Throughout the country, most commonly in lowland areas, near forest edges, grasslands, and farmlands.

Mealy Parrot (Amazona farinose) Called *loro* or *loro verde*, this large, vocal parrot is common in lowland tropical rainforests on both coasts. Almost entirely green, it has a touch of blue on the top of its head, and small red and blue accents on its wings. *Loro* means parrot, and *verde* means green, so you and locals alike may confuse this parrot with any number of other local species. **Prime Viewing:** Lowland rainforests on the Caribbean and Pacific coasts.

Ferruginous Pygmy Owl (Glaucidium brasilianum) Unlike most owls, this small (about 38cm/15-in.) grayish brown or reddish brown owl is most active during the day. **Prime Viewing:** In wooded areas, forest edges, and farmlands of low and middle elevations along the northern Pacific slope.

Clay-Colored Robin (Turdus grayi) In a country with such a rich variety of spectacularly plumaged bird species, this plain brown robin is an unlikely choice to be Costa Rica's national bird. However, it is extremely widespread and common, especially in urban areas of the Central Valley, and it has a wide range of pleasant calls and songs. Known locally as the *yiguirro*, it has uniform brown plumage, with a lighter brown belly and yellow bill. **Prime Viewing:** Low and middle elevations nationwide, especially in clearings, secondary forests, and amid human settlements.

Amphibians

Frogs and toads are actually some of the most beguiling, beautiful, and easy-to-spot residents of tropical forests. Of the 175 species of amphibians, a solid 85% are frogs.

Marine Toad (Bufo marinus) The largest toad in the Americas, the 20cm (8-in.) wart-covered marine toad is also known as the cane toad, or *sapo grande* (giant toad). Females are mottled in color, while males are uniformly brown. These voracious toads have been known to eat small mammals, other toads, lizards, and just about any insect within range. They have a very strong chemical defense mechanism. Glands spread across their back and behind their eyes secrete a powerful toxin when threatened. **Prime Viewing:** Despite the misleading name, this terrestrial toad is not found in marine environments, but can be found in forests and open areas throughout Costa Rica.

Red-Eyed Tree Frog (Agalychnis callidryas) The colorful 7.6cm (3-in.) red-eyed tree frog usually has a pale or dark green back, sometimes with white or yellow spots, with blue-purple patches and vertical bars on the body, orange hands and feet, and deep red eyes. This nocturnal amphibian is also known as the gaudy leaf frog or red-eyed tree frog. **Prime Viewing:** This arboreal amphibian is most frequently found on the undersides of broad leaves, in

Marine Toad.

Red-Eyed Tree Frog.

Green and Black Poison Dart Frog.

low- and middle-elevation wet forests throughout Costa Rica. If you don't find this beautiful, distinctive-looking frog in the wild, you will certainly see its image on T-shirts and postcards.

Green and Black Poison Dart Frog (Dendrobates auratus) Also called the harlequin poison dart frog, the small green and black poison dart frog ranges between 2.5 and 4cm (1–1¹/₂ in.) in length. It has distinctive markings of iridescent green mixed with deep black. **Prime Viewing:** On the ground, around tree roots, and under fallen logs, in low- and middle-elevation wet forests on the Caribbean and southern Pacific slopes.

Fer-de-Lance.

Reptiles

Costa Rica's 225 or so reptile species range from the frightening and justly feared fer-de-lance pit viper and massive American crocodile to a wide variety of less terrifying turtles and lizards. *Note:* Sea turtles are included in the "Sea Life" section below.

Mussurana.

Fer-de-Lance (Bothrops atrox) Known as *terciopelo* in Costa Rica, the aggressive fer-de-lance can grow to 2.4m (8 ft.) in length. Beige, brown, or black triangles flank either side of the head, while the area under the head is a vivid yellow. These snakes begin life as arboreal but become increasingly terrestrial as they grow older and larger. **Prime Viewing:** Predominantly lower elevation forests, but has spread to almost all regions up to 1,300m (4,265 ft.), including towns and cities in agricultural areas.

Tropical Rattlesnake.

Mussurana (Clelia clelia) This bluish black, brown, or grayish snake grows to 2.4m (8 ft.) in length. While slightly venomous, this snake has rear fangs and is of little danger to humans. In fact, it is prized and protected by locals, since its primary prey happens to be much more venomous pit vipers, like the fer-de-lance. **Prime Viewing:** Open forests, pastures, and farmlands across Costa Rica.

Basilisk.

American Crocodile.

Litter Skink.

Tropical Rattlesnake (Crotalus durissus) Known as *cascabel* in Costa Rica, this pit viper has a triangular head, a pronounced ridge running along the middle of its back, and (of course) a rattling tail. It can reach 1.8m (6 ft.) in length. **Prime Viewing:** Mostly found in low elevation dry forests and open areas of Guanacaste.

Basilisk (Basiliscus vittatus) The basilisk can run across the water's surface for short distances on its hind legs, holding its body almost upright; thus its alternate name, "Jesus Christ lizard." **Prime Viewing:** In trees and on rocks located near water in wet forests throughout the country.

American Crocodile (Crocodylus acutus) Although an endangered species, environmental awareness and protection policies have allowed the massive American crocodile to mount an impressive comeback in recent years. While these reptiles can reach lengths of 6.4m (21 ft.), most are much smaller, usually less than 4m (13 ft.). **Prime Viewing:** Near swamps, estuaries, large rivers, and coastal lowlands, countrywide. Guaranteed viewing from the bridge over the Tárcoles River, on the coastal highway to Jacó and Manuel Antonio.

Litter Skink (Sphenomorphus cherriei) This small, brown lizard has a proportionally large head and neck, and short legs. A black stripe extends off the back of its eyes and down its sides, with a yellowish area below. **Prime Viewing:** Common on the ground and in leaf litter of low- and middle-elevation forests throughout the country.

Boa Constrictor (Boa constrictor) Adult boa constrictors (*bécquer* in Costa Rica) average about 1.8 to 3m (6–10 ft.) in length and weigh over 27kg (60 lb.). Their coloration camouflages them. Look for patterns of cream, brown, gray, and black ovals and diamonds. **Prime Viewing:** Low- and middle-elevation wet and dry forests, countrywide. They often live in the rafters and eaves of homes in rural areas.

Green Iguana (Iguana iguana) Despite its name, the green iguana comes in a range of coloring. Individuals can vary in color, ranging from bright green to a dull grayish green, with quite a bit of red and orange mixed in. Predominantly arboreal, it often perches on a branch overhanging a river and will plunge into the water when threatened. **Prime Viewing:** All lowland regions of the country, living near rivers and streams, along both coasts.

Slender Anole (Anolis [norops] limifrons) This thin, olive-colored lizard can reach 5.1cm (2 in.) in length. There are some 25 related species of *anolis* or *norops* lizards. **Prime Viewing:** Lowland rainforests nationwide.

Sea Life

Boasting over 1,290km (780 miles) of shoreline on both the Pacific and Caribbean coasts, Costa Rica has a rich diversity of underwater flora and fauna.

Whale Shark (Rhincodon typus) Although the whale shark grows to lengths of 14m (45 ft.) or more, its gentle nature makes swimming with them a special treat for divers and snorkelers. **Prime Viewing:** Can occasionally be spotted off Isla del Caño, and more frequently off Isla del Coco.

Whale Shark.

Green Turtle (Chelonia mydas) A large sea turtle, the green turtle has a teardrop-shaped carapace that can range in color from dull green to dark brown. Adults reach some 1.5m (4.9 ft.) and weigh an average of 200kg (440 lb.). **Prime viewing:** Carribean coast around Tortuguero National Park, from July through mid-October, with August through September their peak period.

Green Turtle.

Leatherback Sea Turtle (Dermochelys coriacea) The world's largest sea turtle (reaching nearly 2.4m/8 ft. in length and weighing more than 544kg/1,200 lb.), the leatherback sea turtle is now an endangered species. Unlike most other turtle species, the leatherback's carapace is not a hard shell, but rather a thick, leathery skin. **Prime Viewing:** Playa Grande, near Tamarindo, is a prime nesting site from early October through mid-February; also nests off Tortuguero in much lesser numbers from February through June, peaking during the months of March and April.

Leatherback Sea Turtle.

Olive Ridley Sea Turtle (Lepidochelys olivacea) Also known as *tortuga lora*, the olive ridley sea turtle is the most common of Costa Rica's sea turtles, famous for its massive group nestings, or *arribadas*. **Prime Viewing:** Large *arribadas* occur from July through December, and to a lesser extent from

Olive Ridley Sea Turtle.

January through June. Playa Nancite in Santa Rosa National Park and Playa Ostional, north of Nosara, are the prime nesting sites.

Humpback Whale (Megaptera novae-angliae) The migratory humpbacked whale spends the winters in warm southern waters and has been increasingly spotted close to the shores of Costa Rica's southern Pacific coast. These mammals have black backs and whitish throat and chest areas. Females have been known to calve here. **Prime Viewing:** Most common in the waters off Drake Bay and Isla del Caño, from December through April.

Humpback Whale.

Bottle-Nosed Dolphin (Tursiops truncates) A wide tail fin, dark gray back, and light gray sides identify bottle-nosed dolphins. Dolphins grow to lengths of 3.7m (12 ft.) and weigh up to 635kg (1,400 lb.). **Prime Viewing:** Along both coasts and inside the Golfo Dulce.

Bottle-Nosed Dolphins.

Moray Eel (Gymnothorax mordax) Distinguished by a swaying serpent-head and teeth-filled jaw that continually opens and closes, the moray eel is most commonly seen with only its head appearing from behind rocks. At night, however, it leaves its home along the reef to hunt for small fish, crustaceans, shrimp, and octopus. **Prime Viewing:** Rocky areas and reefs off both coasts.

Manta Ray (Manta birostris) The manta is the largest species of ray, with a wingspan that can reach 6m (20 ft.) and a body weight known to exceed 1,360kg (3,000 lb.). Despite its daunting appearance, the manta is quite gentle. If you are snorkeling or diving, watch for one of these extraordinary and graceful creatures. **Prime Viewing:** All along the Pacific coast.

Brain Coral (Diploria strigosa) The distinctive brain coral is named for its striking physical similarity to a human brain. **Prime Viewing:** Reefs off both coasts.

Invertebrates

Creepy-crawlies, biting bugs, spiders, and the like give most folks the chills. But this group, which includes moths, butterflies, ants, beetles, bees, and even crabs, features some of the most abundant, fascinating, and easily viewed fauna in Costa Rica. In fact, Costa Rica has over 300,000 recorded species of invertebrates, with more than 9,000 species of butterflies and moths alone.

Blue Morpho.

Blue Morpho (Morpho peleides) The large blue morpho butterfly, with a wingspan of up to 15cm (6 in.), has brilliantly iridescent blue wings when opened. Fast and erratic fliers, they are often glimpsed flitting across your peripheral vision in dense forest. **Prime Viewing:** Countrywide, particularly in moist environments.

Leafcutter Ants.

Leafcutter Ants (Atta cephalotes) You can't miss the miniature rainforest highways formed by these industrious red ants carrying their freshly cut payload. The ants do not actually eat the leaves, but instead feed off a fungus that grows on the decomposing leaves in their massive underground nests. **Prime Viewing:** Can be found in most forests countrywide.

Golden Silk Orb-Weaver.

Golden Silk Orb-Weaver (Nephila clavipes) The common Neotropical golden silk spider weaves meticulous webs that can be as much as .5m (2 ft.) across. The adult female of this species can reach 7.6cm (3 in.) in length, including the legs, although the males are tiny. The silk of this spider is extremely strong and is being studied for industrial purposes. **Prime Viewing:** Lowland forests on both coasts.

Mouthless Crab.

Mouthless Crab (Gecarcinus quadratus) The nocturnal mouthless crab is a distinctively colored land crab with bright orange legs, purple claws, and a deep black shell or carapace. **Prime Viewing:** All along the Pacific coast.

Sally Lightfoot Crab.

Sally Lightfoot Crab (Grapsus grapsus) Known simply as *cangrego* or "crab," this is the most common crab spotted in Costa Rica. It is a midsize crab with a colorful carapace that can range from dark brown to deep red to bright yellow, with a wide variation in striations and spotting. **Prime Viewing:** On rocky outcroppings near the water's edge all along both coasts.

FLORA
Trees

Despite the idiom to the contrary, it's often a good thing to be able to identify specific trees within a forest. The following are some of the more prominent and important tree species you are likely to see in Costa Rica.

Ceiba (Ceiba pentandra) Also known as the kapok tree, the ceiba tree is typically emergent (its large umbrella-shape crown emerges above the forest canopy), reaching as high as 60m (197 ft.); it is among the tallest trees of Costa Rica's tropical forest. The ceiba tree has a thick columnar trunk, often with large buttresses. Sometimes called the silk cotton tree in English, the ceiba's seed pod produces a light, airy fiber that is resilient, buoyant, and insulating. Throughout history this fiber has been used for bedding, and as stuffing for pillows, clothing, and even life jackets. Ceiba trees may flower as infrequently as once every 5 years, especially in wetter forests. **Prime Viewing:** Tropical forests throughout Costa Rica.

Guanacaste (Enterolobium cyclocarpum) The Guanacaste gives its name to Costa Rica's northwestern-most province, and is the country's national tree. With a broad and pronounced crown, the Guanacaste can reach heights of over 39m (130 ft.), and its trunk can measure more than 1.8m (6 ft.) in diameter. Guanacaste is prized as a shade tree, and is often planted on pasture lands to provide relief to cattle from the hot tropical sun. **Prime Viewing:** Low elevation forests and plains throughout Costa Rica. Most commonly viewed in the open plains and savannas of Guanacaste.

Strangler Fig (Ficus aurea) This parasitic tree gets its name from the fact that it envelops and eventually strangles its host tree. The *matapalo*, or strangler fig, begins as an epiphyte, whose seeds are deposited high in a tree's canopy by

Ceiba.

Guanacaste.

Strangler Fig.

COSTA RICA'S NATURAL WORLD

Flora

bats, birds, or monkeys. The young strangler then sends long roots down to the earth. The sap is used to relieve burns. **Prime Viewing:** Primary and secondary forests countrywide.

Cecropia (Cecropia obtusifolia) Several Cecropia (trumpet tree) species are found in Costa Rica. Most are characterized by large, handlike clusters of broad leaves, and a hollow, bamboolike trunk. They are "gap specialists," fast-growing opportunists that can fill in a gap caused

Cecropia.

by a tree fall or landslide. Their trunks are usually home to Aztec ants. **Prime Viewing:** Primary and secondary forests, rivers, and roadsides, countrywide.

Gumbo Limbo (Bursera simaruba) The bark of the gumbo limbo is its most distinguishing feature: A paper-thin red outer layer, when peeled off the tree, reveals a bright green bark. In Costa Rica, the tree is called *indio desnudo* (naked Indian). In other countries, it is the "tourist tree." Both names refer to its reddish, flaking outer bark. The bark is used as a remedy for gum disease; gumbo limbo–bark tea allegedly alleviates hypertension. **Prime Viewing:** Primary and secondary forests, countrywide.

Flowers & Other Plants

Costa Rica has an amazing wealth of tropical flora, including some 1,200 orchid species, and over 2,000 bromeliad species.

Guaria Morada (Cattleya skinneri) The guaria morada orchid is the national flower of Costa Rica. Sporting a purple and white flower, this plant is also called the "Easter orchid" as it tends to flower between March and April each year. **Prime Viewing:** Countrywide from sea level to 1,220m (4,000 ft.). While usually epiphytic, it also is found as a terrestrial plant.

Guaria Morada.

Heliconia.

Heliconia (Heliconia collinsiana) More than 40 of the world's species of tropical heliconia are found in Costa Rica. The flowers of this species are darkish pink in color, and the underside of the plant's large leaves are coated in white wax. **Prime Viewing:** Low to middle elevations countrywide, particularly in moist environments.

Hotlips (Psychotria poeppigiana) Related to coffee, hotlips is a forest flower that boasts thick red "lips" that resemble the Rolling Stones logo. The small white flowers (found inside the red "lips") attract a variety of butterflies and hummingbirds. **Prime Viewing:** In the undergrowth of dense forests countrywide.

Ornamental Red Ginger (Alpinia purpurata) The red ginger plant has an impressive elongated red bract, often mistaken for the flower. Small white flowers actually emerge out of this bract. Originally a native to Indonesia, it is now quite common in Costa Rica, and is used as both an ornamental plant and cut flower. **Prime Viewing:** Countrywide, particularly in moist environments and gardens.

Poor Man's Umbrella (Gunnera insignis) The poor man's umbrella, a broad-leaved rainforest ground plant, is a member of the rhubarb family. The massive leaves are often used, as the colloquial name suggests, for protection during rainstorms. **Prime Viewing:** Low- to middle-elevation moist forests countrywide. Commonly seen in Poás National Park and Braulio Carrillo National Park.

Hotlips.

Red Ginger.

Poor Man's Umbrella.

5

THE BEST SPECIAL-INTEREST TRIPS

A ctive and adventure travelers will have their hands full and hearts pumping in Costa Rica. While it's possible to stay clean and dry, most visitors want to spend at least some time getting their hair wet, their feet muddy, and their adrenaline flowing. Opportunities range from bird-watching to scuba diving to kiteboarding, and beyond. Other special-interest options for visitors to Costa Rica include language learning programs, volunteer opportunities, and medical and dental tourism trips.

This chapter lays out your options, from tour operators who run multiactivity package tours that often include stays at ecolodges, to the best places in Costa Rica to pursue active endeavors (with listings of tour operators, guides, and outfitters that specialize in each). I also list some educational and volunteer travel options for those of you who desire to actively contribute to the country's social welfare, or assist Costa Rica in the maintenance and preservation of its natural wonders. For information on Costa Rica's top national parks and private reserves, see p. 67.

ORGANIZED ADVENTURE TRIPS

Because many travelers have limited time and resources, organized ecotourism or adventure-travel packages, arranged by tour operators in either Costa Rica or the United States, are a popular way of combining several activities. Bird-watching, horseback riding, rafting, and hiking can be teamed with, say, visits to Monteverde Cloud Forest Biological Reserve and Manuel Antonio National Park.

Traveling with a group has several advantages over traveling independently: Your accommodations and transportation are arranged, and most (if not all) meals are included in the package cost. If your tour operator has a reasonable amount of experience and a decent track record, you should proceed to each of your destinations quickly without snags and long delays. You'll also have the opportunity to meet like-minded souls who are interested in nature and active sports. Of course, you'll pay more for the convenience of having all your arrangements handled in advance.

In the best cases, group size is kept small (10–20 people), and tours are escorted by knowledgeable guides who are either naturalists or biologists. Be sure to ask about difficulty levels when you're choosing a tour. Most companies offer "soft adventure" packages that those in moderately good, but not phenomenal, shape can handle; others focus on more hard-core activities geared toward only seasoned athletes or adventure travelers.

Costa Rican Tour Agencies

Because many U.S.-based companies subcontract portions of their tours to established Costa Rican companies, some travelers like to cut out the middleman and set up their tours directly with these companies. That means that these packages are often less expensive than those offered by U.S. companies, but it doesn't mean they are cheap. You're still paying for the convenience of having your arrangements handled for you.

Scores of agencies in San José offer a plethora of options. These agencies can arrange everything from white-water rafting to sightseeing at one of the nearby volcanoes or a visit to a butterfly farm. Although it's generally quite easy to arrange a day trip at the last minute, other tours are offered only on set dates or when enough people are interested. Contact a few of the companies before you leave home and find out what they might be doing when you arrive. These local operators tend to be a fair share less expensive than their international counterparts, with 10-day tours generally costing in the neighborhood of $1,500 to $4,000 per person, not including airfare to Costa Rica.

ACTUAR ★★ (✆ 866/393-5889 in the U.S., or 2290-7514 in Costa Rica; www.actuarcostarica.com) is a great option for budget travelers and anyone looking to get a taste of real, rural Costa Rica. These folks bring together a network of small, rural lodges and tour operators. In many cases, accommodations are quite rustic. Bunk beds and thin foam mattresses are common. However, all the hotels, lodges, and tour operators are small-scale and local. In many cases, they are family operations.

Coast to Coast Adventures ★ (✆ 2280-8054; www.ctocadventures.com) has a unique excursion involving no motor vehicles. The company's namesake 12-day trip spans the country, with participants traveling on rafts, by mountain bike, and on foot. Custom-designed trips (with a minimum of motorized transport) of shorter duration are also available. They also offer family-friendly adventure tours and student tours.

Costa Rica Expeditions ★★ (✆ 2257-0766; www.costaricaexpeditions.com) offers everything from 10-day tours covering the entire country to 3-day/2-night and 2-day/1-night tours of Monteverde Cloud Forest Biological Reserve and Tortuguero National Park, where they run their own lodges. It also offers 1- to 2-day white-water rafting trips and other excursions. Its tours are some of the most expensive in the country, but it is the most consistently reliable outfitter as well (and its customer service is excellent). If you want to go out on your own, Costa Rica Expeditions can supply you with just transportation from place to place.

Costa Rica Sun Tours ★ (✆ 866/271-6263 in the U.S. and Canada, or 2296-7757 in Costa Rica; www.crsuntours.com) offers a wide range of tours and adventures and specializes in multiday tours that include stays at small country lodges for travelers interested in experiencing nature.

Horizontes ★★, Calle 32 between avenidas 3 and 5 (✆ 888/786-8748 in the U.S. and Canada, or 2222-2022 in Costa Rica; www.horizontes.com), is not a specifically adventure-oriented operator, but it offers a wide range of individual, group, and package tours, including those geared toward active and adventure travelers, as well families and even honeymooners. The company hires responsible and knowledgeable guides, and is a local leader in sustainable tourism practices.

International Tour Operators

These agencies and operators specialize in well-organized and coordinated tours. Many travelers prefer to have everything arranged and confirmed before arriving in Costa Rica, and this is a good idea for first-timers and during the high season. *Be warned:* Most of these operators are not cheap, with 10-day tours generally costing in the neighborhood of $3,000 to $5,000 per person, not including airfare to Costa Rica.

U.S.-BASED TOUR OPERATORS

Abercrombie & Kent ★★ (© 800/554-7016; www.abercrombiekent.com) is a luxury-tour company that offers upscale trips around the globe, and it has several tours of Costa Rica on its menu. It specializes in 8-day highlight tours hitting Monteverde, Arenal, and Tortuguero, and also has an excellent family tour. Service is personalized and the guides are top-notch.

Costa Rica Experts ★ (© 800/827-9046 or 773/935-1009; www.costaricaexperts.com) offers a large menu of a la carte and scheduled departures, as well as day trips and adventure packages, and has decades of experience organizing tours to the country.

Nature Expeditions International ★ (© 800/869-0639; www.naturexp.com) specializes in educational and "low intensity adventure" trips tailored to independent travelers and small groups. These folks have a steady stream of programmed departures or can customize a trip to your needs.

Overseas Adventure Travel ★★ (© 800/955-1925; www.oattravel.com) provides good-value natural-history and "soft adventure" itineraries with optional add-on excursions. Tours are limited to 16 people and are guided by naturalists. All accommodations are in small hotels, lodges, or tent camps, and they offer up very good bang for your buck.

Southern Explorations ★ (© 877/784-5400; www.southernexplorations.com) has a range of nature and adventure-oriented guided excursions, as well as set itinerary self-guided tours, for individuals, groups, and families.

Tauck ★★ (© 800/788-7885; www.tauck.com) is a soft-adventure company catering to higher-end travelers. They offer various Costa Rica options, including a family tour, and Costa Rica–Panama Canal package.

In addition to these companies, many environmental organizations, including the **Sierra Club** (© 415/977-5522; www.sierraclub.org) and the **Smithsonian Institute** (© 855/330-1542; www.smithsonianjourneys.org), regularly offer organized trips to Costa Rica.

U.K.-BASED TOUR OPERATORS

Imaginative Traveller (© 44/1728-885-561 outside the U.K., www.imaginative-traveller.com) is a good-value operator specializing in budget student, group, and family travel. Their offerings in Costa Rica focus on nature and adventure travel, and often include other countries in Central America. These trips range in duration from 12 to 32 days.

Journey Latin America ★ (© 020/3603-8045 in the U.K., www.journeylatinamerica.co.uk) is a large British operator specializing in Latin American travel. They offer a range of escorted tours around Latin America, including a few that touch down in Costa Rica. They also design custom itineraries, and often have excellent deals on airfare.

PLANNING A COSTA RICAN wedding

Getting married in Costa Rica is simple and straightforward. In most cases, all you need are current passports. You'll have to provide some basic information, including a copy of each passport, your dates of birth, your occupations, your current addresses, and the names and addresses of your parents. Two witnesses are required to be present at the ceremony. If you're traveling alone, your hotel or wedding consultant will provide the required witnesses.

Things are slightly more complicated if one or both partners were previously married. In such a case, the previously married partner must provide an official copy of the divorce decree.

Most travelers who get married in Costa Rica do so in a civil ceremony officiated by a local lawyer. After the ceremony, the lawyer records the marriage with Costa Rica's National Registry, which issues an official marriage certificate. This process generally takes between 4 and 6 weeks. Most lawyers or wedding coordinators then have the document translated and certified by the Costa Rican Foreign Ministry and at the embassy or consulate of your home country within Costa Rica before mailing it to you. From here, it's a matter of bringing this document to your local civil or religious authorities, if necessary.

Because Costa Rica is more than 90% Roman Catholic, arranging for a church wedding is usually easy in all but the most isolated and remote locations. To a lesser extent, a variety of denominational Christian churches and priests are often available to perform or host the ceremony. If you're Jewish, Muslim, Buddhist, or a follower of some other religion, bringing your own officiant is a good idea.

Tip: Officially, the lawyer must read all or parts of the Costa Rican civil code on marriage during your ceremony. This is a rather uninspired and somewhat dated legal code that, at some weddings, can take as much as 20 minutes to slog through. Most lawyers and wedding coordinators are quite flexible and can work with you to design a ceremony and text that fits your needs and desires. Insist on this.

Most of the higher-end and romantic hotels in Costa Rica have ample experience in hosting weddings. Many have an in-house wedding planner. Narrowing the list is tough, but I'd say the top choices include **Hotel Punta Islita** (p. 285), **Villa Caletas** (p. 357), **Makanda by the Sea** (p. 382), **Florblanca Resort** (p. 276), and the **Four Seasons Resort** (p. 213). If you want a remote, yet luxurious, rainforest lodge to serve as host and backdrop, try **La Paloma Lodge** (p. 417), **Bosque del Cabo Rainforest Lodge** (p. 429), or **Lapa Ríos** (p. 429).

If you're looking for service beyond what your hotel can offer, or if you want to do it yourself, check out www.weddings.co.cr, www.weddingscostarica.net, www.liquidweddings.com, www.costaricaweddingcelebrations.com, or www.tropicaloccasions.com.

ACTIVITIES A TO Z

Each listing in this section describes the best places to practice a particular sport or activity and lists tour operators and outfitters. If you want to focus on only one active sport during your Costa Rican stay, these companies are your best bets for quality equipment and knowledgeable service.

Adventure activities and tourism, by their very nature, carry certain risks and dangers. Over the years, there have been several deaths and dozens of minor injuries in activities ranging from mountain biking to white-water rafting to canopy tours. Here, I try to list only the most reputable and safest of companies. However, if you ever have any doubt as to the safety of the guide, equipment, or activity, it's better to be safe than sorry. Moreover, know your limits and abilities, and don't try to exceed them.

Biking

Costa Rica has several significant regional and international touring races each year, but as a general rule the major roads are dangerous and inhospitable for cyclists. Roads are narrow and without a shoulder, and most drivers show little care or consideration for those on two wheels. The options are much more appealing for mountain bikers and off-track riders. If you plan to do a lot of biking and are very attached to your rig, bring your own. However, several companies in San José and elsewhere rent bikes, and the quality of the equipment is improving all the time. I list rental shops in each of the regional chapters that follow.

The area around **Lake Arenal** and **Arenal Volcano** wins my vote as the best place for mountain biking in Costa Rica. The scenery's great, with primary forests, waterfalls, and plenty of trails. And the hot springs at nearby Tabacón Grand Spa Thermal Resort are a perfect place for those with aching muscles to unwind at the end of the day. However, the new **Rio Perdido** ★★ (© **2673-3600;** www.rioperdido.com) offers many of the same attractions, including incredible hot springs. But it also features the country's best specifically designed and built mountain bike park, with an extensive network of trails and different level circuits. See chapters 8 & 10 for full details.

TOUR OPERATORS & OUTFITTERS

Bike Arenal ★ (© **866/465-4114** in the U.S. and Canada, or 2479-7150; www.bikearenal.com) is based in La Fortuna and specializes in 1-day and multi-day trips around the Arenal area.

Coast to Coast Adventures ★ (© **2280-8054;** www.ctocadventures. com) offers mountain-biking itineraries among its many tour options.

Lava Tours (© **8836-8258;** www.lava-tours.com) conducts a variety of fixed-date-departure and custom mountain-bike tours all over Costa Rica.

Serendipity Adventures ★ (© **877/507-1358** in the U.S. and Canada, or 2556-5852 in Costa Rica; www.serendipityadventures.com) offers several mountain-biking trips among its many other expeditions.

Ruta de los Conquistadores

Each year, Costa Rica hosts what many consider to be the most challenging and grueling mountain-bike race on the planet. **La Ruta de los Conquistadores** (The Route of the Conquerors; www. adventurerace.com) retraces the path of the 16th-century Spanish conquistadores from the Pacific Coast to the Caribbean Sea—all in 4 days. The race usually takes place in mid-November, and draws hundreds of competitors from around the world.

Bird-Watching

With more than 850 species of resident and migrant birds identified throughout the country, Costa Rica abounds with great bird-watching sites. Lodges with the best bird-watching include **Savegre Lodge,** in Cerro de la Muerte, off the road to San Isidro de El General (quetzal sightings are almost guaranteed); **La Paloma Lodge** in Drake Bay, where you can sit on the porch of your cabin as the avian parade goes by; **Arenal Observatory Lodge,** on the flanks of Arenal Volcano; **La Selva Biological Station,** in Puerto Viejo de Sarapiquí; **Aviarios del Caribe** and **Selva Bananito Lodge,** both just north of Cahuita; **Lapa Ríos** and **Bosque del Cabo,** on the Osa Peninsula; **Playa Nicuesa Rainforest Lodge,** along the Golfo Dulce; **La Laguna del Lagarto Lodge,** up by the Nicaraguan border; and **Tiskita Lodge,** down by the Panamanian border.

Some of the best parks and preserves for serious birders are **Monteverde Cloud Forest Biological Reserve** (for Resplendent Quetzals and hummingbirds); **Corcovado National Park** (for scarlet macaws); **Caño Negro Wildlife Refuge** (for wading birds, including jabiru storks); **Wilson Botanical Gardens** and **Las Cruces Biological Station,** near San Vito (the thousands of flowering plants here are bird magnets); **Guayabo, Negritos,** and **Pájaros Islands biological reserves** in the Gulf of Nicoya (for magnificent frigate birds and brown boobies); **Palo Verde National Park** (for ibises, jacanas, storks, and roseate spoonbills); **Tortuguero National Park** (for great green macaws); and **Rincón de la Vieja National Park** (for parakeets and curassows). Rafting trips down the **Corobicí and Bebedero rivers** near Liberia, boat trips to or at **Tortuguero National Park,** and hikes in any cloud forest also provide good bird-watching opportunities.

In San José, your best bets are to head toward the lush grounds and gardens of the **University of Costa Rica,** or to **Parque del Este,** a little farther east in the foothills just outside of town.

COSTA RICAN TOUR AGENCIES

Costa Rica Expeditions ★★ (℅ **2221-6099;** www.costaricaexpeditions. com) and **Costa Rica Sun Tours** ★ (℅ **866/271-6263** in the U.S. and Canada, or 2296-7757 in Costa Rica; www.crsuntours.com) are well-established companies with very competent and experienced guides who offer a variety of tours to some of the better birding spots in Costa Rica.

INTERNATIONAL TOUR OPERATORS

Costa Rican Bird Route ★★ (℅ **608/698-3448** in the U.S. and Canada; www.costaricanbirdroute.com) is a bird-watching and conservation effort that has created several bird-watching specific itineraries, which they offer up as guided tours, or self-guided adventures.

Field Guides (℅ **800/728-4953** in the U.S. and Canada; www.field guides.com) is a specialty bird-watching travel operator. Its 16-day tour of Costa Rica covers a lot of ground, and group size is limited to 12 participants.

Tropical Birding ★ (℅ **800/348-5941** in the U.S. and Canada; www. tropicalbirding.com), specializing in birding tours around the world, happens to be based in Ecuador. These folks excel at small group tours, with highly skilled guides, and run periodic trips to Costa Rica.

Victor Emanuel Nature Tours ★★ (℅ **800/328-8368** in the U.S. and Canada; www.ventbird.com) is a well-respected, longstanding small group tour operator specializing in bird-watching trips.

WHERE TO SEE THE resplendent quetzal

Revered by pre-Columbian cultures throughout Central America, the Resplendent Quetzal has been called the most beautiful bird on earth. Ancient Aztec and Maya Indians believed that the robin-size quetzal protected them in battle. The males of this species have brilliant red breasts; iridescent emerald green heads, backs, and wings; and white tail feathers complemented by a pair of iridescent green tail feathers that are more than .5m (1³/₄ ft.) long.

The belief that these endangered birds live only in the dense cloud forests cloaking the higher slopes of Central America's mountains was instrumental in bringing many areas of cloud forest under protection as quetzal habitats. (Since then, researchers have discovered that the birds do not, in fact, spend their entire lives here.) After nesting between March and July, Resplendent Quetzals migrate down to lower slopes in search of food. These lower slopes have not been preserved in most cases, and now conservationists are trying to salvage enough lower-elevation forests to help the quetzals survive.

Although for many years **Monteverde Cloud Forest Biological Reserve** was *the* place to see quetzals, throngs of people crowding the reserve's trails now make the pursuit more difficult. Other places where you can see quetzals are in the **Los Angeles Cloud Forest Reserve** near San Ramón, in **Tapantí National Wildlife Refuge,** and in **Chirripó National Park.** Perhaps the best place to spot a quetzal is at one of the specialized lodges located along the **Cerro de la Muerte** between San José and San Isidro de El General.

WINGS ★ (© 866/547-9868 in the U.S. and Canada; www.wingsbirds.com) is a specialty bird-watching travel operator with more than 30 years of field experience. Group size is usually between 4 and 16 people.

Camping

Heavy rains, difficult access, and limited facilities make camping a challenge in Costa Rica. Nevertheless, a backpack and tent will get you far from the crowds and into some of the most pristine and undeveloped nooks and crannies of the country. Camping is forbidden in some national parks, so read the descriptions for each park carefully before you pack a tent.

If you'd like to participate in an organized camping trip, contact **Coast to Coast Adventures** ★ (© 2280-8054; www.ctoadventures.com) or **Serendipity Adventures** ★ (© 888/226-5050 in the U.S. and Canada, or 2556-2222 in Costa Rica; www.serendipityadventures.com).

In my opinion, the best places to pop up a tent on the beach are in **Santa Rosa National Park** and **Ballena Marine National Park.** The best camping trek is, without a doubt, a hike through **Corcovado National Park** or a climb up **Mount Chirripó.**

Canopy Tours

Canopy tours are all the rage in Costa Rica, largely because they are such an exciting and unique way to experience tropical rainforests. It's estimated that some two-thirds of a typical rainforest's species live in the canopy (the uppermost, branching layer of the forest). From the relative luxury of Rain Forest Aerial Tram's high-tech funicular to the rope-and-climbing-gear rigs of zip-line operations, a trip into the canopy will give you a bird's-eye view of a Neotropical forest. Canopy-tour operations are now in or close to nearly every major tourist destination in the country, including Monteverde, Manuel Antonio, La Fortuna, Tabacón, Montezuma, Punta Islita, Villablanca, and Rincón de la Vieja, as well as on Tortuga Island and around Guanacaste and the Osa Peninsula. See the individual destination chapters for specific recommendations on canopy tours around the country.

Most canopy tours involve strapping yourself into a climbing harness and being winched up to a platform some 30m (100 ft.) above the forest floor, or doing the work yourself. Many of these operations have a series of treetop platforms connected by taut cables. Once up on the first platform, you click your harness into a pulley and glide across the cable to the next (slightly lower) platform, using your hand (protected by a thick leather glove) as a brake. When you reach the last platform, you usually rappel down to the ground. (Don't worry—they'll teach even the most nervous neophyte.)

Although this can be a lot of fun, do be careful because these tours are popping up all over the place and there is precious little regulation of the activity. Some of the tours are set up by fly-by-night operators (I don't list any of those). Be especially sure that you feel comfortable and confident with the safety standards, guides, and equipment before embarking. Before you sign on to any tour, ask whether you have to hoist yourself to the top under your own steam, and then make your decision accordingly. Most canopy tours run between $45 and $65 per person.

Top Canopy Tours

Arenal Hanging Bridges, Arenal Volcano area (p. 303)

Canopy Safari, Manuel Antonio (p. 377)

Cartagena Canopy Tour, Northern beach area, Guanacaste (p. 241)

Chiclets Tree Tour, Playa Hermosa (p. 360)

Congo Trail Canopy Tour, Northern beach area, Guanacaste (p. 220)

Hacienda Guachipelín, Rincón de la Vieja, Guanacaste (p. 204)

Hacienda Pozo Azul, Puerto Viejo de Sarapiquí (p. 342)

Rainforest Aerial Tram Atlantic, en route to Puerto Viejo de Sarapiquí (p. 150)

Rio Perdido, Bagaces area, near the Miravalles Volcano (p. 203)

Selvatura Park, Monteverde area (p. 331)

Sky Adventure, Arenal Volcano area (p. 303) and Monteverde area (p. 332)

Vista Los Sueños Canopy Tour, Playa Herradura (p. 354)

Waterfall Canopy Tour, Montezuma (p. 268)

Witch's Rock Canopy Tour, Papagayo Peninsula, Guanacaste (p. 213)

monkey BUSINESS

No trip to Costa Rica would be complete without at least one monkey sighting. Home to four distinct species of primates, Costa Rica offers the opportunity for one of the world's most gratifying wildlife-viewing experiences. Just listen for the deep guttural call of a howler or the rustling of leaves overhead—telltale signs that monkeys are in your vicinity.

Costa Rica's most commonly spotted monkey is the white-faced or **capuchin monkey** (*mono cara blanca* in Spanish), which you might recognize as the infamous culprit from the film "Outbreak." Contrary to that film's plot, however, capuchins are native to the New World Tropics and do not exist in Africa. Capuchins are agile, medium-size monkeys that make good use of their long, prehensile tails. They inhabit a diverse collection of habitats, ranging from the high-altitude cloud forests of the central region to the lowland mangroves of the Osa Peninsula. It's almost impossible not to spot capuchins at Manuel Antonio (chapter 11), where they have become a little too dependent on fruit and junkfood feedings by tourists. Please do not feed wild monkeys (and try to keep your food away from them—they're notorious thieves), and boycott establishments that try to attract both monkeys and tourists with daily feedings.

Howler monkeys (*mono congo* in Spanish) are named for their distinct and eerie call. Large and mostly black, these monkeys can seem ferocious because of their physical appearance and deep, resonant howls that can carry for more than a mile, even in dense rainforest. Biologists believe that male howlers mark the bounds of their territories with these deep, guttural sounds. In the presence of humans, however, howlers are actually a little timid and tend to stay higher up in the canopy than their white-faced cousins. Howlers are fairly common and easy to spot in the dry tropical forests of coastal Guanacaste and the Nicoya Peninsula (see chapter 8).

Even more elusive are **spider monkeys** (*mono araña* in Spanish). These long, slender monkeys are dark brown to black and prefer the high canopies of primary rainforests. Spiders are very adept with their prehensile tails but actually travel through the canopy with a hand-over-hand motion frequently imitated by their less graceful human cousins on playground monkey bars around the world. I've had my best luck spotting spider monkeys along the edges of Tortuguero's jungle canals (see chapter 13), where howlers are also quite common.

The rarest and most endangered of Costa Rica's monkeys is the tiny **squirrel monkey** (*mono tití* in Spanish). These small, brown monkeys have dark eyes surrounded by large white rings, white ears, white chests, and very long tails. In Costa Rica, squirrel monkeys can be found only at Manuel Antonio (see chapter 11) and the Osa Peninsula (see chapter 12). These seemingly hyperactive monkeys are predominantly fruit eaters and often feed on bananas and other fruit trees near hotels in both of the above-mentioned regions. Squirrel monkeys usually travel in large bands, so if you do see them, you'll likely see quite a few.

THE BEST SPECIAL-INTEREST TRIPS

Activities A to Z

Canyoning Tours

Canyoning tours are even more adventurous than canopy tours. Hardly standardized, most involve hiking down along a mountain stream, river, and/or canyon, with periodic breaks to rappel down the face of a waterfall, or swim in a jungle pool. The best canyoning operations in Costa Rica are offered by **Pure Trek Canyoning ★★** (p. 304) and **Desafío Expeditions ★★** (p. 304), both in La Fortuna; **Explornatura ★★** (p. 187), in Turrialba; and **Psycho Tours ★★★** (p. 422), outside Puerto Jiménez. The latter is arguably my favorite adventure tour in the country.

Diving & Snorkeling

Many islands, reefs, caves, and rocks lie off the coast of Costa Rica, providing excellent spots for underwater exploration. Visibility varies with season and location. Generally, heavy rainfall tends to swell the rivers and muddy the waters, even well offshore. Rates run from $70 to $150 per person for a two-tank dive, including equipment, and $35 to $75 per person for snorkelers. Most of the dedicated dive operators listed throughout this book also offer certification classes.

Banana plantations and their runoff have destroyed most of the Caribbean reefs, although **Isla Uvita,** just off the coast of Limón, and **Manzanillo,** down near the Panamanian border, still have good diving. Most divers choose Pacific dive spots such as **Isla del Caño, Bat Island,** and the **Catalina Islands,** where you're likely to spot manta rays, moray eels, white-tipped sharks, and plenty of smaller fish and coral species. But the ultimate in Costa Rican dive experiences is 7 to 10 days on a chartered boat, diving off the coast of **Isla del Coco** (see "Diving Trips to Isla del Coco [Cocos Island]," on p. 259).

Snorkeling is not incredibly common or rewarding in Costa Rica. The rain, runoff, and wave conditions that drive scuba divers well offshore tend to make coastal and shallow-water conditions less than optimal. If the weather is calm and the water is clear, you might just get lucky. Ask at your hotel or check the different beach listings in this book to find snorkeling options and operators up and down Costa Rica's coasts. The best snorkeling experience to be had in Costa Rica is on the reefs off **Manzanillo Beach** in the southern Caribbean coast, particularly in the calm months of September and October.

DIVING OUTFITTERS & OPERATORS

In addition to the companies listed below, check the listings at specific beach and port destinations in the regional chapters.

Aggressor Fleet Limited ★★ (ⓒ 800/348-2628 in the U.S. and Canada; www.aggressor.com) runs the 36m (118-ft.) *Okeanos Aggressor* on regular trips out to Isla del Coco.

Diving Safaris de Costa Rica ★★ (ⓒ 2670-0603; www.costaricadiving.net) is perhaps the largest, most professional, and best-established dive operation in the country. Based out of Playa Hermosa, this outfitter is also a local pioneer in Nitrox diving.

Undersea Hunter ★★ (ⓒ 800/203-2120 in the U.S., or 2228-6613 in Costa Rica; www.undeerseahunter.com) offers the *Undersea Hunter* and its sister ship, the *Sea Hunter,* two pioneers of the live-aboard diving excursions to Isla del Coco.

Fishing

Anglers in Costa Rican waters have landed over 100 world-record catches, including blue marlin, Pacific sailfish, dolphin, wahoo, yellowfin tuna, *guapote*, and snook. Whether you want to head offshore looking for a big sail, wrestle a tarpon near a Caribbean river mouth, or choose a quiet spot on a lake to cast for *guapote*, you'll find it here. You can raise a marlin anywhere along the Pacific coast, while feisty snook can be found in mangrove estuaries along both coasts.

Many of the Pacific port and beach towns—Quepos, Puntarenas, Playa del Coco, Tamarindo, Flamingo, Golfito, Drake Bay, Zancudo—support large charter fleets and have hotels that cater to anglers; see chapters 7 and 9 to 12 for recommended boats, captains, and lodges. Fishing trips usually range between $400 and $2,500 per day (depending on boat size) for the boat, captain, tackle, drinks, and lunch, so the cost per person depends on the size of the group.

> ### Top Fishing Lodges
>
> **Aguila de Osa Inn,** Drake Bay (p. 417)
> **Río Colorado Lodge,** at the Barra del Colorado National Wildlife Refuge (p. 451)
> **Silver King Lodge,** at Barra del Colorado (p. 451)
> **Zancudo Lodge,** in Playa Zancudo (p. 435)

Costa Rican law requires all fishermen purchase a license. The cost is $30, and the license is good for 1 year from the date of purchase, and covers both saltwater and fresh-water fishing. All boats, captains, and fishing lodges listed here and throughout the book will help you with the technicalities of buying your license.

Costa Rica Outdoors ★ (�C 800/308-3394 in the U.S. and Canada or 2231-0306 in Costa Rica; www.costaricaoutdoors.com) is a well-established operation founded by local fishing legend and outdoor writer Jerry Ruhlow, specializing in booking fishing trips around the country.

Golfing

Costa Rica is not one of the world's great golfing destinations. Currently, seven regulation 18-hole courses are open to the public and visitors. These courses offer some stunning scenery, and almost no crowds. However, be prepared—strong seasonal winds make playing most of the Guanacaste courses very challenging from December through March.

The most spectacular course in Costa Rica is at **Four Seasons Resort ★★★** (p. 213), but it is open only to hotel guests. Greens fees run around $250.

Another very lovely option is the **Reserva Conchal** course **★★** at the **Westin Playa Conchal Resort & Spa** (p. 228) up in Guanacaste. Greens fees here are $150, including a cart. With advance notice and depending on available tee times, this course is currently open to guests.

Hacienda Pinilla ★★ (p. 242) is an 18-hole links-style course located south of Tamarindo. This might just be the most challenging course in the country, and the facilities, though limited, are top-notch. Currently, the course is open to golfers staying at hotels around the area, with advance reservations. Greens fees run around $185 for 18 holes, including a cart.

The **Papagayo Golf & Country Club ★** (p. 220), on the outskirts of Playa del Coco, offers up a full 18-hole course, with a pro shop, driving range, and rental equipment. It costs $100 in greens fees, including a cart.

Another major resort course is at the **Los Sueños Marriott Ocean & Golf Resort** ★★ in Playa Herradura (p. 356). Greens fees, including a cart, run around $169 for the general public, and guests pay slightly less.

Down along the Central Pacific coast, south of Dominical, the **San Buenas Golf Resort** (www.sbgr.com) has 18 holes. Greens fees, including a cart, run around $115.

Currently, the best option for golfers staying in and around San José is **Parque Valle del Sol** ★ (© 2282-9222; www.vallesol.com; p. 158), an 18-hole course in the western suburb of Santa Ana. Greens fees are $95, including a cart.

Golfers who want the most up-to-date information, or those who are interested in a package deal that includes play on a variety of courses, should contact **Costa Rica Golf Adventures** ★ (© 888/536-8510 in the U.S. and Canada; www.golfcr.com) or **Tee Times Costa Rica** (© 866/448-3182 in the U.S. and Canada; www.teetimescostarica.com).

Hang Gliding, Paragliding & Ballooning

Based out of Jacó, **Hang Glide Costa Rica** (© 8353-5514; www.hangglidecr.com) offers a half-hour of gentle hang gliding in a tandem rig, which begins with a tow by an ultralight, for $99 to $149 per person.

Paragliding is taking off (pardon the pun) in the cliff areas around Caldera, just south of Puntarenas, as well as other spots around the Central Pacific coast. If you're looking to paraglide, check in with the folks at **Grandpa Ninja's B&B** (© 908/545-3242 in the U.S. and 2200-4824 in Costa Rica; www.paraglide costarica.com). These folks cater to paragliders, and offer lessons or tandem flights. Lessons run around $120 per day, including equipment, while a 30- to 45-minute tandem flight with an experienced pilot will run you around $85.

Serendipity Adventures ★ (© 888/226-5050 in the U.S. and Canada, or 2556-2222 in Costa Rica; www.serendipityadventures.com) will take you up, up, and away in a hot-air balloon near Arenal Volcano. A basic flight costs around $345 per passenger, with a two-person minimum, and a five-person or 800-pound maximum.

Horseback Riding

Costa Rica's rural roots are evident in the continued use of horses for real work and transportation throughout the country. Visitors will find that horses are easily available for riding, whether you want to take a sunset trot along the beach, ride through the cloud forest, or take a multiday trek through the northern zone.

Most travelers simply saddle up for a couple of hours, but those looking for a more specifically equestrian-based visit should check in with the following folks. Rates run between $15 to $30 per hour, depending upon group size and the length of the ride.

Serendipity Adventures ★ (© 888/226-5050 in the U.S. and Canada, or 2556-2222 in Costa Rica; www.serendipityadventures.com) offers horseback treks and tours. Their main stable is just outside La Fortuna.

Motorcycling

Visiting bikers can either cruise the highways or try some off-road biking around Costa Rica. All the caveats about driving conditions and driving customs in Costa Rica apply equally for bikers. If you want to rent a Harley-Davidson for

cruising around the country, **Rent A Moto CR-LTD** (☎ **2289-5552;** www.
rentamotocr.com) conducts guided bike tours and rents well-equipped late-
model Harleys by the day or the week. If your tastes run to off-road riding, both
Wild Riders (☎ **305/407-3637** in the U.S., or 2258-4604 in Costa Rica;
www.wild-rider.com) and **MotoAdventures** (☎ **440/256-8508** in the U.S., or
2228-8494 in Costa Rica; www.motoadventuring.com) rent dirt bikes and run
guided multiday tours. To rent a street bike, you will need a Costa Rican motorcycle license or foreign equivalent; no special motorcycle license is required for
the off-road bikes. In both instances, the rental company will want you to show
sufficient experience and proficiency before letting you take off on their bike.

Rock Climbing

Although this is a nascent sport in Costa Rica, the possibilities are promising,
with several challenging rock formations close to San José and along the Cerro de
la Muerte, as well as great climbing opportunities on Mount Chirripó. The folks
at **Tropical Bungee** (☎ **2248-2212;** www.bungee.co.cr) are the most dependable operators in this field, and they regularly organize climbing outings. Alternatively, you could visit **Mundo Aventura** (☎ **2221-6934;** www.maventura.com),
an adventure- and climbing-gear store with an indoor climbing wall and in-house
tour company. A full-day guided climbing trip should cost you around $70 to $90,
including equipment and lunch.

Spas & Yoga Retreats

Overall, prices for spa treatments in Costa Rica are generally less expensive than
those in the United States or Europe, although some of the fancier options, like
the Four Seasons or Tabacón Grand Spa Thermal Resort, rival the services, facilities, and prices found anywhere on the planet.

The **Four Seasons Resort ★★★** (p. 213) on the Papagayo Peninsula has
ample and luxurious facilities and treatment options, as well as scheduled classes
in yoga, pilates, and other disciplines.

Florblanca Resort ★★★ (p. 276) in Santa Teresa, has some of the most
beautiful boutique spa facilities that I have ever seen. Two large treatment rooms
are set over a flowing water feature.

Luna Lodge ★★ (p. 430) is a gorgeous lodge located on a hillside overlooking Playa Carate, on the border with Corcovado National Park. These folks
run a fairly full schedule of dedicated yoga and wellness programs and have a
good little spa on-site.

Pranamar Villas & Yoga Retreat ★★★, Santa Teresa (p. 276), is a new,
upscale, beachfront resort, with a beautiful, open air-yoga space. A range of daily
classes are offered, and a steady stream of visiting teachers and groups use the
spot for longer retreats and seminars.

Samasati ★, Puerto Viejo de Talamanca (p. 479), is a lovely yoga retreat in
some dense forest on a hillside above the Caribbean. Accommodations range
from budget to rustically luxurious.

Tabacón Grand Spa Thermal Resort ★★★, Tabacón (p. 311), is a top-
notch spa with spectacular hot springs, lush gardens, and a volcano view. A complete range of spa services and treatments is available at reasonable prices.

Xandari Resort & Spa ★★, Alajuela (p. 168), is a unique and distinctive
little luxury hotel that has some top-notch spa facilities and services. This is a
good choice if you're looking for a day or two of pampering, or for day treatments
while staying in San José.

Surfing

Significant sections of "Endless Summer II," the sequel to the all-time surf classic, were filmed in Costa Rica. All along Costa Rica's immense coastline are point and beach breaks that work year-round. **Playas Hermosa, Jacó,** and **Dominical,** on the Central Pacific coast, and **Tamarindo** and **Playa Guiones,** in Guanacaste, are mini surf meccas. **Salsa Brava** in Puerto Viejo is a steep and fast wave that peels off both right and left over shallow coral. It has a habit of breaking boards, but the daredevils keep coming back for more. Beginners and folks looking to learn should stick to the mellower sections of **Jacó** and **Tamarindo**— surf lessons are offered at both beaches. Crowds are starting to gather at the more popular breaks, but you can still stumble onto secret spots on the **Osa** and **Nicoya peninsulas** and along the northern **Guanacaste** coast. Costa Rica's signature wave is still at **Playa Pavones,** which is reputed to have one of the longest lefts in the world. The cognoscenti, however, also swear by places such as **Playa Grande, Playa Negra, Matapalo, Malpaís,** and **Witch's Rock.** An avid surfer's best bet is to rent a dependable four-wheel-drive vehicle with a rack and take a surfin' safari around Guanacaste.

If you're looking for an organized surf vacation, contact **Tico Travel** (© **800/493-8426** in the U.S. and Canada, or 2257-7118 in Costa Rica; www.ticotravel.com), or check out **www.crsurf.com**. For swell reports, general surf information, live wave-cams, and great links pages, point your browser to **www.surfline.com**. Although killer sets are possible at any particular spot at any time of the year, depending upon swell direction, local winds, and distant storms, in broad terms, the northern coast of Guanacaste works best from December to April; the central and southern Pacific coasts work best from April to November; and the Caribbean coast's short big-wave season is December through March. Surf lessons, usually private or in a small group, will run you anywhere from $20 to $40 per hour, including the board.

White-Water Rafting, Kayaking & Canoeing

Whether you're a first-time rafter or a world-class kayaker, Costa Rica's got some white water suited to your abilities. Rivers rise and fall with the rainfall, but you can get wet and wild here even in the dry season. Full-day rafting trips run between $75 and $110 per person.

The best white-water rafting ride is still the scenic **Pacuare River;** although there has been talk about damming it to build a hydroelectric plant, the project has thankfully failed to materialize. If you're just experimenting with river rafting, stick to Class II and III rivers, such as **Reventazón, Sarapiquí, Peñas Blancas,** and **Savegre.** If you already know which end of the paddle goes in the water, you'll have plenty of Class IV and V sections to run.

Die-hard river rats should get **"Chasing Jaguars: The Complete Guide to Costa Rican Whitewater,"** by Lee Eudy, a book loaded with photos, technical data, and route tips on almost every rideable river in the country.

Canoe Costa Rica (© **732/736-6586** in the U.S., or 2282-3579; www.canoecostarica.com) is the only outfit I know of that specializes in canoe trips; it works primarily with custom-designed tours and itineraries, although it does have several set departure trips each year.

Aventuras Naturales ★★ (© **888/680-9031** in the U.S., or 2225-3939 in Costa Rica) is a major rafting operator that runs daily trips on the most popular rivers in Costa Rica. Its **Pacuare Jungle Lodge** ★★★ (p. 188) is very plush, and a great place to spend the night on one of its 2-day rafting trips.

Activities A to Z

THE BEST SPECIAL-INTEREST TRIPS

IN SEARCH OF turtles

Few places in the world have as many sea-turtle nesting sites as Costa Rica. Along both coasts, five species of these huge marine reptiles come ashore at specific times of the year to dig nests in the sand and lay their eggs. Sea turtles are endangered throughout the world due to over-hunting, accidental deaths in fishing nets, development on beaches that once served as nesting areas, and the collection and sale (often illegally) of their eggs. International trade in sea-turtle products is already prohibited by most countries (including the U.S.), but sea-turtle numbers continue to dwindle.

Among the species of sea turtles that nest on Costa Rica's beaches are the **olive ridley** (known for their mass egg-laying migrations, or *arribadas*), **leatherback, hawksbill, green,** and **Pacific green turtle.** Excursions to see nesting turtles have become common, and they are fascinating, but please make sure that you and/or your guide do not disturb the turtles. Any light source (other than red-tinted flashlights) can confuse female turtles and cause them to return to the sea without laying their eggs. In fact, as more development takes place on the Costa Rican coast, hotel lighting may cause the number of nesting turtles to drop. Luckily, many of the nesting beaches have been protected as national parks.

Here are the main places to see nesting sea turtles: **Santa Rosa National Park** (near Liberia, olive ridleys nest here from July–Dec, and to a lesser extent from Jan–June), **Las Baulas National Marine Park** (near Tamarindo, leatherbacks nest here from early Oct through mid-Feb), **Ostional National Wildlife Refuge** (near Playa Nosara, olive ridleys nest from July–Dec, and to a lesser extent from Jan–June), and **Tortuguero National Park** (on the northern Caribbean coast, green turtles nest here from July through mid-Oct, with Aug–Sept their peak period. In lesser numbers, leatherback turtles nest here from Feb–June, peaking during Mar and Apr).

See the regional chapters for descriptions of the resident turtles and their respective nesting seasons, as well as listings of local tour operators and companies that arrange trips to see sea turtles nesting.

Exploradores Outdoors ★ (© 646/205-0828 in the U.S. and Canada, or 2222-6262 in Costa Rica; www.exploradoresoutdoors.com) is another good company run by a longtime and well-respected river guide. They run the Pacuare and Reventazón rivers, and even combine a 1-day river trip with onward transportation to or from the Caribbean coast, or the Arenal Volcano area, for no extra cost.

Río Locos (© 2556-6035; www.whiteh2o.com) is a small company based in Turrialba. These folks are a good option for hard-core kayakers, small custom group tours, and folks who find themselves in Turrialba.

Ríos Tropicales ★★ (© 866/722-8273 in the U.S. and Canada, or 2233-6455 in Costa Rica; www.riostropicales.com) is one of the major operators in Costa Rica, with tours on most of the country's popular rivers. Accommodations options include a very comfortable lodge on the banks of the Río Pacuare for the 2-day trips.

Windsurfing & Kiteboarding

Windsurfing is not very popular on the high seas here, where winds are fickle and rental options are limited, even at beach hotels. However, **Lake Arenal** is considered one of the top spots in the world for high-wind boardsailing. During the winter months, many of the regulars from Washington's Columbia River Gorge take up residence around the nearby town of Tilarán. Small boards, water starts, and fancy gibes are the norm. The best time for windsurfing on Lake Arenal is between December and March. The same winds that buffet Lake Arenal make their way down to **Bahía Salinas** (also known as Bolaños Bay), near La Cruz, Guanacaste, where you can get in some good windsurfing. Both spots also have operations offering lessons and equipment rentals in the high-action sport of kiteboarding. Board rentals run around $55 to $85 per day, while lessons can cost between $50 to $100 for a half-day private lesson. See "La Cruz & Bahía Salinas," in chapter 8, and "Along the Shores of Lake Arenal," in chapter 10, for details.

STUDY & VOLUNTEER PROGRAMS

Language Immersion

As more people travel to Costa Rica with the intention of learning Spanish, the number of options for Spanish immersion vacations increases. You can find courses of varying lengths and degrees of intensiveness, and many that include cultural activities and day excursions. Many of these schools have reciprocal relationships with U.S. universities, so, in some cases, you can even arrange for college credit. Most Spanish schools can arrange for homestays with a middle-class Tico family for a total-immersion experience. Classes are often small, or even one-on-one, and can last anywhere from 2 to 8 hours a day. Listed below are some of the larger and more established Spanish-language schools, with approximate costs. Most are in San José, but schools are also in Monteverde, Manuel Antonio, Playa Flamingo, Malpaís, Playa Nosara, and Tamarindo. A 1-week class with 4 hours of class per day, including a homestay, tends to cost between $350 and $500. (I'd certainly rather spend 2 weeks or a month in one of these spots than in San José.) Contact the schools for the most current price information.

Adventure Education Center (AEC) Spanish Institute ★ (© 800/237-2730 in the U.S. and Canada, or 2556-4614 in Costa Rica; www.adventurespanishschool.com) has branches in Dominical and Turrialba, and specializes in combining language learning with adventure activities.

Centro Panamericano de Idiomas (CPI) ★ (© 877/373-3116 in the U.S., or 2265-6306; www.cpi-edu.com) has three campuses: one in the quiet suburban town of Heredia, another in Monteverde, and one at the beach in Playa Flamingo.

Costa Rican Language Academy ★ in San José (© 866/230-6361 in the U.S., or 2280-1685 in Costa Rica; www.spanishandmore.com) has intensive programs with classes held Monday to Thursday to give students a chance for longer weekend excursions. The academy also integrates Latin dance and Costa Rican cooking classes into the program.

Escuela D'Amore ★ (© 877/434-7290 in the U.S. and Canada, or 2777-0233 in Costa Rica; www.academiadamore.com) is situated in the lush surroundings of Manuel Antonio.

Wayra Instituto de Español (© 2653-0359; www.spanish-wayra.co.cr) is a longstanding operation located in the beach town of Tamarindo.

Alternative Educational Travel

Adventures Under the Sun ★★ (© 866/897-5578 in the U.S. and Canada, or 2289-0404 in Costa Rica; www.adventuresunderthesun.com) is a Costa Rican–based outfit specializing in adventure and volunteer-focused teen travel. Their strong suit is organizing custom group itineraries, but they also run periodic "summer day camps" and set itineraries.

Costa Rica Rainforest Outward Bound School ★★ (© 800/676-2018 in the U.S., or 2278-6062 in Costa Rica; www.crrobs.org) is the local branch of this well-respected international adventure-based outdoor-education organization. Courses range from 2 weeks to a full semester, and offerings include surfing, kayaking, tree climbing, and learning Spanish.

Eco Teach (© 800/626-8992 in the U.S. and Canada; www.ecoteach. com) works primarily to facilitate educational trips for high school and college student groups. Trips focus on Costa Rican ecology and culture. Costs run around $1,500 to $2,000 per person for a 10-day trip, including lodging, meals, classes, and travel within the country. Airfare to Costa Rica is extra.

The **Institute for Central American Development Studies** ★ (© 2225-0508; www.icads.org) offers internship and research opportunities in the areas of environment, agriculture, human rights, and women's studies. An intensive Spanish-language program can be combined with work-study or volunteer opportunities.

The **Monteverde Institute** ★ (© 2645-5053; www.mvinstitute.org) offers study programs in Monteverde and also has a volunteer center that helps in placement and training of volunteers.

The **Organization for Tropical Studies** ★★ (© 919/684-5774 in the U.S., or 2524-0607 in Costa Rica; www.threepaths.co.cr) represents several Costa Rican and U.S. universities. This organization's mission is to promote research, education, and the wise use of natural resources in the Tropics. Research facilities include La Selva Biological Station near Braulio Carrillo National Park and Palo Verde, and the Wilson Botanical Gardens near San Vito. Housing is provided at one of the research facilities. The wide variety of programs range from full-semester undergraduate programs to specific graduate courses (of varying duration) to tourist programs. (These are generally sponsored/run by established operators such as Costa Rica Expeditions or Elderhostel.) Programs range in duration from 3 to 10 days, and costs vary greatly. Entrance requirements and competition for some of these courses can be demanding.

Sustainable Volunteer Projects

Below are some institutions and organizations that are working on ecology and sustainable development projects in Costa Rica.

APREFLOFAS (Association for the Preservation of the Wild Flora and Fauna; © 2240-6087; www.apreflofas.or.cr) is a pioneering local conservation organization that accepts volunteers and runs environmentally sound educational tours around the country.

Asociación de Voluntarios para el Servicio en las Areas Protegidas ★ (**ASVO;** © 2258-4430; www.asvocr.org) organizes volunteers to work in Costa Rican national parks. A 2-week minimum commitment is required, as is an ability to adapt to basic conditions basic ability to converse in Spanish. Housing is provided at a basic ranger station; a $245 weekly fee covers lodging, logistics, and food, which is basic Tico fare.

Sea Turtle Conservancy (© **800/678-7853** in the U.S. and Canada, or 2278-6058 in Costa Rica; www.cccturtle.org) is a nonprofit organization dedicated to sea turtle research, protection, and advocacy. Formerly known as the **Caribbean Conservation Corporation,** their main operation in Costa Rica is headquartered in Tortuguero, where volunteers can aid in various scientific studies, as well as nightly patrols of the beach during nesting seasons to prevent poaching.

Global Volunteers (© **800/487-1074** in the U.S. and Canada; www.globalvolunteers.org) is a U.S.-based organization that offers a unique opportunity to travelers who've always wanted a Peace Corps–like experience but can't make a 2-year commitment. For 2 to 3 weeks, you can join one of its working vacations in Costa Rica. A certain set of skills, such as engineering or agricultural knowledge, is helpful but by no means necessary. Each trip is undertaken at a particular community's request, to complete a specific project. However, *be warned:* These "volunteer" experiences do not come cheap. You must pay for your transportation as well as a hefty program fee, around $2,600 for a 2-week program.

Habitat for Humanity International (© **2296-3436;** www.habitatcostarica.org) has several chapters in Costa Rica and sometimes runs organized Global Village programs here.

Vida (© **2221-8367;** www.vida.org) is a local nongovernmental organization working on sustainable development and conservation issues; it can often place volunteers.

MEDICAL & DENTAL TOURISM

Costa Rica is an increasingly popular destination for dental and medical tourists. Facilities and care are excellent, and prices are quite low compared to the United States and other private care options in the developed world. Travelers are coming for everything from a simple dental checkup and cleaning to elective cosmetic surgery or a triple heart bypass operation. In virtually every case, visitors can save money on the overall cost of care and get a Costa Rican vacation thrown into the bargain. In some cases, the savings are quite substantial.

The country's two top hospitals have modern facilities and equipment, as well as excellent doctor and nursing corps, many of whom speak English. **Clínica Bíblica,** Avenida 14 between calles Central and 1 (© **2522-1000;** www.clinicabiblica.com), is conveniently close to downtown while the **Hospital CIMA** (© **2208-1000;** www.hospitalcima.com) is in Escazú on the Próspero Fernández Highway, which connects San José and the western suburb of Santa Ana. The latter has the most modern facilities in the country. An annex of the Hospital CIMA has even opened in the outskirts of Liberia, close to the beaches of Guanacaste.

The United States embassy in Costa Rica maintains a fairly comprehensive list of recommended doctors, dentists, and other specialists at **http://costarica.usembassy.gov/medical.html**.

6

SAN JOSÉ

CALDERON
DE LA BARCA

F or as long as I've written this book, my stock advice to tourists has been to get in and out of San José as quickly as possible. In most cases, this remains good counsel. Still, San José is the country's only major urban center, with varied and active restaurant and nightlife scenes, several museums and galleries worth visiting, and a steady stream of theater, concerts, and other cultural events that you won't find elsewhere in the country.

At first blush, San José comes across as little more than a chaotic jumble of cars, buses, buildings, and people. The central downtown section of the city exists in a near-constant state of gridlock. Antiquated buses spewing diesel fumes and a lack of emission controls have created a brown cloud over the city's sky. Sidewalks are poorly maintained and claustrophobic, and street crime is a serious problem. Most visitors quickly seek the sanctuary of their hotel room and the first chance to escape the city.

Founded in 1737, San José was a forgotten backwater of the Spanish empire until the late 19th century, when it boomed with the coffee business. At 1,125m (3,690 ft.) above sea level, San José enjoys springlike temperatures year-round and its location in the Central Valley—the lush Talamanca Mountains rise to the south, the Poás, Barva, and Irazú volcanoes to the north—makes it both stunning and convenient as a base of exploration

This chapter helps you plan whatever time you intend for the capital and ease your way through the pitfalls inherent in such a rough-and-tumble little city.

THE BEST SAN JOSÉ EXPERIENCES

o **Taking In the Riches at the Gold Museum:** With more than 2,000 pieces spread over three floors, the Gold Museum provides a fascinating look into the pre-Columbian artistry that inspired colonial-era quests, conquests, and excesses. See p. 121.

o **Catching a Show at the National Theater:** Completed in 1897, and fronting the downtown Plaza de la Cultura, the National Theater is a beautiful and well-preserved turn-of-the-20th-century theater. It features a stunning marble entryway, a series of marble sculptures, and intricate paintings and murals throughout. It also hosts concerts, theater performances, and special events. See p. 144.

> ### San José's Top Sustainable Hotels
>
> **Aurola Holiday Inn** (p. 129)
> **Crowne Plaza Corobicí** (p. 131)
> **Hotel Grano de Oro** (p. 131)

o **Basking in Tropical Opulence at a Boutique Hotel:** Throughout the late 18th and early 19th centuries, newly rich coffee barons built beautiful

PREVIOUS PAGE: **The Teatro Nacional.**

A panoramic view of San José.

mansions around downtown San José. Today, many of these have been converted into charming boutique hotels. See "Where to Stay," below.

o **Visiting the Costa Rican Art Museum and La Sabana Park:** Inhabiting the country's first airport terminal building, the Costa Rican Art Museum houses the country's greatest art collection—from colonial times to the present. Just outside its doors lies La Sabana Park, where you can spend the afternoon relaxing in the grass or practicing any number of sports and activities, alongside some newly made Tico friends. See p. 123 and 125.

o **Getting out on the Dance Floor:** San José is teeming with dance clubs, and most nights the city's dance floors are packed to overflowing. Choose between an old-school salsa dance hall with a live band, or a more contemporary club blasting the latest electronica. See p. 144.

ORIENTATION
Arriving
BY PLANE
Juan Santamaría International Airport (✆ **2437-2626** for 24-hr. airport information; www.fly2sanjose.com; airport code SJO) is near the city of Alajuela, about 20 minutes from downtown San José. A taxi into town costs between ₡14,000 and ₡28,000, and a bus is only ₡585. The Alajuela–San José buses run frequently and will drop you off anywhere along Paseo Colón or at a station near the Parque de la Merced (downtown, btw. calles 12 and 14 and avs. 2 and 4). There are two separate lines: **Tuasa** (✆ **2442-6900**) buses are red; **Station Wagon** (✆ **2442-3226**) buses are beige/yellow. At the airport, the bus stop is directly in front of the main terminal, beyond the parking structure. Be sure to ask whether the bus is going to San José, or you'll end up in Alajuela. If you have a lot of luggage, you probably should take a cab.

Most car-rental agencies have desks and offices at the airport, although if you're planning to spend a few days in San José itself, I personally think a car is a liability. (If you're heading off immediately to the beach, though, it's much easier to pick up your car here than at a downtown office.)

Tip: Chaos and confusion greet arriving passengers the second they step out of the terminal. You must abandon your luggage carts just before exiting the building and then face a gauntlet of aggressive taxi drivers, shuttle drivers waving signs, and people offering to carry your bags. Fortunately, the official airport taxi service (see below) has a booth inside the calm area just before the terminal exit. And official airport porters also hang out in this area. Still, there's often really nowhere for them to have to carry your bags to because the line of waiting taxis and shuttles is just steps away. Keep a very watchful eye on your bags: Thieves have historically preyed on newly arrived passengers and their luggage. You should tip porters about C200 to C300 per bag.

In terms of taxis, you should probably stick with the official airport taxi service, **Taxis Unidos Aeropuerto** (℗ 2221-6865; www.taxiaeropuerto.com), which operates a fleet of orange vans and sedans. These folks have a kiosk in the no man's land just outside the exit door for arriving passengers. Here they will assign you a cab. These taxis use meters, and fares to most downtown hotels should run between C14,000 and C28,000. Despite the fact that Taxis Unidos has an official monopoly at the airport, you will usually find a handful of regular cabs (in traditional red sedans) and "pirate" cabs, driven by freelancers using their own vehicles. You could use either of these latter options ("pirate" cabs tend to charge a dollar or two less), but I recommend using the official service for safety and standardized prices.

You have several options for **exchanging money** when you arrive at the airport. An ATM in the baggage claim area is connected to both the PLUS and Cirrus networks. A **Global Exchange** (℗ 2431-0686; www.globalexchange. co.cr) money exchange booth is just as you clear Customs and Immigration. It's open whenever flights arrive; however, these folks exchange at more than 10% below the official rate. A branch of **Banco de San José** is inside the main terminal, on the second floor across from the airline check-in counters, as well as a couple more ATMs up there. Most taxis and all rental-car agencies accept U.S. dollars. See "Money & Costs," in chapter 14, for more details.

Tip: There's really no pressing need to exchange money the minute you arrive. Taxis Unidos accepts dollars. You can wait until after you settle into your hotel, and see if the hotel will give you a good rate of exchange, or use one of the many downtown banks or ATMs.

If you arrive in San José via private aircraft, or another small commuter or charter airline, you might find yourself at the **Tobías Bolaños International Airport** in Pavas (℗ 2232-2820; airport code SYQ). This small airport is on the western side of downtown San José, about 10 minutes by car from the center. The airport has no car-rental desks, so unless you have a car or a driver waiting for you here, you will have to take a cab into town, which should cost between C8,000 and C18,000.

BY BUS

If you're coming to San José by bus, where you disembark depends on where you're coming from. (The different bus companies have their offices, and thus their drop-off points, all over downtown San José. When you buy your ticket, ask where you'll be let off.) Buses arriving from Panama pass first through Cartago and San Pedro before letting passengers off in downtown San José; buses arriving from Nicaragua generally enter the city on the west end of town, on Paseo Colón. If you're staying here, you can ask to be let off before the final stop.

BY CAR

For those of you intrepid readers arriving by car, you'll enter San José via the Interamerican Highway. If you arrive **from Nicaragua and the north,** the highway brings you first past the airport and the city of Alajuela, to the western edge of downtown, right at the end of Paseo Colón, where it hits Parque La Sabana (La Sabana Park). The area is well marked with large road signs that direct you either to downtown (centro) or to the western suburbs of Rohrmoser, Pavas, and Escazú. If you're heading toward downtown, follow the flow of traffic and turn left on Paseo Colón.

For those of you entering **from Panama and the south,** things get a little more complicated. The Interamerican Highway first passes through the city of Cartago and then through the San José suburbs of Curridabat and San Pedro before reaching downtown. This route is relatively well marked, and if you stick with the major flow of traffic, you should find San José without any problem.

Visitor Information

The **Costa Rican National Tourism Chamber (CANATUR; ✆ 2440-1676;** www.canatur.org) has a desk at the Juan Santamaría International Airport, the baggage claims area, just before Customs. You can pick up maps and browse brochures, and they might even lend you a phone to make or confirm a reservation. It is usually open for all arriving flights.

City Layout

Downtown San José is laid out on a grid. *Avenidas* (avenues) run east and west, while *calles* (streets) run north and south. The center of the city is at **Avenida Central** and **Calle Central.** To the north of Avenida Central, the avenidas have odd numbers beginning with Avenida 1; to the south, they have even numbers beginning with Avenida 2. Likewise, calles to the east of Calle Central have odd numbers, and those to the west have even numbers. The main downtown artery

A colonial-era building in San José.

SEARCHING FOR addresses

This is one of the most confusing aspects of visiting Costa Rica in general, and San José in particular. Although downtown San José often has street addresses and building numbers for locations, they are almost never used. Addresses are given as a set of coordinates such as "Calle 3 between avenidas Central and 1." It's then up to you to locate the building within that block, keeping in mind that the building could be on either side of the street. Many addresses include additional information, such as the number of meters from a specified intersection or some other well-known landmark. (These "meter measurements" are not precise but are a good way to give directions to a taxi driver. In basic terms, 100m = 1 block, 200m = 2 blocks, and so on.) These landmarks are what become truly confusing for visitors to the city because they are often simply restaurants, bars, and shops that would be familiar only to locals.

Things get even more confusing when the landmark in question no longer exists. The classic example of this is "the Coca-Cola," one of the most common landmarks used in addresses in the blocks surrounding San José's main market. The trouble is, the Coca-Cola bottling plant that it refers to is no longer there; the edifice is long gone, and one of the principal downtown bus depots stands in its place. Old habits die hard, though, and the address description remains. You might also try to find someplace near the *antiguo higuerón* ("old fig tree") in San Pedro. This tree was felled over a decade ago. In outlying neighborhoods, addresses can become long directions, such as "50m (½ block) south of the old church, then 100m (1 block) east, then 20m (two buildings) south." Luckily for visitors, most downtown addresses are more straightforward.

Oh, and if you're wondering how letter carriers manage, well, welcome to the club. Some folks actually get their mail delivered this way, but most people and businesses in San José use a post office box. This is called an *apartado* and is abbreviated "Apdo." or "A.P." in mailing addresses.

is **Avenida 2,** which merges with Avenida Central on either side of downtown. West of downtown, Avenida Central becomes **Paseo Colón,** which ends at Parque La Sabana and feeds into the highway to Alajuela, the airport, Guanacaste, and the Pacific coast. East of downtown, Avenida Central leads to San Pedro and then to Cartago and the Interamerican Highway heading south. **Calle 3** takes you out of town to the north, onto the Guápiles Highway that leads to the Caribbean coast.

The Neighborhoods in Brief

San José is divided into dozens of neighborhoods, known as *barrios.* Most of the listings in this chapter fall within the main downtown area, but you'll need to know about a few outlying neighborhoods. In addition, the nearby suburbs of Escazú and Santa Ana are so close that they could almost be considered part of San José. For more information on these towns, see chapter 7.

DOWNTOWN   In San José's busy downtown, you'll find most of the city's museums, as well as a handful of small urban parks and open-air plazas, and the city's

The sculpture garden at Parque La Sabana.

main cathedral. Many tour companies, restaurants, and hotels are located here. Unfortunately, traffic noise and exhaust fumes make this one of the least pleasant parts of the city. Streets and avenues are usually bustling and crowded with pedestrians and vehicular traffic, and street crime is most rampant here. Still, the sections of Avenida Central between calles 6 and 7, as well as Avenida 4 between calles 9 and 14, have been converted into pedestrian malls, greatly improving things on these stretches.

BARRIO AMÓN/BARRIO OTOYA   These two picturesque neighborhoods, just north and east of downtown, are the site of the greatest concentration of historic buildings in San José. Some of these have been renovated and turned into boutique hotels and atmospheric restaurants. If you're looking for character and don't mind the noise and exhaust fumes from passing cars and buses, this neighborhood makes a good base for exploring the city.

LA SABANA/PASEO COLÓN   Paseo Colón, a wide boulevard west of downtown, is an extension of Avenida Central and ends at Parque La Sabana. It has several good, small hotels and numerous restaurants. This is also where several of the city's car-rental agencies have their in-town offices. Once the site of the city's main airport, the Parque La Sabana (La Sabana Park) is San José's largest public park, with ample green areas, sports and recreation facilities, the National Stadium, and the Museo de Arte Costarricense (Costa Rican Art Museum).

SAN PEDRO/LOS YOSES   Located east of downtown San José, Los Yoses is an upper-middle-class neighborhood that is home to many diplomatic missions and embassies. San Pedro is a little farther east and is the site of the University of Costa Rica. Numerous college-type bars and restaurants are all around the edge of the campus, and several good restaurants and small hotels can be found in both neighborhoods.

GETTING AROUND
By Bus

Bus transportation around San José is cheap—the fare is usually somewhere around C150 to C465—although the Alajuela/San José buses that run in from the airport cost C585. The most important buses are those running east along Avenida 2 and west along Avenida 3. The **Sabana/Cementerio** bus runs from Parque La Sabana to downtown and is one of the most convenient buses to use. You'll find a bus stop for the outbound Sabana/Cementerio bus near the main post office on Avenida 3 near the corner of Calle 2, and another one on Calle 11 between avenidas Central and 1. This bus also has stops all along Avenida 2. **San Pedro** buses leave from the end of the pedestrian walkway on Avenida Central between calles 9 and 11, and take you out of downtown heading east.

You pay as you board the bus. The city's bus drivers can make change, although they don't like to receive large bills. Be especially mindful of your wallet, purse, or other valuables, because pickpockets often work the crowded buses.

By Taxi

Although taxis in San José have meters (*marías*), the drivers sometimes refuse to use them, particularly with foreigners, so you'll occasionally have to negotiate the price. Always try to get them to use the meter first (say *"ponga la maría, por favor"*). The official rate at press time is C570 per kilometer (¹/₂ mile). If you have a rough idea of how far it is to your destination, you can estimate how much it should cost from this figure. Wait time is charged at C3,145 per hour, and is prorated for smaller increments.

Depending on your location, the time of day, and the weather (rain places taxis at a premium), it's relatively easy to hail a cab downtown. You'll always find

A bus stop in San José.

taxis in front of the Teatro Nacional (albeit at high prices) and around the Parque Central at Avenida Central and Calle Central. Taxis in front of hotels and the El Pueblo tourist complex usually charge more than others, although this is technically illegal. Most hotels will gladly call you a cab, either for a downtown excursion or for a trip back out to the airport. You can also get a cab by calling **Coopetaxi** (☎ 2235-9966), **Coopeirazu** (☎ 2254-3211), **Coopetico** (☎ 2224-7979), or **Coopeguaria** (☎ 2226-1366). **Cinco Estrellas Taxi** (☎ 2228-3159) is based in Escazú but services the entire metropolitan area and airport, and claims to always have an English-speaking operator on call.

On Foot

Downtown San José is very compact. Nearly every place you might want to go is within a 15-by-4-block area. Because of traffic congestion, you'll

Pedestrians walking along Avenida Central.

often find it faster to walk than to take a bus or taxi. Be careful when walking the streets any time of day or night. Flashy jewelry, loosely held handbags or backpacks, and expensive camera equipment tend to attract thieves. **Avenida Central** is a pedestrian-only street from calles 6 to 7, and has been redone with interesting paving stones and the occasional fountain in an attempt to create a comfortable pedestrian mall. A similar pedestrian-only walkway runs along **Avenida 4,** between calles 9 and 14.

By Train

San José has very sporadic and minimal urban commuter train service, and it is geared almost exclusively to commuters. One line connecting the western neighborhood of Pavas with the eastern suburb of San Pedro passes right through the downtown, with prominent stops at, or near, the U.S. Embassy, Parque La Sabana, the downtown court area, and the Universidad de Costa Rica (University of Costa Rica) and Universidad Latina (Latin University). The train runs commuter hours roughly every $1^1/_2$ hours between 5 and 8:30am and 4:10 and 8pm. Another line runs between downtown San José and Heredia. This train runs roughly every 15 minutes between 5:30 and 8:30am, and again between 4:30 and 7:30pm, with much less frequent service during non-commuter hours. Fares range from C200 to C650, depending on the length of your ride.

By Car

It will cost you between $45 and $150 per day to rent a car in Costa Rica (the higher prices are for 4WD vehicles). Many car-rental agencies have offices at the airport. If not, they will usually either pick you up or deliver the car to any San

Car-Rental Advice

If you plan to rent a car, I recommend reserving it in advance from home. All the major international agencies and many local companies have toll-free numbers and websites. Sometimes you can even save a bit on the cost by reserving in advance. Costa Rica's car-rental fleet is not sufficient to meet demand during the high season when rental rates run at a premium. Sometimes this allows agencies here to gouge last-minute car-rental shoppers.

José hotel. If you decide to pick up your rental car in downtown San José, be prepared for some very congested streets.

The following companies have desks at Juan Santamaría International Airport, as well as offices downtown: **Alamo** (℃ 2242-7733; www.alamocostarica.com), **Adobe Rent A Car** (℃ 2542-4800; www.adobecar.com), **Avis** (℃ 800/230-4898 in the U.S. and 800/272-5871 in Canada, or 2293-2222 central reservation number in Costa Rica; www.avis.com), **Budget** (℃ 800/472-3325 in the U.S. and Canada, or 2255-4240 in San José; www.budget.com), **Dollar** (℃ 800/800-6000 in the U.S. and Canada, or 2257-1585 in San José; www.dollar.com), **Hertz** (℃ 800/654-3131 in the U.S. and Canada, or 2221-1818 in San José; www.hertz.com), **National Car Rental** (℃ 877/222-9058 in the U.S. and Canada, 2242-7878 in San José; www.nationalcar.com), and **Payless Rent A Car** (℃ 800/729-5377 in the U.S. and Canada, or 2432-4747 in Costa Rica; www.paylesscar.com).

Dozens of other smaller, local car-rental agencies are in San José, and most will arrange for airport or hotel pickup or delivery. Two of the more dependable agencies are **Hola! Rent A Car** (℃ **2520-0100;** www.hola.net) and **Toyota Rent A Car** (℃ **2256-5713;** www.toyotarent.com).

For more advice on renting cars, see "Getting Around: By Car," in chapter 14.

[Fast FACTS] SAN JOSÉ

ATMs/Banks You'll find an extensive network of banks and ATMs around San José. Banks are usually open Monday through Friday from 9am to 4pm, although many have begun to offer extended hours. Post offices are generally open Monday through Friday from 8am to 5:30pm, and Saturday from 7:30am to noon. Due to crime directed at folks just as they are withdrawing cash from an ATM, some of the banks have taken to disabling their ATM networks at night.

Dentists Call your embassy, which will have a list of recommended dentists. Bilingual dentists often advertise in the *Tico Times.* Because treatments are so inexpensive in Costa Rica, dental tourism has become a popular option for people needing extensive work.

Doctors Contact your embassy for information on doctors in San José, or see "Hospitals," below.

Drugstores San José has countless pharmacies and drugstores. Many of them deliver at little or no extra cost. The pharmacy at the **Hospital Clínica Bíblica,** Avenida 14 between calles Central and 1 (℃ **2522-1000**), is open daily 24 hours, as is the

Hospital **CIMA** pharmacy (© **2208-1080**) in Escazú. **Farmacia Fischel** (© **800/ 347-2435** toll-free in Costa Rica; www.fischel.co.cr) has scores of branches around the metropolitan area.

Embassies & Consulates
See chapter 14.

Emergencies
In case of any emergency, dial © **911** (which should have an English-speaking operator); for an ambulance, call © **1028;** and to report a fire, call © **1118.**

Hospitals
Clínica Bíblica, Avenida 14 between calles Central and 1 (© **2522-1000;** www. clinicabiblica.com), is conveniently close to downtown and has several English-speaking doctors. The **Hospital CIMA** (© **2208- 1000;** www.hospitalcima. com), located in Escazú on the Próspero Fernández Highway, which connects San José and the western suburb of Santa Ana, has the most modern facilities in the country.

Internet Access
Internet cafes are all over San José. Rates run between C400 and C3,000 per hour. Many hotels have their own Internet cafe or allow guests to send and receive e-mail. And many have added Wi-Fi, either for free or a small charge.

Maps
The information desks at the airport are usually stocked with decent maps of both Costa Rica and San José. Also try **Librería Lehmann,** Avenida Central between calles 1 and 3 (© **2522-4848**); and **Librería Universal,** Avenida Central and calles Central and 1 (© **2222-2222**). Perhaps the best map to have is the waterproof country map of Costa Rica put out by **Toucan Maps** (www. mapcr.com), which can be ordered directly from their website or any major online bookseller, like Amazon. com.

Police
Dial © **911** or 2295-3272 for the police. They should have someone available who speaks English.

Post Office
The main post office (correo) is on Calle 2 between avenidas 1 and 3 (© **2223-9766;** www. correos.go.cr). See "Mail," on p. 508, for more information.

Restrooms
Public restrooms are rare to nonexistent, but most big hotels and public restaurants will let you use their restrooms. Downtown, you can find public restrooms at the entrance to the Museos del Banco Central de Costa Rica (p. 121).

Safety
Pickpockets and purse slashers are rife in San José, especially on public buses, in the markets, on crowded sidewalks, near hospitals, and lurking outside bank offices and ATMs. Leave most of your money and other valuables in your hotel safe, and carry only as much as you really need when you go out. If you do carry anything valuable with you, keep it in a money belt or special passport bag around your neck. Day packs are a prime target of brazen pickpockets throughout the city. One common scam involves someone dousing you or your pack with mustard or ice cream. Another scamster (or two) will then quickly come to your aid—they are usually much more interested in cleaning you out than cleaning you up.

Stay away from the red-light district northwest of the Central Market. Also be advised that the Parque Nacional is not a safe place for a late-night stroll. Other precautions include walking around corner vendors, not between the vendor and the building. The tight space between the vendor and the building is a favorite spot for pickpockets. Never park a car on the street, and never leave anything of value in a car, even if it's in a guarded parking lot. Don't even leave your car unattended by the curb in front of a hotel while you dash in to check on your reservation. With these precautions in mind, you should have a safe visit to San José. Also, see "Safety," in chapter 14.

Time Zone
San José is on Central Standard Time (same as Chicago and St. Louis), 6 hours behind Greenwich Mean Time. For the exact time (in Spanish), call © **1112.**

Useful Telephone Numbers   For directory assistance, call ℂ 1113; for international directory assistance, call ℂ 1024.

Weather   The weather in San José (including the Central Valley) is usually temperate, never getting extremely hot or cold. May through November is the rainy season, although the rain usually falls only in the afternoon and evening.

EXPLORING SAN JOSÉ

Most visitors to Costa Rica try to get out of the city as fast as possible so they can spend more time on the beach or off in the rainforests. But San José has some of the best and most modern museums in Central America, with a wealth of fascinating pre-Columbian artifacts. Standouts include the Museo de Jade Marco Fidel Tristán (Jade Museum) and the Museo de Arte Costarricense (Costa Rican Art Museum), featuring a top-notch collection of Costa Rican art, and a beautiful, open-air sculpture garden.

Just outside San José in the Central Valley are also several great things to see and do. With day trips out of the city, you can spend quite a few days in this region. See chapter 7 for additional touring ideas.

The Top Attractions

DOWNTOWN SAN JOSÉ

Catedral Metropolitano (Metropolitan Cathedral) ★ CATHEDRAL
San José's principal Catholic cathedral was built in 1871. Rather plain from the outside, the large neoclassical church features a pretty mix of stained-glass works, tile floors, and assorted sculptures and bas-reliefs. It also has a wonderfully restored 19th-century pipe organ. A well-tended little garden surrounds the church and features a massive marble statue of Pope Juan Paul II carved by celebrated Costa Rican sculptor Jorge Jiménez Deredia, who also has a work at the Vatican. The cathedral is just across from the downtown Parque Central (Central Park).

Av. 2 and Calle Central. ℂ **2221-3820.** Free admission. Mon–Sat 6am–6pm; Sun 6am–9pm.

Museo Nacional de Costa Rica.

Centro Nacional de Arte y Cultura (National Center of Art and Culture) ★ ART MUSEUM   Housed in what was formerly the National Liquor Factory (FANAL), this complex of museums and performance spaces is also home to the Ministry of Culture. The best museum here is the Museum of Contemporary Art and Design (MADC), which has several very large exhibition spaces and features rotating shows of predominantly local and regional artists, with the occasional exhibition from the rest of the world. The theaters, as well as the central courtyard amphitheater, often host a wide range of cutting-edge Costa Rican drama, dance, and musical performances, as well as talks, conferences, and workshops. This place takes up a full city block between the Parque España and Parque Nacional, and just a half-block away from the Jade Museum (p. 122).

Calle 13, btw. avs. 3 and 5. 𝄐 **2257-7202.** www.madc.ac.cr. Admission $3, free for children and seniors, and free on Mon for everybody. Mon–Sat 9:30am–5pm.

Museos del Banco Central de Costa Rica (Gold Museum) ★★ MUSEUM   Housing some 1,600 gold pieces dating from 500 B.C.E. to 1500 C.E. and spread over three floors, this museum is directly underneath the downtown Plaza de la Cultura. Admirers of gold and jewels will definitely want to stop here. This museum is actually one of three housed in this complex (there are numismatic and philatelic museums here as well), and your admission gets you in to all three. Admission is free every Wednesday.

A gold artifact at the Museos del Banco Central.

Calle 5, btw. avs. Central and 2, underneath the Plaza de la Cultura. 𝄐 **2243-4202.** www. museosdelbancocentral.org. Admission C5,500 adults, C4,000 students, free for children 11 and under. Free admission Wed. Daily 9:15am–5pm. Closed Jan 1, May 1, Dec 25, Holy Thurs, Good Fri, Easter Sun.

Museo Nacional de Costa Rica (National Museum) ★★ MUSEUM Sitting atop the Plaza de la Democracia, this museum provides a great, all-around sampling of the archaeological, historical, and natural wonders of Costa Rica from pre-Columbian times to the present. Housed in a large, former army barracks, the building features turrets and outside walls that still bear the bullet marks from fighting in the 1948 civil war. Exhibits include gold and jade artifacts like those you'd see at the Gold Museum (see below) or Jade Museum (see below), but obviously not in the quantity that you'd find in either of those two more specifically oriented institutions. In addition to all the historical exhibits, this place also has a large butterfly garden with more than 25 species of this lovely insect cavorting about. I'd plan on around 2 hours to really get a good feel for this museum.

Calle 17, btw. avs. Central and 2, on Plaza de la Democracia. 𝄐 **2257-1433.** www.museocosta rica.go.cr. Admission $8 adults, $4 students and children 11 and under. Tues–Sat 8:30am–4:30pm; Sun 9am–4:30pm. Closed Jan 1, May 1, Dec 25, Holy Thurs, Good Fri, Easter Sun.

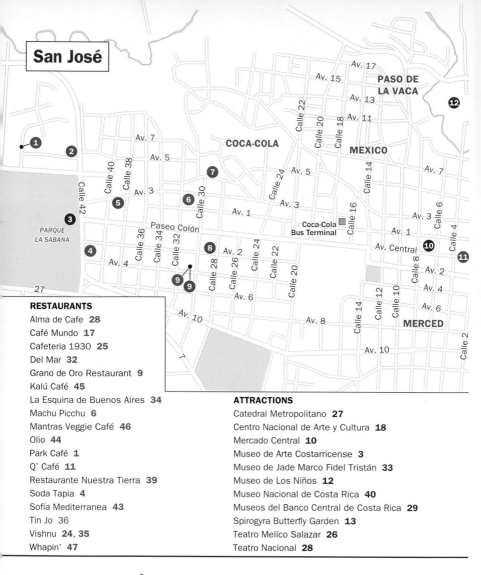

San José

COCA-COLA

PASO DE LA VACA

MEXICO

MERCED

Av. 17
Av. 15
Av. 13
Av. 11
Av. 7
Av. 5
Av. 3
Av. 1
Av. 7
Av. 5
Av. 3
Av. 1
Av. Central
Av. 2
Av. 4
Av. 6
Av. 2
Av. 4
Av. 6
Av. 8
Av. 10

Calle 22
Calle 20
Calle 18
Calle 14
Calle 16
Calle 24
Calle 40
Calle 38
Calle 42
Calle 30
Calle 36
Calle 34
Calle 32
Calle 28
Calle 26
Calle 24
Calle 22
Calle 20
Calle 14
Calle 12
Calle 10
Calle 8
Calle 6
Calle 4
Calle 2

PARQUE LA SABANA

Paseo Colón

Coca-Cola Bus Terminal

27

RESTAURANTS

Alma de Cafe **28**
Café Mundo **17**
Cafeteria 1930 **25**
Del Mar **32**
Grano de Oro Restaurant **9**
Kalú Café **45**
La Esquina de Buenos Aires **34**
Machu Picchu **6**
Mantras Veggie Café **46**
Olio **44**
Park Café **1**
Q' Café **11**
Restaurante Nuestra Tierra **39**
Soda Tapia **4**
Sofía Mediterranea **43**
Tin Jo **36**
Vishnu **24, 35**
Whapin' **47**

ATTRACTIONS

Catedral Metropolitano **27**
Centro Nacional de Arte y Cultura **18**
Mercado Central **10**
Museo de Arte Costarricense **3**
Museo de Jade Marco Fidel Tristán **33**
Museo de Los Niños **12**
Museo Nacional de Costa Rica **40**
Museos del Banco Central de Costa Rica **29**
Spirogyra Butterfly Garden **13**
Teatro Melíco Salazar **26**
Teatro Nacional **28**

BARRIO AMÓN/BARRIO OTOYA

Museo de Jade Marco Fidel Tristán (Jade Museum) ★★ MUSEUM
This museum houses a beautiful and fascinating collection of pre-Columbian jade artifacts, as well as other archaeological finds and relics, dating from around 500 B.C. to 1,500 A.D. Set on the western edge of the Plaza de la Democracia, this new five-story building has more than 7,000 sq. m (75,000 sq. ft.) of exhibition space, which for the first time ever, is enough to display the museum's impressive 7,000 piece collection. Check out the skulls and teeth bearing jade implants, as well as jewelry and functional objects and tools, all made of this precious stone. Everything is well presented, and explanations are in both English and Spanish.

HOTELS

Aldea Hostal 8	Hotel Doña Inés 37
Aurola Holiday Inn 23	Hotel Grano de Oro 9
Costa Rica Backpackers 41	Hôtel Le Bergerac 42
Crowne Plaza Corobicí 2	Hotel Presidente 30
Gran Hotel Costa Rica 25	Hotel Rincón de San José 16
Hostel Pangea 21	Hotel Santo Tomás 22
Hotel Aranjuez 14	Kap's Place 15
Hotel Cacts 7	Pensión de la Cuesta 32
Hotel Colonial 38	Sleep Inn 19
Hotel Don Carlos 20	Tryp Sabana by Windham 5

Calle 13, btw. avenidas 2 and Central. © **2287-6034.** Admission $15; free for children 11 and under. Daily 10am–5pm.

LA SABANA/PASEO COLÓN

Museo de Arte Costarricense (Costa Rican Art Museum) ★★ ART MUSEUM   Originally the main terminal of San José's first international airport, this museum houses the largest and most important collection of works by Costa Rican artists from the colonial time to the present. The museum's permanent collection has over 6,000 pieces, including works by Juan Manuel Sánchez, Max Jiménez, Francisco "Paco" Zuñiga, Francisco Amighetti, Lola Fernández, and more. In the back patio—which used to lead to the tarmac—is a large and lovely

Art displays at Museo de Jade Marco Fidel Tristán.

sculpture garden. This museum is free, and anchors the eastern edge of the large La Sabana city park, making it easy to combine a visit here, with a stroll through the park.

Calle 42 and Paseo Colón, Parque La Sabana Este. © **2256-1281.** www.musarco.go.cr. Free admission. Tues–Sun 9am–4pm.

A sculpture at Museo de Arte Costarricense.

ON THE OUTSKIRTS OF DOWNTOWN

Spirogyra Butterfly Garden ZOO This butterfly garden is smaller and less elaborate than the Butterfly Farm (p. 471), but it provides a good introduction to the life cycle of butterflies. It's also a calm and quiet oasis in a noisy and crowded city, yet quite close to downtown. You'll be given a self-guided-tour booklet when you arrive, and an 18-minute video runs continuously throughout the day. Spirogyra is near El Pueblo, a short taxi ride from San José's center.

100m (1 block) east and 150m (1½ blocks) south of El Pueblo Shopping Center. © **2222-2937.** www.butterflygardencr.com. Admission $7 adults, $6 students, and $5 children 11 and under. Daily 8am–4pm.

Especially for Kids

Museo de Los Niños (Children's Museum) MUSEUM   This massive museum is fun and informative for the whole family. Interactive exhibits and educational displays describe everything from the rainforest, to pre-Columbian village life to the interior of a space ship (in honor of Costa Rican astronaut Franklin Chang). The simulated earthquake exhibit is always a favorite. This museum is in a former prison, and if anyone in your family is acting out, you can actually lock them in a former prison cell to set them straight. The museum is also home to the National Auditorium, and often features temporary exhibitions of contemporary art, as well. You can easily spend 2 to 3 hours at this museum. You'll definitely want to take a taxi here, as the museum sits just in from a rather seedy section of the city's red-light district.

Calle 4 and Av. 9. ✆ **2258-4929.** Admission C1,500 adults, C900 students and children 17 and under. Daily 9am–5pm.

Outdoor Activities & Spectator Sports

Because of the chaos and pollution, you'll probably want to get out of the city before undertaking anything too strenuous. But if you want to brave the elements, San José does have a few outdoor activities to enjoy. For information on horseback riding, hiking, and white-water rafting trips from San José, see "Side Trips from San José," later in this chapter.

Parque La Sabana ★★ (La Sabana Park, at the western end of Paseo Colón), formerly San José's international airport, is the city's center for active sports and recreation. Here you'll find jogging trails, a banked bicycle track, soccer fields, a roller-rink, a few public tennis courts, and the massive National Stadium. Aside from events at the National Stadium, all the facilities are free and open to the public. On weekends, you'll usually find free, public aerobic, yoga, or dancercise classes taking place. Families gather for picnics, people fly kites, pony rides are available for the kids, and everyone strolls through the outdoor

A butterfly at the Spirogyra Butterfly Garden.

sculpture garden. On Sunday mornings, hundreds of folks gather here for free aerobics, dance, and zumba classes. If you really want to experience the local culture, try getting into a pickup soccer game. However, be careful in this park, especially at dusk or after dark, when it becomes a favorite haunt for youth gangs and muggers.

BIRD-WATCHING   Serious birders will certainly want to head out of San José, but it is still possible to see quite a few species in the metropolitan area. Two of the best spots for urban bird-watching are the campus at the **University of Costa Rica,** in the eastern suburb of San Pedro, and **Parque del Este ★**, located a little farther east on the road to San Ramón de Tres Ríos. You'll see a mix of urban species, and if you're lucky, you might spy a couple of humming-birds or even a blue-crowned motmot. To get to the university campus, take any San Pedro bus from Avenida Central between calles 9 and 11. To get to Parque del Este, take the San Ramón/Parque del Este bus from Calle 9 between aveni-das Central and 1.

BULLFIGHTING   Although I hesitate to call it a sport, **Las Corridas a la Tica (Costa Rican bullfighting)** is a popular and frequently comic stadium event. Instead of the blood-and-gore/life-and-death confrontation of traditional bull-fighting, Ticos just like to tease the bull. In a typical *corrida* (bullfight), anywhere from 50 to 150 *toreadores improvisados* (literally, "improvised bullfighters") stand in the ring waiting for the bull. What follows is a slapstick scramble to safety whenever the bull heads toward a crowd of bullfighters. The braver bullfighters try to slap the bull's backside as the beast chases down one of his buddies.

You can see a bullfight during the various Festejos Populares (City Fairs) around the country. The country's largest Festejos Populares are in Zapote, a sub-urb east of San José, during Christmas week and the first week in January. Admis-sion is C5,000 to C10,000. This is a purely seasonal activity and occurs in San José only during the Festejos. However, nearly every little town around the

Parque La Sabana.   A Costa Rican bullfight.

Saprissa fans at a fútbol match.

country has yearly *festejos*. These are spread out throughout the year. Ask at your hotel; if your timing's right, you might be able to take in one of these.

HOTEL SPAS & WORKOUT FACILITIES　Most of the city's higher-end hotels have some sort of pool and exercise facilities. If you're looking for a good, serious work-out, I recommend the **Multispa ★** (✆ **2231-5542;** www.multispa.net), in the Crowne Plaza Corobicí (p. 131). Even if you're not a guest at the hotel, you can use the facilities here and join in any class for $20 per day. Multispa has five other locations around the Central Valley.

JOGGING　Try **Parque La Sabana,** mentioned above, or head to **Parque del Este,** east of town in the foothills above San Pedro. Take the San Ramón/Parque del Este bus from Calle 9 between avenidas Central and 1. It's never a good idea to jog at night, on busy streets, or alone. Women should be particularly careful about jogging alone. And remember, Tico drivers are not accustomed to joggers on residential streets, so don't expect drivers to give you much berth.

SOCCER (FÚTBOL)　Ticos take their *fútbol* seriously. Costa Rican professional soccer is some of the best in Central America, and the national team, or *Sele* (*selección nacional*), qualified for the World Cup in 2002 and 2006. Although they failed to qualify for the 2010 World Cup in South Africa, they did qualify for the 2014 in Brazil—and did quite well considering the odds.

　　The local professional soccer season runs from August through June, with a break for Christmas and New Year's, and separate championship playoffs every December and July. The main San José team is Saprissa (affectionately called El Monstruo, or "The Monster"). **Saprissa's stadium** is in Tibás (✆ **2240-4034;** www.saprissa.co.cr; take any Tibás bus from Calle 2 and Av. 5). Games are often held on Sunday at 11am, but occasionally they are scheduled for Saturday after-noon or Wednesday evening. Check the local newspapers for game times and locations.

　　International and other important matches are held in the **National Sta-dium** on the northeastern corner of Parque La Sabana.

Aside from major international matches at the National Stadium, you don't need to buy tickets in advance. Tickets generally run between C1,000 and C7,500. It's worth paying a little extra for *sombra numerado* (reserved seats in the shade). This will protect you from both the sun and the more rowdy aficionados. Costa Rican soccer fans take the sport seriously, and periodic violent incidents, both inside and outside the stadiums, have marred the sport here, so be careful. Other options include *sombra* (general admission in the shade), *palco* and *palco numerado* (general admission and reserved mezzanine), and *sol general* (general admission in full sun).

It is possible to buy tickets to most sporting events in advance from **E-Ticket** (www.eticket.cr), however the site is entirely in Spanish.

SWIMMING   If you aren't going to get to the beach anytime soon and your hotel doesn't have a pool, you can use the pool at the Multispa facility at the hotel **Crowne Plaza Corobicí** (p. 131) for $20.

WHERE TO STAY

San José offers up a wide range of hotel choices, from plush boutique hotels to budget pensións and backpacker hangouts. Many downtown hotels and small inns are housed in beautifully converted and restored old mansions. The vast majority of accommodations—and the best deals—are in the moderate price range, where you can find everything from elegant little inns to contemporary business class chains. Staying in San José puts you in the center of the action, and close to all of the city's museums, restaurants, and nightlife venues. However, it also exposes you to many urban pitfalls, including noise, traffic, pollution, and street crime.

The prices quoted here are for hotels' rack rates, the maximum that they charge; it is, however, not always necessary to pay that rate. You can typically find discounts of up to 20% for rooms when booking directly, or through websites such as Hotels.com or Expedia.com (see "Tips on Where to Stay," p. 502, for more tips). **Note:** Quoted discount rates almost never include breakfast, local taxes, or other applicable hotel fees.

Downtown San José/Barrio Amón

The urban center of San José is the city's heart and soul, with a wide range of hotels and restaurants and easy access to museums and attractions. It also has several popular public parks and plazas, and the atmospheric Barrio Amón, a charming neighborhood home to the city's greatest concentration of colonial-era architecture. The neighborhood's biggest drawbacks are the street noise, bus fumes, gridlock traffic, and petty crime.

MODERATE

In addition to the hotels listed below, the **Sleep Inn,** Av. 3, between calles 9 and 11 (© **2521-6500;** www.sleepinnsanjose.com), is a modern, American-style chain hotel in the heart of downtown, while **Hotel Colonial ★**, Calle 11, between avenidas 4 and 6 (© **2223-0109;** www.hotelcolonialcr.com); **Hotel Doña Inés** (© **2222-7443;** www.donaines.com), on Calle 11, between avenidas 2 and 6; and **Hotel Rincón de San José** (© **2221-9702;** www.hotelrinconde sanjose.com), on the corner of Avenida 9 and Calle 15, are all solid boutique options.

Aurola Holiday Inn ★ At 17 stories tall, this is the only high rise hotel in San José, and it naturally has some excellent city views, especially from the higher floors. The hotel is wonderfully located fronting the Parque Morazán, and close walking distance to a host of restaurants, bars, and several of the city's better museums. The hotel has an indoor pool and Jacuzzi, and a fairly good exercise room. The Holiday Inn was awarded "4 Leaves" by the CST Sustainable Tourism program.

Av. 5 and Calle 5, San José. ℂ **800/465-4329** in the U.S. and Canada, or 2523-1000. www. holiday-inn.com. 200 units. $87–$157 double; $127–$327 suite. Discounts for reservations made online. Free parking. **Amenities:** 2 restaurants; bar; poolside snack bar; executive-level rooms; exercise room; Jacuzzi; indoor pool; room service; sauna; smoke-free rooms; free Wi-Fi.

Hotel Don Carlos ★★ If you're looking for colonial-era charm and an unmistakably Costa Rican ambience, this is a good choice. The converted downtown home once belonged to a former Costa Rican president. The rooms and hallways are decorated with a wealth of local art and crafts, as well as lush potted ferns, palms and orchids. The hotel has beautiful tile work throughout, and some of the restaurant dining is on a lovely covered patio, with wrought iron chairs and marble tables. The food is pretty good as well. The rooms here can vary tremendously in size, so ask before you book. The hotel's Boutique Annemarie gift shop (p. 142) is one of the most extensive and best stocked in the country.

779 Calle 9, btw. avs. 7 and 9, San José. ℂ **866/675-9259** in the U.S. and Canada, or 2221-6770 in Costa Rica. www.doncarloshotel.com. 33 units. $80–$90 double. Rates include continental breakfast. Free parking. **Amenities:** Restaurant; bar; Jacuzzi; room service; free Wi-Fi.

Hotel Presidente ★ Set right on Avenida Central, the city's bustling commercial center, this well-run mid-range option offers up easy walking access to shops and restaurants. In fact, the hotel sits right on a busy corner, with one side fronting a popular pedestrian mall. Rooms are well maintained and feature understated, yet sharp contemporary decor. The suites are larger and the spa suites come with a private Jacuzzi. You'll pay a little more for rooms with views here, but I think it's worth it.

Av. Central and Calle 7, San José. ℂ **877/540-1790** in the U.S. and Canada, or 2010-0000 in Costa Rica. www.hotel-presidente.com. 100 units. $80–$100 double; $115–$180 suite. Rates include full breakfast buffet. Free parking. **Amenities:** Restaurant; bar; casino; small gym; rooftop Jacuzzi and sauna; room service; free Wi-Fi.

INEXPENSIVE

In addition to the places listed below, **Kap's Place** (ℂ **2221-1169;** www.kaps place.com), across from the Hotel Aranjuez on Calle 19 between avenidas 11 and 13, is another good choice, while real budget hounds might want to try **Hostel Pangea ★** (ℂ **2221-1992;** www.hostelpangea.com), on Avenida 7 and Calle 3, or **Costa Rica Backpackers** (ℂ **2221-6191;** www.costaricaback packers.com), on Avenida 6 between calles 21 and 23.

Gran Hotel Costa Rica I love the location and historic charm of this downtown hotel. Opened in 1930 and set right on the Plaza de la Cultura and cattycorner to the Teatro Nacional, this is a great place to base yourself for some city explorations. The rooms are certainly adequate but feel a bit bare and dated, although that's partly due to their attempt at historical accuracy. In fact, history buffs might be interested in the JFK Presidential suite, where President John F.

Kennedy stayed during his 1963 visit. Breakfasts are served on the 5th floor mezzanine; grab a balcony table if you can, you'll enjoy it with a great view. Meanwhile, down on the ground floor, the hotel's **Cafeteria 1930** is a great place for a cup of coffee and some people-watching.

Av. 2, btw. calles 1 and 3, San José. 🕐 **800/949-0592** in the U.S., or 2221-4000. www.grandhotel costarica.com. 103 units. $60–$95 double; $140–$190 suite. Rates include breakfast buffet. Parking nearby. **Amenities:** 2 restaurants; bar; small gym; room service; free Wi-Fi.

Hotel Aranjuez ★ Set on a quiet side street in the Barrio Amón neighborhood, five adjacent houses have been joined in an enjoyable maze of hallways and courtyards to create one of the best and most unique budget lodgings in the country. Rooms vary greatly in size and isolation; some of the nearly century-old walls in these homes are fairly thin, and noise can be a problem for some. The massive buffet breakfast is a real plus, and the staff and owners are extremely pleasant and helpful.

Calle 19, btw. avs. 11 and 13. 🕐 **2256-1825.** www.hotelaranjuez.com. 35 units, 6 with shared bathroom. $35 double with shared bathroom; $50–$58 double with private bathroom. Rates include breakfast buffet and taxes. Free parking. **Amenities:** Several lounges; free Wi-Fi.

Hotel Santo Tomás ★ This quaint boutique hotel is in the heart of downtown in a restored coffee-baron mansion. Owner Thomas (Tomás) Douglas runs a tight ship. All rooms are clean and well maintained, although it's worth the splurge for the deluxe rooms, which have more space and a better location inside the building (a few even have balconies). There's a small pool and Jacuzzi in a courtyard garden, and the restaurant here is excellent.

Av. 7, btw. calles 3 and 5. 🕐 **2255-0448.** www.hotelsantotomas.com. 30 units. $72–$81 double. Rates include breakfast buffet. $12 parking nearby. **Amenities:** Restaurant; bar; lounge; exercise room; Jacuzzi; small outdoor pool; all rooms smoke-free; free Wi-Fi.

Pensión de la Cuesta This place is a slight step up from your typical hostel, if not so much in terms of facilities and amenities, at least in terms of artistic and cultural cache. Located next to a well-known art gallery (Galeria Jacobo Karpio) this place as well as the neighboring warren of low-rent apartments was once home to a bevy of local and expatriate artists, including Otto Apuy, Diedre Hyde, and Guillermo Conte, as well as other assorted poets, writers and filmmakers. In fact, I spent a month or two on a couch in what was affectionately known as "el barrio" back in 1992, soon after landing in San José. You have your choice of bunk-bed dorm rooms and private rooms with shared baths, as well as private rooms with private bathrooms. Guests have access to a fully functional kitchen.

1332 Cuesta de Núñez, Av. 1, btw. calles 11 and 15, San José. 🕐 **2256-7946.** www.pensionde lacuesta.com. 14 units, 4 with private bathroom. $10–$12 per person in a dorm room; $33 double with shared bath; $43 double with private bath. Rates include continental breakfast and taxes. Parking nearby. **Amenities:** Lounge w/cable TV; free Wi-Fi.

La Sabana/Paseo Colón

Located on the western edge of downtown, La Sabana Park is San José's largest city park, and Paseo Colón is a broad commercial avenue heading straight into the heart of the city. Stay in this neighborhood if you're looking for fast, easy access to the highways heading to Escazú, Santa Ana, the Pacific coast, and the airport and northern zone. Since it's on the edge of town, the area can be pretty dead at night.

EXPENSIVE

In addition to the hotel below, **Tryp Sabana by Windham** ★ (✆ **800/422-1115** in the U.S. and Canada, or **2547-2323** in Costa Rica; www.tryphotels.com), inside the Centro Colón building on Avenida 3, between calles 38 and 40, is a well-located business class hotel, with a very good restaurant and excellent amenities.

Crowne Plaza Corobicí ★   Set on the northeastern corner of La Sabana park, this 11-story business class hotel has unique exterior architecture that makes it look like a cross between a pyramid, an air-traffic control tower and a Soviet-era housing block. Inside, you'll find a huge lobby and open interior, well-maintained rooms, a pleasant and attentive staff, several dining options, a casino, and an excellent gym and spa. A recent remodel has given the rooms a fresh and contemporary feel, and each comes with a 37"-flat screen television. This hotel is not only convenient to La Sabana Park, but also the National Stadium and Costa Rican Art Museum, and is a short cab ride away from a host of restaurants, shops and the heart of downtown.

Autopista General Cañas, Sabana Norte, San José. ✆ **800/227-6963** in the U.S. and Canada, or 2543-6000 in Costa Rica. www.crowneplaza.com. 213 units. $90–$135 double; $135–$250 suite; $445 presidential suite. Free parking. **Amenities:** 2 restaurants; bar; lounge; casino; extensive health club and spa; Jacuzzi; midsize outdoor pool; room service; sauna; Wi-Fi (small fee).

Hotel Grano de Oro ★★★   This is the standard-bearer for luxury boutique hotels in San José and the owners Eldon and Lori Cook support a range of social and environmental causes. A combination of restoration and expansion has transformed this colonial-era mansion into a refined oasis in the center of a busy city. As an added plus, this hotel also boasts one of the city's best restaurants (p. 136). All rooms are elegantly decorated to evoke a bygone era. I think it's worth the

The Jacuzzi terrace at the Hotel Grano de Oro.

splurge for one of the deluxe rooms or suites, which will definitely get you more space, and may also come with a garden patio or private Jacuzzi. The hotel's rooftop patio has two large Jacuzzi spas for those who don't have one in their room.

Calle 30, no. 251, btw. avs. 2 and 4, 150m (1¹/₂ blocks) south of Paseo Colón. ☎ **2255-3322.** www.hotelgranodeoro.com. 40 units. $140–$255 double; $225–$455 suite. Free parking. **Amenities:** Restaurant; bar; lounge; concierge; 2 rooftop Jacuzzis; room service; all rooms smoke-free; spa services; free Wi-Fi.

INEXPENSIVE

In addition to the place mentioned below, **Aldea Hostal** (☎ 2233-6365; www. aldeahostelcostarica.com), is a solid budget hostel option, with a popular little pizza restaurant attached.

Hotel Cacts ★ This is a solid budget option housed in a converted home on a side street about 2 blocks in from the busy Paseo Colón. There's a hostel-like vibe to the operation, but you also get things like a small pool and Jacuzzi. The staff is incredibly friendly and helpful. My favorite feature here, however, is the open-air rooftop patio, which has some chairs and chaise lounges, and offers up a spectacular view of the city and surrounding mountains.

Av. 3 bis, no. 2845, btw. calles 28 and 30, San José. ☎ **2221-2928** or 2221-6546. www.hotelcacts. com. 25 units. $63–$70 double. Rates include breakfast buffet. Free parking. **Amenities:** Lounge; Jacuzzi; small outdoor pool; all rooms smoke-free; free Wi-Fi.

San Pedro/Los Yoses

Located just east of downtown, Los Yoses is home to numerous foreign embassies and consulates, and was one of the city's early upper-class outposts, while San Pedro is home to the University of Costa Rica, and offers up a distinct college town vibe. Staying here, you'll be close to much of the city's action but still enjoy some peace and quiet. If you've rented a car, be sure your hotel provides secure parking or you'll have to find (and pay for) a nearby lot.

MODERATE

Hôtel Le Bergerac ★★ On a residential side street off the busy Avenida Segunda, about midway between downtown and the university district of San Pedro, the Hôtel Le Bergerac is a delightful boutique hotel, exuding a sense of understated elegance. Three contiguous houses have been joined to create this hotel. Rooms are spacious, and most feature bright, varnished wood floors and either plenty of windows or a set of French doors opening onto a patio or balcony.

Calle 35, avenida 0 y 8, San José. ☎ **2234-7850.** www.bergerachotel.com. 28 units. $97–$157 double. Rates include full breakfast. Free parking. **Amenities:** Restaurant; lounge; free Wi-Fi.

Hotel Milvia ★ Housed in a converted old wooden plantation home, this boutique hotel is the handiwork of Steve Longrigg and Florencia Urbina. Steve has decades in the hospitality industry in Costa Rica, and Florencia is one of the country's more prominent artists and the former director of the Costa Rican Art Museum (p. 123). Rooms, hallways and common areas feature a varied and striking collection of contemporary Costa Rican art by Urbina and her friends and cohorts. Rooms are large and well-kept, with plenty of natural light. Most let out onto a veranda or common courtyard sitting area. This hotel is close to the Universidad Latina and one of the city's few train lines, so street noise can be a problem for some.

1 block north and 2 blocks east of the Muñoz y Nanne Supermarket, San Pedro. © **2225-4543.** www.hotelmilvia.com. 9 units. $65–$80 double. Rates include continental breakfast. **Amenities:** Lounge, TV, Wi-Fi.

WHERE TO DINE

San José has an excellent variety of restaurants serving cuisines from all over the world. You can find superb French, Italian, and contemporary fusion restaurants around the city, as well as Peruvian, Japanese, Swiss, and Spanish spots. The greatest concentration and variety of restaurants is in the downtown area, as well as in the nearby Central Valley suburbs of Escazú and Santa Ana (p. 161). If you're looking for cheap eats, you'll find them all across the city in little restaurants known as *sodas,* which are the equivalent of diners in the United States.

Fruit vendors stake out spots on almost every street corner in downtown San José. If you're lucky enough to be in town between April and June, you can sample more varieties of mangoes than you ever knew existed. I like buying them already cut up in a little bag; they cost a little more this way, but you don't get nearly as messy. Be sure to try a green mango with salt and chili peppers—it's guaranteed to wake up your taste buds. Another common street food is *pejibaye,* a bright orange palm nut about the size of a plum. They're boiled in big pots on carts; you eat them in much the same way you eat an avocado, and they taste a bit like squash.

San José has a few 24-hour restaurants for real late-night partiers. In addition to **Restaurante Nuestra Tierra** (see below), your best bet is **Del Mar** (© 2257-7800; Avenida 1 and Calle 9), with stained-glass windows and efficient service; it belongs to and is across from the infamous Hotel Del Rey and its very active sex worker scene. There's also a 24-hour **Denny's** (© 2520-2500; www.dennyscostarica.com), at the Best Western Irazú, on the highway out to the airport, and another is beside the Hampton Inn at the airport.

Downtown San José
EXPENSIVE

La Esquina de Buenos Aires ★★ ARGENTINE/STEAKHOUSE Frankly, the Argentines do steak much better than the Ticos, and this Argentine-themed steakhouse is one of the best restaurants in the city. The decor and ambience are pure Porteño, and the extensive menu features a long list of grilled meats, some

A vendor selling *pejibaye.*

very good pastas, and various seafood and poultry offerings. This place is festive and almost always filled to brimming. Reservations are essential most nights.

Calle 11 and Av. 4. © **2223-1909.** www.laesquinadebuenosaires.com. Reservations recommended. Main courses C7,000–C18,500. Mon–Fri 11:30am–3pm and 6–10:30pm; Sat–Sun noon–10pm.

MODERATE

Restaurante Nuestra Tierra COSTA RICAN   This place was built for and is geared towards tourists. Designed to recreate the feel of an old Costa Rican homestead kitchen, you'll find the wait staff in traditional garb, heavy wooden tables and bench seating, bunches of bananas and onions and scores of painted enamel coffee mugs hung from wooden columns and beams. Typical Costa Rican meals are served on banana leaves set over large plates. The prices are high for what you get. On the plus side, service is prompt and pleasant, portions are large and it does give one the feel of a typical Costa Rican restaurant from a bygone era.

Av. 2 and Calle 15. © **2258-6500.** Main courses C6,000–C15,000. Daily 24 hr.

Tin Jo ★★★ CHINESE/PAN-ASIAN   This has long been one of the best and most popular restaurants in the city. Costa Rica has a long history of Chinese immigration and this family restaurant is on its second generation. However, the menu here wanders far and wide, with more traditional Szechuan and Cantonese plates sharing the menu with a mix of Thai, Japanese, Indian, and even Malay dishes. Each of the various rooms here features unique decor from one of the aforementioned countries or regions. The multiple vegetarian options are all clearly marked as to whether they are vegan and/or gluten free.

Calle 11, btw. avs. 6 and 8. © **2221-7605** or 2257-3622. www.tinjo.com. Reservations recommended. Main courses C6,000–C14,000. Mon–Fri 11:30am–2:30pm and 6–10pm (Fri until 11pm); Sat noon–3pm and 6–11pm; Sun noon–9pm.

INEXPENSIVE

In addition to the places listed below, the **Q'Café** (© **2221-0707;** www.que cafe.com) is a delightful little European-style cafe with a pretty perch above the busy corner of Avenida Central and Calle 2. Try to grab a seat overlooking the action on the street below.

Alma de Café ★ CAFE/COFFEEHOUSE   Housed in an anteroom off the main lobby of the neo-baroque National Theater (Teatro Nacional), this simple coffee shop and restaurant is a great place for a light lunch or to sit over a cup of Costa Rican java and some dessert. The menu features healthful salads, a selection of quiches, sandwiches, and lasagna. There are marble tables and floors, as well as elaborate ceiling murals, and regularly rotating exhibits of contemporary local artists. This place often stays open later on theater performance nights.

In the Teatro Nacional, Av. 2, btw. calles 3 and 5. ✆ **2010-1119.** Sandwiches C3,000–C6,000; main courses C4,000–C6,500. Mon–Sat 9am–7pm; Sun 9am–6pm.

Vishnu VEGETARIAN   This mini-chain was a pioneer in providing vegetarian cooking to the Costa Rican masses. I find their cooking a bit uninspired, but it's a safe and popular bet for folks looking for vegetarian and vegan options in San José. The fresh fruit juices and smoothies here are great, and they do a pretty decent vegetarian burger. A second branch (✆ **2223-3095**) is on the north side of Avenida 8, between calles 11 and 9, as well as outlets in Heredia and Alajuela.

Av. 1, btw. calles 1 and 3. ✆ **2256-6063.** Main courses C3,500–C5,000. Mon–Sat 7am–9pm; Sun 9am–7:30pm.

Barrio Amón/Barrio Otoya

MODERATE

Café Mundo ★ INTERNATIONAL   This popular spot serves good food in a lovely old building with a lively atmosphere and fabulous ambience. Tables and chairs are spread through several rooms, hallways, patios, and terraces in this rambling former residence. The menu features a solid selection of salads, pizzas, pastas, and a range of main dishes running the gamut from seafood-stuffed tenderloin to chicken in a honey-mustard sauce. The largest dining room here features floor to ceiling flowers painted by Costa Rican artist Miguel Casafont.

Calle 15 and Av. 9, 200m (2 blocks) east and 100m (1 block) north of the INS Building. ✆ **2222-6190.** Reservations recommended. Main courses C4,500–C15,000. Mon–Thurs 11am–10:30pm; Fri 11am–11:30pm; Sat 5–11:30pm.

Kalú ★★★ CAFE/BISTRO   Costa Rican-born chef Camille Ratton, trained at the Cordon Bleu, has created a wonderfully casual little bistro restaurant and gallery in a converted old home in a quiet neighborhood. The menu features a range of light and healthful options, as well as pizzas, panini, burgers, and more, including noodle dishes from Thailand and curries from India. Don't miss out on the desserts, which, to my mind, are Camille's specialty. The attached **Kiosco** (p. 143) is one of the better and more creative gift shops in the city.

Calle 31 and Av. 5. ✆ **2221-2081.** www.kalu.co.cr. Reservations recommended. Main courses C4,850–C10,500. Mon–Tues noon–8pm; Wed–Fri noon–10pm; Sat 8am–10pm.

La Sabana/Paseo Colón

VERY EXPENSIVE

Park Café ★★ FUSION   While the Grano de Oro (see below) thrives on elegance and consistency, this place can be a little rougher around the edges—but the payoff from British chef Richard Neat, who ran a two-star Michelin restaurant in London before moving to Costa Rica, can also be substantial. The restaurant is spread throughout the interior courtyard and garden of a stately old home that functions as an antiques and decorative arts shop by day. The menu changes seasonally, but always features creative, contemporary creations with sometimes dazzling presentations.

Sabana Norte, 1 block north of Rostipollos. © **2290-6324.** www.parkcafecostarica.blogspot. com. Reservations recommended. Main courses C15,000–C21,000. Tues–Sat 5:30pm–9pm.

EXPENSIVE

Grano de Oro Restaurant ★★★ INTERNATIONAL   It's no accident that the city's most elegant boutique hotel (p. 131) also has one of its best restaurants. The folks here take fine dining seriously, and it shows from the lovely turn-of-the-20th-century decor to the large and well-stocked wine cellar. Start things off with their trio of savory "crème brûleés"—Gorgonzola, porcini, and goat cheese. For main dishes, I recommend the roasted lamb chops with cilantro sauce and sautéed fennel. Be sure to leave room for dessert, as these also rise to the occasion. You can't miss here for breakfast, brunch, or lunch, either.

Calle 30, no. 251, btw. avs. 2 and 4, 150m (1½ blocks) south of Paseo Colón. © **2255-3322.** www.hotelgranodeoro.com. Reservations recommended. Main courses C8,500–21,000. Daily 7am–10pm.

MODERATE

Machu Picchu ★ PERUVIAN/INTERNATIONAL   This longstanding local institution serves up excellent Peruvian cuisine in a converted old home just off of Paseo Colón. The menu is extensive, with a wide range of ceviches and other cold and hot appetizers. The *parihuela* is a delicious seafood soup almost big and rich enough for a full meal. The *corvina* Machu Picchu is a filet of sea bass served in a seafood and brandy sauce. The house drink is the classic Peruvian pisco sour, made in a blender with pisco, lime juice, ice, and an egg white. A second branch of this restaurant is in San Pedro (© **2283-3679**), as well as a sister operation **Pikeo** (© **2203-6374**), which serves up a more specialized tapas-style menu with outdoor seating on a large covered patio with a fantastic view, located on the old road between Escazú and Santa Ana.

Calle 32, btw. avs. 1 and 3, 150m (1½ blocks) north of the KFC on Paseo Colón. © **2222-7384.** www.restaurantemachupicchu.com. Reservations recommended. Main courses C5,500–C13,000. Mon–Sat 11am–10pm; Sun 11am–6pm.

INEXPENSIVE

Soda Tapia ★ COSTA RICAN   This Costa Rican classic mixes the menu and cuisine of a classic Tico soda with the vibe and styling of a 1950s American diner. Bright lights and Formica tables abound. Still, this is a great place to come for some *típico* cooking. Its extended hours make it a good choice for a late-night bite. The main branch is just across from the popular La Sabana park and Museo de Arte Costarricense (p. 123). Other branches are around the Central Valley, including ones in Santa Ana (Centro Comercial Vistana Oeste, across from MATRA;©**2203-7175**), Heredia (Centro Comercial Paseo de las Flores;©**2238-1340**), and Alajuela (Centro Comercial Plaza Real Alajuela; © **2441-6033**).

Calle 42 and Av. 2, across from the Museo de Arte Costarricense. © **2222-6734.** www.soda tapia.com. Sandwiches C2,000–C4,500; main dishes C3,000–C5,000. Mon–Thurs 6am–2am; Fri–Sat 24 hr.; Sun 6am–2am.

San Pedro/Los Yoses

In addition to the restaurants listed below, local and visiting vegetarians swear by the little **Comida Para Sentir Restaurante Vegetariano San Pedro** (© 2224-1163), located 125m (1¼ blocks) north of the San Pedro Church. Despite the massive size and popularity of the nearby **Il Pomodoro** (© 2224-0966), I prefer **Pane E Vino** (© 2280-2869; www.paneevino.co.cr), an excellent pasta-and-pizza joint on the eastern edge of San Pedro, with other outlets around town, as well. If you're hankering for sushi, try **Ichiban** ★ (© 2253-8012; www.ichibanrestaurante.com) in San Pedro, or **Matsuri** ★ (© 2280-5522), a little farther east in Curridabat. Both of these sushi places have outlets on the west side of town as well.

EXPENSIVE

Donde Carlos ★★ ARGENTINE/STEAK   While **La Esquina de Buenos Aires** (see above) has the better and more authentic Argentine ambience and vibe, this place gets my vote as the best Argentine-style steakhouse in the city, if not the country. The cuts of meat are thick, tender and perfectly prepared. You'll pass the large, open, charcoal grill just inside the front door of this converted former home in an upscale residential neighborhood. Head upstairs for the better seating, and if it's a nice night try to grab one of the outdoor balcony tables. For dessert, the apple pancake is a well-deserved house specialty, and big enough to be shared.

1 block north of the Fatima Church in Los Yoses. © **2225-0819.** www.dondecarlos.com. Main courses C9,000–C18,000. Mon–Thurs noon–3pm and 6:30 10:30pm; Fri noon–3pm and 6.30–11pm; Sat noon–11pm; Sun noon–7pm.

MODERATE

Olio ★ MEDITERRANEAN   This dimly lit and cozy place has an intimate and romantic vibe, and features predominantly Mediterranean cuisine. A laundry list of classic Greek, Italian, and Spanish dishes is served in tapas-size portions, alongside more hearty pasta and main-course options. The wine list ventures beyond the immediate shores of the Mediterranean to include offerings from Chile, Argentina, and even Bulgaria.

Barrio California, 200m (2 blocks) north of Bagelman's. © **2281-0541.** Reservations recommended. Main courses $7–$20. Mon–Wed noon–11pm; Thurs–Fri noon–midnight; Sat 6pm–midnight.

Whapin' ★ COSTA RICAN/CARIBBEAN   It's hard to find authentic Costa Rican Caribbean cooking away from the coast, but this humble place does a good job. You can get a wide range of specialties more commonly served up in Cahuita and Puerto Viejo. They've always got the seafood and root vegetable stew *rondon* on the menu (see "That Run-Down Feeling," on p. 483), as well as rice and beans cooked in coconut milk and served with your choice of chicken, meat or fish. For dessert you can get a piece of coconut pie. They've also go their spicy version of jerk chicken, as well as whole fried red snapper. Most dishes come with a side of fresh fried plantain or *patacones*.

Barrio Escalante, 200m (2 blocks) east of El Farolito. © **2283-1480.** Main courses C5,000–C13,000. Mon–Fri 8am–10pm; Sat 11:30am–10pm.

INEXPENSIVE

Mantras Veggie Café and Tea House ★★ VEGETARIAN   This place gets my vote as the best dedicated vegetarian restaurant in the city. Housed in a converted home in a plush residential neighborhood, the cafe has both indoor and garden patio seating. I especially like the garden seating, under bright red canvas umbrellas. The menu features a broad mix of soups, salads, wraps, sandwiches, and main dishes. There are both vegan and raw offerings. Signature dishes here include their raw zucchini pasta with pesto and their pad Thai.

2 blocks east of El Farolito, in Barrio Escalante. ℂ **2253-6715.** Main courses C3,000–C6,500. Mon–Sat 8:30am–5pm.

Sofía Mediterranea MIDDLE EASTERN   This popular restaurant is a great option for some traditional Middle Eastern cuisine. You can start things off with several of the regional classics, including hummus and tabbouleh, as well as delicious stuffed grape leaves. For a main course, I recommend the *Begendili Kuzu*, slow braised lamb shoulder served with an eggplant purée, or the beef tenderloin that comes with a wine and blackberry reduction. The grilled squid is also excellent. At around $8, their daily lunch special is a great deal, featuring a main course, soft drink, and dessert. At night, there's sometimes a belly dance performance or some live music.

Calle 33 and Av. 1, 2 blocks north of Bagleman's, in Barrio Escalante. ℂ **2224-5050.** Main courses C3,500–C9,500. Tue–Sat noon–11pm; Sun noon-5pm.

SHOPPING

Serious shoppers will be disappointed in San José. Aside from coffee and oxcarts, there isn't much that's distinctly Costa Rican. To compensate for its own relative lack of goods, San José (and all of Costa Rica) does a brisk business in selling crafts and clothes imported from Guatemala, Panama, and Ecuador.

San José's central shopping corridor is bounded by avenidas 1 and 2, from about Calle 14 in the west to Calle 13 in the east. For several blocks west of the Plaza de la Cultura, **Avenida Central** is a pedestrian-only street mall where you'll find store after store of inexpensive clothes for men, women, and children. Depending on the mood of the police that day, you might find a lot of street vendors as well. Most shops in the downtown district are open Monday through Saturday from about 8am to 6pm. Some shops close for lunch, while others remain open (it's just the luck of the draw for shoppers). You'll be happy to find that sales and import taxes have already been figured into display prices.

MARKETS

Several markets are near downtown, but by far the largest is the **Mercado Central** ★ (see below), located between avenidas Central and 1 and calles 6 and 8.

Plaza de la Democracia ★★   Two long rows of outdoor stalls sell T-shirts, Guatemalan and Ecuadorian handicrafts and clothing, small ceramic *ocarinas* (a small musical wind instrument), and handmade jewelry. The atmosphere here is much more open than at the Mercado Central, which I find just a bit too claustrophobic. You might be able to bargain prices down a bit, but bargaining is not a traditional part of the vendor culture here, so you'll have to work hard to save a few colones. On the west side of the Plaza de la Democracia, Calle 13 bis, btw. avs. Central and 2. No phone.

MODERN MALLS

With globalization and modernization taking hold in Costa Rica, much of the local shopping scene has shifted to large megamalls. Modern multilevel affairs with cineplexes, food courts, and international brand-name stores are becoming ubiquitous. The biggest and most modern of these malls include the **Mall San Pedro, Multiplaza** (one each in Escazú and the eastern suburb of Zapote), and **Terra Mall** (on the outskirts of downtown on the road to Cartago). Although they lack the charm of small shops found around San José, they are a reasonable option for one-stop shopping; most contain at least one or two local galleries and crafts shops, along with a large supermarket, which is always the best place to stock up on local coffee, hot sauces, liquors, and other nonperishable foodstuffs.

Shopping A to Z
ART GALLERIES

Galería Jacobo Karpio   This excellent gallery handles some of the more adventurous modern art to be found in Costa Rica. Karpio has a steady stable of prominent Mexican, Cuban, and Argentine artists, as well as some local talent. Av. 1, casa no. 1352, btw. calles 13 and 15. 50m (164 ft.) west of the Legislative Assembly. ℂ **2257-7963.**

Galería Kandinsky   Owned by the daughter of one of Costa Rica's most prominent modern painters, Rafa Fernández, this small gallery usually has a good selection of high-end contemporary Costa Rican paintings, be it the house collection or a specific temporary exhibit. Centro Comercial Calle Real, San Pedro. ℂ **2234-0478.**

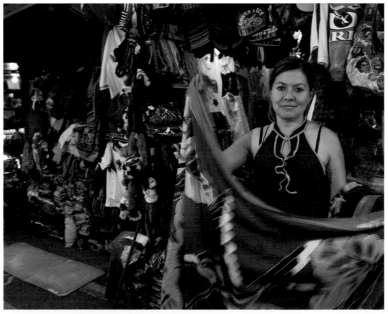

A vendor at the Plaza de la Democracia market.

joe **TO GO**

Two words of advice: Buy coffee. Lots of it.

Coffee is the best shopping deal in all of Costa Rica. Although the best Costa Rican coffee is allegedly shipped off to North American and European markets, it's hard to beat the coffee that's roasted right in front of you here. Best of all is the price: One pound of coffee sells for around $4 to $7. It makes a great gift and truly is a local product.

Café Britt is the big name in Costa Rican coffee. These folks have the largest export business in the country, and, although high-priced, their blends are very dependable. Café Britt is widely available at gift shops around the country, and at the souvenir concessions at both international airports. My favorites, however, are the coffees roasted and packaged in Manuel Antonio and Monteverde, by **Café Milagro** and **Café Monteverde,** respectively. If you visit either of these places, definitely pick up their beans.

In general, the best place to buy coffee is in any supermarket. Why pay more at a gift or specialty shop? If you buy prepackaged coffee in a supermarket in Costa Rica, the whole beans will be marked either *grano* (grain) or *grano entero* (whole bean). If you opt for ground varieties *(molido),* be sure the package is marked *puro;* otherwise, it will likely be mixed with a good amount of sugar, the way Ticos like it.

One good coffee-related gift to bring home is a coffee sock and stand. This is the most common mechanism for brewing coffee beans in Costa Rica. It consists of a simple circular stand, made out of wood or wire, which holds a sock. Put the ground beans in the sock, place a pot or cup below it, and pour boiling water through. You can find the socks and stands at most supermarkets and in the Mercado Central. In fancier crafts shops, you'll find them made out of ceramic. Depending on its construction, a stand will cost you between $1.50 and $15; socks run around 30¢, so buy a few spares.

Galería Valanti ★★   This is a gorgeous, well-lit, and expertly curated gallery. The collection here is ever evolving, but always includes a good mix of contemporary and classic Costa Rican and Latin American artists. Av. 11 #3395, btw. calles 33 and 35, Barrio Escalante. *©* **2253-1659.** www.galeriavalanti.com.

TEORetica ★★   This small downtown gallery was founded by one of the more adventurous and internationally respected collectors and curators in Costa Rica, the late Virginia Pérez-Ratton. It's still one of the best galleries in the country, and you'll usually find very interesting and cutting-edge exhibitions here. Calle 7, btw. avs. 9 and 11. *©* **2233-4881.** www.teoretica.org.

BOOKS

Librería Internacional This is the closest Costa Rica has to a major book retailer. Most of the books here are in Spanish, but they do have a small-to-modest selection of English-language contemporary fiction, nonfiction, and natural history texts. Librería Internacional has various outlets around San José, including in most of the major modern malls. Av. Central, ³/₄ block west of the Plaza de la Cultura. ✆ **2257-2563.** www.libreriainternacional.com.

CHOCOLATE

Sibu Chocolate Building on the success of their organic chocolate production and tour operation in the hills of Heredia (p. 170), the folks from Sibu Chocolate have opened a small storefront in the Sabana Norte neighborhood. This is a great place to pick up a mix of their wonderful truffles and bonbons, as well as cacao powder, chocolate bars, and cacao nibs, which my family loves to sprinkle on cereal and granola in the morning. This is also a great place to grab a cup of hot chocolate (or coffee) and a pastry. 2 blocks north of Rostipollos in Sabana Norte. ✆ **2220-0050.** www.sibuchocolate.com.

HANDICRAFTS

The range and quality of craftworks for sale here has improved greatly in recent years. In addition to the places listed below, you might want to check out the works of Lil Mena, a local artist who specializes in working with and painting on handmade papers and rough fibers, and **Cecilia "Pefi" Figueres ★★**, who specializes in brightly colored abstract and figurative ceramic bowls, pitchers, coffee mugs, and more. Both Mena and Figueres are sold at some of the better gift shops around the city. Another artist to look out for is **Barry Biesanz ★★**,

Finely crafted artworks form colorful displays at Galería Namu.

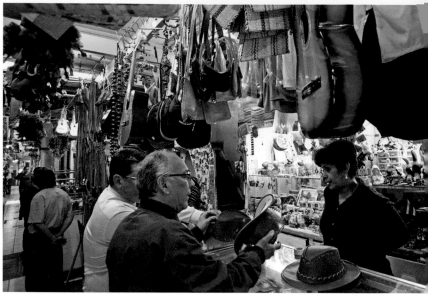

A stall at the Mercado Central.

whose bowls and boxes are works of art. Biesanz's works are also carried at fine gift shops around San José, as well as in his workshop and gallery in the hills above Escazú (p. 163). Vendors at the Plaza de la Democracia market (see above) also sell handicrafts.

Boutique Annemarie ★ Occupying two floors at the Hotel Don Carlos (p. 129), this shop has an amazing array of wood products, leather goods, papier-mâché figurines, paintings, books, cards, posters, and jewelry. You'll see most of this stuff at the city's other shops, but not in such quantities or in such a relaxed and pressure-free environment. At the Hotel Don Carlos, Calle 9, btw. avs. 7 and 9. ⓒ **2233-5343.**

Chietón Morén ★★★ "Chietón Morén" means "fair deal" in the Boruca language. This place features arts and craft works from a dozen or so different Costa Rican indigenous communities displayed in a space that is part museum and part showroom and market. Operating as a nonprofit and certified "fair trade," all the profits are given directly back to the artisans and their communities. Offerings include a wide range of textiles, carved masks, prints, and jewelry. Calle 1, btw. avs. 10 and 12. ⓒ **2221-0145.** www.chietonmoren.org.

Galería Namu ★★★ Galería Namu has some very high-quality arts and crafts, specializing in truly high-end indigenous works, including excellent Boruca and Huetar carved masks and "primitive" paintings. It also carries a good selection of more modern arts and craft pieces, including the ceramic work of Cecilia "Pefi" Figueres. This place organizes tours to visit various indigenous tribes and artisans as well. Av. 7, btw. calles 5 and 7. ⓒ **2256-3412.** www.galerianamu. com.

La Casona Just off Avenida Central, in the heart of downtown, La Casona is a 3-story warren of crafts and souvenir stalls. The various stalls sell similar craft and souvenir works imported from Guatemala, Ecuador, Panama, and even China. On a rainy day, this is a great alternative to the outdoor market on the Plaza de la Democracia (see above). Calle Central btw. avs. Central and 1. © **2222-7999.**

Mercado Central ★   Although this tight maze of stalls is primarily a food market, vendors also sell souvenirs, leather goods, musical instruments, and many other items. Be especially careful with your wallet, purse, and prominent jewelry, as skilled pickpockets frequent the area. All the streets surrounding the Mercado Central are jammed with produce vendors selling from small carts or loading and unloading trucks. It's always a hive of activity, with crowds of people jostling for space on the streets. Your best bet is to visit on Sunday or a weekday; Saturday is particularly busy. Btw. avs. Central and 1 and calles 6 and 8, San José. No phone.

JEWELRY

Kiosco ★★   Attached to the restaurant Kalú (p. 135), this place features a range of original and one-off pieces of functional, wearable, and practical pieces made by contemporary Costa Rican and regional artists and designers. While the offerings are regularly changing, you'll usually find a mix of jewelry, handbags, shoes, dolls, furniture, and knickknacks. Often the pieces are made with recycled or sustainable materials. Calle 31 and Av. 5, Barrio Escalante. www.kioscosjo.com. © **2258-1829.**

Studio Metallo ★★   The outgrowth of a jewelry-making school and studio, this shop has some excellent handcrafted jewelry made in a range of styles, using everything from 18-karat white and yellow gold and pure silver, to some less exotic and expensive alloys. Some works integrate gemstones, while many others focus on the metalwork. 6½ blocks east of the Iglesia Santa Teresita, Barrio Escalante. © **2281-3207.** www.studiometallo.com.

LEATHER GOODS

Del Río ★   This local leather goods manufacturer has several storefronts around the city, and in most of the country's modern malls. Works are high quality and fairly priced, and range from wallets and belts to briefcases, boots, and fancy leather jackets and pants. Del Río also offers free hotel pickup and transfer to its factory outlet in Heredia (© **2262-1415**). Av. Central, btw. calles 3 and 5, fronting the Plaza de la Cultura. © **2255 0203.** www.delrio.cr.

LIQUOR

The best prices I've seen for liquor are at the city's large supermarkets, such as **Más × Menos.** A Más × Menos store is on Paseo Colón and Calle 26, and another is on Avenida Central at the east end of town, just below the Museo Nacional de Costa Rica.

ENTERTAINMENT & NIGHTLIFE

Catering to a mix of tourists, college students, and just generally party-loving Ticos, San José has a host of options to meet the nocturnal needs of visitors and residents alike. You'll find plenty of interesting clubs and bars, a wide range of theaters, and some very lively discos and dance salons.

   To find out what's going on in San José while you're in town, go to **www. ticotimes.net**, or pick up the *La Nación* (Spanish). The former is a good place to find out where local expats are hanging out; the latter's "Viva" and "Tiempo Libre" sections have extensive listings of discos, movie theaters, and live music.

Tip: Several very popular nightlife venues are in the upscale suburbs of Escazú and Santa Ana, as well as in Heredia (a college town) and Alajuela. See "The Central Valley" chapter for more details on nightlife in these areas.

The Performing Arts

Visiting artists stop in Costa Rica on a regular basis. Recent concerts have featured hard rockers Aerosmith, Red Hot Chili Peppers, and Metallica, Mexican crooner Lila Downs, pop legend Elton John, Colombian sensation Shakira, and Latin heartthrob Marc Anthony. These performances take place at one of San José's performing arts theaters or one of the city's large sporting stadiums.

The **National Symphony Orchestra** is respectable by regional standards, although its repertoire tends to be rather conservative. Symphony season runs March through November, with concerts roughly every other weekend at the Teatro Nacional. Tickets cost between $3 and $30 and can be purchased at the box office.

Costa Rica's cultural panorama changes drastically every March when the country hosts large arts festivals. In odd-numbered years, El Festival Nacional de las Artes reigns supreme, featuring purely local talent. In even-numbered years, the month-long fete is **El Festival Internacional de las Artes,** with a nightly smorgasbord of dance, theater, and music from around the world. Most nights of the festival offer between 4 and 10 shows. Many are free, and the most expensive ticket is usually around $5. For exact dates and details, you can contact the **Ministry of Youth and Culture** (𝄞 **2221-2022;** www.mcjdcr.go.cr), although information is in Spanish.

It is possible to buy tickets to many cultural events and concerts in advance from **E-Ticket** (www.eticket.cr), however the site is entirely in Spanish.

Auditorio Nacional   Housed inside the Museo de Los Niños (p. 125) this is the city's most modern performing arts theater, with the best seats and sound system. However, it gets much less use than the more classic Teatro Nacional and Teatro Melico Salazar. Calle 4 and Av. 9. 𝄞 **2256-5876.**

Teatro Melico Salazar   Built in 1928, this baroque theater is larger than the nearby Teatro Nacional. The facility is owned by the Costa Rican Ministry of Culture and houses the National Theater Company and National Dance Company. A regular slate of concerts and dance and theater performances are offered. Av. 2 btw. calles Central and 2. 𝄞 **2233-5424** or 2257-6005. www.teatromelico.go.cr.

Teatro Nacional (National Theater) ★★   Costa Rica's most elegant and elaborate theater, the Teatro Nacional was opened in 1897. Funded with a special tax on coffee, and modeled on the Paris Opera House, this neo-baroque theater features marble floors and columns, numerous sculptures, and a beautiful painted fresco on the main auditorium's ceiling. It is home base for the National Symphony Orchestra, and site of numerous other cultural events. Av. 2 btw. calles 3 and 5. 𝄞 **2221-5341.** www.teatronacional.go.cr.

The Club, Music & Dance Scene

You'll find plenty of places to hit the dance floor in San José. Salsa and merengue are the main beats that move people here, and many of the city's dance clubs, discos, and salons feature live music on the weekends. You'll find a pretty limited selection, though, if you're looking to catch some small-club jazz, rock, or blues performances.

The Teatro Nacional.

The daily "Viva" and Friday's "Tiempo Libre" sections of *La Nación* newspaper have weekly performance schedules. Some dance bands to watch for are Gaviota, Chocolate, Son de Tikizia, Taboga Band, and La Orquestra Son Mayor. While Ghandi, Akasha, and El Parque are popular local rock groups, Marfil is a good cover band, and the Blues Devils, Chepe Blues, and the Las Tortugas are outfits that play American-style hard driving rock and blues. If you're looking for jazz, check out Editus, El Sexteto de Jazz Latino, or pianist and Minister of Culture Manuel Obregón. For a taste of something eclectic, look for Santos y Zurdo, Sonámbulo Psicotrópical, or Amarillo, Cyan y Magenta.

Most of the places listed below charge a nominal cover charge; sometimes it includes a drink or two.

Castro's ★   This is a classic Costa Rican dance club. The music varies throughout the night, from salsa and merengue to reggaeton and occasionally electronic trance. The rooms and various types of environments include some intimate and quiet corners, spread over a couple of floors. It's open daily from noon to anytime between 3 and 6am. Av. 13 and Calle 22, Barrio Mexico. ℂ **2256-8789.**

Salsa 54   This is the place to watch expert salsa dancers and to try some steps yourself. You can take Latin dance classes here, or you might learn something just by watching. This place is popular with Ticos, and tourists are a rare commodity here—tourists who can really dance salsa, even more so. It's open on weekends 'til 4am. Calle 3, btw. avs. 1 and 3. ℂ **2233-3814.**

Vértigo ★★   Tucked inside a nondescript office building and commercial center on Paseo Colón, this club remains one of the more popular places for rave-style late-night dancing and partying. The dance floor is huge and the ceilings are

Salsa dancing at a San José club.

high, and electronic music rules the roost. It's open Friday and Saturday till 6am. Edificio Colón, Paseo Colón. ✆ **2257-8424.** www.vertigocr.com.

The Bar Scene

San José has something for every taste. Lounge lizards will be happy in most hotel bars downtown, while students and the young at heart will have no problem mixing in at the livelier spots around town. Sports fans have plenty of places to catch the most important games of the day, and a couple of brewpubs are drastically improving the quality and selection of the local suds.

The best part of the varied bar scene in San José is something called a *boca*, the equivalent of a tapa in Spain: a little dish of snacks that arrives at your table when you order a drink. Although this is a somewhat dying tradition, especially in the younger, hipper bars, you will still find *bocas* alive and well in the older, more traditional San José drinking establishments. The most traditional of these are known locally as *cantinas*. In most, the *bocas* are free, but in some, where the dishes are more sophisticated, you'll have to pay for the treats. You'll find drinks reasonably priced, with beer costing around $2 to $3 a bottle, and mixed drinks costing $4 to $10.

El 13 ★ Having quickly outgrown their original location, this place continues to draw a wide ranging crowd of punks, bohos, artists, and assorted revelers. A simple cafe and sandwich shop during the day, it really gets going at night, with a steady lineup of DJs, special events, and the occasional live band. This place is proudly LGBT friendly. It's open Tuesday to Saturday from 4pm to 1am. Calle 9, btw. avs. 12 and 14. ✆ **2221-7228.** http://el13cafebar.com.

El Cuartel de la Boca del Monte ★★ This popular bar, one of San José's best, began life as an artist-and-bohemian hangout, and has evolved into a massive melting pot, attracting everyone from the city's young and well-heeled, to foreign exchange students and visitors. Artists still come, too. Live music is usually Monday, Wednesday, and Friday nights, when the place is packed shoulder to shoulder. From Monday to Friday it's open for lunch and again in the evenings;

on weekends it opens at 6pm. On most nights it's open till about 1am, although the revelry might continue till about 3am on Friday or Saturday. Av. 1, btw. calles 21 and 23 (50m/¹/₂ block west of the Cine Magaly). © 2221-0327. www.elcuartel.net.

El Observatorio ★★ It's easy to miss the narrow entrance to this hot spot across from the Cine Magaly. Owned by a local filmmaker, its decor includes a heavy dose of cinema motifs. The space is large, with high ceilings, and one of the best (perhaps only) smoke extraction systems of any popular bar, making the place bearable, even though most of the clientele are chain-smoking. Mondays tend to be for salsa dancing, while Wednesdays often feature stand-up comedy. There's occasional live music and movie screenings and a decent menu of appetizers and main dishes drawn from various world cuisines. It's open 10:30am to 2pm and 6pm to 2am daily. Calle 23, btw. avs. Central and 1. © 2223-0725. www.elobservatorio.tv.

El Sótono ★★ "El Sótono" translates as "the basement." And that's just where you'll find this tiny bar and performance space. Most nights some of the city's best jazz and blues players hold down the scene, and Tuesdays they host an open jam session. There's a small menu of bar food and sandwiches. When there's no live band, the house music is entirely played from vinyl. Upstairs from El Sótono is a separate bar and lounge space, El Solar. It's open 6pm to 2am daily. Calle 3, btw. avs. 9 and 11. © 2221-2302.

El Steinvorth ★ This is one of San José's trendiest clubs, and one of the only places you might find a line to get in, or be turned away because the doorman doesn't like how you're dressed or think you're cool enough. Still, plenty of people like that sort of thing. Housed in an old brick building with a crumbling facade, inside you'll find a large contemporary space with several rooms, art hanging on the walls and a second-floor balcony area that looks down on one of the main dance spaces. El Steinvorth is open Wednesday through Saturday from 9pm until at least 4am. Calle 1, btw. avs. Central and 1. No phone. www.elsteinvorth.com.

Key Largo ★ This meticulously restored downtown mansion is also one of San José's top prostitute pickup bars. Housed in a beautiful old building just off Parque Morazán in the heart of downtown, Key Largo is worth a visit if only to take in the scene and admire the dark-stained carved wood ceilings. There are a couple of pool tables, usually a live band, and always working women—however, this is still an acceptable place for visiting couples and those not actively shopping the wares. It's open 8pm to 2:30am daily. Calle 7, btw. avs. 1 and 3. © 2257-7800.

Rayuela ★★ Named after a classic Julio Cortazar novel, this small, dark, cozy bar oozes boho charm. Poets and folk singers often hold court, and a simple menu of drinks and light bites is offered. If this place is too mellow or artsy for you, its sister spot next door, **El Lobo Estepario,** is larger and has a livelier club feel, with dance music and regular concerts. Av. Central, btw. calles 13 and 15. © 8376-1409. http://enrayuela.blogspot.com.

HANGING OUT IN SAN PEDRO

The funky 2-block stretch of **San Pedro ★★** just south of the University of Costa Rica has been dubbed La Calle de Amargura, or the "Street of Bitterness," and it's the heart and soul of this eastern suburb and college town. Bars and cafes are mixed in with bookstores and copy shops. After dark the streets are packed with teens, punks, students, and professors barhopping and just hanging around. You can walk the strip until someplace strikes your fancy—or you can try one of the places listed below. *Note:* La Calle de Amargura attracts a certain unsavory element. Use caution here. Try to visit with a group, and try not to carry large amounts of cash or wear flashy jewelry.

You can get here by heading out (east) on Avenida 2, and following the flow of traffic. You will first pass through the neighborhood of Los Yoses before you reach a large traffic circle with a big fountain in the center (La Fuente de la Hispanidad). The Mall San Pedro is located on this traffic circle. Heading straight through the circle, you'll come to the Church of San Pedro, about 4 blocks east of the circle. The church is the major landmark in San Pedro. You can also take a bus here from downtown.

Jazz Café ★   The Jazz Café is one of the more happening spots in San Pedro, and consistently a great spot to find live music. It remains one of my favorites, although low ceilings and poor air circulation make it almost unbearably smoky most nights. Wrought iron chairs, sculpted busts of famous jazz artists, and creative lighting give the place its ambience. Most nights feature live music. It's open daily till about 2am. Sister club **Jazz Café Escazú** (© **2288-4740**) is on the western end of town. Next to the Banco Popular on Av. Central. © **2253-8933.** www.jazzcafecostarica.com.

Mundoloco El Chante ★★   This club is the brainchild of DJ, radio host, and musician Bernal Monestel. A relaxed and casual vibe pervades this place, with live music or DJs most nights. Bands tend to be eclectic, with a tendency toward electronic and world music, in addition to homegrown rock and reggae outfits. Its concert area is smoke-free, although smoking is permitted at the bar and the open-air terrace. Southeast corner of the Banco Popular on Av. Central. © **2253-4125.** www.facebook.com/MundolocoElChante.

One of the many bars on La Calle de Amargura in San Pedro.

Terra U Set on a busy corner in the heart of the university district, this two-story joint is one of the most popular bars in the area. Part of this is due to the inviting open-air street-front patio area, which provides a nice alternative to the all-too-common smoke-filled rooms found at most other trendy spots. It's open daily 'til 2am. 200m (2 blocks) east and 150m (1¹/₂ blocks) north of the church in San Pedro. ℂ **2225-4261.**

The Gay & Lesbian Scene

Because Costa Rica is such a conservative Catholic country, the gay and lesbian communities here are rather discreet. Homosexuality is not generally under attack, but many gay and lesbian organizations guard their privacy, and the club scene is changeable and not well publicized.

The most established and happening gay and lesbian bar and dance club in San José is **La Avispa ★**, Calle 1 between avenidas 8 and 10 (ℂ **2223-5343;** www.laavispa.com). It is popular with both men and women, although it sometimes sets aside certain nights for specific persuasions. There's also **Pucho's Bar** (ℂ **2256-1147**), on Calle 11 and Avenida 8; and **El Bochinche** (ℂ **2221-0500**), on Calle 11 between avenidas 10 and 12.

For a more casual and mixed scene, check out **El 13** (see above).

Casinos

Gambling is legal in Costa Rica, with casinos at virtually every major hotel. However, as with Tico bullfighting, some idiosyncrasies are involved in gambling *a la Tica.*

If blackjack is your game, you'll want to play "rummy." The rules are almost identical, except that the house doesn't pay 1¹/₂ times on blackjack—instead, it pays double on any three of a kind or three-card straight flush.

If you're looking for roulette, what you'll find here is a bingolike spinning cage of numbered balls. The betting is the same, but some of the glamour is lost.

You'll also find a version of five-card-draw poker, but the rule differences are so complex that I advise you to sit down and watch for a while and then ask questions before joining in. That's about all you'll find. There are no craps tables or baccarat.

There's some controversy over slot machines—one-armed bandits are currently outlawed—but you will be able to play electronic slots and poker games. Most casinos here are casual and small by international standards. You may have to dress up slightly at some of the fancier hotels, but most are accustomed to tropical vacation attire.

DAY TRIPS FROM SAN JOSÉ

San José makes an excellent base for exploring the beautiful Central Valley. For first-time visitors, the best way to make the most of these excursions is usually to take a guided tour, but if you rent a car, you'll have greater independence. Some day trips also can be done by public bus.

Tip: Virtually every attraction, tour, and activity described in "The Central Valley" chapter makes for an easy day trip out of San José.

In addition, to the tours and attractions offered around the Central Valley, a few other tours and activities just a little bit farther afield are popular and convenient for day trips out of San José. These include the following.

Bungee jumping.

The Rain Forest Aerial Tram Atlantic.

BUNGEE JUMPING There's nothing unique about bungee jumping in Costa Rica, but the site here is quite beautiful. If you've always had the bug, **Tropical Bungee** ★ (© **2248-2212;** www.bungee.co.cr) will let you jump off an 80m (262-ft.) bridge for $75; two jumps cost $120. Transportation is provided free from San José twice daily. Someone should be there from 9am to 3pm every day. They prefer for you to have a reservation, but if you show up on your own, they'll probably let you jump, unless huge groups are booked ahead of you. These folks also offer paragliding tours.

CANOPY TOURS & AERIAL TRAMS Getting up into the treetops is a big trend in Costa Rican tourism, and scores of such tours are around the country. You have several options relatively close to San José.

The most popular canopy-style day trip destination from San José is the **Rainforest Aerial Tram Atlantic** ★ (© **866/759-8726** in the U.S. and Canada, or 2257-5961 in Costa Rica; www.rainforesttram.com), built on a private reserve bordering Braulio Carrillo National Park. This pioneering tramway is the brainchild of rainforest researcher Dr. Donald Perry, whose cable-car system through the forest canopy at Rara Avis helped establish him as an early expert on rainforest canopies. On the 90-minute tram ride through the treetops, visitors have the chance to glimpse the complex web of life that makes these forests unique. Additional attractions include a butterfly garden, serpentarium, and frog collection. They also have their own zip-line canopy tour, and the grounds feature well-groomed trails through the rainforest and a restaurant—with all this on offer, a trip here can easily take up a full day. If you want to spend the night, 10 simple but clean and comfortable bungalows cost $160 per person per day (double occupancy), including three meals, a guided hike, taxes, the signature tram ride, and unlimited use of the rest of the facilities.

The cost for a full-day tour, including both the aerial tram and canopy tour, as well as all the park's other attractions, is $109; students and anyone under 18 pay $65. Packages, including round-trip transportation and lunch, are also available. Alternatively, you can drive or take one of the frequent Guápiles buses—they leave every half-hour throughout the day and cost C1,650—from the Caribbean bus terminal (Gran Terminal del Caribe) on Calle Central, 1 block north of Avenida 11. Ask the driver to let you off in front of the teleférico. If you're driving, head out on the Guápiles Highway as if driving to the Caribbean coast. Watch for the tram's roadside welcome center—it's hard to miss. Because this is a popular tour for groups, I highly recommend that you get an advance reservation in the high season and, if possible, a ticket; otherwise you could wait a long time for your tram ride or even be shut out. The tram handles only about 80 passengers per hour, so scheduling is tight; the folks here try to schedule as much as possible in advance.

For a zip-line style tour, the folks at **Original Canopy Tour** ★ (© **2291-4465;** www.canopytour.com) have their **Mahogany Park** operation about an hour outside of San José. The tour features nine platforms, and at the end you have the choice of taking a cable to a ground station or doing an 18m (60-ft.) rappel down to finish off. The tour takes about 2 hours and costs $45. Package tours with transportation from San José are also available.

DAY CRUISES Several companies offer cruises to lovely Tortuga Island in the Gulf of Nicoya. These full-day tours generally entail an early departure for the $1^1/_2$-hour chartered bus ride to Puntarenas, where you board your vessel for a $1^1/_2$-hour cruise to Tortuga Island. Then you get several hours on the uninhabited island, where you can swim, lie on the beach, play volleyball, or try a canopy tour, followed by the return journey.

The original and most dependable company running these trips is **Calypso Tours** ★ (© **800/887-1969** in the U.S. and Canada, or 2256-2727 in Costa Rica; www.calypsocruises.com). The tour costs $139 per person and includes

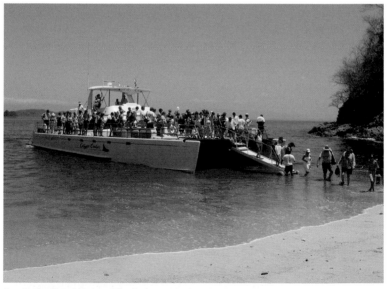

A cruise landing at Tortuga Island.

Aerial view of Tortuga Island.

round-trip transportation from San José, Jacó, or Manuel Antonio, a buffet break-fast before embarking on the boat, all drinks on the cruise, and an excellent buffet lunch on the beach at the island. The Calypso Tours main vessel is a massive motor-powered catamaran. They also run a separate tour to a private nature reserve at **Punta Coral ★**. The beach is much nicer at Tortuga Island, but the tour to Punta Coral is more intimate, and the restaurant, hiking, and kayaking are all superior here. These folks provide daily pickups from San José, Manuel Antonio, Jacó, and Monteverde, and you can use the day trip on the boat as your transfer or transportation option between any of these towns and destinations.

HIKING   Most of the tour agencies listed above offer 1-day guided hikes to a variety of destinations. In general, I recommend taking guided hikes to really see and learn about the local flora and fauna.

RAFTING, KAYAKING & RIVER TRIPS   Cascading down Costa Rica's mountain ranges are dozens of tumultuous rivers, several of which are very popular for white-water rafting and kayaking. If I had to choose just one day trip out of San José, it would be a white-water rafting trip. For between $75 and $120, you can spend a day rafting through lush tropical forests; multiday trips are also available. Some of the most reliable rafting companies are **Aventuras Naturales ★★** (*(C)* **888/680-9031** in the U.S., or 2225-3939 in Costa Rica; www.adventure costarica.com), **Exploradores Outdoors ★** (*(C)* **646/205-0828** in the U.S. and Canada, or 2222-6262 in Costa Rica; www.exploradoresoutdoors.com), and **Ríos Tropicales ★★** (*(C)* **866/722-8273** in the U.S. and Canada, or 2233-6455 in Costa Rica; www.riostropicales.com). These companies all ply a number of rivers of varying difficulties, including the popular Pacuare and Reventazón rivers. For details, see "White-Water Rafting, Kayaking & Canoeing," in chapter 5.

VOLCANO VISITS   The **Poás, Irazú** (see chapter 7 for more details), and **Arenal** volcanoes are three of Costa Rica's most popular destinations, and the first two are easy day trips from San José. Although numerous companies offer day trips to Arenal, I don't recommend them because travel time is at least 3¹/₂ hours in each direction. You usually arrive when the volcano is hidden by clouds and leave before the night's darkness shows off its glowing eruptions. For more information on Arenal Volcano, see chapter 10.

Guided Tours & Adventures

A number of companies offer a wide variety of primarily nature-related day tours out of San José. The most reputable include **Costa Rica Expeditions ★★** (② **2257-0766**; www.costaricaexpeditions.com), **Costa Rica Sun Tours ★** (② **866/271-6263** in the U.S. and Canada, or 2296-7757 in Costa Rica; www. crsuntours.com), **Horizontes Tours ★★** (② **2222-2022**; www.horizontes. com), and **Swiss Travel Service** (② **2282-4898**; www.swisstravelcr.com). Prices range from around $35 to $70 for a half-day trip, and from $70 to $150 for a full-day trip.

Before signing on for a tour of any sort, find out how many fellow travelers will be accompanying you, how much time will be spent in transit and eating lunch, and how much time will actually be spent doing the primary activity. I've had complaints about tours that were rushed, that spent too much time in a bus or on secondary activities, or that had a cattle-car, assembly-line feel to them. You'll find many tours that combine two or three different activities or destinations.

Poás Volcano National Park.

7

THE CENTRAL VALLEY

K
nown locally as La Meseta Central or El Valle Central, the long, thin, doglegging Central Valley is Costa Rica's most densely populated region. In addition to San José, it is home to both Alajuela and Heredia, numerous smaller cities, suburbs and towns, and the country's principal international airport. Most visitors start and end their Costa Rican vacations in the Central Valley.

The hills, mountains, and volcanoes that ring the Central Valley are an agricultural wonderland, with farms, fields, and plantations growing a wide range of crops, most prominently coffee. These towns, cities, hillsides, and volcanoes are home to a wide range of compelling attractions, from volcanic national parks and La Paz Waterfall Gardens, to pre-Colombian ruins and colonial-era churches. And this is a perfect place to tour a working coffee farm. Although technically one valley over, the colonial-era capital city of Cartago is included in this chapter, because of its general geographic location and proximity to San José. With its ornate and locally revered Basilica, earthquake-damaged Central Park ruins, and the lovely, neighboring Orosi Valley, this is an area well worth exploring.

THE BEST CENTRAL VALLEY EXPERIENCES

o **Dining at a Mirador:** Grab a window seat at a *mirador*, and enjoy your meal with the lights of San José at your feet. You'll find *miradores* set up on most of the foothills surrounding the Central Valley. See "Dining Under the Stars," p. 162.

o **Visiting a Volcano:** Several of Costa Rica's most impressive and accessible volcanoes are found in the mountains that define the Central Valley. These include Poás, Irazú, and Turrialba, all active volcanoes with their own namesake national parks. See p. 166, 181, and 187.

o **Visiting La Paz Waterfall Gardens:** This place is akin to a Costa Rican tropical theme park. I enjoy combining a visit here with a stay in their luxurious on-site Peace Lodge (p. 168). Its multiple attractions also make this a great day-trip option. See p. 166.

o **Touring the Orosi Valley:** Arguably one of the most picturesque drives in Costa Rica, a trip around the Orosi Valley offers up stunning vistas, ancient ruins, charming small towns and several top-notch attractions. See p. 183.

The Central Valley's Top Sustainable Hotels

Casa Turire (p. 188)
Finca Rosa Blanca (p. 173)
Hotel Bougainvillea (p. 173)
Pacuare Lodge (p. 188)
Xandari Resort & Spa (p. 168)

○ **Getting Wet & Wild in Turrialba:** This small, rural city is Costa Rica's main base for white-water rafting and kayak guides. From here, trips leave on both the Pacuare and Reventazón rivers. You'll also find a thrilling canyoning operation, and plenty of opportunities for other adventure activities. See p. 186.

ESCAZÚ & SANTA ANA

Escazú: 5.5km (3½ miles) W of San José; Santa Ana: 13km (8 miles) W of San José

Located just west of San José, these affluent suburbs have boomed in recent years, as the metropolitan area continues to grow and expand. Escazú and Santa Ana are popular with the Costa Rican professional class, as well as North American retirees and expatriates. Quite a few hotels have sprung up to cater to their needs. Both have large modern malls, endless little strip malls, and important business parks. It's easy to commute between Escazú or Santa Ana and downtown San José via car, bus, or taxi. And the area is about the same distance from the airport as downtown San José.

Essentials

GETTING THERE & DEPARTING   By Car: Head west out of San José along Paseo Colón. Turn left when you hit La Sabana Park, and turn right a few blocks later, at the start of the Próspero Fernández Highway (CR27). You will see well-marked exits for both Escazú and Santa Ana along this highway.

By Bus: Escazú- and **Santa Ana–bound** buses leave from the Coca-Cola bus station, as well as from Avenida 1 between calles 24 and 28. Alternatively, you can pick up both the Escazú and Santa Ana buses from a busy bus stop at the start of the Próspero Fernández Highway (CR27) on the southeast corner of the Parque La Sabana, next to the Gimnasio Nacional. Buses leave roughly every 5 to 10 minutes from 5am until 8pm, and less frequently during off hours. A bus costs between C285 and C365.

By Taxi: Taxi fare should run around C4,000 to C8,000, each way between San José and Escazú, and another C5,000 to C7,500 or so between Escazú and Santa Ana.

VISITOR INFORMATION   Escazú News ★★ (www.escazunews.com) is an excellent bilingual resource for information on the Escazú and Santa Ana areas. The site has forums, classified ads, maps, restaurant reviews, real estate info, and general advice on the area.

ORIENTATION   Both Escazú and Santa Ana are former farming towns that have been swallowed up by metro San José's urban sprawl. Each has a small downtown core built around an old church, with ever-expanding rings of residential and commercial development radiating off this core. Both also have numerous little satellite towns, such as San Antonio de Escazú, San Rafael de Escazú, and Pozos de Santa Ana.

FAST FACTS   You'll find banks, ATMs, and Internet cafes all over Escazú and Santa Ana, especially in the many malls and shopping centers.

Exploring Escazú & Santa Ana

Escazú and Santa Ana have few traditional tourism attractions, but both offer easy access to the attractions and activities offered up in San José and elsewhere around the Central Valley.

The Central Valley

Ark Herb Farm **8**
Café Britt Farm **12**
Catedral de Alajuela **10**
Catedral de la Inmaculada Concepción **14**
CATIE **18**
Chaverri Oxcart Factory **2**
Doka Estate **7**

Else Kientzler Botanical Garden **1**
Finca Rosa Blanca Coffee Plantation Tour **9**
Golden Bean Coffee Tour **17**
Guayabo National Monument **21**
INBIO Park **16**
Irazú Volcano **19**
Juan Santamaría Museum of Cultural History **10**
La Paz Waterfall Gardens **6**

Museo de Cultura Popular **13**
Poás Volcano **5**
Refugio Herpetologico **11**
Sibu Chocolates **15**
Templo de la Musica **14**
Turrialba Volcano National Park **20**
World of Snakes **3**
Zoo Ave **4**

See Cartago Orosi & Irazú map

One of the exceptions to the above rule is the **Refugio Herpetologico** ★ (*© 2282-4614*; http://refugioherpetologico. com), a family-run reptile and wildlife exhibition. In addition to a couple of dozen snakes, both venomous and nonvenomous, the center has a few other rehabilitating animals, including a crocodile, iguanas, and a spider monkey. It's open from 9am to 4pm, Tuesday to Sunday, and admission is $14 for adults; $11 for students, and $7 for seniors and children 6 through 11.

If you are in downtown Santa Ana, do take a few minutes to visit the town's main **cathedral,** a lovely old stone church, with thick wooden beams, colorful stained-glass windows, and a red-clay tile roof.

And while most folks don't come to Costa Rica to see movies, if you do decide to go, head

Santa Ana's cathedral.

for the **Nova Cinemas** (*© 2299-7485*; www.novacinemas.cr) multiplex, with the country's only IMAX theater and several other VIP salas, in the Avenida Escazú shopping complex.

GOLF & TENNIS   Some of the best Central Valley facilities for visiting golfers and tennis players can be found at **Parque Valle del Sol** ★ (*© 2282-9222*; www.vallesol.com), in Santa Ana. The 18-hole course here is open to the general public. Greens fees are $70, including unlimited balls on the driving range. A golf cart will run you an extra $30. The tennis courts here cost $5 per hour weekdays and $10 per hour weekends. Reservations are essential. The golf course at the Cariari Country Club is not open to the general public.

HORSEBACK RIDING   Options are nearly endless in the mountains and along the coasts, but it's more difficult to find a place to saddle up in the Central Valley. **La Caraña Riding Academy** (*© 2282-6754*; www.lacarana.com) and **Centro Ecuestre del Sol** (Equestrian Sun; *© 2282-1070*; www.equestriansun. com) are both in Santa Ana, and offer riding classes. But your best bet is to head a little further west to Ciudad Colón, where **Finca Caballo Loco** ★★ (*© 7010-1771*; www.fincacaballoloco.com) offers up trail rides through some beautiful rural terrain.

Where to Stay

VERY EXPENSIVE

Real InterContinental San José ★★   Located just across the street from one of the country's largest shopping malls and movie multiplexes, this high rise business-class hotel offers cozy, contemporary luxury rooms and excellent

The Western Central Valley

0 ———— 2 mi
0 ———— 2 km

HOTELS
Alta Hotel **14**
Beacon Escazú **22**
Casa de Flores Hotel & Villa **7**
Casa de las Tías **21**
Courtyard by Marriott **4**
Courtyard San José **15**
Doubletree Cariari By Hilton **10**
Finca Rosa Blanca Coffee
 Plantation & Inn **5**

Holiday Inn Express **4**
Hotel Bougainvillea **8**
Marriott Costa Rica Hotel **9**
Posada Nena **13**
Pura Vida Hotel **3**
Real InterContinental
 San José **16**
Residence Inn San José
 Escazú **17**
Studio Hotel **12**
Xandari Resort & Spa **1**

130

125

1

Alajuela
2

3

4

5

6

7
Barva

126

3

1
Juan
Santamaria
International
Airport

San Antonio de Belén
9

San Pablo
112

Heredia

8
Santo
Domingo

10 106

11

15
15

17

16

14

27

166

12 Santa Ana
13

13

239

18

19

21

22 San Antonio
de Escazú

San José
★

20

San Sebastian

RESTAURANTS
Bacchus **13**
Cantina La Cava **19**
Chancay **15**
El Chante Vegano **2**
El Tigre Vestido **5**
Il Panino **18**
Jalapeños Central **2**
L'Ile de France **17**
La Lluna de Valencia **6**

Le Monestère **19**
Mirador Ram Luna **23**
Mirador Tiquicia **20**
Product-C **11, 17**
Saga **17**
Salatto Bistro **2**
Samurai Fusion **15**
Terraza Toscana **17**
Trattoria Bell'Italia **18**
Tutti Li **15**

23
↓

NICARAGUA
CARIBBEAN
SEA

SAN JOSÉ ★

Map
Area

PACIFIC
OCEAN

PANAMA

Oxcart Derby

This area's agricultural heritage shines each year on **El Día del Boyero** (Oxcart Drivers' Day), which is celebrated on the second Sunday of March. The small town of San Antonio de Escazú is the center of the celebrations, with a street fair, and a large collection of colorfully painted ox-drawn carts parading through the streets.

service. The Inter features a large beautiful outdoor pool, and boasts one of the best equipped spas and gyms in the city. The hotel has several excellent dining options, and a score or more are just across the street. This place is very popular for meeting and convention groups.

Autopista Próspero Fernández, across from the Multiplaza mall, Escazú. ℂ **877/860-1371** in the U.S. and Canada, or 2208-2100 in Costa Rica. www.ichotelsgroup.com. 372 units. $230–$370 double; $580 and up suite. Free parking. **Amenities:** 3 restaurants; 2 bars; lounge; concierge; good-size health club and spa; Jacuzzi; large free-form outdoor pool; room service; smoke-free rooms; outdoor tennis court; free Wi-Fi.

EXPENSIVE

The **Beacon Escazú** ★ (ℂ **866/978-6168** in the U.S. and Canada, or 2228-3110; www.mybeaconescazu.com) is a luxurious boutique hotel in downtown Escazú, just a block from the town's central park. The restaurant and wine bar here are both excellent.

Alta Hotel ★   This elegant option is set on the side of a steep hill between Escazú and Santa Ana. The views here, especially at night, are spectacular. Rooms are lovely, with a minimalist decor featuring white walls adorned with antique black-and-white photos, and most of them feature wonderful private balconies, set to take in the view. Because of the odd shape of the building, a few of the rooms do, unfortunately, feature small bathrooms. The La Luz restaurant here is excellent.

Alto de las Palomas, old road to Santa Ana. ℂ **888/388-2582** in the U.S. and Canada, or 2282-4160. www.thealtahotel.com. 23 units. $150–$180 double; $240–$300 suite. Rates include continental breakfast. Free parking. **Amenities:** Restaurant; bar; concierge; small exercise room; Jacuzzi; midsize outdoor pool; room service; sauna; smoke-free rooms; free Wi-Fi.

MODERATE

In addition to the hotel below, the **Courtyard San José** (ℂ **888/236-2427** in the U.S. and Canada, or 2208-3000; www.marriott.com), **Residence Inn San José Escazú** (ℂ **888/236-2427** in the U.S. and Canada, or 2588-4300; www.marriott.com), and **Holiday Inn Express** (ℂ **800/052 11 00** in the U.S. and Canada, or 2506-5000 in Costa Rica; www.hiexpress.com) are all modern business-class hotels a few miles from each other, right on the western Próspero Fernández Highway connecting Santa Ana and Escazú with San José.

Casa de las Tías ★   The Escazú and Santa Ana areas are awash in modern, business-class chain hotels and upscale boutique options, but this cozy little converted home offers up something special for those looking for a real Costa Rican experience at a reasonable price. Owners Xavier and Pilar live on site and are very hands-on hosts. The hotel is just a block or so away from a bustling Escazú intersection, yet feels a world apart with its large garden and quiet, secure grounds.

San Rafael de Escazú. ℂ **2289-5517.** www.casadelastias.com. 5 units. $100–$110 double. Rates include full breakfast. **Amenities:** Free Wi-Fi.

Studio Hotel ★   Art lovers will love this small contemporary hotel. The lobby, common areas and rooms all feature a wealth of original works by major contemporary and historical Costa Rican artists, including Rafa Fernandez, Isidor Con Wong, and Edgar Zuñiga. The Katowa restaurant here serves up excellent Costa Rican fusion cuisine. However, my favorite feature at this hotel is the third-floor rooftop pool and lounge area, set under a soaring white canvas tent structure, with wonderful views. The hotel sits on a busy intersection at the entrance to Santa Ana, with a host of other restaurant and bar options a short walk away.

Santa Ana. ✆ **866/978-8123** in the U.S. and Canada, or 2282-0505 in Costa Rica. www.costa ricastudiohotel.com. 82 units. $120–$170 double. Rates include full breakfast. **Amenities:** Restaurant; small exercise room; rooftop pool; smoke-free rooms; free Wi-Fi.

INEXPENSIVE

Posada Nena   This place is great for folks visiting friends or family in Santa Ana. Previously called Casa Alegre, this hotel is housed in a converted home, just 2 blocks from the beautiful stone church and central park of this once quiet farming town. The rooms are bright and cheerful. A sunken Jacuzzi sits in the center of a small central garden area, and these folks offer a wide range of tours and services.

Santa Ana. ✆ **2282-1173.** www.posadanena.com. 9 units. $66 double. Rates include breakfast and taxes. **Amenities:** Restaurant; bar; Jacuzzi; free Wi-Fi.

Where to Dine

These two suburbs have the most vibrant restaurant scenes in San José. In addition to the places listed below, **Trattoria Bell'Italia** ★ (✆ **2588-2833**) is a great option for Italian cuisine, and also like **Il Panino** ★ (✆ **2228-3126;** www. ilpanino.net), an upscale sandwich shop and cafe. Both of these are located in the Centro Comercial El Paco.

Two great one-stop options to consider are **Plaza Itskatzú,** just off the highway and sharing a parking lot with the Courtyard San José, and **Avenida**

A *mirador* **outside San José.**

DINING UNDER THE stars

One of my favorite unique Costa Rican experiences is dining on the side of a volcano with the lights of San José shimmering below. These hanging restaurants, called *miradores*, are a resourceful response to the city's topography. Because San José is set in a broad valley surrounded on all sides by volcanic mountains, people who live in these mountainous areas have no place to go but up—so they do, building roadside cafes vertically up the sides of the volcanoes.

The food at most of these establishments is not spectacular, but the views often are, particularly at night, when the wide valley sparkles in a wash of lights. The town of **Aserrí,** 10km (6¼ miles) south of downtown San José, is the king of *miradores*, and **Mirador Ram Luna** (*(C)* **2230-3022;** www.restauranteramluna. com) is the king of Aserrí. Grab a window seat and, if you've got the fortitude, order a plate of *chicharrones* (fried pork rinds). There's often live music. You can hire a cab for around C7,500 or take the Aserri bus at Avenida 6 between calles Central and 2. Just ask the driver where to get off.

Miradores are also in the hills above Escazú and in San Ramón de Tres Ríos and Heredia. The most popular is **Le Monestère** (*(C)* **2289-4404;** www. monastere-restaurant.com; closed Sun), an elegant converted church serving somewhat overrated French and Belgian cuisine in a spectacular setting above the hills of Escazú. I recommend coming here just for the less formal **Cantina La Cava** ★ (see above). I also like **Mirador Tiquicia** ★ (*(C)* **2289-5839;** www.mirador tiquicia.com), which occupies several rooms in a sprawling old Costa Rican home and has live folkloric dance shows on Thursday.

Escazú, which is anchored by the Marriott Residence Inn and is located next to the CIMA Hospital. My favorite options at Plaza Itskatzú include **Tutti Li** ★ (*(C)* **2588-2405**), a good Italian restaurant and pizzeria; **Chancay** ★ (*(C)* **2588-2327;** www.chancay.info), which serves Peruvian and Peruvian/Chinese cuisine; and **Samurai Fusion** ★ (*(C)* **2588-2240**), a fine sushi and teppanyaki joint.

Over on Avenida Escazú, you'll find **Saga** ★ (*(C)* **2289-6615;** www.sagarestaurant.com), with a contemporary-casual bistro menu; **Terraza Toscana** ★★ (*(C)* **4000-2220;** www.terrazzatoscanacr.com) an excellent and elegant Italian restaurant; and **L'Ile de France** ★★ (*(C)* **2289-7533**), a top-notch, high-end French restaurant.

EXPENSIVE

Bacchus ★★ ITALIAN   Set in an adobe home built in 1870, this elegant restaurant is one of the best Italian options in the city. Paper-thin pizzas come out of the wood-burning oven that highlights the open kitchen, and the pastas and raviolis are homemade. Of these, I really like the papardelle with white wine, arugula, carrots, and crabmeat. Desserts are creative and delicious. Try the banana and apple croquetes made of Philo dough and topped with a Gran Marnier sauce. Regularly rotating art exhibits adorn the walls of the dining rooms and an ample open-air covered patio that overlooks the open kitchen and pizza oven.

Downtown Santa Ana. *(C)* **2282-5441.** www.bacchus.cr. Reservations required. Main courses C5,000–C18,500. Mon–Thurs 5–11pm; Fri noon–3pm and 6–11pm; Sat noon–11pm; Sun noon–9pm.

Cantina La Cava ★ COSTA RICAN/STEAK   This cozy spot sits underneath and shares a view with the overpriced and somewhat pretentious Le Monestère restaurant (it's still rather pricey, but the ambience is much more inviting). In fact, this place started out as Le Monestère's wine cellar before being converted into a stylish bar and grill. A wide range of meat, poultry, fish, and game are served. The best seats line a picture window with stunning views of the city at night, and the attached bar has live music most nights.

1.5km (1 mile) south of Centro Comercial Paco; follow the signs to Le Monestère. © **2228-8515.** Reservations recommended. Main courses C7,500–30,000. Mon–Thurs 6pm–midnight; Fri–Sat 6pm–1:30am.

MODERATE

Product-C ★★ SEAFOOD   Although San José is inland, this fish market and restaurant prides itself on daily pre-dawn runs to Puntarenas and other coastal supply points to get the freshest catch possible. They even set up the first and only oyster farm in Costa Rica, producing small, yet very tasty oysters. The daily chalkboard menu features a range of specials that complements the simple menu here. Feel free to check out the display case and choose whatever fish or seafood strikes your fancy, and have it cooked to order in any number of styles.

Av. Escazú. © **2288-5570.** www.product-c.com. Reservations recommended. Main courses C4,300–C13,000. Mon–Sat noon–11pm; Sun noon–5pm.

Shopping

One of the country's best and largest megamalls, **Multiplaza Escazú,** is located along the Próspero Fernández Highway (CR27), just west of downtown Escazú. In the same general area, you'll find two other smaller malls, **Avenida Escazú** and **Plaza Itskatzú,** each of which has an attractive mix of high-end shops, boutiques, restaurants, and art galleries.

Biesanz Woodworks ★★   Biesanz makes a wide range of high-quality wood items, including bowls, jewelry boxes, humidors, and some wonderful sets of chopsticks. The company is actively involved in local reforestation, too. Bello Hori-

Woodwork by Barry Biesanz.

zonte, Escazú. ✆ **2289-4337.** www. biesanz.com. Call for directions and off-hour appointments.

Galería 11–12 ★★★ This outstanding gallery deals mainly in high-end Costa Rican art, from neoclassical painters such as Teodorico Quirós to modern masters such as Francisco Amighetti and Paco Zuñiga, to current stars such as Rafa Fernández, Rodolfo Stanley, Fernando Carballo, and Fabio Herrera. Plaza Itzkatzú, off the Próspero Fernández Hwy., Escazú. ✆ **2288-1975.**

Entertainment & Nightlife

Escazú has a handful of popular bars and clubs. These are especially popular with the Central Valley's well-heeled urban youth. A couple of my favorites include **Henry's Beach Club** ★ (✆ **2289-6250;** on the Guachipelin road in Escazú) has an upbeat casual vibe; and the **Jazz Café Escazú** ★★ (Próspero Fernández Hwy.; ✆ **2288-4740;** www.jazzcafecostarica.com) is a top spot for live music.

Musicians at Jazz Café Escazú.

ALAJUELA, POÁS ★★ & THE AIRPORT AREA

Airport: 15km (9¼ miles) NW of San José; Alajuela: 18½km (11½ miles) NW of San José; Poás Volcano: 37km (23 miles) northwest of San José

Most folks visiting Costa Rica land at the Juan Santamaría International Airport in Alajuela. The downtown area of Costa Rica's second largest city is just a mile or so north of the airport. The city itself is of little interest to most tourists, although it is the gateway to the Poás Volcano, and several more of the Central Valley's top attractions.

Essentials

GETTING THERE & DEPARTING   By Car: Head northwest out of San José on the Interamerican Highway (CR1).

By Bus: Two separate lines make the run between San José and Alajeula: **Tuasa** (✆ **2442-6900**) buses are red; **Station Wagon** (✆ **2441-1181**) buses are beige/yellow. Buses leave roughly every 10 minutes between 5am and 11pm, and less frequently in off hours. The fare is C550.

By Train: A commuter train runs between downtown San José and Heredia. This train runs roughly every 15 minutes between 5:30 and 8:30am, and again between 4:30 and 7:30pm, with much less frequent service during non-commuter hours. Fares range from C200 to C400, depending on the length of your ride.

ORIENTATION Downtown Alajuela is a tight jumble of one-way streets, often choked to a standstill with gridlock traffic. Most folks will be heading up into the hills from downtown. The best way to find the route out of town is usually to follow signs for the Poás Volcano, or some other well-known attraction.

FAST FACTS You'll find banks, ATMs, and Internet cafes all over Alajuela, especially in the central downtown area, and nearby malls and shopping centers. The **Hospital San Rafael de Alajuela** (© **2436-1001**) is large, modern, and well-equipped. If you need a taxi, call **COOTAXA** (© **2443-3030**) or **Taxi Radio Liga** (© **2441-1212**).

Exploring Alajuela

Alajuela's main church, the **Catedral de Alajuela** (Alajuela Cathedral; © **2441-4665**) is a large, relatively ornate Catholic church, with a striking white-washed exterior, beautiful ceiling frescos, and a gold-leaf painted interior dome. The cathedral, which fronts the city's central park, received a major renovation in 2010. Mass is held Monday to Friday at 9am and 5pm; Saturday at 9am and 7pm; and Sunday at 9 and 11am and 5 and 7pm.

The **Museo Historico Cultural Juan Santamaría (Juan Santamaría Museum of Cultural History),** Avenida 3 between calles Central and 2 (© **2441-4775;** www.museojuansantamaria.go.cr), commemorates Costa Rica's national hero, Juan Santamaría, who gave his life defending the country against a small army led by William Walker, a U.S. citizen who invaded Costa Rica in 1856, attempting to set up a slave state. Housed in a sprawling two-story downtown building with a large open central courtyard, the museum features permanent exhibits about Santamaría and Walker's filibuster exploits, as well as regularly changing temporary expositions, and evening concerts and theater performances. The museum is open Tuesday through Saturday from 10am to 5:30pm; admission is free.

Catedral de Alajuela.

NEARBY ATTRACTIONS

Doka Estate ★ FARM   This large and long-standing coffee estate/farm in Alajuela offers up a tour that takes you from "seed to cup." Along the way, you'll get a full rundown of the processes involved in the growing, harvesting, curing, packing, and brewing of their award-winning coffee. This coffee tour is similar to that offered at **Café Britt** (p. 171), but is a little more down-home in feel. These folks also have a butterfly garden, Bonsai tree, and orchid exhibit on-site. Allow about 2¹/₂ hours for the full tour.

Sabanilla de Alajuela. ✆ **2449-5152.** www.dokaestate.com. Admission $20 adults, $15 students with valid ID, $12 children 6–11, free for children 5 and under. Packages including transportation and breakfast or lunch available. Tours daily at 9, 10, and 11am; 1:30 and 2:30pm. Reservations required.

La Paz Waterfall Gardens ★★ NATURAL ATTRACTION   The original attraction here consists of a series of trails through primary and secondary forests alongside La Paz River, with lookouts over a series of powerful falls, including the namesake La Paz Fall. In addition to the orchid garden and a hummingbird garden, you must visit their huge butterfly garden, which is easily the largest in Costa Rica. A small serpentarium, featuring a mix of venomous and nonvenomous native snakes, several terrariums containing various frogs and lizards, and a section of wild cats and local monkey species in large enclosures are added attractions. While the admission fee is a little steep, everything is wonderfully done, and the trails and waterfalls are beautiful. This is a good stop after a morning visit to the Poás Volcano. Plan to spend 3 to 4 hours here. The hotel rooms here at **Peace Lodge** (p. 168) are some of the nicest in the country.

6km (3³/₄ miles) north of Varablanca on the road to San Miguel. ✆ **2482-2100.** www.waterfallgardens.com. Admission $36 adults, $22 children 3–12, free for children 2 and under. Daily 8am–5pm. There is no easy or regular bus service here, so you will need to come in a rental car or taxi, or arrange transport with the gardens.

Poás Volcano ★★ NATURAL ATTRACTIONS   From San José, narrow roads wind through a landscape of fertile farms and dark forests to this active volcano. A paved road leads right to the top, although you'll have to hike in about 1km (.5 mile) to reach the crater. The volcano stands 2,640m (8,659 ft.) tall and is located within a national park, which preserves not only the volcano but also dense stands of virgin forest. The Poás crater, said to be the second largest in the

La Paz Waterfall Gardens.

Poás Volcano.

world, is more than a 1.6km (1 mile) across. Geysers in the crater sometimes spew steam and muddy water 180m (590 ft.) into the air, making this the largest geyser in the world.

The information center shows a slideshow about the volcano, and well-groomed and marked hiking trails through the cloud forest ring the crater. About 15 minutes from the parking area, along a forest trail, is an overlook onto beautiful Botos Lake, which has formed in one of the volcano's extinct craters.

Be prepared when you come to Poás: This volcano is often enveloped in dense clouds. If you want to see the crater, it's best to come early and during the dry season. Moreover, it can get cool up here, especially when the sun isn't shining, so dress appropriately.

Poás de Alajuela. 37km (23 miles) from San José. ℂ **2482-2165.** Admission $10. Daily 8.30am–3.30pm.

Zoo Ave ★ ZOO   Dozens of scarlet macaws, reclusive owls, majestic raptors, several different species of toucans, and a host of brilliantly colored birds from Costa Rica and around the world make this one exciting place to visit. In total, over 115 species of birds are on display, including some 80 species found in Costa Rica. Bird-watching enthusiasts will be able to get a closer look at birds they might have seen in the wild. Other critters to observe include iguana, deer, tapir, ocelot, puma, and monkey—and look out for the 3.6m (12-ft.) crocodile. Zoo Ave houses only injured, donated, or confiscated animals. It takes about 2 hours to walk the paths and visit all the exhibits here.

La Garita, Alajuela. ℂ **2433-8989.** www.zooavecostarica.org. Admission $20, $15 students with valid ID. Daily 9am–5pm. Catch a bus to Alajuela on Av. 2 btw. calles 12 and 14. In Alajuela, transfer to a bus to Atenas and get off at Zoo Ave before you get to La Garita. Fare is 60¢.

DIY: Poás Volcano

If you don't have a rental car and don't want to sign on for an organized tour, a daily bus (ℂ **2442-6900** or 2222-5325) from Avenida 2 between calles 12 and 14 leaves for the volcano at 8:30am and returns at 2pm. The fare is around C3,850 round-trip. The bus is often crowded, so arrive early. If you're driving, head for Alajuela and continue on the main road through town and follow signs for Fraijanes. Just beyond Fraijanes, you will connect with the road between San Pedro de Poás and Poasito; turn right toward Poasito and continue to the rim of the volcano.

Where to Stay in & Around Alajuela

Of the following hotels, the **Doubletree Cariari by Hilton, Holiday Inn Express, Marriott Costa Rica Hotel, Courtyard by Marriott Alajuela,** and **Pura Vida Hotel** are the closest to the airport.

VERY EXPENSIVE

Peace Lodge ★★★ Part of the popular **La Paz Waterfall Gardens** (p. 166), Peace Lodge is about 45 minutes from the airport, near the Poás Volcano. The rooms and villas are huge and feature faux rustic decor, including massive four-poster log beds and river stone fireplaces. All come with a Jacuzzi on their private balcony, but the deluxe rooms also feature an immense bathroom with a second indoor Jacuzzi backed by a full wall of orchids, flowers, and bromeliads, with a working waterfall. The steep rates here get you not only these fanciful rooms, but also unlimited access to the attached Waterfall Gardens.

6km (3³/₄ miles) north of Varablanca on the road to San Miguel. ℂ **954/727-3997** in the U.S., or 2482-2720 in Costa Rica. www.waterfallgardens.com. 17 units. $315–$500 double; $495–$840 villa. Rates include entrance to La Paz Waterfall Gardens. **Amenities:** Restaurant; bar; Jacuzzi; 2 outdoor pools; free Wi-Fi.

Xandari Resort & Spa ★★ On a stunning hillside, artists and owners Sherrill and Charlene Broudy have crafted a unique boutique hotel overflowing with architectural and artistic whimsy. All the rooms here are large, individual villas set along the hillside with large windows and private patios designed to take in the expansive views of the Central Valley. The well-equipped and luxurious spa here is its own little "village," featuring individual thatch-roof treatment bungalows. A network of trails leads through beautiful gardens, along jungle rivers, and to waterfall swimming holes. The restaurant serves excellent spa cuisine, alongside more decadent fare. **GPS:** Latitude 10°3'26.87"N; Longitude 84°12'43.86"W.

Alajuela. ℂ **866/363-3212** in the U.S., or 2443-2020. www.xandari.com. 24 villas. $265–$550 villa for 2. Rates include continental breakfast. $25 for extra person; children 3 and under stay free in parent's room. **Amenities:** Restaurant; bar; lounge; several Jacuzzis; 3 pools; full-service spa; free Wi-Fi.

EXPENSIVE

Doubletree Cariari By Hilton ★★ One of the older resort-style hotels built near the airport, the Cariari is still an excellent choice. The rooms and facilities have been well maintained and updated over the years. The whole complex has an open, airy feel, with covered exterior walkways and stone walls connecting the rooms and various spurs of the rambling building. The hotel has a small casino, as well as several restaurants. Moreover, just in front is a small mall with another handful of good dining options.

Autopista General Cañas, Ciudad Cariari, San José. ℂ **800/222-8733** in the U.S. and Canada, or 2239-0022. www.cariarisanjose.doubletree.com. 222 units. $199–$259 double; $300 suite. Free parking. **Amenities:** 2 restaurants; 2 bars; lounge; casino; babysitting; concierge; small exercise room; large outdoor pool w/swim-up bar; room service; smoke-free rooms; free Wi-Fi.

Marriott Costa Rica Hotel ★★★ Designed to resemble a colonial-era mansion, this is the best large-scale resort hotel in the city. The hotel is close enough to the airport to be considered an "airport hotel," yet it feels like an isolated country retreat. The entryway lets out on to a massive central courtyard meant to mimic Havana's Plaza de Armas. Rooms are large and beautifully done, with views to the surrounding hillsides and city lights. There are several distinct dining choices, and their Casa de Café coffee house and restaurant actually fronts a small working coffee field. Be sure to check their online booking engine, as there are frequently good deals offered there.

San Antonio de Belén. ✆ **888/236-2427** in the U.S. and Canada or 2298-0000 in Costa Rica. www.marriott.com. 299 units. $229–$249 double; $279–$329 executive level; $420 master suite; $850 presidential suite. Valet parking. **Amenities:** 3 restaurants; bar; lounge; free airport transfers; concierge; golf driving range; small but well-appointed health club; Jacuzzi; 2 outdoor pools; room service; sauna; 2 tennis courts; smoke-free rooms; Wi-Fi.

MODERATE

If you want a classic airport hotel, with regular shuttle service, both the **Courtyard by Marriott** (✆ **888/236-2427** in the U.S. and Canada or 2429-2700 in Costa Rica; www.marriott.com) and **Holiday Inn Express** (✆ **888/052-1100** in the U.S. and Canada, or 2506-5000 in Costa Rica; www.hiexpress.com) are solid U.S.–chain hotels located right across from the airport.

Vista del Valle Plantation Inn ★★   Surrounded by coffee farms and set on the edge of a deep river gorge, this boutique hotel is a great choice just 20 minutes or so from the Juan Santamaría International Airport. Rooms are either individual or duplex villas scattered around the well-tended grounds and gardens. Most of the villas feature plenty of varnished woodwork and Japanese design or decor. The best offer stunning views down to the river canyon. A few options, including the newer Deluxe Nature Villas feature a full kitchen or kitchenette, a nice touch for families traveling with young children or planning a longer stay. That said, the restaurant here is excellent, as is the personalized service and attention. You can take a strenuous hike down to a beautiful jungle waterfall, and join the horseback riding and coffee tours on offer.

Marriott Costa Rica Hotel.

Rosario de Naranjo, Alajuela. ☎ **2450-0800** or 2451-1165. www.vistadelvalle.com. 20 units. $145–$185 double. Rates include full breakfast. **Amenities:** Restaurant; Jacuzzi; midsize outdoor pool w/interesting fountain/waterfall; room service; free Wi-Fi.

INEXPENSIVE

Pura Vida Hotel ★★   Located just 10 minutes from the airport, this homey little inn is run by the very genial couple of Bernie Jubb and Nhi Chu. Rooms and private *casitas* ("little houses") are spread around a spacious compound and lush gardens. The two-bedroom casitas are great for families. Nhi is an amazing chef specializing in Asian cuisine, but her dinner menus range far and wide to almost universal acclaim. The hotel is located just a kilometer or two north of downtown Alajuela. **GPS:** 10 01 50" N and 84 13' 33" W

Tuetal de Alajuela. ☎ **2430-2630** or 2430-2929. www.puravidahotel.com. 6 units. $79–$160 double. Rates include full breakfast and one-way airport transfer. **Amenities:** Restaurant; Jacuzzi; free Wi-Fi.

Where to Dine

If you're looking for good Italian food in Alajuela, try **Salatto Bistro** (☎ **2441-6672**) in the Plaza Real strip mall. Vegetarians should definitely head to **El Chante Vegano** (☎ **8911-4787**; www.elchantevegano.com) a tasty and thoughtful vegan restaurant, in the heart of downtown, a half-block south of the Post Office.

A longtime favorite up toward the Poás Volcano is **Chubascos** ★ (☎ **2482-2280**; www.chubascos.co.cr), which serves excellent versions of Costa Rican classics in a cozy mountain setting. In addition, the restaurants at **Xandari Resort & Spa, Marriott Costa Rica Hotel,** and **Vista del Valle Plantation Inn** are all excellent.

Jalapeños Central ★ MEXICAN/TEX MEX   Also known as "Norman's Jalapeño" this downtown favorite was opened more than 10 years ago by Norman Flores, a U.S. expat and world traveler. The burritos and chimichangas are the most sought after dishes on the menu, but it's worth trying the sopa Azteca, or tortilla soup. Vegetarians have several options to choose from. This place has a strong local following and it's sometimes hard to get a table in this tiny little spot.

½ block south of the Post Office, downtown Alajuela. ☎ **2430-4027.** Main courses C3,500–C10,000. Mon–Sat 11:30am–9pm; Sun 11:30am-8pm.

HEREDIA

8.8km (5½ miles) north of San José

Founded in 1706 on the flanks of the impressive Barva Volcano, Heredia is affectionately known as "The City of Flowers." Of all the cities in the Central Valley, Heredia has the most colonial feel to it—you'll still see adobe buildings with Spanish tile roofs along narrow streets. Heredia is also the site of the **National University,** and you'll find some nice coffee shops and bookstores near the school.

Surrounding Heredia is an intricate maze of picturesque villages and towns, including Santa Bárbara, Santo Domingo, Barva, and San Joaquín de Flores. The hills and fields surrounding these towns contain some of the best and most fertile coffee plantations in Costa Rica.

Essentials

GETTING THERE & DEPARTING   **By Car:** The road to Heredia turns north off the Interamerican Highway (CR1) between San José and the airport.

By Bus: Buses (ⓒ 2233-8392) leave for Heredia every 5 minutes between 5am and 11pm from Calle 1 between avenidas 7 and 9, or from Avenida 2 between calles 12 and 14. Bus fare is C490.

CITY LAYOUT   Coming from San José, the most common route passes first through Santo Domingo de Heredia, although another popular route leads into downtown Heredia from San Joaquín de los Flores. The **Universidad Nacional Autonoma (National Autonomous University)** sits on the eastern edge of the city.

Exploring Heredia

The colonial **Catedral de la Inmaculada Concepción** ★ (Church of the Immaculate Conception; ⓒ 2237-0779), inaugurated in 1763, stands guard over Heredia's central park—the stone facade leaves no questions as to the age of the church. The altar inside is decorated with neon stars and a crescent moon surrounding a statue of the Virgin Mary.

In the middle of the palm-shaded central park is a large gazebo, known as **El Templo de la Musica (The Music Temple).** Live music is frequently performed here. Across the street, beside several red tile-roofed municipal buildings, is **El Fortin,** the tower of an old Spanish fort.

Anyone with an interest in medicinal herbs should plan a visit to the **Ark Herb Farm ★★** (ⓒ 8922-7599 or 2269-4847; www.arkherbfarm.com). These folks offer guided tours of their gardens, which feature more than 300 types of medicinal plants, as well as a beekeeping operation. The tour costs $15 per person, and includes a light snack and refreshments. Reservations are required.

Chocolate lovers will definitely want to visit **Sibu Chocolates ★★★** (ⓒ 2268-1335; www.sibuchocolate.com). This gourmet organic chocolate maker has a lovely small cafe, gift shop and offers tours of its production facility. Their shop and production facility is open Tuesday through Saturday from 8am to 5pm. The tasting tours are offered on these days at 10:30am. Reservations are essential, and the tour costs $24. The tour includes an informative presentation about the history and techniques of chocolate making, as well as several tempting tastings.

While on the road to Barva, you'll find the small **Museo de Cultura Popular** (ⓒ 2260-1619; www.museo.una.ac.cr), which is open Monday through Friday from 8am to 4pm and Sunday from 10am to 5pm; admission is C1,000.

TOP ATTRACTIONS

Café Britt Farm ★ FARM   Café Britt is one of the largest coffee producers in Costa Rica, and the company has put together an interesting tour and stage production at its farm, which is 20 minutes outside of San José. Here, you'll see how coffee is grown. You'll also visit the roasting and processing plant to learn how a coffee "cherry" is turned into a delicious roasted bean. Tasting sessions are offered for visitors to experience the different qualities of coffee. The farm also has a restaurant and a store where you can buy coffee and coffee-related gift items. The entire tour, including transportation, takes about 3 to 4 hours. Allow some extra time and an extra $10 for a visit to their nearby working plantation and mill. You can even strap on a basket and go out coffee picking during harvest time.

North of Heredia on the road to Barva. © **2277-1600.** www.coffeetour.com. Admission $22 adults, $17 children 6–11; $39 adults and $34 children, including transportation from downtown San José and a coffee drink. Add $17 for a buffet lunch. Tour daily at 11am (and at 3pm during high season). Store and restaurant daily 8am–5pm.

Finca Rosa Blanca Coffee Plantation Tour ★★ FARM   This gorgeous boutique hotel (p. 173) in Heredia also has its own organic coffee plantation, with some 16 hectares (40 acres) of shade-grown Arabica under cultivation. The hotel offers up daily coffee tours led by a very knowledgeable guide. I recommend combining the coffee tour with lunch at the open-air restaurant here; sitting under the shady gazebos, you'll enjoy a wonderful view of the Central Valley along with some fine healthy dining. The good in-house spa offers several treatments featuring homemade, coffee-based products.

Santa Bárbara de Heredia. © **2269-9392.** www.fincarosablanca.com. Admission $35 adults, free for children 11 and under. Reservations required.

INBio Park ★★   Run by the National Biodiversity Institute (Instituto Nacional de Biodiversidad, or INBio), this place is part museum, part educational center, and part nature park. In addition to watching a 15-minute informational video, visitors can tour two large pavilions explaining Costa Rica's biodiversity and natural wonders, and hike on trails that re-create the ecosystems of a tropical rainforest, dry forest, and premontane forest. A 2-hour guided hike is included in the entrance fee, and self-guided-tour booklets are also available. There's a good-size butterfly garden, as well as a Plexiglas viewing window into the small lagoon. One of my favorite attractions is the series of wonderful animal sculptures donated by one of Costa Rica's premiere artists, José Sancho. A simple cafeteria-style restaurant is on-site for lunch, as well as a coffee shop and gift shop. You can easily spend 2 to 3 hours here.

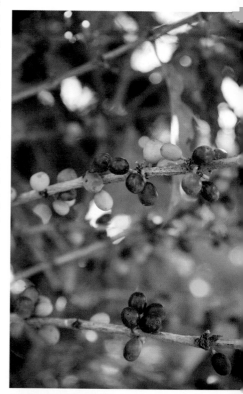

400m (4 blocks) north and 250m (2½ blocks) west of the Shell station in Santo Domingo de Heredia. © **2507-8107.** www.inbioparque. com. Admission $24 adults, $14 children 12 and under. Fri 9am–3pm (admission closes at 2pm); Sat–Sun 9am–4pm.

Where to Stay

While I don't recommend any hotels right in the city center, the small towns and agricultural villages surrounding Heredia are home to one of the country's finest boutique inns. In addition to the places listed below, you might want to check out the lovely little B&B, **Casa de Flores Hotel and Villa**

A coffee tree at Café Britt.

INBio Park.

(www.casadefloreshotel.com; © **2560-4982**), high in the hills above Heredia, near the Barva Volcano.

VERY EXPENSIVE

Finca Rosa Blanca Coffee Plantation & Inn ★★★ This fanciful boutique hotel overflows with artistic touches and architectural whimsy. All rooms here are either junior suites, suites, or villas, and no two are alike. Set on a high hillside on the flank of the Barva volcano, the inn maintains 14 hectares (35 acres) of prize-winning organic coffee under cultivation, and they offer an excellent in-house coffee tour. Organic gardens and greenhouses supply the produce for their wonderful restaurant, **El Tigre Vestido.** As the name implies, an award-winning organic coffee plantation is on site, and excellent, informative tours and tastings are offered (see above). The owners here are committed environmentalists and leaders in the local sustainable tourism field. **GPS:** 10°02'44.91"N 84°09'03.86"W.

Santa Bárbara de Heredia. © **305/395-3042** in the U.S., or © 2269-9392 in Costa Rica. www.fincarosablanca.com. 15 units. $305–$660 double. Rates include breakfast. Free parking. **Amenities:** Restaurant; bar; lounge; concierge; small free-form pool set in the hillside; room service; full-service spa; all rooms smoke-free; free Wi-Fi.

MODERATE

Hotel Bougainvillea ★ This well-run midsize hotel, about 15 to 20 minutes from the airport, has the feel and facilities of a larger resort hotel, but at a very affordable price. The signature features here are the large, lush, and varied gardens that surround the hotel. Rooms are large and well kept. Most come with a small, private balcony overlooking either the gardens or the city below. Nice extras include a lovely pool and two lighted tennis courts.

In Santo Tomás de Santo Domingo de Heredia, 100m (1 block) west of the Escuela de Santo Tomás, San José. © **866/880-5441** in the U.S. and Canada, or 2244-1414 in Costa Rica. www.hb.co.cr. 81 units. $110–$120 double; $140 suite. Free parking. **Amenities:** Restaurant; bar; midsize pool in attractive garden; sauna; smoke-free rooms; 2 lighted tennis courts; free Wi-Fi.

Finca Rosa Blanca Coffee Plantation & Inn.

Where to Dine

It's also worth making the winding drive to San Pedro de Barva de Heredia to stop in at **La Lluna de Valencia** ★★ (📞 **2269-6665;** www.lallunadevalencia. com), a delightful rustic Spanish restaurant with amazing paella, delicious sangria, and a very colorful and amiable host.

El Tigre Vestido ★★ INTERNATIONAL/VEGETARIAN   This is the in-house restaurant for the lovely Finca Rosa Blanca Coffee Plantation & Inn (see above). Owners Glenn and Teri Jampol are foodies and environmentalists. Much of the fruits and vegetables are grown organically on the grounds and in the greenhouses here. As much as possible of the remaining ingredients are locally sourced. The menu here seeks to jazz up traditional Costa Rican classics and create new dishes out of local ingredients. You'll find their homegrown coffee finding its way into rubs and sauces and desserts. The indoor dining room is lovely, but my favorite seats are on the deck, set under tall trees overlooking the city lights of the Central Valley below.

At Finca Rosa Blanca, Santa Bárbara de Heredia. 📞 **305/395-3042** in the U.S., or 2269-9392 in Costa Rica. http://eltigrevestido.com. Main courses $16–$22. Daily 7am–10pm.

Entertainment & Nightlife

Home to the National Autonomous University, the center of Heredia is chock-full of bars and clubs frequented by college kids. Of these, **Bulevar Relax** (📞 **2237-1832**), **Fresas** (📞 **2262-5555**), and **La Choza** (📞 **2237-1553**), all right near each other on Avenida Central, are the best. Down along the Interamerican Highway, in San Joaquín de los Flores, **Club 212** (📞 **2265-1079**) is a massive dance club with regular contemporary DJs, heavy beats, and occasional live acts.

GRECIA, SARCHÍ & ZARCERO

All these towns are northwest of San José and can be combined into a long day trip (if you have a car), perhaps in conjunction with a visit to Poás Volcano and/or the Waterfall Gardens. The scenery here is rich and verdant, and the small towns and scattered farming communities are truly representative of Costa Rica's agricultural heartland and *campesino* tradition. This is a great area to explore on your own in a rental car, if you don't mind getting lost a bit (roads are narrow, winding, and poorly marked). If you're relying on buses, you'll be able to visit any of the towns listed below, but probably just one or two per day.

If you're heading out to this area and want some adventure mixed in, you might consider taking a leap with the folks at **Tropical Bungee** (p. 150), which is just off the Interamerican Highway, a little bit beyond the Grecia exit.

Grecia

9km (12 miles) NW of Alajuela; 37 km (23 miles) NW of San José

The picturesque little town of Grecia is noteworthy for its unusual **metal church,** which is painted a deep red with white gingerbread trim, and is just off the town's central park. About 1km (¹/₂ mile) outside of Grecia, on the old road to Alajuela, you will find the **World of Snakes** (© **2494-3700;** www.theworldofsnakes.com). Open daily from 8am to 5pm, this serpentarium has more than 150 snakes representing more than 50 species. Admission, which includes a guided tour, is $12 for adults and $6 for children 7 to 14.

GETTING THERE: By Car: Grecia is located just off the Interamerican Highway (CR1), on the way from San José to Puntarenas.

By Bus: Tuan (© **2258-2004**) buses leave San José every half-hour for Grecia from Calle 18 between avenidas 3 and 5 (on the east side of the Abonos Agros building). The fare is C1,050.

Sarchí ★

7km (4 miles) NW of Grecia; 44km (27 miles) NW of San José

Sarchí is Costa Rica's main artisan town. The colorfully painted miniature **oxcarts** that you see all over the country are made here. Oxcarts such as these were once used to haul coffee beans to market. Today, although you might

An oxcart factory in Sarchí.

occasionally see oxcarts in use, most are purely decorative. However, they remain a well-known symbol of Costa Rica. In addition to miniature oxcarts, many carved wooden souvenirs are made here with rare hardwoods from the nation's forests. The town has dozens of shops, and all have similar prices. Perhaps your best one-stop shop in Sarchí is the large and long-standing **Chaverri Oxcart Factory** ★ (℗ **2454-4411;** www.sarchicostarica.net), which is right in the center of things, but it never hurts to shop around and visit several of the stores.

Built between 1950 and 1958, the town's main **church** ★ is painted pink with aquamarine trim and looks strangely like a child's birthday cake. It's definitely worth a quick visit.

Close-up of a typical Costa Rican oxcart.

GETTING THERE   By Car: If you're going to Sarchí from San José, head north on the Interamerican Highway (CR1), and take the exit for Grecia. From Grecia, the road to Sarchí heads off to the left as you face the main church, but because of all the one-way streets, you'll have to drive around the church. Rural roads connect Sarchí to Naranjo, San Ramón, and Zarcero.

By Bus: Tuan (℗ **2258-2004**) buses leave San José about three times throughout the day for Sarchí from Calle 18 between avenidas 3 and 5. The fare is C985. Alternatively, you can take any Grecia bus from this same station. In Grecia, they connect with the Alajuela-Sarchí buses, leaving every 30 minutes from Calle 8 between avenidas Central and 1 in Alajuela.

Else Kientzler Botanical Garden ★★ GARDEN   Located on the grounds of an ornamental flower farm, on the outskirts of the tourist town Sarchí, these are extensive, impressive, and lovingly laid-out botanical gardens. Over 2.5km (1.5 miles) of trails run through a collection of more than 2,000 species of flora. All the plants are labeled with their Latin names, with some further explanations around the grounds in both English and Spanish. On the grounds are a topiary labyrinth, as well as a variety of lookouts, gazebos, and shady benches. A children's play area features some water games, jungle gym setups, and a child-friendly, little zip-line canopy tour. Over 40% of the gardens are wheelchair accessible.

About 6 blocks north of the central football (soccer) stadium in the town of Sarchí, Alajuela. ℗ **2454-2070.** www.elsegarden.com. Admission C6,600 adults, C3,550 students with valid ID and children 5–12. A guided tour costs an extra C6,000 guide per hour. Advance reservations are necessary for guided tours. Daily 8am–4pm.

Where to Stay & Dine

While Sarchí itself has no noteworthy accommodations, the plush **El Silencio Lodge & Spa** (see below) is about a 35-minute drive away in a beautiful mountain setting.

El Silencio Lodge & Spa ★★ This isolated luxury nature lodge features large individual bungalows scattered over a forested hillside with great views and an unmistakable sense of having finally "gotten away from it all." Each bungalow suite comes with a King bed, a large sitting area with built-in couches that convert to two twin beds, a spacious balcony and private outdoor Jacuzzi with privacy provided by artistic bamboo screening. The newer two-bedroom family suites are the only units here that come with televisions. There are trails around the grounds and private reserve, as well as a top notch spa and gorgeous open-air yoga studio. On-site organic gardens supply the wonderful kitchen which specializes in healthy spa cuisine. El Silencio has earned "5 Leaves" in the CST Sustainable Tourism program, the highest rating.

To get here, you must first drive to the town of Sarchí. From the Pali supermarket in the center of town, head north and follow the signs. El Silencio is some 22km (13 miles) outside of Sarchí.

Bajos del Toro, Alajuela. 🕿 **2231-6122** reservations office in San José, or 2476-0303 at the hotel. www.elsilenciolodge.com. 20 units. $250–$550 double; $620–$700 two-bedroom suites. Rates include breakfast. **Amenities:** Restaurant; bar; small spa; Wi-Fi.

Zarcero

60km (38 miles) NW of San José

Beyond Sarchí, on picturesque roads lined with cedar trees, is the town of Zarcero. In a small park in the middle of town is a **menagerie of sculpted shrubs** that includes a monkey on a motorcycle, people and animals dancing, an

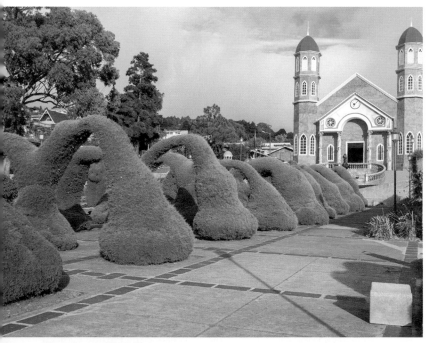

The topiary gardens in Zarcero.

ox pulling a cart, a man wearing a top hat, and a large elephant. Behind all the topiary is a wonderful rural **church.** It's not really worth the drive just to see this park, but it's a good idea to take a break in Zarcero to walk the gardens, on the way to La Fortuna and Arenal Volcano.

GETTING THERE   By Car: Zarcero is located along the popular route from San José to La Fortuna. Take the Interamerican Highway (CR1) north to Naranjo, and follow signs to Ciudad Quesada and Zarcero.

By Bus: Daily buses (✆ **2255-0567**) for Zarcero leave from San José hourly from the Atlántico del Norte bus station at Avenida 9 and Calle 12. This is actually the Ciudad Quesada–San Carlos bus. Just tell the driver that you want to get off in Zarcero, and keep an eye out for the topiary. The ride takes around 1¹⁄₂ hours, and the fare is around C1,050.

CARTAGO ★

24km (15 miles) SE of San José

Cartago is the original capital of Costa Rica. Founded in 1563, it was Costa Rica's first city—and was, in fact, the *only* city for almost 150 years. Irazú Volcano rises up from the edge of town, and although it's quiet these days, it has not always been so peaceful. Earthquakes have damaged Cartago repeatedly over the years, so today few of the old colonial buildings are left standing. In the center of the city, a public park winds through the ruins of a large church that was destroyed in 1910 before it could be finished.

Essentials

GETTING THERE & DEPARTING   By Car: Head east out of San José on Avenida 2, toward the suburbs of Los Yoses and San Pedro, continuing on through Curridabat. As you exit Curridabat, you will see signs to Cartago, putting you on the Interamerican Highway (CR2) to Cartago. This section of the highway is also known locally as the Florencio del Castillo Highway. There's a C75 toll charged in one direction, as you leave Curridabat heading toward Cartago.

By Bus: Lumaca buses (✆ **2537-2320**) for Cartago leave San José every 3 to 5 minutes between 4:30am and 9pm, with slightly less frequent service until midnight, from Calle 3 and Avenida 2. You can also pick up one en route at any of the little covered bus stops along Avenida Central in Los Yoses and San Pedro. The length of the trip is 45 minutes; the fare is C450.

By Train: San José's scenic, but sporadic main train line runs all the way from the western suburb of Pavas to downtown Cartago, with major stops in downtown San José, and at the Universidad de Costa Rica (University of Costa Rica) and Universidad Latina (Latin University). The train runs commuter hours roughly every 1¹⁄₂ hours between 5 and 8:30am and 4:10 and 8pm. Fair to Cartago is about C650 each way.

ORIENTATION   The main route into town from the highway, Avenida 2, enters downtown Cartago from the west and leads right to the center of town, and the central park and ruins. The Basilica is 6 blocks farther east, near where you pick up the road out to Paraiso and the Orosi Valley.

Exploring Cartago

Cartago is a quiet city, with little going on or of interest to tourists, aside from the Basilica (see below). If you spend time in the city, head to the **Parque Central**

HOTELS
Ambrosia en la Montaña **6**
Orosi Lodge **5**

RESTAURANTS
La Casona del Cafetal **9**

ATTRACTIONS
Basílica de Nuestra Señora
  de los Angeles **3**
Irazú Volcano **10**
La Casa del Soñador **8**
Lankester Gardens **4**
Las Ruinas **2**
Museo Municipal
  de Cartago **1**
Orosi Church & Religious
  Art Museum **5**
Ujarrás **7**

Cartago, Orosi & Irazú

Irazú Volcano
Diego de la Haya Crater **10**
Volcán Irazú Nat'l Park

Rancho Redondo
Laguna
Llano Grande
San Juan de Chicoa
San Gerardo
Banderilla
Tierra Blanca
Pacayas
Pascón
Ochomogo
Cot
Capira
Cervantes
Taras
See map below
San Rafael
Cartago
Caballo Blanco
Tobosí
Dulce Nombre
Birrisito
Cachí Dam
Tejar
San Francisco
Paraíso
San Juan
Finca
San Isidro
Lourdes
Ujarrás **7**
Cachí **8** **9**
Navarro
Loáiza
Cangreja
Muñeco
Orosí
Río Macho
To San Isidro del General
Estrella
Río Navarro y Río Sombrero Protected Area
Palomas
Tapantí
Purisil

NICARAGUA
CARIBBEAN SEA
SAN JOSÉ
Map Area
PACIFIC OCEAN
PANAMA

0   3 mi
0   3 km

Lago de Chací
Valle de Orosí
Paloma

Cartago
Avenida 6
Avenida 2
Avenida 1
Avenida 3
Avenida 5
Av 7
Av 9
Av 11
Avenida 3
Calle 10

1
2
3

0   1/2 mi
0   0.5 km

Las Ruinas.

(Central Park), also known as **Las Ruinas (the Ruins)** ★. This is the site of the city's ill-fated original cathedral. Begun in 1575, the church was devastated by a series of earthquakes. Despite several attempts, construction was abandoned after the massive 1910 quake, and today the stone and mortar ruins sit at the heart of a neatly manicured park, with quiet paths and plenty of benches. The ruins themselves are closed off, but the park itself is lovely.

You might want to stop in at the **Museo Municipal de Cartago** (Cartago Municipal Museum; ✆ **2591-1050**), on Avenida 6 between calles 2 and 4. Located in a former, and wonderfully restored military barracks, the museum houses a series of local historical displays, as well as a range of changing exhibits, including some featuring local artists. The museum is open Tuesday to Saturday, 9am to 4pm and Sunday till 3pm, free admission. Cartago (and the Orosi Valley) is also a good stop along the way to visit one of the quetzal-viewing lodges in the Dota and Cerro de la Muerte region (p. 404).

Since there's no real reason to stay in Cartago, and no highly recommendable hotels right in the city, I suggest picking a hotel in the Orosi Valley or Turrialba region if you're looking to stay in the area.

Basílica de Nuestra Señora de los Angeles ★★★ CHURCH Dedicated to the patron saint of Costa Rica, the impressive Basilica of Our Lady of the Angels anchors the east side of the city. Within the walls of this Byzantine-style church is a shrine containing the tiny carved figure of **La Negrita,** the Black Virgin, which is nearly lost amid its ornate altar. The walls of the shrine are covered with a fascinating array of tiny silver images left in thanks for cures affected by La Negrita. Amid the plethora of diminutive silver arms and legs, are also hands, feet, hearts, lungs, kidneys, eyes, torsos, breasts, and—peculiarly—guns, trucks, beds, and planes. Outside the church, vendors sell a wide selection of these trinkets, as well as little candle replicas of La Negrita.

Calle 16, btw. avs. 2 and 4. ✆ **2551-0465.** Free admission. Daily 6:30am–5pm.

La Negrita

Legend has it that Juana Pereira stumbled upon the statue of La Negrita sitting atop a rock, while gathering wood. Juana took it home, but the next morning it was gone. She went back to the rock, and there it was again. This was repeated three times, until Juana took her find to a local priest. The priest took the statue to his church for safekeeping, but the next morning it was gone, only to be found sitting upon the same rock later that day. The priest eventually decided that the strange occurrences were a sign that the Virgin wanted a temple or shrine built to her upon the spot. And so work was begun on what would eventually become today's impressive Basilica.

Miraculous healing powers have been attributed to La Negrita, and, over the years, parades of pilgrims have come to the shrine seeking cures for their illnesses and difficulties. August 2 is her patron saint's day. Each year, on this date, tens of thousands of Costa Ricans and foreign pilgrims walk to Cartago from San José and elsewhere in the country in devotion to this powerful statue.

Attractions Around Cartago

Irazú Volcano ★★ NATURAL ATTRACTION   The 3,378m (11,080-ft.) Irazú Volcano is historically one of Costa Rica's more active volcanoes, although it's relatively quiet these days. It last erupted on March 19, 1963, the day that President John F. Kennedy arrived in Costa Rica. The landscape here is often compared to that of the moon. A good paved road leads right to the rim of the crater, where a desolate expanse of gray sand nurtures few plants and the air smells of sulfur. The drive up from Cartago has magnificent views of the fertile Meseta Central and Orosi Valley, and if you're very lucky, you might be able to see both the Pacific Ocean and the Caribbean Sea. Clouds usually descend by noon, so get here as early in the day as possible. Dress in layers; this might be the Tropics, but it can be cold up at the top if the sun's not out.

A short trail leads to the rim of the volcano's two craters, their walls a maze of eroded gullies feeding onto the flat floor far below. A 2km (1.25-mile) trail loops around the rim of the Playa Hermosa Crater. The visitor center up here has information on the volcano and natural history. The park restaurant, at an elevation of 3,022m (9,912 ft.), with

The interior of Cartago's Basilica.

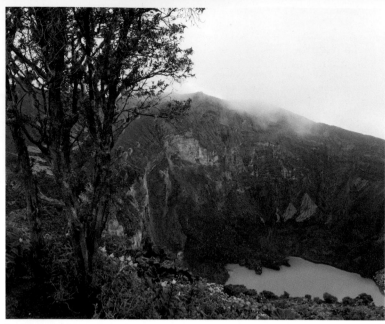

Irazú Volcano.

walls of windows looking out over the valley far below, claims to be the highest restaurant in Central America.

Irazú de Cartago, 52km (32 miles) east of San José. ✆ **2200-5615.** Admission $10. Daily 8am–4pm.

Lankester Gardens ★★ GARDEN   Costa Rica has more than 1,400 varieties of orchids, and almost 800 species are cultivated and on display at this botanical garden in Cartago province. Created in the 1940s by English naturalist Charles Lankester, the gardens are now administered by the University of Costa Rica. The primary goal is to preserve the local flora, with an emphasis on orchids and bromeliads. Paved, well-marked trails meander from open, sunny gardens into shady forests. In each environment different species of orchids are in bloom. An information center and a gift shop are also on site. Plan to spend between 1 and 3 hours here if you're interested in flowers and gardening; you could run through it more quickly if you're not. You can easily combine a visit here with a tour at Cartago and/or the Orosi Valley and Irazú Volcano.

1km (½ mile) east of Cartago, on the road to Paraíso de Cartago. ✆ **2511-7939.** www.jbl.ucr.ac.cr. Admission $7.50 adults, $5 children 6–16. Daily 8:30am–4:30pm.

> ### DIY: Irazú Volcano
>
> If you don't have a rental car and don't want to sign on for an organized tour, buses leave San José for Irazú Volcano daily at 8am from Avenida 2 between calles 1 and 3 (across the street from the entrance to the Gran Hotel Costa Rica). The fare is C4,500 round-trip, with the bus leaving the volcano at 12:30pm. This company is particularly fickle. To make sure that the buses are running, call ✆ **2530-1064,** although that might not help much, since they often don't answer their phone, and speak only Spanish.

THE OROSI VALLEY ★★

The Orosi Valley, southeast of Cartago, is generally considered one of the most beautiful valleys in Costa Rica. The Reventazón River meanders through this steep-sided valley until it collects in the lake formed by the Cachí Dam. A well-paved road winds a near-perfect loop around the lake, allowing for easy access to all of the attractions listed below. Scenic overlooks are near the town of Orosi, at the head of the valley, and in Ujarrás, on the banks of the lake.

GETTING THERE & DEPARTING   If you're driving, take the road to Paraíso from Cartago, head toward Ujarrás, continue around the lake, and then pass through Cachí and on to Orosi. From Orosi, the road leads back to Paraíso. It is difficult to explore this whole area by public bus because this is not a densely populated region and connections are often infrequent or unreliable. However, regular buses do run from Cartago to the town of Orosi and around the entire loop. These buses run roughly every half-hour and leave the main bus terminal in Cartago. The trip takes 30 minutes, and the fare runs between C250 to C500, depending upon where you get off the bus.

Exploring the Orosi Valley

Near **Ujarrás** are the ruins of Costa Rica's oldest church, which was built in 1693. Little remains beyond the worn brick and adobe facade of the church, but the gardens are a great place to sit and gaze at the surrounding mountains.

Along the main road around the valley, especially near the town of Orosi, are several **scenic overlooks;** take the time to pull over and admire the views and snap a photo or two. In the town of **Orosi** itself is yet another **colonial church** (see below) and convent worth visiting.

An orchid in bloom at Lankester Gardens.

From the Orosi Valley, it's a quick shot to the entrance to the **Tapantí National Park ★** (✆ **2206-5615**), where you'll find some gentle and beautiful hiking trails, as well as riverside picnic areas. The park is open daily from 8am to 4pm; admission is $10.

TOP ATTRACTIONS

La Casa del Soñador COMMERCIAL ART GALLERY   The "House of the Dreamer" is the home and gallery of the late sculptor Macedonio Quesada. Quesada earned fame with his primitive sculptures of La Negrita (see "La Negrita," p. 181) and other religious and secular characters carved on coffee tree roots and trunks. You can see some of Macedonio's original work here, including his version of "The Last Supper" carved onto one of the walls of the main building. Today,

The Orosi Valley.

his sons carry on the family tradition. You can shop among their collection of small sculptures, carved religious icons, and ornate walking sticks.

1km ('/₂ mile) south of Cachí. © **2577-1186.** Daily 8am–4pm.

Orosi Church & Religious Art Museum ★ CHURCH/ART MUSEUM
The beautiful Orosi river valley is home to Costa Rica's oldest still-functioning church. The church, which was first built by Franciscan monks in the mid–18th century, features well-maintained traditional adobe walls that have weathered centuries, and several major earthquakes. Off to the side you'll find a small museum with a collection of religious paintings and artifacts, as well as original antique furniture and period clothing exhibits.

West side of the soccer field, Orosi. © **2533-3051.** Admission C500. Tues–Fri 1–5pm; Sat–Sun 9am–5pm.

Where to Stay & Eat

If you're interested in staying out here, check out the charming little **Orosi Lodge** ★ (© **2533-3578;** www.orosilodge.com), on the south side of the tiny town of Orosi, right next to some simple hot-spring pools. A little farther out of town is **Ambrosia en la Montaña** ★ (© **2533-2336** or 8385-7609; www.ambrosiaenlamontana.com), a pretty little inn, with two individual wooden cabins, great views, and an excellent restaurant.

La Casona del Cafetal COSTA RICAN   This is a dependable lunch stop for your drive around the Orosi Valley. This long-standing institution is set on expansive grounds overlooking Lake Cachi. Tables are spread around patios and verandas designed to take in the view, and a few heavy concrete tables are around the lawn. The restaurant serves up hearty and authentic traditional Costa

LEFT: **The Ujarrás ruins.**
RIGHT: **Iglesia de San José de Orosi.**

Rican cuisine. Local ladies are always on hand forming and cooking up fresh corn tortillas. They also offer an all-you-can eat Sunday buffet for around $22, including tax and tip.

Cachí. ✆ **2577-1414.** www.lacasonadelcafetal.com. Main courses C4,500–C18,000. Daily 11am–6pm.

Sculptures at La Casa del Soñador.

TURRIALBA ★★

53km (33 miles) E of San José

This attractive little town is best known as the starting point and home base for many popular white-water rafting trips. Turrialba is a hot spot for active and adventure travelers. However, it's also worth a visit if you have an interest in pre-Columbian history or tropical botany.

Turrialba is situated in the heart of a rich agricultural region. Coffee and sugar cane are the principal crops. The area is lower in elevation than San José and much of the rest of the Central Valley, and for visitors (and the happy crops) this translates into generally higher temperatures. See "The Central Valley" map on p. 157.

Turrialba sits on the old transit route between San José and the Caribbean port city Limón. This makes Turrialba an excellent stop as part of an itinerary taking you to or from the Caribbean coast.

Essentials

GETTING THERE & DEPARTING By Car: If you're driving, follow the directions to Cartago (p. 178), and then take the road from Cartago to Paraíso, through Juan Viñas, and on to Turrialba. It's pretty well marked. (Alternatively you can head toward the small town of Cot, on the road to Irazú Volcano, and then through the town of Pacayas on to Turrialba, another well-marked route.)

By Bus: Transtusa buses (✆ **2222-4464** or 2557-5050; www.transtusacr.com) leave San José at least once every hour for Turrialba between 5:15am and 10pm from Calle 13 between avenidas 6 and 8. The fare is C1,300.

Around three buses also head to Guayabo daily from the main bus terminal in Turrialba. The fare is C535.

A view of the Turrialba Valley.

CITY LAYOUT   Turrialba itself is a bit of a jumble, and you will probably have to ask directions to get to locations in, around, and outside of town. Guayabo is about 20km (12 miles) beyond Turrialba on a road that is paved the entire way except for the last 3km (1³/₄ miles).

Exploring Turrialba

Most of the white-water rafting companies in Costa Rica have an operational base in Turrialba, and the put-in points for several of the more popular river trips are nearby. See chapter 5 for more information on rafting trips and operators.

In addition to rafting and kayaking, **Explornatura** ★★ (✆ 866/571-2443 in the U.S. and Canada, or 2556-0111 in Costa Rica; www.explornatura.com) is an excellent local adventure tour operator that offers up a range of trips and activities, including canopy and canyoning tours, horseback riding, hiking, and mountain biking. Their **canyoning tour** ★★ is a wet adventure that includes several rappels down the face of rainforest waterfalls.

Guayabo National Monument ★ (✆ 2559-1220) is one of Costa Rica's only pre-Columbian sites open to the public. It's 19km (12 miles) northeast of Turrialba and preserves a town site that dates from between 1000 b.c. and a.d. 1400. Archaeologists believe that Guayabo might have supported a population of as many as 10,000 people, but no clues yet explain why the city was eventually abandoned only shortly before the Spanish arrived in the New World. Excavated ruins at Guayabo consist of paved roads, aqueducts, stone bridges, and house and temple foundations. The site also has gravesites and petroglyphs. The monument is open daily from 8am to 3:30pm. This is a national park, and admission is $10 at the gate.

Hovering over the town, the **Turrialba Volcano National Park** ★★ boasts nearly 1,600 hectares (3,950 acres) of lush rainforest, as well as its namesake 3,340m (10,955-ft.) volcano. The volcano is in a fairly active phase, and the park trails are sometimes closed to the public. When it's open, it is possible to hike to the volcano's summit, which offers fantastic views. It's best to visit as part of a tour, since the final 8km (5 miles) to the park entrance is on a rough gravel road.

Botanists and gardeners will want to pay a visit to the **Center for Agronomy Research and Development** (**CATIE;** ✆ 2556-2700; www.catie.ac.cr), which is located 5km (3 miles) southeast of Turrialba on the road to Siquirres. This center is one of the world's foremost facilities for research into tropical agriculture. Among the plants on CATIE's 810 hectares (2,000 acres) are hundreds of varieties of cacao and thousands of varieties of coffee. The plants here have been collected from all over the world. In addition to trees used for food and other purposes, other plants grown here are strictly for ornamental purposes. CATIE is open Monday through Friday from 7am to 4pm. Guided tours are available with advance notice for $15 per person.

If you're a java junkie, you'll want to take the **Golden Bean Coffee Tour** ★ (✆ 2531-2008 or 8701-2637), a comprehensive and informative tour of a working coffee plantation. The mill and processing facilities here have been in operation for almost a century. The tour takes around 2 hours, and operates daily at 9am and 2pm. It costs $22 per person.

Where to Stay & Eat

In addition to the places listed below, you might want to check out **Turrialtico** ★ (✆ 2538-1111; www.turrialtico.com), a simple hotel with a beautiful open-air restaurant on a hill overlooking the Turrialba Valley. The view here is one of the finest in the area, with lush greenery far below and volcanoes in the distance. The Costa Rican food is good and reasonably priced, and a double room in the rambling old wooden building will cost you $52 to $75, including breakfast and taxes. This place is popular with rafting companies that bring groups here for meals and for overnights before, during, and after multiday rafting trips.

Casa Turire ★   This lakefront boutique hotel was built to resemble a majestic old plantation home, replete with a long entrance driveway lined with tall Royal palms. Casa Turire was actually built before the nearby hydroelectric dam created Lake Angostura, which now laps gently just below the hotels well-tended gardens and grounds. The restaurant, which focuses on locally sourced organic produce and proteins, is excellent. The hotel has earned "4 Leaves" in the CST Sustainable Tourism program.

1.5km (1 mile) from the Cruce de Atirro, Turrialba. ✆ **2531-1111** in Costa Rica. www.hotelcasa turire.com. 16 units. $145–$160 double; $250–$420 suite. Rates include full breakfast. **Amenities:** Restaurant; bar; Jacuzzi; outdoor pool; small spa; smoke-free rooms; free Wi-Fi.

Pacuare Lodge ★★★   Set on the edge of the roaring Pacuare river, this luxurious raft in-raft out jungle lodge is a marvel. The first time I rafted the Pacuare river more than 20 years ago, it was with Aventuras Naturales (p. 152), the owners of this lodge. We camped in tents on this very spot. Today the lodge rooms and private suites are some of the most plush nature lodge rooms you'll find in the country. A couple even come with private plunge pools. Of these, the remote honeymoon suite is the real star, reached by a long private suspension bridge over the forest and river. For a really unique experience here, be sure to reserve a meal in the treetop "El Nido" platform. The Pacuare Lodge has received the highest "5 Leaves" rating from the CST Sustainable Tourism program.

On the banks of the Pacuare River. ✆ **800/963-1195** in the U.S. and Canada, or 2224-0505 in Costa Rica. www.pacuarelodge.com. 19 units. Rates begin at $420 per person for a 2-day/1-night package, including 3 meals, transportation to and from San José, 2 days on the river, a guided hike, and all taxes. **Amenities:** Restaurant; bar; outdoor solar heated pool; spa; all rooms smoke-free.

GUANACASTE:

THE GOLD COAST

G uanacaste is Costa Rica's "Gold Coast"—and not because this is where the Spanish Conquistadors found vast quantities of the brilliant metal ore. Instead, it's because more and more visitors to Costa Rica are choosing Guanacaste as their first—and often only— stop. Beautiful beaches abound along this coastline. Several are packed with a mix of hotels and resorts, some are still pristine and deserted, and others are backed by small fishing villages. Choices range from long, broad sections of sand stretching on for miles, to tiny pocket coves bordered by rocky headlands.

This is Costa Rica's most coveted vacation destination and the site of its greatest tourism development. The international airport in Liberia receives daily direct flights from several major U.S. and Canadian hub cities, allowing tourists to visit some of Costa Rica's prime destinations without having to go through San José.

This is also Costa Rica's driest region. The rainy season starts later and ends earlier, and overall it's more dependably sunny here than in other parts of the country. Combine this climate with a coastline that stretches south for hundreds of miles, from the Nicaraguan border, all the way to the Nicoya Peninsula, and you have an equation that yields beach bliss.

One caveat: During the dry season (mid-Nov–Apr), when sunshine is most reliable, the hillsides in Guanacaste turn browner than the chaparral of Southern California. Dust from dirt roads blankets the trees in many areas, and the vistas are far from tropical. Driving these dirt roads without air-conditioning and the windows rolled up tight can be extremely unpleasant.

On the other hand, if you happen to visit this area in the rainy season (particularly from May–Aug), the hillsides are a beautiful, rich green, and the sun usually shines all morning, giving way to an afternoon shower—just in time for a nice siesta.

Inland from the beaches, Guanacaste remains Costa Rica's "Wild West," a land of dry plains populated with cattle ranches and cowboys, who are known here as *sabaneros*, a name that derives from the Spanish word for "savanna" or "grassland." If it weren't for those rainforest-clad volcanoes in the distance, you might swear you were in Texas.

Guanacaste is home to several active volcanoes and some beautiful national parks, including **Santa Rosa National Park ★**, the site of massive sea turtle nestings and of a major battle to maintain independence; **Rincón de la Vieja National Park ★★**, which features hot springs and bubbling mud pots, pristine waterfalls, and an active volcanic crater; and **Palo Verde National Park ★**, a beautiful expanse of mangroves, wetlands, and savanna.

PREVIOUS PAGE: **Witch's Rock.**

THE BEST GUANACASTE EXPERIENCES

o **Barefoot Dining with Your Feet in the Sand:** Beachfront dining options range from the fine seared tuna and Belgian fries found at **Lola's** (p. 250) to the just-grilled daily catch at a simple Costa Rican *soda*. See the "Where to Dine" sections of the various destinations below for recommendations.

o **Catching Your First Wave:** All up and down the Guanacaste coast are excellent breaks, and many are perfect for beginners. See the "Exploring" sections of the various destinations below for surf school recommendations.

o **Taking a Sailboat Cruise:** Most of the beach towns and destinations in Guanacaste boast a small fleet of charter boats. Trips often include lunch and a snorkel stop or two. Some stop at deserted beaches, or linger at sea for the sunset. See the "Exploring" sections of the various destinations below for boat recommendations.

o **Taking a Sunset Stroll on the Beach:** What could be more peaceful or romantic than a leisurely stroll on a Guanacaste beach in the late afternoon, as the sun sets into the Pacific? I prefer more isolated stretches of sand, like Playa Avellanas or Playa Grande, but it's hard to go wrong almost anywhere along this coastline.

o **Checking Out Rincón de la Vieja's Hot Springs, Hiking & Adventures:** Even if you're staying at one of the region's beach resorts, Rincón de la Vieja National Park's namesake volcano and fabulous trails are definitely worth a visit. Also worth seeing are the hot springs just outside the park and the amazing Hacienda Guachipelín's adventure tours. See "Rincón de la Vieja National Park" below.

LIBERIA

217km (135 miles) NW of San José; 132km (82 miles) NW of Puntarenas

Founded in 1769, Liberia is the capital of Guanacaste province, and although it can hardly be considered a bustling metropolis, it is growing rapidly, in large part as a business center to feed the growing coastal boom. Hardware stores, warehouses, malls, and shipping companies are setting up shop in Liberia, and the city serves as a housing hub for the many workers needed to man the construction and tourism boom along the coast here.

Guanacaste's Top Sustainable Hotels

Hacienda Guachipelín (p. 204)
Four Seasons Resort (p. 213)
Bahía del Sol Beachfront & Boutique Hotel (p. 233)
Hotel Las Tortugas (p. 236)
Hotel Playa Hermosa Bosque del Mar (p. 215)
Hotel Capitán Suizo (p. 244)

That said, Liberia offers up more colonial atmosphere than almost any other city in the country. Its narrow streets are lined with charming old adobe homes, many of which have ornate stone accents on their facades, carved wooden doors, and aged red-tile roofs. Many have beautiful large, shuttered windows (some don't even have iron bars for protection) opening onto the narrow streets. The central plaza, which occupies

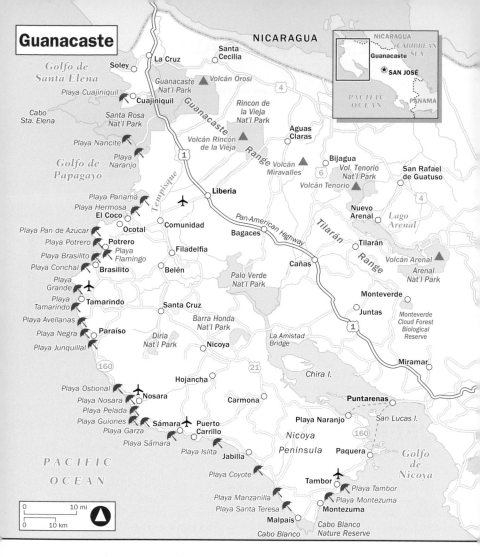

Guanacaste

NICARAGUA

Golfo de
Santa Elena

Cabo
Sta. Elena

Golfo de
Papagayo

PACIFIC
OCEAN

Soley

La Cruz

Santa
Cecilia

Volcán Orosí

Guanacaste
Nat'l Park

Cuajiniquil

Playa Cuajiniquil

Rincon de
la Vieja
Nat'l Park

Aguas
Claras

Santa Rosa
Nat'l Park

Volcán Rincón
de la Vieja

Playa Nancite

Playa
Naranjo

Volcán
Miravalles

Bijagua

Vol. Tenorio
Nat'l Park

San Rafael
de Guatuso

Volcán Tenorio

Playa Panamá

Playa Hermosa
El Coco

Liberia

Nuevo
Arenal

Lago
Arenal

Playa Pan de Azúcar

Ocotal

Comunidad

Bagaces

Pan-American Highway

Tilarán

Playa Potrero

Potrero

Playa Brasilito

Playa
Flamingo

Filadelfia

Volcán Arenal

Arenal
Nat'l Park

Playa Conchal

Brasilito

Belén

Cañas

Palo Verde
Nat'l Park

Playa
Grande

Playa
Tamarindo

Tamarindo

Santa Cruz

Barra Honda
Nat'l Park

Monteverde

Juntas

Monteverde
Cloud Forest
Biological
Reserve

Playa Avellanas

Playa Negra

Paraíso

Diria
Nat'l Park

La Amistad
Bridge

Nicoya

Playa Junquillal

Miramar

Hojancha

Chira I.

Playa Ostional

Nosara

Carmona

Puntarenas

Playa Nosara

Playa Pelada

Playa Guiones

Sámara

Puerto
Carrillo

Playa Naranjo

San Lucas I.

Playa Garza

Nicoya
Peninsula

Paquera

Golfo
de
Nicoya

Playa Sámara

Playa Islita

Jabilla

PACIFIC
OCEAN

Playa Coyote

Tambor

Playa Tambor

Playa Manzanilla

Playa Santa Teresa

Playa Montezuma

Montezuma

Malpaís

Cabo Blanco

Cabo Blanco
Nature Reserve

0   10 mi
0   10 km

---

2 square blocks in front of the church, remains the city's social hub and principal gathering spot.

Liberia can serve as a base for exploring this region or as an overnight stop in a longer itinerary. You'll find several moderately priced hotels in the city and its outskirts. Still, all things considered, it's usually preferable to base yourself either at the beach or at a mountain lodge, and to visit the city on a day trip.

Essentials

GETTING THERE & DEPARTING   By Plane: The **Daniel Oduber International Airport** (© **2668-1010;** airport code LIR) in Liberia receives a steady stream of scheduled commercial and charter flights throughout the year. Major North American airlines have direct links to Liberia; check the list on p. 496. In

Liberia's central park.

addition, numerous commercial charter flights from various North American cities fly in throughout the high season. Check with your travel agent.

Sansa (✆ **877/767-2672** in the U.S. and Canada, or 2290-4100 in Costa Rica; www.flysansa.com) and **Nature Air** (✆ **800/235-9272** in the U.S. and Canada, or 2299-6000; www.natureair.com) both have several flights daily to Liberia. Fares run between $100 and $145 each way. Flight duration is around 50 minutes.

The following car rental companies all have local agencies: **Adobe** (✆ 2667-0608), **Alamo** (✆ 2668-1111), **Avis** (✆ 2668-1196), **Budget** (✆ 2668-1118), **Dollar** (✆ 2243-2950), **Hertz** (✆ 2668-1048), Thrifty (✆ 2665-0787), and **Toyota** (✆ 2668-1212). You can also reserve with these and most major international car rental companies via their San José and international offices (see "Getting Around," in chapter 6).

The airport is 13km (8 miles) from downtown Liberia. Taxis await all incoming flights; a taxi into town should cost around $10. The ride takes around 10 minutes.

By Car: From San José, you can either take the Interamerican Highway (CR1) north all the way to Liberia from downtown San José, or first head west out of the city on the San José–Caldera Highway (CR27). When you reach Caldera, follow the signs to Puntarenas, Liberia, and the Interamerican Highway (CR1). This will lead you to the unmarked entrance to CR1. You'll want to pass under the bridge and follow the on-ramp, which will put you on the highway heading north. This latter route is a faster and flatter drive. Depending upon which route you take and traffic conditions, it's a 3- to 4-hour drive.

By Bus: Pulmitan express buses (✆ **2222-1650** in San José, or 2666-0458 in Liberia; www.pulmitandeliberia.com) leave San José roughly every hour between 6am and 8pm from Calle 24 between avenidas 5 and 7. The ride to Liberia takes around 4 hours. A one-way fare costs C3,300.

Gray Line (© 800/719-3105 in the U.S. and Canada, or 2220-2126 in Costa Rica; www.graylinecostarica.com) and Interbus (© 4100-0888; www.interbusonline.com) both have two daily buses leaving San José for Liberia and all beaches in this area, one in the morning and one in the afternoon. The fare is around $47. The morning bus (for either company) makes connections to Rincón de la Vieja and Santa Rosa national parks. Both companies will pick you up at most San José–area hotels, and provide connections to and from most other destinations in Costa Rica.

Buses depart for San José and most of the area beaches and national parks from the Liberia bus station on the edge of town, 200m (2 blocks) north and 100m (1 block) east of the main intersection on the Interamerican Highway. Express buses for San José leave roughly every hour between 3am and 8pm.

CITY LAYOUT Liberia's small city center lies just to the east of the main intersection of the Interamerican Highway and the road to the beaches. On the southern outskirts of the city is a modern shopping mall, the place to come for a food court fix or to catch a semi-late-run movie at the local multiplex. Smaller, contemporary strip malls and shopping centers can be found near the airport, and right at the major intersection near the entrance to town.

FAST FACTS Several state and private bank offices are clustered around downtown Liberia, as well as a branch of the **Banco de Costa Rica** inside the airport. The local **police** number is © 2690-0129, and the **Liberia Hospital** number is © 2690-2300. If you need a taxi, dial © 2666-3330. A host of Internet cafes are on the blocks surrounding and just off the central plaza.

Exploring the Town

The central plaza in Liberia is a great place to people-watch, especially in the early evenings and on weekends. Grab a seat on one of the many concrete benches, or join the families and young lovers as they leisurely stroll around. On

An Interesting Stop on Your Way to Liberia

If you're driving to or from Guanacaste, be sure to take a brief break to check out the **Iglesia de Cañas (Cañas Church)** ★ ★ in Cañas. Well-known painter, installation artist, and local prodigal son Otto Apuy has designed and directed the envelopment of the entire church in colorful mosaic. The work uses whole and broken tiles in glossy, vibrant colors to depict both religious and abstract themes. The church's nearly 30m-tall (100-ft.) central tower is entirely covered in mosaics. It is estimated that more than a million pieces of ceramic were used in the work. The church is located in the center of town, just a few blocks off the highway.

the northern edge of the Plaza Central, the **Iglesia de la Inmaculada Concepción** is Liberia's main house of worship. The church was built in 1972 and features a tall A-frame–style central nave and a separate clock tower that rises up sharply—a contemporary concrete obelisk. The main church is generally open from 6am to 6pm, though it's sometimes open later for masses.

Just off the northwest corner of the main central plaza, the **Museo de Guanacaste** (Guanacaste Museum; ✆ **2665-7114**) occupies the city's former military barracks and prison. There's no real permanent collection, but the public space is often used for traveling exhibits and various cultural events—concerts, lectures, recitals. Inaugurated in 1940, the building takes up a full city block, and is known locally as either the Comandancia de Plaza de Liberia, or El Cuartel.

A colonial-era building in Liberia.

If you venture for a few blocks down **Calle Real** ★, you'll see fine examples of the classic Spanish colonial adobe buildings with ornate wooden doors, heavy beams, central courtyards, and faded, sagging, red-tile roofs.

While the Catholic church that anchors the central plaza is unspectacular, if you head several blocks east of the plaza, you will come to **Iglesia La Ermita de la Agonía** ★ (✆ **2666-0518**). Built in 1865, this whitewashed stone church is in surprisingly good shape. Inside it is plain and bare, but it is the only remaining colonial-era church to be found in Guanacaste. The visiting hours are seriously limited (daily 2:30–3:30pm), but not to worry: Local tour agencies can sometimes arrange visits during off hours. Even if you can't enter, you'll still get a good feel for the place by checking out its whitewashed stucco exterior.

Outdoor Adventures near Liberia

In addition to the activities listed below, Liberia is a major jumping-off point for Rincón de la Vieja National Park (p. 199).

LLANO DE CORTES WATERFALL ★

Located about 25km (16 miles) south of Liberia, the **Llanos del Cortés Waterfall** ★ is a beautiful and wide jungle waterfall with an excellent pool at the base for cooling off and swimming. At roughly 12m (40 ft.) wide, the falls are actually slightly wider than they are tall. This is a great spot for a picnic. The turnoff for the dirt road to the falls is well marked and about 3km (1¾ miles) north of the crossroads for Bagaces. From the turnoff, you must drive a rough dirt road to the parking area and then hike down a short steep trail to the falls. Admission is C1,000 and goes to support the local school. Even though guards are on duty, be careful about leaving anything of value in your car.

Shady Business

This province gets its name from the abundant Guanacaste *(Enterolobium cyclocarpum)*, Costa Rica's national tree. This distinctive tree is known for its broad, full crown, which provides welcome shade on the Guanacaste's hot plains and savannas. The Guanacaste is also known as the elephant-ear tree, because of the distinctive shape of its large seedpods. Its fragrant white flowers bloom between February and April.

BIRDING

The **Río Tempisque Basin ★**, southwest of town, is one of the best places in the country to spot marsh and stream birds by the hundreds. This area is an important breeding ground for gallinules, jacanas, and limpkins, as well as numerous heron and kingfisher species and the roseate spoonbill. Several tour operators offer excursions and a wide range of tours in the region. **Swiss Travel Services** (© **2282-4898;** www.swisstravelcr.com) is the largest and most reliable of the major operators here.

One of the most popular tours is a boat tour down the Bebedero River to **Palo Verde National Park ★**, which is south of Cañas and is best known for its migratory bird populations. Some of the best bird-watching requires no more than a little walking around the Biological Station in the park.

You can get a similar taste of these waterways and bird-watching opportunities at **El Viejo Wetlands** (p. 229) and **Rancho Humo** (p. 283).

RAFTING TRIPS

Leisurely raft trips (with little white water) are offered by **Ríos Tropicales ★★** (© **2233-6455;** www.riostropicales.com), about 40km (25 miles) south of Liberia. Its 2-hour ($55) float trips are great for families and bird-watchers. Along the way you may see many of the area's more exotic animal residents: howler monkeys, iguanas, caimans, coatimundis, otters, toucans, parrots, motmots, trogons, and many other species of birds. Aside from your binoculars and camera, a bathing suit and sunscreen are the only things you'll need. Ríos Tropicales is based out of the Restaurant Rincón Corobicí, which is located right on the Interamerican Highway (CR1).

For a much wetter and wilder ride, the folks at **Hacienda Guachipelín** (see below) offer white-water inner-tube trips on the narrow Río Negro.

ESPECIALLY FOR KIDS

Since the landscape is postcard-perfect, especially in the dry season, you shouldn't be too surprised to see antelopes, zebras, giraffes, and elands roaming the grassy plains of Guanacaste. **Africa Mia** (**MyAfrica;** © **2666-1111;** http://africamiacr.com) offers safari-style open-jeep tours through its 100-hectare (247-acre) private reserve

Africa Mia.

A capuchin monkey in Palo Verde National Park.

populated with a wide range of nonnative (predominantly African) species. All the animals are herbivores, so don't expect to see any lions, hyenas, or cheetahs. The trip does provide some sense of being on the Serengeti or some other African plain, and the animals have plenty of room to roam. Admission, which is C9,000 for adults, and C6,000 for children 11 and under, includes a 90-minute guided tour. Other more extensive tours include a chance to get closer to the animals, and the opportunity to feed a giraffe. Africa Mia is located just off the Interamerican Highway, 8km (5 miles) south of Liberia. The park is open daily from 9am to 5pm.

Where to Stay

MODERATE

Hilton Garden Inn Liberia Airport ★ Located directly across the two-lane Highway 21 from the Daniel Oduber International Airport (LIR), this five-story contemporary chain hotel is a popular choice for folks with late arrivals or early departures. Still, with drive times of between 30 minutes to an hour to most nearby beach hotels, I debate how useful or necessary staying this close to the airport really is. Everything is what you'd expect from a Hilton Garden Inn. There's a free airport shuttle, as well as a small shopping mall adjacent to the hotel with a few restaurant options.

Across from the airport, Liberia, Guanacaste. ℂ **877/STAY-HGI** (7829-444) in the U.S. and Canada, or 2690-8888 in Costa Rica. www.hilton.com 169 units. $129–$149 double; $159–$229 suite. Rates include breakfast buffet. **Amenities:** Restaurant; bar; exercise room; Jacuzzi; outdoor pool; room service; all rooms smoke-free; free Wi-Fi.

INEXPENSIVE

El Punto Bed & Breakfast ★★ This cheery little B&B is a solid choice in Liberia. The seven rooms are set in a converted home, located in a residential neighborhood just off the main intersection of the Interamerican Highway and the road to the coast. The rooms feature cool white tile floors, colorful artwork and lots of natural light. The common areas are similarly inviting, with various sitting areas and shade covered hammocks for whiling away the time.

$1^1/_2$ blocks south of the intersection of CR1 and CR21, Liberia, Guanacaste. ☏ **2665-2986** or 8877-3949. www.elpuntohotel.com. 7 units. $65–$110 double. Rates include full breakfast and taxes. **Amenities:** Restaurant; bar; free Wi-Fi.

Hotel Liberia   Budget travelers should check this place out first. Located in an old home on the historic Calle Real, this colonial-era adobe home was first pressed into service as a hotel back in 1918. All of the rooms are spacious and kept meticulously clean. I recommend the La Casona rooms off the main central hallway, with a broad shady shared veranda. The restaurant here is excellent, with both indoor and outdoor courtyard seating.

Calle Real, $^3/_4$ block south of the old Government building, Liberia, Guanacaste. ☏ **2666-0161.** www.hotelliberiacr.com. 18 units. $15 per person, dorm room; $35–$40 double. Rates include taxes. **Amenities:** Restaurant; bar; free Wi-Fi.

Where to Dine

Liberia has plenty of standard Tico dining choices. For some local flavor, choose one of the *sodas* around the central park. The best of these is **Restaurante Paseo Real ★** (☏ 2666-3455). Another option for Costa Rican cuisine is **La Choza de Laurel** (☏ 2668-1019; www.lachozadelaurel.com), located along the main highway, about 800m (2,624 ft.) east of the Liberia airport entrance. Another popular alternative is **Pizzería Pronto** (☏ 2666-2098), which serves a wide range of wood-oven pizzas and assorted pasta dishes, in a restored old colonial home.

For seafood and a good bar scene, try **LIB** (☏ 2665-0741), which some-times features live music and dancing at night, and is in the Centro Comercial Santa Rosa, at the main highway crossroads.

For American-style fast food, head to the main intersection of the Intera-merican Highway and the road to the beaches, or the food court at the mall on the southern outskirts of town. Both spots sport a handful of fast food outlets.

INEXPENSIVE

El Café Liberia ★★   INTERNATIONAL/COSTA RICAN   From filling breakfasts, to cool afternoon fruit smoothies and iced coffee drinks, to gourmet dinners and desserts, this happening local hotspot is the best and most creative restaurant in town. Rustic wooden tables and chairs are spread around a couple of rooms and an open garden courtyard of an old historic colonial-era home. You can get sandwiches, burgers and delicious *ceviche,* as well as light snacks such as spinach dip with parmesan cheese and pita chips. At dinner time, the menu gets much more sophisticated, with artful presentations and world cuisine influences. Dessert lovers will want to save room for their "lava flow" molten chocolate cake and vanilla crème brûlée.

Calle Real. $1^1/_5$ blocks south of the Central Plaza. ☏ **2665-1660.** Main courses $5–$17. Mon 3pm–9pm; Tues–Sat 9am–9pm.

Shopping

On the road to the beaches, just west of the airport, are several large souvenir shops. These are popular stopping points on organized tours throughout this region. The best of the bunch for a one-stop shop is **La Gran Nicoya** (☏ 2667-0062; www.lagrannicoya-cr.com). However, you might find better selections and prices, especially for Guaitíl pottery, at some of the smaller makeshift roadside kiosks that line the road between Liberia and the Guanacaste beaches.

For something different, check out the **Hidden Garden Art Gallery ★★** (© **8386-6872;** http://hiddengarden.thevanstonegroup.com), a well-stocked contemporary art gallery, with a large stable of prominent Costa Rican and expatriate artists, and regularly changing special exhibitions. This place is located 5km (3 miles) west of the Liberia airport, on the road to the beaches.

RINCÓN DE LA VIEJA NATIONAL PARK

242km (151 miles) NW of San José; 25km (16 miles) NW of Liberia

This sprawling national park begins on the flanks of the Rincón de la Vieja Volcano and includes this volcano's namesake active crater. Down lower is an area of geothermal activity similar to that of Yellowstone National Park in the United States. Fumaroles, geysers, and hot pools cover this small area, creating a bizarre, otherworldly landscape. In addition to hot springs and mud pots, you can explore waterfalls, a lake, and volcanic craters. The bird-watching here is excellent, and the views across the pasturelands to the Pacific Ocean are stunning.

ESSENTIALS

GETTING THERE   By Car: Follow the directions to Liberia (p. 193). When you reach Liberia, head straight through the major intersection, following signs to Peñas Blancas and the Nicaraguan border.

To reach the **Las Pailas (Las Espuelas) entrance,** drive about 5km (3 miles) north of Liberia and turn right on the dirt road to the park. The turnoff is well marked. In about 12km (7½ miles), you'll pass through the small village of

Rincón de la Vieja National Park mud pots.

Curubandé. Continue on this road for another 6km (3¾ miles) until you reach the Hacienda Guachipelín. The lodge is private property, and the owners charge vehicles a C700 toll to pass through their gate and continue on to the park. I'm not sure if this is legal or mandatory, but it's not worth the hassle to protest. Pay the toll, pass through the gate, and continue for another 4km (2½ miles) until you reach the park entrance.

> ### What's in a Name?
>
> Rincón de la Vieja translates literally as "the old lady's corner." In this case, "la vieja" has the connotation of a witch or hag, while "rincón" is better interpreted as a "lair" or "hangout." The smoking, belching volcanic crater and mud pots gave rise to this name.

Two routes lead to the **Santa María entrance.** The principal route heads out of the northeastern end of Liberia toward the small village of San Jorge. This route is about 25km (16 miles) long and takes about 45 minutes. A four-wheel-drive vehicle is required. Alternatively, you can reach the entrance on a turnoff from the Interamerican Highway at Bagaces. From here, head north through Guayabo, Aguas Claras, and Colonia Blanca. Though the road is paved up to Colonia Blanca, a four-wheel-drive vehicle is required for the final, very rough 10km (6¼ miles) of gravel road.

Exploring Rincón de la Vieja National Park ★★

Rincón de la Vieja National Park has several excellent trails. The easiest hiking is the gentle **Las Pailas loop ★**. This 3km (1.75-mile) trail is just off the Las Espuelas park entrance and passes by several bubbling mud pots and steaming fumaroles. Don't get too close, or you could get scalded. Happily, the strong sulfur smell given off by these formations works well as a natural deterrent. This gentle trail crosses a river, so you'll have to either take off your shoes or get them wet. The whole loop is 3.2km (2 miles) and takes around 2 hours at a leisurely pace.

My favorite hike here is to the **Blue Lake** and **La Cangrejo Waterfall ★★**. Along this well-marked 9.6km (6-mile) round-trip trail, you will pass through several different ecosystems, including tropical dry forest, transitional moist forest, and open savanna. You are likely to spot a variety of birds and mammals and have a good chance of coming across a group of coatimundi—a raccoonlike local mammal. While not requiring any great climbs or descents, the hike is nonetheless arduous. Pack a lunch; at the

La Cangrejo Waterfall.

end of your 2-hour hike in, you can picnic at the aptly named Blue Lake, where a 30m (98-ft.) waterfall empties into a small pond whose crystal-blue hues are amazing.

Due to volcanic activity and the extreme nature of the hike, the summit trail was closed to visitors for most of 2013 and early 2014. If it's open, more energetic hikers can tackle the **summit** ★ and explore the several craters and beautiful lakes up here. On a clear day, you'll be rewarded with a fabulous view of the plains of Guanacaste and the Pacific Ocean below. The trail is 16.6km (10.3 miles) round-trip and should take about 7 hours (the trail head is at the ranger station). It heads pretty much straight up the volcano and is pretty steep in places. Along the way, you'll pass through several different ecosystems, including sections of tropical moist and tropical cloud forests, while climbing some 1,000m (3,280 ft.) in altitude. After about 6km (3.7 miles), the trail splits. Take the right-hand fork to the Crater Activo (Active Crater). Filled with rainwater, this crater is some 700m (2,300 ft.) in diameter and still active. Off to the side is the massive Laguna Jigueros. Because this crater emits large amounts of sulfur and acid gases, it's not recommended that you linger here long. If you have the energy, a side trail leads to the Von Seebach Crater.

The park entrance fee is $10 per person per day, and the park is open Tuesday to Sunday from 7am to 3pm.

Camping will cost you an extra $2 per person per day. There are actually two entrances and camping areas here: **Santa María** and **Las Pailas** (also called Las Espuelas; ✆ **2666-5051**) ranger stations. Las Pailas is by far the more popular and accessible, and it's closer to the action. These small camping areas are near each other. I recommend the one closer to the river, although the restroom and shower facilities are about 90m (295 ft.) away, at the other site. For those seeking a less rugged tour of the park, several lodges are around the park perimeter and offer guided hikes and horseback rides into the park.

Other Adventures Around Rincón de la Vieja

ONE-STOP ADVENTURE SHOP

Hacienda Guachipelín (p. 204) offers up a range of adventure tour options, including horseback riding, hiking, white-water river inner-tubing, a waterfall canyoning and rappel tour, and a more traditional zip-line canopy tour. The most popular is the hacienda's **1-Day Adventure pass** ★★, which allows you to choose as many of the hotel's different tour options as you want and fit them into 1 adventure-packed day. The price for this is $80, including a buffet lunch and transportation. Almost all Guanacaste beach hotels and resorts offer day trips here, or you can book directly with the lodge. *Be forewarned:* During the high season, the whole operation has a bit of a cattle-car feel, with busloads of day-trippers coming in from the beach. Also, I have found the inner-tube adventure to be fairly dangerous when the river is high, particularly during or just after the rainy season.

HOT SPRINGS & MUD BATHS

The active Rincón de la Vieja Volcano has blessed this area with several fine hot springs and mud baths. Even if you're not staying at the **Hacienda Guachipelín** (p. 204) or the **Hotel Borinquen Mountain Resort** (p. 203), you can take advantage of their hot spring pools and hot mud baths. Both have on-site spas offering massages, facials, and other treatments.

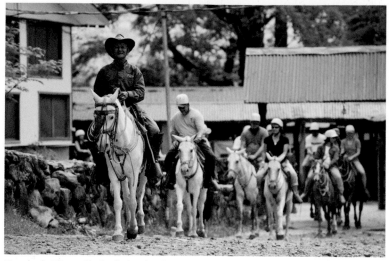

Horseback riding at Hacienda Guachipelín.

Up the road from their lodge, Hacienda Guachipelín has opened the **Río Negro Hot Springs** ★★ (℃ **2666-8075**). A $15 entrance fee gets you access to the pools and an application of the hot volcanic mud. For $50 you can do a horseback ride from the main lodge to the springs. A wide range of massages, mud wraps, facials, and other treatments are available at reasonable prices.

At the **Hotel Borinquen Mountain Resort,** a $30 entrance fee allows you access to their range of **hot spring–fed pools** ★, which vary from tepid to very hot, as well as their fresh volcanic mud bath area, and large freshwater pool.

Finally, **Vandara Hotsprings** ★★ (℃ **4000-0660;** www.vandarahot springs.com) is an excellent spa and adventure center run by the folks at Buena Vista Lodge, with a lovely manmade pool fed by natural hot springs. Unlike the other pools mentioned above, this one has no sulfuric smell. Entrance to the pool runs $30, but various packages, with a canopy tour, horseback ride, or other adventure activity, are available. Meals and spa treatments are also on offer.

Río Celeste & the Tenorio Volcano

A crystalline turquoise pool at the foot of a forest waterfall, with nearby hot springs and volcanic mud, make the **Río Celeste** ★★ a must-see. Offering similar attractions and activities to Rincón de la Vieja, this is a much less visited and more remote-feeling area. Río Celeste, which means "Blue River," is inside the **Parque Nacional Volcán Tenorio** (Tenorio Volcano National Park; ℃ **2206-5369**). The hike there takes about 2 hours each way, and is steep in places. Above the main pool and waterfall, a loop trail will take you along the river to a few spots where underground hot springs bubble up into the blue waters. Locals have made some well-worn pools at the spots best for soaking. Along the river banks here, you can find volcanic mud deposits perfect for a free, mid-hike facial treatment. The park is open daily from 8am until 4pm, and the entrance fee is $10.

If you want easy access to the Tenorio Volcano and Río Celeste, I recommend the humble, yet delightful, **La Carolina Lodge** ★ (℃ **2466-6393**; www.lacarolinalodge.com), which is on a working farm, next to a clear flowing river. Another good option is the **Celeste Mountain Lodge** ★ (℃ **2278-6628**; www.celestemountainlodge.com), a beautiful, sustainable lodge, with great views of the surrounding volcanoes. Finally, the most luxurious option in these parts is the **Río Celeste Hideaway** ★★ (℃ **800/320-3541** in the U.S. and Canada, or 2206-5114 in Costa Rica; www.riocelestehideaway.com), which is actually located on the "back side" of the Tenorio National Park, and reached via the road connecting Upala to the small town of Guatuso.

Getting There: Tenorio National Park is located near the small town of Bijagua. The road to Bijagua (CR6) heads north off of the Interamerican Highway about 5km (3 miles) northwest of Cañas. From here, it's another 30km (18¹/₂ miles) to Bijagua, and another 12km (7¹/₂ miles) to the park entrance. The last part of this is on rough dirt roads.

Near the Miravalles Volcano

Part of a string of active volcanos running down the spine of the country, the **Miravalles Volcano** has long been a major energy supplier for the country's electric grid, but a rather forgotten and undiscovered area for tourism. **Rio Perdido** ★★ (℃ **2673-3600**; www.rioperdido.com) aims to change all that. With a beautiful setting among rolling hills and striking rock formations, this hotel, spa and adventure center features lovely rooms, and a gorgeous hot spring complex. The hot springs here range from a modern pool structure fed by warm mineral waters up near the main lodge, to a beautiful natural river with pools of clear water and varied temperatures. The lodge also has a zip-line canyon tour, an extensive mountain bike park, and offers white water river tubing.

Where to Stay & Dine Around the Rincón de la Vieja National Park

In addition to the hotels listed below, a couple of other good choices are by the park. On the Cañas Dulces road, **Buena Vista Lodge** ★ (℃ **2690-1414**; www.buenavistalodgecr.com) is set on the edge of the national park and offers a wide range of activities and attractions, including its own water slide and canopy tour.

Another good choice for adventure tourists is the **Canyon Lodge** (℃ **2665-3161**; www.thecanyonlodge.com), located just 3km (2 miles) inland from the main highway (CR1) on the outskirts of Liberia.

Over in the area around Aguas Claras, **Finca La Anita** ★★ (℃ **8388-1775** or 2466-0228; laanitarainforestranch.com) is a remote and rustic, yet very cozy lodge, with a series of wooden cabins set on a working farm, on the edge of lush rain and cloud forests. The area around the lodge is home to several hot springs, and this area also provides easy access to the seldom used Santa Maria sector of Rincón de la Vieja National Park.

EXPENSIVE

Hotel Borinquen Mountain Resort ★★   Large private and duplex bungalows are spread over rolling hills above a lovely natural hot springs bordering thick forest. The well-appointed rooms all feature private balcony or deck areas with beautiful views. Many of the rooms are a good, vigorous hike away from the restaurant and pool areas, and while golf cart rides are offered, they are not always prompt or ready when you are. A wide range of tours and activities are offered, including horseback riding and zip-lining, but most guests are content to spend most of their time lounging by the pools, and covering themselves with volcanic mud harvested regularly from bubbling mud pots just steps from the hotel's little hot spring complex.

Cañas Dulces, Guanacaste. © **2690-1900.** www.borinquenresort.com. 39 units. $185 double villa; $194–$286 double bungalow; $323 junior suite. Rates include breakfast and unlimited use of the hot springs, sauna, and mud baths. Drive 12km (7½ miles) north of Liberia along the Interamerican Hwy. (CR1), take the turnoff toward Cañas Dulces, and follow the signs. The hotel is approximately 21km (13 miles) from the highway, along a mostly rugged dirt road. **Amenities:** Restaurant; bar; large outdoor pool; small spa; all rooms smoke-free; Wi-Fi.

MODERATE

Hacienda Guachipelín ★★ This working cattle and horse ranch is my favorite lodge for easy access to the hiking and adventures and vistas offered up in the Rincón de la Vieja area. Most of the rooms are housed in a large horseshoe around an ample garden and lawn area a short walk from the main lodge and restaurants. The rooms themselves are large and airy, although simple and plain. A few standard rooms are still housed in some of the ranch's older buildings. Plenty of hikes, tours, and adventure activities are offered—see "One-Stop Adventure Shop," above. These folks even run a free shuttle several times a day to the national park entrance, as well as to their own, wonderful hot springs. The owners are deeply committed to sustainable tourism and the conservation of this region.

Rincón de la Vieja (23km/14 miles northeast of Liberia). © **888/730-3840** in the U.S. and Canada, or 2690-2900 for reservations in Costa Rica, or 2666-8075 at the lodge. www.guachipelin.com. 54 units. $88 double; $98 superior double; $153 suite. Rates include breakfast. Rates higher during peak periods. Follow the directions/signs to Curubandé and Rincón de la Vieja National Park. **Amenities:** Restaurant; outdoor pool; small spa; Wi-Fi.

LA CRUZ & BAHÍA SALINAS

277km (172 miles) NW of San José; 59km (37 miles) NW of Liberia; 20km (12 miles) S of Peñas Blancas

Near the Nicaraguan border, La Cruz is a tiny hilltop town that has little to offer beyond a fabulous view of Bahía Salinas (Salinas Bay), but it does serve as a gateway to the nearly deserted beaches down below, a few mountain lodges bordering the nearby Santa Rosa and Guanacaste national parks, and the Nicaraguan border crossing at Peñas Blancas.

There's little reason to stay in La Cruz, but if you must, check out **Hotel La Mirada Inn** (www.hotellamirada.com; © **2679-9702**), a simple, well-kept local hotel. However, instead of staying in town, stay on the shores of the beaches listed below.

Essentials

GETTING THERE & DEPARTING **By Plane:** The nearest airport with regular service is in Liberia (see "Liberia," earlier in this chapter).

By Car: Follow the directions for driving to Liberia (p. 193). When you reach Liberia, head straight through the major intersection, following signs to Peñas Blancas and the Nicaraguan border. Allow approximately 5 hours to get from San José to La Cruz.

On to Nicaragua

Guanacaste is a popular jumping-off point for trips into Nicaragua. The main border point is at Peñas Blancas, Costa Rica. Several tour agencies and hotel desks arrange day trips to Nicaragua from resorts and hotels around Guanacaste.

Costa Rica charges no fees for entering or leaving, while Nicaragua charges $13 to enter and $3 to leave. Though it's by no means necessary, it's somewhat common to hire a helper or *gavilan* (literally, seagull), to expedite the process. These locals can occasionally cut lines, alleviate confusion, and speed up the process slightly. On the Costa Rican side, expect to spend about $5 for a bilingual *gavilan*, whereas on the Nicaraguan side, the cost should be around $3.

By Bus: Transportes Deldú buses (🕾 **2256-9072** in San José, or 2679-9323 in La Cruz; www.transportesdeldu.com) leave San José roughly every 2 hours (more frequently during the middle of the day) between 4am and 7pm for **Peñas Blancas** from Calle 20 and Avenida 1. These buses stop in La Cruz and will also let you off at the entrance to Santa Rosa National Park if you ask. The ride to La Cruz takes 5½ hours; a one-way fare costs between C4,250 and C5,000. Additional buses are often added on weekends and holidays.

Local buses (🕾 **2666-0517**) leave Liberia for Peñas Blancas periodically throughout the day. The ride to La Cruz takes about 1 hour and costs C1,450. Buses depart for San José from Peñas Blancas daily between 5am and 6.30pm, passing through La Cruz about 20 minutes later. Daily buses leave Liberia for San José roughly every hour between 3am and 8pm.

CITY LAYOUT   The highway passes slightly to the east of town. You'll pass the turnoffs to Santa Rosa National Park and Playa Caujiniquil before you reach town. For the Bahía Salinas beaches, head into La Cruz and take the road that runs along the north side of the small central park and then follow the signs down to the water.

Exploring Santa Rosa National Park

Known for its remote, pristine beaches (reached by several kilometers of hiking trails or a 4WD vehicle), **Santa Rosa National Park ★** (🕾 **2666-5051;** www.acguanacaste.ac.cr) is a great place to camp on the beach, surf, bird-watch, or (if you're lucky) watch sea turtles nest. Located 30km (19 miles) north of Liberia and 21km (13 miles) south of La Cruz on the Interamerican Highway, Costa Rica's first national park blankets the Santa Elena Peninsula. Unlike other national parks, it was founded not to preserve the land but to save a building, known as **La Casona,** which played an important role in Costa Rican independence. It was here, in 1856, that Costa Rican forces fought the decisive Battle of Santa Rosa, forcing the U.S.-backed soldier of fortune William Walker and his men to flee into Nicaragua. La Casona was completely destroyed by arson in 2001, but it has been rebuilt, very accurately mimicking the original building, and now houses a small museum, detailing the political history of the ranch house and housing rotating temporary art exhibits. The museum descriptions, however, are in Spanish only.

La Casona has few nearby hiking trails. The best for most visitors is the **Indio Desnudo (Naked Indian) trail.** This 2.6km (1.5-mile) loop trail should

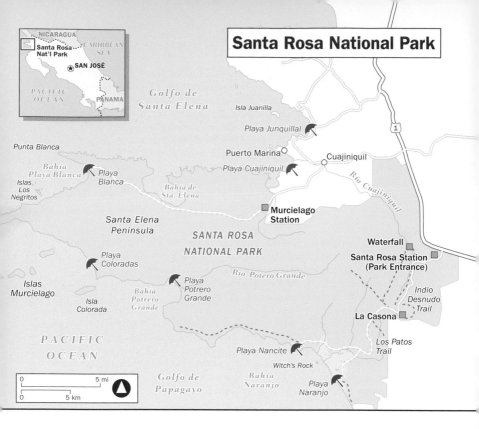

Santa Rosa National Park

take you about 45 minutes. It leads through a small patch of tropical dry forest and into overgrown former pastureland. If you're lucky, you might spot a white-tailed deer, coatimundi, black guan, or mantled howler monkey along the way.

It costs $10 per person to enter the park; day visitors can access the park daily from 8am to 4pm. Camping is allowed at several sites within the park. A campsite costs C1,000 per person per day. Camping is near the entrance, the principal ranger station, La Casona, and down by playas Naranjo and Nancite.

THE BEACHES ★★ Eight kilometers (5 miles) west of La Casona, down a rugged road that's impassable during the rainy season (it's rough on 4WD vehicles even in the dry season), is **Playa Naranjo.** Four kilometers (2¹/₂ miles) north of Playa Naranjo, along a hiking trail that follows the beach, you'll find **Playa Nancite. Playa Blanca** is 21km (13 miles) down a dirt road from Caujiniquil, which itself is 20km (12 miles) north of the park entrance. None of these three beaches has shower or restroom facilities. (Playa Nancite does have some facilities, but they're in a reservation-only camping area.) Bring along your own water, food, and anything else you'll need, and expect to find things relatively quiet and deserted.

Playa Nancite is known for its *arribadas* ("arrivals," grouped egg-layings) of olive ridley sea turtles, which come ashore to nest by the tens of thousands each year in October. Playa Naranjo is legendary for its perfect surfing waves. In fact, this spot is quite popular with day-trippers who come in by boat from the Playa del Coco area to ride the waves that break around **Witch's Rock,** which lies just offshore.

On the northern side of the peninsula is **Playa Blanca,** a beautiful, remote white sand beach with calm waters. This beach is reached by way of the small village of Caujiniquil and is accessible only during the dry season.

If you reach Caujiniquil and then head north on a rugged dirt road for a few kilometers, you'll come to a small annex to the national park system at **Playa Junquillal** ★ (© **2666-5051**), not to be confused with the more-developed beach of the same name farther south in Guanacaste. This is a lovely little beach that is also often good for swimming. You'll have to pay the park entrance fee ($10) to use the beach, and $2 more to camp here. There are basic restroom and shower facilities.

Fun on & over the Waves

The waters of Bahía Salinas are buffeted by serious winds from mid-November through mid-May, and this area is a prime spot for windsurfing and kiteboarding. The folks at **Ecoplaya Beach Resort** (see below) have a good windsurfing operation and rent equipment. If you want to try your hand at the sport of kiteboarding, check in with the folks at the **Kitesurfing Center,** who operate out of the **Blue Dream Hotel** (© **8826-5221** or 2676-1042; www.bluedreamhotel.com) in Playa Copal.

Beach lovers should head to the far western tip of the Bahía Salinas, where you will find **Playa Rajada** ★★, a beautiful little white sand beach, with gentle surf and plenty of shade trees.

La Casona at Santa Rosa National Park.

Note: If you're coming to this area and aren't interested in windsurfing or kitesurfing, the winds can make your beach time rather unpleasant during the peak wind months. If you're just looking for a beach resort vacation, I recommend heading to one of the beaches farther south in Guanacaste.

Where to Stay & Dine near La Cruz

To get to either of these hotels from La Cruz, take the dirt road that heads toward Bahía Salinas and Playa Soley, and then follow signs to the hotels. This is a very rough, washboard dirt road most of the year.

MODERATE

Ecoplaya Beach Resort This place is your best choice in the area if you want to be right on the beach. The hotel is no longer a part of the Best Western brand. The resort has two distinct sections: The standard hotel rooms are in a two-story concrete building on one side of the property,

Witch's Rock.

while a set of individual villas with kitchenettes and living areas is on the other. The hotel primarily caters to windsurfers, especially between December and March when the winds up here howl. The hotel is fairly isolated and there's not much else going on in this area. The beach itself opens up on to Salinas Bay, and is comprised of dark sand which is wide and calm and great for walking at low tide, but almost entirely disappears at high tide.

La Coyotera Beach, Salinas Bay. ☎ **2676-1010.** www.ecoplaya.com. 44 units. $100–$200 double; $114–$280 villa. Rates include taxes. From La Cruz, take the dirt road that heads toward Bahía Salinas and Playa Soley, and then follow signs to the hotel. **Amenities:** Restaurant; bar; 2 Jacuzzis; midsize outdoor pool; extensive watersports equipment rental.

Recreo ★ A series of private homes and villas are scattered over rolling hills at this remote little resort. These homes and villas are all fairly new and very well equipped, and have either a pool or plunge pool. Some have fabulous ocean views. Meals aren't included and the property lacks a restaurant, but you can have a private chef or meals brought to your villa as part of the services offered here. The resort itself is not right on the water, but is just a few minutes away from the gorgeous and almost always semi-deserted Playa Rajada. You've pretty much reached the end of the road when you get here, and Playa Rajada is a perfect payback. The resort is about an hour and a half from the Liberia airport, and a rental car is highly recommended.

El Jobo Beach, Salinas Bay. ☎ **877/268-2911** in the U.S. and Canada, or 8378-6364 in Costa Rica. www.recreocostarica.com. 8 units. $225–$750 villa. **Amenities:** Bar; small, well-equipped exercise room; 5 outdoor pools; tennis court; free Wi-Fi.

PLAYA HERMOSA, PLAYA PANAMÁ & PAPAGAYO ★

258km (160 miles) NW of San José; 40km (25 miles) SW of Liberia

While most of Costa Rica's coast is highly coveted by surfers, the beaches here are mostly protected and calm, making them good destinations for families with kids. **Playa Hermosa ★** means "beautiful beach," which is an apt moniker for this pretty crescent of sand. Surrounded by steep forested hills, this curving gray sand beach is long and wide and the surf is usually quite gentle. Fringing the beach is a swath of trees that stays surprisingly green even during the dry season. The shade provided by these trees, along with the calm protected waters, is a big part of the beach's appeal. Rocky headlands jut out into the surf at both ends of the beach, and at the base of these rocks are fun tide pools to explore.

Beyond Playa Hermosa, you'll find **Playa Panamá ★** and, farther on, the calm waters of **Bahía Culebra ★**, a large protected bay dotted with small, private patches of beach and ringed with mostly intact dry forest. Around the north end of Bahía Culebra is the **Papagayo Peninsula ★**, home to two large all-inclusive resorts and one championship golf course. This peninsula has a half-dozen or so small to midsize beaches, the nicest of which might just be **Playa Nacascolo ★★★**, which is inside the domain of the Four Seasons Resort here—but all beaches in Costa Rica are public, so you can still visit, albeit after passing through security and parking at the public parking lot.

Essentials

GETTING THERE & DEPARTING   By Plane: The nearest airport with regularly scheduled service is in Liberia (p. 192). From there you can arrange a taxi to bring you the rest of the way. The ride takes about 25 minutes and should cost $40 to $60.

By Car: Follow the directions for getting to Liberia (p. 193). When you reach the main intersection in Liberia, take a left onto CR21, which heads toward Santa Cruz and the beaches of Guanacaste. The turnoff for the Papagayo Peninsula is prominently marked 8km (5 miles) south of the Liberia airport. At the corner here, you'll see a massive Do It Center hardware store and lumberyard.

If you are going to a hotel along the Papagayo Peninsula, turn at the Do It Center and follow the paved road out and around the peninsula. If you are going

Playa Hermosa.

HOTELS
El Velero Hotel **1**
Hotel Playa Hermosa Bosque del Mar **6**
Villa del Sueño Hotel **7**

RESTAURANTS
El Quijole **3**
Ginger **4**
Los Sueños **7**
Upper Deck Sport's Bar **8**

ATTRACTIONS
Aqua Sport **5**
Diving Safaris de Costa Rica **2**
Spa Aguas de Hermosa **9**

Playa Hermosa

Bahía
Playa
Hermosa

To Playa Panamá

Playa Hermosa

NICARAGUA
Papagayo Peninsula
Playa Hermosa
CARIBBEAN
SEA
SAN JOSÉ
PACIFIC
OCEAN
PANAMA

Playa Pedregosa

151

To Playa del Coco

0   1/4 mi
0   0.25 km

to Playa Panamá or Playa Hermosa, you should also turn here and take the access road shortcut that leads from a turnoff on the Papagayo Peninsula road, just beyond the Do It Center, directly to Playa Panamá. When you reach Playa Panamá, turn left for Playa Hermosa, and turn right for the Hilton Papagayo Resort (p. 214).

To get to Playa Hermosa, you can also continue on a little farther west on CR21, and, just past the village of Comunidad, turn right. In about 11km (6¾ miles) you'll come to a fork in the road; take the right fork.

These roads are all relatively well marked, and a host of prominent hotel billboards should make it easy enough to find the beach or resort you are looking for. The drive takes about 4 to 4½ hours from San José.

By Bus: A **Tralapa** express bus (© **2221-7202**) leaves San José daily at 3:30pm from Calle 20 and Avenida 3, stopping at Playa Hermosa and Playa Panamá, 3km (1¾ miles) farther north. One-way fare for the 5-hour trip is around C5,000.

Gray Line (© **800/719-3105** in the U.S. and Canada, or 2220-2126 in Costa Rica; www.graylinecostarica.com) and **Interbus** (© **4100-0888**; www.interbusonline.com) both have two daily buses leaving San José for all beaches in this area, one in the morning and one in the afternoon. The fare is around $47.

210

Papagayo Peninsula

Golfo de Papagayo

Bahía Zapotillal

Playa Nacascolito

To Liberia

Islas Palmitas

Culebra

Bahía Huevos

Playa Sombrero

Iguanita

Bahía Pochote

Playa Iguanita

Four Seasons Golf Club

Playa Nacascolo

Bahía Culebra

Bahía Prieta

Bahía Virador

Cerro Pando

Playa Venado

Punta Mostrenco

Playa Monte del Barco

Bahía Impace

Punta Mala

Bahía Impace

Punta Arenilla

Playa Panamá

To Playa Hermosa (3 miles)

0   1 mi
0   1 km

HOTELS
Allegro Papagayo Resort 3
Anda Peninsula Papgayo 4
Casa Conde del Mar 9
El Mangroove Resort 8
Four Seasons Resort
    Costa Rica 1
Hilton Papagayo Resort 6
Occidental Grand
    Papagayo 7

ATTRACTIONS
Playa Nacascolo 2
Resort Divers 6
Witch's Rock Canopy Tour 5

Both companies will pick you up at most San José–area hotels, and offer connections to most other major tourist destinations in Costa Rica.

You can take a bus from San José to Liberia (see "Essentials," earlier in this chapter), and then take a bus from Liberia to Playa Hermosa and Playa Panamá. **Transportes La Pampa** buses (© **2665-7520**) leave Liberia for Playa Hermosa and Playa Panamá at least a half-dozen times daily between 4:30am and 5:30pm. The trip lasts 40 minutes because the bus stops frequently to drop off and pick up passengers. The one-way fare costs C750. These bus schedules change from time to time, so it's always best to check in advance. During the high season and on weekends, extra buses from Liberia are sometimes added. You can also take a bus to Playa del Coco, from which playas Hermosa and Panamá are a relatively quick taxi ride away. Taxi fare should run C8,000.

One direct bus departs for San José daily at 5am from Playa Panamá, with a stop in Playa Hermosa along the way. Buses to Liberia leave Playa Panamá regularly between 6am and 7pm, stopping in Playa Hermosa a few minutes later. Ask at your hotel about current schedules, and where to catch the bus.

AREA LAYOUT   From the well-marked turnoff for the Papagayo Peninsula (near the prominent Do It Center hardware store), a paved road leads around to the Allegro Papagayo and Four Seasons resorts. If you are heading to the beaches a

A sunset over the Golfo de Papagayo.

little farther south, continue on to the well-marked turnoff for Playa del Coco and Playa Hermosa. This road forks before reaching Playa del Coco. You'll come to the turnoff for Playa Hermosa first. Playa Panamá is a few kilometers farther along the same road. The road ends at the Hilton Papagayo Resort. A road connects the Papagayo Peninsula road and Playa Panamá. This 11km (6³/₄-mile) shortcut is definitely your quickest route to Playa Panamá.

Playa Hermosa is about a 450m (1,476-ft.) stretch of beach, with all the hotels laid out along this stretch. From the main road, which continues on to Playa Panamá, three access roads head off toward the beach. All the hotels are well marked, with signs pointing guests down the right access road. Playa Panamá is the least developed of the beaches out here. Somewhat longer than Playa Hermosa, it also has several access roads heading in toward the beach from the main road, which is slightly inland.

Exploring Playa Hermosa, Playa Panamá & Papagayo

Most of the beaches up here are usually quite calm and good for swimming. If you want to do some diving, check in with **Diving Safaris de Costa Rica** ★★ (② **2672-1259;** www.costaricadiving.net), on the principal access road into Playa Hermosa, about 137m (450 ft.) before you hit the beach. This is a long-established and respected dive operation. It has a large shop and offers a wide range of trips to numerous dive spots, and it also offers night dives, multiday packages, certification classes, and Nitrox dives. These folks also offer multiday live-aboard and dive trips on their 14m (48-ft.) yacht.

Alternatively, you can check out **Resort Divers** (② **2672-0106;** www. resortdivers-cr.com), which has set up shop at the Hilton Papagayo Resort.

Both of the above-mentioned companies will accept divers from any of the hotels in the area, and can arrange transport. A two-tank dive should run between

$70 and $140 per person, depending primarily on the distance traveled to the dive sites.

In the middle of Playa Hermosa, **Aqua Sport** (℃ 2672-0050) is where to go for watersports equipment rental. Kayaks, sailboards, canoes, bicycles, beach umbrellas, snorkel gear, and parasails are available at fairly reasonable rates. You'll also find a small supermarket, public phones, and a restaurant.

Because the beaches in this area are relatively protected and generally flat, surfers should look into boat trips to nearby **Witch's Rock ★★** and **Ollie's Point ★** (p. 222). **Costa Rica Surf Charters** (℃ 8935-2538; www.crsurf charters.com), **Hotel La Finisterra** (℃ 2672-0227), and **Aqua Sport** (℃ 2672-0050) all offer trips for up to six surfers for around $60 to $120 per hour.

Most of the companies mentioned above also offer fishing trips for $250 to $600 for groups of two to four anglers. Or you can check in with **Dream On Sportfishing ★★** (℃ 855/415-5500 in the U.S. and Canada, or 8735-3121 in Costa Rica; www.dreamonsportfishing.com) or **North Pacific Tours ★** (℃ 2670-1564; www.northpacifictours.com).

If you're interested in wind power, check in with the folks at the **El Velero Hotel** (see below), or any of the sailboat charter options listed in the Playa del Coco section below. All offer a range of full- and half-day tours, with snorkel stops, as well as sunset cruises.

Other Options

Both **Charlie's Adventures ★** (℃ 2672-0317; www.charliesadventure.com) and **Swiss Travel Service** (℃ 2668-1020; www.swisstravelcr.com) offer a wide range of activities and tours, including trips to Santa Rosa or Rincón de la Vieja national parks, and rafting on the Corobicí River. Both of these operations have desks at several of the hotels around here and will pick you up at any hotel in the area.

The best zip-line canopy tour in this area is the **Witch's Rock Canopy Tour ★★** (℃ 2696-7101; www.witchsrockcanopytour.com), just before the Allegro Papagayo Resort. The $1^{1}/_{2}$-hour tour covers 3km ($1^{3}/_{4}$ miles) of cables touching down on 24 platforms and crossing three suspension bridges. The tour costs $75.

Finally, the Arnold Palmer–designed championship course at the Four Seasons Resort (see below) is hands-down the most beautiful and challenging **golf course** in the country. However, it is open only to Four Seasons' guests.

If you're looking for some pampering, whether it be a massage, facial, or body scrub, check out **Spa Aguas de Hermosa** (℃ 2672-1386), in the Hermosa Heights Resort Community, and offers up a wide range of treatment options.

Where to Stay

VERY EXPENSIVE

In addition to the Four Seasons, **El Mangroove Resort** (℃ 2291-7750; www.elmangroove.net) and the **Andaz Peninsula Papagayo Resort** (℃ 800/233-1234 in the U.S. and Canada, or 2690-1234 in Costa Rica; http://papagayo.andaz.hyatt.com) are two new luxury resorts on the Papagayo Peninsula.

Four Seasons Resort Costa Rica ★★★   This is hands-down Costa Rica's premier luxury resort hotel. The hotel itself is set near the narrowest point along a long peninsula with beautiful, white sand beaches on either side.

Four Seasons Resort Costa Rica.

Ronald Zucher's architecture is meant to evoke the forms and shapes of turtles and armadillos, particularly the roof lines. Rooms are large and plush, as you would expect, but you can also choose from a range of suite and villa options. Four restaurants offer up the top-notch dining experience you'd expect from the Four Seasons—and their famed service remains peerless. The Arnold Palmer–designed golf course is my favorite in the country, with ocean views from 15 of its 18 holes. In addition to providing all this luxury, the Four Seasons has also been awarded "4 Leaves" by the CST Sustainable Tourism program.

Papagayo Peninsula, Guanacaste. © **800/332-3442** in the U.S., or 2696-0000. www.four seasons.com/costarica. 154 units. $725–$950 double; $1,075 and up suites and villas. Children stay free in parent's room. **Amenities:** 4 restaurants; 2 bars; lounge; babysitting; children's programs; concierge; championship 18-hole golf course; 3 free-form outdoor pools; room service; smoke-free rooms; full-service spa; 5 tennis courts; watersports equipment; Wi-Fi.

EXPENSIVE

Over on Playa Panamá, **Casa Conde del Mar** ★ (© **2227-4232** or 2672-1001; www.grupocasaconde.com) is a pretty, boutique resort, with plush rooms and lush grounds.

Hilton Papagayo Resort ★★ This large all-inclusive is a solid bet. I find the rooms and food offerings far better than those at the Occidental Grand Papagayo or Allegro Papagayo resorts (see below). The rooms feature marble floors, contemporary furnishings and minimalist decor, a host of amenities and either a private balcony or private patio. Most are found in a series of single story duplex units spread across a large contoured area with undulating hillsides and tall trees. Papagayo suites are larger, and are located on the highest point of the property, with the best views. While the King junior suites come with private plunge pools. The beach here is very calm and protected, and there are both adult-only and family pool areas. The resort also has a very lovely and well-equipped spa area.

Playa Panamá, Guanacaste. ☎ **800/445-8667** in the U.S. and Canada, or 2672-0000 in Costa Rica www.hiltonpapagayoresort.com. 202 units. $350–$600 double; $750–$1,200 suite. Rates include food, drinks, a range of activities, and taxes. **Amenities:** 3 restaurants; 2 bars; babysitting; children's programs; well-equipped health center and spa; Jacuzzi; 3-tiered main outdoor pool, small lap pool, and resistance lap pool; tennis court; watersports equipment; free Wi-Fi.

Hotel Playa Hermosa Bosque del Mar ★★★

Sitting on the quiet southern end of Playa Hermosa, this is my favorite beachfront boutique hotel in the area. Rooms are large and modern and spread around the free-form pool amid the shade of tall, old-growth trees. The owners took great care to preserve these trees (which are inhabited by iguanas and troops of monkeys), and employ sound sustainable and environmental policies at every turn. The oceanfront suites come with a Jacuzzi on their private balcony and are clearly the best rooms in the house, although all the rooms are contemporary and comfortable. On the third floor of the main lobby is a three-bedroom penthouse complex that can be rented whole or broken up, and is a good option for groups or families.

Playa Hermosa, Guanacaste. ☎ **2672-0046.** www.hotelplayahermosa.com. 32 units. $148–$245 junior suite; $196–$345 suite; $250 and up penthouse suites. **Amenities:** Restaurant; bar; Jacuzzi; pretty outdoor pool w/sculpted waterfall; free Wi-Fi.

Occidental Grand Papagayo ★

Converted into an adult-only resort in late November 2013, this sprawling, large all-inclusive is set on a hilly point of land overlooking the Papagayo Peninsula and Pacific Ocean, although not all rooms here boast sea views. Rooms are spacious and well maintained, and most feature red or white tile floors, bright white linens and a small private balcony. Wildlife abounds in the trees spread around the property, and you're almost guaranteed to spot monkeys right on the hotel grounds. At the base of the hotel's property you'll find a small beach that is broad and calm at low tide, but recedes up to the tree line at high tide.

Papagayo Peninsula, Guanacaste. ☎ **855/565-5147** in the U.S. and Canada, 2672-0191 for reservations inside Costa Rica. www.occidentalhotels.com. 169 units. $250–$300 double occupancy; $360-$700 Royal Club room double. Rates include food, drinks, a range of activities, and taxes. **Amenities:** 4 restaurants; 4 bars; lounge; large health club and spa; 2 large free-form outdoor pools; smoke-free rooms; 1 lighted tennis court; watersports equipment; free Wi-Fi.

MODERATE

Allegro Papagayo Resort This family-friendly resort is a sister to the Occidental Grand Papagayo (see above). It is a large, all-inclusive that offers great value—but that value comes with some downsides. The food is passable, housekeeping can be a little lax, and the rooms and facilities show their wear and tear. The resort is set on a steep hillside and regular shuttles run around the property every 10 to 15 minutes. All rooms are exactly the same size, and come with either one king or two twin beds, and a small private balcony. The "premium" rooms here have the best views. The dark sand beach right at the resort is has very calm and protected waters, but they also shuttle folks at regular intervals to and from a nearby white sand beach that is much prettier. The massive free-form pool has a popular swim-up bar. A wide range of organized activities and non-motorized watersports equipment are included as part of the all-inclusive packages here.

Playa Manzanillo, Guanacaste ☎ **855/565-5147** in the U.S. and Canada, or 2690-9900 at the resort. www.occidentalhotels.com. 300 units. $140–$180 double occupancy. Rates include food, drinks, a range of activities, and taxes. **Amenities:** 3 restaurants; 3 bars; babysitting; children's programs; small fitness center; 2 Jacuzzis; large free-form outdoor pool; watersports equipment; free Wi-Fi.

INEXPENSIVE

El Velero Hotel ★   This longstanding hotel is a solid option just steps from the sand on Playa Hermosa. Rooms are all very spacious, if somewhat spartan, but all come with air-conditioning. I recommend those on the second floor, which have high ceilings. The design motif here is Mediterranean, with white-washed walls and interior archways. There's a small plunge pool and a popular restaurant and bar. El Velero means "the sailboat" and these folks do, indeed, have a sailboat for charter.

Playa Hermosa, Guanacaste. ℂ **2672-1017.** www.costaricahotel.net. 22 units. $69–$89 double. **Amenities:** Restaurant; bar; small outdoor pool; free Wi-Fi.

Villa del Sueño Hotel ★★   This midsize hotel and condo project offers up cool, clean, and well-priced rooms a block inland from the sand. The plentiful shaded and grassy areas are a welcome respite from the dusty and sandy streets all around. Suites feature kitchenettes and family-size options. The hotel has a couple of pools here and an excellent little restaurant, which sometimes features live music.

Playa Hermosa, Guanacaste. ℂ **800/378-8599** in the U.S., or 2672-0026 in Costa Rica. www.villadelsueno.com. 46 units. $65–$140 double; $109–$310 suite. Free for children 12 and under. **Amenities:** Restaurant; bar; 2 outdoor pools; free Wi-Fi.

Where to Dine

In addition to the places listed below, you'll find good restaurants at both the **El Velero Hotel** (see above) and the **Hotel Playa Hermosa Bosque del Mar** (see above). I've also gotten good reports about the fresh seafood and lively ambiance at **El Quijote** (ℂ 2672-0172) located along the second entrance road towards the beach.

Abbocato ★★★ FUSION/BISTRO   This amazing little restaurant far outshines its rather odd setting in the clubhouse of an ongoing hotel-and-planned-community development. Husband-wife chefs Andrea and Paola create two distinct nightly tasting menus. One typically features Asian-inspired flavors and preparations, and the other is Mediterranean in style. Everything is sublime. On the Asian side, you might get some home-smoked fresh tuna in a light ginger dressing with homemade pickles; on the Mediterranean side, it could be home-made mushroom sausage in a phyllo quiche shell with pesto and Fontina cheese. An excellent wine list and cellar complete the experience, but do try their signature cocktail, which features vodka, cognac, jalapeño, ginger, and passion fruit. Abbocato is also open for lunch and tapas.

Inside Hacienda del Mar, 1km (½ mile) inland from Playa Panamá. ℂ **2672-0073** or 8820-2576. www.abbocatocr.com. Reservations necessary for dinner. Main courses $10–$35. Prix-fixe dinner $45. Tues–Sat noon–9pm.

Ginger ★★ INTERNATIONAL/TAPAS   From the angular open architecture of Victor Cañas to the creative cocktails and wide-ranging tapas menu, this is easily the hippest place to drink and dine in the Papagayo area. The menu demonstrates international influences as diverse and distinct as Thailand, Spain, and Italy. I especially like the firecracker shrimp and the shredded pork lettuce wraps in a mango-tamarind sauce. Friday night is "Martini Night," featuring $3 martinis.

On the main road, Playa Hermosa. ℂ **2672-0041.** www.gingercostarica.com. Tapas $5–$13. Tues–Sun 5–10pm.

Los Sueños ★ INTERNATIONAL   This is the excellent in-house restaurant of the Villa del Sueño Hotel and condo complex (see above). The open-air restaurant also features outdoor tables and chairs which are delightful on clear evenings. The French-Canadian owners serve up fresh and healthy fare featuring local ingredients and favorites blended with contemporary Continental cuisine. You can get a thick steak with pepper sauce, or some fresh red snapper in a local shrimp sauce. Throughout the high season, a house band or visiting performer usually plays.

At the Villa del Sueño Hotel. ℂ **2672-0026.** Main courses $12–$25. Daily 7am–9:30pm.

Entertainment & Nightlife

Most of the large resorts here have a variety of bars, and a few feature nightly entertainment revues or live bands. For U.S.-style bar food and entertainment, try the **Upper Deck Sports Bar** (ℂ **2672-1276**), just off the main road. For a mellow cocktail scene on an open-air deck, head for **Ginger** (see above). Outside of the large resorts, find out whether the **Los Sueños** restaurant (see above) has live music.

PLAYA DEL COCO & PLAYA OCOTAL

253km (157 miles) NW of San José; 35km (22 miles) W of Liberia

Playa del Coco is one of Costa Rica's busiest and most developed beach destinations. A large modern mall and shopping center anchor the eastern edge of town. You'll pass through a tight jumble of restaurants, hotels, and souvenir shops for several blocks before you hit the sand and sea; homes, condos, and hotels

Playa Ocotal.

have sprouted up along the beach in either direction. This has long been, and remains, a popular destination with middle-class Ticos and weekend revelers from San José. It's also a prime jumping-off point for some of Costa Rica's best scuba diving. The beach, which has grayish-brown sand and gentle surf, is quite wide at low tide and almost nonexistent at high tide. The crowds that come here like their music loud and late, so if you're in search of a quiet retreat, stay away from the center of town. Still, if you're looking for a beach with a wide range of hotels, lively nightlife, and plenty of cheap food and beer close at hand, you'll enjoy Playa del Coco.

More interesting still, in my opinion, is **Playa Ocotal ★**, which is a couple of miles to the south. This tiny pocket cove features a small salt-and-pepper beach bordered by high bluffs and is quite beautiful. When it's calm, good snorkeling can be had around some rocky islands close to shore.

Essentials

GETTING THERE & DEPARTING **By Plane:** The nearest airport with regularly scheduled flights is in Liberia (p. 192). From there, you can arrange for a taxi to take you to Playa del Coco or Playa Ocotal, which is about a 25-minute drive, for $35 to $60.

By Car: From Liberia, head west on CR21 toward Santa Cruz. Just past the village of Comunidad, turn right. In about 11km (6¾ miles), you'll come to a fork in the road. Take the left fork. The right fork goes to Playa Hermosa. The drive takes about 4 hours from San José.

By Bus: Pulmitan express buses (✆ **2222-1650** in San José, or 2670-0095 in Playa del Coco; www.pulmitandeliberia.com) leave San José for Playa del Coco at 8am and 2 and 4pm daily from Calle 24 between avenidas 5 and 7. Allow 5 hours for the trip. A one-way ticket is C4,250. From Liberia, buses (✆ **2666-0458**) to Playa del Coco leave regularly throughout the day between 5am and 7pm. A one-way ticket for the 40-minute trip costs around C750. These bus schedules change frequently, so it's always best to check in advance. During

Panoramic view of Playa del Coco and Ocotal.

Playa del Coco & Playa Ocotal

Punta Miga
Playita Blanca
Bahía El Coco
Bahía Jicote
Punta Centinela
Playa del Coco
EL COCO
Bahía Ocotal
Cerro La Flor
Playa Ocotal
OCOTAL
To Route 51, Route 21

NICARAGUA
Playa del Coco & Playa Ocotal
CARIBBEAN SEA
SAN JOSÉ
PACIFIC OCEAN
PANAMA

0   1/2 mi
0   0.5 km

HOTELS

Coco Beach Hotel & Casino **8**
El Ocotal Beach Resort **2**
Hotel Villa Casa Blanca **1**
The Suites at Café de Playa **14**

RESTAURANTS

Café de Playa **14**
Citron **10**
Donde Claudio & Gloria **12**
Father Rooster **3**
Papagayo Seafood **7**
Papagayo Steak House **7**
Papagayo Sushi Boat **7**
Soda Mediterranea **13**

NIGHTLIFE

Beach Bums Bar & Grill **11**
Coconutz **6**
La Vida Loca **4**
Lizard Lounge **9**
Zi Lounge **5**

the high season and on weekends, extra buses from Liberia are sometimes added. The direct bus for San José leaves Playa del Coco daily at 4 and 8am and 2pm. Local buses for Liberia leave daily between 5am and 7pm.

Depending on demand, the Playa del Coco buses sometimes go as far as Playa Ocotal; it's worth checking beforehand. Otherwise, a taxi should cost around C3,000 to C5,000.

Gray Line (✆ **800/719-3105** in the U.S. and Canada, or 2220-2126 in Costa Rica; www.graylinecostarica.com) and **Interbus** (✆ **4031-0888;** www. interbusonline.com). The fare is $47. Both companies will pick you up at most San José–area hotels, and have connections to most other tourist destinations around Costa Rica.

Depending on demand, the Playa del Coco buses sometimes go as far as Playa Ocotal; it's worth checking beforehand. Otherwise, a taxi should cost around C3,000 to C4,000.

GETTING AROUND You can rent cars from any number of rental companies. Most are based in Liberia, or at the airport. See "Essentials," under "Liberia," for details and contact information.

If you can't flag down a **taxi** on the street, call ☎ **2670-0408.**

CITY LAYOUT Playa del Coco is a compact and busy beach town. At the center of town, running for a few hundred meters in either direction is a seafront walkway, or *malecón.* You'll find benches spread along this walkway, as well as patches of grass and a basketball court. Most of its hotels and restaurants are either on the water, on the road leading into town, or on the road that heads north, about 100m (328 ft.) inland from and parallel to the beach.

Playa Ocotal, which is south of Playa del Coco on a paved road that leaves the main road about 183m (600 ft.) before the beach, is a small collection of vacation homes, condos, and a couple of hotels. It has one bar and one restaurant on the beach.

FAST FACTS The nearest major hospital is in Liberia (☎ **2690-2300**). For the local **health clinic,** call ☎ **2670-1717;** for the local **pharmacy,** call ☎ **2670-2050.** For the local **police,** dial ☎ **2670-0258.** You'll find several banks and ATMs around town.

Exploring Playa del Coco & Playa Ocotal

Plenty of boats are anchored at Playa del Coco, and that means plenty of opportunities to go fishing, diving, or sailing. Still, the most popular activities, especially among the hordes of Ticos who come here, are lounging on the beach, walking along the *malecón,* hanging out in the *sodas,* and cruising the bars and discos at night. If you're interested, you might be able to join a soccer match. (The soccer field is in the middle of town.) You can also arrange horseback rides; ask at your hotel.

BEACH CLUB If you're staying at a hotel without a pool, or just want a sense of exclusivity on the beach, you might check out **Café de Playa Beach & Dining Club** (☎ **2670-1621;** www.cafedeplaya.com). In addition to having an excellent restaurant (see above), this place offers day passes for $15 that allow access to their pool and private grassy lawn fronting the beach, which is filled with comfortable teak chaise lounges. They also have a host of watersports equipment rental and tour options, and a small spa.

CANOPY TOUR The **Congo Trail Canopy Tour** ★ (☎ **2666-4422** or 2697-1801) is on the outskirts of Playa del Coco, along a dirt road that leads to Playa Pan de Azúcar. This place is set in a stand of thick, tropical dry forest. In addition to the zip-line canopy tour, these folks have a small butterfly farm, and a few zoo-enclosures, with some monkeys, and reptiles. The tour runs every day from 8am to 5pm, and costs $40 for the canopy tour, and an extra $5 to see the animals.

GOLF Located about 10km (6¼ miles) outside Playa del Coco, the **Papagayo Golf & Country Club** ★ (☎ **2697-0169;** www.papagayo-golf.com) is a full 18-hole course, with a pro shop, driving range, and rental equipment. It costs $100 in greens fees, including a cart, and access to the pool area before or after your round. Tee time reservations are necessary on weekends. It's closed on Mondays during the off season.

Boats at anchor, Playa del Coco.

GYM   If you want to work out while in town, head to the **Coco Gym** (📞 2670-2129), which is on the road between Playa del Coco and Ocotal. Weights, cardio machines, and a range of classes are offered. A day pass here costs just $5.

HORSEBACK RIDING   You can't ride on the beaches here, but the folks at **Haras del Mar** (📞 8816-2970; harashorses@gmail.com) offer great trail and country riding at on well-tended and perfectly trained horses about 20 minutes outside of Playas del Coco.

SAILING   Several cruising sailboats and longtime local salts offer daily sailing excursions. The 47-foot ketch-rigged **"Kuna Vela"** (📞 8301-3030; www.kuna-vela.com) and the 45-foot ketch **"Seabird"** (📞 8880-6393; www.seabird sailingexcursions.com) both ply the waters off Playa del Coco. They also offer half- and full-day and sunset sailing options, with snorkel stops and an open bar.

SCUBA DIVING   Scuba diving is the most popular watersport in the area, and dive shops abound. **Ocotal Diving** (📞 2670-0321; www.ocotaldiving.com), **Summer Salt ★** (📞 2670-0308; www.summer-salt.com), and **Rich Coast Diving ★★** (📞 2670-0176; www.richcoastdiving.com) are the most established and offer equipment rentals and dive trips. A two-tank dive, with equipment, should cost between $65 and $150 per person, depending on the distance to the dive site. The more distant dive sites visited include the Catalina Islands and Bat Island. All of these operators also offer PADI certification courses.

SPORTFISHING   Full- and half-day sportfishing excursions can be arranged through any of the hotel tour desks, or with **Costa Rican Sport Fishing** (📞 8882-8943; www.costaricansportfishing.com) or **Dream On Sportfishing ★★** (📞 855/415-5500 in the U.S. and Canada, or 8735-3121 in Costa Rica; www.dreamonsportfishing.com). A half-day of fishing, including the boat, captain,

Charlie Don't Surf, but Ollie Does

Ollie's Point is named after Oliver North, the famous and felonious former lieutenant colonel at the center of the Iran-Contra scandal. The beaches and ports of northern Guanacaste were a staging ground for supplying the Nicaraguan Contra rebels. Legend has it that during a news broadcast of an interview with North, some surfers noticed a fabulous point break going off in the background. Hence, the discovery and naming of Ollie's Point.

food, and tackle, should cost $500 to $800 for two to four passengers; a full day should run $700 to $1200.

SURFING   Playa del Coco has no surf whatsoever, but it is a popular jumping-off point for daily boat trips to Witch's Rock or Roca Bruja, and Ollie's Point up in Santa Rosa National Park (p. 205). Most of the above-mentioned sportfishing and dive operations also ferry surfers up to these two isolated surf breaks. A boat that carries five surfers for a full day, including lunch and beer, should run around $350 to $600. **Note:** Both Witch's Rock and Ollie's Point are technically within Santa Rosa National Park. Permits are sometimes required, and boats without permits are sometimes turned away. If you decide to go, be sure your boat captain is licensed and has cleared access to the park. You may also have to pay the park's $10 fee. Alternately, you can contact **Pacific Coast Stand Up Paddle & Surf Trips** (© **8359-8115;** www.pacificcoastsuptours.com). The calm waters off of Playa del Coco are great for stand up paddling. These folks offer lessons and guided outings for both traditional surfing, and for those looking to try out stand up paddling.

Where to Stay
EXPENSIVE

El Ocotal Beach Resort ★   This small resort has an enviable location, perched on a steep hillside overlooking the Pacific Ocean and a series of tiny offshore islands. The views are mesmerizing all day, and the sunsets are spectacular. Most rooms enjoy these wonderful views. If you get one that doesn't, the open-air deck off the main restaurant and bar is a prime ocean view spot. The rooms and facilities here are a mixed bag, and service and upkeep can be lax at times. Some of the rooms are quite well done and well kept, while others show their age. These folks have one of the best and longest running dive operations in the area.

Playa del Coco, Guanacaste. © **2670-0321.** www.ocotalresort.com. 42 units. 12 bungalows, 5 suites. $185–$220 double; $230–$265 bungalow and suite. Rates include full breakfast. Free for kids under 12. **Amenities:** 2 restaurants; exercise room; Jacuzzi; 3 outdoor pools and 3 plunge pools; lighted tennis court; free Wi-Fi.

MODERATE

Coco Beach Hotel & Casino   If you want to be in the center of the action, this is the place for you. Set right in the heart of Playa del Coco's busiest restaurant, bar and commercial strip, this place features clean, cool, contemporary rooms. A small strip mall separates the rooms from the street and also help to block the blazing Guanacaste sun, which was a problem when this place first opened. The beach is about 2 blocks away.

Playa del Coco, Guanacaste. ☏ **2670-0494.** www.cocobeachhotelandcasinocr.com. 32 units. $100–$175 double. Rates include full breakfast. **Amenities:** Restaurant; bar; casino; small outdoor pool; small spa; free Wi-Fi.

The Suites at Café de Playa ★ You can't beat this intimate boutique hotel and restaurant if you're looking for beachfront digs right on Playa del Coco. Guest rooms are simple and minimalist in style, and none have ocean views, but they are cool, clean, and roomy, with either one or two queen-size beds. Still, the biggest draw here is the fact that you are right on the beach.

Playa del Coco, Guanacaste. ☏ **2670-1621.** www.cafedeplaya.com. 5 units. $100–$180 double. Rates include full breakfast. **Amenities:** Restaurant; outdoor pool; small spa; free Wi-Fi.

INEXPENSIVE

Hotel Villa Casa Blanca ★ Set slightly uphill from Playa Ocotal, this hotel is set in a converted home with red clay tile floors and whitewashed walls. Separate villas and suites are set behind the main building. These are larger and have the best views. The hotel has lush gardens, resident parrots, and ample common areas for mingling with fellow guests, or settling down with a good book. The new owners are from Spain, and have put some serious effort into updating the installations and improving the service.

Playa Ocotal, Guanacaste. ☏ **2670-0448.** www.hotelvillacasablanca.com. 11 units. $75–$120 double; $100–$130 double suite. Rates include breakfast buffet. **Amenities:** Outdoor lounge and bar; Jacuzzi; small outdoor pool; free Wi-Fi.

Where to Dine

A clutch of basic open-air *sodas* is at the traffic circle in the center of El Coco village. These restaurants serve Tico standards, with an emphasis on fried fish. Prices are quite low—and so is the quality, for the most part.

You can get excellent Italian food at **Soda Mediterránea ★** (☏ **8425-4136**), in the little El Pueblito strip mall on the road running north and parallel to the beach, and a good mix of Mediterranean and Peruvian cuisine at the beachfront **Donde Claudio & Gloria ★** (☏ **2670-1514**).

Right on the main strip, you'll also find the various Papagayo operations. Building on the success of their seafood restaurant, **Papagayo Seafood ★** (☏ **2670-0298**), **Papagayo Steak House ★** (☏ **2670-0605**), and **Papagayo Sushi Boat ★** (☏ **2670-0298**), in an attempt to cover all possible bases.

Café de Playa ★★ FUSION/INTERNATIONAL If you're looking for a casual table overlooking the ocean, this is the place. The menu ranges from burgers and fish-and-chips to Thai beef salad and a range of Mediterranean-inspired pasta dishes. For more local flavor, try the fresh sea bass in a coconut-milk sauce. The ambiance is casual chic both day and night, with heavy teak tables and lounge seating spread on a large, open-air wooden deck and out onto the grassy lawn.

On the beach, Playa del Coco. ☏ **2670-1621.** www.cafedeplaya.com. Reservations recommended. Main courses C5,500–C16,000. Daily 8am–10pm.

Citron ★★★ FUSION/INTERNATIONAL Even though it's set in a small contemporary strip mall, a bit removed from the heart of Playa del Coco, this is easily the town's most elegant and creative restaurant. The decor features a central bar, beautiful masonry work along one whole wall, creative lighting, a water feature, and a caña brava (a local cane) ceiling. The menu is equally inventive. I especially like the tenderloin and Portobello risotto in red-wine reduction. Be sure to save room for their desserts, especially the vanilla crème brûlée, made with local organic vanilla.

In the Pacifico mall, on the main road into town. Playa del Coco. © **2670-0942.** www.citron coco.com. Main courses $12–$19. Mon–Sat 5:30–10pm.

Father Rooster ★ SEAFOOD/BAR This casual, open-air beachfront bar sits just a few steps from the water on tiny Playa Ocotal. You can get burgers and tacos and beer-battered fish or shrimp, as well as nachos and other typical bar fare. The building itself is a rustic wood affair painted a haphazard mix of colors. A pool table is in one room, and seating is all around the veranda and out onto the sand. On the weekends, you'll sometimes catch a live band here.

On the beach, Playa Ocotal. © **2670-1246.** Main courses C6,500–C9,000. Daily 11:30am–10pm.

En Route: Playas del Coco & Playa Flamingo

Hotel Sugar Beach ★★ If you're looking for an isolated boutique getaway in Guanacaste, you can't beat this place. The hotel is spread over a gently curved, forested hillside that cradles Playa Pan de Azúcar (Sugar Beach). Rooms are all very spacious and well maintained, with plenty of modern conveniences. The grounds are rich in wildlife, and it's not uncommon to find troops of howler monkeys in the trees here—so be prepared for some unrequested early wake-up calls. While there are no private beaches in Costa Rica, for all intents and purposes the beach here is the nearly exclusive playground of the hotel guests.

Playa Pan de Azúcar, Guanacaste. © **2654-4242.** www.sugar-beach.com. 28 units. $155–$190 double; $270–$310 suite; $575–$671 3-bedroom villa. Rates include breakfast and taxes. **Amenities:** Restaurant; bar; small kidney-shaped pool set on the hillside; watersports equipment rental; free Wi-Fi.

RIU Guanacaste This massive all-inclusive resort boasts over 700 hundred rooms, and does a brisk business in Canadian, European and American charter travel. Throughout the high season, the bars, buffets and pool bars are brimming with sunburned revelers looking to take as much advantage as they can of all the free food, booze and activities on offer. The rooms are large and well equipped and most offer at least a bit of a sea view from their private balcony. Next door you'll find the 538-room, all suite **RIU Palace Guanacaste,** a similar sister resort with more upscale rooms and more attentive service. The dark sand beach is rocky in places, and the construction of these properties were mired in environmental complaints and controversies.

Playa Matapalo, Guanacaste. © **800/748-4990** in the U.S. and Canada, or 2681-2300 at the hotel. www.riu.com. 701 units. $240–$350 double RIU Guanacaste; $290–$600 RIU Palace. Rates include all meals, drinks, taxes, a wide range of activities, and use of non-motorized land and watersports equipment. Spa services extra. **Amenities:** 8 restaurants; 7 bars; 2 lounges; casino; discotheque; babysitting; free bike usage; children's programs; concierge; extensive exercise facilities and spa; large free-form outdoor pool w/several Jacuzzis, smoke-free rooms; lighted tennis court; watersports equipment rental; Wi-Fi.

Entertainment & Nightlife

Playa del Coco is one of Costa Rica's liveliest beach towns after dark. Most of the action is centered along a 2-block section of the main road into town, just before you hit the beach. Here you'll find the **Lizard Lounge ★** (© 2670-0307), which has a raucous party vibe. Just across the street is the large, open-air **Zi**

Lounge ★★ (© 2670-1978). Those looking for a gringo-influenced sports bar hangout can try **Coconutz** ★ (© 2670-1982; www.coconutz-costarica.com).

Just off the beach, at the center of town you'll find **Beach Bums Bar & Grill** ★ (© 2671-0110). This is a very popular spot, with frequent live bands and DJs.

On the south end of the beach, reached via a rickety footbridge over the estuary, you'll find **La Vida Loca** ★ (© 2670-0181), a lively beachfront bar with a pool table, Ping-Pong table, foosball table, and live bands.

If you head north on the dirt road running parallel to the beach, you'll find **Café de Playa** (see above), which has a laid-back Euro-chic feel to it.

PLAYAS CONCHAL & BRASILITO

280km (174 miles) NW of San José; 67km (42 miles) SW of Liberia

Playa Conchal ★★ is the first in a string of beaches stretching north along this coast. This beach is almost entirely backed by the massive Westin Playa Conchal resort and Reserva Conchal condominium complex. The unique beach here was once made up primarily of soft crushed shells—a shell-collectors' heaven. Unfortunately, as Conchal has developed and its popularity spread, unscrupulous builders have brought in dump trucks to haul away the namesake seashells for landscaping and construction, and the impact is noticeable.

Just beyond Playa Conchal to the north, you'll come to **Playa Brasilito,** a tiny beach town and one of the few real villages in the area. The soccer field is the center of the village, and around its edges are a couple of little *pulperías* (general stores). The long stretch of gray sand beach has a quiet, undiscovered feel to it.

Essentials

GETTING THERE & DEPARTING **By Plane:** The nearest airport with regularly scheduled flights is in Tamarindo (see "Playa Tamarindo & Playa Langosta: Getting There & Departing: By Plane," later) although it is also possible to fly into Liberia (p. 192). From either of these places, you can arrange for a taxi to drive you to any of these beaches. Playas Brasilito and Conchal are about 25 minutes from Tamarindo and 40 minutes from Liberia. A taxi from Tamarindo should cost around $35 to $50, and between $50 and $70 from Liberia.

By Car: Two major routes go to the beaches. The most direct is by way of the La Amistad Bridge over the Tempisque River. Take the Interamerican Highway west from San José. Forty-seven kilometers (29 miles) past the turnoff for Puntarenas, you'll see signs for the turnoff to the bridge. After crossing the Tempisque River, follow the signs for Nicoya, continuing north to Santa Cruz. About 16km (10 miles) north of Santa Cruz, just before the village of Belén, take the turnoff for playas Conchal, Brasilito, Flamingo, and Potrero. After another 20km (12 miles), at the town of Huacas, take the right fork to reach these beaches. The drive takes about 41/2 hours.

Alternatively, you can drive here via Liberia. When you reach Liberia, turn west and follow the signs for Santa Cruz and the various beaches. Just beyond the town of Belén, take the turnoff for playas Flamingo, Brasilito, and Potrero, and continue following the directions given above. This route takes around 5 hours.

By Bus: Tralapa express buses (© 2221-7202 in San José, or 2654-4203 in Flamingo) leave San José daily at 8 and 10:30am and 3pm from Calle 20

Dining on the beach at Playa Brasilito.

between avenidas 3 and 5, stopping at playas Brasilito, Flamingo, and Potrero, in that order. The ride takes around 5 hours. A one-way ticket costs C6,250.

Alternatively, the same company's buses to Santa Cruz (© **2680-0392**) connect with one of the several buses from Santa Cruz to Playa Potrero. Buses depart San José for Santa Cruz roughly every 2 hours daily between 7am and 6pm from Calle 20 between avenidas 3 and 5. The trip duration is around 4 hours; the fare is C5,200. From Santa Cruz, the ride is about 90 minutes; the fare is C1,500.

Gray Line (© **800/719-3105** in the U.S. and Canada, or 2220-2126 in Costa Rica; www.graylinecostarica.com) and **Interbus** (© **4031-0888;** www. interbusonline.com) both have two daily buses leaving San José for the beaches in this area, one in the morning and one in the afternoon. The fare is $47. Both companies will pick you up at most San José–area hotels, and offer connections to most other tourist destinations in the country.

Express buses depart **Playa Potrero** for San José at 3 and 9am and 2pm, stopping a few minutes later in playas Flamingo and Brasilito. Ask at your hotel where to catch the bus. Buses to **Santa Cruz** leave Potrero at regular intervals throughout the day and take about 90 minutes. If you're heading north toward Liberia, get off the bus at Belén and wait for a bus going north. Buses leave Santa Cruz for San José roughly every other hour between 6am and 6pm.

ORIENTATION The pavement ends just beyond Playa Conchal as you leave the small village of Brasilito.

Exploring Playas Conchal & Brasilito

Playa Conchal ★★, which is legendary for its crushed seashells, is also stunningly beautiful, but the drop-off is quite steep, making it notorious for its strong riptides. However, the water at **Playa Brasilito** is often fairly calm, which makes it a good swimming choice. This is also a great jumping-off point for visiting other nearby and less popular beaches, like **Playa La Penca** ★★ and **Playa Pan de Azúcar** ★★, both of which are north of here.

All of the hotels here have tour desks offering a range of tour and activity options, including those available in the Flamingo and Potrero area (see below).

Tip: All beaches in Costa Rica are public property. But the land behind the beaches is not, and the Westin hotel owns almost all of it in Playa Conchal, so

HOTELS
Bahía del Sol **14**
Camping Brasilito **2**
Casa Melray **16**
Conchal Hotel **4**
Flamingo Beach Resort **9**
Flamingo Marina Resort
    Hotel and Club **12**
Hotel Brasilito **3**
Hotel Sugar Beach **17**
Maiyra's **7**
RIU Guanacaste **18**
Westin Playa Conchal
    Resort & Spa **1**

RESTAURANTS
Angelina's **10**
Camarón Dorado **6**
Coco Loco **8**
El Coconut Beach Club **13**
Happy Snapper **5**
Marie's **10**
Papaya **4**

NIGHTLIFE
Amberes **11**
Angelina's **10**
Flamingo Beach Resort **9**
Happy Snapper **5**
La Terraza de los Mariscos **15**

Playa Danta

Is. Pitahayas
Playa Pan de Azúcar

Playa Prieta

Is. Choyocas
Playa La Penca
Potrero

Isla Plata

Bahía de
Potrero

Punta Salinas

Playa Potrero

Playa Flamingo

Bahía
Brasilito
I. Loras

Playa Brasilito

Brasilito

Playa
Conchal

Playa
Las Minas

Playa Nombre
de Jesús

Playa Real

NICARAGUA
CARIBBEAN
SEA
Playas Flamingo,
Brasilito
& Conchal
SAN JOSÉ
PACIFIC
OCEAN
PANAMA

0   1 mi
0   1 km

To Huacas,
Tamarindo

**Playas Flamingo,
Brasilito & Conchal**

the only public access is along the soft-sand road that follows the beach south from Brasilito. Before the road reaches Conchal, you'll have to ford a small river and then climb a steep, rocky hill, so four-wheel-drive is recommended.

GOLF   The **Westin Playa Conchal Resort & Spa ★★** (© **2654-4123**) is home to the excellent **Reserva Conchal Golf Course.** This Robert Trent Jones–designed resort course features broad open fairways, fast greens, and a few wonderful views of the ocean. It costs $160 in greens fees for 18 holes and $100 for 9 holes. If you tee off after 1pm, the price drops to $95 for all the rounds you can squeeze in.

WATERSPORTS   You can rent jet skis and Wave Runners on the beach in Playa Conchal, from **Dorado Jet Ski Tours** (© **8824-4293**). These folks also offer guided snorkel tours out to the Catalina Islands, as well as wet and wild "Banana Boat" rides, where a group of friends and family get pulled behind a speed boat on a giant, inflatable banana boat.

Where to Stay
VERY EXPENSIVE
Westin Playa Conchal Resort & Spa ★★★   This is easily the best large-scale, all-inclusive resort in Costa Rica, and it sits on one of the country's prettiest beaches, to boot. The massive, free-form swimming pool is also a marvel. Every room here is considered a suite and comes with either one king-size or two double beds, set in a raised sleeping room. Only a handful of the rooms actually have ocean views, however. You choose from restaurants, but a steady stream of food, beverages, and organized activities is on tap all day and night.

Playa Conchal, Guanacaste. © **800/937-8461** in the U.S., or 2654-3500. www.westinplaya conchal.com. 406 units. $400–$850 double; $650 and up deluxe double; children 3–12 add $90–$145 per child per day; kids 13 and up charged as adults; kids under 3 free. Rates include all meals, drinks, taxes, a wide range of activities, and use of non-motorized land and watersports

The village of Playa Brasilito.

A Day Trip Destination: El Viejo Wetlands

Located a bit inland from the Guanacaste agricultural town of Filadelfia and bordering the Palo Verde National Park, **El Viejo Wildlife Refuge & Wetlands** ★★ (© **2296-0966;** www.elviejowetlands. com) is a unique and intriguing option for a day tour. The principal attraction here is the wildlife, which is abundant, and viewed both from open-air safari-style vehicles and small boats on the Tempisque River. You'll certainly see scores of water birds, and most probably a crocodile or two. The main hacienda-style building at the heart of this operation dates to 1870, and is where they serve up excellent Costa Rican lunches. Additional tour options here include a zip-line canopy tour, and a tour of the on-site organic farm and sugar cane processing "trapiche." Rates run from $60 to $130, depending upon how many activities or tours you take, and whether or not you want lunch.

equipment. Golf and spa services extra. **Amenities:** 6 restaurants; 5 bars; 2 lounges; casino; babysitting; bike rental; children's programs; concierge; Robert Trent Jones II–designed 18-hole golf course and pro shop; modest exercise facilities and spa; massive free-form outdoor pool w/ several Jacuzzis, another large outdoor pool for Royal Level suites; room service; all rooms smoke-free; 4 lighted tennis courts; watersports equipment rental; free Wi-Fi.

INEXPENSIVE

A string of inexpensive cabinas line the main road leading into Brasilito, just before you hit the beach. It's also possible to camp on playas Potrero and Brasilito. At the former, contact **Maiyra's** (© **2654-4213**); at the latter, try **Camping Brasilito** (© **2654-4452**). Both of these places offer some budget rooms as well. Each charges around C3,000 per person to make camp and use the basic restroom facilities or around C5,000 to C10,000 per person to stay in a rustic room.

Conchal Hotel ★★   Burned to the ground in early 2013, this place was quickly rebuilt and is better than ever. The complex is anchored by a central pool and garden area. Rooms are spacious and feature sturdy steel bed frames, white linens and whitewashed walls offset with bright primary accents. Superior rooms come with large, flat-screen televisions and more space. Most rooms open on to a private or shared balcony or veranda fronting the pool and gardens. Despite its name, this hotel really should be considered part of Playa Brasilito. Owners Simon and Hilda are delightful and very hands-on. Service is very attentive and personal, and the hotel's Papaya restaurant (see below) is one of the best in the area.

Playa Brasilito, Guanacaste. © **347/298-9356** in the U.S., or **2654-9125** in Costa Rica. www. conchalcr.com. 9 units. $75–$120 double. Rates include continental breakfast and taxes. Seriously reduced rates available in the off season. **Amenities:** Restaurant; bar; small pool; free Wi-Fi.

Hotel Brasilito   This longstanding budget hotel offers clean, well-kept rooms in a pair of two-story wood buildings just a stone's throw from the water right on Playa Brasilito. Snag a room with a balcony and you'll be in budget heaven. These folks have an excellent in-house tour operation and their open-air restaurant, El Oasis, is equally recommendable.

Playa Brasilito, Guanacaste. © **2654-4237.** www.hotelbrasilito.com. 15 units. $35–$74 double. **Amenities:** Restaurant; free Wi-Fi.

Where to Dine

You'll find good fresh seafood and international fare at the **Happy Snapper** (© **2654-4413**) in Brasilito.

Camarón Dorado ★ SEAFOOD   The quintessential beach restaurant, complete with plastic lawn furniture set in the sand and Tiki torches. You can also sit in an open-air, but covered, dining area on a concrete slab if you don't want sand in your shoes. The menu is extensive, but heavy on seafood. Everything is very well prepared, although the success this place enjoys has led them to jack up the prices a bit above what you should be paying in what is really a simple, beachfront fish shack.

Playa Brasilito. © **2654-4028.** Reservations recommended in high season. Main courses C5,000–C16,000. Daily 11am–10pm.

Papaya ★★★ INTERNATIONAL/SEAFOOD   A great spot for any meal of the day, this is easily the best restaurant in the Brasilito/Conchal area. After some temporary time at a nearby roadside location, the restaurant is once again back at the Conchal Hotel (see above), in a lovely, open-air space on the second floor, overlooking the pool area. The fresh, vibrant food and friendly, personal service remains the same. Pacific Rim fusion and Nuevo Latino flavors stand out on the small menu, which is always augmented with daily specials. My faves include fresh mahi-mahi in a coconut crust and local lobster tails seasoned with Chinese five spice.

Playa Brasilito. © **2654-9125.** Main courses C8,500–C14,000. Thurs–Tues 7am–9pm.

Entertainment & Nightlife

Pretty much all of the nightlife in Playa Conchal happens at the large Westin resort (see above), which has a range of bars, nightly entertainment, and a casino. Over in Brasilito, you might see if there's any live music or sporting events on the televisions at the **Happy Snapper** (see above).

PLAYAS FLAMINGO ★★ & POTRERO

285km (176 miles) NW of San José; 71km (44 miles) SW of Liberia

Playa Flamingo is one of the prettiest beaches in the region. A long, broad stretch of pinkish white sand, it is on a long spit of land that forms part of Potrero Bay. At the northern end of the beach is a high rock outcropping upon which most of Playa Flamingo's hotels and vacation homes are built. This rocky hill has great views.

If you continue along the road from Brasilito without taking the turn for Playa Flamingo, you'll come to **Playa Potrero,** which sits in a broadly curving bay, protected by the Flamingo headlands. The sand here is a brownish gray, but the beach is long, clean, deserted, and very calm for swimming. You can see the hotels of Playa Flamingo across the bay. Drive a little farther north and you'll find the still-underdeveloped beaches of **Playa Prieta ★**, **Playa La Penca ★** and, finally, **Playa Pan de Azúcar ★★**, or Sugar Beach.

Playa Flamingo.

Essentials

GETTING THERE & DEPARTING   **By Plane:** The nearest airport with regularly scheduled flights is in Tamarindo (see "Playa Tamarindo & Playa Langosta: Getting There & Departing: By Plane," below), although it is also possible to fly into Liberia (p. 192). From either, you can arrange for a taxi to drive you to any of these beaches. Playas Flamingo and Potrero are about 30 minutes from Tamarindo and 45 minutes from Liberia. A taxi from Tamarindo should cost around $35 to $55, and between $50 and $75 from Liberia.

By Bus: For information on reaching these beaches by bus, see "Essentials: Getting There & Departing" for Playas Conchal & Brasilito above.

By Car: See the information for driving to Playas Conchal and Brasilito above. Playa Flamingo is the first beach you'll come to beyond Playa Brasilito. Two prominent turnoffs on your left will take you to the beach, whereas if you continue straight, and follow signs bearing right, you'll soon come to Playa Potrero.

GETTING AROUND   Economy Rent A Car (℡ 2654-4543) has an office in Playa Flamingo.

Exploring Playas Flamingo & Potrero

Playa Flamingo ★★ is a long and beautiful stretch of soft white sand, although the surf can sometimes get a bit rough here. The beach doesn't have much shade, so be sure to use plenty of sunscreen and bring an umbrella if you can. If you're not staying here, parking spots are all along the beach road where you can park your car for the day—although do not leave anything of value inside. **Playa Potrero** has much gentler surf and, therefore, is the better swimming beach. However, the beach is made up of hard-packed dark sand that is much less appealing than Playa Flamingo.

A BEACH CLUB   If your hotel doesn't have a pool or beach access, you can always head to **El Coconut Beach Club** (℡ 2654-4300;

www.elcoconut-tamarindo.com). Located right on Playa Potrero, these folks have a pool and a mess of chaise lounges and chairs. You can enjoy the facilities, as long as you eat and drink at their excellent restaurant, a sister to **El Coconut** in Tamarindo (p. 246).

HORSEBACK RIDING   You can arrange a horseback ride with the **Flamingo Equestrian Center** (© 8846-7878) or **Casagua Horses** (© 2653-8041; www.paintedponyguestranch.com). Depending on the size of your group, it should cost between $25 and $40 per person per hour.

LANGUAGE LEARNING   The **Centro Panamericano de Idiomas** (© 2265-6306; www.cpi-edu.com), which has schools in San José and Monteverde, has a branch in Flamingo, across from the Flamingo Marina, facing Potrero Bay. A 1-week program with 4 hours of class per day and a homestay with a Costa Rican family costs $525.

Playa Pan de Azúcar.

SCUBA DIVING   Scuba diving is quite popular here. **Costa Rica Diving** (© 2654-4148; www.costarica-diving.com) has a shop in Flamingo and offers trips to the Catalina Island for around $85. Alternatively, you can check in at the **Flamingo Marina Resort Hotel and Club** (p. 234).

WATERSPORTS   You can rent jet skis, boogie boards, skim boards, and stand up paddle boards on Playa Flamingo from **Playa Vida** (© 2654-4444). These folks are on the south side of the Flamingo Beach resort (p. 234), and offer guided snorkel tours out to the Catalina Islands in addition to renting out beach chairs and shade umbrellas.

If you're interested in stand up paddling, surfing or surf lessons, check in with the folks at **Point Break Surf School** (© 8866-4413; www.pointbreak surf.com).

SPORTFISHING & SAILBOAT CHARTERS   Although the Flamingo Marina remains in a state of legal limbo and turmoil (see box above), you still have plenty of sport-fishing and sailboat charter options here. Jim McKee, the former force behind

---

Flamingo Marina

In 2004, the Flamingo marina was closed down by the municipal and county authorities for operating without proper permits (it had been built and set up a decade or so earlier). Currently, it remains tied up in a slow and convoluted process of public bidding, and there's been no word on when or if it will reopen. The harbor just outside the marina break wall is big, deep, and well protected; all boats are just working from there, and are kept at anchor, instead of at dock.

the Flamingo Marina, manages a fleet of boats. Contact him via his company, **Oso Viejo** (© **8827-5533** or 2653-8437; www.flamingobeachcr.com). A full-day fishing excursion costs between $700 and $2,200, depending on the size and quality of the boat, and distance traveled to the fishing grounds. Half-day trips cost between $500 and $700.

If you're looking for a full- or half-day sail or sunset cruise, check in with Oso Viejo to see what boats are available, or ask about the 52-foot cutter **Shannon.** Prices range from around $50 to $120 per person, depending on the length of the cruise. Multiday trips are also available.

Alternatively, you can ask at the **Flamingo Marina Resort Hotel and Club** (p. 234).

Where to Stay

In addition to the places mentioned below, **Casa Melray** ★ (© **2654-4316;** www.casamelray.com) is a luxury, beachfront bed-and-breakfast in Playa Potrero.

If you plan to be here for a while or are coming down with friends or a large family, you might consider renting a condo or house. For information and reservations, contact the folks at **ETS Costa Rica** (© **2653-7444;** www.etscr.net).

EXPENSIVE

Bahía del Sol Beachfront & Boutique Hotel ★★   I like the low-key vibe and intimate feel of this small resort. The hotel is set on a grassy patch of land just in from the center of Playa Potrero, a calm and protected beach with hard-packed, dark gray sand. The rooms are simple and plain, but very well kept and a good value. Studio apartments and suites with kitchenettes are good for families or for longer stays, but a good restaurant is also on the property. A small spa is set in a patch of thick gardens smack in the center of the resort. This hotel has received "4 Leaves" in the CST Sustainable Tourism program.

A sailboat cruise near Tamarindo.

Playa Potrero, Guanacaste. ☏ **866/223-2463** in the U.S. and Canada, or 2654-4671 in Costa Rica. www.bahiadelsolhotel.com. 28 units. $180–$260 double; $330–$410 suite. Rates include breakfast. **Amenities:** Restaurant; bar; Jacuzzi; outdoor pool; room service; spa; free Wi-Fi.

Flamingo Beach Resort ★ This is the only true beachfront hotel in Playa Flamingo. And what it lacks in style, flair, and pizzazz, it makes up for in location. Set just across a dirt road from a beautiful section of this white sand beach, the hotel is built in a horseshoe shape around its large central pool, with the whole thing facing the ocean. That said, the hotel does have plenty of "forest" and "mountain" view rooms, so if you want an ocean view, be sure to specify. The rooms are large, with tile floors and modern furnishings, although they do feel a bit Spartan. Some of the suites and family rooms come with kitchenettes.

Playa Flamingo, Guanacaste. ☏ **877/856-5519** in the U.S. and Canada, or 2654-4444 in Costa Rica. www.resortflamingobeach.com. 120 units. $145–$190 double; $290–$455 suite. **Amenities:** Restaurant; 2 bars; casino; exercise room; large outdoor pool; room service; small spa; outdoor lighted tennis court; watersports equipment rental; free Wi-Fi.

MODERATE

Flamingo Marina Resort Hotel and Club Set on a steep hillside overlooking Flamingo Bay and Playa Potrero, this complex features a mix of hotel rooms and condo units. This is one of the older resorts in the area, and despite periodic updates and renovations, many of the rooms feel a bit worn and tired. Many of the rooms have excellent views, from an inviting private balcony. The resort has a popular bar and restaurant, just off the main pool area, as well as a tennis court. It's a bit of a walk, or short car ride, to the Flamingo or Potrero beaches.

Playa Flamingo, Guanacaste. ☏ **940/440-8310** in the U.S., or 2654-4141 in Costa Rica. www.flamingomarina.com. 30 units, 60 condo units. $125 double; $160–$195 suite; $230–$320 condo. Standard rooms include continental breakfast. **Amenities:** 2 restaurants; bar; Jacuzzi; 5 small outdoor pools; tennis court; watersports equipment rental; Wi-Fi.

Where to Dine

You also can't go wrong with the California-style and Asian fusion cuisine and fresh baked pizzas at **Angelina's ★★** (☏ **2654-4839;** www.angelinasplayaflamingo.com), on the second floor of La Plaza shopping center, or at **El Coconut Beach Club** (☏ **2654-4300;** www.elcoconut-tamarindo.com; see "A Beach Club," above).

Coco Loco ★★★ COSTA RICAN/SEAFOOD While many still bemoan the closing of Mar y Sol, there's plenty of reason to rejoice, now that chef Jean-Luc Taulere has opened up a wonderful, casual beachfront bar and restaurant. Teak wood tables under white canvas umbrellas are spread out on the sand at the far southern end of Playa Flamingo. The menu features a blackened swordfish wrap, and fresh yellow fin tuna tacos. Meat lovers can opt for the slow-cooked pork ribs in a pineapple barbeque sauce. This is a great spot for sunsets with the extensive bar and cocktail menu; stay through the evening as they often host live music or DJs at night.

South end of Playa Flamingo. ☏ **2654-6242.** www.cocolococostarica.com. Main courses C3,400–C5,700. Daily 11am–9pm.

Marie's ★★ COSTA RICAN/SEAFOOD Marie has been serving up good, fresh, fairly priced food here for decades, and her restaurant is justifiably popular. You can get a typical casado, or blue plate special, as well as burritos and quesadillas, or some simple grilled fish or chicken. Be sure to check for daily specials. The large, open-air restaurant features extremely high ceilings pocked with slow-turning ceiling fans.

Playa Flamingo. ✆ **2654-4136.** www.mariesrestaurantincostarica.com. Main courses C3,800–C13,000. Daily 6:30am–9:30pm.

Entertainment & Nightlife

With both a disco and casino, **Amberes** (✆ **2654-4001**), just slightly up the hill at the north end of town, is the undisputed hot spot in this area; however, **Flamingo Beach Resort** (see above) also has a casino. You'll find a mellower bar and lounge scene at the bar of **Angelina's** ★ (see above), or on the beach at **Coco Loco** (see above).

Over in Potrero, the rooftop bar at **La Terraza de los Mariscos** (✆ **2654-4379**) sometimes has live music.

PLAYA GRANDE ★★

295km (183 miles) NW of San José; 70km (43 miles) SW of Liberia

Playa Grande is one of the principal nesting sites for the giant leatherback turtle, the largest turtle in the world. This beach is often too rough for swimming, but the well-formed and consistent beach break here is very popular with surfers. The beach is a long, straight stretch of soft, golden sand, with very little development at the moment. I almost hate to mention places to stay in Playa Grande because the steady influx of tourists and development is severely threatening it as a turtle nesting site. For help locating the below hotels, restaurants, and attractions, see the map "Around Tamarindo," on p. 241.

Essentials

GETTING THERE & DEPARTING   By Plane: The nearest airport with regularly scheduled flights is in Tamarindo (see "Tamarindo & Playa Langosta: Getting There & Departing: By Plane," below), although it is also possible to fly into Liberia (p. 192). From either of these places, you can arrange for a taxi to drive you to Playa Grande. Playa Grande is about 15 minutes from Tamarindo and 45 minutes from Liberia. A taxi from Tamarindo should cost around $25 to $40, and between $50 and $75 from Liberia.

By Car: See the information for driving to Tamarindo below. The dirt and gravel entrance roads to Playa Grande are located along CR155 between Tamarindo and Huacas.

Exploring Playa Grande

Leatherback sea turtles nest on Playa Grande between early October and

Leatherback turtle hatchlings on Playa Grande.

mid-February. The turtles come ashore to lay their eggs only at night. During the nesting season, you'll be inundated with opportunities to sign up for nightly tours, which usually cost $35 to $50 per person. No flash photography or flash-lights are allowed because any sort of light can confuse the turtles and prevent them from laying their eggs; guides must use red-tinted flashlights.

Note: Turtle nesting is a natural, unpredictable, and increasingly rare event. Moreover, things have gotten worse here over the years. All indications are that excessive building and lighting close to the beach are the culprits. Even during heavy nesting years, you sometimes have to wait your turn for hours, hike quite a way, and even accept the possibility that no nesting mothers will be spotted that evening.

If your hotel can't set a tour up for you, you'll see signs all over town offering tours. Make sure you go with someone licensed and reputable. Do-it-yourselfers can drive over to Playa Grande and book a $25 tour directly with the **National Parks Service** (© 2653-0470). The Parks Service operates out of a small shack just before the beach, across from the Hotel Las Tortugas (see below). It opens each evening at around 6pm to begin taking reservations. They sometimes answer their phone during the day, and it's best to make a reservation in advance because only a limited number of people are allowed on the beach at one time. Spots fill up fast, and if you don't have a reservation, you may have to wait until really late, or you may not be able to go out onto the beach.

Where to Stay

In addition to the places listed below, **Hotel Bula Bula** ★ (© 877/658-2880 in the U.S. and Canada, or 2653-0975 in Costa Rica; www.hotelbulabula.com) is another excellent inland option, while the **Playa Grande Surf Camp** (© 2653-1074; www.playagrandesurfcamp.com) is geared toward surfers and budget travelers.

Hotel Las Tortugas ★   Louis Wilson came to Costa Rica decades ago for the waves. He's stayed and still surfs, but has also been a leading figure in creating a protected habitat for the nesting sea turtles here in Playa Grande. The hotel sits right at the center of Playa Grande, near some of the best breaks, and is quite popular with surfers. Some guests complain about the lack of ocean view at this beachfront hotel. However, the reason is simple, a natural barrier of trees and shrubs is a deliberate measure to block manmade lighting from reaching the beach, as it confuses and scares off potential nesting turtles. Rooms here vary greatly in size and comfort level. The hotel also rents and manages several fully equipped apartments and condominiums.

Playa Grande, Guanacaste. © **2653-0423** or 2653-0458. www.lastortugashotel.com. 11 units. $26–$60 economy room double; $50–$105 double; $85–$130 suite. **Amenities:** Restaurant; bar; Jacuzzi; small outdoor pool; free Wi-Fi.

Rip Jack Inn ★   I find these to be the most comfortable and best equipped rooms in Playa Grande, particularly the deluxe rooms and suites. The hotel itself is about a block or so in from the beach. Daily yoga and Pilates classes are offered in the large yoga space here. There's a refreshing lap pool, and the hotel's second-floor restaurant is one of the better dining options in town.

Playa Grande, Guanacaste. © **800/808-4605** in the U.S. and Canada, or 2653-0480 in Costa Rica. www.ripjackinn.com. 20 units. $80–$155 double; $150–$250 suite. **Amenities:** Restaurant; bar; lap pool; Wi-Fi.

Where to Dine

Dining options are pretty limited in Playa Grande. I like **Upstairs ★**, the restaurant at the Rip Jack Inn (see above), or the **Great Waltini's ★**, at the Hotel Bula Bula (see above). Both are excellent restaurants serving fresh seafood and prime meats, cooked with care and creativity. You might also try the **Taco Star** (no phone) a simple open-air beachfront joint serving up fresh fish tacos and other Mexican favorites.

PLAYA TAMARINDO ★ & PLAYA LANGOSTA ★★

295km (183 miles) NW of San José; 73km (45 miles) SW of Liberia

Tamarindo is the biggest boomtown in Guanacaste—and in some ways, I think the boom has gone a bit too far, a bit too fast. The main road into Tamarindo is a helter-skelter jumble of strip malls, surf shops, hotels, and restaurants. Ongoing development is spreading up the hills inland from the beach and south to Playa Langosta. None of it seems regulated or particularly well planned out.

Still, the wide range of accommodations, abundant restaurants, and active nightlife, along with very dependable surf, have established Tamarindo as one of the most popular beaches on this coast. The beautiful beach here is a long, wide swath of white sand that curves gently from one rocky headland to another. Fishing boats bob at their moorings and brown pelicans skim the water's surface just beyond the breakers. A sandy islet off the southern end of the beach makes a great destination if you're a strong swimmer; if you're not, it makes a great foreground for sunsets. Tamarindo is very popular with surfers, who ply the break right here or use the town as a jumping-off place for beach and point breaks at playas Grande, Langosta, Avellanas, and Negra.

Surfing in Tamarindo.

Essentials

GETTING THERE & DEPARTING **By Plane:** Both **Nature Air** (© 800/235-9272 in the U.S. and Canada, or 2299-6000; www.natureair.com) and **Sansa** (© 877/767-2672 in the U.S. and Canada, or 2290-4100 in Costa Rica; www.flysansa.com) have several daily direct flights throughout the day to the small airstrip on the outskirts of Tamarindo. Fares run $95 to $150. During the high season, additional flights are sometimes added. Nature Air also connects Tamarindo and Arenal, Liberia, and Quepos.

Whether you arrive on Sansa or Nature Air, a couple of cabs or minivans are always waiting for arriving flights. It costs C3,000 to C5,000 for the ride into town.

If you're flying into Liberia, a taxi should cost around $80. Alternatively, you can use **Tamarindo Shuttle** (© 2653-4444; www.tamarindoshuttle.com), which charges $20 per person, one-way. These folks also offer a variety of tours and transfer services.

By Car: The most direct route is by way of the La Amistad bridge. From San José, you can either take the Interamerican Highway (CR1) north from downtown San José, or first head west out of the city on the San José–Caldera Highway (CR27). This latter route is a faster and flatter drive. When you reach Caldera on this route, follow the signs to Puntarenas, Liberia, and the Interamerican Highway (CR1). This will lead you to the unmarked entrance to CR1. You'll want to pass under the bridge and follow the on-ramp, which will put you on the highway heading north. Forty-seven kilometers (29 miles) north of the Puntarenas exit on the Interamerican Highway, you'll see signs for the turnoff to the bridge. After crossing the river, follow the signs for Nicoya and Santa Cruz. Continue north out of Santa Cruz, until just before the village of Belén, where you will find the turnoff for Tamarindo. In another 20km (12 miles), take the left fork for Playa Tamarindo at Huacas and continue on until the village of Villareal, where you make your final turn into Tamarindo. The trip should take around 4 hours.

You can save a little time, especially in the dry season, by taking a more direct but rougher route: You turn left just after passing the main intersection for Santa Cruz at the turnoff for playas Junquillal and Ostional. The road is paved until the tiny village of Veintesiete de Abril. From here, it's about 20km (12 miles) on a rough dirt road until the village of Villareal, where you make your final turn into Tamarindo.

Alternatively, you can drive here via Liberia. When you reach Liberia, turn west and follow the signs for Santa Cruz and the various beaches. Just beyond the town of Belén, take the turnoff for playas Flamingo, Brasilito, and Tamarindo, and then follow the directions for the second option above. This route takes around 5 hours.

By Bus: Alfaro express buses (© 2222-2666 in San José, or 2653-0268 in Tamarindo; www.empresaalfaro.com) leave San José daily for Tamarindo at 11:30am and 3:30pm, departing from Calle 14 between avenidas 3 and 5. **Tralapa** (© 2221-7202) also has two daily direct buses to Tamarindo leaving at 7:15am and 4pm from their main terminal at Calle 20 between avenidas 3 and 5. The trip takes around 5 hours, and the one-way fare is around C5,800.

You can also catch a bus to Santa Cruz from either of the above bus companies. Buses leave both stations for Santa Cruz roughly every 2 hours between 6am and 6pm. The 4-hour, one-way trip is around C5,300. Buses leave Santa

Tamarindo

HOTELS
15 Love B&B **23**
Cabinas Marielos **24**
El Diriá **22**
Hostel La Botella de Leche **8**
Hotel & Villas Cala Luna **4**
Hotel Arco Iris **7**
Hotel Capitan Suizo **5**
Hotel Pasatiempo **12**
Hotel Pueblo Dorado **30**
Hotel Zully Mar **18**
Sueño del Mar **3**
Villa Alegre **2**
Witch's Rock Surf Camp **25**

RESTAURANTS
Bamboo Sushi Club **20**
Carlos & Carlos **6**
Dragonfly Bar & Grill **9**
El Coconut **27**
Green Papaya Taco Bar **10**
La Baula **11**
Pangas Beach Club **29**
Nogui's Café **17**
Patagonia **19**
Season's by Shlomy **7**
Wok N Roll **16**

NIGHTLIFE
Aqua **26**
Bar 1 **13**
Barcelo Langosta Casino **1**
Crazy Monkey Bar **28**
Dragonfly Bar & Grill **9**
El Garito **13**
Sharky's **15**
Voodoo Lounge **14**

SHOPPING
Automercado **31**
Azul Profundo **21**
Garden Plaza **31**

239

Cruz for Tamarindo roughly every 1½ hours between 5:45am and 10pm; the one-way fare is C680.

Gray Line (© 800/719-3105 in the U.S. and Canada, or 2220-2126 in Costa Rica; www.graylinecostarica.com) and **Interbus** (© 4031-0888; www.interbusonline.com) both have two daily buses leaving San José for Tamarindo (one in the morning, one in the afternoon); the fare is $47. Both companies will pick you up at most San José–area hotels, and offer connections to most other major tourist destinations in Costa Rica.

Direct buses leave Tamarindo for San José daily at 3:30 and 5:30am (except on Sun) and 2 and 4pm. Buses to Santa Cruz leave roughly every 2 hours between 4:30am and 8:30pm. In Santa Cruz, you can transfer to one of the frequent San José buses.

GETTING AROUND   Adobe (© 2667-0608), **Alamo** (© 2653-0727), **Budget** (© 2436-2000), **Economy** (© 2653-0752), **Hertz** (© 2653-1358), and **Thrifty** (© 2653-0829) have rental car offices in Tamarindo.

The town itself is very compact and you should be able to walk most places. Heck, it's not even that far a walk from Playa Langosta. Still, a large fleet of taxis are usually cruising around town, or hanging out at principal intersections and meeting points. If you need to, you can contact **PDQ Taxi** (© 8918-3710; www.tamarindo-taxi.com).

If you need a ride to either the Tamarindo airstrip or Liberia international airport, contact **Tamarindo Shuttle & Tours** ★ (© 2653-4444; www.tamarindoshuttle.com).

CITY LAYOUT   The road leading into town runs parallel to the beach and ends in a small cul-de-sac just past Zully Mar. A major side road off this main road leads farther on, to Playa Langosta, from just before Zully Mar. A variety of side roads branch off this road. To reach playas Avellanas, Negra, and Junquillal, you have to first head out of town and take the road toward Santa Cruz.

FAST FACTS   The local **police** can be reached at © 2653-0283.

A **Banco Nacional** branch is at the little mall across from El Diria, and a branch of the **Banco de Costa Rica** is in the Plaza Conchal mall. Several Internet cafes and a couple of pharmacies are also in town. You'll find **Back Wash Laundry** (© 2653-0870) just past the turnoff for Playa Langosta.

Exploring Tamarindo

Tamarindo is a long, white sand beach. Still, you have to be careful when and where you swim. The calmest water and best swimming are always down at the far southern end of the beach, toward Punta Langosta. Much of the sea just off the busiest part of the town is best for surfing. When the swell is up, you'll find scores of surfers in the water here. *Be careful:* Rocks are just offshore in several places, some of which are exposed only at low tide. An encounter with one of these rocks could be nasty, especially if you're bodysurfing. I also advise that you

---

Yo Quiero Hablar Español

If you want to try an intensive immersion program or just brush up on your rusty high school Spanish, check in with the folks at **Wayra Instituto de Español**

(© 2653-0359; www.spanish-wayra.co.cr). This place is located up a side street from the dirt road that connects Tamarindo to Playa Langosta.

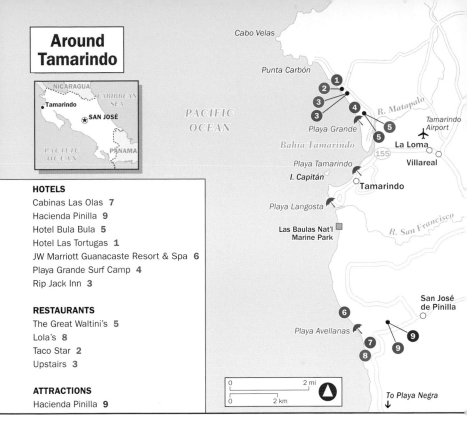

Around Tamarindo

Cabo Velas

Punta Carbón

PACIFIC OCEAN

1
2
3
3 **4** *R. Matapalo*
Playa Grande
5 Tamarindo Airport
Bahía Tamarindo **5** La Loma
Playa Tamarindo Villareal
I. Capitán 155
Tamarindo
Playa Langosta

Las Baulas Nat'l
Marine Park

R. San Francisco

San José de Pinilla

6
Playa Avellanas
7 **9** **9**
8

0 ——————— 2 mi
0 ——————— 2 km

To Playa Negra ↓

NICARAGUA
CARIBBEAN SEA
Tamarindo
SAN JOSÉ
PACIFIC OCEAN
PANAMA

HOTELS
Cabinas Las Olas 7
Hacienda Pinilla 9
Hotel Bula Bula 5
Hotel Las Tortugas 1
JW Marriott Guanacaste Resort & Spa 6
Playa Grande Surf Camp 4
Rip Jack Inn 3

RESTAURANTS
The Great Waltini's 5
Lola's 8
Taco Star 2
Upstairs 3

ATTRACTIONS
Hacienda Pinilla 9

avoid swimming near the estuary mouth, where the currents can carry you out away from the beach.

Tamarindo has a host of good tour operators. My favorites include **Xplore CR ★** (✆ **2653-4130;** www.xplorecostarica.com), **Tamarindo Shuttle & Tours ★** (✆ **2653-4444;** www.tamarindoshuttle.com) and **Iguana Surf** (✆ **2653-0613;** www.iguanasurf.net). All offer a range of half- and full-day trips, including outboard or kayak tours through the nearby estuary and mangroves, excursions to Santa Cruz and Guaitíl, raft floats on the Corobicí River, and tours to Palo Verde and Rincón de la Vieja national parks. Rates run between $40 and $150, depending on the length of the tour and group size.

All of the hotel desks and tour operators here offer **turtle nesting tours** to Playa Grande (p. 235), in season, or you can contact **ACOTAM** (✆ **2653-1687**), a specialized local operator.

BIKING   Bikes are available for rent at several locations in Tamarindo. Check around; you'll probably find the best bikes at the **Blue Trailz Bike Shop ★** (✆ **2653-1705;** www.bluetrailz.com), which rents high-end Trek and Specialized mountain bikes for around $20 per day. These folks also offer guided mountain bike tours and excursions, as well as surf lessons and trips.

CANOPY TOURS   No canopy tour is available right in Tamarindo, but the **Monkey Jungle Canopy Tour** (✆ **2653-1172;** www.canopymonkeyjungle.com) and **Cartagena Canopy Tour ★** (✆ **2675-0801;** www.canopytourcartagena.

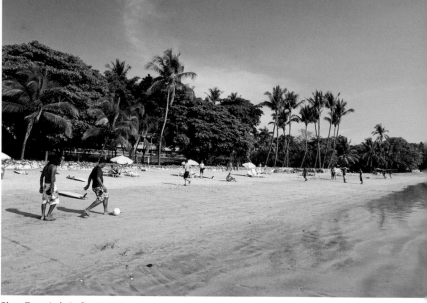

Playa Tamarindo in Guanacaste.

com) are nearby. Both charge $45 per person and include transportation from Tamarindo. Of these two, the Monkey Jungle operation is much closer, but I prefer the Cartagena tour, which has a much more lush forest setting. Still, I think your best bet is to take a day trip to Hacienda Guachipelín (p. 204) and do the zip-line and canyoning tours there.

FOUR-WHEELING Arenas Adventure Tours (© 2653-0108; http://aa.arenascr.com) offers a variety of guided ATV tours from 1 to 3 hours from $45 to $130 per person. This company also rents dirt bikes, snorkel equipment, surf and boogie boards, and jet skis and offers a full menu of other guided tours around the region.

GOLF Hacienda Pinilla ★★ (© 2681-4505; www.haciendapinilla.com) is a beautiful 18-hole links-style course located south of Tamarindo. The course is currently accepting golfers staying at all of the hotels around the area, with advance reservation. Greens fees run around $175 for 18 holes, including a cart, with discounts for guests staying at Hacienda Pinilla or the JW Marriott resort. Many folks staying in Tamarindo also play at the **Westin Playa Conchal Resort & Spa ★★**, an excellent resort course (p. 228).

HORSEBACK RIDING Although some will be disappointed, I think it's a very good thing that horses are no longer allowed on the beach. Fortunately, you'll find plenty of opportunities to ride in the hills and forests around Tamarindo. Most local tour operators offer horseback riding options, but I recommend you go riding with **Casagua Horses ★** (© 2653-8041; www.paintedponyguestranch.com). Rates for horse rental, with a guide, are around $30 to $65 per hour.

SAILBOAT CHARTERS Several boats offer cruises offshore from Tamarindo; the 40-foot catamaran **"Blue Dolphin" ★** (© 855/842-3204 in the U.S., or 8842-3204 in Costa Rica; www. http://bluedolphinsailing.com) and 66-foot catamaran

"**Marlin del Rey**" (© 877/827-8275 in the U.S., or 2653-1212 in Costa Rica; www.marlindelrey.com) are both good choices. A half-day snorkel or shorter sunset cruise should cost $70 to $85 per person, and a full day should run between $100 and $150 per person. This usually includes an open bar and snacks on the half-day and sunset cruises, and all of that plus lunch on the full-day trip.

SCUBA DIVING For scuba diving or snorkeling, check in with **Agua Rica Diving Center ★** (© 2653-0094). These folks are the best and longest running operators in Tamarindo, and have a full-service dive shop. They offer day trips, multiday dive cruises, and standard resort and full-certification courses.

SPORTFISHING A host of captains offer anglers a chance to go after the "big ones" that abound in the offshore waters. From the Tamarindo estuary, it takes only 20 minutes to reach the edge of the continental shelf, where the waters are filled with mostly marlin and sailfish. Although fishing is good all year, the peak season for billfish is between mid-April and August. Contact **Tamarindo Sportfishing** (© 2653-0090; www.tamarindosportfishing.com), **Capullo Sportfishing★** (©2653-0048; www.capullo.com), or **Osprey Sportfishing** (©8754-9292; www.osprey-sportfishing.com).

TENNIS You can rent court time and equipment at the **Tamarindo Tennis Club** (© 2653-0898), which features two lighted outdoor courts on the back road on the way to the Hotel El Jardín del Edén. It is open daily from 7:30am to 8pm, and court time runs $10 per day. You can also play at Hacienda Pinilla (see "Golf" above) for $5 per hour during the day, and $10 per hour at night.

WATERSPORTS If you want to try snorkeling, surfing, or sea kayaking in Tamarindo, **Agua Rica Diving Center, Iguana Surf,** and **Arenas Adventure Tours** (see above) rent all the necessary equipment. They have half-day and hourly rates for many of these items.

The Hacienda Pinilla golf course.

Tamarindo has a host of surf shops and surf schools, if you want to learn to catch a wave while in town. Tamarindo's got a great wave to learn on, although it can get very crowded at the popular beginners' breaks. You can shop around town, or check in with the **Tamarindo Surf School** (© **2653-0923;** www.tamarindo surfschool.com), **Kelly's Surf Shop** ★ (© **888/710-4746** in the U.S. and Canada, or 2653-1355 in Costa Rica; www.kellyssurfshop.com), or **Witch's Rock Surf Camp** ★ (© **888/318-7873** in the U.S. and Canada, or 2653-1262 in Costa Rica; www.witchsrocksurfcamp.com).

WELLNESS CENTERS Most of the higher-end hotels have their own spas, and most hotels can call you a massage therapist. But if you're looking for a local day spa experience, try **Cocó Day Spa** (© **2653-2562;** www.cocobeautyspa.com), which has a wide range of treatments and packages, from facials and pedicures to hot stone massages. Alternately, you can head about 15 to 20 minutes inland to **Los Altos de Eros** ★ (© **8850-4222;** www.losaltosdeeros.com) for one of their signature, full-day spa experiences.

For a good yoga session, contact **Ser Om Shanti Yoga Studio** (© **8346-8005;** www.seryogastudio.com)

Especially For Kids

If your kids have had too much beach or pool time, you can head to **Bolas Locas Mini Golf** (© **2653-1178;** http://bolaslocas.com), located next to Dragonfly Bar & Grill (see above). Open daily from 9am until 11pm, this 18 hole course features a wave wall, as a well as a waterfall and traditional Costa Rican ox cart as obstacles. A round of golf costs $7 for adults, and $5 for children under 10.

Where to Stay

In addition to the hotels listed below, Tamarindo, Playa Langosta, and Playa Grande have a wide range of beach houses and condos for rent by the night, the week, or the month. For more information on this option, check out **RE/MAX Tamarindo** (© **866/976-8898** in the U.S. and Canada, or 2653-0073 in Costa Rica; www.remax-oceansurf-cr.com) or **RPM Vacation Rentals** (© **2653-0738;** www.rpmvacationrentals.com).

VERY EXPENSIVE

Cala Luna Boutique Hotel & Villas ★★   This is by far the best equipped and most luxurious option in Tamarindo. The deluxe rooms are beautiful contemporary hotel rooms with subtle design touches and plenty of amenities. However, the real draw here are the two- and three-bedroom villas. Each comes with a private kidney-shaped swimming pool, a large fully equipped kitchen, ample living and dining areas, and a washer and dryer. Playa Langosta is reached via a short private path across a dirt road, and Tamarindo beach is a short taxi ride, or 15 minute walk away. The hotel's grounds and gardens are very lush and beautifully landscaped.

Playa Langosta, Guanacaste. © **800/210-0919** in the U.S. and Canada, or 2653-0214 in Costa Rica. www.calaluna.com. 20 units, 16 villas. $295 double; $500–$700 villa. Rates for rooms, but not villas, include breakfast. Rates slightly higher during peak weeks. **Amenities:** 2 restaurants; bar; babysitting; large free-form pool w/poolside bar; room service; watersports equipment rental; free Wi-Fi.

Hotel Capitán Suizo ★★★   This is my favorite hotel in Tamarindo. Right on the beach at the quieter far southern end, the grounds are lush and beautiful, service is top-notch, and the rooms are large, well kept, and thoroughly inviting. The hotel's free-form pool is one of the largest and best in town. This hotel is great for families and honeymooners alike. The rooms don't have TVs, if that matters, and about half are cooled simply by fans and well-designed cross-ventilation.

Playa Tamarindo, Guanacaste. © **2653-0075** or 2653-0353. www.hotelcapitansuizo.com. 24 units and 7 bungalows. $175–$260 double; $250–$415 bungalow; $330–$415 suite. Rates include breakfast buffet. **Amenities:** Restaurant; bar; small exercise room; midsize outdoor pool and children's pool; spa; Wi-Fi.

EXPENSIVE

El Diriá This massive complex sits right in the center of Tamarindo. The original hotel rooms and pool are right on the beach, and are my favorites. I especially like the third-floor sunset rooms, which offer up beautiful ocean and sunset views from their private balconies. However, most of the rooms and suites, as well as several other pools are located just inland in a series of high-rise buildings. Frankly, I find this resort has grown a bit too big and service and upkeep can suffer at times.

Playa Tamarindo, Guanacaste. © **866/603-4742** in the U.S. and Canada, or 2653-0032 in Costa Rica. www.tamarindodiria.com. 240 units. $180–$275 double. Rates include breakfast buffet. **Amenities:** 2 restaurants; 2 bars; 3 outdoor pools; free Wi-Fi.

Sueño del Mar ★★ This intimate bed-and-breakfast has built a loyal following and gained plenty of local fame with its well-designed rooms, personalized service, gorgeous sunsets, and spectacular breakfasts. A quiet setting on Playa Langosta doesn't hurt, either. The second-floor Luna Suite is the prime room in the house and is worth the splurge if it's available. The standard rooms feature cute open-air showers with small gardens and plantings providing privacy.

Playa Langosta, Guanacaste. © **2653-0284.** www.sueno-del-mar.com. 4 units, 2 casitas. $155–$240 double; $185–$340 suite or casita. Rates include full breakfast. No children 11 and under. **Amenities:** Small outdoor pool; free use of snorkel equipment and boogie boards; free Wi-Fi.

Villa Alegre ★ In a converted home bordering a small private reserve, this intimate bed-and-breakfast is an excellent, friendly option. The rooms and small villas are all cozy and each is decorated in a distinct country theme. The villas feature small kitchenettes and private balconies. The Mexico room, with its large outdoor shower is my favorite option, and considered their top honeymoon choice. Copious and varied breakfasts are served family-style on a shaded patio, and the personable owners, Barry and Suzye Lawson are usually part of the party. A short path leads to a lookout point and rugged wooden bench set on a small bluff over Playa Langosta, just a few steps above the beach and one of the best sunset spots in the area.

Playa Langosta, Guanacaste. © **2653-0270.** www.villaalegrecostarica.com. 5 units, 2 villas. $150–$185 double; $195–$230 villa. Rates include breakfast. **Amenities:** Midsize outdoor pool; free Wi-Fi.

MODERATE

In addition to the places listed here, **Hotel Pueblo Dorado** (© 2653-0008; www.pueblodorado.com) is a well-located option just across from the beach, while tennis lovers (and anyone else) might want to check out the **15 Love Bed & Breakfast** (© 2653-0898; www.15lovebedandbreakfast.com), attached to the Tamarindo Tennis Club (p. 243).

Hotel Arco Iris ★★   Set about 300m (100 ft.) inland from the beach, this small complex of rooms and bungalows sits in shady grounds. It's worth a small splurge for the larger deluxe rooms. The American owner Richard is frequently on hand and makes sure everything is in great shape. There's a small pool, and the restaurant here, **Season's By Shlomy** (see below), is excellent.

Playa Tamarindo, Guanacaste. ✆ **2653-0330.** www.hotelarcoiris.com. 13 units. $99–$170 double. Rates include breakfast. **Amenities:** Restaurant; bar; small outdoor pool; free Wi-Fi.

Hotel Pasatiempo ★★   This lovely small resort, located a few blocks inland from the water, offers rooms that are spacious and well maintained, with cool tile floors and a relaxed, tropical decor. The central pool is quite inviting, featuring a broad deck area all around it, with tall shade trees. The hotel's bar and restaurant is one of the livelier spots in town. Wednesday nights are especially fun with an open mic.

Playa Tamarindo, Guanacaste. ✆ **2653-0096.** www.hotelpasatiempo.com. 18 units. $89–$99 double; $129–$169 suite. Rates include continental breakfast. **Amenities:** Restaurant; bar; pool; free Wi-Fi.

INEXPENSIVE

In addition to the hotels listed below, **Hostel La Botella de Leche** ★ (✆ **2653-0189;** www.labotelladeleche.com) bills itself as a "5 star" hostel and is a popular backpacker option. The beachfront **Witch's Rock Surf Camp** ★ (✆ **888/318-7873** in the U.S. and Canada, or 2653-1238 in Costa Rica; www. witchsrocksurfcamp.com) caters to young, budget-minded surfers.

Cabinas Marielos ★   This longstanding, family-run budget hotel is located right across from the beach near the entrance to town. Owner Maria de los Angeles ("Marielos") Gonzalez and her children run a tight ship. Rooms come either with fans or air-conditioning. A few even have kitchenettes. The best rooms here are the second-floor units with private balconies. Although right near the center of all the action and just steps from the sand, the gardens and grounds here create a quiet oasis amid all the tumult of Tamarindo.

Playa Tamarindo, Guanacaste. ✆ **2653-0141** or 2653-0954. www.cabinasmarieloscr.com. 24 units. $40–$65 double. Rates include taxes. **Amenities:** Surfboard rentals.

Hotel Zully Mar ★   With an enviable location on a prominent corner right in the heart of Tamarindo, this family-run operation delivers clean, cozy rooms at great prices. It's worth the small splurge for a room with air-conditioning and television. You can enjoy a small, free-form pool for cooling off, but the beach is literally just steps away, across the street. Still, be forewarned, this hotel is located right on the busiest corner of Tamarindo, so this is not a good choice for those seeking a quiet getaway or a peaceful retreat.

Playa Tamarindo, Guanacaste. ✆ **2653-0140.** www.zullymar.com. 22 units. $46–$69 double. **Amenities:** Small outdoor pool, free Wi-Fi.

Where to Dine

Tamarindo has a glut of excellent restaurants. **El Coconut** ★ (✆ **2653-0086;** www.elcoconut-tamarindo.com), right on the main road into town, is a longstanding option, with a wide-ranging menu, specializing in fresh seafood, with a European-influenced flair.

Nogui's Café ★ (✆ **2653-0029;** http://noguistamarindo.com) is one of the more popular places in town—and rightly so. This simple open-air cafe just off the beach on the small traffic circle serves hearty breakfasts and well-prepared salads, sandwiches, burgers, and casual meals. They even have a few tables and chairs on the beach, in front of the main restaurant.

Wok N Roll ★ (© 2653-0156), a half-block inland from Zully Mar along the road that leads to Playa Langosta, is a lively, open-air affair, with a big menu of healthy, fresh Asian cuisine. For pizzas, I recommend La Baula ★ (© 2653-1450), a delightful open-air place, on the road to Dragonfly (see below), and for Mexican fare and good breakfast burritos, try Green Papaya Taco Bar (© 2653-0863), just across the street. If you want sushi, head to the Bamboo Sushi Club ★ (© 2653-4519), on the main road, near the turnoff for Langosta. And, for good steaks and Argentinean fare, try Patagonia (© 2653-0612), located right across from the Tamarindo Diria Hotel.

Finally, if you're staying in a condo, or just too lazy to head out for a meal, Tico To Go (© 800/8426-8646; http://ticotogo.com) offers up delivery service from a wide range of local restaurants, with both phone and online ordering possibilities.

Carlos & Carlos ★ ITALIAN   This place is the sister to a Chicago area staple that has been in Costa Rica for a few years, but only moved from its Playa Flamingo location to Tamarindo in late 2013. The menu is heavy on Northern Italian pastas and main dishes, but also shows some Spanish and Mediterranean influences as well. The black Angel Hair pasta with shrimp and lobster is one of the most popular items on the menu, as is the fresh mahi-mahi. For meat lovers, the veal with porcini mushrooms is excellent. And for dessert try their take on the local favorite Tres Leches ("Three Milks"), a sweet cake soaked in plain milk, condensed milk and caramelized *dulce de leche*. The restaurant is one of the few enclosed and air-conditioned options in town.

On the road to Playa Langosta. © **2653-0862.** Reservations recommended during the high season. Main courses $14–$28. Mon–Sat 5–10pm.

Dragonfly Bar & Grill ★★ INTERNATIONAL/FUSION   Set down a back street a little bit away from the action, this open-air restaurant has a casual chic vibe. The menu features spices and flavors from around the world with prominent influences from the Pacific Rim and southwestern United States. The thick-cut pork loin comes crusted in panko and served with a brandy-Dijon cream sauce. Portions are large. The bar serves up good contemporary cocktails, and there's occasionally live music.

Down a dirt road behind the Hotel Pasatiempo. © **2653-1506.** www.dragonflybarandgrill.com. Reservations recommended. Main courses C6,000–C11,200. Mon–Sat 6–9:30pm.

Pangas Beach Club ★★★ SEAFOOD/INTERNATIONAL   Chef Jean-Luc Taulere had a very successful run at Mar y Sol in Playa Flamingo, but real estate issues forced him to close up shop there—much to the betterment of the dining scene in Tamarindo. Located on the main road near the northern end of town, this place lets out on to the beach, right about where the ocean meets the estuary. Heavy wooden tables are spread on hard-packed sand under tall coconut trees, which are strung with simple lights to give this place a tropically romantic feel by night. While fresh seafood is the specialty here, folks love the steak tenderloin served on a hot volcanic stone to be cooked at the table. Breakfast and lunch are also served.

On the waterfront, north end of Tamarindo. © **2653-0024.** Reservations recommended. Main courses C8,000–C14,000. Daily 8am–10pm.

Pretty Pots

The lack of any longstanding local arts and crafts tradition across Costa Rica is often lamented. One of the outstanding exceptions to this rule is the small village of Guaitíl, located on the outskirts of the provincial capital of Santa Cruz. The small central plaza—actually a soccer field—of this village is ringed with craft shops and artisan stands selling a wide range of ceramic wares. Most are low-fired relatively soft clay pieces, with traditional Chorotega indigenous design motifs. All of the local tour agencies offer day trips to Guaitíl, or you can drive there yourself, by heading first to Santa Cruz, and then taking the well-marked turnoff for Guaitíl, just south of the city, on the road to Nicoya.

Season's by Shlomy ★★ INTERNATIONAL   Cordon Bleu–trained chef and owner Shlomy Koren began his time in Tamarindo at Pachangas. But for the past 5 years or so he's been serving up his tasty Mediterranean-inspired cuisine out of a small kitchen at the Hotel Arco Iris (p. 246). I recommend pretty much anything and everything on the menu, but find myself going back for the rice-paper-wrapped red snapper with a sun-dried-tomato tapenade and lemon-chili sauce. Still, it's hard to get too attached to any one dish, as the menu changes regularly, with new specials and seasonal variations.

Inside the Hotel Arco Iris. ✆ **8368-6983.** www.seasonstamarindo.com. Reservations recommended. Main courses $18–$19. No credit cards. Mon–Sat 6–10pm.

Shopping

Tamarindo's main boulevard is awash in souvenir stands, art galleries, jewelry stores, and clothing boutiques. For original beachwear and jewelry, try **Azul Profundo** ★ (✆ **2653-0395**), in the Plaza Tamarindo shopping center. The modern **Garden Plaza** shopping center, near the entrance to town, has several high-end shops, as well as a massive **Automercado** (supermarket).

Entertainment & Nightlife

As a popular surfer destination, Tamarindo has a sometimes raging nightlife. The most happening bars in town are **Bar 1** ★★ (✆ **2653-2686**) and **El Garito** ★★ (✆ **2653-2017**), both housed in the same building about a block inland, on the road leading toward Playa Langosta, and **Aqua** ★ (✆ **2653-2782**), on the main road through town. Other popular spots throughout the week include the **Crazy Monkey Bar** at the Best Western Tamarindo Vista Villas (✆ **2653-0114**), and the **Dragonfly Bar & Grill** (p. 247). For a chill-out dance scene, try the **Voodoo Lounge** (✆ **2653-0100**), while those looking for a rocking sports bar can head to **Sharky's** (✆ **8918-4968**). These latter two places are just across from each other, a little up the road that heads to Playa Langosta.

The best casino in town is at the **Barceló Playa Langosta** (✆ **2653-0363**) resort down in Playa Langosta.

En Route South: Playa Avellanas & Playa Negra

Heading south from Tamarindo are several as-yet-undeveloped beaches, most of which are quite popular with surfers. Beyond Tamarindo and Playa Langosta are **Playa Avellanas** and **Playa Negra,** both with a few basic surfer cabinas, and

8

GUANACASTE | Playa Tamarindo & Playa Langosta

248

little else. To locate the hotels and restaurants listed below, see the map "Around Tamarindo," on p. 241.

WHERE TO STAY

The **Mono Congo Lodge** (© 2652-9261; www.monocongolodge.com), just outside of Playa Negra, is a rustically plush option in a lush, forested setting a few hundred yards from the water.

About a 15- to 20-minute drive inland is **Los Altos de Eros** ★ (© 8850-4222; www.losaltosdeeros.com), a small, adults-only, luxury hotel and spa.

In addition to the JW Marriott (see below), the large golf, residential, and vacation resort complex of **Hacienda Pinilla** (© 2681-4318; www.haciendapinilla.com) features a couple of small hotels and condo rental units.

Very Expensive

JW Marriott Guanacaste Resort & Spa ★★★ This beautifully designed large resort is built around a massive pool and fronts a gorgeous—but decidedly small and rocky—patch of white sand beach. The rooms are cozy and well equipped, and all come with a large balcony or patio. Some of the patios, however, open on to heavily trafficked walkways. The best rooms have ocean and sunset views. The hotel runs a regular shuttle to nearby Playa Langosta, where guests have access to a small beach club, with a pool, showers, bathrooms, restaurant, and bar.

Hacienda Pinilla, Guanacaste. © **888/236-2427** in the U.S. and Canada, or 2681-2000. www.marriott.com. 310 units. $250–$830 double; $400 and up suite. **Amenities:** 4 restaurants; 3 bars; lounge; babysitting; children's programs; concierge; championship 18-hole golf course nearby; large, modern health club and spa; massive free-form outdoor pool; room service; smoke-free rooms; tennis courts nearby; watersports equipment; Wi-Fi for a fee.

Moderate

In addition to the places listed below, **Villa Deevena** (© 2653-2328; www.villadeevena.com) offers up six cool, comfortable and well-appointed rooms in a quiet setting, a few hundred yards from the beach at Playa Negra.

Cabinas Las Olas This is the only hotel in Playa Avellanas with direct beach access. This place definitely caters to surfers as a range of excellent beach breaks stretch up and down a white sand beach in each direction. However, the five duplex buildings that house the rooms are actually located a hundred yards or so inland under tall native trees and reached via a raised walkway through a mangrove reserve. The rooms themselves are fairly plain and basic, but they are very spacious, and feature a private little veranda with hammock that is perfect for an afternoon siesta.

Playa Avellanas, Guanacaste. © **2652-9315.** www.cabinaslasolas.co.cr. 10 units. $90–$110 double. **Amenities:** Restaurant; bar; bike rentals; limited watersports equipment rentals; free Wi-Fi.

Hotel Playa Negra This small collection of thatch-roofed concrete bungalows is just steps away from Playa Negra, a legendary right-handed point break that was made famous in the surf film classic "Endless Summer II." As with Cabinas Las Olas (above), this place caters to surfers, and the rooms and services offered are rather spartan. Most of the beds are built-in concrete affairs, although the mattresses are firm and comfortable. The wave here is particularly good for experienced surfers, and the take-off point can get crowded at times. The tables at the simple restaurant and bar have prime views of the wave and action.

Playa Negra, Guanacaste. © **2652-9134.** www.playanegra.com. 17 units. $90–$100 bungalow; $120–$155 bungalow suite. Rates higher during peak periods. **Amenities:** Restaurant; bar; midsize outdoor pool; Wi-Fi.

WHERE TO DINE

In addition to the place listed below, the restaurants inside the **JW Marriott** resort (p. 249) are excellent, and open to the general public, while the restaurant at **Villa Deevena** (see above), in Playa Negra, is also excellent.

Lola's ★★★ INTERNATIONAL/SEAFOOD   This quintessential beach bar and restaurant sits on a patch of land and sand fronting the quiet and underdeveloped Playa Avellanas beach. The Belgian and American owners serve up solid, healthful, fresh food on homemade heavy wooden tables and chairs underneath the shade of palm trees and large linen umbrellas. The fresh, seared tuna can come as a sandwich on thick, freshly baked focaccia, or on top of a large salad. This place is extremely popular, especially on weekends, so be prepared to wait occasionally for food or a table (sorry, no reservations). When you're finished, and if you're really lucky, you might snag a siesta in one of the hammocks strung between the many coconut palms.

On the beach, Playa Avellanas. © **2652-9097.** Main courses C3,900–C7,500. No credit cards. Tues–Sun 8am–sunset.

PLAYA JUNQUILLAL ★

30km (19 miles) W of Santa Cruz; 20km (12 miles) S of Tamarindo

A long, windswept beach that, for most of its length, is backed by grasslands, Playa Junquillal remains a mostly undiscovered gem on an increasingly crowded coast. With no village to speak of here and a rough road, this is a good place to get away from it all and enjoy some unfettered time on a nearly deserted beach. The long stretch of white sand is great for strolling, and the sunsets are superb. When the waves are big, this beach is great for surfing, but can be a little dangerous for swimming. When it's calm, jump right in.

Essentials

GETTING THERE & DEPARTING   By Plane: The nearest airport with regularly scheduled flights is in Tamarindo (p. 238). You can arrange a taxi from the airport to Playa Junquillal. The ride should take around 40 minutes and cost about $50 to $70.

By Car: From San José, you can either take the Interamerican Highway (CR1) north from downtown San José, or first head west out of the city on the San José–Caldera Highway (CR27). This latter route is a faster and flatter drive. When you reach Caldera on this route, follow the signs to Puntarenas, Liberia, and the Interamerican Highway (CR1). This will lead you to the unmarked entrance to CR1. You'll want to pass under the bridge and follow the on-ramp, which will put you on the highway heading north. Forty-seven kilometers (29 miles) past the Puntarenas on-ramp, you'll see signs and the turnoff for the La Amistad Bridge. After crossing the river, follow the signs for Nicoya and Santa Cruz. Just after leaving the main intersection for Santa Cruz, you'll see a marked turnoff for Playa Junquillal, Ostional, and Tamarindo. The road is paved for 14km (8½ miles), until the tiny village of Veintesiete de Abril. From here, it's another rough 18km (11 miles) to Playa Junquillal.

Playa Junquillal.

From Liberia, head south to Santa Cruz on the main road to all the beach towns, passing through Filadelfia and Belén. Then follow the directions above from Santa Cruz.

By Bus: To get here by bus, you must first head to Santa Cruz and, from there, take another bus to Playa Junquillal. Buses depart San José for Santa Cruz roughly every 2 hours between 6am and 6pm from the **Tralapa** bus station (© **2221-7202**) at Calle 20 between avenidas 3 and 5, and from the **Alfaro** bus station (©**2222-2750**) at Calle 14 between avenidas 3 and 5. The 4-hour trip is C5,300.

Buses leave Santa Cruz for Junquillal about 6 times daily, roughly every 2 hours between 5am and 6pm from the town's central plaza. The ride takes about 1 hour, and the one-way fare is C1,100. Buses depart Playa Junquillal for Santa Cruz daily pretty much just after they arrive.

Always check with your hotel in advance as the schedule of buses between Junquillal and Santa Cruz is notoriously fickle. If you miss the connection, or there's no bus running, you can hire a taxi for the trip to Junquillal for $30 to $50. From Tamarindo, a taxi should cost $50 to $70.

Exploring Playa Junquillal

Other than walking on the beach, surfing, swimming when the surf isn't too strong, and exploring tide pools, there isn't much to do here—which is just fine with me. This beach is ideal for anyone who wants to relax without any distractions. Bring a few good books. If you have a car, you can explore the coastline just north and south of here.

Junquillal is a nesting site for both olive ridley and leatherback turtles, although conservation efforts and organized turtle watching tours are both in their infancy here.

For surfers, the Junquillal beach break is often pretty good. I've also heard that if you look hard enough, a few hidden reef and point breaks are around. However, be careful here, as the beach and rip currents are often a bit rough for casual swimming.

Several sportfishing boats operate out of Playa Junquillal. Inquire at your hotel or ask at the Iguanazul Hotel. To rent a mountain bike, you can also check in at the Iguanazul. If you want to ride a horse on the beach, call **Paradise Riding** (© **2658-8162;** www.paradiseriding.com). The cost is $55 per person for a 2-hour ride and $65 per person for a 3-hour ride.

Where to Stay & Dine

In addition to two hotels mentioned below, **Hotel & Pizzería Tatanka** (☎ 866/498-0824 in the U.S. and Canada, or 2658-8426 in Costa Rica; www.hotel tatanka.com), offers up well done rooms at very reasonable rates, as well as excellent wood-oven pizzas and fresh seafood. It's near the Iguanazul Hotel on your left as you come into Junquillal, and also has good ocean and sunset views.

INEXPENSIVE

In addition to the hotel listed below, **Camping Los Malinches** (☎ 2658-8429) has wonderful campsites on fluffy grass amid manicured gardens set on a bluff above the beach. Camping costs C3,500 per person, and includes restroom and shower privileges. You'll see a sign on the right as you drive toward Playa Junquillal, a little bit beyond the Iguanazul Hotel. The campground is about 1km ($^1/_2$ mile) down this dirt road. These folks also have some simple, rustic rooms.

Iguanazul Hotel   This intimate and isolated hotel has always had one of my favorite settings, on a high, flat bluff and steep grassy cliff overlooking the Pacific Ocean at the north end of Playa Junquillal. The pretty, free-form pool is surrounded by tall palm trees. They've thankfully abandoned their short transformation into an all-inclusive resort. Unfortunately, the rooms are very spartan and the whole operation is in need of a major overhaul. Still, you can't beat the views, especially around sunset, and everything here is fairly priced.

Playa Junquillal, Guanacaste. ☎ **2658-8123.** www.iguanazul.com. 24 units. $60–$120 double. Rates include breakfast. **Amenities:** Restaurant; bar; outdoor pool; small spa; free Wi-Fi.

Hotel Hibiscus   This longstanding, German-owned hotel is located just a few hundred feet or so from the beach at Playa Junquillal. The shady grounds, lush gardens and cozy rooms are all immaculately maintained. The rooms themselves feature bright white walls and polished red-tile floors. The good restaurant offers a range of international and local fare.

Playa Junquillal, Guanacaste. ☎ **2658-8437.** www.hibiscus-info.com. 5 units. $40–$60 double. Rates include taxes. **Amenities:** Restaurant.

9

PUNTARENAS
& THE NICOYA
PENINSULA

The beaches of the Nicoya Peninsula don't get nearly as much attention or traffic as those to the north in Guanacaste. However, they are just as stunning, varied, and rewarding. Montezuma, with its jungle waterfalls and gentle surf, is the original beach destination out this way. However, it's eclipsed by the up-and-coming hot spots of Malpaís and Santa Teresa.

Farther up the peninsula lie the beaches of **Playa Sámara** and **Playa Nosara.** With easy access via paved roads and the time-saving La Amistad Bridge, Playa Sámara is one of the coastline's more popular destinations, especially with Ticos looking for a quick and easy weekend getaway. Just north of Sámara, Nosara and its neighboring beaches remain remote and sparsely visited, thanks in large part to the horrendous dirt road that separates these distinctly different destinations. However, Nosara is widely known and coveted as one of the country's top **surf spots,** with a host of different beach and point breaks from which to choose.

Nearby **Puntarenas** was once Costa Rica's principal Pacific port. The town bustled and hummed with commerce, fishermen, coffee brokers, and a weekend rush of urban dwellers enjoying some sun and fun at one of the closest beaches to San José. Today, Puntarenas is a run-down shell of its former self. Still, it remains a major fishing port, and the main gateway to the isolated and coveted beaches of the Nicoya Peninsula.

THE BEST PUNTARENAS & THE NICOYA PENINSULA TRAVEL EXPERIENCES

o **Taking a Dip in the Pool at the Foot of Montezuma Waterfall:** Nestled in thick forest, the **Montezuma waterfall** features a large, deep, and cool pool at its base—perfect for swimming. The hike in is pretty awesome as well. See p. 267.

o **Getting Your Yoga on:** The Nicoya Peninsula is home to several of the country's top yoga retreat centers. **Pranamar Villas & Yoga Retreat** (p. 276) in Santa Teresa, **Anamaya Resort** (p. 269) in Montezuma, and the **Nosara Yoga Institute** (p. 290) are all top-notch choices. See below for even more options.

o **Having Playa Barrigona (Almost) to Yourself:** Access is a bit rough, especially in the rainy season, but if you're feeling adventurous, head to Playa Barrigona, a largely undiscovered gem of white sand and clear waters. You'll probably need local help in finding the unmarked entrance, but it's worth it. See p. 282.

PREVIOUS PAGE: **Curú Wildlife Refuge.**

- **Going Deep (Underground) at Barra Honda:** Strap on a headlamp and some climbing gear and descend into the underworld at **Barra Honda National Park.** After exploring the nooks and crannies of Terciopelo Cave, take a refreshing dip in La Cascada. See p. 283.

- **Mingling with the Hip & Famous in Malpaís & Santa Teresa:** Arguably the most happening of Costa Rica's beach hot spots, **Malpaís and Santa Teresa** are the country's best destinations for

Top Sustainable Hotels
Cristal Azul (p. 279)
Florblanca Resort (p. 276)
The Harmony Hotel & Spa (p. 290)
Hotel Punta Islita (p. 285)
Lagarta Lodge (p. 291)
Pranamar Villas & Yoga Retreat (p. 276)
Ylang Ylang Beach Resort (p. 255)

celebrity sightings. Even if you don't bump into Leo DiCaprio, Flea, or Tom & Giselle, you can wander the miles of nearly deserted beaches and enjoy the beautiful sunsets. See p. 273.

PUNTARENAS

115km (71 miles) W of San José; 191km (118 miles) S of Liberia; 75km (47 miles) N of Playa de Jacó

They say you can't put lipstick on a pig, and this has proven true for Puntarenas. Despite serious investment and the steady influx of cruise ship passengers, Puntarenas can't seem to shed its image as a rough-and-tumble, perennially run-down port town. While the seafront **Paseo de los Turistas (Tourist Walk)** has a string of restaurants and souvenir stands, this town has little to interest visitors, and the beach here pales in comparison to almost any other beach destination in the country.

Puntarenas's Catholic church.

A 16km (10-mile) spit of land jutting into the Gulf of Nicoya, Puntarenas was once Costa Rica's busiest port, but that changed drastically when the government inaugurated nearby Puerto Caldera, a modern container port facility. After losing its shipping business, the city has survived primarily on commercial fishing.

You can reach Puntarenas (on a good day, with little traffic) in little more than an hour by car from San José, which makes it one of the closest beaches to the capital. A long, straight stretch of sand with gentle surf, the beach is backed for most of its length by the Paseo de los Turistas. Across a wide boulevard from the Paseo de los Turistas are hotels, restaurants, bars, discos, and shops. The sunsets and the views across the Gulf of Nicoya are quite beautiful, and a cooling breeze usually blows in off the water. All around town, you'll find unusual old buildings, reminders of the important role that Puntarenas once played in Costa Rican history. It was from here that much of the Central Valley's coffee crop was once shipped, and while the coffee barons in the highlands were getting rich, so were the merchants of Puntarenas.

Puntarenas is primarily popular as a weekend holiday spot for Ticos from San José and is liveliest on weekends. Puntarenas is also where you must pick up the ferries to the southern Nicoya Peninsula, and some folks like to arrive the night before and get an early start.

Essentials

GETTING THERE & DEPARTING   By Car: Head west out of San José on the San José–Caldera Highway (CR27). When you reach Caldera, follow the signs to Puntarenas. The drive takes a little over 1 hour. To reach Puntarenas from Liberia, just take the Interamerican Highway south, to the well-marked exit for Puntarenas.

By Bus: Empresarios de Unidos Puntarenas express buses (✆ **2222-0064** or 2261-3138) leave San José daily every hour between 6am and 7pm from Calle 16 and Avenida 12. The trip duration is 2 hours; the fare is C2,540. Buses to San José leave the main station daily every hour between 6am and 7pm.

The main Puntarenas bus station is cater-cornered to the main pier on the Paseo de los Turistas. Buses to Quepos and Manuel Antonio (✆ **2777-0743**) leave the main station daily at 5, 8, and 11am and 12:30, 2:30, and 4:30pm. The trip's duration is 1 hour; the fare is C1,250. There are also about three daily buses between Puntarenas and Monteverde and Santa Elena.

By Ferry: See "Playa Tambor" or "Playa Montezuma," below, for information on crossing to and returning from Puntarenas from Paquera or Naranjo on the Nicoya Peninsula.

GETTING AROUND   If you need a taxi, call **Coopetico** (✆ **2663-2020**).

CITY LAYOUT   Puntarenas is built on a long, narrow sand spit that stretches 16km (10 miles) out into the Gulf of Nicoya and is marked by only five streets at

---

A Colorful Festival

If you're in Puntarenas on the Saturday closest to July 16, you can witness the **Fiesta del Virgen del Mar (Fiesta of the Virgin of the Sea).** During this festival, a regatta of colorfully decorated boats carries a statue of Puntarenas's patron saint. Boats run all along the waterfront, but the Paseo de los Turistas makes for a good place to catch the port town pageantry.

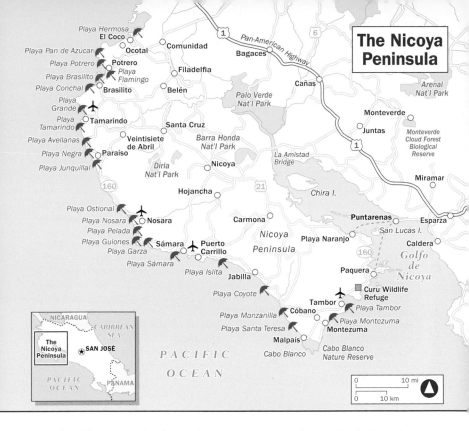

The Nicoya Peninsula

Playa Hermosa
El Coco
Playa Pan de Azúcar
Ocotal
Comunidad
Bagaces
Pan-American Highway
Cañas
Arenal Nat'l Park
Playa Potrero
Potrero
Playa Brasilito
Playa Flamingo
Filadelfia
Playa Conchal
Brasilito
Belén
Palo Verde Nat'l Park
Monteverde
Juntas
Monteverde Cloud Forest Biological Reserve
Playa Grande
Playa Tamarindo
Tamarindo
Santa Cruz
Playa Avellanas
Veintisiete de Abril
Barra Honda Nat'l Park
La Amistad Bridge
Playa Negra
Paraíso
Diria Nat'l Park
Nicoya
Miramar
Playa Junquillal
160
Hojancha
21
Chira I.
Playa Ostional
Playa Nosara
Nosara
Carmona
Puntarenas
Esparza
San Lucas I.
Playa Pelada
Nicoya
Playa Naranjo
Caldera
Playa Guiones
Sámara
Puerto Carrillo
Peninsula
160
Golfo de Nicoya
Playa Garza
Playa Sámara
Paquera
Playa Islita
Jabilla
Curú Wildlife Refuge
Playa Coyote
Tambor
Playa Tambor
Playa Manzanilla
Cóbano
Playa Montezuma
Playa Santa Teresa
Montezuma
Malpaís
Cabo Blanco
Cabo Blanco
Cabo Blanco Nature Reserve

NICARAGUA
CARIBBEAN SEA
The Nicoya Peninsula
SAN JOSÉ
PACIFIC OCEAN
PANAMA

PACIFIC OCEAN

0   10 mi
0   10 km

its widest. The north side of town faces an estuary, and the south side faces the mouth of the gulf. The Paseo de los Turistas is on the south side of town, beginning at the pier and extending out to the point. The ferry docks for the Nicoya Peninsula are near the far end of town, as are the bus station and market.

FAST FACTS Several banks, Internet cafes, and general markets are all within a 2-block radius of the town's small church and central park. The town's main post office can be found here as well.

The **Hospital Monseñor Sanabria** (© 2663-0033), on the outskirts of downtown, is the largest and best equipped hospital in this region. However, it was severely damaged in a 2013 earthquake, and reparations are slow going. Still, the hospital is up and running.

Exploring Puntarenas

Take a walk along the **Paseo de los Turistas,** which feels a bit like a Florida beach town out of the 1950s. The hotels here range in style from converted old wooden homes with bright gingerbread trim to modern concrete monstrosities to tasteful Art Deco relics that need a new coat of paint.

If you venture into the center of the city, be sure to check out the **central plaza around the Catholic church.** The large, stone church itself is interesting because it has portholes for windows, reflecting the city's maritime tradition. In addition, it's one of the few churches in the country with a front entry facing east (most face west). Here you'll also find the city's cultural center, **La Casa de la Cultura** (© **2661-1394**). In addition to rotating exhibits and the occasional theater performance or poetry reading, this place houses the **Museo Histórico** (© **2661-1394**), a small museum on the city's history, especially its maritime history, with exhibits in both English and Spanish. Admission is free, and it's open Monday to Saturday from 8am to 4pm. If you're looking for a shady spot to take a break, some inviting benches are in a little park off the north side of the church.

The largest attraction in town is the **Parque Marino del Pacífico** (**Pacific Marine Park;** © **2661-5272;** www.parquemarino.org), a collection of saltwater aquariums highlighting the sea life of Costa Rica. Of the 23 separate tanks, the largest re-creates the undersea environment of Isla del Coco. Still, this park has a neglected and run-down feel to it. It's 2 blocks east of the main cruise ship terminal and is open Tuesday through Sunday from 9am to 4:30pm. Admission is $10 for adults and $5 for children 11 and under.

If you want to go swimming, the gulf waters in front of Puntarenas are perfectly safe (pollution had been a problem for many years), although the beach is still not very attractive. Some folks choose to head a few kilometers south of town, to **Playa Doña Aña,** a popular local beach with picnic tables, roadside vendors, and a couple of *sodas* (diners). If you head a little farther south, you will come to **Playa Tivives,** which is virtually unvisited by tourists, but quite popular with Ticos, many of whom have beach houses up and down this long, brown-sand beach. Surfers can check out the beach break here or head to the mouth of the Barranca River, which boasts an amazingly long left break. Still, surfers and swimmers should be careful; crocodiles live in both the Barranca and Tivives river mouths, and I'd be wary of pollution in the waters emptying out of the rivers here.

If you don't want to swim in the gulf and your hotel doesn't have a pool, or you simply want to mix with some locals, head to the **San Lucas Beach Club** (© **2661-3881;** www.sanlucasbeachclub.com). This misleadingly named local attraction is actually a landlocked recreation complex with a large free-form pool, small snack bar, and some conference rooms used for corporate incentive activities. At the end of the peninsula, with a view of the gulf, it is open Thursday through Sunday from 9am until 5pm. Admission is C4,000.

Puntarenas isn't known as one of Costa Rica's prime sportfishing ports, but a few charter boats are usually available. Check at your hotel or head to the docks and ask around. Rates (for up to six people) are usually between $400 and $600 for a half-day and between $800 and $1,800 for a full day.

You can also take a yacht cruise through the tiny, uninhabited islands of the Guayabo, Negritos, and Pájaros Islands Biological Reserve. These cruises include a lunch buffet and a relaxing stop on beautiful and undeveloped **Tortuga Island ★,** where you can swim, snorkel, and sunbathe. The water is clear blue, and the sand is bright white. However, this trip has surged in popularity, and many of the tours have a cattle-car feel. Several San José–based companies offer these excursions, with round-trip transportation from San José, but if you're already in Puntarenas, you might receive a slight discount by boarding here.

Calypso Tours ★ (© **855/855-1975** in the U.S. and Canada, or 2256-2727 in Costa Rica; www.calypsocruises.com) is the most reputable company that cruises out of Puntarenas. In addition to **Tortuga Island** trips, Calypso Tours takes folks to its own private nature reserve at **Punta Coral** and even on a sunset cruise that includes dinner and some guided stargazing. Either cruise will run you $139 per person. These prices are the same whether you join them in

DIVING TRIPS TO isla del coco (COCOS ISLAND)

This little speck of land located some 480km (300 miles) off the Pacific coast was a prime pirate hide-out and refueling station. Robert Louis Stevenson most likely modeled "Treasure Island" on Cocos. Sir Francis Drake, Captain Edward Davis, William Dampier, and Mary Welch are just some of the famous corsairs who dropped anchor in the calm harbors of this Pacific pearl. They allegedly left troves of buried loot, although scores of treasure hunters over several centuries have failed to unearth more than a smattering of the purported bounty. The Costa Rican flag was first raised here on September 15, 1869. Throughout its history, Isla del Coco has provided anchorage and fresh water to hundreds of ships and has entertained divers and dignitaries. (Franklin Delano Roosevelt visited it three times.) In 1978 it was declared a national park and protected area.

The clear, warm waters around Cocos are widely regarded as one of the most rewarding **dive destinations** ★★★ on the planet. This is a prime place to see schooling herds of scalloped hammerhead sharks. On my shallow-water checkout dive—normally, a perfunctory and uninspiring affair—I spotted my first hammerhead lurking just 4.5m (15 ft.) below me within 15 seconds after flipping into the water. Soon there were more, and soon they came much, much closer.

Other denizens of the waters around Isla del Coco include white- and silver-tipped reef sharks; marbled, manta, eagle, and mobula rays; moray and spotted eels; octopi; spiny and slipper lobsters; hawksbill turtles; squirrel fish, trigger fish, and angelfish; surgeon fish, trumpet fish, grouper, grunts, snapper, jack, and tangs; and more. Two of the more spectacular underwater residents here include the red-lipped batfish and the frogfish.

Most diving at Cocos is relatively deep (26–35m/85–115 ft.), often with strong currents and choppy swells to deal with—not to mention all those sharks. This is not a trip for novice divers.

The perimeter of Isla del Coco is ringed by steep, forested cliffs punctuated by dozens of majestic waterfalls cascading down in stages or steady streams for hundreds of feet. The island itself has a series of trails that climb its steep hills and wind through its rainforested interior. Several endemic bird, reptile, and plant species here include the ubiquitous Cocos finch, which I spotted soon after landing onshore, and the wild Isla del Coco pig.

With just a small ranger station housing a handful of national park guards, Isla del Coco is essentially uninhabited. Visitors these days come on private or charter yachts, fishing boats, or one of the few live-aboard dive vessels that make regular voyages out here. It's a long trip: Most dive vessels take 30 to 36 hours to reach Cocos. Sailboats are even slower.

Both **Aggressor Fleet Limited** (☏ **800/348-2628;** www.aggressor.com) and **Undersea Hunter** (☏ **800/203-2120** in the U.S., or 2228-6613 in Costa Rica; www.underseahunter.com) regularly run dive trips to Isla del Coco from Puntarenas.

San José or Puntarenas. These folks provide daily pickups from San José, Manuel Antonio, Jacó, and Monteverde, and you can use the day trip on the boat as your transfer or transportation option between any of these towns and destinations.

If you ask around at the docks, you might find some other boats that ply the waters of the Nicoya Gulf. Some of these companies also offer sunset cruises with live music, snacks, and a bar.

Where to Stay

In addition to the places mentioned below, the **Double Tree Resort by Hilton Puntarenas** (✆ **800/445-8667** in the U.S. and Canada, or 2663-0808 in Costa Rica; www.puntarenas.doubletree.com) is an all-inclusive resort set on a decidedly unspectacular patch of sand, just south of the Puntarenas peninsula. While the accommodations and service are certainly acceptable, it's still not a top beach resort pick in my book.

MODERATE

Apartotel Alamar ★   This is probably the best hotel along the Paseo de los Turistas and my top choice for an overnight in Puntarenas. They offer a mix of standard hotel rooms, as well as one- and two-bedroom condo-style units with full kitchens. The hotel is located out toward the western end of the peninsula, directly across the street from the beach, and walking distance to several good restaurants. There's a small, rectangular pool and unheated Jacuzzi that is fed by a concrete waterfall that is usually turned off at the center of the small central courtyard area here.

Paseo de los Turistas, Puntarenas. ✆ **2661-4343.** www.alamarcr.com. 34 units. C72,000–C105,000 double. Rates include buffet breakfast. **Amenities:** Restaurant; bar; Jacuzzi; small outdoor pool; free Wi-Fi.

Hotel Las Brisas   Right next to the Apartotel Alamar, this is another good choice. One of the original hotels catering to the tourism and ferry trade here, this place has been well maintained over the years. There's a touch of a Greek theme to some of the design elements and menu items here, thanks to the owners mix of American and Greek heritage. The rooms are simple, but spacious and comfortable. The hotel has plenty of secure parking, if your waiting for the next day's ferry, as well as a refreshing small pool in the center of the complex.

Paseo de los Turistas, Puntarenas. ✆ **2661-4040.** www.lasbrisashotelcr.com. 25 units. C79,000–C99,000 double. Rates include taxes and breakfast. **Amenities:** Restaurant; bar; small outdoor pool; free Wi-Fi.

INEXPENSIVE

Hotel La Punta   This is easily the best budget option in Puntarenas and one of the closest hotels to the ferry docks. Rooms are cozy and well-kept, as are the grounds and gardens. Rustic wooden beds and red tile floors give the place a hint of colonial era charm. A small kidney-shaped pool with a broad surrounding deck and tall palm trees for shade, offers some cooling respite from the grueling mid-day heat here.

Puntarenas (½ block south of the ferry terminal). ✆ **2661-0696.** www.hotellapunta.net. 8 units. C40,000 double. **Amenities:** Small outdoor pool.

Where to Dine

You're in a seaport, so try some of the local catch. Corvina (sea bass) is the most popular offering, and it's served in various forms and preparations. My favorite dish on a hot afternoon is *ceviche,* and you'll find that just about every restaurant in town serves this savory marinated seafood concoction.

A Frosty Churchill

No one should leave Puntarenas without trying a "Churchill." Sold by scores of vendors out of makeshift carts, food trucks and kiosks all along the Paseo de los Turistas, these concoctions are made from freshly shaved ice smothered with a wide range of toppings. Without fail a Churchill will have some sweet syrup, condensed milk and fruit salad. Some also come with ice cream and some sort of sweet cookie or cracker. Most of the itinerant sellers serve them up in plastic cups, but if you look around, you might find them in large soda fountain style glasses, which I prefer. Dating to at least the 1940s, the local legend claims that the original creator of these refreshing sweet treats bore a striking resemblance to the then British Prime Minister.

The most economical option is to pull up a table at one of the many open-air *sodas* along the Paseo de los Turistas, serving everything from sandwiches, drinks, and ice cream to fish. Sandwiches are priced at around $2, and a fish filet with rice and beans should cost around $4. If you want some seafood in a slightly more formal atmosphere, try the **Jardin Cervecero, Capitan Moreno, Casa de los Mariscos,** or the open-air **Restaurant Aloha,** all located on the Paseo de los Turistas.

La Yunta Steakhouse ★ STEAK/SEAFOOD   This is my go-to restaurant in Puntarenas. Set right on the Paseo de los Turistas and overlooking the beach, this is a simple, open-air restaurant serving up dependable fare. Despite the name, there's probably more seafood than meat on the menu here, and both are good choices. The front patio of this old wooden former residence has been given a terraced affect, with tables and chairs on several levels, and almost all of them offering up a good view of the water.

Paseo de los Turistas. ② **2661-3216.** Reservations recommended in high season and on Fri–Sat. Main courses C3,500–C15,000. Daily 10am–midnight.

PLAYA TAMBOR

150–168km (93–104 miles) W of San José (not including ferry ride); 20km (12 miles) S of Paquera; 38km (24 miles) S of Naranjo

Playa Tambor was the site of Costa Rica's first large-scale all-inclusive resort, the Barceló Playa Tambor Beach Resort. Despite big plans, the resort and surrounding area have never really taken off. Today, Tambor has a forgotten, isolated feel to it.

Part of the blame lies with the beach itself. Playa Tambor is a long, gently curving stretch of beach protected on either end by rocky headlands. These headlands give the waters ample protection from Pacific swells, making this a good beach for swimming. However, the sand is a rather unattractive, dull gray-brown color, which often receives a large amount of flotsam and jetsam brought in by the sea. Playa Tambor pales in comparison to the beaches located farther south along the Nicoya Peninsula.

However, Tambor is the site of the only major commuter airport on the southern Nicoya Peninsula, and you'll be arriving and departing here if you choose to visit Montezuma, Malpaís, or Santa Teresa by air.

Essentials

GETTING THERE & DEPARTING By Plane: Sansa (☎ 877/767-2672 in the U.S. and Canada, or 2290-4100 in Costa Rica; www.flysansa.com) and **Nature Air** (☎ 800/235-9272 in the U.S. and Canada, or 2299-6000 in Costa Rica; www.natureair.com) both have several flights daily to a small airstrip in **Tambor airport** (airport code: TMU; no phone). The flight is about 30 minutes, and fares range from $90 to $110, one-way.

By Car: The traditional route here is to drive to Puntarenas and catch the ferry to either Naranjo or Paquera. Tambor is about 30 minutes south of Paquera and about an hour and 20 minutes south of Naranjo. The road from Paquera to Tambor is paved and taking the Paquera ferry will save you time and some rough, dusty driving.

Playa Tambor.

The road from Naranjo to Paquera is all dirt and gravel and often in very bad shape. For directions on driving to Puntarenas, see p. 256.

Naviera Tambor (☎ 2661-2084; www.navieratambor.com) car ferries to Paquera leave Puntarenas roughly every 2 to 3 hours daily between 9am and 8:30pm, with one early trip at 5am. The trip takes 1½ hours. The fare is C11,400 per car, including the driver; C810 for each additional adult, and C485 for children. I recommend arriving early during the peak season and on weekends because lines can be long; if you miss the ferry, you'll have to wait 2 hours or more for the next one. Moreover, the ferry schedule changes frequently, with fewer ferries during the low season, and the occasional extra ferry added during the high season to meet demand. It's always best to check in advance.

The car ferry from Paquera to Puntarenas leaves roughly every 2 to 3 hours between 6am and 8pm. **Note:** If you have to wait for the ferry, do not leave your car unattended, since break-ins are common.

The **Naranjo ferry** (☎ 2661-1069; www.coonatramar.com) leaves daily at 6:30 and 10am and 2:30 and 7:30pm. The trip takes 1½ hours. Return ferries leave Naranjo for Puntarenas daily at 8am and 12:30, 5:30, and 9pm. The fare is C9,000 per car, including the driver; C1,005 for each additional adult; and C600 for children.

Another option is to drive via La Amistad Bridge over the Tempisque River. I recommend this route only when the ferries are on the fritz, or when the wait for the next car ferry is over 3 hours. (When the lines are long, you may not find room on the next departing ferry.) Although heading farther north and crossing the bridge is more circuitous, you will be driving the whole time, which beats waiting around in the midday heat of Puntarenas. To go this route, take the Interamerican Highway west from San José. Forty-seven kilometers (29 miles) past the turnoff for Puntarenas, turn left for La Amistad Bridge. After you cross the Tempisque River, head to Quebrada Honda and then south to Route 21, following signs for San Pablo, Jicaral, Lepanto, Playa Naranjo, and Paquera.

To drive to Tambor from Liberia, head out of town on the main road to the Guanacaste beaches, passing through Filadelfia, Santa Cruz, and Nicoya on your way toward the turnoff for La Amistad Bridge. Continue straight at this turnoff, and follow the directions for this route as listed above.

By Bus & Ferry: Transportes Cobano (© 2642-1112) runs two daily direct buses between San José and Cóbano, dropping passengers off in Tambor en route. The buses leave from the Coca-Cola bus terminal at Calle 12 and Avenida 5 at 6am and 2pm. The fare is C6,900, including the ferry ride, and the trip takes a little over 4 hours.

Alternatively, it takes two buses and a ferry to get to Tambor. **Empresarios Unidos de Puntarenas** express buses (© 222-9840) leave San José daily every hour between 6am and 7pm from Calle 16 and Avenida 12. Trip duration is 2 hours; the fare is C2,540. From Puntarenas, take the car ferry to Paquera mentioned above. A bus south to Montezuma (this will drop you off in Tambor) will be waiting to meet the ferry when it arrives in Paquera. The bus ride takes about 40 minutes; the fare is around C1,100. Be careful not to take the Naranjo ferry because it does not meet with regular onward bus transportation to Tambor.

When you're ready to head back, buses originating in Montezuma, Cóbano, or Malpaís pass through Tambor roughly every 2 hours between 6am and 4:30pm. Theoretically, these should connect with a waiting ferry in Paquera. Total trip duration is 3½ hours. Buses to San José leave Puntarenas daily every hour between 5am and 8pm.

ORIENTATION   Although there's a tiny village of Tambor, through which the main road passes, the hotels themselves are scattered along several kilometers, with Tango Mar (p. 264) definitively outside Tambor proper. You'll see signs for all these hotels as the road passes through and beyond Playa Tambor.

If you need a bank, pharmacy, or post office, you'll have to head to nearby Cóbano.

Exploring Tambor

Curú Wildlife Refuge ★★ (© 2641-0100; www.curuwildliferefuge.com), 16km (10 miles) north of Tambor, is a private reserve that has several pretty, secluded beaches, as well as forests and mangrove swamps. This area is extremely rich in wildlife. Mantled howler and white-faced monkeys are often spotted here, and quite a few species of birds. You will usually see scarlet macaws, as the refuge is actively involved in a macaw protection and repopulation effort. Horses are available to rent in the refuge for $10 per hour. Typically, the horse rentals work like this: You'll ride, with a guide, for about an hour to a lovely beach, hang out on the sand for about an hour, and then ride back. Happily, you only get charged for the time you're actually on horseback, so trips run about $20. If you'd like to take a

A woodpecker at Curú Wildlife Refuge.

longer ride, simply ask if they'll accommodate you. Admission for the day is $10 per person. Some very rustic cabins are available with advance notice for $30 per person per day. Meals are $10. If you don't have a car, you should arrange pickup with the folks who manage this refuge. Or you can contact **Turismo Curú** (© **2641-0004;** www.curutourism.com), which specializes in guided tours to the refuge, as well as kayaking trips and other area adventures.

Both the hotels listed below offer horseback riding and various tours around this part of the peninsula and can arrange fishing and dive trips.

Where to Stay & Dine

Aside from the hotels listed here, a few inexpensive cabinas are available near the town of Tambor, at the southern end of the beach. Most are very rustic and basic, and charge around $10 per person. Another option is **Costa Coral ★** (© **2683-0105;** www.hotelcostacoral.com), a very attractive place with a good restaurant. This place would be my top choice in Tambor, except it's unfortunately set right off the busy main road here, several hundred meters from the beach.

The **Barceló Playa Tambor Beach Resort** (© **2683-0303;** www.barcelo tamborbeach.com) was Costa Rica's first all-inclusive resort, but its beach is mediocre at best, and the Barceló company has been accused of violating Costa Rica's environmental laws, ignoring zoning regulations, and mistreating workers. Although this resort is a major presence here, I don't recommend it; much better all-inclusive options are available farther north in Guanacaste.

Tambor Tropical ★   This is easily the best hotel right on the beach in Playa Tambor. The individual and two-story bungalows are huge with walls, floors, ceilings, and furnishings of brightly varnished local hardwoods. I prefer the second-floor rooms which feature huge wrap-around verandas facing the sea and offering up wonderful morning sunrise views. All rooms are classified as suites, and come with full kitchens. A small free-form pool is set under tall coconut palms and the beach is just a stone's throw away. The restaurant and bar are housed under a soaring thatch roof and serve up excellent fresh seafood, continental cuisine, and cocktails.

Tambor, Puntarenas. © **866/890-2537** in the U.S., or 2683-0011 in Costa Rica. www.tambor tropical.com. 14 units. $160–$220 double. Rates include continental breakfast. No children 15 and under. **Amenities:** Restaurant; bar; small free-form outdoor pool and Jacuzzi; small spa; Wi-Fi.

Tango Mar Resort ★★   Set a few kilometers southwest of Tambor, roughly midway between Tambor and Montezuma, this isolated resort features lovely rooms in a range of styles spread around its sprawling beachfront grounds. I think it's worth the slight splurge for a deluxe beachfront room, but for views, you can't beat the Tropical Suites, which are set on a high bluff. Tango Mar fronts a beautiful white-sand beach, and is a short walk from a picturesque waterfall that empties into a pool formed by a rock formation adjacent to the sea. Of the several pools here, one particularly gorgeous one is set just a few steps away from the surf. The resort also has a 9-hole, par-3 golf course and two tennis courts. In addition to the hotel rooms and suites, these folks also rent out a range of private homes and villas spread around the grounds.

Playa Tambor, Puntarenas. © **800/297-4420** in the U.S., or 2683-0001 in Costa Rica. www.tango mar.com. 45 units. 17 tropical suites, 6 deluxe, 5 bungalows, and 2 villas. $220–$250 double; $295 suite; $500–$1,150 villa. Rates include breakfast. **Amenities:** 2 Restaurants; bar; bike rental; 9-hole par-3 and 4 golf course ($40 full-day greens fee) w/wonderful sea views; 4 small outdoor pools; room service; small spa; 2 lighted tennis courts.

PLAYA MONTEZUMA ★★

166–184km (103–114 miles) W of San José (not including the ferry ride); 36km (22 miles) SE of Paquera; 54km (33 miles) S of Naranjo

For decades, this remote village and its surrounding beaches, forests, and waterfalls have enjoyed near-legendary status among backpackers, UFO seekers, hippie expatriates, and European budget travelers. Although it maintains its alternative vibe, Montezuma is a great destination for all manner of travelers looking for a beach retreat surrounded by some stunning scenery. Active pursuits abound, from hiking in the Cabo Blanco Absolute Nature Reserve to horseback riding to visiting a beachside waterfall. The natural beauty, miles of almost abandoned beaches, rich wildlife, and jungle waterfalls here are what first made Montezuma famous, and they continue to make this one of my favorite beach towns in Costa Rica.

Essentials

GETTING THERE & DEPARTING   By Plane: The nearest airport is in Tambor, 17km (11 miles) away (see "Playa Tambor," above, for details). Some of the hotels listed below might pick you up in Tambor for a reasonable fee. If not, you'll have to hire a taxi, which could cost anywhere between $30 and $50. **Taxis** are generally waiting to meet most regularly scheduled planes, but if they aren't, you can call **Gilberto Rodríguez** (© **8826-9055** or 2642-0241; gilbertotaxi@gmail.com).

Sunset at Playa Montezuma.

By far the fastest route is the daily speedboat shuttle between Montezuma and Jacó (actually Playa Herradura). This 1-hour shuttle departs Montezuma for Playa Herradura at 9am and makes the return trip from Playa Herradura to Montezuma at 11am. The folks at **CocoZuma**

Traveller (© **2642-0911;** www.coco zuma.com) can help book this, including connecting shared shuttle service to or from San José, Manuel Antonio, Malpaís, and other destinations. The boat shuttle itself is $40 per person, one-way.

By Car: The traditional route here is to first drive to Puntarenas and catch the ferry to either Naranjo or Paquera. Montezuma is about 30 minutes south of Tambor, 1 hour south of Paquera, and about 2 hours south of Naranjo. The road from Paquera to Tambor is paved, and taking the Paquera ferry will save you time and some rough, dusty driving. The road from Naranjo to Paquera is all dirt and gravel and often in very bad shape.

For info on car ferries, see p. 262. For driving directions to Puntarenas, see p. 256.

To drive to Montezuma from Liberia, head out of town on the main road to the Guanacaste beaches, passing through Filadelfia, Santa Cruz, and Nicoya on your way toward the turnoff for La Amistad Bridge. Continue straight at this turnoff, and follow the directions for this route as listed above.

By Bus & Ferry: Transportes Cobano (© **2642-1112**) runs two daily direct buses between San José and Montezuma. The buses leave from the Coca-Cola bus terminal at Calle 12 and Avenida 5 at 6am and 2pm. The fare is C7,500, including the ferry ride, and the trip takes a little over 5 hours.

Alternatively, it takes two buses and a ferry ride to get to Montezuma. **Empresarios Unidos de Puntarenas** express buses (© **2222-0064**) to Puntarenas leave San José daily every hour between 6am and 7pm from Calle 16 and Avenida 12. The trip takes 2 hours; the fare is C2,540. From Puntarenas, you can take the ferry to Paquera, mentioned on p. 262. A bus south to Montezuma will be waiting to meet the ferry when it arrives in Paquera. The bus ride takes about 1½ hours; the fare is C1,800. Be careful not to take the Naranjo ferry because it does not meet with regular onward bus transportation to Montezuma.

Buses are met by hordes of locals trying to corral you to one of the many budget hotels. Remember, they are getting a commission for everybody they bring in, so their information is biased. Not only that, they are often flat-out lying when they tell you the hotel you wanted to stay in is full.

When you're ready to head back, direct buses leave Montezuma daily at 6:20am and 2:20pm. Regular local buses to Paquera leave Cóbano roughly every 2 hours throughout the day starting around 6:30am. Buses to San José leave Puntarenas daily every hour between 6am and 7pm.

CITY LAYOUT   As the winding mountain road that descends into Montezuma bottoms out, you turn left onto a small dirt road that defines the village proper. On this 1-block road, you will find El Sano Banano Village Cafe and, across from it, a small shaded park with plenty of tall trees, as well as a basketball court and children's playground. The bus stops at the end of this road. From here, hotels are scattered up and down the beach and around the village's few sand streets.

9

PUNTARENAS & THE NICOYA PENINSULA | Playa Montezuma

Around the center of town are several tour agencies and Internet cafes among the restaurants and souvenir stores.

Exploring Montezuma

The ocean here is a gorgeous royal blue, and beautiful beaches stretch out along the coast on either side of town. Be careful, though: The waves can occasionally be too rough for casual swimming, and you need to be aware of stray rocks at your feet. Be sure you know where the rocks and tide are before doing any bodysurfing. Given the prevailing currents and winds here, Montezuma also has experienced several severe and long-lasting red tide episodes in recent years. During these periods of massive algae bloom, the ocean is reddish-brown in color and not recommended for swimming.

The best places to swim are a couple of hundred meters north of town in front of **El Rincón de los Monos,** or several kilometers farther north at Playa Grande.

If you're interested in more than simple beach time, head for the **Montezuma waterfall** ★★ just south of town—it's one of those tropical fantasies where water comes pouring down into a deep pool. It's a popular spot, and it's a bit of a hike up the stream. Along this stream are a couple of waterfalls, but the upper falls are by far the more spectacular. You'll find the trail to the falls just over the bridge south of the village (on your right just past Las Cascadas restaurant). At the first major outcropping of rocks, the trail disappears and you have to scramble up the rocks and river for a bit. A trail occasionally reappears for short stretches. Just stick close to the stream and you'll eventually hit the falls.

Note: Be very careful when climbing close to the rushing water, and also if you plan on taking any dives into the pools below. The rocks are quite slippery, and several people each year get very scraped up, break bones, and otherwise hurt themselves here.

Another popular local waterfall is **El Chorro** ★, located 8km (5 miles) north of Montezuma. This waterfall cascades down into a tide pool at the edge of the ocean. The pool here is a delightful mix of fresh- and seawater, and you can bathe while gazing out over the sea and rocky coastline. When the water is clear and calm, this is one of my favorite swimming holes in all of Costa Rica. However, a massive landslide in 2004 filled in much of this pool and also somewhat lessened the drama and beauty of the falls. Moreover, the pool here is dependent upon the tides—it disappears entirely at very high tide. It's about a 2-hour hike along the beach to reach El Chorro. Alternatively, you can take a horseback tour here with any of the tour operators or horseback riding companies in town.

BUTTERFLY GARDEN   For an intimate look at the life cycle and acrobatic flights-of-fancy of butterflies, head to the **Mariposario Montezuma Gardens** (© **2642-1317** or 8888-4200; www.monte-zumagardens.com). This is perhaps the most wild and natural feeling of all the butterfly gardens in Costa Rica. Wooden walkways wind through thick vegetation under black screen meshing. Most of the butterflies in the enclosure are self-reproducing. You can also see butterflies and other wildlife on trails through open forested

Buy the Book . . . or Just Borrow It

If you came unprepared or ran out of reading material, check in at **Librería Topsy** (© **2642-0576**), which, in addition to selling books, runs a lending library and serves as the local post office. These folks also have a branch up in Cabuya.

areas outside the enclosure. Along the dirt road heading up the hill just beyond the entrance to the waterfall trail, this place is open daily from 8am to 4pm. Admission is $4. These folks also have a few pretty rooms they rent out, or give to volunteers in exchange for work around the gardens.

A UNIQUE CANOPY TOUR One popular tour option here is the **Waterfall Canopy Tour** ★ (© 2642-0808; www.montezumatraveladventures.com), which is built right alongside Montezuma's famous falls. The tour, which features nine cables connecting 13 platforms, includes a swim at the foot of the falls and costs $40 per person. Tours are offered daily at 9am and 1 and 3pm.

HORSEBACK RIDING Several people around the village will rent you horses for around $10 to $20 an hour, although most people choose to do a guided 4-hour horseback tour for $30 to $50. Any of the hotels or tour agencies in town can arrange it for you, or you can contact Marvin at **El Pinto Expeditions** (© 8849-8569; www.elpintoexpeditions.com). Another good option is **Finca Los Caballos** ★ (© 2642-0124; www.naturelodge.net; p. 269), which is up the hill on the road leading into Montezuma.

OTHER ACTIVITIES Some shops in the center of the village rent bicycles by the hour or day, as well as boogie boards and snorkeling equipment (although the water must be very calm for snorkeling).

A range of guided tour and adventure options is available in Montezuma. **CocoZuma Traveller** (© 2642-0911; www.cocozuma.com) and **Sun Trails** (© 2642-0808; www.montezumatraveladventures.com) can both arrange horseback riding, boat excursions, scuba-dive and snorkel tours, ATV outings, and rafting trips; car and motorcycle rentals; airport transfers; international phone, fax, and Internet service; and currency exchange.

An Excursion to Cabo Blanco Absolute Nature Reserve

As beautiful as the beaches around Montezuma are, the beaches at **Cabo Blanco Absolute Nature Reserve** ★★ (© 2642-0093), 11km (6¾ miles) south of the village, are even more stunning. At the southernmost tip of the Nicoya Peninsula, Cabo Blanco is a national park that preserves a nesting site for brown pelicans, magnificent frigate birds, and brown boobies. The beaches are backed by a lush tropical forest that is home to howler monkeys. The main trail here, Sendero Sueco (Swiss Trail), is a rugged and sometimes steep hike through thick rainforest. The trail leads to the beautiful Playa Balsita and Playa Cabo Blanco, two white-sand stretches that straddle either side of the namesake Cabo Blanco point. The beaches are connected by a short trail. It's 4km (2.5 miles) to Playa Balsita. Alternately, you can take a shorter 2km (1.25-mile) loop trail through the primary forest here. This is Costa Rica's oldest official bioreserve and was set up thanks to the pioneering efforts of conservationists Karen Mogensen and Nicholas Wessberg. Admission is $10; the reserve is open Wednesday through Sunday from 8am to 4pm.

On your way out to Cabo Blanco, you'll pass through the tiny village of **Cabuya.** There are a couple of private patches of beach to discover in this area, off some of the deserted dirt roads, and a small offshore island serves as the town's picturesque cemetery. Snorkel and kayak trips to this island are offered out of Montezuma.

Shuttle buses head from Montezuma to Cabo Blanco roughly every 2 hours beginning at 8am, and then turn around and bring folks from Cabo Blanco to

Cabo Blanco Absolute Nature Reserve.

Montezuma; the last one leaves Cabo Blanco around 5pm. The fare is $3 each way. These shuttles often don't run during the off season. Alternatively, you can share a taxi: The fare is around $15 to $20 per taxi, which can hold four or five passengers. Taxis tend to hang around Montezuma center. One dependable *taxista* is **Gilberto Rodríguez** (© **8826-9055** or 2642-0241).

Where to Stay

EXPENSIVE

In addition to the places mentioned below, the **Anamaya Resort** ★ (© **866/ 412-5350** in the U.S. and Canada, or 2642-1289 in Costa Rica; www. anamayaresort.com) is a lovely and luxe option on a high hillside above Montezuma. Anamaya specializes in yoga and wellness retreats.

Ylang Ylang Beach Resort ★★ This small rainforest resort does an excellent job of blending tropical fantasy with some lovely perks and hints of luxury. The whole complex is set just off the beach in a dense patch of forest and flowering gardens. Lodging options range from glamping-style tent cabins to individual bungalows and geodesic domes. There are no roads, nor regular vehicular access to the resort, so check-in is done at the sister El Sano Banano Village Cafe (see below) in the town, and you and your bags are shuttled in via Jeep or dune buggy. The owners, Lenny and Patricia, have been here for decades and have done much to promote and protect the area.

Montezuma, Cóbano de Puntarenas. © **888/795-8494** in the U.S. and Canada, or 2642-0636 in Costa Rica. www.ylangylangbeachresort.com. 22 units. $140–$365 double. Rates include breakfast and dinner. **Amenities:** Restaurant; bar; midsize outdoor pool; spa; free Wi-Fi.

MODERATE

Nature Lodge Finca Los Caballos ★ Set on a high hillside above Montezuma this place was originally a horse ranch and operation, but has lately focused primarily on casual tourists. The rooms are relatively plain, but come with some nice design and decorative touches that liven things up. If you want an ocean view, be sure to get one of the Superior Pacific rooms. Most of the rest feature jungle or garden views. Still, you can always enjoy the stunning vista of the Pacific Ocean over rolling forested hills from the pool and other common areas.

3km (1³/₄ miles) outside of Montezuma, on the way to Cóbano de Puntarenas. ℗ **2642-0124.** www.naturelodge.net. 12 units. $86–$146 double. Rates include breakfast buffet. **Amenities:** Restaurant; small outdoor pool; spa; free Wi-Fi in the restaurant area.

INEXPENSIVE

In addition to the places mentioned below, **El Pargo Feliz** (℗ 2642-0064) and **Cabinas Mar y Cielo** (℗ 2642-0261) are two good budget options right in the center of town.

The folks at Ylang Ylang (see above) also run the in-town **El Sano Banano B&B** (℗ 866/332-3590 in the U.S. and Canada, or 2642-0636 in Costa Rica; www.elbanano.com), just off their popular restaurant (see below). The rooms here feature air-conditioning (which, because of the design, you are basically forced to use) and satellite televisions. Double rooms are $65 to $95.

Amor de Mar ★★   This hotel has an idyllic setting, with a wide expanse of neatly trimmed grass sloping down to the sea, tide pools (one of which is as big as a small swimming pool), and hammocks slung from the mango trees. The rooms are housed in a two-story building, which abounds in varnished hardwoods. Although simply appointed, most rooms have plenty of space and receive lots of sunlight. However, a couple of the less expensive rooms are a bit small and dark. My favorite room is no. 5, which has exclusive access to a long second-floor balcony with a superb ocean view. Breakfast and lunch only are served on a beautiful open-air patio overlooking the sea. These folks also rent out a large fully equipped two-story, four-bedroom house next to the hotel.

Montezuma, Cóbano de Puntarenas. ℗ **2642-0262.** www.amordemar.com. 11 units. $90–$150 double; $250–$270 villa. **Amenities:** Restaurant; Wi-Fi.

El Jardín   As you descend the steep hill that leads into Montezuma, you'll find this place on your right, just before the main crossroads of the village. Rooms here are clean and tidy, but rather spartan. They are spread up the hillside and some offer up excellent views. Rooms furthest from the road and reception require a bit of a steep hike, but the view from some of these is definitely worth it. The hotel's pool and Jacuzzi area is its best feature. I also enjoy the location, which provides easy access to the town, yet feels a bit removed.

Montezuma, Cóbano de Puntarenas. ℗ **2642-0074.** www.hoteleljardin.com. 17 units. $65–$85 double; $95–$115 villa. Prices include taxes. **Amenities:** Jacuzzi; small outdoor pool; Wi-Fi.

Hotel La Aurora   Just to the left as you enter the village of Montezuma, you'll find this long-standing budget hotel. The rooms are spread out over three floors in two neighboring buildings fronting the village's small park and playground. All rooms are clean and well-kept. A two-room apartment on the third floor has a private balcony and a bit of an ocean view through the treetops. The hotel also features a couple of common sitting areas, a small lending library, some hammocks and comfortable chairs for chilling out in, a communal kitchen, and flowering vines growing up the walls. In fact, the plants and vines all over La Aurora keep things cool and give the place a fitting tropical feel. Fresh coffee, tea, and hearty breakfasts are served each morning.

Montezuma, Cóbano de Puntarenas. ℗ **2642-0051.** www.hotelaurora-montezuma.com. 18 units. $40–$75 double. Rates include taxes. **Amenities:** Lounge; communal kitchen; free Wi-Fi.

HOTELS
Amor de Mar **5**
Anamaya Resort **22**
Cabinas Mar y Cielo **16**
El Jardin **9**
El Pargo Feliz **18**
El Sano Banano Village
  Bed & Breakfast **12**
Hotel La Aurora **10**
Hotel Lucy **6**
Nature Lodge Finca
  Los Caballos **22**
Ylang Ylang
  Beach Resort **21**

RESTAURANTS
Bakery Café **19**
Cocolores **17**
El Sano Banano
  Village Cafe **12**
Hotel Moctezuma **13**
Orgánico **15**
Pizzería L'Angulo Allegro **11**
Playa de los Artistas **7**
Puggo's **8**
Ylang Ylang **21**

ATTRACTIONS
Cabo Blanco Absolute
  Nature Reserve **4**
El Chorro **20**
Mariposario Montezuma
  Gardens **1**
Montezuma Waterfall **3**
Waterfall Canopy Tour **2**

NIGHTLIFE
Chico's Bar **14**
Hotel Moctezuma **13**
El Sano Banano
  Village Cafe **12**

Hotel Lucy

For a budget hotel, this place has some serious location cache. Set right on the beach a short walk south of the village and close to the Montezuma Waterfall trail entrance, the rooms here are incredibly basic and sporadically maintained, and the service and personal attention provided are minimal. Still it's very inexpensive, and right on the beach. You have the option of private bathrooms or shared dorm-style affairs. Spend a few extra dollars for the private bath.

Montezuma, Cóbano de Puntarenas. ℂ **2642-0273.** 17 units, 6 with bathroom. $24 double with shared bathroom; $27 double with private bathroom. **Amenities:** Smoke-free rooms.

Where to Dine

In addition to the places listed below, you'll find several basic *sodas* and casual restaurants right in the village. My favorite of these is the **Pizzería L'Angolo Allegro** (ℂ **2642-1111**), which is at the crossroads into town and serves good thin-crust pizzas, calzones, and pastas. You might also want to check out the Spanish cuisine and fabulous setting at the downtown **Hotel Moctezuma** (ℂ **2642-0657**), or the varied international fare at **Cocolores** (ℂ **2642-0348**). Just outside of downtown proper, the Israeli owned **Puggo's ★** (ℂ **2642-0325**) serves up an eclectic menu that ranges from falafel to *ceviche* to focaccia and beyond.

For breakfast, coffee, and light meals, **Orgánico ★** (ℂ **2642-1322**) is a good option, with a range of healthy sandwiches, daily specials, and freshly baked goods. The **Bakery Café** (☎ **2642-0458**) is another good choice, serving everything from gourmet coffee drinks to full meals from their massive menu.

El Sano Banano Village Cafe ★★ INTERNATIONAL/VEGETARIAN Delicious vegetarian meals, including nightly specials, sandwiches, and salads, are the specialty of this perennially popular Montezuma restaurant, although there's also a variety of fish and chicken dishes. Lunches feature hefty sandwiches on whole-wheat bread and filling fish and vegetarian *casados*. The natural yogurt fruit shakes are fabulous, but I like to get a little more decadent and have one of the mocha chill shakes. El Sano Banano also doubles as the local movie house. Nightly DVD releases are projected onto a large screen; the selection ranges from first-run to quite artsy films culled from a growing library of more than 1,000 movies. The movies begin at 7:30pm and require a minimum purchase of $6.

On the main road into the village. ☎ **2642-0944.** Main courses $6–$15. Daily 7am–10pm.

Playa de los Artistas ★★★ ITALIAN/MEDITERRANEAN This open-air restaurant is housed in the back garden of an old house fronting the beach, and only has a few tables, so arrive early. If you don't get a seat and you feel up to it, try the low wooden table surrounded by tatami mats on the sand. Meals are served in large creative plates, in broad wooden bowls set on ceramic-ringed coasters, or on large wooden planks lined with banana leaves. The menu changes nightly but always features several fish dishes. The fresh grouper in a black-pepper sauce is phenomenal, as is the *moscardini* polenta, a tasty appetizer of polenta topped with grilled calamari tentacles and pecorino cheese. The outdoor brick oven and grill turns out consistently spectacular grilled seafood. All meals come with plenty of fresh bread for soaking up the delicious sauces.

Across from Hotel Los Mangos. ☎ **2642-0920.** Reservations recommended. No credit cards. Main courses C6,000–C10,000. Mon–Sat 5pm–9:30pm. **Note:** Hours here are very seasonal, with lunch sometimes served during the high season.

Ylang Ylang ★★ INTERNATIONAL/VEGETARIAN This is the main restaurant at the wonderful Ylang Ylang Beach Resort (see above). A large, but covered open-air dining room lets out onto an open patio fronting a small patch of lawn that fronts the beach and ocean beyond. My favorite tables are set on this patio with white canvas umbrellas offering protection from the sun. The menu features quite a few vegan, gluten-free, and raw options, as well as sushi and a range of Asian-inspired dishes. Presentations are artistic, and there are plenty of meat, chicken and seafood dishes for those seeking to indulge those guilty pleasures.

At the Ylang Ylang Beach Resort. ☎ **2642-0402.** Reservations recommended. Main courses $12–$26. Daily 7am–9pm.

Entertainment & Nightlife

Montezuma has had a tough time coming to terms with its nightlife. For years, local businesses banded together to force most of the loud, late-night activity out of town. This has eased somewhat, allowing for quite an active nightlife in Montezuma proper. The local action seems to base itself either at **Chico's Bar** ★ (☎ **2642-0526**) or at the bar at the **Hotel Moctezuma** (☎ **2642-0058;** www. hotelmoctezuma.com). Both are located on the main strip in town facing the water. If your evening tastes are mellower, **El Sano Banano Village Cafe** (see above) doubles as the local movie house, with nightly late-run features projected on a large screen.

MALPAÍS & SANTA TERESA ★★

150km (93 miles) W of San José; 12km (7¹/₂ miles) S of Cóbano

Malpaís (or Mal País) translates as "badlands," and, while this may have been an apt moniker several years ago, it no longer accurately describes this booming beach area. Malpaís is a bucket term often used to refer to a string of neighboring beaches running from south to north, and including Malpaís, Playa Carmen, Santa Teresa, Playa Hermosa, and Playa Manzanillo. To a fault, these beaches are long, wide expanses of light sand dotted with rocky outcroppings. This is one of Costa Rica's hottest spots, and development continues at a dizzying pace, especially in Santa Teresa. Still, it will take some time before this place is anything like more developed destinations Tamarindo or Manuel Antonio. In Malpaís and Santa Teresa today, you'll find a mix of beach hotels and resorts, restaurants, shops, and private houses, as well as miles of often deserted beach, and easy access to some nice jungle and the nearby **Cabo Blanco Absolute Nature Reserve** (p. 268).

Essentials

GETTING THERE & DEPARTING   By Plane: The nearest airport is in Tambor (see "Playa Tambor," p. 261, for flight details). The airport is about 22km (14 miles) from Malpaís; the ride takes around 20 to 25 minutes. Some of the hotels listed below might be willing to pick you up in Tambor for a reasonable fee. If not, you'll have to hire a taxi, which could cost anywhere between $40 and $60. **Taxis** are generally waiting to meet most regularly scheduled planes, but if they aren't, you can call **Richard** (☎ **8360-8166** or 2640-0003) for a cab.

   By Car: Follow the directions above to Montezuma (see "Playa Montezuma," earlier in this chapter). At Cóbano, follow the signs to Malpaís and Playa Santa Teresa. It's another 12km (7¹/₂ miles) down a rough dirt road that requires four-wheel-drive much of the year, especially during the rainy season.

   To drive to Malpaís from Liberia, head out of town on the main road to the Guanacaste beaches, passing through Filadelfia, Santa Cruz, and Nicoya on your way toward the turnoff for La Amistad Bridge. Continue straight at this turnoff, and follow the directions for this route as listed above.

   By Bus & Ferry: Transportes Cobano (☎ **2642-1112**) has two daily buses to Malpaís and Santa Teresa departing from from Avenida 9 and Calle 12. The buses leave at 6am and 2pm, and the fare is C7,535, including the ferry passage. The ride takes around 6 hours. The return buses leave Santa Teresa at 5:15am and 2pm.

   Alternatively, you can follow the directions above for getting to Montezuma, but get off in Cóbano. From Cóbano, there are several daily buses for Malpaís and Santa Teresa running throughout the day. The fare is C900. **Be forewarned:** These bus schedules are subject to change according to demand, road conditions, and the whim of the bus company.

Surfing in Santa Teresa.

Malpaís & Santa Teresa

To Manzanillo
To Manzanillo
Playa Cocal del Peñón
Santiago
To Cóbano
El Peñón
160
San Isidro
Santa Teresa
Playa Santa Teresa
Quebrada Carmen
Río Montezuma
Río Eumedio

HOTELS
Beija Flor Resort **15**
Casa Chameleon **14**
Florblanca Resort **4**
Hotel Moana **13**
Latitude 10 **3**
Malpaís Surf Camp & Resort **12**
Pranamar Villas & Yoga Retreat **1**
Tranquilo Backpackers **8**
Trópico Latino Lodge **7**

RESTAURANTS
Artemis Café **11**
Beija Flor Resort **15**
Brisas del Mar **9**
El Rey Patricio **2**
Mary's **16**
Nectar **4**
Product C **11**
Ume Sushi **11**

NIGHTLIFE
Coco Loco **6**
Frank's Place **10**
La Lora Amarilla **5**
Malpaís Surf Camp **12**

ATTRACTIONS
Canopy del Pacífico **17**

Playa Carmen
"El Cruce"
Malpaís
160

PACIFIC OCEAN

NICARAGUA
CARIBBEAN SEA
SAN JOSÉ
Malpaís & Santa Teresa
PACIFIC OCEAN
PANAMA

Punta Barrigona
Playa Malpaís
Punta Cuevas
Playa Cuevas

0   1 mi
0   1 km

Cabo Blanco Nature Reserve
Playa San Miguel
Punta Coquitas
To Cabuya

If you miss the bus connection in Cóbano, you can hire a cab to Malpaís for around $20 to $25.

GETTING AROUND   If you need a taxi, call **Richard** (© **8317-7614** or 2640-0003). If you want to do the driving yourself, you can contact the local offices of **Alamo** (© **2640-0526;** www.alamocostarica.com) or **Budget Rent A Car** (© **2640-0500;** www.budget.co.cr). Or you can head to **Quads Rental Center** (© **2640-0178**), which has a large stock of ATVs.

VILLAGE LAYOUTS   Malpaís and Santa Teresa are two tiny beach villages. As you reach the ocean, the road forks; Playa Carmen is straight ahead, Malpaís is to your left, and Santa Teresa is to your right. If you continue beyond Santa Teresa, you'll come to the even-more-deserted beaches of playas Hermosa and

Manzanillo (not to be confused with beaches of the same names to be found elsewhere in the country). To get to playas Hermosa and Manzanillo, you have to ford a couple of rivers, which can be tricky during parts of the rainy season.

Exploring Malpaís & Santa Teresa

If you decide to do anything here besides sunbathe on the beach and play in the waves, your options include nature hikes, horseback riding, ATV tours, scuba diving, and snorkeling, which most hotels can help arrange. Surfing is a major draw, with miles of beach breaks to choose from and a few points to boot. If you want to rent a board or take a lesson, you can find a host of surf shops in Malpaís, Playa Carmen, and Santa Teresa, all of which rent boards and offer lessons. I recommend **Costa Rica Surf & SUP** (✆ **2640-0328;** www.costa ricasurfandsup.com) and **Del Soul Surf School** (✆ **8878-0880;** www.surf vacationcostarica.com).

If you've gotten beat up by the waves, or are sore from paddling out, you'll find several excellent spas in town. The best and most extensive (and most expensive) of these is at the **Florblanca Resort** (see below). But you might also check in to the **Pranamar Villas & Yoga Retreat** (see below), which is located on the beach, at the northern end of Santa Teresa.

For canopy adventures, head to **Canopy del Pacífico** (✆ **2640-0360;** www.canopydelpacifico.com), which is toward the southern end of Malpaís and just slightly inland. A 2-hour tour over the nearly 2km (1 mile) of cables touches down on 11 platforms, features two rappels, and offers good views of both the

Santa Teresa.

forest and the ocean below. The cost is $45. Round-trip transportation from an area hotel is just another $5 per person.

Finally, any hotel in the area can arrange a horseback-riding or ATV trip into the hills and along the beaches of this region, a guided hike through **Cabo Blanco Nature Reserve,** a sportfishing excursion out onto the high seas, or a trip over to Montezuma.

Where to Stay
VERY EXPENSIVE

In addition to the places listed below, **Casa Chameleon** ★★ (☎ 888/705-0274 in the U.S. and Canada, or 2288-2879 in Costa Rica; www.hotelcasa chameleon.com) is a collection of four plush, individual villas, each with a private pool, set on a steep hillside overlooking Malpaís.

Florblanca Resort ★★★   This is the premier boutique luxury beach resort in this area, which is saying a lot. A collection of massive private villas are spread around lush and exuberant gardens. The best units here have ocean views. Those that don't are surrounded by lush and abundant gardens and old-growth trees. About half are designed for couples, and the rest feature a separate bedroom for families—although no children under 6 are allowed. All feature a massive living room that lets out on to an equally spacious private patio area, as well as large, open-air bathrooms with outdoor showers and tubs. The resort has a gorgeous full-service spa; a large, two-tier swimming pool; and spacious wood-floored yoga studio with regular classes and workshops. The Nectar restaurant here (see below) is also excellent.

Playa Santa Teresa. ☎ 2640-0232. www.florblanca.com. 11 units. $400–$500 double; $575–$725 2-bedroom villa for 4; $775–$925 honeymoon house. No children under 6. **Amenities:** Restaurant; bar; bike rental; small open-air gym; outdoor pool; room service; spa; watersports equipment rental; free Wi-Fi.

Latitude 10 ★★   If you're looking for an intimate and exclusive beachfront getaway it's hard to beat this beautiful little resort. With only five independent bungalows and one main lodge room, this place never gets crowded, and quite often is rented out entirely by a family or group. The bungalows are built from local hardwoods and show heavy Indonesian and Balinese influences in both the design and decor. With sliding wooden doors and slatted windows they are designed to be entirely open, especially during the day. This may be a bit too close to nature for some folks, and there's even a prominent and important "Is Latitude 10 for Me" tab on their web site. The resort fronts a gorgeous section of Santa Teresa beach, with just a pool, a patch of well-manicured lawn and a string of coconut palms separating it from the sand and sea.

Playa Santa Teresa, Cóbano de Puntarenas. ☎ 8309-2943. www.latitude10resort.com. 6 units. $250 double; $330–$430 junior suite; $610 master suite. Rates include breakfast. Rates lower in the off season. **Amenities:** Restaurant, bar; outdoor pool; all rooms smoke-free; Wi-Fi.

Pranamar Villas & Yoga Retreat ★★   Having first started out building the intimate Sueño del Mar (p. 245) hotel in Tamarindo, Susan and Greg Money went on to design and build the nearby Florblanca Resort (see above), before claiming to have finally settled down with this gorgeous beach resort and yoga retreat. As is common on this coast, there's a heavy dose of Balinese, Thai and Indonesian artwork, crafts and furnishings, but mixed in with elements from Mexico, Guatemala, and Ecuador, as well. As the name suggests, yoga is an

Florblanca Resort.

integral part of the program here, with regular daily classes, visiting workshops and a large and lovely yoga studio. The hotel's Buddha Eyes restaurant is excellent, and specializes in healthy and vegetarian cuisine. This hotel is located on the far northern edge of Santa Teresa, where it becomes Playa Hermosa.

Playa Santa Teresa, Cóbano de Puntarenas. ℭ **2640-0852.** www.pranamarvillas.com. 10 units. $250–$370 double. Rates include breakfast and daily yoga class. Rates lower in the off season; higher during peak periods. **Amenities:** Restaurant; bar; saltwater pool; all rooms smoke-free; spa treatments; free Wi-Fi.

MODERATE

In addition to the hotels listed below, **Beija Flor Resort ★** (ℭ **2640-1007;** www.beijaflorresort.com) is a cozy little resort with an excellent restaurant in Malpaís.

Hotel Moana ★　This is an excellent small hotel spread over a steep mountainside just a little inland from the beach towards the northern end of Malpaís. The best rooms and the hotel's excellent restaurant are on the highest points of the property, but this also means they require a bit of exercise to reach. It's definitely worth the effort, once you take in the spectacular views of the Pacific Ocean, rugged coastline, and beautiful forested hills. Many of the rooms sport African inspired design and decor. These folks also rent out a spectacular 5-bedroom independent house, Casa Moana, located above the hotel, perfect for larger groups or families.

Malpaís, Cóbano de Puntarenas. ℭ **888/865-8032** in the U.S. and Canada, or 2640-0230 in Costa Rica. www.moanalodge.com. 10 units. $130–$160 double; $220–$325 suite; $550–$1,250 house. Rates include breakfast and taxes. **Amenities:** Restaurant, bar; Jacuzzi; outdoor pool; all rooms are smoke-free; free Wi-Fi.

Trópico Latino Lodge ★★　This is a wonderful little beachfront resort set on a prime patch of sand in Santa Teresa. You can opt for the large and economical garden units, or splurge for a beachfront room or bungalow. The expansive grounds here are covered with tall pochote trees that are often frequented by roaming bands of howler monkeys. The lodge has a small pool and beautiful oceanfront yoga studio and spa; their Shambala restaurant is excellent.

Playa Santa Teresa, Cóbano, Puntarenas. ✆ **800/724-1235** in the U.S. and Canada, or 2640-0062 in Costa Rica. www.hoteltropicolatino.com. 22 units. $95–$135 double; $155–$240 deluxe rooms and bungalows; $350–$695 suite. **Amenities:** Restaurant; bar; Jacuzzi; small free-form outdoor pool; small spa; free Wi-Fi.

INEXPENSIVE

Hardcore budget travelers can check out **Tranquilo Backpackers** ★ (✆ 2640-0589; www.tranquilobackpackers.com), a bit inland off the road running toward Santa Teresa and has a mix of dorm-style and private rooms.

Malpaís Surf Camp & Resort ★   This is a great, multifaceted, budget-conscious resort with a wide range of rooms and price points. You can opt for everything from bunk-bed rooms with shared bathrooms to private poolside villas. You can also pitch a tent here, if you so desire. A good-size, free-form pool sits at the center of the complex, which itself is about a 5-minute walk from the waves.

Malpaís, Cóbano de Puntarenas. ✆ **2640-0031.** www.malpaissurfcamp.com. 16 units, 8 with shared bathroom. $10 per person, camping; $35 double with shared bathroom; $65 double with private bathroom and $100 villa. **Amenities:** Restaurant; bar; small exercise room; midsize outdoor pool; watersports equipment rental; free Wi-Fi.

Where to Dine

In addition to the places listed below, you might try **Mary's** (✆ 2640-0153; www.maryscostarica.com), a very popular open-air joint that features wood-oven baked pizzas and fresh seafood, and is toward the northern end of Malpaís. The fresh creative cooking at the **Beija Flor Resort** (✆ 2640-1006; www.beijaflor resort.com) is another good option in Malpaís.

On the far northern end of Playa Santa Teresa, **El Rey Patricio** (✆ 2640-0248; www.elreypatricio.com) is a great place to come for tapas, drinks and a sunset view.

Right at the Playa Carmen Commercial Center, at the crossroads at the entrance to town, you'll find a small food court with a wide range of options, including the bistro-style **Artemis Café** (✆ 2640-0579; www.artemiscafe. com) and the somewhat pricey sushi joint **Ume Sushi** (✆ 2640-0968). My favorite, however, is **Product C** ★★ (✆ 2640-1026; www.product-c.com), a seafood retail outlet that also cooks up the daily catch, makes fresh *ceviche*, and serves fresh, farm-grown, local oysters.

VERY EXPENSIVE

Nectar ★★★ FUSION   This is the flagship restaurant at Florblanca Resort, and consistently one of the top fine dining experiences in the country. Chef Norman Roqhuett Mata has continued and built upon a long tradition of fine chefs at the helm of the kitchen here. Start things off with a tuna tartar tower featuring mango and avocado. Main courses run the gamut from a fresh-caught jumbo shrimp risotto to perfectly grilled steaks. Those looking for lighter fare can peruse the sushi and tapas menus. Meals are served in an elegant open-air dining area overlooking the pool and beach. Be sure to save room for dessert. Their signature sweet treat is the ice cream sandwich, featuring all homemade and fresh ice cream between two chocolate chip cookies.

At Florblanca Resort in Santa Teresa. © **2640-0232.** Reservations recommended. Main courses $10–$29. Daily 7am–9pm.

EXPENSIVE

Brisas del Mar ★★★ FUSION   The small, nightly menu at this open-air, hilltop restaurant changes regularly. The British-born chef might serve up some chipotle-lime-marinated mahi-mahi or grilled chicken served over linguine with a Roquefort, brandy, and green peppercorn sauce. Dessert might feature a chocolate-banana bread pudding with single-malt infused crème anglaise. Seating is on a broad wooden deck with fabulous ocean and sunset views. Be sure to have reservations, or come early, as this place fills up fast.

On a hillside, just north of main crossroads in Malpaís. © **2640-0941.** Reservations recommended. Main courses $10–$24. No credit cards. Tues–Sun 8–11am and 4–10pm.

Entertainment & Nightlife

The most popular bar in the area is **Coco Loco ★** (© **6097-2557**), which is right on the beach in Santa Teresa and features a mix of live bands and DJs, with weekly reggae and Latin nights, as well as a monthly full moon party. Also in Santa Teresa, **La Lora Amarilla** (© 2640-0132) is a classic local nightspot. This is definitely the place to come on Saturday night to dance some salsa and merengue with the locals. For a mellower scene, travelers tend to gather in the evenings at **Frank's Place** (© 2640-0096), at the crossroads of Malpaís and Playa Carmen, and the **Malpaís Surf Camp** (see above).

A Truly Remote Beach: Undiscovered, for Now

The Nicoya Peninsula coastline between Santa Teresa and Playa Sámara is perhaps the last, long undeveloped stretch of Costa Rican coastline. The following hotel is roughly midway between Santa Teresa and Playa Sámara. It can be reached year round by rough, mostly unmarked dirt roads, so it is best to carefully coordinate your transportation with the hotel.

Cristal Azul ★   You'll need a four-wheel drive vehicle to reach this isolated hilltop hotel and its four individual cabins. They are simple, almost to the point of austere, but they all offer up fabulous views out on to the ocean. Down below, Playa San Miguel is a quiet and virtually undiscovered piece of Pacific coast sand. Hosts Zene and Henner Morales are very personable and attentive, and their commitment to local tourism, conservation and social programs has helped earn the hotel "4 Leaves" from the CST Sustainable Tourism program.

Playa San Miguel, Guanacaste. © **888/822-7369** in the U.S. and Canada, or 2655-8135 in Costa Rica. www.cristalazul.com. 4 units. $140–$225 double. Rates include full breakfast. **Amenities:** Restaurant; bar; midsize outdoor pool; Wi-Fi.

PLAYA SÁMARA ★

35km (22 miles) S of Nicoya; 245km (152 miles) W of San José

Playa Sámara is a long, broad beach on a gently curved horseshoe-shape bay. Unlike most of the other beaches along this stretch of the Pacific coast, the water here is usually calm and perfect for swimming because an offshore island and rocky headlands break up most of the surf. Playa Sámara is popular both with Tico families seeking a quick and inexpensive getaway and with young Ticos looking to do some serious beach partying. On weekends, in particular, Sámara can get crowded and rowdy. Still, the calm waters and steep cliffs on the far side of the bay make this a very attractive spot, and the beach is so long that the crowds are usually well dispersed. Moreover, if you drive along the rugged coastal road in either direction, you'll discover some truly spectacular and isolated beaches.

Essentials

GETTING THERE & DEPARTING By Car: Head west out of San José on the San José–Caldera Highway (CR27). When you reach Caldera, follow the signs to Puntarenas and the Interamerican Highway (CR1). You will actually follow signs for Liberia and San José, which are, in fact, leading you to the unmarked entrance to CR1. This road (CR23) ends when it hits the Interamerican Highway. You'll want to pass

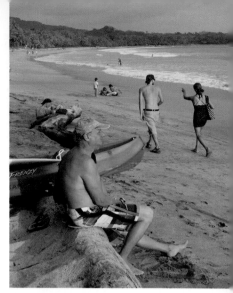

Playa Sámara.

under the bridge and follow the on-ramp, which will put you on the highway heading north. Forty-seven kilometers (29 miles) after you get on the Interamerican Highway heading north, you'll see signs and the turnoff for La Amistad Bridge (CR18). After crossing the bridge, continue on CR18 until it hits CR21. Take this road north to Nicoya. Turn in to the town of Nicoya, and head more or less straight through town until you see signs for Playa Sámara. From here, it's a well-marked and paved road (CR150) all the way to the beach.

To drive to Sámara from Liberia, head out of town on the main road to the Guanacaste beaches, passing through Filadelfia, Santa Cruz, and Nicoya. Once you reach Nicoya, follow the directions outlined above.

By Bus: Alfaro express buses (✆ **2222-2666;** www.empresaalfaro.com) leave San José daily at noon from Avenida 5 between calles 14 and 16. The trip lasts 5 hours; the one-way fare is C4,700. Extra buses are sometimes added on weekends and during peak periods, so it's always wise to check.

Alternatively, you can take a bus from this same station to Nicoya and then catch a second bus from Nicoya to Sámara. **Alfaro** buses leave San José nearly every hour between 6am and 5pm. The fare is C4,250. The trip can take between 4 and 5½ hours, depending if the bus goes via Liberia or La Amistad Bridge. The latter route is much faster and much more frequent. **Empresa Rojas** (✆ **2685-5032**) buses leave Nicoya for Sámara and Carrillo regularly throughout the day, between 5am and 9pm. The trip's duration is 1½ hours. The fare to Sámara is C1,135; the fare to Carrillo is C1,300.

Express buses to San José leave daily at 4 and 8am. Buses for Nicoya leave throughout the day between 5am and 6pm. Buses leave Nicoya for San José nearly every hour between 3am and 5pm.

Interbus (✆ **4100-0888;** www.interbusonline.com) has a daily bus that leaves San José for Playa Sámara at 8am. The fare is $49, and they will pick you up at most San José–area hotels.

GETTING AROUND   If you need a ride around Sámara, or to one of the nearby beaches, have your hotel call you a taxi. Rides in town should cost $2 to $5; rides to nearby beaches might run $10 to $25, depending upon the distance.

VISITOR INFORMATION   The website **www.samarabeach.com** is an excellent, all-around resource for information about Playa Sámara and the vicinity.

CITY LAYOUT   Sámara is a busy little town at the bottom of a steep hill. The main road heads straight into town, passing the soccer field before coming to an end at the beach. Just before the beach is a road to the left that leads to most of the hotels listed below. This road also leads to Playa Carrillo (see below) and the **Hotel Punta Islita** (p. 285). If you turn right 3 blocks before hitting the beach, you'll hit the coastal road that goes to playas Buena Vista, Barrigona, and eventually Nosara.

FAST FACTS   To reach the local police, dial ℂ **2656-0436.** Sámara has a small **medical clinic** (ℂ **2656-0166**). A branch of **Banco Nacional** (ℂ **2656-0089**) is on the road to Playa Buena Vista, just as you head out of town. For full-service laundry, head to **Green Life Laundry** (ℂ **2656-1051**), about 3 blocks west of the Banco Nacional.

Exploring Playa Sámara

Aside from sitting on the sand and soaking up the sun, the main activities in Playa Sámara seem to be hanging out in the bars and *sodas* and dancing into the early morning hours. But if you're looking for something more, there's horseback

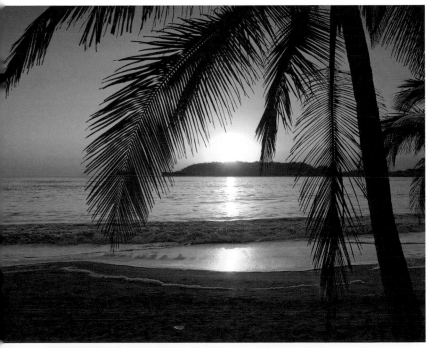

Playa Carrillo.

9

PUNTARENAS & THE NICOYA PENINSULA

Playa Sámara

riding either on the beach or through the bordering pastureland and forests. Other options include sea kayaking in the calm waters off Playa Sámara, sport-fishing, snorkeling, scuba diving, boat tours, mountain biking, and tours to Playa Ostional to see the mass nesting of olive ridley sea turtles. You can inquire about and book any of these tours at your hotel.

You'll find that the beach is nicer and cleaner down at the south end. Better yet, head about 8km (5 miles) south to **Playa Carrillo** ★★, a long crescent of soft, white sand. With almost no development here, the beach is nearly always deserted. Loads of palm trees provide shade. If you've got a good four-wheel-drive vehicle, ask for directions at your hotel and set off in search of the hidden gems of **Playa Buena Vista** and **Playa Barrigona** ★★, which are north of Sámara, less than a half-hour drive away.

e can help you arrange any number of tour options, including horseback rides, boat trips, sea kayaking, scuba diving, and snorkeling outings. You might also contact **Carrillo Adventures** (𝄞 2656-0606; www.carrilloadventures. com), an excellent all-around local tour company.

CANOPY TOURS   The folks at **Wingnuts Canopy Tours** (𝄞 2656-0153; www.wingnutscanopy.com) offer zip-line and harness "canopy tours". The 2-hour outing costs $60 per person or $40 for those under 12. If you want to repeat the adventure, these folks offer a 50% discount on your second tour. You'll find their office by the giant strangler fig tree, or matapalo, toward the southern end of the beach.

SPORT FISHING   Almost every hotel in the area can arrange sportfishing trips, or you can contact **Kingfisher** ★ (𝄞 2656-0091; www.costaricabillfishing.com). Rates run from $300 to $800 for a half-day and $700 to $1,400 for a full day outing.

SURFING   The waves hitting Playa Sámara are somewhat muffled by an offshore reef and headlands on each side. For some this makes it a great wave to learn on. For lessons or to rent a board, check in with **C&C Surf Shop and School**

Scuba diving.

(© **5006-0369;** http://cncsurfsamara.webs.com) or **Choco's Surf School** (© **8937-5246;** www.chocossurfschool.com). Surfboard rentals run around $12 to $15 per day. Private lessons cost $30 to $50 per hour.

ULTRALIGHT FLYING For a bird's-eye view of the area, head over to the **Flying Crocodile** (© **8330-3923;** www.flying-crocodile.com) in Playa Buena Vista. The folks here also offer flights on a two-seat (one for you, one for the pilot) Gyrocopter, the ultralight equivalent of a helicopter. Although it might feel like little more than a modified tricycle with a nylon wing and lawnmower motor, these winged wonders are very safe. A 20-minute flight will run you $110, while an hour-long tour costs $230.

WILDLIFE VIEWING Located near Barra Honda National Park (see below), **Rancho Humo** ★★ (© **2233-2233;** www.ranchohumo.com) is a private wildlife reserve that offers fabulous bird-watching and wildlife viewing opportunities along the Tempisque River basin and surrounding wetlands. The area is rich in waterbird species, shore lizards, and crocodiles. A full-day tour ($95) here includes a river boat trip, a tour of the reeds and lowland forest in a motorized safari-style vehicle, and a tour of the neighboring cattle ranching operations, as well as lunch. Transportation can be provided, and you can choose a half-day tour that takes in only one or two of the elements of the full-day tour.

Learn the Language

If you want to acquire or polish some language skills while here, check in with the **Sámara Language School** (© **866/978-6813** in the U.S. and Canada, or 2656-3000 in Sámara; www.samaralanguageschool.com). These folks offer a range of programs and private lessons and can arrange for a homestay with a local family. The facility even features classes with ocean views, although that might be a detriment to your language learning.

Going Down Under

Spelunkers will want to head 62km (38 miles) northeast of Playa Sámara on the road to La Amistad Bridge. If you don't have a car, your best bet is to get to Nicoya, which is about a half-hour away by bus, and then take a taxi to the park, which should cost about $20. Here, at **Barra Honda National Park** ★ (© **2659-1551** or 2685-5267), is an extensive system of caves, some of which reach more than 200m (656 ft.) in depth. Human remains and indigenous relics have been found in other caves, but those are not open to the public. The park is open daily from 8am to 5pm and admission is $10.

If you plan to descend the one publicly accessible cave, you'll need to hire a local guide at the park entrance station. These guides are always available, and will provide harnesses, helmets, and flashlights. Depending upon your group size and bargaining abilities, expect to pay between $20 to $40 per person for a visit to the **Terciopelo Cave,** including the guide, harness, helmet, and flashlight. Furthermore, the cave is open only during the dry season (mid-Nov to Apr). You begin the roughly 3-hour tour with a descent of 19m (62 ft.) straight down a wooden ladder with a safety rope attached. Inside you'll see plenty of impressive stalactites and stalagmites while visiting several chambers of varying sizes. Even if you don't descend, the trails around Barra Honda and its prominent limestone plateau are great for hiking and bird-watching. Be sure to make a stop at **La Cascada,** a gentle waterfall that fills and passes through a series of calcium and limestone pools, some of them large enough to bathe in. The entire operation is slightly reminiscent of Ocho Rios in Jamaica.

Where to Stay

MODERATE

Fenix Hotel ★
These beachfront studio apartments are a great value. Set towards the middle section of the long, gentle Playa Sámara, they have a wonderful location—just a short walk from most of the restaurants, clubs, and downtown activity—and yet are quiet and slightly removed. Set in a tight ring around the hotel's small pool, each unit features a full kitchen. The beach is just steps away, and there's a series of hammocks strung from coconut palms perfectly positioned right between the pool and sea. The owners are very hands-on and run a tight, yet friendly, ship.

Playa Sámara, Nicoya, Guanacaste. ✆ **2656-0158.** www.fenixhotel.com. 6 units. $114–$145 double. Children 17 and under stay free in parent's room. **Amenities:** Small outdoor pool; free Wi-Fi.

The Hideaway Hotel ★★
This two-story boutique hotel has the feel of a converted home. The guest rooms are all large, contemporary, and cool, featuring bold colors and pleasant design touches. There's an inviting pool and well-kept gardens, and the food and service are excellent. The hotel is set about a block or so inland from the far southern end of Playa Sámara.

Playa Sámara, Nicoya, Guanacaste. ✆ **2656-1145.** www.thehideawayplayasamara.com. 12 units. $89–$179 double. Rates include full breakfast. **Amenities:** Restaurant; bar; outdoor pool; free Wi-Fi.

Hotel Guanamar ★
It helps to have a rental car if you're staying here, but the ocean views and easy access to Playa Carrillo make this a great choice if you do. The best rooms are set into a steep hillside, with private, ocean-view balconies. The hotel's main restaurant and pool are set on the property's highest point, which also enjoys some fabulous vistas.

Puerto Carrillo. ✆ **2656-0054.** www.guanamarhotel.com. 37 units. $110–$140 double. Rates include taxes and breakfast. **Amenities:** Restaurant; bar; large outdoor pool; room service; free Wi-Fi.

Sámara Tree House Inn ★★
This small hotel is set right on the sand in the heart of Playa Sámara. The four raised-stilt wooden cabins that give this place its name are set in a tight line facing the ocean. They have wonderful views from their large sitting rooms, although the rest of the unit does feel a bit small and spartan by comparison, and there's no air-conditioning. However, every unit here does come with a full kitchenette, and there's a postage stamp–size pool at the center of the complex.

Playa Sámara, Guanacaste. ✆ **2656-0733.** www.samaratreehouse.com. 6 units. $89–$165 double. Rates include breakfast. **Amenities:** Jacuzzi; small outdoor pool; free Wi-Fi.

INEXPENSIVE

In addition to the hotels listed below, **Tico Adventure Lodge ★** (✆ 2656-0628; www.ticoadventurelodge.com) is another good option, about 2 blocks from the beach, in the heart of town. A slew of very inexpensive places to stay are along the road into town and around the soccer field. Many of the rooms at these places are less accommodating than your average jail cell.

Casa del Mar   This is my favorite budget option in Playa Sámara. The rooms are spacious, clean and comfortable, and the beach is just a few steps away across the street. The pool is just a hair bigger and deeper than a fountain, but it will cool you off on a hot day.

Playa Sámara, Nicoya, Guanacaste. © **2656-0264.** www.casadelmarsamara.net. 17 units, 11 with private bathroom. $45–$50 double with shared bathroom; $65–$105 double with private bathroom and A/C. Rates include taxes. Breakfast included for private bathroom rates year round. Breakfast included for shared bathroom rates in off season. **Amenities:** Bar; unheated outdoor pool/Jacuzzi; free Wi-Fi.

Hotel Belvedere ★   This long-standing German-run option is a few blocks inland and uphill from the beach. Rooms are housed in the older main building, and a newer annex, another block or so inland. Those in the annex feature modern split A/C units, one queen and one twin bed, a coffeemaker, and little fridge. The rooms in the older section are somewhat more basic, although everything is well maintained and immaculate. Some have a small kitchenette, and so are geared toward longer stays and families. Each of the building sites has a pool. Only breakfast is served, although they run a snack bar throughout most of the day and an honor bar system for beverages.

Playa Sámara. www.belvederesamara.net. © **2656-0213.** 24 units. $50–$85 double. Rates include breakfast. **Amenities:** Lounge; Jacuzzi; 2 outdoor pools; free Wi-Fi.

A NEARBY LUXURY HOTEL

Hotel Punta Islita ★★★   This exclusive and remote luxury resort sits on a hilltop above the beach. Most of the rooms are private bungalows or villas, and many come with either a private Jacuzzi or plunge pool. The larger villas and

Hotel Punta Islita.

private homes make great bases for families and small groups. The beach is a 10-minute or so hike away, but the hotel runs regular shuttle services. My favorite way to get to the beach here however is via the hotel's in-house canopy tour. The resort's main pool is up on the hillside, with a gorgeous infinity effect, and another pool and bar and grill are down by the beach. Punta Islita actively supports a range of local social, artistic, and conservation projects. In 2014, Punta Islita was added to the Marriott hotel chain's exclusive Autograph Collection. These folks have a sister mountain lodge El Silencio (p. 315) that can be bundled together to give you the best of two worlds inside Costa Rica.

Playa Islita. ☎ **866/446-4053** in the U.S. and Canada, or 2231-6122 in Costa Rica. www.hotel puntaislita.com. 34 units, 22 villas. $280–$330 double; $476–$528 suite or casita; $613–$723 villas 4 people. Rates include breakfast. **Amenities:** 2 restaurants; 2 bars; 9-hole golf course and driving range; small exercise room and spa; Jacuzzi; small tile outdoor pool and lap pool; room service; smoke-free rooms; 2 lit tennis courts; free Wi-Fi.

Where to Dine

Sámara has numerous inexpensive *sodas,* and most of the hotels have their own restaurants. In addition to the places mentioned below, **El Ancla** (☎ **2656-0716**), located a bit south of downtown, serves up good, simple meals, with an excellent view of the beach and waves.

El Lagarto ★ STEAK/GRILL   A massive fire churns out a stream of hot coals to feed the large, long grill stations at this beachfront restaurant and bar. The setting is beautiful, with heavy wooden furniture set under tall trees and dim lighting. Grilled meats, seafood, and other goodies are the heart of the long menu here. Everything is served on huge, heavy crosscut blocks of wood, which adds to the rustic, homey vibe.

On the beach, north end of Playa Sámara. ☎ **2656-0750.** www.ellagartobbq.com. Reservations recommended. Main courses $8–$32. Daily 3–11pm.

Gusto Beach ★★ ITALIAN/BISTRO   This simple, Italian-run restaurant is basically a beachfront trattoria—and then some. Three meals daily are served at a mix of tables, chairs, couches, and bar stools at high cocktail tables all set in the sand underneath coconut palms strung with rope lighting. You can get excellent pastas, panini, and thin-crust pizzas, as well as sushi, sashimi, and curries. There's often live music or DJs. A sister restaurant, **Gusto Creativo,** fronts the soccer field in the center of town.

On the beach, north end of Playa Sámara. ☎ **2656-0252.** Reservations recommended. Main courses C4,000–C10,500. Daily 9am–11pm.

Entertainment & Nightlife

After dark the most happening place in town is **Bar Arriba** ★ (☎ 2656-0487 or 8996-3954), a second-floor affair with a contemporary vibe a couple of blocks inland from the beach on the main road into town. You might also check out what's going on at **Gusto Beach** ★ (see above), **La Vela Latina** (☎ 2656-2286), or **Tabanuco** (☎ 2656-1056), all on the beach or fronting the water, right near the center of the action, on the main road running parallel to the beach off the center of town.

PLAYA NOSARA ★★

55km (34 miles) SW of Nicoya; 266km (165 miles) W of San José

As is the case in Malpaís, **Playa Nosara** is a bucket term used to refer to several neighboring beaches, spread along an isolated stretch of coast. In addition to the namesake beach, **Playa Guiones, Playa Pelada, Playa Garza,** and (sometimes) **Playa Ostional** are also lumped into this area. In fact, the village of Nosara itself is several kilometers inland from the beach. Playa Nosara marks the northern limit of the Nicoya Peninsula.

Playa Guiones is one of Costa Rica's most dependable beach breaks, and surfers come here in good numbers throughout the year. However, the waves are still much less crowded than you would find in and around Tamarindo.

The best way to get to Nosara is to fly, but, with everything so spread out, that makes getting around difficult after you've arrived. The roads to, in, and around Nosara are almost always in very rough shape, with little sign that this will improve anytime soon.

Essentials

GETTING THERE & DEPARTING By Plane: **Sansa** (✆ 877/767-2672 in the U.S. and Canada, or 2290-4100 in Costa Rica; www.flysansa.com) and **Nature Air** (✆ 800/235-9272 in the U.S. and Canada, or 2299-6000 in Costa Rica; www.natureair.com) both have several flights daily to **Nosara airport** (airport code: NOB; no phone). Fares run between $100 and $145 each way.

It's usually about a 5- to 10-minute drive from the airport to most hotels. Taxis wait for every arrival, and fares range between C3,000 and C6,000 to most hotels in Nosara.

By Car: Follow the directions for getting to Playa Sámara (see "Playa Sámara," earlier in this chapter), but watch for a well-marked fork in the road a few kilometers before you reach that beach. The right-hand fork leads to Nosara over another 22km (14 miles) of rough dirt road.

By Bus: An **Alfaro** express bus (✆ 2222-2666 in San José, or 2682-0064 in Nosara; www.empresaalfaro.com) leaves San José daily at 5:30am from Avenida 5 between calles 14 and 16. The trip's duration is 5¹/₂ hours; the one-way fare is C4,805.

You can also take an Alfaro bus from San José to Nicoya and then catch a second bus from Nicoya to Nosara. **Alfaro** buses leave San José nearly every hour between 6am and 5pm. The fare is C3,950. The trip can take between 4 and 5¹/₂ hours, depending on whether the bus goes via Liberia or La Amistad Bridge. The latter route is much faster and much more frequent. **Empresa Rojas** buses (✆ 2685-5352) leave Nicoya for Nosara daily at 4:45 and 10am, 12:30pm, and 3 and 5:30pm. The trip is about 2 hours, and the one-way fare is C1,870. Return buses leave Nosara for Nicoya at 5, 6, and 7am, noon and 3:30pm

A direct Alfaro bus from Nosara to San José leaves daily at 12:45pm. Buses to Nicoya leave Nosara daily at 4:45 and 10am, noon, and 3 and 5:30pm. Buses leave Nicoya for San José nearly every hour between 3am and 5pm.

GETTING AROUND If you want to rent a car, both **Economy** (✆ 877/326-7368 in the U.S. and Canada, or 2582-1246 in Costa Rica; www.economyrentacar.com) and **National** (✆ 2242-7878; www.natcar.com) have offices here.

PUNTARENAS & THE NICOYA PENINSULA | Playa Nosara

Because demand often outstrips supply, I recommend you reserve a car in advance. Alternatively, you can rent an ATV from several operators around town, including **Iguana Expeditions** (see below) and **Boca Nosara Tours** (see below). If you need a taxi, call **Taxi Freddy** (*©* **8662-6080**) or **Gypsy Cab Company** (*©* **8302-1903;** www.nosaracab.com).

VILLAGE LAYOUT The village of Nosara is about 5km (3 miles) inland from the beach. The small airstrip runs pretty much through the center of town; however, most hotels listed here are on or near the beach itself.

This area was originally conceived and zoned as a primarily residential community. The maze of dirt roads and lack of any single defining thoroughfare can be confusing for first-time visitors. Luckily, a host of hotel and restaurant signs spread around the area help point lost travelers in the direction of their final destination.

FAST FACTS You'll find the post office and police station (*©* **2682-1130**) right at the end of the airstrip. An EBAIS medical clinic (*©* **2682-0266**)

Playa Guiones.

and a couple of pharmacies are in the village as well. Both Banco Popular and Banco Nacional have offices in Nosara with ATMs. There's even a tiny strip mall at the crossroads to Playa Guiones.

An Internet cafe is in the village, and others are at **Café de Paris** (p. 292), **Frog Pad** (*©* **2682-4039**), and **Harbor Reef Surf Resort** (p. 291).

Exploring Playa Nosara

Among the several beaches at Nosara are the long, curving **Playa Guiones ★★**, **Playa Nosara ★**, and the diminutive **Playa Pelada ★**. Because the village of Nosara is several miles inland, these beaches tend to be clean, secluded, and quiet. Surfing and bodysurfing are good here, particularly at Playa Guiones, which is garnering quite a reputation as a consistent and rideable beach break. Pelada is a short white-sand beach with three deep scallops, backed by sea grasses and mangroves. There isn't too much sand at high tide, so you'll want to hit the beach when the tide's out. At either end of the beach, rocky outcroppings reveal tide pools at low tide.

When the seas are calm, you can do some decent snorkeling around the rocks and reefs just offshore. Masks, snorkels, and fins can be rented at **Café de Paris** (p. 292) or **Coconut Harry's** (p. 289). Bird-watchers should explore the mangrove swamps around the estuary mouth of the Río Nosara. Just walk north from Playa Pelada and follow the riverbank; then explore the paths into the mangroves. In addition to numerous water, shore, and sea bird species, you're apt to spot a range of hawks and other raptors, as well as toucans and several parrot species.

FISHING   All the hotels in the area can arrange fishing charters for $200 to $500 for a half-day, or $400 to $1,200 for a full day. These rates are for one to four people and vary according to boat size and accouterments.

HIKING & WILDLIFE VIEWING   Located on land surrounding the Nosara river mouth, the **Nosara Biological Reserve** (✆ **2682-0035;** www.lagarta.com) features a network of trails and raised walkways through tropical transitional forests and mangrove swamps. More than 270 species of birds have been spotted here. This private reserve is owned and managed by the folks at the **Lagarta Lodge** (see below), and the trails start right at the hotel. Admission is $6. Guided tours and guided boat tours are also available.

HORSEBACK RIDING & QUAD TOURS   The folks at **Boca Nosara Tours** (✆ **2682-0280;** www.bocanosaratours.com) have a large stable of well-cared-for horses and a range of beach, jungle, and waterfall rides to choose from. They also run similar tours on motorized off-road quads. Rates run between $50 and $90 per person, depending on the size of your group and the length of the tour.

KAYAK TOURS   Based out of the Gilded Iguana hotel and restaurant, **Iguana Expeditions** ★ (✆ **2682-4089;** www.iguanaexpeditions.com) offers a range of full- and half-day tours around the area. Explore the inland coastal mangroves by kayak or hike to a stunning waterfall. These folks can also arrange inexpensive fishing outings in a *panga* (small craft) with a local fisherman. The kayaking expedition costs $50, and the waterfall hike is $25.

SEA TURTLE–WATCHING   If you time your trip right, you can do a night tour to nearby **Playa Ostional** to watch nesting olive ridley sea turtles. These turtles come ashore by the thousands in a mass egg-laying phenomenon known as an *arribada.* The *arribadas* are so difficult to predict that no one runs regularly scheduled turtle-viewing trips, but when the *arribada* is in full swing, several local guides and agencies offer tours. These *arribadas* take place 4 to 10 times between July and December; each occurrence lasts between 3 and 10 days. Consider yourself very lucky if you happen to be around during one of these fascinating natural phenomena. Your best bet is to ask the staff at your hotel or check in with **Iguana Expeditions** ★ (✆ **2682-4089;** www.iguanaexpeditions.com). Tours are generally run at night, but because the turtles come ashore in such numbers, you can sometimes catch them in the early morning light as well. Even if it's not turtle-nesting season, you might want to look into visiting Playa Ostional just to have a long, wide expanse of beach to yourself. However, be careful swimming here because the surf and riptides can be formidable. During the dry season (mid-Nov to Apr), you can usually get here in a regular car, but during the rainy season you'll need four-wheel-drive. This beach is part of **Ostional National Wildlife Refuge** (✆ **2682-0428**). At the northwest end of the refuge is **India Point,** which is known for its tide pools and rocky outcrops.

SURFING   With miles of excellent beach breaks and relatively few crowds, this is a great place to surf or learn how to surf. If you want to try to stand up for your first time, check in with the folks at **Coconut Harry's Surf Shop** (✆ **2682-0574;** www.coconutharrys.com), **Del Mar Surf Camp** (✆ **855/833-5627** in the U.S. and Canada, or 2682-1433 in Costa Rica; www.delmarsurfcamp.com), or **Safari Surf School** (✆ **866/433-3355** in the U.S. and Canada, or 2682-0874 in Costa Rica; www.safarisurfschool.com). All of the above offer hourly solo or group lessons, multiday packages with accommodations and meals included, and board rental.

YOGA & MORE If you want to spend some time getting your mind and body together, check in with the **Nosara Yoga Institute** ★★ (☏ **866/439-4704** in the U.S. and Canada, or 2682-0071 in Costa Rica; www.nosarayoga. com), which offers intensive and daily yoga classes, teacher trainings, and a host of custom-designed "retreat" options. This is an internationally recognized retreat and teacher training center. Their daily 90-minute classes are open to the public and cost just $15, and they even provide a mat.

You might also check in to see if anything is being offered up at the Harmony Hotel & Spa (see below).

Where to Stay

In addition to the places listed below, the **Nosara Beach House** ★ (☏ **2682-0019;** www.thenosarabeachhouse.com), on Playa Guiones, has clean, comfortable rooms and a swimming pool—and it's right on the beach, to boot. For an intimate option that's also a very good deal, check out the **Nosara B&B** ★ (☏ **2682-0209;** www.nosarabandb.net).

VERY EXPENSIVE

The Harmony Hotel & Spa ★★★ With an enviable setting right on Playa Guiones, this is by far the best hotel option in Nosara. The "Coco" rooms are all spacious, with queen-size beds and a private, enclosed garden deck area featuring an outdoor shower with massive rainwater-style shower head. The bungalows are even larger, with king beds. A short path leads to the shore, and the hotel has a shower and fresh towels for guests right where the property lets out on to the beach. There's an excellent onsite spa and yoga facility, and the restaurant serves top-notch local fare and healthful spa cuisine. This hotel was awarded "5 Leaves" from the CST Sustainable Tourism program, thanks to a comprehensive commitment to environmental protection, social responsibility, and other sustainable practices.

Playa Guiones. ☏ **2682-4114.** www.harmonynosara.com. 24 units. $200–$300 double; $270–$370 bungalow; $490–$590 2-bedroom suite. Rates include breakfast and 1 yoga class. **Amenities:** Restaurant; bar; complimentary use of bikes; midsize outdoor pool; spa; surfboard rental; free Wi-Fi.

L'Acqua Viva ★ This is the most upscale and best equipped hotel in Nosara, and it features some unique and beautiful architectural touches, including a wide range of pools and water features—thus the name, which is Italian for "Living Water." However, the L'Acqua Viva is located a good deal inland from the beach. Moreover, Nosara's main road, a dusty unpaved thoroughfare, wraps around the property, blanketing the rooms and buildings closest to the road in thick dust throughout most of the high season.

Playa Guiones. ☏ **888/273-1977** in the U.S., or 2682-1087 in Costa Rica. www.lacquaviva.com. 35 units. $170 double; $255–$275 suite; $425–$595 villa. Rates include continental breakfast. **Amenities:** Restaurant; bar; Jacuzzi; large outdoor pools; room service; full-service spa; Wi-Fi.

MODERATE

Harbor Reef Surf Resort ★ This sprawling miniresort features a mix of rooms and suites at excellent prices, and is quite popular with the surf crowd. All of the rooms are spacious and clean, if on the spartan side. Some of the suites come with full kitchens, and these folks also rent out several fully equipped houses for longer stays. The grounds feature tall trees and lush gardens and two swimming pools. Hammocks are strung from some of those tall trees. The beach and popular surf break at Playa Guiones is about a 3-minute walk away. These folks have a well-stocked convenience store attached and rent bicycles, ATVs and golf carts.

Playa Guiones. ℂ **2682-5049.** www.harborreef.com. 23 units. $110–$185 double; $220–$250 suite. Rates include continental breakfast. **Amenities:** Restaurant; bar; 2 small outdoor pools; watersports equipment rental; free Wi-Fi.

INEXPENSIVE

In addition to the places mentioned below, **Kaya Sol** ★ (ℂ **2682-1459**; www. nosarahotelkayasol.com) is a popular budget option and surfer hangout.

The Gilded Iguana ★ Located in the heart of Playa Guiones, about 200m (600 ft.) inland from the beach, this place features a mix of rooms, a refreshing kidney-shaped pool, and one of the best restaurant and bar scenes in the area (see below). The most economical rooms here are simple and road-worn. I think it's worth a splurge for the newer rooms with air-conditioning. The downside to the restaurant and bar's popularity is that it can be noisy here, especially when there's a live band or major sporting event going on.

Playa Guiones. ℂ **2682-0450.** www.thegildediguana.com. 12 units. $50–$60 double; $75–$95 suite. **Amenities:** Restaurant; bar; midsize outdoor pool; free Wi-Fi.

Lagarta Lodge ★★ Geared slightly more to nature lovers than surfers, this small lodge sits on a high hilltop overlooking the Nosara River. Rooms are simple, but clean and cozy. Some of the rooms, as well as the small restaurant here, enjoy fabulous views over the river and rainforests and beyond to the long stretch of Ostional Beach in the distance. It's only a 10- to 15-minute jaunt down to the beach, but it's a pretty steep and strenuous hike back up to the hotel. The owners of this hotel own 35 hectares (86 acres) of land bordering the Nosara River, which they've converted into a private reserve. Guests here get unlimited access to the trails of the reserve, which pass through tropical lowland rainforests and mangrove forests.

Playa Nosara. ℂ **2682-0035.** www.lagarta.com. 12 units. $55–$150 double. **Amenities:** Restaurant; bar; midsize outdoor pool; Wi-Fi.

Where to Dine

In addition to the places mentioned below, **Marlin Bill's** (ℂ **2682-0458**) is a popular and massive open-air haunt on the hillside on the main road, just across from **Café de Paris** (see below). You can expect to get good, fresh seafood and American classics here. For Italian, **La Dolce Vita** ★★ (ℂ **2682-0107**), on the outskirts of town on the road to Playa Sámara, serves up good Italian fare nightly.

If you're looking to beat the heat, head to **Robin's Ice Cream** ★ (ℂ **2682-0617**; www.robinsicecream.com) for some homemade ice cream. This popular place also serves breakfast, lunch, and dinner.

For local flavor, **Doña Olga's** (no phone) is a simple Costa Rican *soda* right on the beach in Playa Pelada.

Café de Paris ★ BAKERY/BISTRO I like to stop here for a freshly baked croissant and cup of coffee before an early morning surf session—and I often return for a full breakfast afterwards. But it's also worthwhile for lunch (think burgers, nachos, or wraps) or dinner—both the steak au poivre and fish curry are excellent. A pool and children's play set just off the main dining area make this a good choice for families with young kids. It's located right at the main crossroads for access to Playa Guiones.

On the main road into Nosara. ℂ **2682-1036.** www.cafedeparis.net. Main courses C6,500–C9,900. Daily 7am–5pm.

The Gilded Iguana ★★ SEAFOOD/GRILL With excellent food and fresh fish perfectly prepared, this casual, open-air spot is one of the most popular in the Nosara area. The food here is bar-food-plus, with all the regular bar-food staples you'd expect—burgers, nachos, quesadillas, fajitas, and wings—as well as more substantial (chicken Parmesan) or eclectic (Thai shrimp) fare. The menu also features vegetarian, gluten-free, and low-calorie options. There's live music here Tuesdays and Fridays.

About 90m (295 ft.) inland from the beach at Playa Guiones. ℂ **2682-0259.** www.thegilded iguana.com. Main courses C3,500–C8,500. Daily 7:00am–9:30pm.

La Luna ★★ INTERNATIONAL This funky, oceanfront bistro enjoys the best setting of any restaurant in Nosara. From the grassy perch right above Playa Pelada, you can watch surfers just below from one of the outdoor tables. This is also a great place to catch the sunset. Wood oven–fired pizzas and Mediterranean fare are the specialties here, but nightly chalkboard specials might feature anything from pad Thai to chicken curry. Start things off with the feta quinoa salad, fresh ceviche, or some tuna tartare. For lunch, I really like their fish tacos.

Playa Pelada. ℂ **2682-0122.** Main courses C6,600–C10,500. Daily Noon–9pm.

Entertainment & Nightlife

When evening rolls around, don't expect a major party scene. **Kaya Sol** (ℂ **2682-1459**) has a lounge-style scene popular with surfers, and the **Gilded Iguana** (see above) often has live music. In "downtown" Nosara, you'll probably want to check out either the **Tropicana** (ℂ **2682-0140**), the town's long-standing local disco, or the **Legends Bar** (ℂ **2682-0184**), an American–style bar with big-screen TVs and pool and foosball tables.

North of Nosara

Just north of Nosara lies Playa Ostional, famous for its massive nestings of olive ridley sea turtles (see above). This is a very underdeveloped beach village with only a few hotels. The best of these is **Hotel Luna Azul** ★ (ℂ **2682-1400;** www.hotellunaazul.com), which features beautiful individual bungalows and a great view of the ocean—although the beach is a good distance away. If you come to Ostional to surf, try the **Ostional Turtle Lodge** (ℂ **2682-0131;** www.surfing ostional.com), a basic hostel-type affair right on the beach near the center of the village.

A baby sea turtle on Playa Ostional.

THE NORTHERN ZONE:

MOUNTAIN LAKES, CLOUD FORESTS & A VOLCANO

10

C osta Rica's northern zone is a fabulous destination for all manner of adventurers, naturalists, and down-to-earth travelers. The region is home to several prime ecotourist destinations, including the majestic **Arenal Volcano ★★** and the misty **Monteverde Cloud Forest Biological Reserve ★★★**. Changes in elevation create unique microclimates and ecosystems throughout the region. You'll find rainforests and cloud forests, jungle rivers and waterfalls, mountain lakes, lowland marshes, and an unbelievable wealth of birds and other wildlife. In addition to these natural wonders, this region also provides an intimate glimpse into the rural heart and soul of Costa Rica. Small, isolated lodges flourish, and towns and villages remain predominantly small agricultural communities.

This area is also a must for adventure travelers. The northern zone has one of the best windsurfing spots in the world, on **Lake Arenal ★**, as well as excellent opportunities for mountain biking, hiking, canyoning, and river rafting. Zip-line canopy tours and suspended forest bridges abound. And if you partake in any number of adventure activities, you'll also find several soothing natural hot springs in the area where you can soak your tired muscles.

THE BEST NORTHERN ZONE TRAVEL EXPERIENCES

o **Soaking in a Hot Spring at the Foot of Arenal Volcano:** Although the eruptions have subsided, Arenal Volcano remains the source of several natural hot springs, ranging from the over-the-top splendor of Tabacón Grand Spa Thermal Resort, to the simple forest enshrouded pools at the family-run Eco Termales. See p. 301.

o **Rappelling Down the Face of a Rainforest Waterfall:** Canyoning is a wet and wild adventure sport that is thriving in Costa Rica's northern zone. A mix of hiking, river wading, and rappelling, these tours are offered in La Fortuna and Monteverde. See p. 303 and 331.

The Northern Zone's Top Sustainable Hotels

Arenal Observatory Lodge (p. 312)
Caño Negro Natural Lodge (p. 316)
El Silencio Lodge & Spa (p. 315)
Hotel Poco a Poco (p. 336)
La Quinta de Sarapiquí Country Inn (p. 346)
La Selva Biological Station (p. 345)
Monteverde Lodge & Gardens (p. 336)
Rara Avis (p. 346)
Selva Verde Lodge (p. 345)
Tabacón Grand Spa Thermal Resort (p. 311)
Villa Blanca Cloud Forest & Spa (p. 316)

PREVIOUS PAGE: **Arenal Volcano.**

Arenal Volcano's cooled lava flows.

○ **Hiking the Trails of a Cloud Forest:** The well-groomed network of trails at the Monteverde Cloud Forest Biological Reserve reveals its rich mysteries with stunning regularity. Walk through gray mist and peer up at the dense tangle of epiphytes and vines, looking for exotic birds and troops of monkeys. See p. 328.

○ **Climbing Over Cooled-off Lava at Arenal National Park:** This area has tons of great hiking, but I especially like scrambling over the volcano's old lava flows. Most are on the relatively flat flanks of the volcano, so there's not too much climbing involved. See p. 302.

○ **Riding a Horse or Mountain Bike Along a Rural Back Road:** The dirt roads and ox-trails of this rural zone provide a wealth of great opportunities for mountain biking and horseback riding. See the "Exploring" sections of individual destinations throughout this chapter.

ARENAL VOLCANO & LA FORTUNA ★★

140km (87 miles) NW of San José; 61km (38 miles) E of Tilarán

In July 1968, Arenal Volcano, which had lain dormant for hundreds of years, surprised everybody by erupting with sudden violence. The nearby village of Tabacón was destroyed, and nearly 80 of its inhabitants were killed. At 1,607m (5,271-ft.) high, Arenal was for many decades afterward one of the world's most regularly active volcanoes. Sometime around December 2010, it entered into a relatively quiet phase. No one knows how long this may last. Still, rising to a near-perfect cone, the volcano itself remains majestic to gaze upon. And the area offers up a rich variety of primary rainforests, rushing jungle rivers and waterfalls, lush natural hot springs, and a wide range of adventure activities.

The Northern Zone

NICARAGUA

Los Chiles

Caño Negro

Caño Negro
Nat'l Wildlife
Refuge 35

San Jorge

San Juan

San Rafael
de Guatuso

Carlos

Boca Tapada

Trinidad

Vol. Tenorio
Nat'l Park

Volcán Tenorio

Guatuso
Indian Res.

Santa Rosa

San

Gloria

Veracruz

Puerto Viejo
de Sarapiquí

Nuevo Arenal

Lago
Arenal

La Fortuna

Muelle

Pital

Chilamate

La Selva
Biological
Station

Tilarán

142

Volcán Arenal

141

La Virgen

Aguas Zarcas

San Miguel

Horquetas

Arenal
Nat'l Park

Florencia

140

Volcán Platanar

Monteverde

Monteverde
Cloud Forest
Biological Reserve

Ciudad Quesada

Juntas

Juan Castro
Blanco
Nat'l Park

Vol. Poás
Nat'l Park

Braulio
Carrillo
Nat'l Park

10 mi

10 km

The Northern Zone

San Ramon

Zarcero

Volcán Poás

Naranjo

La Paz
Waterfall Gardens

San Pedro

Volcán Barva

Central Range

Road Closed

Sarapiquí

Frio

SAN JOSÉ

The
Northern
Zone

PACIFIC
OCEAN

Lying at the eastern foot of this natural spectacle is the town of **La Fortuna.** Once a humble little farming village, La Fortuna has become a magnet for
volcano watchers, adventure tourists, and assorted travelers from around the
world.

Essentials

GETTING THERE & DEPARTING **Nature Air** (✆ **800/235-9272** in the U.S.
and Canada, or 2549-7534 in Costa Rica; www.natureair.com) flies to Arenal/La
Fortuna from Juan Santamaría International Airport in San José (airport code:
SJO).

Taxis are sometimes waiting for arriving flights. If not, you can call one at
✆ **2479-9605.** The fare to La Fortuna runs around C6,000. Alternatively,
Nature Air can arrange to have a van waiting for you, for $62 for up to six
people.

By Car: Several routes connect La Fortuna and San José. The most popular
is to head west on the Interamerican Highway (CR1) from San José and then
turn north at Naranjo, continuing north through Zarcero to Ciudad Quesada on
CR141. From Ciudad Quesada, CR141 passes through Florencia, Jabillos, and
Tanque on its way to La Fortuna. This route offers wonderful views of the San
Carlos valley as you come down from Ciudad Quesada; Zarcero, with its topiary

La Fortuna and Arenal Volcano.

gardens and quaint church, makes a good place to stop, stretch your legs, and snap a few photos (see chapter 7, "The Central Valley," for more information).

You can also stay on the Interamerican Highway (CR1) until San Ramón (west of Naranjo) and then head north through La Tigra on CR142. This route is very scenic and passes the Villa Blanca Cloud Forest & Spa (p. 316). The travel time on any of the above routes is roughly 3 to 3½ hours.

By Bus: Buses (© **2255-0567** or 2255-4318) leave San José for La Fortuna at 6:30, 8:30, and 11:30am from the **Atlántico del Norte** bus station at Avenida 9 and Calle 12. The trip lasts 4 hours; the fare is C2,800. The bus you take might be labeled tilarán. Make sure it passes through Ciudad Quesada. If so, it passes through La Fortuna; if not, you'll end up in Tilarán via the Interamerican Highway, passing through the Guanacaste town of Cañas, a long way from La Fortuna.

Alternatively, you can take a bus from the same station to Ciudad Quesada and transfer there to another bus to La Fortuna. These buses depart roughly every 30 minutes between 5am and 7:30pm. The fare for the 2½-hour trip is C2,500. Local buses between Ciudad Quesada and La Fortuna run regularly through the day, although the schedule changes frequently, depending on demand. The trip lasts an hour; the fare is C1,200.

Buses depart **Monteverde/Santa Elena** for Tilarán every day at 7am. This is a journey of only 35km (22 miles), but the trip lasts 2½ hours because the road is in rough shape. People with bad backs should think twice about making the trip, especially by bus. The return bus from Tilarán to Santa Elena leaves at 12:30pm. The fare is C1,250. Buses from Tilarán to La Fortuna depart daily at 7am and 12:20 and 4:30pm, and make the return trip at 8am and 12:15 and 5:30pm. The trip is 2 to 3 hours; the fare is C1,600.

Buses depart La Fortuna for San José roughly every 2 hours between 5am and 6pm; in most instances, you will have to transfer in Ciudad Quesada to one of the frequent buses to San José.

Arenal National Park

La Fortuna

HOTELS
Arenal Backpackers Resort 26
Arenal Kioro 5
Arenal Kokoro 9
Arenal Observatory Lodge 20
Cabinas Los Guayabos 6
Hotel La Fortuna 37
Hotel Las Colinas 36
Hotel Magic Mountain 25
Hotel Royal Corin 14
Hotel Silencio del Campo 12
Nayara Hotel, Spa
  & Gardens 10
Tabacón Grand Spa Thermal
  Resort 3
The Springs Resort & Spa 8
Volcano Lodge 11

RESTAURANTS
Anch'io 27
Don Rufino 39
El Novillo de Arenal 7
Gecko Gourmet 31
La Choza de Laurel 29
Las Brasitas 28
Lava Lounge 32
Los Tucanes 3
Rancho La Cascada 34
Restaurante Nene's 38

ATTRACTIONS
Arenal Hanging Bridges 1
Arenal National Park 18
Athica Canopy 2
Baldi Hot Springs 16
Eco Termales 15
Ecoglide 17
La Fortuna Catholic Church 35
La Pradera 23
Río Fortuna Waterfall 21
Sky Tram 19
Tabacón Hot Springs 4
Termales Los Laureles 13

SHOPPING
Art Shop Onirica 33
Original Grand Gallery 24

NIGHTLIFE
Don Rufino 39
Luigi's Casino 30
One Love Lounge 22

Gray Line (📞 **800/719-3105** in the U.S. and Canada, or 2220-2126 in Costa Rica; www.graylinecostarica.com) and **Interbus** (📞 **4031-0888;** www.interbusonline.com) both have two buses daily leaving San José for La Fortuna. The fare is around $49. Both companies will pick you up at most San José–area hotels. And both companies also run routes from La Fortuna with connections to most other major destinations in Costa Rica.

Both companies will pick you up at most San José–area hotels. And both companies also run routes from La Fortuna with connections to most other major destinations in Costa Rica.

CITY LAYOUT As you enter La Fortuna from the east, you'll see the massive volcano directly in front of you. The main road into town, CR142, passes through the center of the La Fortuna and then out of toward Tabacón and the volcano. La

boats, **HORSES & TAXIS**

You can travel between La Fortuna and Monteverde by boat and taxi, or on a combination of boat, horseback, and taxi. A 10- to 20-minute boat ride across Lake Arenal cuts out hours of driving around its shores. From La Fortuna to the put-in point is about a 25-minute taxi ride. It's about a 1½-hour four-wheel-drive taxi ride between the Río Chiquito dock on the other side of Lake Arenal and Santa Elena. These trips can be arranged in either direction for between $30 and $50 per person, all-inclusive.

You can also add on a horseback ride on the Santa Elena/Monteverde side of the lake. Several routes and rides are on offer. The steepest heads up the mountains and through the forest to the town of San Gerardo, only a 30-minute car ride from Santa Elena. Other routes throw in shorter sections of horseback riding along the lakeside lowlands. With the horseback ride, this trip runs around $85 per person.

Warning: The riding is often rainy, muddy, and steep. Many find it much more arduous than awe-inspiring. Moreover, I've received numerous complaints about the condition of the trails and the treatment of the horses, so be very careful and demanding before signing on for this trip. Find out what route you will be taking, as well as the condition of the horses, if possible. **Desafío Expeditions** ★★ (© 855/818-0020 in the U.S. and Canada, or 2479-0020 in Costa Rica; www.desafiocostarica.com) is one of the more reputable operators. They will even drive your car around for you while you take the scenic (and sore) route.

If you're looking to make the ride just by taxi and boat, check in with **Jeep Boat Jeep** (© 2479-9955), which has a daily fixed departures in each direction at 8am and 2pm for $25 per person.

Fortuna is only a few streets wide, with almost all the hotels, restaurants, and shops clustered along the main street and around the small central park, which fronts the Catholic church.

VISITOR INFORMATION   Desafío Expeditions ★★ (© 855/818-0020 in the U.S. and Canada, or 2479-0020 in Costa Rica; www.desafiocostarica.com), **Jacamar Tours** (© 2479-9767; www.arenaltours.com), and **Pure Trek Canyoning** ★★ (© 866/569-5723 in the U.S. and Canada, or 2479-1313 in Costa Rica; www.puretrek.com) are the main tour operators in the area. All of these companies offer most of the tours listed in this section, as well as fishing and sightseeing excursions on the lake, and transfers to and from other destinations around Costa Rica.

GETTING AROUND   If you don't have a car, you'll need to either take a cab or go on an organized tour if you want to visit the hot springs or view the volcano. La Fortuna has tons of taxis (you can flag one down practically anywhere, or dial © 2479-9605), and a line of them is always ready and waiting along the main road beside the central park. Another alternative is to rent a car when you get here. **Alamo** (© 2479-9090; www.alamocostarica.com) has an office in downtown La Fortuna.

Several places to rent scooters and ATVs are around town. I like Moto Rental (© 2479-7376), which rents scooters and off-road motorcycles. Provided it's not raining too heavily, this is a good way to get around. Rates run around $45 to $60 per day for a scooter. They also offer up a 2¹/₂-hour ATV tour. The cost is $70 per person.

SPECIAL EVENTS   Each year, starting around February 1, La Fortuna pulls out all the stops for a 2-week celebration of the town's *Fiestas Civicas,* or Civic Celebrations. There are horse parades, bull fights, mechanical rides, food stands, and concerts.

FAST FACTS   You'll find several information and tour-booking offices and Internet cafes, as well as a couple of pharmacies, general stores, banks, and laundromats within a few blocks' radius of the town's central park and church. If you need assistance, call the Tourist Police at *©* **2479-7257.**

Exploring Arenal Volcano & La Fortuna

While in the town of La Fortuna, be sure to spend some time simply people-watching from a bench or grassy spot on the central plaza. It's also worth a quick visit to tour the town's **Catholic church.** This contemporary church was designed by famous Costa Rican artist Teodorico Quirós, and features an interesting soaring concrete front steeple and clock tower.

EXPERIENCING THE VOLCANO ★★★

As I mention earlier, for the past couple of years, the Arenal Volcano has been very quiet, with no loud eruptions or pyroclastic blasts. Still, the actual volcano remains a stunning sight to behold and the natural park, and surrounding trails and activities make this a fabulous destination. That said, Arenal is surrounded by cloud forests and rainforests, and the volcano's cone is often socked in by clouds and fog. Many people come to Arenal and never see the exposed cone.

Note: Although it's counterintuitive, the rainy season is often a better time to see the exposed cone of Arenal Volcano, especially at night. I don't know why this is, but I've had excellent volcano-viewing sessions at various points during the rainy season; during the dry season, the volcano can often be shrouded for

Arenal Volcano looms over La Fortuna church.

days at a time. The bottom line is that catching a glimpse of the volcano's cone is never a sure thing.

Despite its current state of dormancy, climbing Arenal Volcano is neither common nor recommended. Over the years, many daredevil climbers have lost their lives, and others have been severely injured. The most recent fatalities occurred in August 2000. This is still a very "alive" volcano, with steam vents and a molten core.

Arenal National Park

Arenal National Park ★★ (© 2461-8499) constitutes an area of more than 2,880 hectares (7,114 acres), which includes the viewing and parking areas closest to the volcano. The park is open daily from 8am to 3:30pm and charges $15 admission per person. The trails through forest and over old lava flows inside the park are gorgeous and fun. (Be careful climbing on those volcanic boulders, though.)

The principal trail inside the park, **Sendero Coladas (Lava Flow Trail)** ★★, is just under 2km (1.25 miles) long and passes through secondary forest and open savanna. At the end of the trail, a short natural stairway takes you to a broad, open lava field left in the wake of a massive 1992 eruption. Scrambling over the cooled lava is a real treat, but be careful, as the rocks can be sharp in places. Many spots throughout the park offer great views of the volcano, but the closest view can be found at **El Mirador (The Lookout)** ★, where you not only can see the volcano better, but also can hear it rumble and roar on occasion. From the parking lot near the trail head for the Lava Flow Trail, you have the option of hiking or driving the 1km (.6 mile) to El Mirador.

NEARBY ATTRACTIONS

BUTTERFLY GARDEN Located 2km (a little over a mile) beyond the Arenal dam out beyond the Arenal Hanging Bridge, the **Mot Mot Jungle** (© 2479-1170) has a large enclosure, where they breed and display a wide variety of local butterfly species. They also have some gentle paths planted with local flowers that attract a number of free flying butterflies, as well as hummingbirds. A tour here includes an explanation and exhibit of the insect's entire life cycle. It's open daily from 8am to 4pm, admission is $8.

COOKING CLASSES If you want to learn a little about Costa Rican cuisine, try the **Tropical Cooking Class** ★ (© 2479-1569; www.costaricacooking.com), offered up by the folks at Lava Lounge. The 3¹/₂-hour class is held at a beautiful lookout and open-air kitchen near the **Río Fortuna waterfall.** Advance reservations are necessary. The cost is $125 per person.

ESPECIALLY FOR KIDS

Located a couple of miles outside of La Fortuna, the **Ecocentro Danaus** ★ (© 2479-7019; www.ecocentrodanaus.com) is a private biological reserve and sustainable tourism project, which offers educational and engaging tours. Among the attractions here are a butterfly garden and reproduction center, botanical and medicinal plant gardens, and a small museum honoring the local Maleku indigenous culture. It's open daily from 8am to 4pm, and admission is $17, including a 90-minute guided tour; or $12 for a self-guided visit. Night tours ($37) are offered by reservation. Children 5 to 10 get a 50% discount, and children 4 and under are free.

Set along the banks of the Arenal River, **Club Rio** ★★ (© 954/727-8333 in the U.S. and Canada, or 2401-3313 in Costa Rica; www.thespringscostarica.

A Sky Tram canopy tour.

com) is a wonderful playground for parents and kids alike. You can go inner tubing on the river, ride a horse through the forest trails, visit their midsize zoo, and take a shot at their three-story climbing wall. There's also a series of naturally fed hot springs sculpted alongside the river, as well as a restaurant and some simple chaise lounges for relaxing. It's part of **The Springs Resort and Spa** (p. 311), but you don't have to be staying at the resort to enjoy the activities and facilities here. A day pass ($99 adult; $75 for children 12 and under) gets you access to the facilities and two of the above-mentioned adventure activities, as well as a full lunch and free run of all the pools and waterslides at the resort itself. It also allows for re-entry to enjoy the pools and springs the following day.

OUTDOOR ACTIVITIES

Aside from the impressive volcanic activity, the area around Arenal Volcano is packed with other natural wonders.

ATV La Pradera (© 2479-8444; www.lapraderadelarenal.com) offers a 3-hour adventure through the forests and farmlands around La Fortuna. The tour includes a stop at a riverside swimming hole where you can cool off as well as lunch. You get good views of the volcano, as well as La Fortuna Waterfall. The cost is $85 per ATV. A second rider on the same ATV costs $30.

CANOPY TOURS & CANYONING You have numerous ways to get up into the forest canopy here. Perhaps the simplest is to hike the trails and bridges of **Arenal Hanging Bridges ★** (© 2290-0469; www.hangingbridges.com). Located just over the Lake Arenal dam, this attraction is a complex of gentle trails and suspension bridges through a beautiful tract of primary forest. It's open daily from 7:30am to 4pm; admission is $24.

Another option is the **Sky Tram ★★** (© 2479-4100; www.skyadventures. travel), an open gondola-style ride that begins near the shores of Lake Arenal and rises up, providing excellent views of the lake and volcano. From here, you can hike their series of trails and suspended bridges. In the end, you can hike down, take the gondola, or strap on a harness and ride their zip-line canopy tour down to the bottom. The zip-line tour here features several very long and very fast sections, with some impressive views of the lake and volcano. The cost is $112 for the combined tram ride up, a guided hike to the trails and hanging bridges, and the zip-line tour back down. It's $44 to ride the tram round-trip. The tram runs daily from 7:30am to 3pm. These folks also have butterfly and orchid garden exhibits on-site.

Ecoglide ★ (© 2479-7120; www.arenalecoglide.com) and Athica Canopy (© 2479-1405; www.athicacanopy.com) are two other good zip-line canopy tour operations close to La Fortuna.

If you'd like a bigger rush than the canopy tours offer, you could go "canyoning" with Pure Trek Canyoning ★★ (© 866/569-5723 in the U.S. and Canada, or 2479-1313; www.puretrek.com) and Desafío Expeditions ★★ (© 855/818-0020 in the U.S. and Canada, or 2479-0020 in Costa Rica; www.desafio costarica.com). This adventure sport is a mix of hiking through and alongside a jungle river, punctuated with periodic rappels through and alongside the faces of rushing waterfalls. Pure Trek's trip is probably better for first-timers and families with kids, while Desafío's tour is just a bit more rugged and adventurous. The former charges $98. The latter charges $95. Both of these companies offer various combination full-day excursions, mixing canyoning with other adventure tours, and tend to have two to three daily departures.

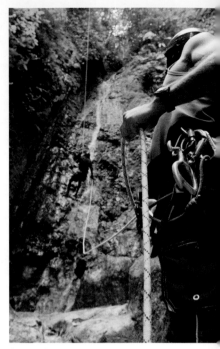
A canyoning tour.

FISHING   With Lake Arenal just around the corner, fishing is a popular activity here. The big fish to catch is *guapote,* a Central American species of rainbow bass. However, you can also book fishing trips to Caño Negro, where snook, tarpon, and other game fish can be stalked. Most hotels and adventure-tour companies can arrange fishing excursions. Costs run around $150 to $250 per boat, and a full day goes for around $250 to $500.

HIKING & HORSEBACK RIDING   Horseback riding is a popular activity in this area, with scores of good rides on dirt backroads and through open fields and dense rainforest. Volcano and lake views come with the terrain on most rides. Horseback trips to the Río Fortuna waterfall are perhaps the most popular, but remember, the horse will get you only to the entrance; from there, you'll have to hike a bit. A horseback ride to the falls should cost between $30 and $45, including the entrance fee. Alternately, you can check in with the folks at Cabalgata Don Tobias (© 2479-1780; www.cabalgatadontobias.com), which runs a 2½-hour tour on their private land—a mix of farmland and forest, with some great views of the volcano. Two tours leave daily at 8:30am and 1:30pm, and the cost is $65 per person.

El Silencio Mirador y Senderos ★ (© **2479-9900;** www.miradorel
silencio.com) is a great place for hiking outside of the national park. This private
reserve has four well-marked and well-groomed trails, one of which takes you to
a patch of the 1968 lava flow. There's a pretty pond, and excellent views of the
volcano, as well. It's open daily from 7am to 7pm, and admission is $8.

If you're looking for a more strenuous hike, sign up to climb **Cerro
Chato** ★★, a dormant volcanic cone on the flank of Arenal with a beautiful
little crater lake. **Desafío Expeditions** ★★ (© **855/818-0020** in the U.S. and
Canada, or 2479-0020 in Costa Rica www.desafiocostarica.com;) leads a 5- to
6-hour hike for $75, including lunch.

LA FORTUNA FALLS Leading the list of side attractions in the area is the impressive **Río Fortuna Waterfall** ★★ (© **2479-8338;** www.arenaladifort.com),
about 5.5km (3½ miles) outside of town in a lush jungle setting. A sign in town
points the way to the road out to the falls. You can drive or hike to just within
viewing distance. When you get to the entrance to the lookout, you'll have to pay
a $10 entrance fee to actually check out the falls. It's another 15- to 20-minute
hike down a steep and often muddy path to the pool formed by the waterfall. The
hike back up will take slightly longer. You can swim, but stay away from the tur-
bulent water at the base of the falls—several people have drowned here. Instead,
check out and enjoy the calm pool just around the bend, or join the locals at the
popular swimming hole under the bridge on the paved road, just after the turnoff
for the road up to the falls. The trail to the falls is open daily from 8am to 5pm.

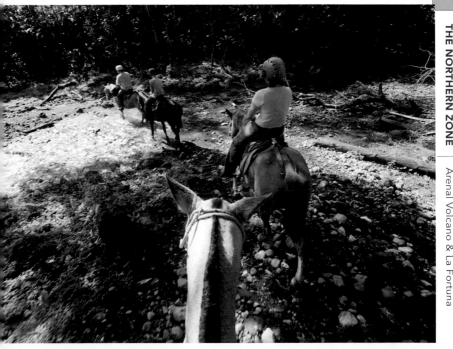

Horseback riding to Cerro Chato.

What's SUP?

Stand Up Paddling (SUP) is a booming sport and fitness craze, and you can practice it on the lovely Lake Arenal, in the shadow of the lake's namesake volcano, with the folks at Desafío Expeditions (see below).

It's also possible to reach the falls by horseback. Most tour operators in town, as well as the waterfall folks themselves, offer this option for around $45. The tour generally lasts around 3 to 4 hours.

MOUNTAIN BIKING   This region is very well suited for mountain biking. Rides range in difficulty from moderate to extremely challenging. You can combine a day on a mountain bike with a visit to one or more of the popular attractions here. **Bike Arenal ★** (© 866/465-4114 in the U.S. and Canada, or 2479-7150 in Costa Rica; www.bikearenal.com) offers up an excellent collection of top notch bikes and equipment and a wide range of tour possibilities.

Hardcore bikers will want to come in March for the **Vuelta al Lago ★** (© 2695-5297; www.vueltaallago.net), an annual 2-day race around the lake.

WHITE-WATER RAFTING, CANOEING & KAYAKING   For adventurous tours of the area, check out **Desafío Expeditions ★★** (© 855/818-0020 in the U.S. and Canada, or 2479-0020 in Costa Rica; www.desafiocostarica.com), or **Wave Expeditions ★★** (© 888/224-6105 in the U.S. and Canada, or 2479-7262 in Costa Rica; www.waveexpeditions.com).

Both companies offer daily raft rides of Class I to II, III, and IV to V on different sections of the Toro, Peñas Blancas, and Sarapiquí rivers. If you want a wet and personal ride, try Desafío's tour in inflatable kayaks, or "duckies." For

White-water rafting the Río Toro.

families, a gentle safari float on the Peñas Blancas is probably your best bet. A half-day float trip on a nearby river costs between $55 to $65 per person; a full day of rafting on some rougher water costs around $85 to $100 per person, depending on what section of river you ride. Both companies also offer mountain biking and local guided trips.

A more laid-back alternative is to take a canoe tour with **Canoa Aventura** (✆ **2479-8200;** www. canoa-aventura.com), which offers half-, full-, and multiday excursions on a variety of rivers in the region, which range from $47 to $155 per person.

DAY TRIPS

La Fortuna is a great place from which to make a day trip to the **Caño Negro National Wildlife Refuge** ★. This vast network of marshes and rivers (particularly the Río Frío) is 100km (62 miles) north of La Fortuna near the town of Los Chiles. This refuge is best known for

10

Watch for spider monkeys in Caño Negro National Wildlife Refuge.

its amazing abundance of bird life, including roseate spoonbills, jabiru storks, herons, and egrets, but you can also see caimans and crocodiles. Bird watchers should not miss this refuge, although keep in mind that the main lake dries up in the dry season (mid-Apr to Nov), which reduces the number of wading birds. Full-day tours to Caño Negro average between $60 and $70 per person. However, most of the tours run out of La Fortuna that are billed as Caño Negro never really enter the refuge but instead ply sections of the nearby Río Frío, which features similar wildlife and ecosystems. If you're interested in staying in this area and really visiting the refuge, check out the **Caño Negro Natural Lodge** (p. 316).

You can also visit the **Venado Caverns,** a 45-minute drive away. In addition to plenty of stalactites, stalagmites, and other limestone formations, you'll see bats and cave fish. Tours cost around $65. All of the tour agencies and hotel tour desks can arrange or directly offer trips to Caño Negro and Venado Caverns.

Where to Stay in La Fortuna
MODERATE
Hotel La Fortuna ★ I've been around long enough to remember when this was a simple, two-story, wood-and-zinc hostel. But a fire changed all of that, and now it's a modern, five-story property in the heart of downtown La Fortuna. The best rooms have volcano-facing balconies; of these, the top floors are obviously the best. The restaurant here is only open for breakfast, but you are right in the heart of downtown and close to all of the restaurants and shops of La Fortuna.

Tabacón Grand Spa Thermal Resort ★★★ (© 2519-1900; www.tabacon.com) is the most luxurious, extensive, and expensive spot in the area to soak your tired bones. A series of variously sized pools, fed by natural springs, are spread out among lush gardens. One of the stronger streams flows over a sculpted waterfall, with a rock ledge underneath that provides a perfect place to sit and receive a free hydraulic shoulder massage. The extensive grounds are worth exploring, but the pools and springs closest to the volcano are the hottest—makes sense, doesn't it? The resort also has an excellent spa on the grounds, offering professional massages, mud masks, and other treatments, as well as yoga classes (appointments required). Most of the treatments are conducted in lovely open-air gazebos surrounded by the rich tropical flora. The spa here even has several permanent sweat lodges, based on a Native American traditional design. A full-service restaurant, garden grill, and a couple of bars are available for those seeking sustenance.

Admission is $60 for adults and $10 for children 11 and under. A range of packages, including meals, are available. The hot springs are open daily from 10am to 10pm. The pools are busiest between 2 and 6pm. After 6pm, you can enter for $45, not including any meals. Management enforces a policy of limiting visitors, so reservations (which can be made online or by phone) are recommended.

Baldi Hot Springs (© 2479-2190; www.baldihotsprings.cr) are the first hot springs you'll come to as you drive from La Fortuna toward Tabacón. This place

1 block south of the gas station, downtown La Fortuna, San Carlos. © **415/315-9595** in the U.S. and Canada or 2479-9197 in Costa Rica. www.fortunainn.com. 44 units. $61–$86 double. Rates include continental breakfast and taxes. **Amenities:** Restaurant; free Wi-Fi.

Hotel Magic Mountain ★   This is a good option if you want great views, large, clean and contemporary rooms and close proximity to the restaurants and shops of La Fortuna. Every room comes with a private balcony or patio with a volcano view. The junior suites are much larger and come with a private volcano-view Jacuzzi. I'd try to land a room on the second or third floor if possible, and the end units are especially well-placed. Some of the ground-floor rooms have their volcano views blocked by the gardens and foliage. The beautiful pool area has a couple of Jacuzzis, for those who don't splurge on a junior suite. "Lina's" restaurant here is quite good, and there's also a separate sports bar.

La Fortuna, San Carlos. © **2479-7246.** www.hotelmagicmountain.com. 42 units. $130 double; $180 junior suite. Rates include buffet breakfast. **Amenities:** Restaurant; bar; 2 Jacuzzis; outdoor pool; spa; Wi-Fi.

more intimate than Tabacón, this series of pools set amid lush forest and gardens is almost as picturesque and luxurious, although it has far fewer pools, lacks a view of the volcano, and the spa services are much less extensive. Reservations are absolutely necessary here, and admissions are limited so that it never gets crowded. The admission fee is $34. These folks have added a restaurant serving basic local fare, but I recommend just coming for the springs.

Termales Los Laureles (✆ **2479-1395;** www.termalesloslaureles.com) is located between Baldi and Eco Termales and Tabacón. This is the area's most local feeling spot, and by far the most economical, charging just C6,000 for adults.

Finally, you can also enjoy the hot springs, pools, and facilities at the **Springs Resort & Spa ★★** (see below). In addition to the main pools by the hotel, they have a few more at a beautiful riverfront area about one kilometer away. The Springs is open to day visitors from 8am to 9pm, and admission is $40 per person.

has grown substantially over the years, with many different pools, slides, and bars and restaurants spread around the expansive grounds. They have recently even added some rooms. However, I find this place far less attractive than the other options mentioned here. Baldi has much more of a party vibe, with loud music often blaring at some of the swim-up bars. Admission is $31.

Just across the street from Baldi Hot Springs is the unmarked entrance of my current favorite local hot spring, **Eco Termales ★★** (✆ **2479-8484;** www.ecotermalesfortuna.cr). Smaller and

INEXPENSIVE

Right in La Fortuna you'll find a score of budget options. If you have time, it's worth checking out a couple. One of the better options is **Arenal Backpackers Resort** (✆ **2479-7000;** www.arenalbackpackersresort.com), which bills itself as a "five-star hostel"—even backpackers get to enjoy the large pool, Wi-Fi, and volcano views. It has both shared-bathroom dorm rooms, and more upscale private rooms.

A couple of places both in town and right on the outskirts of La Fortuna allow camping, with access to basic bathroom facilities, for around $5 to $10 per person per night. If you have a car, drive a bit out of town toward Tabacón and you'll find several more basic cabins and camping sites, some that even offer views of the volcano.

Hotel Las Colinas This centrally located three-story hotel is a great value. The less expensive rooms here are all clean and cozy, while for a bit more you can upgrade and get a private volcano-view balcony and in-room Jacuzzi. Even if you don't, there's a gorgeous, large open-air second-floor terrace with perfect views of the Arenal Volcano. This common area, really is the highlight and social center of the hotel. While the rooms all come with televisions, most of these are small, antiquated tube versions, and some are inconveniently hung in a far, high corner. Still, the service at this family-run operation is friendly, attentive and knowledgeable.

La Fortuna, San Carlos. ☎ **2479-9305.** www.lascolinasarenal.com. 21 units. $52 budget room double; $69–$75 double; $83–$86 suite. Rates include breakfast and taxes. **Amenities:** Restaurant.

Where to Stay near the Volcano

While La Fortuna is the major gateway town to Arenal Volcano, for my money, the best places to stay are on the road between La Fortuna and the National Park.

One other very unique alternative is to stay aboard the *Rain Goddess* (☎ **866/593-3168** in the U.S., or 2231-4299; www.bluwing.com). This luxurious houseboat has four staterooms, ample lounge and dining areas, and cruises around Lake Arenal.

VERY EXPENSIVE

Arenal Kioro ★ This is one of the closest hotels to the volcano, offering fabulous views. The rooms themselves are very large and most feature two Queen-size beds or one King bed set facing a full wall of windows with a sliding glass door that lets out onto a private balcony or patio with a perfect volcano view. Most rooms also come with a large in-room spa Jacuzzi, which I find to be superfluous and unnecessary. And even though they don't use chlorine, there's still an unmistakable odor from the water and its treatment system. I much prefer using the beautiful on-site outdoor hot springs. The restaurant has a great open-air view, although the food can be a bit disappointing. This hotel has earned "4 Leaves" in the CST Sustainable Tourism program.

On the main road btw. La Fortuna and Lake Arenal, 10km (6 miles) from La Fortuna. ☎ **2479-1700.** www.hotelarenalkioro.com. 53 units. $295 double. Rates include buffet breakfast. **Amenities:** 2 restaurants; bar; exercise room; small hot spring complex; large outdoor pool; small spa.

Hotel Royal Corin ★★ I really like the pool, sauna, steam and hot spring complex at this contemporary option. The five-story main building is built in a horseshoe around the pool complex and all of the rooms are set on the inside with a private balcony looking out over the pools to the Arenal Volcano. The rooms themselves are clean and modern. They feature white tile floors, white walls and ceilings, with splashes of color provided by a piece of artwork here and some patterned linens and throw pillows there. The junior and master suites come with private Jacuzzi tubs and larger balconies. An excellent little spa is attached to the hotel, and the restaurant here is quite good.

On the main road btw. La Fortuna and Lake Arenal, 4km (2¹/₂ miles) from La Fortuna. ☎ **877/642-6746** in the U.S. and Canada, or 2479-2201 in Costa Rica. www.royalcorin.com. 54 units. $318 double; $400–$431 suite. Rates include buffet breakfast. **Amenities:** Restaurant; bar; babysitting; exercise room; 6 Jacuzzis; large outdoor complex of pools and hot springs; room service; small spa; sauna.

Nayara Hotel, Spa & Gardens ★★★ This is the best choice for those looking for an intimate, romantic, and pampered experience. The individual cabins are all large and luxurious, with private volcano-facing balconies featuring a large, two-person Jacuzzi. Lush gardens provide privacy and good bird-watching. The dining options are varied and all well executed, from the classy wine and tapas bar to the Peruvian-influenced sushi bar to the main international restaurant. However, unlike most of the other offerings in this price category, the hotel does not have a natural hot springs on site. For a real splurge and sense of luxury and your own natural spring-fed hot pool, these folks have opened the neighboring **Nayara Springs Resort** (www.nayarasprings.com). These huge villas are stunning, and each features a spring-fed private pool and personal concierge service.

On the main road btw. La Fortuna and Lake Arenal. © **888/332-2961** in the U.S. and Canada, or 2479-1600 in Costa Rica. www.arenalnayara.com. 50 units. $285 deluxe; $395 suite, $590 Springs villas. Rates includes buffet breakfast. **Amenities:** 4 restaurants; 3 bars; small spa; exercise room; large outdoor pools; 3 Jacuzzis; room service; smoke-free rooms; free Wi-Fi.

The Springs Resort & Spa ★★★ This massive complex features huge, well-appointed and luxurious rooms, as well as a wide range of on-site attractions and activity options, including an extensive collection of hot and temperate pools, a jungle waterslide near the main hotel, and a separate "Club Rio" adventure park (p. 302) a short shuttle ride away on the banks of the Arenal River. All rooms are oriented to offer views of the Arenal Volcano over lush farmlands and forests. This is a great option for families, thanks to all of the on-site attractions and activities, and there are several family-suites and private villas with connecting rooms and either kitchenettes or full kitchens. The restaurants, spa, and overall service here are top notch.

Off the main road btw. La Fortuna and Lake Arenal, 10km (6 miles) from La Fortuna. © **954/727-8333** in the U.S. or 2401-3313 in Costa Rica. www.thespringscostarica.com. 45 units. $515–$625 double; $425–$595 suite; $750–$880 2-bedroom suite; $990 and up villa for 4–6 people. **Amenities:** 5 restaurants; 5 bars; large, modern spa and exercise room; series of outdoor pools and hot springs; room service; free Wi-Fi.

Tabacón Grand Spa Thermal Resort ★★★ This is a great luxury hotel, with the added bonus of being just across the street from the best, most beautiful, and extensive hot springs in the area (see "Taking a Soothing Soak in Hot Springs," on p. 308). Staying at the resort gets you unlimited access to the Tabacón hot spring complex, as well as slightly extended hours. If you take into account the hefty entrance fee to the springs, this place is practically a bargain. Not all of the rooms have volcano views, and they maddeningly won't guarantee a volcano-view room, no matter how hard you beg. On the plus side, management has a deep commitment to locally sustainable development and environmental conservation.

On the main road btw. La Fortuna and Lake Arenal, Tabacón. © **877/277-8291** in the U.S. and Canada, 2519-1999 for reservations in San José, or 2479-2020 at the resort. www.tabacon.com. 114 units. $240–$425 double; $475–$850 suite. **Amenities:** 2 restaurants; 2 bars; exercise room; Jacuzzi; large pool w/swim-up bar; room service; all rooms smoke-free; extensive hot springs and spa facilities across the street; free Wi-Fi.

EXPENSIVE

Hotel Silencio del Campo ★★ This friendly, family-run resort features a small collection of individual cabins oriented to take in the volcano view. All are quite spacious and perfectly maintained. All feature air-conditioning, television, and a minifridge. They are a little bit close together, but not entirely cramped, and large tropical flowers and palms planted all around give them a sense of privacy and isolation. Still try for one furthest from the main road and parking area. The best feature here is their lovely pool and hot spring complex, by far the best hotel hot spring complex in this price range. Service is extremely personalized and attentive.

On the main road btw. La Fortuna and Lake Arenal. ☏ **2479-7055.** www.hotelsilenciodel campo.com. 24 units. $164–$182 double. Rates include full breakfast. **Amenities:** Restaurant; bar; pool and hot spring complex; free Wi-Fi.

Volcano Lodge and Springs Most of the rooms at this sprawling midsize resort offer beautiful, unobstructed views of the Arenal Volcano. This place has steadily grown over the years, and now features two pool areas and two separate restaurants, as well as its own little hot spring complex, hiking trails and children's playground. The gardens here are lush and well-tended, and the service is very attentive and accommodating, despite the fact that they often cater to large tour groups.

On the main road btw. La Fortuna and Lake Arenal. ☏ **800/649-5913** in the U.S. or 2479-1717. www.volcanolodge.com. 62 units. $205 double. Rates include taxes and breakfast buffet. **Amenities:** 2 restaurants; 2 bars; 2 Jacuzzis; 2 outdoor pools; small spa; free Wi-Fi.

MODERATE

Arenal Kokoro ★ This place gets my vote for best bang for your buck in this area. The individual Eco-Cabinas are spacious, cozy, and inviting. Most are free-standing individual cabins that have volcano views and a small private balcony. The Casona rooms are a bit more basic and housed in two-story blocks of four rooms. It's definitely worth the slight splurge for an Eco-Cabina. The hotel has a pool as well as a small, natural hot springs complex, as well as extensive and lush gardens and grounds. The staff is very friendly and helpful.

On the main road btw. La Fortuna and Lake Arenal. ☏ **800/649-5913** in the U.S. and Canada, or 2479-1717 in Costa Rica. www.arenalkokoro.com. 30 units. $95–$140 double. Rates include breakfast. **Amenities:** Restaurant; bar; outdoor pool; small hot springs complex and spa; free Wi-Fi.

Arenal Observatory Lodge ★★ Originally a scientific observatory associated with the Smithsonian to monitor volcanic activity, this is one of the closest hotels to the Arenal Volcano. The views are simply spectacular. The lodge is a bit isolated from the rest of the hustle and bustle of this busy region, and is graced with a large, private reserve and an excellent network of trails. The best rooms and views are found in the suites and private villas set below the main lodge building and restaurant.

On the flanks of Arenal Volcano. To get here, head to the national park entrance, stay on the dirt road past the entrance, and follow the signs to the Observatory Lodge. A 4WD vehicle is not essential, although you'll always be better off with the clearance afforded by one. ☏ **877/804-7732** in the U.S. and Canada or 2290-7011 for reservations in San José, or 2479-1070 at the lodge. www.arenalobservatorylodge.com. 48 units. $97 La Casona double; $133 standard double; $171 Smithsonian; $195 junior suite. Rates include breakfast buffet and taxes; rates reduction in off-season. **Amenities:** Restaurant; bar; Jacuzzi; midsize outdoor pool; free Wi-Fi.

INEXPENSIVE

While the hotels along the road between La Fortuna and the National Park tend to be geared toward higher-end travelers, more budget-conscious travelers do have a few choices. In addition to the inexpensive options in La Fortuna, if you have a car, **Cabinas Los Guayabos** (✆ **2479-1444;** www.cabinaslosguayabos. com) is a good value, with views and a location that rival the more expensive lodgings listed above.

Where to Dine in & Around La Fortuna

Dining in La Fortuna is nowhere near as inspired or inspiring as the area's natural attractions and activities, but, given the town's booming tourist business, options abound. For a casual breakfast or lunch, I like **Gecko Gourmet** ★ (✆ **2479-8905;** www.geckogourmet.com), located behind the church.

Other options include **Rancho La Cascada** (✆ **2479-9145**), **La Choza de Laurel** (✆ **2479-7063**), and **Restaurante Nene's** (✆ **2479-9192**) for Tico fare, and **Las Brasitas** (✆ **2479-9819;** www.lasbrasitas.com) for Mexican. For good pizza and Italian cuisine, try **Anch'io** (✆ **2479-7560**), just beyond Las Brasitas, on the road towards Tabacón and the national park entrance.

Finally, for some fine and fancy dining, you can try **Los Tucanes** ★★ (✆ **2479-2020**) restaurant at the Tabacón Grand Spa resort (p. 311).

Don Rufino ★★ COSTA RICAN   Don Rufino is the semi-official social center of town, with a popular open-air bar overlooking the main street through La Fortuna. The decor has rustic touches, but this is clearly a hopping restaurant with Costa Rican roots and fusion flourishes at every turn. In addition to great steaks and local staples, the long menu features everything from Szechuan chicken to Cajun shrimp pasta. Prices are on the high end for La Fortuna, but, in my mind, are worth it.

Main road through downtown La Fortuna, 2 blocks east of the church. ✆ **2479-9997.** www. donrufino.com. Main courses $10–$50. Daily 11am–11pm. Reservations recommended during the high season.

El Novillo del Arenal ★ COSTA RICAN/STEAKHOUSE   If you want some local steaks or grilled chicken, but don't need the fancier ambience and or accouterments of the other places listed here, this is your spot. Portions are hearty and the price is right. The restaurant is a simple affair set on a plain concrete slab under a very high, open-air, corrugated-zinc-roof structure. When it's clear, you get an excellent view of the volcano.

On the road to Tabacón, 10km (6¼ miles) outside of La Fortuna. ✆ **2479-1910.** Main courses C4,000–C10,000. Daily 11:00am–10pm.

Lava Lounge ★ INTERNATIONAL   California meets Costa Rica at this popular downtown restaurant. The menu here ranges from glorified bar food— think nachos, quesadillas, wings, and wraps—to a hearty Costa Rican blue-plate special, or casado, with dishes such as a thick-cut grilled pork chop or coconut shrimp with spicy mango salsa. There are also burgers, pizzas, and nightly specials.

Downtown La Fortuna, on the main road. ✆ **2479-7365.** www.lavaloungecostarica.com. Main courses $9–$25. Daily 11am–11pm.

Shopping

La Fortuna is chock-full of souvenir shops selling standard tourist fare. However, one of my favorite craft shops is also here. As you leave the town of La Fortuna toward Tabacón, keep your eye on the right-hand side of the road. When you see a massive collection of wood sculptures and a building reading **Original Grand Gallery** (✆ **8946-0928**), slow down and pull over. This local artisan and his family produce works in a variety of styles and sizes. They specialize in faces, many of them larger than a typical home's front door. You can also find a host of animal figures, ranging in style from purely representational to rather abstract. Another good shop, which features original oil paintings and acrylics, as well as other one-off jewelry and jade pieces, is **Art Shop Onirica** (✆ **2479-7589;** www.galeriaoniricacr.com), located next to La Fortuna's post office.

Entertainment & Nightlife

Now that the volcano is not throwing up lava with any real frequency, the after-dark activities around La Fortuna and the Arenal Volcano have cooled off as well. (If the volcano does wake up again, however, be sure to get in on some after-dark volcano viewing.) Perhaps the only true club in the area, with a good dance scene, live DJs and occasional live bands is the **One Love Lounge** (✆ **8872-9703**), behind Vagabundo Pizza on the outskirts of downtown, heading towards the National Park. In town, the folks at Luigi's Hotel have a midsize **casino** (✆ **2479-9909**) next door to their hotel and restaurant, while the open-to-the-street bar at **Don Rufino** (p. 313) is a popular spot for a drink. Finally, a cozy sports bar with a pool table and flatscreen televisions is on the second floor at the **Hotel Magic Mountain** (p. 308).

Where to Stay & Dine Farther Afield

All the hotels listed in the following four sections are at least a half-hour drive from La Fortuna and the volcano. Most, if not all, offer both night and day tours to Arenal and Tabacón, but they also hope to attract you with their own natural charms.

EAST OF LA FORTUNA

The broad, flat San Carlos valley spreads out to the east of La Fortuna. This is agricultural heartland, with large plantations of yuca, papaya, and other cash crops. The popular Ciudad Quesada route to, or from, La Fortuna will take you through this area.

In addition to the places listed below, **Leaves & Lizards** (✆ **888/ 828-9245** in the U.S. and Canada, or 2478-0023 in Costa Rica; www.leaves andlizards.com), near El Muelle, wins high praise as an intimate, isolated getaway.

Termales del Bosque ★ The name of this place translates to "Hot Springs in the Forest," and that's exactly what you'll find at this simple collection of rooms and bungalows on a large former farm. The rooms themselves are basic, but do have air-conditioning and TVs. The bungalows are

Termales del Bosque.

two-bedroom units with a full kitchen, good for families and longer stays. The namesake hot springs are the real draw, though, featuring a series of pools built alongside a rushing creek in the midst of dense rainforest. There's a rustic, natural steam room and pools in a range of temperatures, and you can always cool off in the creek. A host of tours and activities are offered, including horseback riding. If you're not staying at the hotel, you can visit the hot springs with a $12 admission.

On the road from San Carlos to Aguas Zarcas, just before El Tucano. Ciudad Quesada, San Carlos. (C) **2460-1356** or 2640-1356. www.termalesdelbosque.com. 46 units. $110 double; $150 bungalow. Rates include full breakfast, unlimited use of the hot springs, and taxes. **Amenities:** 2 restaurant; bar; several hot springs pools set beside a forest river; limited spa services; free Wi-Fi.

Tilajari Resort Hotel ★ This is a low-key small resort and nature lodge set on the banks of the San Carlos River. Rooms are found in a row of two-story buildings that run parallel to the water, and most have a private patio or balcony with a river view. This is a wonderful hotel for bird-watching and wildlife viewing. The river is home to crocodiles, lizards, turtles and perfect habitat for a great variety of bird species. Popular with tour groups and Costa Rican families, this place has extensive facilities, including multiple indoor and lit tennis courts, soccer fields, game rooms, an orchid garden, a butterfly garden and a medicinal herb garden. The hotel lies about 35 minutes from La Fortuna and the Arenal Volcano, but also provides good access to attractions in Aguas Zarcas.

Muelle, San Carlos. (C) **2462-1212.** www.tilajari.com. 76 units. $112–$122 double; $128–$136 suite. Rates include full breakfast and taxes. **Amenities:** Restaurant; bar; exercise room; Jacuzzi; large outdoor pool; sauna; 6 lighted tennis courts (2 indoors); free Wi-Fi.

SOUTH OF LA FORTUNA

In addition to the places listed below, **Finca Luna Nueva Lodge ★★** (C) **800/ 903-3470** in the U.S. and Canada, or 2468-4006 in Costa Rica; www.fincaluna nuevalodge.com) is a fascinating sustainable farm and tourism project, and proud local advocate for the international "Slow Foods" movement.

Chachagua Rainforest Hotel & Hacienda ★★ This boutique rainforest lodge is set on 100 hectares (247 acres) of land, much of which is primary rainforest. While the rooms are certainly comfortable and cozy, I recommend splurging a bit more for one of the individual wooden bungalows, which are much roomier, and come with their own large, covered-deck area. If you need modern conveniences like a TV and Jacuzzi tub, opt for one of the deluxe bungalows. The rainforest here has miles of excellent trails, as well as a host of adventure tours and activities.

The small village of Chachagua sits 10km (6 miles) south of La Fortuna, on the road to San Ramón. The lodge itself is another 2km (1¼ miles) along a dirt road from the village. The entrance is well-marked and easy to spot.

Chachagua, Alajuela. (C) **2468-1011.** www.chachaguarainforesthotel.com. 28 units. $209 double, $259–$299 bungalows. Rates include breakfast. **Amenities:** Restaurant; bar; concierge; large outdoor pool; small spa; mountain bike rental, free Wi-Fi.

El Silencio Lodge & Spa ★★ This is a lovely and remote boutique rainforest lodge and spa set in a seldom visited valley near the Bajos del Toro waterfall. The rooms are all large individual cabins spread over the rolling hills that rise around the main lobby and restaurant area. Each comes with a king bed, separate sitting area, private balcony and private outdoor Jacuzzi. The two-bedroom villas are perfect for families. The most popular activity here is hiking their network of trails, which lead through thick rainforest to several wonderful waterfalls and lookouts. There's also a luscious and pampering spa, as well as a fine attention to the culinary arts. This lodge is owned and run by the folks from Punta Islita (p. 285) and has earned "5 Leaves" from the CST Sustainable Tourism program.

Bajos del Toro, Alajuela. ℂ 866/446-4053 in the U.S. and Canada, or 2231-6122 in Costa Rica. www.elsilenciolodge.com. 16 units. $295–$342 double, $660–$688 2-bedroom villa for up to 6 people. Rates include breakfast and 1 hike. **Amenities:** Restaurant; bar; outdoor pool, small spa; free Wi-Fi.

Villa Blanca Cloud Forest & Spa ★★   Once the country retreat and family-run hotel of former Costa Rican President Rodrigo Carazo Odio, this lovely little mountain retreat features a series of individual little houses, or casitas, with clay-tile roofs, whitewashed stucco walls, rustic tile floors, and open-beam and cane ceilings. Each casita has a working wood-burning fireplace, which comes in handy in the cool, moist climate here. The deluxe casitas and suites come with their own Jacuzzi tubs. The hotel's own private reserve borders the Los Angeles Cloud Forest Reserve, a lush area and ecosystem, very similar to that found in Monteverde. In fact, lucky visitors even have spotted the elusive Resplendent Quetzal here. A member of the "Green Hotels of Costa Rica," this lodge has earned "5 Leaves" in the CST Sustainable Tourism program.

To reach this hotel, you must first drive to the mountain city of San Ramón, which sits on the Interamerican Highway (CR1), northwest of San José. From here, you'll drive north on CR142 towards Los Angeles, following signs to Villa Blanca.

San Ramón, Alajuela. ℂ **877/256-8399** in the U.S. and Canada, or 2461-0300 in Costa Rica. www.villablanca-costarica.com. 36 units. $255 double; $205 superior; $230 deluxe. Rates include full breakfast. **Amenities:** Restaurant; bar; small spa; free Wi-Fi.

NORTH OF LA FORTUNA

Caño Negro Natural Lodge ★   Serious bird watchers, nature lovers, and fishermen might consider this very remote little spot, in the tiny lagoon-side village of Caño Negro. Bordering the area's namesake Caño Negro Wildlife Refuge, this simple lodge offers easy access to the lakes, lagoons, and waterways of this beautiful, low-lying wetlands area. The rooms themselves are large, clean, and cool, and the expansive grounds feature lovely, well-tended gardens. To get there, drive towards Los Chiles, and just before reaching the town of Los Chiles, follow the well-marked signs for Caño Negro Natural Lodge and the wildlife refuge. The final 18km (11 miles) is on a flat, but rugged, dirt road.

Caño Negro. ℂ **2265-3302** for reservations in San José, or 2471-1426 direct to the lodge. www.canonegrolodge.com. 42 units. $125 double. Rates include continental breakfast. **Amenities:** Restaurant; bar; midsize outdoor pool; free Wi-Fi.

A REALLY REMOTE NATURE LODGE

This is a very remote region, right along the San Carlos River, near the Nicaraguan border. The roads up here are rough and poorly maintained. In addition to the place listed below, **Manquenque Ecolodge ★** (ℂ **2479-8200;** www.maquenqueecolodge.com) is another great option for spotting the green macaw in the wild and getting to know this area.

Tip: To get here, you head first to Pital and then continue on dirt roads to the town of Boca Tapada. It's also possible, albeit difficult, to get here on public transportation (ask your lodge for directions), or you can arrange for the lodge to handle your transportation from San José or La Fortuna (for a cost). Since anyone with four-wheel-drive can make the trip here independently, though, you're best off driving on your own.

La Laguna del Lagarto Lodge   This place is not exactly at the end of the road, but it certainly feels like it. Tucked into a far northern section of Costa Rica, close to the San Carlos River and the Nicaraguan border, this is a simple nature lodge that caters primarily to bird watchers and nature lovers. The bird count here tops 390 species, and this is one of the best places in Costa Rica to observe the endangered and rare Green Macaw. The lodge features two man-made lakes set just below the main lodge and keeps a fleet of canoes available for guest use at their leisure. They also have an extensive network of hiking trails and offer a range of active adventure tours and guided hikes around the area.

7km (3³/₄ miles) north of Boca Tapada. ℂ **2289-8163.** www.lagarto-lodge-costa-rica.com. 20 units. $75 double. **Amenities:** Restaurant; bar.

ALONG THE SHORES OF LAKE ARENAL ★

200km (124 miles) NW of San José; 20km (12 miles) NW of Monteverde; 70km (43 miles) SE of Liberia

Despite its many charms, this remains one of the least-developed tourism regions in Costa Rica. Lake Arenal, the largest lake in Costa Rica, is the centerpiece here. A long, beautiful lake, it is surrounded by rolling hills that are partly pastured and partly forested. Loads of activities and adventures are available both on the lake and in the surrounding hills and forests. While the towns of Tilarán and Nuevo Arenal remain quiet rural communities, several excellent hotels spread out along the shores of the lake.

Locals here used to curse the winds, which often come blasting across this end of the lake at 60 knots or greater. However, since the first sailboarders caught wind of Lake Arenal's combination of warm, fresh water, steady blows, and spectacular scenery, things have been changing quickly. Even if you aren't a fanatical sailboarder, you might enjoy hanging out by the lake, hiking in the nearby forests, riding a mountain bike on dirt farm roads and one-track trails, and catching glimpses of Arenal Volcano.

The lake's other claim to fame is its rainbow-bass fishing. These fighting fish are known in Central America as *guapote* and are large members of the cichlid family. Their sharp teeth and fighting nature make them a real challenge.

Essentials

GETTING THERE & DEPARTING   By Car: From San José, you can either take the Interamerican Highway (CR1) north all the way from San José to Cañas, or first head west out of San José on the San José–Caldera Highway (CR27). When you reach Caldera, follow the signs to Puntarenas and the Interamerican Highway (CR1). You will actually follow signs for Liberia and San José, which are, in fact, leading you to the unmarked entrance to CR1. This road (CR23) ends when it hits the Interamerican Highway. You'll want to pass under the bridge and follow the on-ramp, which will put you on the highway heading north. This latter route is a faster and flatter drive, with no windy mountain switchbacks to contend with. In Cañas, turn east on CR142 toward Tilarán. The drive takes 3 to 4 hours. If you're continuing on to Nuevo Arenal, follow the signs in town, which will put you on the road that skirts the shore of the lake. Nuevo Arenal is about a half-hour drive from Tilarán. You can also drive here from La Fortuna, along a scenic road that winds around the lake. From La Fortuna, it's approximately 1 hour to Nuevo Arenal and 1$^1/_2$ hours to Tilarán.

By Bus: Transportes Tilarán buses (✆ **2222-3854**) leave San José for Tilarán roughly five times throughout the day between 7:30am and 6:30pm from Calle 20 and Avenida 3. The trip lasts from 4 to 5$^1/_2$ hours, depending on road conditions; the fare is C4,000.

Morning and afternoon buses connect **Puntarenas** to Tilarán. The ride takes about 3 hours; the fare is C1,750. (For details on getting to Puntarenas, see "Puntarenas," in chapter 9.) The daily bus from **Monteverde** (Santa Elena) leaves at 7am. The fare for the 2$^1/_2$-hour trip is C1,250. Buses from **La Fortuna** leave for Tilarán daily at 8am and 12:15 and 5:30pm, returning at 7am and 12:20 and 4:30pm. The trip takes around 2 to 3 hours; the fare is C1,600.

Direct buses to San José leave from Tilarán beginning at 5am. Buses to Puntarenas leave at 6am and 1pm daily. The bus to Santa Elena (Monteverde) leaves daily at 12:30pm. Buses also leave regularly for Cañas, and can be caught heading north or south along the Interamerican Highway.

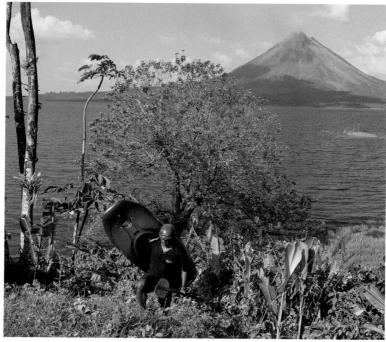

Lake Arenal and Arenal Volcano.

Along the Shores of Lake Arenal

0		4 mi
0	4 km	

HOTELS

Chalet Nicholas **7**
La Mansion Inn Arenal **12**
Lake Arenal Hotel **3**
Lucky Bug B&B **9**
Mystica **4**
Villa Decary **11**

RESTAURANTS

Cabinas Mary **1**
Gingerbread **10**
Hotel La Carreta **1**
La Huerta **3**
Mystica **4**
Tom's Pan German
 Bakery **8**
Willy's Caballo Negro **9**

ATTRACTIONS

Arenal Fishing Tours **2**
Tico Wind **5**

SHOPPING

Casa Delagua **6**
Lucky Bug Gallery **9**

GETTING AROUND   Both Tilarán and Nuevo Arenal are very small towns, and you can easily walk most places in the compact city centers. If you need a taxi to get to a lodge on Lake Arenal, call **Taxis Unidos Tilarán** (© **2695-5324**) in Tilarán, or **Taxis Nuevo Arenal** (© **2694-4415**) in Nuevo Arenal.

Exploring Along the Shores of Lake Arenal

ARTS, CRAFTS & DOWN-HOME COOKING   About halfway between Nuevo Arenal and Tilarán is **Casa Delagua ★** (© **2692-2101**), the studio, gallery, and coffee shop of Costa Rican artist Juan Carlos Ruiz. These folks also have a good used book and DVD collection on sale.

The **Lucky Bug Gallery ★★** is an excellent roadside arts-and-crafts and souvenir shop, attached to the Lucky Bug Bed & Breakfast (p. 320). This place features a host of locally produced functional and decorative pieces.

FISHING   Ask at your hotel if you want to try your hand at fishing for *guapote*. A half-day fishing trip should cost around $150 to $250 per boat, and a full day goes for around $250 to $500. The boats will usually accommodate up to three people fishing. If you're interested in fishing, I recommend you check in with **Captain Ron** at **Arenal Fishing Tours** (© **2694-4678;** www.arenalfishing.com).

HORSEBACK RIDING   Any of the hotels in the area can hook you up with a horseback-riding tour for around $10 to $20 per hour.

SWIMMING   You can certainly swim in Lake Arenal, although it can get a bit rough in places, especially during peak windsurfing season. Up above Lake Arenal on the far side of the lake from Tilarán, you'll find the beautiful little heart-shaped **Lake Coter.** This lake is surrounded by forest and has good, protected swimming. (UFO watchers also claim that this is a popular pit stop for extraterrestrials.) A taxi to Lake Coter costs around C15,000.

WINDSURFING & KITEBOARDING   If you want to try windsurfing or kiteboarding, check in with the folks at **Tico Wind ★** (© **2692-2002;** www.ticowind. com), which sets up shop on the shores of the lake each year from December 1 to the end of April, when the winds blow. Rates run around $88 per day, including lunch; multiday and lesson packages are also available. This is also the place to rent standup paddle boards and equipment.

WAKEBOARDING   Lake Arenal is a big lake with plenty of calm quiet corners to practice wakeboarding. If you're interested in lessons, or just a reliable pull on a wakeboard or water skis, contact **Fly Zone** (© **8339-5876;** www.flyzone-cr. com). Simple pulls behind their specialized boat run around $115 per hour, including boards, skis, and any other necessary gear.

Where to Stay

In addition to the places listed below, **La Mansion Inn Arenal** (© **877/660-3830** in U.S. and Canada, or 2692-8018 in Costa Rica; www.lamansionarenal. com) is an upscale option with a great setting and cozy cabins.

MODERATE

Lucky Bug Bed & Breakfast ★

Set back from the road, on a small hill above a small lake, this intimate bed-and-breakfast is a great option in the area. The rooms don't have any view to speak of, but they are spacious, cheery, and creative. All feature handmade furniture, hand-painted tiles, and unique artwork created by the owner and her triplet daughters. The Butterfly and Frog rooms are my favorites, each with small private balconies. Over on the other side of the lake is an excellent restaurant and unique and well-stocked gift shop featuring a host of creations made by your host family.

Nuevo Arenal. © **2694-4515.** www.lucky bugcr.net. 5 units. $89–$109 double. Rates include full breakfast. **Amenities:** Restaurant; free Wi-Fi.

Mystica ★★   This Italian-owned
hilltop retreat is a great place to unwind, or use as a base for kite- and windsurfing during the windy season. Rooms are simple, but immaculate, with painted cement floors, large windows, and a

Windsurfing on Lake Arenal.

The lush forest surrounding Lake Arenal.

shared common lake-view veranda. The best rooms are the private villa and the individual cabin, which offer more space and a greater sense of privacy. Families or small groups can book a two-bedroom house, with a full kitchen and hot tub. The beautiful expansive grounds and gardens include a lovely river-stone pool and open-air yoga platform, as well as a massage room in a tree house. The hotel's in-house restaurant (p. 322) is a real plus here as well.

On the road btw. Tilarán and Nuevo Arenal. © **2692-1001.** www.mysticacostarica.com. 9 units. $120 double; $140–$165 villa or cabin; $275 2-bedroom house. Rates include breakfast, except for the house. **Amenities:** Restaurant; bar; outdoor pool; yoga center and small spa; free Wi-Fi.

Villa Decary ★★   This intimate, lake-view hotel offers up a wonderfully cozy and friendly bed-and-breakfast experience. The rooms in the main building feature large picture windows and private balconies with wonderful views of Lake Arenal over well-tended gardens and patches of forest. There are also three private casitas, or little houses, with full kitchens and more space. These all offer excellent lake views as well. Casitas Latania and Serenoa, in particular, have the prime views. The original owners were hardcore palm enthusiasts, and the grounds and gardens are planted with scores of unique palm species. These lush grounds and gardens make for some fabulous bird- and wildlife-watching without even leaving the hotel.

Nuevo Arenal. © **800/556-0505** in the U.S and Canada, or 2694-4330 in Costa Rica. www.villadecary.com. 5 units, 3 casitas. $109 double; $142–$164 casita for 2. Rates include full breakfast. Extra person $15. **Amenities:** Free Wi-Fi.

INEXPENSIVE
Chalet Nicholas   You'll be made to feel right at home by John and Catherine Nicholas, who have owned and run this intimate bed-and-breakfast for more

than 20 years. All of the rooms are in the main house, and all feature volcano views. If you stay here, you must love dogs—big dogs—as the owner's three Great Danes are an integral part of the experience. The hotel has lovely gardens and backs on to rugged forest.

2.5km (1¹/₂ miles) west of Nuevo Arenal. ℂ **2694-4041.** www.chaletnicholas.com. 3 units. $65–$75 double. Rates include full breakfast. No credit cards.

Lake Arenal Hotel ★ This place has changed hands a couple of times in recent years. Originally the Hotel Tilawa, its most recent incarnation was as the Volcano Brewing Company. Despite the change, a microbrewery and brewpub are still on site, and both are quite good. In fact, the current management seems to be the most engaged and attentive in quite some time. Set on a high hillside overlooking Lake Arenal, this place has always catered primarily to the windsurf and kitesurf crowds. And they later further catered to that crowd by building a skateboard and BMX bike park. Still it's not a bad choice for anyone looking to explore the area, or spend some time taking in an amazing view of Lake Arenal. Rooms are simple and slightly spartan, but most are quite spacious and well-maintained..

On the road btw. Tilarán and Nuevo Arenal. ℂ **2695-5050.** www.lakearenalhotel.com. 21 units. $58–$98 double. Rates include continental breakfast. **Amenities:** 2 Restaurant; 2 bars; surfboard rental, outdoor pool; free Wi-Fi.

Where to Dine

Tilarán has numerous inexpensive places to eat, including the restaurant at **Hotel La Carreta** (ℂ 2695-6593) and **Cabinas Mary** (ℂ 2695-5479). Another couple of good options are the brew pub and **La Huerta** restaurant at the **Lake Arenal Hotel** (see above).

In Nuevo Arenal, **Tom's Pan German Bakery** (ℂ 2694-4547; www.toms pan.com) is a popular spot for breakfast, snacks, lunch, and baked goods.

Gingerbread ★★★ MEDITERRANEAN/INTERNATIONAL This small, lakeside restaurant serves up the best and most creative food in the area. Israeli-born chef Eyal Ben-Menachem is loud, gregarious, and gracious. The menu and offerings change regularly, and Eyal seeks outs the best and freshest local ingredients. Portions are large, and often big enough to share. In fact, depending upon your group size and reservation, you may just be served a family-style meal, with no menu or selections offered—although the food will be abundant, with plenty of variety and pizzazz. The duck quesadillas, seared tuna salad, and shrimp risotto are a few regularly occurring specials. There's both indoor and patio seating, and a bar area, with a large U-shape bar that stays open long after the kitchen has closed down.

On the road btw. Tilarán and Nuevo Arenal. ℂ **2694-0039.** www.gingerbreadarenal.com. Main courses $27–$32. No credit cards. Reservations recommended. Tues–Sat 5–8pm.

Mystica ★★ ITALIAN/PIZZA This intimate and cozy restaurant, dressed in simple, rustic furnishings and decor, serves up excellent brick-oven pizzas and delicious Italian pastas and main dishes. The owners are Italian, and they ensure the food is both authentic and excellent. The menu features several family recipes, including their signature dessert, Cousin Nappe's banana cream pie. Many of the ingredients in their sauces, salads, and sides come straight from the hotel's organic gardens. Take in the great view of the lake through large picture windows.

In the Mystica hotel. On the road btw. Tilarán and Nuevo Arenal. © **2692-1001.** www.mystica costarica.com. Main courses C5,500–C7,000. Dinner by reservation only. Daily 7–9pm.

Willy's Caballo Negro ★ INTERNATIONAL/VEGETARIAN   This popular spot is part and parcel to the Lucky Bug Bed & Breakfast (see above) and their inventive gift shop and art gallery. The Krauskopf family brings some of their German heritage to the table here, offering up Jaeger Schnitzel, Zigeuner Scnitzel, homemade Spaetzle and bratwursts. I especially like the corned beef hash for breakfast. The menu also has some non-German dishes and a host of vegetarian items as well. The eggplant parmesan is a perennial favorite, in fact.

Nuevo Arenal (about 3km/1¾ miles out of town on the road to Tilarán). © **2694-4715.** Main courses $8–$16. Daily 7am–5pm.

MONTEVERDE ★★

167km (104 miles) NW of San José; 82km (51 miles) NW of Puntarenas

Monteverde, which translates to "Green Mountain," is one of world's first and finest ecotourism destinations. The mist-enshrouded and marvelous Monteverde Cloud Forest Biological Reserve and extensive network of neighboring private reserves are both rich and rewarding. Bird watchers flock here for a chance to spot the myth-inspiring Resplendent Quetzal, scientists study its bountiful biodiversity, and a bevy of attractions and adventures await everyone else.

Cloud forests are a mountaintop phenomenon. Moist, warm air sweeping in off the ocean is forced upward by mountain slopes, and as this moist air rises, it cools, forming clouds. The mountaintops around Monteverde are blanketed almost daily in dense clouds, and as the clouds cling to the slopes, moisture condenses on forest trees. This constant level of moisture has given rise to an incredible diversity of innovative life forms and a forest in which nearly every square inch of space has some sort of plant growing. Within the cloud forest, the

Monteverde Cloud Forest Biological Reserve.

branches of huge trees are draped with epiphytic plants: orchids, ferns, and bromeliads. This intense botanical competition has created an almost equally diverse population of insects, birds, and other wildlife. Beyond the **Resplendent Quetzal,** the Monteverde area boasts more than 2,500 species of plants, 450 types of orchids, 400 species of birds, and 100 species of mammals.

Essentials

GETTING THERE & DEPARTING   By Car: The principal access road to Monteverde is located along the Interamerican Highway (CR1); about 20km (12 miles) north of the exit for Puntarenas is a marked turnoff for Sardinal, Santa Elena, and Monteverde. From this turnoff, the road is paved for 15km (9¹/₂ miles), to just beyond the tiny town of Guacimal. From here, it's another 20km (12 miles) to Santa Elena, the gateway town to Monteverde.

From San José, you can either take the Interamerican Highway (CR1) north all the way to the turnoff, or first head west out of San José on the San José–Caldera Highway (CR27). When you reach Caldera, follow the signs to Puntarenas and the Interamerican Highway (CR1). You will actually follow signs for Liberia and San José, which are, in fact, leading you to the unmarked entrance to CR1. This road (CR23) ends when it hits the Interamerican Highway. You'll want to pass under the bridge and follow the on-ramp, which will put you on the highway heading north. This latter route is a faster and flatter drive.

> ### Today's Forecast . . . Misty & Cool
>
> The climatic conditions that make Monteverde such a biological hot spot can leave many tourists feeling chilled to the bone. More than a few visitors are unprepared for a cool, windy, and wet stay in the middle of their tropical vacation, and can find Monteverde a bit inhospitable, especially from August through November.

Another access road to Santa Elena is found just south of the Río Lagarto Bridge. This turnoff is the first you will come to if driving from Liberia. From the Río Lagarto turnoff, it's 38km (24 miles) to Santa Elena, and the road is unpaved the entire way.

Once you arrive, the roads in and around Santa Elena are paved, including all the way to Cerro Plano, and about halfway to the Cloud Forest Preserve.

To drive from Monteverde to La Fortuna, head out of Santa Elena toward Sky Trek and the Santa Elena Cloud Forest Reserve. Follow signs for Tilarán, which are posted at most of the critical intersections. If there's no sign, stick to the most well-worn road. This is a rough dirt road, all the way to Tilarán. From Tilarán, you have mostly well-marked and okay paved roads around the lake, passing first through Nuevo Arenal, and then over the dam and through Tabacón, before reaching La Fortuna.

By Bus: Transmonteverde express buses (✆ **2256-7710** in San José, or 2645-7447 in Santa Elena) leave San José daily at 6:30am and 2:30pm from Calle 12 between avenidas 7 and 9. The trip takes around 4 hours; the fare is C2,900. Buses arrive at and depart from Santa Elena. If you're staying at one of the hotels or lodges near the reserve, arrange pickup if possible, or take a taxi or local bus. Return buses for San José also depart daily at 6:30am and 2:30pm.

Three daily Transmonteverde buses depart Puntarenas for Santa Elena at 7:50am, and 1:50 and 2:15pm. The bus stop in Puntarenas is across the street

Monteverde

See Inset

To San José

NIGHTLIFE
Bar Amigos 7
La Taberna 14

RESTAURANTS
Café Caburé 28
Las Orquideas Café 12
Morpho's Café 10
Sabor Español 3
Sabor Tico 2
Sofia 23
Stella's Bakery 30
The Common Cup 13
Tramonti 29
Trio 6

HOTELS
Arco Iris Lodge 9
El Establo Mountain Hotel 22
El Sol 1
Hidden Canopy Treehouses 4
Hotel Fonda Vela 36
Hotel Heliconia 21
Hotel Poco a Poco 17
La Colina Lodge 35
Monteverde Country Lodge 19
Monteverde Lodge & Gardens 18
Pensión Santa Elena 8

SHOPPING
CASEM 31
Casa de Arte 20

ATTRACTIONS
Bajo del Tigre Trail 26
Bat Jungle 28
Centro Panamericano de Idiomas 27
Chocolate Tour 28
Curicancha Reserve 32
Don Juan Coffee Tour 3
Ecological Sanctuary 25
El Trapiche Tour 3
Finca Modelo Canyoning Tour 37
Frog Pond of Monteverde 16
Monteverde Butterfly Garden 24
Monteverde Cheese Factory 33
Monteverde Cloud Forest Biological Reserve 38
Monteverde Coffee Tour 37
Monteverde Serpentarium 15
Orchid Garden 11
Original Canopy Tour 5
Río Shanti 34
Santa Elena Cloud Forest Reserve 4
Selvatura Park 4
Sky Trek 4
Sky Walk 4

MONTEVERDE CLOUD FOREST BIOLOGICAL RESERVE 38

Park Entrance

SANTA ELENA
Post Office
Gas Station
CERRO PLANO
Quebrada Máquina
Río Guacimal
CASEM

Santa Elena
Bus Terminal

NICARAGUA
CARIBBEAN SEA
Monteverde
★ SAN JOSÉ
PANAMA
PACIFIC OCEAN

MONTEVERDE

1/2 mi
0.5 km

from the main bus station. The fare for the 2¹/₂-hour trip is C1,350. A daily bus from Tilarán (Lake Arenal) leaves at 12:30pm. Trip duration, believe it or not, is 2 hours (for a 40km/25-mile trip); the fare is C1,250. The express bus departs for San José daily at 6:30am and 2:30pm. The buses from Santa Elena to Puntarenas leave daily at 4:30 and 6am and 3pm.

   Gray Line (✆ **800/719-3105** in the U.S. and Canada, or 2220-2126 in Costa Rica; www.graylinecostarica.com) and **Interbus** (✆ **4031-0888;** www. interbusonline.com) both offer two daily buses that leave San José for Monteverde one in the morning and one in the afternoon. The fare is around $49. Both of the above companies will pick you up and drop you off at most San José and

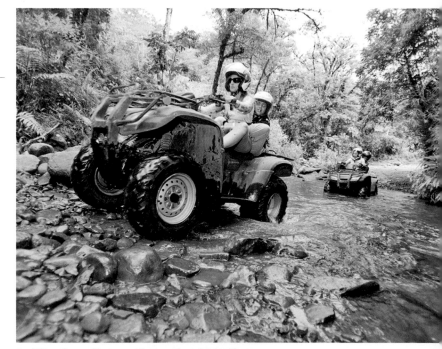

An ATV on the road between Monteverde and Santa Elena.

Monteverde area hotels. Both Gray Line and Interbus offer routes with connections to most major destinations in Costa Rica.

If you're heading to Manuel Antonio, take the Santa Elena/Puntarenas bus and transfer in Puntarenas. To reach Liberia, take any bus down the mountain and get off as soon as you hit the Interamerican Highway. You can then flag down a bus bound for Liberia (almost any bus heading north). The Santa Elena/Tilarán bus leaves daily at 7am.

GETTING AROUND Five or so daily buses connect the town of Santa Elena and the Monteverde Cloud Forest Biological Reserve. The first bus leaves Santa Elena for the reserve at 6:15am and the last bus from the reserve leaves at 4pm. The fare is C500. Periodic van transportation also runs between the town of Santa Elena and the Santa Elena Cloud Forest Reserve. Ask around town and you should be able to find the current schedule and book a ride for around C1,000 per person. A **taxi** (© **2645-6969** or 2645-6666) between Santa Elena and either the Monteverde Reserve or the Santa Elena Cloud Forest Reserve costs around C5,500 for up to four people. Count on paying between C5,000 and C5,500 for the ride from Santa Elena to your lodge in Monteverde. Finally, several places around town rent **ATVs,** or all-terrain vehicles, for around $50 to $75 per day.

CITY LAYOUT The tiny town of **Santa Elena** is the gateway to Monteverde and the Monteverde Cloud Forest Biological Reserve, 6km (3³/₄ miles) outside of town along a windy road that dead-ends at the reserve entrance. As you approach Santa Elena, take the right fork in the road if you're heading directly to Monteverde. If you continue straight, you'll come into the little town center of tiny **Santa Elena,** which has a bus stop, a health clinic, a bank, a supermarket, and a few general stores, and a collection of simple restaurants, budget hotels, souvenir shops, and tour offices. Heading just out of town, toward Monteverde, is a small strip mall with a large and prominent Megasuper supermarket. **Monteverde,** on the other hand, is not a village in the traditional sense of the word. There's no center of town—only dirt lanes leading off from the main road to various farms. This main road has signs for all the hotels and restaurants mentioned here, and it dead-ends at the reserve entrance.

For a map of Monteverde Cloud Forest Reserve, see the inside front cover of this book.

Peace, Love & Ecotourism

Monteverde was settled in 1951 by Quakers from the United States who wanted to leave behind the fear of war, as well as their obligation to support continued militarism through paying U.S. taxes. They chose Costa Rica, a country that had abolished its army a few years earlier, in 1948. Although Monteverde's founders came here to farm the land, they wisely recognized the need to preserve the rare cloud forest that covered the mountain slopes above their fields, and to that end, they dedicated the largest adjacent tract of cloud forest as the Monteverde Cloud Forest Biological Reserve.

If you want an in-depth look into the lives and history of the local Quaker community, pick up a copy of the "Monteverde Jubilee Family Album." Published in 2001 by the Monteverde Association of Friends, this collection of oral histories and photographs is 260 pages of local lore and memoirs. It's very simply bound and printed but well worth the $20 price.

FAST FACTS   The telephone number for the **local clinic** is © **2645-5076**; for the **Red Cross,** © **2645-6128**; and for the **local police,** © **911** or 2645-6248. The **Farmacia Monteverde** (© **2449-5495**) is right downtown. A **Banco Nacional** (© **2645-5610**) is in downtown Santa Elena, and a **Coopemex** (© **2645-6948**) is on the road out to Santa Elena, near Finca Valverde; both have 24-hour ATMs.

Exploring the Monteverde Cloud Forest Biological Reserve ★★★

The **Monteverde Cloud Forest Biological Reserve** (© **2645-5122**; www.reservamonteverde.com) is one of the most developed and well-maintained natural attractions in Costa Rica. The trails are clearly marked, regularly traveled, and generally gentle in terms of ascents and descents. The cloud forest here is lush and largely untouched. Still, keep in mind that most of the birds and mammals are rare, elusive, and nocturnal. Moreover, to all but the most trained of eyes, those thousands of exotic ferns, orchids, and bromeliads tend to blend into one large mass of indistinguishable green. However, with a guide hired through your hotel, or on one of the reserve's official guided 2- to 3-hour hikes, you can see and learn far more than you could on your own. At $18 per person, the reserve's tours might seem like a splurge, especially after you pay the entrance fee, but I strongly recommend that you go with a guide.

Perhaps the most famous resident of the cloud forests of Costa Rica is the quetzal, a robin-size bird with iridescent green wings and a ruby-red breast, which has become extremely rare due to habitat destruction. The male quetzal also has two long tail feathers that can reach nearly .6m (2 ft.) in length, making it one of the most spectacular birds on earth. The best time to see quetzals is early morning to midmorning, and the best months are February through April (mating season).

Other animals that have been seen in Monteverde, although sightings are extremely rare, include jaguars, ocelots, and tapirs. After the quetzal, Monteverde's most famous resident used to be the golden toad (*sapo dorado*), a rare native species. However, the golden toad has disappeared from the forest and is feared extinct. Competing theories of the toad's demise include adverse effects of a natural drought cycle, the disappearing ozone layer, pesticides, and acid rain.

ADMISSION, HOURS & TOURS   The reserve is open daily from 7am to 4pm, and the entrance fee is $18 for adults and $9 for students and children. Because only 220 people are allowed into the reserve at any one time, you might be forced to wait. Most hotels can reserve a guided walk and entrance to the reserve for the

---

Seeing the Forest for the Trees, Bromeliads, Monkeys, Hummingbirds . . .

Because the entrance fee to Monteverde is valid for a full day, I recommend taking an early-morning walk with a guide and then heading off on your own either directly after that hike or after lunch. A guide will certainly point out and explain a lot, but there's also much to be said for walking quietly through the forest on your own or in very small groups. This will also allow you to stray from the well-traveled paths in the park.

10

Monteverde

THE NORTHERN ZONE

A SELF-GUIDED hike THROUGH THE RESERVE

I know I strongly recommend going on a guided tour, but if you're intent on exploring the reserve on your own, or heading back for more, I suggest starting off on the **Sendero El Río (River Trail)** ★★. This trail, which heads north from the reserve office, puts you immediately in the midst of dense primary cloud forest, where heavy layers of mosses, bromeliads, and epiphytes cover every branch and trunk. This very first section of trail is a prime location for spotting a Resplendent Quetzal.

After 15 or 20 minutes, you'll come to a little marked spur leading down to a **catarata,** or waterfall. This diminutive fall fills a small, pristine pond and is quite picturesque, but if you fail in your attempts to capture its beauty, look for its image emblazoned on postcards at souvenir stores all around the area. The entire trek to the waterfall should take you an hour or so.

From the waterfall, turn around and retrace your steps along the River Trail until you come to a fork and the **Sendero Tosi (Tosi Trail).** Follow this shortcut, which leads through varied terrain, back to the reserve entrance.

Once you've got the River Trail and waterfall under your belt, I recommend a slightly more strenuous hike to a lookout atop the Continental Divide. The **Sendero Bosque Nuboso (Cloud Forest Trail)** ★ heads east from the reserve entrance. As its name implies, the trail leads through thick, virgin cloud forest. Keep your eyes open for any number of bird and mammal species, including toucans, trogans, honeycreepers, and howler monkeys. Some great specimens

of massive strangler fig trees are on the trail. These trees start as parasitic vines and eventually engulf their host tree. After 1.9km (1.2 miles), you will reach the Continental Divide. Despite the sound of this, there's only a modest elevation gain of some 65m (213 ft.).

A couple of lookout points on the Divide are through clearings in the forest, but the best is **La Ventana (The Window)** ★, just beyond the end of this trail and reached via a short spur trail. Here you'll find a broad, elevated wooden deck with panoramic views. Be forewarned: It's often misty and quite windy up here.

On the way back, take the 2km (1.2-mile) **Sendero Camino (Road Trail).** As its name implies, much of this trail was once used as a rough all-terrain road. Since it is wide and open in many places, this trail is particularly good for birdwatching. About halfway along, you'll want to take a brief detour to a **suspended bridge** ★. Some 100m (330-ft.) long, this midforest bridge gives you a bird's-eye view of the forest canopy. The entire loop should take around 3 hours.

following day for you, or you can get tickets in advance directly at the reserve entrance.

Some of the trails can be very muddy, depending on the season, so ask about current conditions. Before venturing into the forest, have a look around the information center. Several guidebooks are available, as well as posters and postcards of some of the reserve's more famous animal inhabitants.

Night tours of the reserve leave every evening at 6:15pm. The cost is $17, including admission to the reserve, a 2-hour hike, and, most important, a guide with a high-powered searchlight. For an extra $3, they'll throw in round-trip transportation to and from your area hotel.

Exploring Outside the Reserve

In addition to everything mentioned below, all of the area hotels can arrange a wide variety of other tours and activities, including guided night tours of the cloud forest and night trips to the Arenal Volcano (a tedious 4-hr. ride, each way).

BIRD-WATCHING & HIKING

You'll find ample bird-watching and hiking opportunities outside the reserve boundaries. Avoid the crowds at Monteverde by heading 5km (3 miles) north from the village of Santa Elena to the **Santa Elena Cloud Forest Reserve ★★** (© **2645-5390;** www.reservasantaelena.org). This 310-hectare (765-acre) reserve has a maximum elevation of 1,680m (5,510 ft.), making it the highest cloud forest in the Monteverde area. The reserve has 13km (8 miles) of hiking trails, as well as an information center. Because it borders the Monteverde Reserve, a similar richness of flora and fauna is found here, although quetzals are not nearly as common. The $14 entry fee at this reserve goes directly to support a variety of good causes, including conservation and improving the local schools. The reserve is open daily from 7am to 5pm. Three-hour guided tours are available for $15 per person, not including the entrance fee. (Call the number above to make a reservation for the tour.)

Santa Elena Cloud Forest Reserve.

Located just before the Monteverde Cloud Forest Reserve, and sharing many of the same ecosystems and habitats, the **Curicancha Reserve ★★★** (© **2645-6915;** www.reservacuricancha. com) is an excellent alternative, especially for folks looking to avoid some of the crowds and confusion that can sometimes be found at the area's namesake attraction. The reserve covers some 86 hectares (240 acres), of which almost half is primary cloud forest. The trails here are rich in flora and fauna, and quetzals are frequently spotted here. The reserve is open daily from 7am to 3pm and again from 5:30 to 7:30pm. Entrance is $12 per person, and a 3- to 4-hour guided hike can be arranged for an additional $15 per person. Children under $7 are free.

Sky Walk ★★ (© **2645-5238;** www.skyadventures.travel) is a network of forest paths and suspension bridges that provides visitors with a view previously reserved for birds, monkeys, and the much more adventurous traveler. The bridges reach 39m (128 ft.) above the ground at their highest point, so acrophobia could be an issue. The Sky Walk and its sister attraction, **Sky Trek** (see "Canopy & Canyoning Tours," below), are about 3.5km (2¼ miles) outside the town of Santa Elena, on the road to the Santa Elena Cloud Forest Reserve. The Sky Walk is open daily from 7am to 4pm; admission is $35, which includes a knowledgeable guide. For $89 per person, you can do the Sky Trek canopy tour and Sky Tram, and then walk the trails and bridges of the Sky Walk. Reservations are recommended; round-trip transportation from Santa Elena is just $6.50 per person.

To learn even more about Monteverde, stop in at the **Monteverde Conservation League** (© **2645-5003;** www.acmcr.org), which administers the 22,000-hectare (54,000-acre) private reserve **Bosque Eterno de Los Niños (Children's Eternal Forest),** as well as the Bajo del Tigre Trail. The Conservation League has an information center and small gift shop at the trail head/ entrance to the Bajo del Tigre Trail. In addition to being a good source for information, it also sells books, T-shirts, and cards, and all proceeds go to purchase more land for the Bosque Eterno de Los Niños. The **Bajo del Tigre Trail ★** is a 3.5km (2.3-mile) trail that's home to several different bird species not usually found within the reserve. You can take several different loops, lasting anywhere from 1 hour to several hours. The trail starts a little past the CASEM artisans' shop (see "Shopping," below) and is open daily from 8am to 4pm. Admission is $12 for adults and $10 for students and children under 12. These folks also do a 2-hour night hike that departs at 5:30pm, and costs $22 per adult, and $19 per student. All of this is free for children 6 and under.

Finally, you can walk the trails and grounds of the **Ecological Sanctuary ★★** (© **2645-5305;** www.santuarioecologico.com), a family-run wildlife refuge and private reserve located down the Cerro Plano road. This place has four main trails through a variety of ecosystems, and wildlife-viewing is often quite good. A couple of pretty waterfalls are off the trails. It's open daily from 8am to 7:30pm; admission is $12 for self-guided hiking on the trails, $28 during the day for a 2-hour guided tour, and $22 for the 2-hour guided night tour at 5:30pm.

CANOPY & CANYONING TOURS

Selvatura Park ★★ (© **2645-5929;** www.selvatura.com), located close to the Santa Elena Cloud Forest Reserve, is the best one-stop shop for various adventures and attractions in the area. In addition to an extensive canopy tour, with 13 cables connecting 15 platforms, they also have a network of trails and suspended bridges, a huge butterfly garden, a hummingbird garden, a snake exhibit, and a wonderful insect display and museum. Prices vary depending upon how much you want to see and do. Individually, the canopy tour costs $45; the walkways and bridges, $30; the snake and reptile exhibit, the butterfly garden, and the insect museum, $15 each. Packages to combine the various exhibits are available, although it's definitely confusing, and somewhat annoying, to pick the perfect package. For $132, you get the run of the entire joint, including the tours, lunch, and round-trip transportation from your Monteverde hotel. It's open daily from 7am to 4:30pm.

Another popular option is offered by the folks at **Sky Adventures ★★** (© **2479-4100;** www.skyadventures.travel), which is part of a large complex of aerial adventures and hiking trails. This is one of the more extensive canopy tours in the country, and begins with a cable car ride (or **Sky Tram**) up into the cloud forest, where their zip-line canopy tour commences. This tour features 10 zip-line cables. The longest of these is some 770m (2,525 ft.) long, high above the forest floor. There are no rappel descents here, and you brake using the pulley system for friction. Nearby, their **Sky Walk ★★** operation is a network of forest paths and suspension bridges that provides visitors with a view previously reserved for birds, monkeys, and the much more adventurous traveler. The bridges reach 39m (128 ft.) above the ground at their highest point, so acrophobia could be an issue. These folks have also added a serpentarium and hummingbird garden to their list of attractions. This place is about 3.5km (2¼ miles) outside the town of Santa Elena, on the road to the Santa Elena Cloud Forest Reserve. The Sky Walk is open daily from 7am to 1pm; admission is $35, which includes a knowledgeable guide. For $106 per person, you can do the Sky Trek canopy tour and Sky Tram, and then walk the trails and bridges of the Sky Walk. Reservations are recommended; round-trip transportation from Santa Elena is $4 per person.

One of the oldest canopy tours in the country is run by the **Original Canopy Tour ★** (© **2291-4465;** www.canopytour.com). This is one of the more interesting canopy tours in Costa Rica because the initial ascent is made by climbing up the hollowed-out interior of a giant strangler fig. The tour has 13 platforms and one rappel. The 2- to 2½-hour tours run tree times daily and cost $45 for adults, $35 for students, and $25 for children 12 and under.

Finally, if you want to add a bit more excitement to your adventure, and definitely more water, try the **Finca Modelo Canyoning Tour ★★** (© **2645-5581;** www.familiabrenestours.com). This tour involves a mix of hiking and then rappelling down the face of a series of forest waterfalls. The tallest of these waterfalls is around 39m (130 ft.). You will get wet on this tour. The cost is $50.

Anybody in average physical condition can do any of the adventure tours in Monteverde, but they're not for the fainthearted or acrophobic. Try to book directly with the companies listed above or through your hotel. Beware of touts on the streets of Monteverde, who make a small commission and frequently try to steer tourists to the operator paying the highest percentage.

HORSEBACK RIDING

Monteverde has excellent terrain for horseback riding. **Horse Trek Monteverde ★** (© **2645-5874;** www.costaricahorsebackridingvacations.com) and **Sabine's Smiling Horses ★** (© **2645-6894;** www.smilinghorses.com) are the most established operators, offering guided rides for around $15 to $20 per hour. Horseback/boat trips link Monteverde/Santa Elena with La Fortuna (p. 304).

OTHER ATTRACTIONS IN MONTEVERDE

It seems as if Monteverde has an exhibit or attraction dedicated to almost every type of tropical fauna. It's a pet peeve of mine, but I really wish these folks would band together and offer some sort of general pass. However, as it stands, you'll have to shell out for each individual attraction.

Butterflies abound here, and the long-established **Monteverde Butterfly Garden** ★ (© 2645-5512; www.monteverdebutterflygarden.com), located near the Pensión Monteverde Inn, displays many of Costa Rica's most beautiful species. Aside from seeing the hundreds of preserved and mounted butterflies, you can watch live butterflies in the garden and greenhouse. The garden is open daily from 8:30am to 4pm, and admission, including a guided tour, is $15 for adults, $10 for students, and $5 for kids ages 4 to 6. If you can, visit between 9 and 11am, when the butterflies tend to be most active.

If your taste runs toward the slithery, you can check out the informative displays at the **Monteverde Serpentarium** ★ (© 2645-6002), on the road to the reserve. It's open daily from 9am to 8pm and charges $13 for adults and $11 for students for admission.

The **Frog Pond of Monteverde** ★ (© 2645-6320; www.ranario monteverde.com), a couple of hundred meters north of the Monteverde Lodge, is another good bet. The entrance fee ($13.50 for adults and $12 for students) gets you a 45-minute guided tour, and your ticket is good for 2 days. A variety of amphibians populates a series of glass terrariums. These folks also have a butterfly garden and on-site canopy tour. It's open daily from 9am to 8:30pm. I especially recommend that you stop by at least once after dark, when the tree frogs are active.

The **Bat Jungle** ★★★ (© 2645-7701; www.batjungle.com) provides an in-depth look into the life and habits of these odd flying mammals. A visit here includes several different types of exhibits, from skeletal remains to a large enclosure where you get to see various live species in action—the enclosure and room

A tree frog at the Monteverde Serpentarium.

are kept dark, and the bats have had their biological clocks tricked into thinking that it's night. It's quite an interesting experience. The Bat Jungle is open daily from 9am to 8pm, and the tour lasts around 45 minutes; the last tour starts at 6:45pm. Admission is $12 for adults and $10 for students. Children under 6 are free.

If you've had your fill of birds, snakes, bugs, butterflies, and bats, you might want to stop at the **Orchid Garden ★★** (© **2645-5308;** www.monteverde orchidgarden.net), in Santa Elena across from the Pensión El Tucano. This botanical garden has more than 425 species of orchids. The tour is fascinating, especially given the fact that you need (and are given) a magnifying glass to see some of the flowers in bloom. Admission is $10 for adults, $7 for students and $5 for kids ages 12 to 6. It's open daily from 8am to 5pm.

AGRICULTURAL & CULINARY TOURISM

Several options are available for those looking for a glimpse into the practices and processes of daily life in this region. **Don Juan Coffee Tour ★★** (© **2645-7100;** www.donjuancoffeetour.com) is a local, family-farm operation, which offers a 2-hour tour on their sprawling farm. Coffee is the primary crop and focus of the tour, although these folks also have a range of crops, including macadamia; a trapiche, or sugar cane mill; and small boutique-chocolate production area. As a bonus, you get a snack and coffee tasting, and you may even get to meet the farm's namesake septuagenarian, Don Juan. The tour costs $30 for adults and $12 for children 6 to 12, including transportation.

A sugar cane field.

The **Monteverde Coffee Tour** (✆ 2645-5006; lifemonteverde@gmail. com) is run by the folks at the Cooperativa Santa Elena, a local Fair Trade coffee producer, with a shop right next to CASEMCOOP. They offer a 3-hour tour to a working coffee farm and mill for $30 and $25 students.

El Trapiche Tour ★★ (✆ 2645-7780 or 2645-7650; www.eltrapiche tour.com) is another family-run tour, which gives you insight into the traditional means of harvesting and processing sugar cane, as well as the general life on a farm that includes bananas, macadamia, and citrus groves. Back at the farmhouse, you get to see how the raw materials are turned into cane liquor, raw sugar, and local sweets. The 2-hour tour includes a ride in an ox-drawn cart, and a visit to the family's coffee farm and roasting facility. Depending upon the season, you may even get to pick a bushel of raw coffee beans. Tours run daily at 10am and 3pm, and cost $32 for adults, and $12 for children 6 through 12, and include transportation.

Finally, if you want a detailed explanation of the processes involved in growing, harvesting, processing, and producing chocolate, be sure to stop by Café Caburé (p. 338) for their **Chocolate Tour.** You'll take some chocolate beans right through the roasting, grinding, and tempering processes, in the 45-minute tour. The tour is offered most days at 1:30pm, and by appointment. The cost is $10.

LEARN THE LANGUAGE

The **Centro Panamericano de Idiomas** ★ (✆ 2645-5441; www.cpi-edu. com) offers immersion language classes in a wonderful setting. A 1-week program with 4 hours of class per day and a homestay with a Costa Rican family costs $550. They offer language seminars on topics such as social work, medicine, and security. Be sure to check their website for the dates the seminars are taking place.

LOOSE & LIMBER

If you're interested in a massage treatment or yoga class, head to **Río Shanti** (✆ 2645-6121; www.rioshanti.com). This delightful spot offers regular, open yoga classes, private lessons, and various massage treatments. Their little boutique and shop sells handmade jewelry, clothing, and a range of oils, scents, and lotions, most made with organic local ingredients.

Where to Stay

When choosing a place to stay in Monteverde, be sure to check whether the rates include a meal plan. In the past, almost all the lodges included three meals a day in their prices, but this practice is waning. Check before you assume anything.

VERY EXPENSIVE

El Establo Mountain Hotel ★ I remember when the Beeche family transformed their old horse stable (hence, *el establo*) into a simple roadside budget lodging. Today that original hostel is gone, and in its place is arguably the biggest and most luxurious hotel in Monteverde. Large rooms are spread around expansive grounds that rise up a steep hillside from the main road between Santa Elena and the Monteverde Cloud Forest Reserve. The hotel provides golf cart-style shuttle service to help you get around the hilly property. All rooms have a private balcony or patio, and those on the higher floors of the buildings highest up the hillside have some amazing views out to the Gulf of Nicoya. There are two pools (one under a clear atrium-style roof), two restaurants, a small spa, and an on-site zip-line canopy tour.

Monteverde. ✆ **2645-5110.** www.hotelelestablo.com. 155 units. $215 double; $295–$325 suite. Rates include breakfast and taxes. **Amenities:** 2 restaurants; bar; 2 outdoor pools; all rooms smoke-free; small spa.

Hidden Canopy Treehouses ★★★ If you're looking for an intimate, unique, in-touch-with-nature experience in the Monteverde area, you can't beat this place. While a couple of rooms are off the main lodge building, you'll definitely want one of the individual "tree houses." Set amid the forest canopy these are all large, individual units, awash in varnished hardwoods and featuring large picture windows and a balcony or outdoor deck. You can take in superb sunset views from the main lodge, where afternoon tea is served daily. These folks have excellent in-house guides and provide very personalized service.

On the road to the Santa Elena Cloud Forest Reserve. ✆ **2645-5447.** www.hiddencanopy. com. 7 units. $225 double; $285–$445 double tree house. Rates include breakfast and afternoon tea. Extra person $40. No children 14 or under. 2-night minimum. **Amenities:** Lounge; free Wi-Fi (in main house lounge).

EXPENSIVE

Hotel Poco a Poco ★★ This is a good choice for families with kids. Located on the outskirts of Santa Elena, Poco a Poco has clean, comfortable rooms with all the modern amenities, including TV/DVD systems and access to their massive DVD library. A pool, heated Jacuzzi, and small spa are also on-site. The restaurant is excellent and features live music nightly. These folks take sustainable tourism seriously and have earned "4 Leaves" in the CST Sustainable Tourism program.

Santa Elena. ✆ **855/557-6262** in U.S. and Canada, or 2645-6000 in Costa Rica. www.hotel pocoapoco.com. 30 units. $151–$174 double. Rates include breakfast. **Amenities:** Restaurant; bar; Jacuzzi; small outdoor pool; spa; free Wi-Fi.

Monteverde Lodge & Gardens ★★★ Some things do get better with age, and that's certainly true of this pioneering ecolodge. Rooms are large and cozy, and all of the furnishings, appointments, and decor have been recently updated. Personally, I think it's worth the splurge for a second-floor balcony room. The large, communal hot tub under a soaring atrium has long been a focal point here, but equally appealing are the extensive and well-maintained gardens. These folks also have one of the best guide and tour operations in the area.

Santa Elena. ✆ **2257-0766** San José office, or 2645-5057 at the lodge. www.monteverde lodge.com. 28 units. $198–$228 double. Rates include full breakfast. **Amenities:** Restaurant; bar; Jacuzzi; free Wi-Fi.

MODERATE

In addition to the hotels listed below, **El Sol ★** (✆ **2645-5838;** www.elsol nuestro.com) is a unique little boutique option, on the road to the Interamerican Highway, about 10 minutes south of Santa Elena. Also check out **Monteverde Country Lodge** (✆ **888/936-5696** in U.S and Canada, or 2645-7600 in Costa Rica; www.monteverdecountrylodge.com), a homey, simple hotel run by the folks at Hotel Poco a Poco (see above).

Arco Iris Lodge ★★   This small boutique hotel is actually right in the town of Santa Elena, but you'd never know it. The expansive grounds and gardens give it a great sense of isolation and privacy, while still being a short walk from a host of restaurants, shops, and attractions. The rooms are quite cozy and immaculately kept. Service and attention are also top notch.

Santa Elena. ℂ **2645-5067.** www.arcoirislodge.com. 24 units. $42–$50 budget rooms; $88–$145 double; $195 honeymoon cabin. Rates include taxes. **Amenities:** Lounge; free Wi-Fi.

Hotel Fonda Vela ★★   This longstanding hotel is one of the closest you'll find to the Monteverde Cloud Forest Reserve, just a 15-minute or so walk away. Owner Paul Smith's paintings, stained-glass works, and large sculptures are scattered throughout the hotel and grounds. Rooms, in several separate blocks of buildings, have views over the forests to the Gulf of Nicoya. The junior suites are especially spacious and worth the upgrade. A short walk from the restaurant and rooms is a covered pool, a couple of Jacuzzis, pool and Ping-Pong tables, board games, and a casual bar.

On the road to the Monteverde Cloud Forest Reserve. ℂ **800/270-8091** in the U.S. and Canada, or 2645-5125 in Costa Rica. www.fondavela.com. 40 units. $135 double; $180 junior suite. Extra person $15. Rates include taxes. **Amenities:** 2 restaurants; 2 bars; Jacuzzi; outdoor pool; free Wi-Fi in lobby and restaurant.

Hotel Heliconia   Located right at the Cerro Plano intersection along the road between Santa Elena and the Monteverde Cloud Forest Reserve, this is another local lodging that has steadily grown and expanded over the years. Set on the highest part of the property the newest and largest building is where you'll find the rooms with the best views. Personally, I think the wood paneled walls and carpeted floors give the decor a very dated feel. Five different hot tubs and Jacuzzis are spread around the lush grounds between the hotels several buildings. These folks have a large private cloud forest preserve behind the hotel, and also run the Selvatura canopy tour and adventure center (p. 331).

Monteverde. ℂ **2645-5109.** www.hotelheliconia.com. 55 units. $104 double; $141 suite. Rates include breakfast and taxes. **Amenities:** Restaurant; bar; Jacuzzi.

INEXPENSIVE

In addition to the hotel listed below, quite a few pensións and backpacker specials are in Santa Elena and spread along the road to the reserve. The best is the **Pensión Santa Elena** (ℂ **2645-5051;** www.pensionsantaelena.com).

Finally, it's possible to stay in a room right at the **Monteverde Cloud Forest Biological Reserve** (ℂ **2645-5122;** www.cct.or.cr). A bunk bed, shared bathroom, and three meals per day here run $62 per person. For an extra $11, you can get a room with a private bathroom. Admission to the reserve is included in the price.

La Colina Lodge ★   This is my favorite budget option in the area. The rustic old lodge (originally the Pensión Flor Mar) is fairly close to the Monteverde Cloud Forest Reserve, and it radiates a very friendly, homey vibe. Guests from all over the world gather in the common lounge area, or cook together in the communal kitchen. Rooms are basic, but well-kept and cozy.

Monteverde. ℂ **2645-5009.** www.lacolinalodge.com. 11 units, 7 with private bathroom. $35 double with private bathroom; $25 double with shared bathroom; $15 shared bunk room; $8 per person camping. Rates include taxes. **Amenities:** Restaurant, free Wi-Fi.

Where to Dine

Because most visitors want to get an early start, they usually grab a quick breakfast at their hotel. It's also common for people to have their lodge pack them a bag lunch to take to the reserve, although a decent little *soda* is at the reserve entrance.

In addition to the places listed below, you can get good pizzas and pastas at **Tramonti** ★ (© **2645-6120;** www.tramonticr.com), along the road to the reserve, and great paella and other Spanish specialties at **Sabor Español** ★ (© **2645-5387**), a few miles outside of Santa Elena on the road to Tilarán. Also, the restaurant at the **Hotel Poco a Poco** (© **2645-6000**) gets good marks for its wide range of international dishes.

> ## Take a Break
>
> If all the activities in Monteverde have worn you out, stop in at **Las Orquídeas Café** (© **2645-6850**) or the **Common Cup** ★ (© **2645-6247**), two excellent local coffee shops just off the main drag in Santa Elena. The latter is especially focused on sustainable farming practices and community development.

A popular choice for lunch is **Stella's Bakery** (© 2645-5560), across from the CASEM gift shop. The restaurant is bright and inviting, with lots of varnished woodwork, as well as a few outdoor tables. The selection changes regularly but might include vegetarian quiche, eggplant parmigiana, and different salads. Stella's also features a daily supply of decadent baked goods.

EXPENSIVE

Sofia ★★ COSTA RICAN/FUSION   This is a great choice for a splurge, or for a change from the simple typical Costa Rican cooking you might be getting your fill of. The food here is still based on classic Tico dishes and ingredients, but with interesting twists. I like the tenderloin in chipotle butter salsa and the guava-glazed chicken. Try to grab a seat in the dining room with a large picture window overlooking lush foliage.

Cerro Plano, just past the turnoff to the Butterfly Farm, on your left. © **2645-7017.** Reservations recommended during high season. Main courses $14–$20. Daily 11:30am–9:30pm.

MODERATE

Café Caburé ★★★ INTERNATIONAL/CHOCOLATES   Set on the second floor of a small complex also housing the Bat Jungle (p. 333), with open-air seating on a broad wooden veranda, this is a great spot for lunch, dinner, or a decadent dessert break. The main menu features a wide range of international dishes, with everything from chicken mole to shrimp curry in a coconut-milk broth. You could also choose from the excellent sandwiches, wraps, and fresh empanadas (one of the owners is Argentine). The homemade chocolates and fancy, flavored truffles are a standout. And if you want to learn more about the chocolate-making and -tempering process, be sure to take their Chocolate Tour (p. 335).

On the road btw. Santa Elena and the reserve, at the Bat Jungle. © **2645-5020.** www.cabure. net. Reservations recommended during high season. Main courses $3–$18. Mon–Sat 9am–8:30pm.

Birds at the Hummingbird Gallery.

Trio ★★★ FUSION   This trendy downtown spot serves up excellent creative
cooking. I keep going back for the hamburger, which comes topped with a fig jam
and caramelized onions, and features sundried tomatoes blended into the burger
itself. The braised short ribs are also excellent. For a lighter bite, you could try the
green curry chicken wrap. This place has a good little wine list, as well as some
creative cocktails.

Downtown Santa Elena, below the supermarket. ✆ **2645-7254.** Reservations recommended
during high season. Main courses $10–$17; sandwiches $7–$9. Daily 1–10:30pm.

INEXPENSIVE

Morpho's Restaurant ★ COSTA RICAN/VEGETARIAN   Although it's
moved around over the years, this place is a local institution, serving up hearty
and healthy meals at great prices. The large and varied casado (a local blue-plate
special) is quite popular, as are the fresh fruit smoothies and home-baked desserts. For something a bit fancier, try the thick pork chop in a plum/cherry sauce.
There are also a host of excellent vegetarian selections. You can't miss this place,
with its painted exterior covered with oversize, fluttering blue morpho butterflies.
The hand-painted murals continue inside.

In downtown Santa Elena, next to the Orchid Garden. ✆ **2645-5607.** www.morphos
restaurant.com. Main courses C3,000–C12,000. Daily 11am–9pm.

Sabor Tico ★★ COSTA RICAN   The name of this place translates as "Tico
Flavor," and that's what you get at this family-run, traditional joint. The portions
are huge, and everything is extremely tasty and well prepared, although service
can be slow (but friendly) when they are busy. The casados, arroz con pollo, and
fresh fruit juices are all excellent. I always try to snag one of the few tables on the
front veranda overlooking the town's soccer field. These folks have opened a second location (✆ **2645-5968**) in the Centro Comercial Monteverde shopping

plaza, but I much prefer the more casual and authentic vibe of the original location.

In downtown Santa Elena, across from the soccer field. ✆ **2645-5827.** Main courses C2,700–C4,900. Daily 9am–9pm.

Shopping

The **Monteverde Cloud Forest Biological Reserve** has a well-stocked gift shop, just off their entrance. You'll find plenty of T-shirts, postcards, and assorted crafts here, as well as science and natural history books.

Another good option is **CASEM COOP** ★ (✆ **2645-5190;** http://casemcoop.blogspot.com), on the right side of the main road, just across from Stella's Bakery. This crafts cooperative sells embroidered clothing, T-shirts, posters, and postcards with photos of the local flora and fauna, Boruca weavings, locally grown and roasted coffee, and many other items to remind you of your visit to Monteverde. CASEM COOP is open daily 7am to 5pm.

Over the years, Monteverde has developed a nice little community of artists.

Shopping in Monteverde.

Around town, you'll see paintings by local artists such as Paul Smith and Meg Wallace, whose works are displayed at Hotel Fonda Vela and Stella's Bakery, respectively. You should also check out **Casa de Arte** ★★ (✆ **2645-5275;** www.monteverdearthouse.com), which has a mix of arts and crafts in many media.

Finally, it's worth stopping by the **Monteverde Cheese Factory** (✆ **2645-5150;** www.monteverde.net) to pick up some of the best cheese in Costa Rica. You can even watch cheese being processed and get homemade ice cream. The cheese factory is right on the main road about midway between Santa Elena and the reserve. They offer 1-hour tours at 9am and 2pm, at a cost of $12.

Entertainment & Nightlife

Perhaps the most popular after-dark activities in Monteverde are night hikes in one of the reserves. However, if you want a taste of the local party scene, head to **Bar Amigos** (✆ **2645-5071;** www.baramigos.com), a large and often loud bar in the heart of Santa Elena. You'll find a bunch of flatscreen TVs showing sporting events, a couple of pool tables, and occasional live bands. However, I prefer **La Taberna** ★ (✆ **2645-5883**), on the edge of Santa Elena town, below the Serpentarium. With a more contemporary club vibe, this place attracts a mix of locals and tourists, cranks its music loud, often gets people dancing, and occasionally has live bands.

PUERTO VIEJO DE SARAPIQUÍ ★

82km (51 miles) N of San José; 102km (63 miles) E of La Fortuna

The Sarapiquí region, named for the principal river that runs through this area, lies at the foot of the Cordillera Central mountain range. To the west is the rainforest of **Braulio Carrillo National Park,** and to the east are **Tortuguero National Park ★★** and **Barra del Colorado National Wildlife Refuge ★.** In between these protected areas lay thousands of acres of banana, pineapple, and palm plantations. Here you see the great contradiction of Costa Rica: On the one hand, the country is known for its national parks, which preserve some of the largest tracts of rainforest left in Central America; on the other hand, nearly every acre of land outside of these parks, save a few private reserves, has been clear-cut and converted into plantations—and the cutting continues.

Within the remaining rainforest are several lodges that attract naturalists (both amateur and professional). Two of these lodges, **La Selva** and **Rara Avis,** are famous for the research that's conducted on their surrounding reserves. Birdwatching and rainforest hikes are the primary attractions, but more adventure-oriented travelers will find plenty of other available activities, including canopy tours and boating and rafting trips along the Sarapiquí River.

Essentials

GETTING THERE & DEPARTING   By Car: The Guápiles Highway (CR32), which leads to the Caribbean coast, heads north out of downtown San José on Calle 3.

Howler monkey at La Selva Biological Station.

Turn north before reaching Guápiles on the road to Río Frío (CR4), and continue north through Las Horquetas, passing the turnoffs for Rara Avis, La Selva, and El Gavilán lodges before reaching Puerto Viejo.

A more scenic route goes through Heredia, Barva, Varablanca, and San Miguel before reaching Puerto Viejo. This route passes very close to the Poás Volcano and directly in front of La Paz waterfall. If you want to take this route, head west out of San José, then turn north to Heredia and follow the signs for Varablanca and La Paz Waterfall Gardens.

Tip: If you plan to stop on the way to see **La Paz Waterfall Gardens** (p. 166) or ride the **Rain Forest Aerial Tram** (p. 344), budget at least 2 hours to visit either attraction.

By Bus: Empresarios Guapileños buses (© **2222-0610** in San José, or 2710-7780 in Puerto Viejo) leave San José roughly every hour between 6:30am and 6pm from the **Gran Terminal del Caribe,** on Calle Central, 1 block north of Avenida 11. The trip takes around 2 hours; the fare is C2,500. Buses for San José leave Puerto Viejo roughly every hour between 5:30am and 5:30pm.

CITY LAYOUT Puerto Viejo is a very small town, with a soccer field at its center. If you continue past the soccer field on the main road and stay on the paved road, and then turn right at the Banco Nacional, you'll come to the Río Sarapiquí and the dock, where you can look into arranging a boat trip.

> ## Getting Loopy
>
> If you connect the two routes mentioned above, you get what is sometimes referred to as "The Sarapiquí Loop." This loop is a pretty drive, punctuated with attractions and tour opportunities, and it also connects quite nicely with an alternative route to La Fortuna and the Arenal Volcano area (p. 301).

The local tourism chamber maintains a good, comprehensive website of local businesses and attractions, **www.sarapiquicostarica.com**, although the information is in Spanish only, and some of the bus info is dated.

Exploring Puerto Viejo de Sarapiquí

BOAT TRIPS For the adventurous, Puerto Viejo is a jumping-off point for trips down the Río Sarapiquí to Barra del Colorado National Wildlife Refuge and Tortuguero National Park on the Caribbean coast. A boat for up to 10 people will cost you around $400 to $600 to Barra del Colorado or $500 to $700 to Tortuguero. If you're interested in this trip, it's worth checking at your hotel or with **Oasis Nature Tours** (© **2766-6108**); www.oasisnaturetours.com. Alternatively, you can head down to the town dock on the bank of the Sarapiquí and see if you can arrange a less expensive boat trip on your own by tagging along with another group or, better yet, with a bunch of locals.

In addition to the longer trips, you can take shorter trips on the river for between $10 and $20 per person per hour. A trip down the Sarapiquí, even if it's for only an hour or two, provides opportunities to spot crocodiles, caimans, monkeys, sloths, and dozens of bird species.

CANOPY TOUR & MORE **Hacienda Pozo Azul** ★ (© **877/810-6903** in the U.S. and Canada, or 2438-2616 in Costa Rica; www.pozoazul.com) is a working cattle farm and one-stop shop for a wide range of adventure activities. These folks have an extensive zip-line canopy tour operation, with 17 platforms connected by 12 different cable runs, in addition to offering white-water rafting, horseback riding, and guided hikes. They even run a tent-camp and separate rustic lodge in deep rainforest sites here. Several differently priced combo packages are offered, and the property is open daily from 8am to 6pm.

HIKING & GUIDED TOURS Anyone can take advantage of the 56km (35 miles) of well-maintained **trails at La Selva ★★** (p. 345). If you're not staying there, however, you'll have to take a guided hike, led by experienced and well-informed naturalists. Half- and full-day hikes ($32 and $45, respectively) are offered daily, but you must reserve in advance (✆ **2524-0607**; www.threepaths.co.cr). The tours leave at 8am and 1:30pm daily.

My favorite hike starts off with the Cantarrana ("singing frog") trail, which includes a section of low bridges over a rainforest swamp. From here, you can join up with either the near or far circular loop trails—**CCC** and **CCL**. Another good hiking option is the trails and suspended bridges at the **Centro Neotrópico SarapiquíS.**

For a more orderly introduction to the local flora, head to a botanical garden, like the **Chester Field Biological Gardens** (see below), or the nearby **Heliconia Island** (✆ **2764-5220**; www.heliconiaisland.com), an interesting garden with over 70 varieties of heliconia, on a small island. This place is open daily from 8am to 5pm. Admission is $12 for a self-guided walk, or $18 for a guided tour.

A NATURAL-HISTORY THEME PARK The **Alma Ata Archaeological Park** is a small ongoing dig of a modest pre-Columbian gravesite, that is attached to a local hotel, **SarapiquíS Rainforest Lodge** (✆ **2761-1004**; www.sarapiquis.org). So far, 12 graves, some petroglyphs, and numerous pieces of ceramic and jewelry have been unearthed. The hotel also has a small museum that displays examples of the ceramics, tools, clothing, and carvings found here, as well as other natural-history exhibits. Just across the hotel's driveway, you'll find the Chester Field Biological Gardens, with its well-tended displays of local medicinal and ornamental plants and herbs, as well as food crops. Admission to the archaeological park, museum, and gardens costs $30, and includes lunch. If you just want to visit the museum, the cost is $15; it's open daily from 6am to 5pm. A self-guided walk through the botanical gardens is free.

Across the river from the SarapiquíS Rainforest Lodge is the 300-hectare (741-acre) private **Tirimbina Rainforest Center ★** (✆ **2761-0333**; www. tirimbina.org), with a small network of trails and several impressive suspension bridges, both over the river and through the forest canopy. A self-guided walk of the reserve's bridges and trails costs $15 per person, and a 2-hour guided tour costs $25 per person—definitely worth the extra few bucks. The center is open daily from 7:30am to 5pm, and from 7to 9:30pm for night tours; specialized early morning bird-watching tours are also available.

RAFTING & KAYAKING If you want a fast, wild ride on the river, check in with **Aguas Bravas** (✆ **2292-2072**; www.costaricaraftingvacation.com) or **Aventuras del Sarapiquí ★** (✆ **2766-6768**; www.sarapiqui.com). Both companies run trips on a variety of sections of the Sarapiquí and Puerto Viejo rivers, ranging from Class I to Class IV. Trips cost between $56 and $110 per person. Aventuras del Sarapiquí also runs mountain-biking and horseback-riding tours in the area. They rent kayaks, give kayaking classes, and offer kayak trips for more experienced and/or daring river rats, and offer inner-tube floats for those with lesser skill sets still looking to get wet.

SNAKES UNDER GLASS Just a few blocks west of the Centro Neotrópico SarapiquíS, you'll find **Jardín de Serpientes** (**Snake Garden;** ✆ **2761-1059**;

Eyelash vipers are one of the many reptiles that you'll see at Jardín de Serpientes.

Rafting on Sarapiquí River.

snakegarden@hotmail.com), a collection of over 50 snakes, both venomous and nonvenomous, and other reptiles and amphibians. Two of the prize attractions here, although not native, are a massive, yellow Burmese python and similarly impressive anaconda. There are also caiman and crocodiles. All are kept in clean, well-lit displays. Admission is $30 adults for a guided tour, or $15 adult for a self-guided entrance. Children 4-12 years of age are $20 for the guided tour and $10 for self-guided entrance. This place is open daily from 9am to 5pm. Night tours are also offered with advance reservations.

ONE MAJOR ATTRACTION EN ROUTE   If you're driving to Puerto Viejo de Sarapiquí via the Guápiles Highway, you might want to stop at the **Rain Forest Aerial Tram** ★. You'll see the entrance on your right shortly after passing through the Zurquí tunnel. For more information, see "Side Trips from San José," in chapter 6.

Where to Stay & Dine

All the lodges listed below arrange excursions throughout the region, including boat trips on the Sarapiquí, guided hikes in the rainforest, and horseback or mountain bike rides. Also note that rates for the lodges in the "Expensive" category include all meals, taxes, and usually a tour or two, greatly reducing their real cost. In addition to the hotels listed below, **Peace Lodge** (p. 168), at La Paz Waterfall Gardens, is almost close enough to be considered lodging in this region.

EXPENSIVE

In addition to the places listed below, **Hacienda La Isla** ★ (✆ **2764-2576;** www.haciendalaisla.com) is an intimate boutique hotel near the small town of Las Horquetas.

Selva Verde Lodge ★★ Begun in 1982 by Giovanna Holbrook and Holbrook Travel, this is one of the first ecotourist lodges in Costa Rica and is still running strong. Set in a patch of thick forest on the banks of the Sarapiquí River, these folks have a large private reserve on the other side of the river. A series of raised wooden buildings connected by a maze of covered walkways house the main river lodge rooms. These are all very simple, with varnished wood floors, screen windows, a couple of beds, a fan and bathroom. A few bungalows have air-conditioning, but these are located across the street and a nice little walk away from the main lodge and river. My favorite feature here is the large, open-air main dining room that overlooks the river. In addition to a more typical lodge menu, they also offer buffet dining (aimed primarily at tour groups), as well as pizzas from a wood-burning brick oven. There's a lovely pool area, as well as several swimming holes along the river. A bridge leads across the river to a network of trails through the rainforest, and they also have their own little zip-line.

Chilamate, Sarapiquí. ℂ **800/451-7111** in the U.S. and Canada, or 2761-1800 in Costa Rica. www.selvaverde.com. 40 units, 5 bungalows. $134 double, $163 bungalows. Rates include breakfast and taxes. **Amenities:** 2 restaurants; bar; outdoor pool; smoke-free rooms.

MODERATE

Although I highly recommend you choose one of the more atmospheric nature lodges listed in this section, if you absolutely must (or for some reason prefer to) stay in Puerto Viejo de Sarapiquí proper, **Hotel El Bambú** (ℂ **2766-6005;** www.elbambu.com) is a clean, comfortable, and almost modern option.

In addition to the places outside town that are reviewed below, the **Tirimbina Rainforest Center** ★ (p. 343) also has rooms.

Hotel Hacienda Sueño Azul ★ This place is located fairly close to the Highway 32 which connects San José to the Caribbean coast, on the outskirts of the tiny village of Las Horquetas. You reach the property by crossing a couple of hammock bridges that appear too narrow for most vehicles, but seem to do the job. The rooms are large and feature rustic four-poster wooden beds and private verandas. The best of these are close to and overlooking a river or lagoon. The hotel sits at the meeting point of two rivers, and water features prominently. One of the property's two pools is a very large, river-fed, semi-natural pool. This place often hosts yoga or wellness retreats, but horseback riding, hiking and other active adventures are also offered.

Las Horquetas de Sarapiquí. ℂ **2253-2020** reservation number in San José, 2764-1000 at the lodge. www.suenoazulresort.com. 64 units. $100–$120 double; $152 suite. **Amenities:** Restaurant; bar; Jacuzzi; 2 outdoor pools; small spa; free Wi-Fi.

La Selva Biological Station The name says it all, this is no prissy upscale ecolodge. Built primarily to accommodate biologists, researchers and student groups, this place also accepts everyday tourists. That said, don't expect fine linens, pampering service or memorable meals. There are both very basic bunk bed and dorm style rooms, as well as newer more plush rooms geared towards tourists more than scientists. The better rooms are a good 15 to 20 minute hike from the main lodge, restaurant and research facilities. La Selva, is operated by the Organization for Tropical Studies (OTS) and has more than 1,614 hectares (3,656 acres) of private reserve, and this borders the even larger Braulio Carrillo National Park. These folks maintain a very extensive, well-marked and well-maintained trail system through these forests, and the wildlife viewing and flora here are some of the best in Costa Rica.

A bungalow at Selva Verde Lodge.

Puerto Viejo. www.threepaths.co.cr. © **2524-0607** reservations office in San José, or 2766-6565 at the lodge. 24 units, 16 with shared bathroom. $93 double. Rates include all meals, 1 guided walk and taxes. Rates lower for researchers and student groups. **Amenities:** Restaurant.

La Quinta de Sarapiquí Country Inn ★   Leo and Beatriz run a cozy, laid-back little lodge on the edge of the Sardinal River. Rooms are found in a series of buildings spread around the ample grounds and gardens. The rooms are very simple, but immaculately maintained, with lots of natural light and a cheery feel. The hotel has two separate swimming pools, as well as a butterfly garden and poison dart frog garden. They also operate a separate six room lodge next door, Kinkajou Town, geared more towards students, researchers and itinerant NGO workers. La Quinta was awarded "5 Leaves" by the CST Sustainable Tourism program.

Chilamate, Sarapiquí. © **2761-1052.** www.laquintasarapiqui.com. 40 units. $110 double; $140 suite. Children 11 and under stay free in parent's room. **Amenities:** Restaurant; bar; 2 small outdoor pools.

Rara Avis   Owner Amos Bien is a pioneer and moving force in sustainable tourism. This place is quite rustic and rough around the edges, but those looking for a real nature lodge in the middle of some of Costa Rica's richest rainforests will be greatly rewarded. Aside from the amazing wildlife and lush fauna, the star attraction here is a nearby swimming hole fed by a beautiful two-tiered waterfall. Meals are standard Tico fare and forgettable, although the service and guides are top notch.

    This is not a good place for walk-ins or spur of the moment visits. If you plan to stay here, prior reservations are essential. Be sure to get very specific directions and coordinate closely with the folks here, as the lodge is 15km (10 miles) up a very rugged dirt road and can only be reached via horse, tractor or a very long strenuous hike.

15km (9¹/₃ miles) from Las Horquetas. www.rara-avis.com. ℂ **2764-1111.** 14 units. 10 with private bathroom. $65 per person with shared bathroom; $84 per person with private bathroom. Rates include all meals and 2 guided tours per day. **Amenities:** Restaurant.

INEXPENSIVE

The **Posada Andrea Cristina** (ℂ **2766-6265;** www.andreacristina.com), just on the outskirts of Puerto Viejo, is run by Alex Martínez, an excellent local guide and pioneering conservationist in the region. You may also consider staying at the jungle tent-camp or isolated Magsasay Lodge at **Hacienda Pozo Azul ★** (ℂ **877/810-6903** in the U.S. and Canada, or 2438-2616, www.pozoazul.com).

Gavilán Sarapiquí River Lodge   This longstanding local lodge is fairly basic, but well-run, friendly and relaxed. Most of the rooms are quite large, although some of the bathrooms show their age. Personally, I think it's worth the splurge for one of their six superior rooms. The expansive grounds have beautiful gardens, as well as an unheated Jacuzzi fed by a natural spring. The hotel is set right on a high bank of the Sarapiquí River, but on the other side of the river from town, so it's quiet and feels remote. These folks have their own 49 hectare (120 acre) private reserve, and more than 450 bird species have been spotted in the area.

Puerto Viejo de Sarapiquí. ℂ **2234-9507** reservation office in San José, 2766-7131 or 8343-9480 at the lodge. www.gavilanlodge.com. 20 units. $60 double; $75 superior double. **Amenities:** Restaurant; bar; Jacuzzi, free Wi-Fi.

10

THE CENTRAL PACIFIC COAST:
WHERE THE MOUNTAINS MEET THE SEA

A fter Guanacaste, the beaches of Costa Rica's central Pacific coast are the country's most popular. Options here range from the surfer and snowbird hangout of Jacó, to the ecotourist mecca of Manuel Antonio, to remote and diminutive Dominical, with its jungle-clad hillsides and rainforest waterfalls. Now that a newish modern highway connects San José to the coast, and improvements along the Costanera Sur highway are heading south, this region has gotten even easier to visit.

Jacó and Playa Herradura are the closest major beach destinations to San José. They have historically been the first choice for young surfers and city-dwelling Costa Ricans. Just north of Playa Herradura sits **Carara National Park ★★**, one of the few places in Costa Rica where you can see the disappearing dry forest join the damp, humid forests that extend south down the coast. It's also a great place to see scarlet macaws in the wild.

Just a little farther south, Manuel Antonio is one of the country's foremost ecotourist destinations, with a host of hotel and lodging options and an easily accessible national park that combines the exuberant lushness of a lowland tropical rainforest with several gorgeous beaches. **Manuel Antonio National Park ★★** is home to all four of Costa Rica's monkey species, as well as a wealth of other easily viewed flora and fauna.

If you're looking to get away from it all, **Dominical** and the **beaches south of Dominical ★** should be your top destination on this coast. Still a small village, the beach town of Dominical is flanked by even more remote and undeveloped beaches, including those found inside **Ballena Marine National Park ★★**.

Finally, if you can tear yourself away from the beaches and coastline here, and head slightly inland, you'll find **Chirripó National Park ★★**, a misty cloud forest that becomes a barren páramo (a region above 3,000m/9,840 ft.) at the peak of its namesake, Mount Chirripó—the tallest peak in Costa Rica.

The climate here is considerably more humid than that farther north in Guanacaste, but it's not nearly as hot and steamy as along the southern Pacific or Caribbean coasts.

THE BEST CENTRAL PACIFIC TRAVEL EXPERIENCES

o **Having Miles of Pacific Beach Practically to Yourself:** While Jacó, Manuel Antonio, and Dominical are all bustling tourist beaches, the rest of the long, Central Pacific coastline is almost entirely deserted. Rent a car or hire a taxi to visit any number of isolated and virtually undiscovered beaches. See the individual destination sections below for options.

o **Visiting Carara National Park:** The Tárcoles River crocodiles are best viewed from the bridge just outside the park entrance, and the resident scarlet

PREVIOUS PAGE: **A capuchin monkey.**

The Central Pacific Coast's Top Sustainable Hotels

Arenas Del Mar (p. 380)
Cuna del Angel (p. 396)
Hotel Parador (p. 380)
Gaia Hotel & Reserve (p. 380)
Hacienda Barú (p. 391)

Hotel Sí Como No (p. 380)
La Cusinga Lodge (p. 397)
Monte Azul (p. 403)
Savegre Hotel (p. 404)

macaws can often be seen outside the park as well. Still, I recommend hiking the lush and varied trails inside Carara National Park. You'll be rewarded with rich foliage and the chance to see much more wildlife. See p. 355.

o **Hiking the Trails in Manuel Antonio National Park:** The trails here wind through thick tropical rainforest and periodically offer beautiful ocean views as well as opportunities to spot wildlife—all four of Costa Rica's monkey species call this national park home. You may not knock all four species off your life list, but a visit here almost—I said almost—guarantees you'll see these local primates darting around the tropical treetops. See p. 369.

o **Visiting the Nauyaca Waterfalls Outside of Dominical:** Nestled in a patch of thick tropical rainforest, the Nauyaca Waterfalls are gorgeous, and feature a large and inviting pool at its base. See p. 392.

o **Climbing Mount Chirripó:** The highest mountain in Costa Rica, Mount Chirripó is a challenging, but accessible peak whose summit sometimes offers simultaneous views of the Pacific Ocean and Caribbean Sea. See p. 400.

PLAYA HERRADURA

108km (67 miles) W of San José; 9km (6 miles) NW of Playa de Jacó

Playa Herradura is the first major beach you'll hit as you head south along the Southern Coastal Highway. **Playa Herradura** is a long stretch of brown sand that is home to the massive **Los Sueños Marriott Ocean & Golf Resort ★★** (p. 356) and its attached marina. North of Herradura, you'll find a few other small beaches and resorts, including the elegant boutique hotel **Villa Caletas ★★★** (p. 357).

Essentials

GETTING THERE & DEPARTING   By Car: Head west out of San José on the San José–Caldera Highway (CR27). Just past the toll booth at Pavón, this road connects with the Costanera Sur (CR34), or Southern Coastal Highway. The exit is marked for Jacó and CR34. From here it's a straight and flat shot down the coast to Playa Herradura. The trip should take about an hour.

By Bus: No direct buses run all the way into Playa Herradura. All buses to Jacó will drop off passengers at the entrance to Playa Herradura, which is about 1km (½ mile) or so from the beach and Los Sueños resort complex. See "Playa de Jacó: Getting There & Departing," p. 358, for bus info.

Gray Line (© **800/719-3105** in the U.S. and Canada, or 2220-2126 in Costa Rica; www.graylinecostarica.com) and **Interbus** (© **2283-5573;** www.interbusonline.com) both have two buses daily leaving San José for Jacó, one in

The Central Pacific Coast

En Route to Jacó: An Isolated Boutique Beauty

If you're planning on heading to the beaches of the central Pacific coast via Ciudad Colón and Puriscal, you might consider a stop at **Ama Tierra Retreat & Wellness Center ★** (© **866/659-3805** in the U.S. and Canada, or 2419-0110 in Costa Rica, www.amatierra.com), a lovely little boutique hotel and retreat center about 1¹/₂ hours outside of San José along this route, and approximately 1 hour from Jacó.

the morning and one in the afternoon. The fare is $47. Both companies will pick you up at most San José–area hotels and drop you off at any hotel in or around Playa Herradura. Both also offer connections to most major tourist destinations in the country.

Buses from San José to **Quepos** and Manuel Antonio also pass by Playa Herradura. (They let passengers off on the highway about 1km/¹/₂ mile from town.) However, during the busy months, some of these buses will refuse passengers getting off in Playa Herradura or will accept them only if they pay the full fare to Quepos or Manuel Antonio. For information and departure times of these buses, see p. 371.

LAYOUT Playa Herradura is a short distance off the Southern Coastal Highway. Just before you hit the beach, you'll see the entrance to the Los Sueños resort complex and marina on your right. One dirt road runs parallel to the beach, with a few restaurants and a makeshift line of parking spaces all along its length.

FAST FACTS Playa Herradura has no real town. At the main intersection with the Southern Coastal Highway, you'll find a modern strip mall, with a large Automercado supermarket, and some restaurants, shops, and a couple of ATMs.

Exploring Playa Herradura

Because they're so close, many folks staying in Playa Herradura take advantage of the tours and activities offered out of Jacó and even those offered out of Quepos and Manuel Antonio. See the respective sections below for more details.

BEACHES Playa Herradura is a calm and protected beach, although the dark sand is rocky in places and not very attractive. The calmest section of beach is toward the north end, where you'll find the **Los Sueños Marriott Ocean & Golf Resort.** Aside from sunbathing and swimming, you won't find too much to do here. When the swell is big, the center section of beach can be a good place to body surf, boogie-board, or try some beginning surf moves.

Punta Leona, just a few kilometers north of Playa Herradura, is a cross between a hotel, a resort, and a private country club, and it has some of the nicer beaches in the area. Although they effectively have restricted access to their beaches for years, this is technically illegal in Costa Rica, and you have the right to enjoy both playas **Manta ★** and **Blanca ★**, two very nice white-sand beaches inside the Punta Leona complex. The public access beach road is south of the main Punta Leona entrance and is not very well marked.

In contrast to the dryness of Guanacaste, these are the first beaches on the Pacific coast to have a tropical feel. The humidity is palpable, and the lushness of the tropical forest is visible on the hillsides surrounding town. In hotel gardens, flowers bloom profusely throughout the year.

HOTELS
The Backyard **18**
Cabinas Las Arenas **15**
Cabinas Las Olas **16**
Costanera Bed
    & Breakfast **14**
Los Sueños Marriott
    Ocean & Golf Resort **8**
Pumilio Mountain &
    Ocean Resort **11**
Sandpiper Inn **13**
Surf Inn Hermosa **17**
Villa Caletas **5**
Villa Lapas **2**

RESTAURANTS
Bambu **9**
El Galeón **9**
El Pelícano **10**
Hook Up **9**
Inka Grill **7**
La Linterna **9**

ATTRACTIONS
Carara National Park **1**
Jungle Crocodile
    Safaris **3**
Pura Vida Botanical
    Gardens **4**
Rain Forest Aerial Tram
    Pacific **12**
Villa Lapas **2**
Vista Los Sueños
    Canopy Tour **6**

To San José   Lomas Pizote

Río Grande de Tárcoles

Carara National Park **1**

Quebrada Bonita

Playa Tárcoles

34

Tárcoles

2
2

Cerros Quebrada Bonita

3

Río Tárcolitos

Punta Mala

4

Lomas Camaronal

Golfo de Nicoya

Lomas Pita

Río Camaronal

Playa Agujas

Agujas

Río Agujas

Quebrada Ganado

Playa Limoncito
Punta Leona

Playa Blanca   Playa Mantas

Punta Sucia

34

Cerro Herradura

5

Playa Caletas

PACIFIC

OCEAN

Playa Coyol

6

Playa Matapalo

Herradura

7

Playas Herradura & Hermosa

Punta Conejo

9 **8**

Islote Piña de Arroz

Bahía Herradura

34

11   **12**

Cerro Fresco

10

Río Copey

Río Gloria

Playa Herradura

Fila Quebrada Bonita

Quebrada Cañablancal

Isla de Herradura

Finca Balsal

Playa Balsal

Jacó

Cerro Puntudo

Playa Jacó

Cerro Guapinol

0   2 mi
0   2 km

Punta Guapinol
Playa Hermosa

34

13
14
        15
To Quepos   **16**
            17   **18**

Don't Feed the Crocs

The Costanera Highway passes over the Tárcoles River just outside the entrance to **Carara National Park,** about 23km (14 miles) south of Orotina. This is a popular place to pull over and spot some gargantuan crocodiles. Some can reach 3.7 to 4.6m (12–15 ft.) in length. Usually anywhere from 10 to 20 are easily visible, either swimming in the water or sunning on the banks. But be careful. First, you'll have to brave walking on a narrow sidewalk along the side of the bridge with cars and trucks speeding by. And second, car break-ins are common here, including in the seemingly safe restaurant parking lots at the north end of the

bridge. Although a police post has somewhat reduced the risk, I recommend that you don't leave your car or valuables unguarded for long, or better yet, leave someone at the car and take turns watching the crocs.

CANOPY TOURS Vista Los Sueños Canopy Tour ★ (© 321/220-9631 in the U.S. or 2637-6020 in Costa Rica; www.canopyvistalossuenos.com) is set in the hills above Playa Herradura. This tour features 12 zip-lines, some excellent views, and boasts the longest cable in the area, at nearly a kilometer (almost a half-mile) in length. The cost is $60 per person, and round-trip transportation can be added on. These folks also offer horseback riding tours to a nearby waterfall.

Nearby **Villa Lapas** (p. 357) has two different tours through the treetops outside of Jacó. The better and least expensive option is a guided hike on its network of trails and five suspended bridges ($28 per person). The operator also has a relatively low-adrenaline zip-line canopy tour ($48 per person), with seven platforms connected by six cables.

CROCODILE TOURS If you're staying in any of the nearby beach towns, you might consider taking a boat tour of the river and mangroves. Several companies offer such a tour, and every hotel and tour agency in the area can make arrangements for you. Nearly all the operators bring along plenty of freshly killed chickens to attract the crocs—a practice I cannot endorse. That's why I suggest going with the more responsible tour operator, **Eco Jungle Cruises** ★ (© 2582-0181; www.ecojunglecruisescom). These folks don't believe in feeding the crocs or altering their behaviors. There are still plenty (hundreds, in fact) of crocodiles to be seen along the stretch of river and mangrove they run, and plenty of top notch photo opportunities. The cost of their 2-hour tour is $40 for adults and $30 for children ages 4 to 12 (free for children 3 and under). Transportation from Jacó, Playa Herradura, Manuel Antonio, or San José is available.

GOLF The excellent **La Iguana,** an 18-hole golf course at the Los Sueños Marriott Ocean & Golf Resort (© 2630-9028; www.golflaiguana.com), is open to non-guests. Greens fees are $174. Club and shoe rentals are available. Marriott guests pay slightly less to play here

PURA VIDA GARDENS AND WATERFALLS Just beyond Carara National Park on the Costanera Sur in the direction of Jacó, you'll find the **Pura Vida Gardens**

and Waterfalls ★ (© 2645-1001; www.puravidagarden.com). Admission is $20, and it's open daily from 8am to 5pm. The fee includes free run of the gardens and trails, which lead to a couple of small waterfalls. The gardens also have a good little restaurant, which is a great spot for a meal or some sunset cocktails.

To get here, turn off at the signs for Villa Lapas (p. 357). From there, it's a rough 8km (5 miles) up to the gardens.

SPORTFISHING, SCUBA DIVING & SEABORNE FUN   Since the Los Sueños Marriott Resort (p. 356) and its adjacent 250-slip marina opened, most maritime activity has shifted over here. If you're interested in doing some sportfishing, scuba diving, or any other waterborne activity, I recommend that you check with your hotel or at the marina. Dependable operators that have set up here include **Maverick Sportfishing Yachts** (© 800/405-8206 in the U.S., or 8712-9683 in Costa Rica; www.maverickyachtscostarica.com) and **Costa Rica Dreams** (© 337/205-0665 in the U.S., or 2637-8942 in Costa Rica; www.costarica dreams.com). A half-day fishing trip for four people costs around $700 to $1,200, and a full day costs between $1,000 and $1,800.

Carara National Park ★★

A little more than 17.5km (11 miles) north of Playa Herradura is **Carara National Park** (© 2637-1054 for visitor center), a world-renowned nesting ground for **scarlet macaws.** It has a few kilometers of trails open to visitors. The **Sendero Accesso Universal (Universal Access Trail),** which heads out from the national park office, is broad, flat, and wheelchair-accessible (hence the trail name). The first half of this 1km (.7-mile) stretch leads into the forest and features various informative plaques, in both English and Spanish, pointing out prominent flora. About 10 or 15 minutes into your hike, you'll see that the trail splits, forming a loop (you can go in either direction). The entire loop trail should take you about an hour. The macaws migrate daily, spending their days in the park and their nights among the coastal mangroves. It's best to view them in the early morning when they arrive, or around sunset when they head back to the coast for the evening, but a good guide can usually find them for you during the day. Whether or not you see them, you should hear their loud squawks. Among the other wildlife that you might see are caimans, coatimundis, armadillos, pacas, peccaries, and, of course, hundreds of species of birds.

Be sure to bring along insect repellent or, better yet, wear light cotton long sleeves and pants. (I was once foolish enough to attempt a quick hike while returning from Manuel Antonio, still in beach clothes and flip-flops.) The reserve is open daily from 7am to 4pm. Admission is $10 per person at the gate.

Most hotel desks can arrange for a guided hike to Carara National Park, or you can contact **Jaguar Riders** (© 2643-0180; www.jaguariders.com) in Jacó to set one up. Although you can certainly hike the gentle and well-marked trails of Carara independently, my advice is to take a guided tour; you'll learn a lot more about your surroundings.

Where to Stay

VERY EXPENSIVE

In addition to its hotel rooms, the Los Sueños resort has scores of condominium units for rent. All come with kitchens, access to swimming pools, and rights to use the golf course here. These are excellent options for families who want to do

A scarlet macaw, one of the many birds you might spot in Carara National Park.

some cooking, and for longer stays. If you want to rent a condo here, contact **Stay In Costa Rica** (© **866/439-5922** in the U.S. and Canada, or 2637-2661 in Costa Rica; www.stayincostarica.com) Rates are begin around $250 to $350 nightly for one- and two-bedroom units, to well over $1,000 for some of the more luxurious three-bedroom and larger units.

Los Sueños Marriott Ocean & Golf Resort ★★   This is the premier large resort hotel on the Central Pacific coast, with beautiful rooms, stunning architecture, a lovely 18-hole regulation golf course and one of the largest and most unique pools in the country. This pool, designed to conjure images of Venetian canals, is a complex maze with a host of small bridges connecting islands of chaise lounges and lush gardens, interspersed with secret grottoes and quiet corners. It's a good thing that the pool is so interesting and inviting, as the beach in front of the resort is made of hard-packed dark sand and not particularly appealing for either sunbathing or swimming. A host of good dining options are on site and in the nearby marina.

Playa Herradura © **888/236-2427** in the U.S. and Canada, 2298-000 or 2630-9000 in Costa Rica; www.lossuenosmarriott.com. 201 units. $259–$539 double; $449–$589 suite; $680 and up presidential suite. **Amenities:** 4 restaurants; coffee shop; bar; lounge; children's program; concierge; golf course and pro shop; 9-hole miniature golf course; extensive health club and spa; large outdoor pool; room service; smoke-free rooms; 4 outdoor lit tennis courts; Wi-Fi in most public areas.

Villa Caletas ★★★ This cliff-top collection of private villas and rooms is opulent and elegant. Rooms are all quite large and feature refined neoclassical decor. Most provide impressive views of the Pacific Ocean over the forested hillside below. The separate Zephyr Palace is similar in luxury, but the rooms each feature a unique design theme, ranging from the Egyptian suite to the Imperial suite, with several other distinct cultures and regions represented as well. And while the service and attention are top notch throughout, the Zephyr Palace also offers personal concierge services. The main Greek-inspired amphitheater at Villa Caletas is a very popular spot to catch the sunset.

Btw. Punta Leona and Playa Herradura ✆ **2630-3000.** www.hotelvillacaletas.com. 54 units. $195–$226 double; $268 villa; $352–$557 suite; $347–$1,586 Zephyr Palace suites. Extra person $42 at Villa Caletas; $85 at Zephyr Palace. **Amenities:** 3 restaurants; 2 bars; concierge; 4 midsize outdoor pools; Jacuzzi; spa; free Wi-Fi.

EXPENSIVE

In addition to the place listed below, **Pumilio Mountain & Ocean Hotel** (✆ **2643-5678;** www.hotelpumilio.com) is a boutique hotel and spa, located on a hillside a bit inland, between Playa Herradura and Jacó.

Villa Lapas This is a lovely small resort on the banks of the Tarcolitos River that provides a nice alternative to all the beach resorts and hotels that typically define this region. The lodge is set right on the border of Carara National Park and offers easy access to some wonderful bird watching and wildlife viewing. It's not uncommon to see some namesake *lapas*, or Scarlet Macaws, flying right overhead here. The hotel has its own zip-line canopy tour, hanging bridges and a recreated rural Costa Rican village, replete with a wedding chapel based on the old colonial-era church in Ujarrás (p. 183). If you want to combine a stay here with some beach time, it's just 15 to 25 minutes by car to the beaches of Jacó, Play Hermosa, and Herradura.

Tárcoles. ✆ **2637-0232.** www.villalapas.com. 58 units. $144–$159 per person. Rates include 3 meals daily, drinks, and taxes. **Amenities:** 2 restaurants; 2 bars; small outdoor pool; free Wi-Fi.

Where to Dine

Several restaurants, including some fast-food outlets and the Peruvian chain **Inka Grill** (✆ **2637-8510**), are in the strip mall on the highway near the entrance to the beach. At the Los Sueños Marina you'll find several other options, including **Bambu,** a sushi bar and Pan-Asian restaurant; **La Linterna,** a fancy Italian restaurant; and **Hook Up,** an excellent American-style grill and restaurant, serving great lunch and light fare, with a second-floor perch and good views. You can make reservations at any of the marina restaurants by calling ✆ **2630-4444.**

VERY EXPENSIVE

El Galeón ★★ FUSION Although pricey, this is easily the best restaurant at the Los Sueños Marina. A large, open-air dining room overlooks the marina and Herradura Bay. The menu is broad and creative, and the presentations are artful. On my last visit, I really enjoyed the slider appetizer, which included small buns sporting a mix of thin-sliced prime rib, barbeque pork and beef short ribs, served with Cajun spiced sweet potato fries. For a main dish, you can't go wrong with the Moroccan style lamb tangine, or the whole fried red snapper with a black bean and garlic sauce. This place has one of the most diverse and well-thought out wine lists in the area.

At the marina of the Los Sueños Marriott Resort (p. 356). ✆ **2630-4555.** Reservations recommended. Main courses $24–$65. Daily 5:30–10pm.

MODERATE

El Pelícano ★ SEAFOOD/COSTA RICAN   This is the best local restaurant in Playa Herradura and an excellent beachfront option, to boot. Set just across the single-lane dirt road that runs along the beach, this simple, open-air spot serves up fresh ceviche, fish, and seafood, and other Tico standards. You can also get steak and chicken, but I recommend the seafood that's caught and brought in daily. Most meals come with a visit to their small salad bar.

On the beach in Playa Herradura. ✆ **2637-8910.** Reservations recommended during high season. Main courses C6,500–C38,000. Daily noon–10pm.

PLAYA DE JACÓ

Jacó: 117km (73 miles) W of San José; 75km (47 miles) S of Puntarenas

Playa de Jacó is a long stretch of beach backed by a dense hodgepodge of hotels in all price categories, souvenir shops, seafood restaurants, pizza joints, and rowdy bars. The main strip, running parallel to the shoreline, is an overcrowded and congested collection of restaurants, shops, and small strip malls, where pedestrians, bicycles, scooters, cars, and ATVs vie for right of way both day and night.

The number-one attraction is the surf, and this is definitely a surfer-dominated beach town. Surfers love the consistent beach break; however, the beach itself is not particularly appealing. It consists of dark-gray sand with lots of little rocks, and it's often pretty rough for swimming. Still, given its proximity to San José, Jacó is almost always packed with a mix of foreign and Tico vacationers. Beyond the surf, Jacó is also known for its nightlife. The raging bars here offer everything from live music venues to chill lounge environments to beachfront sports bars with pool and foosball tables.

Essentials

GETTING THERE & DEPARTING   **By Car:** Head west out of San José on the San José–Caldera Highway (CR27). Just past the toll booth at Pavón, this road connects with the Costanera Sur (CR34), or Southern Coastal Highway. The exit is marked for Jacó and CR34. From here, it's a straight and flat shot down the coast to Jacó. The trip should take a little over an hour.

By Bus: Transportes Jacó express buses (✆ 2223-1109; www.transportes jacoruta655.com) leave San José daily every 2 hours between 7am and 7pm from the Coca-Cola bus terminal at Calle 16 between avenidas 1 and 3. The trip takes between 2$\frac{1}{2}$ and 3 hours; the fare is C2,335. On weekends and holidays, extra buses are sometimes added, so it's worth calling to check.

Gray Line (✆ 800/719-3105 in the U.S. and Canada, or 2220-2126 in Costa Rica; www.graylinecostarica.com) and **Interbus** (✆ 4031-0888; www. interbusonline.com) both have two buses daily leaving San José to Jacó, one in the morning and one in the afternoon. The fare is around $49. Both companies will pick you up at most San José–area hotels. Both also offer connections to most major tourist destinations in the country.

A Jacó surf shop.

Buses from San José to **Quepos** and Manuel Antonio also pass by Jacó. (They let passengers off on the highway about 1km/¹/₂ mile from town.) However, during the busy months, some of these buses will refuse passengers getting off in Jacó or will accept them only if they pay the full fare to Quepos or Manuel Antonio. For information and departure times of these buses, see p. 371.

From **Puntarenas,** you can catch daily **Transportes Quepos Puntarenas** (✆ **2777-1617**) Quepos-bound buses at 5, 8, and 11am and 12:30, 2:30, and 4:30pm. The buses drop you off on the highway outside of town. The trip's duration is 1 hour; the fare is C1,100.

The Jacó bus station is at the north end of town, at a small mall across from the Jacó Fiesta Hotel. Buses for San José leave daily every 2 hours between 5am and 5pm. Buses returning to San José from Quepos pass periodically and pick up passengers on the highway. Because schedules can change, it's best to ask at your hotel about current departure times.

CITY LAYOUT   Playa de Jacó is a short distance off the southern highway. One main road runs parallel to the beach, with a host of arteries heading toward the water; you'll find most of the town's hotels and restaurants off these roads.

GETTING AROUND   Almost everything is within walking distance in Jacó, but you can call **Asotaxi** (✆ **2643-2020** or 2643-1919) for a cab.

You can also rent a bicycle or scooter from a variety of different shops and stands along the main street. A bike rental should run you around $10 to $15 per day, and a scooter should cost between $40 and $70 per day. Shop around, and make sure you get a bike that is in good condition and comfortable.

For longer excursions, you can rent a car from **Budget** (✆ **2643-2665**), **Economy** (✆ **2643-1719**), **National** (✆ **2643-3224**), or **Zuma** (✆ **2643-1528**). Expect to pay approximately $50 to $120 for a 1-day rental. You might also consider talking to a local taxi driver, who'd probably take you wherever you want to go for about the same price, saving you some hassle and headache.

FAST FACTS   A handful of state-run and private banks have branches in town on the main road. The **health center** (☎ 2643-3667) and **post office** (☎ 2643-2175) are at the Municipal Center at the south end of town. However, the best-equipped medical center is the **ProSalud** (☎ 2643-5059), located 4 blocks inland from the Pop's ice-cream shop. You'll find a half-dozen or so pharmacies, and a similar number of Internet cafes, along the town's main drag.

A gas station is on the main highway, between Playa Herradura and Jacó, and another station, **El Arroyo,** on the highway on the southern edge of Jacó. Both are open 24 hours.

Exploring Jacó

ATV TOURS   Several operations take folks out on ATV tours through the surrounding countryside. Tours range in length from 2 to 4 hours and cost between $70 and $120 per person. Contact **Jaguar Riders** (☎ 2643-0180; www.jaguariders.com).

BEACHES   Jacó's beach has a reputation for dangerous riptides (as does most of Costa Rica's Pacific coast). Even strong swimmers have been known to drown in the powerful rips. In general, the far southern end of the beach is the calmest and safest place to swim.

As an alternative to Playa de Jacó, you may want to visit other nearby beaches, like **Playa Manta, Playa Blanca, Playa Hermosa, Esterillos,** and **Playa Bejuco.** These beaches are easily reached by car, moped, or even bicycle—if you've got a lot of energy. All are signposted, so you'll have no trouble finding them. These are just south of Jacó. See the sections above and below for more information on these beaches.

CANOPY TOURS   The easiest way to get up into the canopy here is on the **Rain Forest Aerial Tram Pacific** ★ (☎ 866/759-8726; in the U.S. and Canada, or 2257-5961 in Costa Rica; www.rfat.com; see map "Playas Herradura & Hermosa"). A sister project to the original Rain Forest Aerial Tram (p. 150), this attraction features modified ski-lift type gondolas that take you through and above the transitional forests bordering Carara National Park. The $60 entrance fee includes the guided 40-minute tram ride, and a guided 45-minute hike on a network of trails. You can also hike the company's trails for as long as you like. These folks have a zip-line canopy tour, botanical gardens, and serpentarium on the same grounds, and offer guided tours, including transportation from both San José and any hotel in the area. The Aerial Tram is a few kilometers inland from an exit just north of the first entrance into Jacó.

Quite a few zip-line and harness-style canopy tours are in this area. **Chiclets Tree Tour** (☎ 2643-1880) offers up a canopy adventure in nearby Playa Hermosa. This is an adventurous tour, with 16 platforms set in transitional forest, with some sweeping views of the Pacific.

You can also easily use any of the canopy tour options mentioned in the Playa Herradura section above.

GOLF   The excellent **La Iguana,** an 18-hole golf course at the **Los Sueños Marriott Ocean & Golf Resort** (☎ 2630-9028; www.golflaiguana.com), is open to non-guests. See p. 356 for details.

HORSEBACK RIDING   Horseback riding tours give you a chance to get away from all the development in Jacó and see a bit of nature. The best operator in the area, with the best horses, is **Discovery Horseback** (© **8838-7550**; www. horseridecostarica.com), down in Playa Hermosa. It's $75 per person for a 2½-hour tour. These folks offer a variety of options from beach riding to trails through the rainforest with stops at a jungle waterfall.

KAYAKING **Kayak Jacó** (© **2643-1233**; www.kayakjaco.com) runs a couple of different trips. Tours are offered in single and tandem sea kayaks, as well as eight-person outrigger canoes. Along the way, you'll be able to admire the beautiful coastline, and—when conditions permit—take a snorkel break. Kayak fishing tours and sailing trips aboard 25-foot Trimarans are also available. Most options run around 4 hours and include transportation to and from the put-in, as well as fresh fruit and soft drinks during the trip. The tours cost between $55 and $80 per person, depending on the particular trip and group size..

ORGANIZED TOURS FARTHER AFIELD If you'll be spending your entire Costa Rican visit in Jacó but would like to see some other parts of the country, you can arrange tours with **Piko Travel** (© **8833-1772**; www.pikotravel.com) or through the local offices of **Gray Line Tours** (© **2643-3231**), which operates out of the Best Western Jacó Beach Resort (p. 362). Both offer a wide range of day tours, including trips to Arenal and Poás volcanoes; white-water rafting trips; and cruises to Tortuga Island. Rates range from $65 to $180 for day trips. Overnight trips are also available. In addition to the above-mentioned companies, many local operators offer a variety of tour options in **Manuel Antonio,** including trips to the national park, the Rainmaker Nature Refuge, and the Damas Island estuary. See the "Manuel Antonio National Park" section (later in this

Fishing vessels at Los Sueños Marina.

chapter) for more details on the types of tours and activities available there. Thanks to improvements to the road, you can reach Manuel Antonio in about 1 hour from Jacó.

SPA Catleya ★ (© 2643-1624) offers massages, as well as mud packs, face and body treatments, and manicures and pedicures. The spa's Jacó branch is on the first floor, among a tiny little cul-de-sac of shops next to Zuma Rent-A-Car.

SPORTFISHING, SCUBA DIVING & SEABORNE FUN Since the Los Sueños Marriott Resort (p. 356) and its adjacent 250-slip marina opened, most local maritime activity has shifted over there. See p. 355 for information on these activities.

SURFING The same waves that often make Playa de Jacó dangerous for swimmers make it one of the most popular beaches in the country with surfers. Nearby **Playa Hermosa, Playa Tulin,** and **Playa Escondida** are also excellent surfing beaches. Those who want to challenge the waves can rent surfboards and boogie boards, for around $3 an hour or $10 to $20 per day, from any one of the numerous surf shops along the main road. If you want to learn how to surf, try the **Del Mar Surf Camp** ★★ (© 2643-3197; www.delmarsurfcamp.com) or **Jacó Surf School** (© 8829-4697; www.jacosurfschool.com).

Where to Stay

Because Playa Herradura, Playa Hermosa de Jacó (not to be confused with either Playa Hermosa in Guanacaste, or Playa Hermosa on the Nicoya Peninsula), Playa Esterillos, and Playa Bejuco are close, many people choose accommodations in these beach towns as well.

EXPENSIVE

Best Western Jacó Beach Resort This popular all-inclusive hotel has a wonderful location right on the beach on the southern end of Jacó, just a short walk to all of the town's best bars, restaurants, and shops. That said, this is clearly a no-frills type of resort that feels a bit dated and is a bit too popular with large charter groups for my taste. The midsize round main pool is not quite big enough for the resort when it's full, and features an odd waterfall sculpture at its center that just seems to get in the way. Still, room upkeep has been pretty good over the years, and the Best Western offers up decent value for those looking for an affordable all-inclusive option in Jacó.

Playa de Jacó, Puntarenas. © **800/780-7234** in the U.S. and Canada, or 2643-1000 in Costa Rica; www.bestwesternjacobeach.com. 125 units. $180–$260 double. Rates are all-inclusive, featuring meals, drinks, and taxes. **Amenities:** Restaurant; bar; well-equipped gym; 2 circular outdoor pools; tennis and volleyball courts; free calls to the U.S. and Canada.

Club del Mar Condominiums & Resort ★★★ This is my favorite hotel in Playa de Jacó. Located at the far southern end of the beach, this place feels far removed from the crowds and craziness that can sometimes plague Jacó. Most of the accommodations here are one- and two-bedroom condominiums with fully equipped kitchens, although there are some more typical hotel rooms and a lavish penthouse in the main building above the open-air restaurant and bar. The best units are closest to the waves and have great views. The beach here is somewhat protected by the rocky headlands, making a great spot for swimming and beginning surf lessons, and there's also a good, midsize pool. This place caters to and is great for families.

Playa de Jacó

0   1/4 mi
0   0.25 km

To Playa Herradura and San José

Parque Lapa Verde

To Playa Hermosa & Quepos/Manuel Antonio

PACIFIC OCEAN

Soccer Field
Bus Stop
Calle Ancha
Boulevard
Ave. Pastor Díaz
El Bohío
Cocal
Central
Hicaco
Las Brisas
Barahona
Morales
Costanera
Soccer Field

HOTELS

Apartotel Girasol **26**
Best Western Jaco Beach **4**
Canciones del Mar **13**
Club del Mar Condominiums & Resort **31**
Hotel Catalina **21**
Hotel Mar de Luz **9**
Hotel Nine **30**
Hotel Perico Azul **28**
Hotel Poseidon **12**
Pochote Grande **1**

RESTAURANTS

Café del Mar **5**
Caliche's Wishbone **18**
El Barco de Mariscos **21**
El Hicaco **24**
El Recreo **3**
Graffiti **7**
Green Room Café **20**
Lemon Zest **25**
Los Amigos **17**
Taco Bar **16**
The Coffee Shop **19**
Tsunami Sushi **15**

NIGHTLIFE

Bohio Bar **14**
Casino Amapola **27**
Clarita's Beach Bar & Grill **2**
Funky Monkey **8**
Hotel & Casino Cocal **22**

Hotel Copacabana **11**
Hotel Poseidon **12**
Jaco Taco **6**
Le Loft **23**
Tabacón **10**

Playa de Jacó. ℂ **866/978-5669** in the U.S. and Canada, or 2643-3194 in Costa Rica. www.clubdelmarcostarica.com. 27 units. $159 double; $234–$329 condo; $349 penthouse. **Amenities:** Restaurant; bar; babysitting; outdoor pool; room service; small spa; free Wi-Fi.

MODERATE

In addition to the places listed below, the oceanfront **Apartotel Girasol ★** (ℂ **800/923-2779** or 2643-1591; www.girasol.com), with 16 fully equipped one-bedroom apartments, is a good option, especially for longer stays. **Hotel Poseidon** (ℂ **2643-1642;** www.hotel-poseidon.com) is a pretty boutique hotel in the heart of downtown, while **Canciones del Mar** (ℂ **888/260-1523** in the U.S. and Canada, or 2643-3273 in Costa Rica; www.cancionesdelmar.com) and **Hotel Catalina** (ℂ **2643-1237;** www.hotelcatalinacr.com) are two more good beachfront choices.

Hotel Nine ★   This is an intimate and well-run little boutique hotel on a quiet stretch of beach towards the southern end of Jacó. Rooms are clean and contemporary, and come in a range of sizes and prices. A small pool is at the center of the complex and good ocean views can be had from the narrow shared veranda that fronts most rooms. The penthouse suite is quite large and comes with a complete kitchen, living room, and dining room area.

Playa de Jacó, Puntarenas. ℂ **800/477-2486** in U.S. & Canada or 2643-5335 in Costa Rica. www.hotelnine.com. 14 units. $118–$143 double; $273–$398 suite. Rates include continental breakfast. **Amenities:** Restaurant; bar; Jacuzzi; midsize outdoor pool; room service; surfboards; free Wi-Fi.

Pochote Grande This tidy German-run hotel towards the northern end of the beach used to be in an isolated and quiet spot. Nowadays, high-rise condominium construction is going on all around. Still, this remains a very well-kept and quiet option, with lush gardens in the immediate vicinity, and a short stroll to the beach. A cool and refreshing pool is at the center of the compound, and a good little restaurant is on site.

Playa de Jacó, Puntarenas. ✆ **2643-3236.** www.hotelpochotegrande.net. 24 units. $107 double. **Amenities:** Restaurant; bar; outdoor pool; free Wi-Fi.

INEXPENSIVE

In addition to the hotels reviewed below, quite a few budget hotels are around town. Most cater to itinerant surfers, backpackers, and Ticos. If you're looking to stay on the cheap, your best bet is to simply walk the strip and see who's got the best room at the best price.

Hotel Mar de Luz ★★ This family-friendly hotel about a half-block or so inland from the main street feels like an oasis amidst the hustle and bustle of busy Jacó. Owner Victor Keulen runs a tight ship, and provides excellent value. Rooms are kept very clean, and the common areas are cozy and inviting. The hotel has two pools and a small garden area, with a couple of grills for guests' use. The hotel's sister property, **Hotel Playa Bejuco** (see p. 375), is about 20 minutes down the road in remote Playa Bejuco.

Playa de Jacó. ✆ **2643-3000.** www.mardeluz.com. 29 units. $74 bungalow; $84 standard; $120 family room. Rates include breakfast. **Amenities:** Jacuzzi; 2 outdoor small-to-midsize adult pools and children's pool; smoke-free rooms; free Wi-Fi.

Hotel Perico Azul ★★ Located a couple blocks inland from the water, on the south end of Jacó, this hotel is a favorite of surfers, backpackers, and budget travelers of all stripes. Clean, well-kept rooms surround a central courtyard with a popular—albeit small—plunge pool. A couple of rooms come with their own kitchenette, but there's also a communal kitchen for all guests. The best room here is the second-floor one-bedroom studio, with its own private veranda. Owners Mike and Celine are very hands-on, and also run a surf school, Tortuga Surf.

Playa de Jacó, Puntarenas. ✆ **2643-4170.** www.hotelpericoazuljaco.com. 6 units. C35,000–C45,000 double. Rates include taxes. **Amenities:** Small pool; free Wi-Fi.

Where to Dine

Playa de Jacó has a wide range of restaurants, although many cater to surfers and budget travelers. In addition to the places listed below, if you're looking for simply prepared fresh seafood, **El Barco de Mariscos** (✆ 2643-2831) and **El Recreo** (✆ 2643-1172) are both good bets that serve standard Tico beach fare—fresh seafood, sandwiches, chicken, and steak. Sushi lovers should head to **Tsunami Sushi** (✆ 2643-3678), inside the El Galeone strip mall. For a coffee break and newly baked pastries and breads, head to **Café del M@r** (✆ 2643-1250) or the **Coffee Shop** (✆ 2643-3240).

EXPENSIVE

El Hicaco COSTA RICAN/SEAFOOD You can't beat the beachfront location of this popular local seafood spot. I still remember when this was a very humble little fish shack and traditional local soda. However, they've totally rebuilt and remodeled. Now, it's not uncommon to see tour buses parked out front and a line to be seated. Personally, I think the success has gone to their heads. Prices have skyrocketed and service has suffered. You can still get some good fresh seafood, however, and as I said the setting is stellar.

On the beach in downtown Jacó. ✆ **2643-3226.** www.elhicaco.net. Reservations recommended during high season. Main courses C8,750–C26,150. Daily 11am–11pm.

Lemon Zest ★★ SEAFOOD/FUSION   Chef/owner Richard Lemon left a teaching gig at Le Cordon Bleu and moved to Jacó and the local culinary scene is better because of it. His second-floor restaurant serves up excellent and creative contemporary cuisine showing a range of world influences. The Korean barbecue skewers come with homemade banana ketchup, while the local jumbo shrimp are battered, coated in coconut and plantain, and then fried crisp. My biggest complaint here is that the room can get loud at times, but the food and service do much to make up for that.

Downtown Jacó. ✆ **2643-2591.** www.lemonzestjaco.com. Reservations recommended during high season. Main courses $13.50–$26.50. Tues–Sun 5–10pm.

MODERATE

Graffiti Resto Café & Wine Bar ★★★ FUSION   It's a little hard to find this place wedged in the far back corner of a nondescript strip mall near the center of town, but it's worth the search. Graffiti art decorates the interior and each night you'll find a short selection of specials drafted up on a chalkboard, based on the chef's whims and what's fresh. I almost always order one of the specials, but the main menu is also excellent and features Graffiti's signature cacao- and coffee-crusted tenderloin and Asian-spiced seared tuna. They also have a small sushi bar, and—as the name suggests—a good wine list. Occasionally live music is on the menu, and it's worth perusing the attached gift shop, which features hand-carved wooden surfboards and unique body surfing paddles.

Centro Comercial Pacific Center, downtown Jacó. ✆ **2643-1708.** www.graffiticr.com. Reservations recommended during high season. Main courses C5,000–C18,500. Mon–Sat 5–10pm.

Green Room Café ★★ BISTRO/SEAFOOD   This is yet another excellent little restaurant serving creative cuisine making use of fresh local ingredients. They source as much as they can from organic producers and local fisherman. While this borders on fine dining, the atmosphere is decidedly casual. The menu staples feature a range of breakfast and brunch items, and sandwiches, wraps, tacos and burgers, as well as a range of more substantial plates. The nightly specials are where you'll find the most creativity, and might feature anything from mango-shrimp tartar to a thick-cut rib eye steak with gorgonzola butter. I prefer the terrace seating when the weather's nice. On weekend nights there's often live music or a DJ. No credit cards are accepted.

On the Cocal Casino road in Jacó. ✆ **2643-4425.** Reservations recommended during high season. Main courses C3,000–C13,000. Tues–Sun 8:30am–3pm and 6pm–10pm.

INEXPENSIVE

Caliche's Wishbone ★ SEAFOOD/MEXICAN   This place is a local landmark. The brainchild and baby of a local surfing legend, Caliche, it serves up hearty, fresh fare for surfers and landlubbers alike. The menu runs the gamut from pizzas, burritos, and stuffed potatoes to fresh, seared tuna in a soy-wasabi sauce (my favorite). Surf videos play on a few TVs in the main dining room, but I prefer the tables closest to the busy sidewalk, on the covered veranda. On the main road in Jacó. ℂ **2643-3406.** Main courses C3,500–C13,000. Thurs–Tues noon–10pm.

Los Amigos INTERNATIONAL/SEAFOOD   Occupying a prime location on one of the busiest corners in downtown Jacó, this casual spot is a popular social hub. The menu features a mix of typical American-style bar food, fresh seafood, Tex-Mex favorites, and Thai curries, rice bowls and noodle dishes. They advertise and serve some "Big Ass Smoothies" made with fresh local fruits and veggies. There's both indoor and outdoor seating, and on hot days, you'll want to opt for the indoor and air-conditioned dining room. Live sporting events and surf videos are shown on seven flatscreen TVs. On the main road in Jacó. ℂ **2643-2961.** www.losamigosjaco.com. Main courses C4,500–C8,000. Sun–Thurs noon–11pm.

Taco Bar ★ MEXICAN/INTERNATIONAL   This place got so popular that they've opened a couple of branches in San José, and are looking to expand elsewhere around the country. This open-air joint features two long, heavy wooden bars with seating on wooden "swings" supported by heavy ropes. You can choose from more traditional tables and picnic tables. The menu features a wide range of tacos, burritos, and pizzas that you can have with any of several freshly caught fish choices served in any number of sauces. Other possible fillings include shrimp, calamari, grilled chicken, and steak. After choosing the main plate, you also have ample choices at their well-stocked and inventive salad bar. Also open for breakfast. 1/2 block inland from Pop's, central Jacó. ℂ **2643-0222.** www.tacobar.info. Main courses C4,000–C8,000. Mon noon–10pm; Tues–Sun 7:00am–10pm.

Shopping

If you try to do any shopping in Jacó, you'll be overrun with shops selling T-shirts, cut-rate souvenirs, and handmade jewelry and trinkets. Most of the offerings are of pretty poor quality.

Entertainment & Nightlife

Playa de Jacó is the central Pacific's party town, with tons of bars and several discos. I like to start things out with some fish tacos and a sunset view at **Bohio Bar & Bubba's Tacos** ★★, on the beach in the middle of town. **Le Loft** ★, on the main street and near the center of town, attracts a more sophisticated and chic clubbing crowd. For a more casual atmosphere, head to either **Los Amigos** or **Tabacón** ★ on the main street, near the center of town. Tabacón has popular pool and foosball tables, and often has live music.

Other popular bars in town include **Funky Monkey,** with DJs and a large dance floor, and **Jacó Taco,** a two-story affair with regular live bands that is open 24 hours every day of the year. Both of the aforementioned bars are along the main strip through town. *Note:* Jacó has a good amount of prostitution. The most popular pick-up spot is the **Hotel & Casino Cocal** (ℂ **2643-1201;** www. hotelcocalandcasino.com). However, it's not uncommon to find working women at any of the bars around town.

Sports freaks can catch the latest games at **Clarita's Beach Bar & Grill, Hotel Copacabana** (both are right on the beach toward the north end of town), or **Hotel Poseidon** (on a side street near the center of town). The first two serve up good reasonably priced burritos, burgers, and bar food, while the latter offers much the same, as well as some items from its much better restaurant downstairs.

If you're into casino games, head to the **Casino Amapola** (© **2643-1434**) at the Hotel Amapola. The latter is a modest casino situated toward the southern end of the main road through Jacó (Av. Pastor Díaz), about a block beyond where it takes a sharp turn inland toward the Costanera Sur.

Side Trips from Playa de Jacó: Playas Hermosa, Esterillos & Bejuco

South of Jacó, Costa Rica's coastline is a long, almost entirely straight stretch of largely undeveloped beach backed by thick forests and low-lying rice and African palm plantations.

Playa Hermosa ★, 10km (6¼ miles) southeast of Jacó, is the first beach you'll hit as you head down the Southern Coastal Highway. This is primarily a surfers' beach, but it is still a lovely spot to spend some beach time. In fact, even though the surf conditions here can be rather rough and unprotected, and the beach is made of dark volcanic sand, I find Playa Hermosa and the beaches south of it much more attractive than Jacó. Be careful on Playa Hermosa, as the fine dark sand can get extremely hot in the tropical sun; be sure to have adequate footwear and a large towel or mat to lay out on the sand. Aside from a small grouping of hotels and restaurants, most of Playa Hermosa is protected, as **olive ridley sea turtles** lay eggs here from July to December. During turtle nesting season, all of the hotel tour desks and local tour agencies can help you arrange a nighttime turtle nesting tour, for around $40 to $50 per person.

Playa Hermosa is the only beach in this section located right along the Southern Coastal Highway; all of the rest are a kilometer or so in from the road and reached by a series of dirt access roads. If you exit the highway in Playa Hermosa, you can follow a dirt-and-sand access road that runs parallel to the shore along several miles of deserted, protected beach, as Playa Hermosa eventually becomes **Playa Tulin,** near the Tulin River mouth. This is another popular surf spot, but be careful—crocodiles live in the Tulin River.

As you continue down the coastal highway from Playa Hermosa, you will hit Esterillos. **Playa Esterillos,** 22km (14 miles) south of Jacó, is long and wide and almost always nearly deserted. Playa Esterillos is so long, in fact, that it has three separate entrances and sections, Esterillos Oeste, Centro, and Este—West, Center, and East, in order as you head away from Jacó.

If you keep heading south (really southeast), you next come to **Playa Bejuco,** another long, wide, nearly deserted stretch of sand. Playa Bejuco, which features a very narrow strip of land fronting the beach, with mangroves and swampland behind, has very little development.

Note: While beautiful, isolated, and expansive, the beaches of Hermosa, Esterillos, and Bejuco can be quite rough at times and dangerous for swimming. Caution is highly advised here.

WHERE TO STAY IN PLAYA HERMOSA
Moderate
In addition to the place listed below, you might want to check out **Surf Inn Hermosa** (© **2643-7184;** www.surfinnhermosa.com), which offers one-bedroom

Playa Esterillos.

studios with a kitchenette, and two-bedroom fully equipped condo units, or the **Sandpiper Inn** (© **2643-7042;** www.sandpipercostarica.com), a cozy surfer joint. Both of these options are right on the beach.

The Backyard This place sits right in front of the most prized peaks Playa Hermosa has to offer, and is very popular with surfers. The rooms are simple and unadorned. The best rooms are the second-floor units with ocean-view balconies. A small pool is on the side of the hotel, and a palm tree or two with chaise lounges set facing the sand. The restaurant and bar here are quite popular and can be jam packed and noisy most nights, just in case you had any illusions about getting a peaceful night's sleep. Still, during the day, you can grab a table at the restaurant and watch the better surfers work this wave.

Playa Hermosa de Jacó, Puntarenas. © **2643-7011.** www.backyardhotel.com. 8 units. $133–$230 double. **Amenities:** Restaurant; bar; small outdoor pool; free Wi-Fi.

Inexpensive

Playa Hermosa has a host of simple hotels and cabinas catering to surfers. Prices, conditions, and upkeep can vary greatly. If you've got the time, your best bet is to visit a few until you find the best deal on the cleanest room. **Costanera Bed & Breakfast** (© 2643-7044; www.costaneraplayahermosa.com), **Cabinas Las Arenas** (© 8729-4532; www.cabinaslasarenas.com), and **Cabinas Las Olas** (© 2643-7021; www.lasolashotel.com) are three good options.

WHERE TO STAY IN PLAYA ESTERILLOS

If you're looking for something even more remote and undeveloped than the hotel listed below, head to Playa Esterillos Este and the **Pelican Hotel** (© **2778-8105;** www.pelicanbeachfronthotel.com), a simple, homey beachfront bed-and-breakfast.

Very Expensive

Alma del Pacifico Hotel ★★   This upscale boutique hotel is a hidden gem on a very undiscovered patch of sand. Originally built as a sister resort to Xandari (p. 168), the individual villas here feature the same contemporary design and artistic sensibility. All of the villas are large and inviting, with white tile floors, white walls, white bed linens and plenty of natural light, all accented with bold splashes of primary colors found in paintings, mosaic tile works, curtains, and more. The open-air ocean-view restaurant is top notch.

Playa Esterillos Centro, Puntarenas. © **888/960-2562** in the U.S. and Canada, or 2778-7070 in Costa Rica. www.almadelpacifico.com. 20 units. $270–$555 double. Rates include Alma breakfast. **Amenities:** Restaurant; bar; concierge; Jacuzzi; 2 outdoor lap pools; room service; all rooms smoke-free; full-service spa; free Wi-Fi.

WHERE TO STAY IN PLAYA BEJUCO

Moderate

Hotel Playa Bejuco ★   Owned and run by the folks from Mar de Luz hotel in Playa de Jacó (p. 364), this is a small, cozy option in a shady spot a hundred yards or so from the broad and uncrowded sands of Playa Bejuco. Most of the rooms are quite large, and some even feature separate sleeping lofts and multiple bed options, perfect for large groups or families. However, this is a remote and undeveloped area and there's not much else around in terms of dining or entertainment, unless you have a car and feel like driving towards either Jacó or Manuel Antonio.

Playa Bejuco, Puntarenas. © **2779-2000.** www.hotelplayabejuco.com. 20 units. $110–$142 double. Rates include breakfast and taxes. Lower rates in off season. **Amenities:** Restaurant; bar; outdoor pool.

MANUEL ANTONIO NATIONAL PARK ★★

140km (87 miles) SW of San José; 69km (43 miles) S of Playa de Jacó

Manuel Antonio was Costa Rica's first major ecotourist destination and remains one of its most popular. The views from the hills overlooking Manuel Antonio are

An easy trail through Manuel Antonio National Park.

spectacular, the beaches (especially those inside the national park) are idyllic, and its rainforests are crawling with howler, white-faced, and squirrel monkeys, among other forms of exotic wildlife. The downside is that you'll have to share it with more fellow travelers than you would at other rainforest destinations around the country. Moreover, booming tourism and development have begun to destroy what makes this place so special. What was once a smattering of small hotels tucked into the forested hillside has become a string of lodgings along the 7km

369

(4¹/₃ miles) of road between Quepos and the national park entrance. Hotel roofs now regularly break the tree line, and there seems to be no control over zoning and unchecked ongoing construction. A jumble of snack shacks, souvenir stands, and makeshift parking lots choke the beach road just outside the park, making the entrance road look more like a shanty town than a national park.

Still, this remains a beautiful destination, with a wide range of attractions and activities. Gazing down on the blue Pacific from high on the hillsides of Manuel Antonio, it's almost impossible to hold back a gasp of delight. Offshore, rocky islands dot the vast expanse of blue, and in the foreground, the rich, deep green of the rainforest sweeps down to the water. Even cheap cell phone cameras regularly produce postcard-perfect snapshots. It's this superb view that keeps people transfixed on decks, patios, and balconies throughout the area.

One of the most popular national parks in the country, Manuel Antonio is also one of the smallest, covering fewer than 680 hectares (1,680 acres). Its several nearly perfect small beaches are connected by trails that meander through the rainforest. The mountains surrounding the beaches quickly rise as you head inland from the water; however, the park was created to preserve not its beautiful beaches but its forests, home to endangered squirrel monkeys, three-toed sloths, purple-and-orange crabs, and hundreds of other species of birds, mammals, and plants. Once, this entire stretch of coast was a rainforest teeming with wildlife, but now only this small rocky outcrop of forest remains.

Those views that are so bewitching also have their own set of drawbacks. If you want a great view, you aren't going to be staying on the beach—in fact, you probably won't be able to walk to the beach. This means that you'll be driving back and forth, taking taxis, or riding the public bus. Also keep in mind that it's hot and humid here, and it rains a lot. However, the rain is what keeps Manuel Antonio lush and green, and this wouldn't be the Tropics if things were otherwise.

If you're traveling on a rock-bottom budget or are mainly interested in sportfishing, you might end up staying in the nearby town of **Quepos,** which was once a quiet banana port and now features a wide variety of restaurants, souvenir and crafts shops, and lively bars; the land to the north was used by Chiquita to grow its bananas. Disease wiped out most of the banana plantations, and now the land is planted primarily with African oil-palm trees. To reach Quepos by road, you pass through miles of these **oil-palm plantations;** see the box "Profitable Palms," below, for info.

Essentials

GETTING THERE & DEPARTING By **Plane:** Both **Nature Air** (© 800/235-9272 in the U.S. and Canada, or 2299-6000; www.natureair.com) and **Sansa** (© 877/767-2672 in the U.S. and Canada, or 2290-4100 in Costa Rica; www.flysansa.com) offer several daily direct flights to the **Quepos airport** (no phone; airport code: XQP). The flight is 30 minutes long; the fare is $85 to $120 each way.

A tractor on a palm plantation near Quepos.

Travel Tips

Despite the above caveats, Manuel Antonio is still a fabulous destination with a wealth of activities and attractions for all types and all ages. If you plan carefully, you can avoid many of the problems that detract from its appeal. If you steer clear of the peak months (Dec–Mar), you'll miss most of the crowds. If you must come during the peak months, try to avoid weekends, when the beach is packed with families and young Ticos from San José. If you visit the park early in the morning, you can leave when the crowds begin to show up at midday. In the afternoon, you can lounge by your pool or on your patio.

Both **Sansa** (✆ **2777-1912** in Quepos) and **Nature Air** (✆ **2777-2548** in Quepos) provide minivan airport-transfer service coordinated with their arriving and departing flights. The service costs around $8 per person each way, depending on where your hotel is located. Speak to your airline's agent when you arrive to confirm your return flight and coordinate a pickup at your hotel for that day if necessary. Taxis meet incoming flights as well. Expect to be charged between $10 and $20 per car for up to four people, depending on the distance to your hotel.

When you're ready to depart, **Sansa** (✆ **2777-1912** in Quepos) flights begin departing at 8:10am, with the final flight leaving at 3:40pm. **Nature Air** (✆ **2777-2548** in Quepos) flights leave for San José daily at 9am and 3pm.

By Car: From San José, take the San José–Caldera Highway (CR27) west to Orotina. Just past the toll booth at Pavón, this road connects with the Costanera Sur (CR34), or Southern Coastal Highway. The exit is marked for Jacó and CR34. From here, it's a straight and flat shot down the coast to Quepos and Manuel Antonio.

If you're coming from Guanacaste or any point north, take the Interamerican Highway to the Puntarenas turnoff and follow signs to the San José–Caldera Highway (CR27). Take this east toward Orotina, where it connects with the Costanera Sur (CR34). It's about a 4½-hour drive from Liberia to Quepos and Manuel Antonio.

By Bus: Tracopa buses (✆ **2221-4214** or 2290-1308; www.tracopacr. com) to Manuel Antonio leave San José regularly throughout the day between 6am and 7:30pm from Calle 5 between avenidas 18 and 20. Trip duration is around 3 hours; the fare is C4,520. These buses go all the way to the park entrance and will drop you off at any of the hotels along the way.

For your return trip, the **Quepos bus station** (✆ **2777-0263**) is next to the market, located 3 blocks east of the water and 2 blocks north of the road to Manuel Antonio. Buses depart for San José daily between 4am and 5pm.

Gray Line (✆ **800/719-3105** in the U.S. and Canada, or 2220-2126 in Costa Rica; www.graylinecostarica.com) and **Interbus** (✆ **4031-0888;** www. interbusonline.com) both have two buses daily leaving San José for Quepos and Manuel Antonio, one in the morning and one in the afternoon. The fare is around $49. Both companies will pick you up at most San José–area hotels. Both also offer connections to most major tourist destinations in the country.

Many of the buses for Quepos stop to unload and pick up passengers in **Playa de Jacó.** If you're in Jacó heading toward Manuel Antonio, you can try your luck at one of the covered bus stops out on the Interamerican Highway.

Profitable Palms

On any drive to or from Quepos and Manuel Antonio, you will pass through miles and miles of African palm plantations. Native to West Africa, *Elaeis guineensis* was planted along this stretch in the 1940s by United Fruit, in response to a blight that was attacking their banana crops. The palms took hold and soon proved quite profitable, being blessed with copious bunches of plum-size nuts that are rich in oil. This oil is extracted and processed in plantations that dot the road between Jacó and Quepos. The smoke and distinct smell of this processing is often easily noticed. The processed oil is eventually shipped overseas and used in a wide range of products, including soaps, cosmetics, lubricants, and food products.

These plantations are a major source of employment in the area—note the small, orderly "company towns" built for workers—but their presence is controversial. The palm trees aren't native, and the farming practices are thought by some to threaten Costa Rica's biodiversity.

In the busy winter months, tickets sell out well in advance, especially on weekends; if you can, purchase your ticket several days in advance. However, you must buy your Quepos-bound tickets in San José and your San José return tickets in Quepos. If you're staying in Manuel Antonio, you can buy your return ticket for a direct bus in advance in Quepos, and then wait along the road to be picked up. There is no particular bus stop; just make sure you are out to flag down the bus and give it time to stop—you don't want to be standing in a blind spot when the bus comes flying around a tight corner.

Buses leave **Puntarenas** for Quepos daily at 5, 8, and 11am and 12:30, 2:30, and 4:30pm. The ride takes 2 hours; the fare is C1,100. Buses for **Puntarenas** leave daily at 4:30, 7:30, and 10:30am and 12:30, 3, and 5:30pm. Any bus headed for San José or Puntarenas will let you off in Playa de Jacó.

GETTING AROUND   A taxi between Quepos and Manuel Antonio (or any hotel along the road toward the park) costs between C4,000 and C5,000, depending upon the distance. At night or if the taxi must leave the main road (for hotels such as La Mariposa, Parador, Makanda, and Arenas del Mar), the charge is a little higher. If you need to call a taxi, dial © **2777-0425** or 2777-1207. Taxis are supposed to use meters, although this isn't always the case. If your taxi doesn't have a meter, or the driver won't use it, try to negotiate in advance. Ask your hotel desk what a specific ride should cost, and use that as your guide.

The bus between Quepos and Manuel Antonio (© **2777-0318**) takes 15 minutes each way and runs roughly every half-hour from 5:30am to 9:30pm daily. The buses, which leave from the main bus terminal in Quepos, near the market, go all the way to the national park entrance before turning around and returning. You can flag down these buses from any point on the side of the road. The fare is C250.

You can also rent a car from **Adobe** (© 2777-4242), **National/Alamo** (© **2777-3344**), **Economy** (© **2777-5353**), or **Hertz** (© **2777-3365**) for around $45 to $160 a day. All have offices in downtown Quepos or Manuel Antonio, but with advance notice, someone will meet you at the airport with your car for no extra charge.

If you rent a car, never leave anything of value in it unless you intend to stay within sight of the car at all times. Car break-ins are common here. A couple of parking lots just outside the park entrance cost around $3 for the entire day. You should definitely keep your car in one of these while exploring the park or soaking up sun on the beach. And although these lots do offer a modicum of protection and safety, you still should not leave anything of value exposed in the car. The trunk is probably safe, though.

CITY LAYOUT Quepos is a small port city at the mouth of the Boca Vieja Estuary. If you're heading to Manuel Antonio National Park, or any hotel on the way to the park, after crossing the bridge into town, take the lower road (to the left of the high road). In 4 blocks, turn left, and you'll be on the road to Manuel Antonio. This road winds through town a bit before starting over the hill to all the hotels and the national park.

FAST FACTS The telephone number of the **Quepos Hospital** is ℂ 2777-0922. In the event of an emergency, you can also call the **Cruz Roja** (Red Cross; ℂ 2777-0116). For the **local police,** call ℂ 2777-1511.

The **post office** (ℂ 2777-1471) is in downtown Quepos. Several pharmacies are in Quepos, as well as a pharmacy at the hospital, and another close to the park entrance. A half-dozen or so laundromats and laundry services are in town.

Several major Costa Rican banks have branches and ATMs in downtown Quepos, and a couple of ATMs have sprung up along the road to the national park. An ample array of **Internet cafes** can be found around Quepos and along the road to Manuel Antonio, and many hotels have them as well.

Exploring the National Park

Manuel Antonio is a small park with three major trails. Most visitors come primarily to lie on a beach and check out the white-faced monkeys, which sometimes seem as common as tourists. A guide is not essential here, but unless you're experienced in rainforest hiking, you'll see and learn a lot more with one. Personally, I recommend entering the park with a guide. You'll see much more and learn a lot. You can always stay on inside the park after your guided tour is over. A 2- or 3-hour guided hike should cost between $25 and $50 per person. Almost any of the hotels in town can help you set up a tour of the park, if not, contact **Manuel Antonio Expeditions** (ℂ 8365-1057; manuelantonioexpeditions.blogspot.com), run by Juan Brenes, who does a wonderful job. Be careful of touts dressed as guides stopping you on the street and doing a hard sell. Avoid these types of "guides.". If you decide to explore the park on your own, see the trail map on the inside front cover of this book.

ENTRY POINT, FEES & REGULATIONS The park (ℂ 2777-5185) is open Tuesday through Sunday from 7am to 4pm year round. The entrance fee is $16 per person. The **main park entrance** is located almost about 1.5km (almost a mile) inland, at the end of the road that leads off perpendicular to Playa Espadilla just beyond Marlin Restaurant.

Another ranger station and exit point is at the end of the road from Quepos. This ranger station is located across a small, sometimes polluted stream that's little more than ankle-deep at low tide but that can be knee- or even waist-deep at high tide. It's even reputed to be home to a crocodile or two. For years there has been talk of building a bridge over this stream; in the meantime you'll have to either wade it or pay a boatman a small voluntary tip for the very quick crossing.

MINAE, the national ministry that oversees the park, has been frustratingly inconsistent about which entrance visitors must use. For the past year or so, tickets have been sold and entry allowed only at the inland entrance. This requires about 20 to 30 minutes of hiking along an often muddy access road before you get to the beach and principal park trails. You can, however, exit via the much shorter beach trail to Playa Espadilla. **Note:** The Parks Service allows only 800 visitors to enter each day, which could mean that you won't get in if you arrive in midafternoon during the high season. Camping is not allowed.

THE BEACHES   **Playa Espadilla Sur** (as opposed to Playa Espadilla, which is just outside the park; see "Hitting the Water," below) is the first beach within the actual park boundaries. It's usually the least crowded and one of the best places to find a quiet shade tree to plant yourself under. However, if there's any surf, this is also the roughest beach in the park. If you want to explore further, you can walk along this soft-sand beach or follow a trail through the rainforest parallel to the beach. **Playa Manuel Antonio,** which is the most popular beach inside the park, is a short, deep crescent of white sand backed by lush rainforest. The water here is sometimes clear enough to offer good snorkeling along the rocks at either end, and it's usually fairly calm. At low tide, Playa Manuel Antonio shows a very interesting relic: a circular stone turtle trap left by its pre-Columbian residents. From Playa Manuel Antonio, another slightly longer trail leads to **Puerto Escondido,** where a blowhole sends up plumes of spray at high tide.

THE HIKING TRAILS   From either Playa Espadilla Sur or Playa Manuel Antonio, you can take a circular loop trail (1.4km/.9 mile) around a high promontory bluff.

Playa Espadilla.

The highest point on this hike, which takes about 25 to 30 minutes round-trip, is **Punta Catedral** ★★, where the view is spectacular. The trail is a little steep in places, but anybody in average shape can do it. I have done it in sturdy sandals, but you might want to wear good hiking shoes. This is a good place to spot monkeys, although you're more likely to see a white-faced monkey than a rare squirrel monkey. Another good place to see monkeys is the **trail inland** from Playa Manuel Antonio. This is a linear trail and mostly uphill, but it's not too taxing. It's great to spend hours exploring the steamy jungle and then take a refreshing dip in the ocean.

Finally, a trail connects Puerto Escondido (see above) and **Punta Serrucho,** which has some sea caves. Be careful when hiking beyond Puerto Escondido: What seems like easy beach hiking at low tide becomes treacherous to impassable at high tide. Don't get trapped.

> ### Helping Out
>
> If you want to help efforts in protecting the local environment and the severely endangered squirrel monkey (mono titi), make a donation to the **Titi Conservation Alliance** ((✆ **2777-2306;** www.monotiti.org), an organization supported by local businesses and individual donors, or to **Kids Saving The Rainforest** ((✆ **2777-2592;** www.kidssaving therainforest.org), which was started in 1999 by a couple of local children.

Hitting the Water

BEACHES OUTSIDE THE PARK **Playa Espadilla,** the gray-sand beach just outside the park boundary, is often perfect for board surfing and bodysurfing. At times it's a bit rough for casual swimming, but with no entrance fee, it's the most popular beach with locals and visiting Ticos. Some shops by the water rent boogie boards and beach chairs and umbrellas. A full-day rental of a beach umbrella and two chaise lounges costs around $10. (These are not available inside the park.) This beach is actually a great spot to learn how to surf, because several open-air shops renting surfboards and boogie boards are along the beachfront road. Rates run $5 to $10 per hour, and around $20 to $30 per day. If you want a lesson, I recommend the **Blue Horizon Surf School** (✆ **8994-1424;** blueho-rizonsurfschool@gmail.com), which provides excellent attention for individuals, small groups and families.

BOATING, KAYAKING, RAFTING & SPORTFISHING TOURS Iguana Tours (✆ 2777-2051; www.iguanatours.com) is the most established and longest-running tour operator in the area, offering river rafting, sea kayaking, mangrove tours, and guided hikes.

The above company, as well as **Amigos del Río** (✆ **2777-0082;** www. amigosdelrio.net), offer full-day rafting trips for around $85 to $110. Large multiperson rafts are used during the rainy season, and single-person "duckies" are broken out when the water levels drop. Both companies also offer half-day rafting adventures and sea-kayaking trips for around $65. Depending on rainfall and demand, they will run either the Naranjo or Savegre rivers. I very much prefer the **Savegre River** ★★ for its stunning scenery.

Another of my favorite tours in the area is the mangrove tour of the **Damas Island estuary.** These trips generally include lunch, a stop on Damas Island, and roughly 3 to 4 hours of cruising the waterways. You'll see loads of wildlife. The cost is usually around $60 to $80. **Manuel Antonio Expeditions** (✆ 8365-1057; manuelantonioexpeditions.blogspot.com) is my choice operator for this tour.

Among the other boating options around Quepos/Manuel Antonio are excursions in search of dolphins and sunset cruises. **Iguana Tours** (see above) and **Planet Dolphin** ★ (✆ 2777-1647; www.planetdolphin.com) offer these tours for around $80 per person, depending upon the size of the group and the length of the cruise. Most tours include a snorkel break and, if lucky, dolphin sightings. **Jungle Coast Jets** (✆ 888/765-8475 in U.S. & Canada or 2777-7547 in Costa Rica; www.junglecoastjets.com) offers 2-hour jet ski tours for $130 per person on a single jet ski, or $160 for two people on a double. This tour plies the same waters and includes some snorkeling and the possibility of a dolphin encounter.

Quepos is one of Costa Rica's sportfishing centers, and sailfish, marlin, and tuna are all common in these waters. In recent years, fresh- and brackish water fishing in the mangroves and estuaries has also become popular. If you're into sportfishing, try hooking up with **Blue Fin Sportfishing** (✆ 2777-0000; www.bluefinsportfishing.com) or **Luna Tours Sportfishing** (✆ 2777-0725; www.lunatours.net). A full day of fishing should cost between $600 and $1,900, depending on the size of the boat, distance traveled, tackle provided, and amenities. With so much competition here, it pays to stop by the marina and shop around.

SCUBA DIVING & SNORKELING   **Oceans Unlimited** ★ (✆ 2777-3171; www.scubadivingcostarica.com) offers both scuba diving and snorkel outings, as well as certification and resort courses. Because of river run-off and often less-than-stellar visibility close to Quepos, the best trips involve some travel time. Tours around Manuel Antonio run $98 per person for a two-tank scuba dive.

However, **Isla del Caño** (p. 415) is only about a 90-minute ride each way. This is one of the best dive sites in Costa Rica, and I highly recommend it. Trips to Isla del Caño are $125 for snorkeling and $165 for two-tank scuba diving.

LEFT: **A Damas Island boat tour.**
RIGHT: **White-water rafting the Savegre River.**

A Planet Dolphin sailing tour.

Other Activities in the Area

ATV   If you want to try riding a four-wheel ATV (all-terrain vehicle), check in with the folks at **Midworld** ★★ (© 2777-7181; www.midworldcostarica.com), who offer a range of tours through forests and farmlands at their adventure center on the outskirts of Quepos and Manuel Antonio.

BIKING   For mountain biking, contact **Estrella Tour** (© 2777-1286; www.x-trella.org) in downtown Quepos. These folks offer a number of different guided tours according to skill level, for between $45 and $75 per day, as well as multiday expeditions.

BUTTERFLY GARDEN   **Fincas Naturales/Nature Farm Reserve** ★★ (©2777-0777; www.sicomono.com) is just across from (and run by) Hotel Sí Como No (p. 380). A lovely bi-level **butterfly garden** ★ is the centerpiece attraction here, but there is also a private reserve and a small network of well-groomed trails through the forest. A 1-hour guided tour of the butterfly garden costs $15 per person. This is also a good place for a night tour ($39).

CANOPY ADVENTURES   The most adventurous local canopy tour is **Midworld** ★★ (© 2777-7181; www.midworldcostarica.com). Their main zip-line tour features 10 cables, including the longest cables in the area. However they also have a "Superman" cable, which is very long, very fast, and ridden in a prone position, as well as a ropes course. Their ATV tours through the surrounding rainforest stop at a waterfall pool for a dip. **Canopy Safari** ★ (© 888/765-8475 in the U.S. and Canada, or 2777-0100 in Costa Rica; www.canopysafari.com), is another good option, featuring 18 treetop platforms connected by a series of cables and suspension bridges, and the tour features a Tarzan-type swing and two rappels. The on-site butterfly garden and serpentarium are an added bonus. A canopy tour should run between $55 and $75 per person, and up to $130 for a combo package that includes various adventures and lunch.

About 20 minutes outside of Quepos is **Rainmaker Park** (© 8860-3836 or 2777-3565; www.rainmakercostarica.org). The main attraction is a system of connected suspension bridges strung through the forest canopy, crisscrossing a deep ravine. Of the six bridges, the longest is 90m (295 ft.) across. The refuge also has a small network of trails and some great swimming holes. The refuge is open daily from 7am to 5pm. The entrance fee is $15 and $25 additional for a guided tour.

A butterfly at Fincas Naturales.

FOR KIDS   For a good taste of local Tico rural culture, mixed in with some fabulous scenery and adventure, sign up for the **Santa Juana Mountain Tour & Canopy Safari** (© 888/742-6667 in the U.S. and Canada, or 2777-0777 in Costa Rica; www.sicomono.com). This full-day tour starts off with a visit to the Canopy Safari (p. 377) and then takes you to a local farming village in the mountains outside of Quepos. Depending upon your needs and interests, once you arrive in the village, you can tour the surrounding coffee and citrus farms, go for a horseback ride, hike the trails, swim in rainforest pools, fish for tilapia, and see how sugar cane is processed. A typical Tico lunch is included. Rates are $119 to $139 per person, depending upon the size of your group, and $85 for children under 12.

HORSEBACK RIDING   While you can still sometimes find locals renting horses on the beaches outside the national park, I discourage this, as there are just too many crowds, the beach is too short, and the horse droppings are problematic. Better yet, head back into the hills and forests. Both **Finca Valmy** (© 2779-1118; www.valmytours.com) and **Brisas del Nara** (© 2779-1235; www.horsebacktour.com) offer horseback excursions that pass through both primary and secondary forest and feature a swimming stop or two at a jungle waterfall. Full-day tours, including breakfast and lunch, cost between $55 and $90 per person. Finca Valmy also offers an overnight tour for serious riders, with accommodations in rustic, but cozy, cabins in the Santa María de Dota mountains.

PARASAILING   If you want a good view of Manuel Antonio's spectacular scenery, you might want to go parasailing. The folks at **Aguas Azules** (© 2777-9192; www.costaricaparasailing.com) set up shop every morning on Playa Espadilla right in front of the souvenir store Caycosta, and offer parasailing rides behind a speedboat. Prices start at $75 for a single 15-minute ride.

Yo Quiero Hablar Español

Escuela D'Amore (© 877/434-7290 in the U.S. and Canada, or 2777-0233 in Costa Rica; www.academiadamore.com) runs language-immersion programs out of a former hotel with a fabulous view on the road to Manuel Antonio. A 2-week conversational Spanish course, including a homestay and two meals daily, costs $895. Or you can try the **Costa Rica Spanish Institute** (COSI; © 2234-1001 or 2777-0021; www.cosi.co.cr), which charges $1,010 for a similar 2-week program with a homestay.

ONE-STOP ADVENTURE HOT SPOT   The **ADR Adventure Park** ★★ (© **2777-0082;** www.adradventurepark.com) is an excellent one-stop spot for adventure travelers and thrill seekers. Billing itself as a 10-in-1 adventure tour, the 7-hour full-day tour here includes a zip-line canopy tour, waterfall rappels, a high plunge into a jungle river pool, horseback riding, and much more. The cost is $130, and includes transportation and lunch.

SOOTHE YOUR BODY & SOUL   The best of the local day spas are **Raindrop Spa** (© **800/381-3770** in the U.S. and Canada, or 2777-2880 in Costa Rica; www.raindropspa.com) and **Spa Uno** ★ (© **747/200-9005** in the U.S., or 2777-2607 in Costa Rica; www.spauno.com). A wide range of treatments, wraps, and facials are available at both of the above.

   Holis Spa (© **2777-0939**) has open yoga classes ($15) Monday to Friday at 8am and Saturday at 10am in the event center at Hotel Costa Verde and also offer private classes. Sivana Yoga (© **8899-2987**) is another option for private classes.

SPICE UP YOUR LIFE   Located 16km (10 miles) outside of Quepos, **Villa Vanilla** ★★ (© **2779-1155** or 8839-2721; www.rainforestspices.com) offers an informative and tasty tour of their open-air botanical gardens and spice farm. Their on-site commercial vanilla operation is the centerpiece of the show, but you'll also learn about a host of other tropical spices and assorted flora. You'll even sample some sweet and savory treats and drinks made with the on-site bounty. The half-day guided tour runs daily at 9am and 1pm, and costs $50, which includes round-trip transportation from any area hotel. Be sure to stock up at their small shop, which offers pure vanilla, cinnamon, and locally grown pepper.

Where to Stay

Take care when choosing your accommodations in Quepos/Manuel Antonio. You won't have much luck finding a hotel where you can walk directly out of your room and onto the beach, since Manuel Antonio has very few true beachfront hotels. In fact, most of the nicer hotels here are 1km ($\frac{1}{2}$ mile) or so away from the beach, high on the hill overlooking the ocean.

   If you're traveling on a rock-bottom budget, you'll get more for your money by staying in Quepos and taking the bus to the beaches at Manuel Antonio. The rooms in Quepos might be small, but they're generally cleaner and more appealing than those available in the same price category closer to the park.

VERY EXPENSIVE

Buena Vista Villas and Casas ★★ (© **866/569-6241** in the U.S. and Canada, or 2777-0580 in Costa Rica; www.buenavistavillas.net) is the current incarnation of the former Tulemar Resort. It features a wide range of private villas and bungalows in a gated community; each unit has access to Buena Vista's own secluded and protected bit of beach.

   If you're coming for an extended stay with the family or a large group, consider **Escape Villas** ★★★ (© **888/771-2976** in the U.S., or 2203-2158 in Costa Rica; www.escapevillas.com) or **Manuel Antonio Rentals** ★★ (© **985/247-4558** in the U.S., or 8913-9415 in Costa Rica; www.manuelantonio vacationrentals.com). Both outfits rent a broad selection of large and luxurious private villas and homes, with all the amenities and some of the best views in Manuel Antonio.

Arenas del Mar ★★★ This beachfront resort is in a league of its own in Manuel Antonio, with beautiful rooms, fabulous views, great dining, and direct access to not one, but two, beaches. All of the rooms are large and feature antique-style tile floors and sleek, minimalist decor. Most come with a private outdoor Jacuzzi tub on a private balcony. There are two main centers of operation here—one near the highest point of the property, the other down by one of the beaches—and each has its own pool, restaurant, and bar. This property is a leader in sustainable tourism and conservation.

Manuel Antonio. © **888/240-0220** in the U.S. and Canada or 2777-2777 in Costa Rica. www. arenasdelmar.com. 38 units. $350–$470 double; $590–$780 suite. Additional person $70. Rates include full breakfast and free local and international calls. **Amenities:** 2 restaurants; 2 bars; babysitting; concierge; 2 small outdoor pools; room service; spa; free Wi-Fi.

Gaia Hotel & Reserve ★★ Set on a series of rolling hills amidst its own private reserve, this ultra-hip and contemporary hotel offers up the most luxury and pampering possible in the Manuel Antonio area. Every guest enjoys personal concierge services, as well as a complimentary 20-minute spa treatment. Rooms come in a range of sizes and categories, although you'll need to opt for a suite if you want a private balcony, while the deluxe suites boast both a balcony and private rooftop terrace. All of the rooms are modern and equipped with all the latest amenities. The Luna restaurant here is quite good, with beautiful views over the hillsides to the sea. The owners of Gaia are very active in local conservation and social issues, and the hotel has been granted "4 Leaves" by the government-sponsored CST Sustainable Tourism program.

Manuel Antonio. © **800/226-2515** in the U.S., or 2777-9797 in Costa Rica. www.gaiahr.com. 20 units. $290–$395 studio; $425–$590 suite; $850 Gaia suite. Rates include full breakfast. No children 13 and under. **Amenities:** Restaurant; bar; concierge; small gym; multilevel outdoor pool; room service; extensive spa; free Wi-Fi.

Hotel Parador ★★ Located at the end of the road, with more than 4.8 hectares (12 acres) of land and private reserve that take up most of a sizeable peninsula, this resort-style hotel is spread out and quite varied. A wide range of room choices are available in a wide range of buildings. The best suites and views are found in the five-story "Las Suites" building, on a hilltop at the far side of the property. The Parador has several pools, including a large family pool with a concrete crocodile in the shallow end, but no direct beach access. However, the remote and protected Biesanz beach is a short walk away. All the options in the range of restaurant and dining options are quite good. This place was granted "5 Leaves" in the CST Sustainable Tourism program.

Manuel Antonio. © **2777-1414.** www.hotelparador.com. 122 units. $268–$340 double; $374–$412 premium; $512–750, suite. Rates include breakfast buffet. Rates slightly higher during peak weeks. **Amenities:** 4 restaurants; 2 bars; babysitting; concierge; health club and spa; Jacuzzi; 3 outdoor pools including one large free-form pool w/swim-up bar and central fountain; room service; unlit outdoor tennis court.

Hotel Sí Como No ★★ This boutique resort occupies a privileged position on a high ridge about midway between Quepos and the Manuel Antonio National Park. It's all thick rainforest below with beautiful views out to the Pacific Ocean from most of the rooms, which almost all feature private balconies. Monkey sightings are quite common here. There are two restaurants, two pools (one is adults only, the other has a fun little waterslide for the kids), and an air-conditioned theater with nightly movie showings. Sí Como No is an early leader in sustainable

Manuel Antonio & Quepos

To Airport, Hospital & Dominical

To San José

See inset

QUEPOS

Bahía La Ceiba

NICARAGUA
CARIBBEAN SEA

SAN JOSÉ

Manuel Antonio & Quepos

PACIFIC OCEAN

PANAMA

HOTELS
Arenas del Mar **24**
Buena Vista Villas
  & Casas **15**
Best Western Kamuk Hotel **4**
Byblos Resort **25**
El Mono Azul Hotel **11**
Gaia Hotel & Reserve **13**
Hotel Costa Verde **29**
Hotel Parador **23**
Hotel Sí Como No **27**
Hotel Verde Mar **31**
La Posada **33**
La Sirena Hotel **2**
Makanda by the Sea **22**
Villas Nicolás **26**
Widemouth Frog **3**

SHOPPING
Galería Yara **12**
Mot Mot Gallery **4**
Regaláme **27**

RESTAURANTS
Agua Azul **21**
Barba Roja **20**
Café Milagro **19**
El Avion **28**
El Gran Escape **8**
Kapi Kapi **16**
La Luna **13**
Marlin Restaurant **32**
Mar Luna **14**
Pizza de Marco **12**
Playitas **24**
Rafael's Terrazas **30**
Ronny's Place **9**
Sancho's **18**
Sunspot Bar & Grill **22**

NIGHTLIFE
Arco Iris **1**
Bambu Jam **10**
Barba Roja **20**
Billfish Sportbar
  & Grill **25**
Dos Locos **6**
Fish Head Bar **8**
Kamuk Casino **4**
Salsipuedes **17**
Sargento Garcia's **7**
Wacky Wanda's **5**

Playa Espadilla

Bahía Manuel Antonio

Isla Larga o Picuda

Punta Quepos

Punta Catedral

Main Park Entrance

Ranger Station

Playa Espadilla Sur

Playa Manuel Antonio

MANUEL ANTONIO NATIONAL PARK

Laguna Negra

Playa Puerto Escondido

Punta Surrucho

0 — 1/2 mi
0 — 0.5 km

Bahía La Ceiba

Calle 2

Calle Central

Av. 1

Bus Station

Market

Av. Central

Calle 5

Calle 7

Church

0 — 1/8 mile
0 — 100 meters

To Airport, Hospital & Dominical

To Manuel Antonio Nat'l Park

Quepos

381

One of the pools at Arenas del Mar.

tourism in Costa Rica and was awarded "5 Leaves" in the CST Sustainable Tourism program.

Manuel Antonio. ℂ **888/742-6667** in the US or 2777-0777 in Costa Rica. www.sicomono.com. 58 units. $250–$299 double; $320–$365 suite. Rates include full breakfast. Extra person $30. Children 5 and under stay free in parent's room. **Amenities:** 2 restaurants; 2 bars; babysitting; concierge; 2 Jacuzzis; 2 midsize outdoor pools, including 1 w/small water slide; modest spa; free Wi-Fi.

Makanda by the Sea ★★   With just 11 units, this remains my top choice for an intimate and artistic boutique retreat in the Manuel Antonio area. A mix of one bedroom studio units and larger villas are spread around lush gardens and thick forest on a steep hillside. Every option here comes with a full kitchen or kitchenette. All are large and open, with a minimalist Japanese-inspired design aesthetic. Some have gorgeous ocean views over and through the thick rain forest. Breakfasts are delivered every morning to your studio or villa, while, in the evenings, the elegant Sunspot Bar & Grill (see below) is one of the better restaurants in the area.

Manuel Antonio. ℂ **888/625-2632** in the U.S., or 2777-0442 in Costa Rica. www.makanda.com. 11 units. $265–$315 studio; $400 villa. Rates include full breakfast. Children 15 and under are not allowed, unless booking the entire resort. **Amenities:** Restaurant; bar; concierge; Jacuzzi; midsize outdoor pool; room service; free Wi-Fi.

EXPENSIVE

In addition to the place listed below, you might check out **Byblos Resort ★** (ℂ **888/929-2567** in the U.S. and Canada, or 2777-0411 in Costa Rica; www.bybloshotelcostarica.com), which features a mix of rooms, suites, and jungle bungalows. Although they're the oldest and simplest units on the property, I really like the individual bungalows set in deep forest.

Hotel Costa Verde ★ This sprawling complex features everything from rustic rooms and cottages to a converted 727 airplane that serves as a two-bedroom suite, with the cockpit and nose appearing to jut out of the forest. Most of the rooms, however, are in two tall buildings (one for families, one adults only), featuring large balconies with wonderful rainforest and ocean views. The studio and studio-plus rooms all have kitchenettes and flatscreen TVs. Not all of the rooms have air-conditioning or televisions, so be sure to check before making your final choice. The hotel has a series of trails, and is about a 10-minute walk (downhill) to the beach. However, the whole complex is located on a steep hillside, so the return trip from the beach and to some of the rooms can be strenuous. Breakfast is served at the main hotel complex; three additional restaurant locations are across the street.

Manuel Antonio. ✆ **866/854-7958** in the U.S. and Canada, or 2777-0584 in Costa Rica. www.costaverde.com. 70 units. $115–$300 double; $500 727 Fuselage suite. **Amenities:** 4 restaurants; 4 bars; 3 small outdoor pools; free Wi-Fi.

MODERATE

In addition to the hotels mentioned below, the **Best Western Kamuk Hotel** (✆ **2777-0811**; www.kamuk.co.cr) and **La Sirena Hotel** (✆ **2777-0572**; www.lasirenahotel.com) are two dependable options right in downtown Quepos. Both are popular with sportfishing enthusiasts, while **La Posada Private Jungle Bungalows** (✆ **2777-1446**; www.laposadajungle.com) is a good option a few blocks inland from the beach, right near the main entrance to the National Park.

El Mono Azul Hotel Also known as The Blue Monkey, this little hotel has a hostel-like feel and social vibe, with slightly more upscale accommodations. Rooms are on both sides of the main road that runs from Quepos to the national park entrance, and vary quite a bit in size and amenities. Some rooms feel a bit dated. The several pool areas are quite nice, with lush overgrown gardens and plenty of shade. These folks were instrumental in founding Kids Saving the Rainforests, a non-profit conservation and art program, and part of all of their proceeds goes to support the project. The little restaurant here is a hub of activity and great place to meet fellow travelers.

Manuel Antonio. ✆ **800/381-3578** in the U.S., or 2777-1548 in Costa Rica. www.monoazul.com. 32 units. $85–$120 double; $105–$190 villa. **Amenities:** Restaurant; bar; lounge; 3 small outdoor pools; free Wi-Fi.

Hotel Verde Mar This hotel has an enviable location, just a short walk on a raised walkway through shady trees to Playa Espadilla. The rooms are all of good size, and most come with a kitchenette. Given that there's a small free-form pool and overall the staff is friendly and helpful, the hotel provides an excellent value. Still, the rooms, linens, and installations feel in need of a major overhaul and updating.

Manuel Antonio. ✆ **877/872-0459** in the U.S. & Canada or 2777-2122 in Costa Rica. www.verdemar.com. 22 units. $105 double. **Amenities:** Restaurant; small outdoor pool; free Wi-Fi.

Villas Nicolás ★★ Located right next to Sí Como No (see above), this collection of spacious condo units offers up the very same classic Manuel Antonio views, but at bargain prices. Virtually all of the options here come with large, rainforest- and ocean-facing balconies. Some have full kitchens, and many can be combined to accommodate families or groups. The lovely pool is set amidst lush gardens, and the service here is friendly and personal.

Manuel Antonio. ℂ **2777-0481.** www.villasnicolas.com. 19 units. $125–$160 double; $180–$340 suite. Weekly, monthly, and off-season (May–Nov) rates available. Rates include full breakfast. **Amenities:** Restaurant; bar; small outdoor pool; free Wi-Fi.

INEXPENSIVE

Budget hotels are hard to come by in and around Quepos and Manuel Antonio. Your best bet is the **Widemouth Frog** ★ (ℂ 2777-2798; www.widemouthfrog. org), a hostel right in downtown Quepos, which offers everything from bunk-bed dorm rooms with shared bathrooms to cozy double rooms with a private bathroom. It even has its own swimming pool.

Where to Dine

Scores of dining options are available around Manuel Antonio and Quepos, and almost every hotel has some sort of restaurant. For the cheapest meals around, try a simple soda in Quepos, or head to one of the open-air joints on the beach road before the national park entrance. Here, the standard Tico menu prevails, with prices in the C3,000-to-C5,000 range. Of these, **Marlin Restaurant** ★ (ℂ 2777-1134), right in front of Playa Espadilla, is your best bet. For Mexican-style cooking, try **Sancho's** ★ (ℂ 2777-0340), near the soccer field in Manuel Antonio. **Mi Lugar,** or "**Ronny's Place**" ★ (ℂ 2777-5120; www.ronnysplace. com), on the outskirts of Quepos, is another good option. **Mar Luna** (ℂ 2777-5107), on the main road as you climb the hill from Quepos toward Manuel Antonio, is another solid Tico-owned spot specializing in seafood and local cuisine.

For lunch, try the beachfront **Playitas** ★★ at Arenas del Mar (see above); in addition to its great location and secure parking, you get pool privileges for the price of an excellent meal.

EXPENSIVE

Kapi Kapi ★★★ FUSION/NUEVO LATINO   This place is expensive, but if you're looking for a quiet, romantic, and elegant meal, it's hard to beat. The menu and decor both show a strong Asian influence, although both incorporate as much local produce, products, and materials as possible. The local fresh shrimp is skewered on long spikes of sugar cane, grilled, and then bathed in a glaze of rum, tamarind, and coconut; the mahi-mahi is crusted in crushed macadamia nuts, and served with a sweet plum-chili sauce and a side of Jasmine rice. The wide-ranging wine list includes selections from Italy, France, Argentina, and Chile.

On the road btw. Quepos and Manuel Antonio. ℂ **2777-5049.** www.restaurantekapikapi.com. Reservations recommended. Main courses C8,500–C14,500. Daily 4–10pm.

Sunspot Bar & Grill ★ INTERNATIONAL   This small and elegant poolside restaurant is the in-house option at Makanda by the Sea (p. 382). Just a handful of tables are set under a pair of purple temporary tent structures. The menu changes regularly and there are always nightly specials, but grilled to order fresh seafood and prime meats are the perennial stars here. The grilled mahi-mahi may come with a passion fruit glaze, whereas a tenderloin might be bathed in a gorgonzola and cognac sauce. Their molten chocolate cake is a favorite for dessert. As at the hotel, this is an grownups-only environment.

At Makanda by the Sea. ℂ **2777-0442.** Reservations recommended. Main courses C4,500–C18,000. Daily noon–10pm.

MODERATE

Agua Azul ★★ INTERNATIONAL   This popular restaurant has one of the best settings, sitting high above the rainforest with sweeping views over the trees to the Pacific Ocean below. This place serves up excellent fare, with a menu heavy in bar food standards, but often served with a creative twist, like their signature Tuna Margarita, which features seared tuna served over a cucumber salad with a lime vinaigrette, all served in a salt-rimmed margarita glass. You can also get burgers, burritos, nachos, chicken fingers, and a few more substantial plates, like whole snapper in a tamarind sauce, and the chef's nightly pasta special. This place is very popular for sunset drinks, and the prime viewing seats fill up fast.

Manuel Antonio, near Villas del Parque. 🕐 **2777-5280.** www.cafeaguaazul.com. Main courses C8.500–C10.500. Thurs–Tues 11am–9:30pm.

Barba Roja SEAFOOD/INTERNATIONAL   This is another very popular sunset viewing spot, with an equally popular restaurant and bar. On clear nights, you'll want to grab one of the lounge style low tables with couch-like seating set on the broad wooden deck. The menu ranges from Tex-Mex to fresh grilled meats and fish to Asian fusion. They also serve Tico standards, and traditional bar food, and have a pretty good sushi bar to boot.

Manuel Antonio. 🕐 **2777-0331.** www.barbarojarestaurant.com. Reservations recommended in high season. Main courses C5,900–C8,800. Tues–Sun 10am–10pm; Mon 4–10pm.

El Avión SEAFOOD/INTERNATIONAL   This is a fun place to bring the family and the view is beautiful. El Avión, or "the plane," is a former CIA C-123 supply plane that was shot down by the Sandinistas during the Contra War. It now provides shade and cover for the restaurant's tables and chairs, which set on a large wooden deck built under the plane's wings and even more expansive open-air roof structure. You can get fresh seafood, steaks, burgers, and sandwiches. This place's popularity has led to the construction of a whole second-floor dining area. The sunset view here is very sought after and you should reserve in advance if you want a table with a view. The restaurant's bar is inside the old cargo plane's fuselage.

Manuel Antonio. www.elavion.net. 🕐 **2777-3378.** Reservations recommended. Main courses C5,000–C11,000. Daily noon–11pm.

El Gran Escape ★★ SEAFOOD   This longstanding local institution has a new home on the second floor of the commercial space overlooking the Pez Vela Marina. They do seafood wonderfully here, and even have a "you hook 'em, we cook 'em" policy for anyone heading out fishing. Seating is comfortable in a large, open-air, yet covered, patio. I like to start things off with the fresh tuna sashimi, and then usually get the catch of the day, simply grilled. They also do excellent burgers, as well as fish, shrimp, chicken, beef, or Portobello mushroom tacos. The attached Fish Head Bar is popular and lively, and they also do really good breakfasts.

At the Pez Vela Marina. 🕐 **2777-0395.** www.elgranescape.com. Reservations recommended in high season. Main courses C8,000–C19,000. Mon–Sun 11am–10pm.

Milagro ★★★ NUEVO LATINO/FUSION   An institution in Manuel Antonio, Milagro is the nerve center of a bustling little local empire that has grown out of their Café Milagro coffee-roasting business. As you'd expect, this spot is an excellent coffee house with the full range of barista-brewed concoctions. They also serve breakfast, lunch, and dinner. For lunch I like their take on a traditional Cuban sandwich, replacing the pork with fresh, local mahi-mahi. The dinner menu features fusion-inspired Latin fare with everything from jerk chicken to shrimp in a coconut-rum sauce served over mango-infused rice. They have creative, contemporary cocktails, as well as a good list of South American wines.

On the road btw. Quepos and Manuel Antonio. ☎ **2777-0794.** www.cafemilagro.com. Reservations recommended. Main courses C6,300–C13,000. Daily 7am–10pm.

Rafael's Terrazas ★ SEAFOOD/COSTA RICAN   This simple open-air restaurant has a stunning location, clinging to a steep hillside with a perfect view of the Pacific over zinc roofs and a small patch of thick rain forest. The hillside is so steep the dining rooms are terraced (hence the name) and spread over three floors connected by steep steps. The menu features a host of Tico classics and is heavy on fresh seafood. You can get some excellent ceviche as a starter, and a *casado* of fish, chicken or beef for a main course. They also have some more worldly options, including seared tuna with a ginger, soy, and wasabi sauce. Meat lovers should try the bacon-wrapped tenderloin in a fresh mushroom sauce.

On the road btw. Quepos and Manuel Antonio. ☎ **2777-6310.** Reservations recommended. Main courses C5,300–C15,000. Tues–Sun 11am–11pm.

Shopping

If you're looking for souvenirs, you'll find plenty of beach towels, beachwear, and handmade jewelry in a variety of small shops in Quepos and at impromptu stalls down near the national park. The best of these is **Mot Mot Gallery** (☎ **2777-3559;** www.motmotcr.com), located downtown in the first floor of the Best Western Kamuk Hotel.

For higher-end gifts, check out Hotel Sí Como No's **Regálame** (www.regalameart.com) gift shop, which has a wide variety of craft works, clothing, and original paintings and prints, or **Galería Yara** (☎ **2777-4846**), a contemporary, tropical art gallery in the Plaza Yara shopping center.

Manuel Antonio Nightlife & Entertainment

The bars at the **Barba Roja** restaurant, about midway along the road between Quepos and Manuel Antonio, and the **Hotel Sí Como No** (p. 380) are good places to hang out and meet people in the evenings. To shoot some pool, I head to the **Billfish Sportbar & Grill** ★ at the Byblos Resort (on the main road btw. Quepos and the park entrance). For tapas and local *bocas,* try **Salsipuedes** (roughly midway along the road btw. Quepos and the National Park entrance), which translates as "get out if you can." If you want live music, **Bambu Jam** ★ (along the road btw. Quepos and the park entrance) and **Dos Locos** (in the heart of downtown) are your best bets. In downtown Quepos, **Sargento Garcia's, Wacky Wanda's,** and the **Fish Head Bar** at El Gran Escape (see above) are all popular hangouts.

Night owls and dancing fools have several choices here, although the bulldozing of Mar y Sombra down by the beach has really hurt the scene. The live music at **Bambu Jam** is often salsa and merengue, perfect for dancing. For real late-night action, the local favorite appears to be the **Arco Iris,** just before the bridge heading into town. Admission is usually around $3.

The **Best Western Kamuk Hotel** in Quepos and the **Byblos Resort** (see above) both have small casinos and will even foot your cab bill if you try your luck and lay down your money. If you want to see a flick, check what's playing at **Hotel Sí Como No**'s (p. 380) little theater, although you have to eat at the restaurant or spend a minimum at the bar to earn admission.

Side Trip from Manuel Antonio: Playa Matapalo

Playa Matapalo is a long expanse of flat beach that's about midway between Quepos and Dominical. It's an easy but bumpy 26km (16 miles) south of Quepos on the Costanera Sur. It's nowhere near as developed as either of those two beaches, but that's part of its charm. The beach here seems to stretch on forever, and it's usually deserted. The surf and strong riptides frequently make Matapalo too rough for swimming, although surfing and boogie-boarding can be good. Foremost among this beach's charms are peace and quiet.

WHERE TO STAY

Matapalo is a tiny coastal village, although the actual beach is about 1km ($^1/_2$ mile) away. A few very small and intimate lodges are located right on the beach. One of the more interesting is **Bahari Beach Bungalows** (✆ 2787-5014; www.baharibeach.com), which offers deluxe tents with private bathrooms, and more standard rooms, right on the beach, or **Dreamy Contentment** (✆ 2787-5223; www.dreamycontentment.com), a more traditional beachfront hotel. **El Coquito del Pacífico** hotel (✆ 2787-5031; www.elcoquito.com) has a restaurant popular with tourists and locals alike.

For something completely different, you can head into the hills alongside the Savegre River to **Rafiki Safari Lodge** ★ (✆ 2777-2250; www.rafikisafari. com), which features a collection of large safari tents on elevated platforms in a rich forest setting.

DOMINICAL ★

29km (18 miles) SW of San Isidro; 42km (26 miles) S of Quepos; 160km (99 miles) S of San José

With a stunning setting, and miles of nearly deserted beaches backed by rainforest-covered mountains, Dominical and the coastline south of it are excellent places to find uncrowded stretches of sand, spectacular views, remote jungle waterfalls, and everything from abundant budget lodgings to luxurious rainforest villas. The beach at Dominical is one of the prime surf destinations in Costa Rica, with both right and left beach breaks. When the swell is big, the wave here is a powerful and hollow tube, and the town is often packed with surfers. In fact, while the beach at Dominical gets broad, flat, and beautiful at low tide, its primary appeal is to surfers. It is often too rough for casual bathers. However, you will find excellent swimming, sunbathing, and strolling beaches just a little farther south at **Dominicalito, Playa Hermosa,** and inside **Ballena Marine National Park ★★**.

Leaving Manuel Antonio, the road south to Dominical runs by mile after mile of oil-palm plantations. However, just before Dominical, the mountains again meet the sea. From Dominical south, the coastline is dotted with tide pools, tiny coves, and cliff-side vistas. Dominical is the largest village in the area and has several small lodges both in town and along the beach to the south. The village enjoys an enviable location on the banks of Río Barú, right where it widens considerably before emptying into the ocean. The banks of the river and throughout the surrounding forests offer good birding. Along the coast and rivers, you're likely to see numerous shore and sea birds, including herons, egrets, and king-fishers, while the forests are home to colorful and lively tanagers, toucans, and trogons.

Essentials

GETTING THERE & DEPARTING   By Plane: The nearest airport with regular service is in Quepos (see "Essentials" under "Manuel Antonio National Park," earlier in this chapter). From there you can hire a taxi, rent a car, or take the bus.

By Car: The traditional route from San José involves heading east out of town (toward Cartago), and then south on the Interamerican Highway (CR2) to the city of San Isidro de El General. From San Isidro, a well-marked and well-traveled route (CR243) leads to Dominical and the coast. The entire drive takes about 4 hours.

However, it's faster and easier to take the San José–Caldera Highway (CR27) west to Orotina. Just past the toll booth at Pavón, this road connects with the Costanera Sur (CR34), or Southern Coastal Highway. The exit is marked for Jacó and CR34. From here, it's a straight and flat shot down the coast. When you reach Quepos, follow the signs for Dominical. This route should take you just over 3 hours.

The Costanera Sur (CR34) heading south from Dominical to Palmar Norte, passing all the beaches mentioned below, is in excellent shape.

By Bus: To reach Dominical, you must first go to San Isidro de El General or Quepos. Buses leave San José for San Isidro roughly every hour between

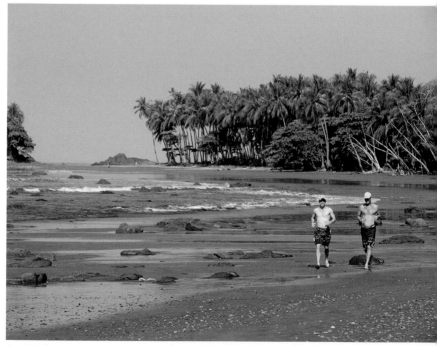

Dominicalito.

4:30am and 5:30pm. See "Getting There & Departing" in "San Isidro de El General: A Base for Exploring Chirripó National Park," later in this chapter. The trip takes 3 hours; the fare is C2,810. The main bus stop in Dominical is in the heart of town, near the soccer field and San Clemente restaurant.

From Quepos, **Transportes Blanco** buses (✆ **2771-4744**) leave daily at 5:30 and 11:30am, and 3:30pm. The trip takes about an hour and costs C1,900.

From San Isidro de El General, **Transportes Blanco** buses (✆ **2771-4744**) leave for Dominical at 7, 9, and 11:30am, and 3:30 and 4pm. The bus station in San Isidro for rides to Dominical is 1 block south of the main bus station and 2 blocks west of the church. The trip duration is 1½ hours; the fare is C1,500.

When you're ready to leave, buses depart Dominical for San Isidro at 6am and 1, 2, and 4:30pm. Buses leave San Isidro for San José roughly every hour between 5:30am and 5:30pm. Buses to Quepos leave Dominical at 8:30am, 1 and 4:30pm.

GETTING AROUND   Taxis tend to congregate in front of the soccer field. If you need a car, **Solid Rental Car** (✆ **2787-0111**) will arrange drop-off and pickup at any area hotel.

SPECIAL EVENTS   Each year, this area hosts the **Envision Festival** ★ (www.envisionfestival.com), a 3-day celebration of art, music, and dance, that's a little bit like Burning Man in the Tropics. The festival usually takes place in late-February or early March.

VILLAGE LAYOUT   Dominical is a small village on the banks of the Río Barú. The village is to the right after you cross the bridge (heading south) and stretches out along the main road parallel to the beach. As you first come into town, you'll see the small Pueblo del Río shopping center dead ahead of you, where the road hits a "T" intersection. On your left is the soccer field and the heart of the village. To the right, a rough road heads to the river and up along the riverbank. If you stay on the Costanera Highway heading south, just beyond the turnoff into town is a little strip mall, **Plaza Pacífica,** with a couple of restaurants, a pharmacy, bank, and a grocery store.

FAST FACTS   You'll find a handful of Internet cafes spread around the village. A branch of the **Banco de Costa Rica,** with an ATM, is located in the Plaza Pacífica.

Exploring the Beaches South of Dominical & Ballena Marine National Park

The open ocean waters just in front of town and toward the river mouth are often too rough for swimming. However, you can swim in the calm waters of the Río Barú, just in from the river mouth, or head down the beach a few kilometers to the little sheltered cove at **Roca Verde.**

If you have a car, you should continue driving south, exploring beaches as you go. You will first come to **Dominicalito,** a small beach and cove that shelters the local fishing fleet and that can be a decent place to swim, but continue on a bit. You'll soon hit **Playa Hermosa,** a long stretch of desolate beach with fine sand. As in Dominical, this beach is unprotected and can be rough, but it's a nicer place to sunbathe and swim than Dominical.

At the village of Uvita, 16km (10 miles) south of Dominical, you'll reach the northern end of the **Ballena Marine National Park ★★**, which protects a

Ballena Marine National Park.

coral reef that stretches from Uvita south to Playa Piñuela and includes the little Isla Ballena, just offshore. To get to **Playa Uvita** (which is inside the park), turn in at the village of Bahía and continue until you hit the ocean. The beach here is actually well protected and good for swimming. At low tide, an exposed sandbar allows you to walk about and explore another tiny island. This park is named for the whales that are sometimes sighted close to shore in the winter months. If you ever fly over this area, you'll also notice that this little island and the spit of land that's formed at low tide compose the perfect outline of a whale's tail. An office at the entrance here regulates the park's use and even runs a small turtle-hatching shelter and program. Entrance to the national park is $10 per person. Camping is allowed here for $2 per person per day, including access to a public restroom and shower.

Dominical is a major surf destination. Its long and varied beach break is justifiably popular. In general, the beach boasts powerful waves best suited for experienced surfers. Nevertheless, beginners should check in with the folks at the **Green Iguana Surf Camp ★** (✆ 8825-1381; www.greeniguanasurfcamp. com), who offer lessons and comprehensive "surf camps." Rates run around $785 to $1,295 per person, based on double occupancy, for a 1-week program including accommodations, lessons, unlimited surfboard use, transportation to various surf breaks, and a T-shirt.

Outdoor & Wellness Activities in the Area

In addition to the activities mentioned below, other adventure activities offered in Dominical include kayak tours of the mangroves, river floats in inner tubes, and day tours to Caño Island and Corcovado National Park. To arrange any of these activities, check in with **Dominical Adventures** (✆ 2787-0431; www. dominicalsurfadventures.com), or the folks at the **Hotel Roca Verde** (✆ 2787-0036; www.rocaverde.net).

DIVING   If you want to take a scuba-diving trip out to the rocky sites off Ballena National Park or all the way out to Isla del Caño, call **Mystic Dive Center** (© 2786-5217; mysticdive@yahoo.com), which has its main office in a small roadside strip mall down toward Playa Tortuga and Ojochal. These folks are only open from December 1 through April 15, and prices for Ballena National Park are $70 for snorkeling and $100 for a two-tank dive; prices for Isla del Caño are $100 for snorkeling and $150 for a two-tank dive.

FISHING   For sportfishing, I recommend the folks at **Sportfishing Dominical** (© 2787-8012; www.sportfishingdominical.co.cr), who are based out of the hotel Cuna del Angel (p. 396).

FLYING   If you're looking for a bird's-eye view of the area, **Skyline Ultralights** (© 2743-8037; www.ultralighttour.com) offers a variety of airborne tours of the area. Near the beach in Uvita, these folks offer options ranging from a 20-minute introductory flight for $110 to a roughly hour-long circuit exploring the Ballena Marine National Park and neighboring mangrove forests for $235.

HIKING & HORSEBACK RIDING   Several local farms offer horseback tours through forests and orchards, and some of these farms provide overnight accommodations. **Hacienda Barú** ★ (© 2787-0003; www.haciendabaru.com) offers several different hikes and tours, including a walk through mangroves and along the riverbank (for some good bird watching), a rainforest hike through 80 hectares (198 acres) of virgin jungle, an all-day trek from beach to mangrove to jungle that includes a visit to some Indian petroglyphs, an overnight camping trip, and a combination horseback-and-hiking tour. The operation, which is dedicated to conservation and reforestation, even has tree-climbing tours and a small canopy platform 30m (98 ft.) above the ground, as well as one of the more common zip-line canopy tours. Tour prices range from $25 for the mangrove hike to $125 to overnight in the jungle. If you're traveling with a group, you'll be charged a lower per-person rate, depending on the number of people. In addition to its eco- and adventure tourism activities, Hacienda Barú also has six comfortable cabins with two bedrooms each, full kitchens, and even a living room (prices range from

---

A Special Snake & Reptile Showcase

For a fun side trip for anyone interested in snakes and other little critters, head to **Parque Reptilandia** ★★ (© 2787-0343; www.crreptiles.com), a few miles outside Dominical on the road to San Isidro. In my opinion, this is the best snake and reptile attraction in Costa Rica. With more than 55 well-designed and spacious terrariums and enclosed areas, the collection includes a wide range of snakes, frogs, turtles, and lizards, as well as crocodiles and caimans. Some of my favorite residents here are the brilliant eyelash pit viper and sleek golden vine snake. Both native and

imported species are on display, including the only Komodo dragon in Central America. For those looking to spice up their visit, Fridays are feeding days. It's open daily from 9am to 4:30pm; admission is $12 adults, and $6 for children 14 and under.

$75–$85 for a double, including breakfast). Hacienda Barú is about 1.5km (1 mile) north of Dominical on the road to Manuel Antonio.

WATERFALLS   The jungles just outside of Dominical are home to two spectacular waterfalls. The most popular and impressive is the **Santo Cristo** or **Nauyaca Waterfalls ★**, a two-tiered beauty with an excellent swimming hole. Most of the hotels in town can arrange for the horseback ride up here, or you can contact **Don Lulo** (© **2787-0541;** www.cataratasnauyaca.com) directly. A full-day tour, with both breakfast and lunch, should cost around $65 per person, including transportation to and from Dominical. The tour is a mix of hiking, horseback riding, and hanging out at the falls. It is also possible to reach these falls by horseback from an entrance near the small village of Tinamaste. (You will see signs on the road.) Similar tours (at similar prices) are offered to the **Diamante Waterfalls,** which are a three-tiered set of falls with a 360m (1,180-ft.) drop, but not quite as spacious and inviting a pool as the one at Santo Cristo.

YOGA   If you want to keep up with your ongoing practice or to take an introductory class, check in with the folks at **Bamboo Yoga Play & Danyasa Eco-Retreat ★★** (© **2787-0229**); www.danyasa.com). They offer a wide range of regular yoga and dance classes, as well as private instruction and longer retreats. A drop-in class costs $14, and weeklong or multi-class deals are offered.

Where to Stay

In addition to the places listed below, a host of beautiful private homes on the hillsides above Dominical regularly rent out rooms. Most come with several bedrooms and full kitchens, and quite a few have private pools. If you're here for an extended stay and have a four-wheel-drive vehicle (a must for most of these), check in with **Paradise Costa Rica** (© **800/708-4552** in the U.S. and Canada; www.paradisecostarica.com) or with the folks at **Villas Alturas ★★** (© **2200-5440;** www.villasalturas.com).

Nauyaca Waterfalls.

Spanish Classes

If you're looking to learn or bone up on your Spanish, **Adventure Education Center** (© **800/237-2730** in the U.S. and Canada, or 2787-0023 in Costa Rica; www.adventurespanishschool.com), located right in the heart of town, offers a variety of immersion-style language programs. A standard, 1-week program including 16 hours of class, homestay, and breakfasts and dinners costs $410. These folks also offer specialized family and medical language courses, and can throw some surf lessons into the package, if you're interested.

EXPENSIVE

Cascadas Farallas Waterfall Villas ★★ This place should probably be listed someplace else, because it's certainly in a category all its own. Specializing in unplugged, vegan yoga retreats and general mind-body rejuvenation, this boutique hotel and wellness retreat center is about 8km (5 miles) outside of Dominical proper. It is set in the midst of thick forest and on the edge of a running river and gorgeous stepped waterfall. A Balinese design aesthetic is obvious in the rooms and common areas. Be prepared for no Wi-Fi, and a kitchen that puts out predominantly vegetarian, vegan and raw foods.

8km (5 miles) northeast of Dominical, on the road to San Isidro © **2787-4137.** www.waterfall villas.com. 6 units. $150–$230 double. Rates include breakfast. **Amenities:** Restaurant; spa.

MODERATE

Hotel Diuwak This surfer-friendly mini-resort is just a half-block away from the waves. Rooms are a bit dated and in need of some upkeep and remodeling, and the service can be slack. But most folks don't seem to care, seeing that as a fair trade off for easy access to the waves and a host of other amenities. The hotel has a very good sized pool area, as well as a restaurant, bar, surf shop and well-stocked convenience store.

Dominical. © **2787-0087.** www.diuwak.com. 36 units. $100–$105 double; $115–$125 deluxe; $170–$180 suites. Rates include full breakfast and taxes. **Amenities:** Restaurant; bar; midsize outdoor pool, free Wi-Fi.

Hotel Roca Verde ★ This is my top beachfront choice in Dominical. The rooms and location are the best to be found in this generally budget oriented surfer town. All rooms come with either a private patio or balcony, but you'll want to try for a second floor unit if possible, as the balconies are a bit nicer to have. Rooms are spacious and well maintained and have hand-painted accents to liven things up. The hotel is set right on a quiet section of beach on its own little cove on the far southern end of Dominical village. The open-air restaurant and bar here are quite popular, and sometimes features live music on weekend nights.

1km (1/2 mile) south of Barú River Bridge in Dominical, just off the coastal hwy. © **2787-0036.** www.rocaverde.net. 10 units. $99 double. Rate include breakfast and taxes. **Amenities:** Restaurant; bar; small outdoor pool; free Wi-Fi.

INEXPENSIVE

As a popular surfer destination, budget lodgings abound in Dominical. I try to list the best below, but if you're really counting pennies, it's always a good idea to walk around and check out what's currently available. Another good budget option is **Montanas de Agua** (© 2787-0200; www.montanasdeagua.com), about a block and a half inland from the beach, across from Domilocos (see below). There are plenty of camping options as well. I recommend **Piramys** (© 2787-0196; piramys@hotmail.com) or **Camping Antorchas** (© 2787-0307; www.campingantorchas.net), both of which offer basic rooms very close to the beach.

Cabinas San Clemente   The simple rooms in this no-frills beachfront hotel are well maintained and a good value. The owner Mike McGigginis is an old-school surfer and pioneer in these parts. The best rooms are the second-floor units with private bathrooms, but you can also opt for dorm rooms with bunk beds and shared baths and access to a communal kitchen. The small Surf Shak restaurant attached to the hotel serves up breakfasts and lunch, as well as the sister San Clemente Restaurant (see below), just a short walk away in the center of town.

Dominical. © **2787-0026** or 2787-0055. 18 units, 12 with private bathroom. $10 per person with shared bathroom; $30–$65 double with private bathroom. **Amenities:** Restaurant; bar; free Wi-Fi.

Domilocos   This place fills an odd niche. The rooms are a bit more comfortable and better kept than those at Diuwak, but you're further from the beach and center of town. That said, you're only 1 block from the waves, and perhaps 5 blocks from the village. So, if you want a little mellower scene than typically found at the surfer hotels around Dominical, this might be your best bet. The rooms all have air-conditioning and windows out on to the central courtyard and shared veranda or walkways. At the center of this central courtyard is a large unheated Jacuzzi. The restaurant here is very good.

Dominical. © **2787-0244**. www.domilocos.com. 26 units. $75–$110 double. Rates include breakfast. **Amenities:** Restaurant; bar; Jacuzzi, room service; free Wi-Fi.

Tortilla Flats   This is the most popular and lively of the beachfront surfer hostels in Dominical, with an excellent and equally popular restaurant attached. Rooms are spread around several buildings in a small complex surrounding the restaurant. They vary a bit in size and amenities. I'd definitely recommend splurging for an air-conditioned unit on the second floor, if possible.

Dominical. © **2787-0033**. 16 units. $30–$50 double. **Amenities:** Restaurant; bar.

Where to Dine

On the beach, **Tortilla Flats** (see above) is the best and most happening spot, and their menu features some excellent fresh-fish dishes and a touch of fusion cuisine. If you head a bit south of town, you can check out the restaurant at the **Hotel Roca Verde** (p. 393), which is usually pretty good for grilled fish, steaks, and burgers.

Soda Nanyoa (© 2787-0164) is a basic Tico restaurant on the main road, just down a bit from the soccer field, serving local food and fresh seafood at good prices.

If you're staying in Dominical and have a car, it's probably worthwhile to head south and sample some of the options mentioned in the next section below.

Maracatú ★ INTERNATIONAL/VEGETARIAN   Located in the heart of Dominical village, right across from the soccer field, this local hotspot specializes in healthy cuisine, particularly vegetarian and vegan fare, although you can also get fresh seafood. Choose from vegetarian fajitas, veggie burgers, a range of pasta dishes, and Middle Eastern classics, like falafel and taboulleh. All of the produce and seafood is locally sourced, and much of it comes from their own organic farm Selva Armonia in the nearby hills. This place also has a lively lounge and bar scene and often features live music or DJs.

Across from the soccer field, Dominical. ⌀ **2787-0091.** Reservations not accepted. Main courses C4,000–C8,000. Daily noon–9:30pm.

San Clemente Bar & Grill ★★ MEXICAN/AMERICAN   This large, open-air restaurant is a local institution. You can't miss it, located next to the soccer field, with a full-sized Volkswagen camper van serving as the restaurant's sign. Folks come for the fresh-made margaritas and generous portions. A wide range of traditional Tex-Mex standards are on offer. Their Taco Tuesdays are a big hit, with low-priced beef, chicken, and fish tacos flowing freely from the kitchen. Be sure to ask for some of their homemade hot sauce. It's delicious stuff and spicy, but not mouth numbingly so. If you bring in a broken surf board to add to their collection, the house will treat you to a bucket of cold beer on ice.

Next to the soccer field, Dominical. ⌀ **2787-0055.** Reservations not accepted. Main courses C3,000–C4,500. Daily 11am–10pm.

Dominical Nightlife & Entertainment

The big party scenes shift from night to night. **Maracatú** (see above) hosts an open jam session every Sunday and a ladies' night every Wednesday. The loud and late-night dancing scene usually takes place Fridays at **San Clemente** (see above), and there's often live music or a rowdy scene at the bar at **Roca Verde** (p. 393). In addition, **Thrusters** in the center of town is a popular surfer bar with pool tables and dartboards.

South of Dominical

The beaches south of Dominical are some of the nicest and most unexplored in Costa Rica. With the paving of the Costanera Sur, hotels and cabinas have begun

Dominical's coastline.

popping up all along this route. This is a great area to roam in a rental car—it's a beautiful **drive ★★**. One good itinerary is to make a loop from San Isidro to Dominical, down the Costanera Sur, hitting several deserted beaches, and then returning along the Interamerican Highway.

Among the beaches you'll find are **Playa Ballena, Playa Uvita, Playa Piñuela, Playa Ventanas,** and **Playa Tortuga.** *Tip:* Most of these beaches are considered part of **Ballena Marine National Park** (p. 389) and are subject to the national park entrance fee of $6 per person. If you're visiting several of these beaches in 1 day, save your ticket—it's good at all of them.

WHERE TO STAY

Just south of Dominical, on a point over Dominicalito beach, **La Parcela** (✆ 2787-0016; www.laparcela.net) offers up four simple, but ideally located individual cabins that sleep up to four people, for $85 per night, while the nearby **Coconut Grove** (✆ 2787-0130; www.coconutgrovecr.com) offers a mix of cottages and guesthouses with direct access to Dominicalito, for between $85 and $135 per double. If you're looking for luxury in this neck of the woods, I'd recommend **Kura Design Villas ★★** (✆ 8848-5744; www.kuracostarica.com) an all-villa, boutique hotel overlooking Ballena National Park and the other beautiful beaches of this area.

Moderate

Costa Paraiso Lodge With lush gardens and tall palm trees, this friendly small boutique hotel sits just above a series of rocky outcroppings and tide pools at the northern end of Dominicalito beach. The rooms are mostly fully equipped studio apartments. The Toucan Nest is the prized room here, a private bungalow in a prime location overlooking the sea. The other units are all part of two separate duplex buildings that primarily overlook the hotel's gardens and parking area. The lodge has a small swimming pool, as well as a handful of cool and shady common areas and gazebos for chilling out. Perhaps the best feature here is their excellent Por Que No? restaurant (see below).

2km (1¼ miles) south of Dominical, just off the coastal hwy., Dominicalito. ✆ **2787-0025.** www. costa-paraiso.com. 5 units. $140–$150 double. **Amenities:** Restaurant; small outdoor pool; free Wi-Fi.

Cuna del Angel ★★ This is a lovely little boutique hotel on a lush piece of property overlooking a gently sloping hill covered in thick rainforest with the Pacific Ocean below. While the standard "Jungle" rooms are perfectly fine, I recommend splurging for one of the "Deluxe" rooms. These are painted in warm ochre and amber tones, with plush linens, and feature either a private balcony or patio. The real splurge here, however, is the 3-bedroom villa "Can Shekinah", which is fully equipped with a top-notch kitchen and private pool. The La Palapa restaurant specializes in healthy cuisine and everything on the menu is gluten free. Every meal also has vegetarian and vegan choices, with most of the produce coming from the hotel's own

Get the Scoop

If you're venturing south of Dominical, you might want to stop in at the **Uvita Tourist Information Center** (✆ 2743-8072; www. uvita.info), right on the Costanera Sur, at the main intersection in Uvita. These folks are a wealth of knowledge, have a tour booking agency and rental car operation, and even function as the local branch of the Costa Rican post office, DHL, and UPS.

organic farm. This hotel has earned "4 Leaves" in the CST Sustainable Tourism program.

9km (5½ miles) south of Dominical, just off the coastal hwy. © **2787-4343.** www.cunadelangel. com. 23 units. $108–$196 double. Rates include buffet breakfast. **Amenities:** Restaurant; bar; Jacuzzi; midsize outdoor pool; sauna; small spa, free Wi-Fi.

La Cusinga Lodge ★   This is a small, sustainable ecolodge set on a lovely hillside with a view to Ballena National Park. Accommodations range from dorm rooms to private cabins. Locally produced reforested lumber and natural stones are used extensively throughout. Folks gather every afternoon in the beautiful open-air common area to take in the spectacular sunsets, while a large, open-air yoga center hosts regular classes and visiting retreat groups. A rugged trail leads down to a secluded beach, about a 10 to 15 minute walk away. The food is predominantly vegetarian and organic.

Bahía Ballena. © **2770-2549.** www.lacusingalodge.com. 10 units. $136–$172 double; $204 suite. Rates include breakfast and taxes. **Amenities:** Restaurant; small spa.

Pacific Edge ★   It's a steep bumpy ride up a dirt road to get here, but the payoff comes quick and lasts long in the form of amazing views. The individual wood cabins all feature spacious private balconies from which to take in the beautiful views. If you get tired of the view from your cabin, you can also enjoy it from the pool area, or climb the nearby lookout tower for even broader vistas. Owners George and Susie Atkisson opened this place more than 20 years ago, and they are still a vibrant and active presence here, and run a tight ship.

Dominical. © **2200-5428.** www.pacificedge.info. 5 units. $70–$110 double. Rates include taxes. No children under 13 years old. **Amenities:** Restaurant; midsize outdoor pool; free Wi-Fi.

Inexpensive

In addition to the place listed below, you'll find a campground at Playa Ballena and a couple of basic cabinas in Bahía and Uvita. The best of these is the **Tucan Hotel** (© **2743-8140;** www.tucanhotel.com), with a mix of private rooms and dorm accommodations and a friendly hostel-like vibe.

However, if you want to be closer to the beach, check out **Canto de Ballenas** (© **2743-8085;** www.hotelcantoballenas.com), an interesting local cooperative with neat rooms located about.7km (a little less than a half-mile) from the national park entrance at Playa Uvita.

Hotel Villas Gaia ★   Down towards the end of the Costanera Sur highway, this quiet place offers up a handful of individual bungalows scattered through lush forests. Each of the bungalows comes with wooden walls, polished concrete floors, and one twin and one Queen bed, as well as a private veranda. Most, but not all, have air-conditioning. The land here heads up from the highway, and the bungalows located at the top of the property, where you'll find the pool and pool bar, have great views over rain forests to the Pacific Ocean. The rest look out into the lush forests. Although do try to get one as far from the roadside and parking area as possible.

Playa Tortuga. © **2244-0316** reservations in San José, or 2786-5044 at the lodge. www.villas gaia.com. 14 units. $75 double. **Amenities:** Restaurant; bar; small outdoor pool.

WHERE TO DINE

In addition to the places mentioned below, in Ojochal you'll also find the charming **Ylang-Ylang ★★** (© **2786-5054**), which serves up Indonesian fare Wednesday through Saturday, for dinner only. Reservations required.

Citrus Restaurante ★★ BISTRO/FUSION This popular local spot mixes culinary influences from far and wide. You can start things off with a Caribbean inspired seafood soup with coconut milk and thyme, or fried calamari with a spicy Asian mayonnaise. For a main course, I recommend the yellow fin tuna with a Panko and wasabi crust served over organic soba noodles, with house-made tamarind-Siracha. There are also daily specials and a great range of cocktails and fresh fruit drinks. Whatever you do, be sure to save room for their basil and orange blossom crème brulee and their Belgian chocolate and brandy mousse. Weekend nights during the high season often feature live music or a DJ.

Just inland from the turnoff for Ojochal, in front of the police station. ✆ **2786-5175.** resto citrus@yahoo.ca. Reservations recommended. Main courses C5,000–C16,000. Daily 11am–10pm. Reduced hours in the off season.

Exotica ★★★ FRENCH/INTERNATIONAL Robert and Lucy's roadside restaurant is the grand dame of Ojochal's unexpectedly vibrant fine dining scene. Only a handful of tables are found under the open-air thatch roof that houses this place and you'll definitely want to have a reservation. This place is the furthest of the bunch from the main road, and you may think you're lost before finding your way here. Although rooted in classic French cuisine, the menu shows a wide range of worldly influences including hints of Thailand, Africa, and Costa Rica. There are daily specials, as well as longstanding favorites, like the namesake Chicken Exotica which comes in a red pepper sauce and is stuffed with bacon, prunes, and blue cheese.

1km (¹/₂ mile) inland from the turnoff for Ojochal. ✆ **2786-5050.** Reservations required. Main courses $8–$34. Mon–Sat 5–9pm.

Por Que No? ★★ FUSION This casual, open-air spot serves up some excellent grub in a lovely setting. The best tables have ocean and coastline views. I especially like the tables in the separate little gazebo furthest away from the main building and closest to the water. This is one of the best breakfast spots in the area, and as the day heats up, they also fire up their outdoor wood-burning brick pizza oven and serve gourmet pizzas for lunch and dinner. Sandwiches and full meals on buns range from jerk chicken to a veggie burger to the house special slow pulled pork with a pineapple barbeque sauce. You can also get a refreshing cold Asian noodle salad, or some blackened mahi-mahi with a coffee and chipotle rub.

At Costa Paraiso Lodge. 2km (1¹/₄ miles) south of Dominical, just off the coastal hwy., Dominicalito. ✆ **2787-0025.** www.cpporqueno.com. Main courses $7–$14; pizzas $16–$24. Tues–Sun 7am–1:30pm and 5–10pm.

SAN ISIDRO DE EL GENERAL: A BASE FOR EXPLORING CHIRRIPÓ NATIONAL PARK

120km (74 miles) SE of San José; 123km (76 miles) NW of Palmar Norte; 29km (18 miles) NE of Dominical

San Isidro de El General is just off the Interamerican Highway in the foothills of the Talamanca Mountains and is the largest town in this region. Although there

Little Devils

If you're visiting the San Isidro area in February, head out to the nearby **Rey Curré** village for the **Fiesta of the Diablitos,** where costumed Boruca Indians perform dances representative of the Spanish conquest of Central America. The 3-day event also includes fireworks and an Indian handicraft market—this is *the* best place in Costa Rica to buy hand-carved Boruca masks. The date varies, so it's best to call the **Costa Rica Tourist Board** (© 866/267-8274 in the U.S. and Canada) for more information.

isn't much to do right in town, this is the jumping-off point for trips to **Chirripó National Park.**

Essentials

GETTING THERE & DEPARTING   By Car: The long and winding stretch of the Interamerican Highway between San José and San Isidro is one of the most difficult sections of road in the country. Not only are there the usual car-eating potholes and periodic landslides, but you must also contend with driving over the 3,300m (10,824-ft.) **Cerro de la Muerte (Mountain of Death).** This aptly named mountain pass is legendary for its dense afternoon fogs, blinding torrential downpours, steep drop-offs, severe switchbacks, and unexpectedly breathtaking views. (Well, you wanted adventure travel, so here you go!) Drive with extreme care, and bring a sweater or sweatshirt—it's cold up at the top. It'll take you about 3 hours to get to San Isidro.

Tip: If you want a break from the road, stop for a coffee or meal at **Mirador Valle del General** (© 8384-4685 or 2200-5465; www.valledelgeneral.com; at Km 119), a rustic roadside joint with a great view, gift shop, hiking trails, and orchid collection. These folks also have a few rustic cabins, as well as a zip-line canopy tour.

By Bus: Musoc buses (© 2222-2422 in San José, or 2771-0414 in San Isidro) leave from their terminal at Calle Central and Avenida 22 roughly hourly between 5:30am and 6:30pm. **Tracopa** (© 2221-4214 or 2771-0468; www.tracopa.com) also runs express buses between San José and San Isidro that leave at 6 and 8:30am and 12:30, 2:30, 4, and 6:30pm from Calle 5, between avenidas 18 and 20. Whichever company you choose, the trip takes a little over 3 hours, and the fare is roughly C3.600. Return buses depart San Isidro for **San José** roughly every hour between 4:30am and 6:30pm.

Buses from **Quepos** to San Isidro leave daily at 5:30 and 11:30am and 3:30pm. The trip duration is 3 hours; the fare is C2,500. Buses to or from **Golfito** and **Puerto Jiménez** will also drop you off in San Isidro.

CITY LAYOUT   Downtown San Isidro is just off the Interamerican Highway. A large church fronts the central park, and you'll find several banks, and a host of restaurants, shops, and hotels within a 2-block radius of this park. The main bus station is 2 blocks west of the north end of the central park.

Exploring Chirripó National Park ★★

At 3,819m (12,526 ft.) in elevation, Mount Chirripó is the tallest mountain in Costa Rica. If you're headed up this way, come prepared for chilly weather. Actually, dress in layers and come prepared for all sorts of weather: Because of the great elevations, temperatures frequently dip below freezing, especially at night. However, during the day, temperatures can soar—remember, you're still only 9 degrees from the equator. The elevation and radical temperatures have produced an environment here that's very different from the Costa Rican norm. Above 3,000m (9,840 ft.), only stunted trees and shrubs survive in páramos. If you're driving the Interamerican Highway between San Isidro and San José, you'll pass through a páramo on the Cerro de la Muerte.

Hiking up to the top of Mount Chirripó is one of Costa Rica's best adventures. On a clear day (usually in the morning), an unforgettable **view ★★★** is your reward: You can see both the Pacific Ocean and the Caribbean Sea from the summit. You can do this trip fairly easily on your own if you've brought gear and are an experienced backpacker. Although it's possible to hike from the park entrance to the summit and back down in 2 days (in fact, some daredevils even do it in 1 day), it's best to allow 3 to 4 days for the trip in order to give yourself time to enjoy your hike fully and spend some time on top, because that's where the glacier lakes and páramos are. For much of the way, you'll be hiking through cloud forests that are home to abundant tropical fauna, including the spectacular **quetzal,** Costa Rica's most beautiful bird. However, quetzal sightings on summit climbs are rare. If you really want to see one of these birds, head to one of the specialized lodges listed below.

Several routes lead to the top of Mount Chirripó. The most popular, by far, leaves from **San Gerardo de Rivas.** However, it's also possible to start your hike from the nearby towns of **Herradura** or **Canaan.** All these places are within less than 2km (a mile) or so of each other, reached by the same major road out of San Isidro. San Gerardo is the most popular because it's the easiest route to the top and has the greatest collection of small hotels and lodges, as well as the National Parks office. Information on all of these routes is available at the parks office.

Movin' On Up

From San Gerardo de Rivas, the 14.5km (9-mile) trail to the summit lodge is well marked and well maintained. The early parts of the trail are pretty steep and will take you through thick cloud forests and rainforests. After about 7.5km (4.7 miles), you will reach the "Water Ridge," a flat ridge that features a small shelter and water spigot. This is roughly the midway point to the lodge and a great place to take a break.

From Water Ridge, three steep uphill sections remain: Cuesta de Agua (Water Hill), Monte Sin Fe (Mountain without Hope), and La Cuesta de los Arrepentidos (The Hill of Regret). As you continue to climb, you will notice the flora changing. The entire elevation gain for this hike is 2,200m (7,215 ft.). La Cuesta de los Arrepentidos, your final ascent, brings you to a broad flat valley, where you'll find the summit lodge. This hike can take anywhere from 6 to 10 hours, depending on how long you linger along the way.

Mount Chirripó.

When you're at the summit lodge, you have a number of hiking options. Just in front of the lodge are Los Crestones (the Crests), an impressive rock formation, with trails leading up and around them. The most popular, however, is to the actual summit (the lodge itself is a bit below the summit itself), which is about a 2-hour hike that passes through the Valle de los Conejos (Rabbit Valley) and the Valle de los Lagos (Valley of Lakes). Other hikes and trails lead off from the summit lodge, and it's easy to spend a couple of days hiking around here. A few trails will take you to the summits of several neighboring peaks. These hikes should be undertaken only after carefully studying an accurate map and talking to park rangers and other hikers.

Warning: It can be dangerous for more inexperienced or out-of-shape hikers to climb Chirripó, especially by themselves. It's not very technical climbing, but it is a long, arduous hike. If you're not sure you're up for it, you can just take day hikes out of San Isidro and/or San Gerardo de Rivas, or ask at your hotel about guides.

ENTRY POINT, FEES & REGULATIONS   Although it's not that difficult to get to Chirripó National Park from nearby San Isidro, it's still rather remote. And to see it fully, you have to be prepared to hike. To get to the trail head, you have three choices: car, taxi, or bus. If you choose to drive, take the road out of San Isidro, heading north toward San Gerardo de Rivas, which is some 20km (12 miles) down the road. Otherwise, you can catch a bus in San Isidro that will take you directly to the trail head in San Gerardo de Rivas. Buses leave daily at 9:30am and 2 and 6:45pm from the bus station beside the central market, a block or so south of San Isidro's central park. It costs C910 one-way and takes 1¹⁄₂ hours. Buses return to San Isidro daily at 5:15 and 11:30am and 4pm. A taxi from town should cost around C15,000 to C20,000. Because the hike to the summit of Mount Chirripó can take between 6 and 12 hours, depending on your physical condition, I recommend taking a taxi, so that you can start hiking when the day is still young. Better still, you should arrive the day before and spend the night in San Gerardo de Rivas (there are several inexpensive cabinas, a couple of mid-range options, and one very nice hotel there) before setting out early the following morning.

Before climbing Mount Chirripó, you must make a reservation and check in with the **National Parks office** (✆ **2742-5083;** reservacioneschirripo@gmail.com) in San Gerardo de Rivas. The office is open from 8am to noon and 1 to 4pm, Monday through Friday for reservations, but opens at 6:30am for hikers and walk-in traffic. Only 25 slots per day are available, and the park service is notoriously fickle about when they open these slots up. Without excellent Spanish skills and persistence, it's very hard to reserve a slot in advance. That said, 10 additional slots are opened up each day for walk-in reservations. If you arrive the day before, you should almost always be able to get a slot to climb and stay in the lodge the following day. In some cases, you may have to wait an extra day. The park service only allows a maximum of 2 nights at the lodge.

Even if you have a reservation, I recommend checking in the day before you plan to climb. Note that camping is not allowed in the park. It's possible to have your gear carried up to the summit by horseback during the dry season (Dec–Apr). **Guides** (✆ **2742-5225**) work outside the park entrance in San Gerardo de Rivas. They charge between $25 and $35 per pack, depending on size and weight. In the rainy season, the same guides work, but they take packs up by themselves, not by horseback. The guides like to take up the packs well before dawn, so arrangements are best made the day before. The entrance fee to the national park is $18 per day.

Note: The park is closed each year from May 15 to 31, and all of October.

STAYING AT THE SUMMIT LODGE Once you get to the lodge, you'll find various rooms with bunk beds, several bathrooms and showers, and a common kitchen area. It has good drinking water. However, blankets, lanterns, and cookstoves are no longer for rent up top, so you have to pack all your own gear, as well as food and water (for the hike up). **Note:** It gets cold up here at night, and the lodge seems to have been designed to be as cold, dark, and cavernous as possible. The showers are freezing. It costs $10 per person per night to stay here.

Other Adventures in & Around San Isidro

If you want to undertake any other adventures while in San Isidro, contact **Costa Rica Trekking Adventures** (✆ **2771-4582;** www.chirripo.com), which offers organized treks through Chirripó National Park, as well as white-water rafting trips and other adventure tours and activities.

Just 7km (4$^1/_3$ miles) from San Isidro is **Las Quebradas Biological Center** (✆ **2771-4131**), a community-run private reserve with 2.7km (1.75 miles) of trails through primary rainforest. The rustic lodge for visitors and researchers is $8 per person (C25,000 per person, if part of group, including three meals and entrance to the center), and camping is also permitted. You can hike the trails and visit the small information center on site for $4. From San Isidro, you can take a local bus to Quebradas, but you'll have to walk the last mile to the entrance. You can also take a taxi for around C7,000. If you're driving, take the road to Morazán and Quebradas.

Where to Stay & Dine in San Isidro

San Isidro doesn't have much of a dining scene. Sure, the town has its fair share of local joints, but most visitors are content at their hotel restaurant. If you do

---

Race to the Top

If simply climbing the tallest peak in Costa Rica is a bit too mundane for you, why not join the annual **Carrera Campo Traviesa Al Cerro Chirripó** (www.carrera chirripo.com). Held the third or fourth Saturday of February, this is a grueling 34km (21-mile) race from the base to the summit and back. The record time, to date, is 3 hours, 15 minutes, and 3 seconds.

---

venture beyond your hotel, I recommend the tacos, nachos, and burritos served up at **Taquería México Lindo** (© 2771-8222), in the Centro Comercial Pedro Perez Zeledon, just across from the central park. Although the food is mediocre, the second-floor, open-air balcony seating at **La Cascada** (© 2771-6479), right in the town center, offers some excellent opportunities for people-watching, and is a great place to mingle with locals. For a coffee break or light meal, I like **Kafe de la Casa ★** (© 2770-4816), which offers up free Wi-Fi, along with its regular breakfast, lunch, and dinner menu, and is located next to the **Thunderbird Hotel & Casino** (© 2770-6230; www.tbrcr.com).

INEXPENSIVE

Hotel Los Crestones   Central San Isidro doesn't have a lot of great hotel choices, but this downtown option is perhaps the best. The three-story building features basic rooms with tile floors and bare white walls. A small television is hung in the corner, and the hotel has a swimming pool and outdoor Jacuzzi for guests to use. This place is on the main road heading out to Dominical, on the south side of the city, near the main soccer stadium.

San Isidro de El General (southwest side of the stadium). © **2770-1200.** www.hotelloscrestones. com. 27 units. $50–$60 double. **Amenities:** Restaurant; outdoor pool; room service.

Where to Stay & Dine Closer to the Trail Head

If you're climbing Mount Chirripó, you'll want to spend the night as close to the trail head as possible. As I mention above, several basic cabinas right in San Gerardo de Rivas charge between $10 and $30 per person. The best of these are **El Descanso** (© 2742-5061; www.hoteleldescansocr.com), **Casa Mariposa** (© 2742-5037; www.hotelcasamariposa.net), and **Roca Dura** (© 2742-5071; hotelrocadura@hotmail.com). If you're looking for a little more comfort and a swimming pool, check out **El Pelicano** (© 2742-5050; www.hotel pelicano.net), the **Río Chirripó Retreat** (© 2742-5109; www.riochirripo. com), or the hotels listed below.

For good general information on the tiny village and its surrounding area, check out www.sangerardocostarica.com.

VERY EXPENSIVE

Monte Azul ★★★   This is one of the most unique, remote and artistic boutique hotels in the country. There are just four individual casitas, or cabins, spread around lush grounds and gardens on the banks of the Chirripó River. Each cabin has a Queen bed, small kitchenette and private garden area. The owners are art collectors and have a huge studio space on the grounds, where they often host visiting artists in residency. They also have an extensive contemporary art and sculpture collection throughout around the hotel. The excellent restaurant is dedicated to using organic and locally produced fruits, vegetables, coffees, meats, and cheeses. They also offer up a range of cooking, baking, and drink mixing classes.

Rivas, San Isidro. (*C*) **2742-5222.** www.monteazulcr.com. 4 units. $368 casita. Rates include full breakfast and dinner. **Amenities:** Restaurant; bar; concierge; free Wi-Fi

INEXPENSIVE

Talari Mountain Lodge This place offers up more comfortable rooms and better grounds than the cluster of backpacker hotels near the Chirripó National Park entrance. This still serves as a good base, either before or after climbing to the summit, but it also caters to bird watching groups and folks looking to get away from it all. The lodge is set on the banks of the Río General, some 8km (5 miles) outside of San Isidro. The rooms are housed in a couple of simple buildings set on plain concrete blocks, and while cozy, certainly feel as if they could use a little upkeep and modernization.

Rivas, San Isidro. (*C*) **2771-0341.** www.talari.co.cr. 14 units. $80 double. Rates include full breakfast. **Amenities:** Restaurant; bar; Jacuzzi; small outdoor pool and separate children's pool; indoor lit tennis court.

Where to See Quetzals in the Wild: Cerro de la Muerte & San Gerardo de Dota ★★

Between San José and San Isidro de El General, the Interamerican Highway climbs to its highest point in Costa Rica and crosses over the **Cerro de la Muerte (the Mountain of Death).** About midway between San Isidro and Cartago, a deep valley descends toward the Pacific coast and the tiny town of San Gerardo de Dota. This area is one of the best places in Costa Rica to see quetzals. March through May is nesting season for these birds, and this is usually the best time to see them. However, it's often possible to spot them year round. On my first visit here, during a 2-hour hike without a guide, my small group spotted eight of these amazing birds. I was hooked.

If you plan on spending any time in the region and want to take an organized tour, contact **Santos Tours ★** ((*C*) **8855-9386;** www.santostour.net), a local, community tourism project that offers a range of active adventures, including waterfall hikes, coffee plantation tours, and even a canopy tour.

In addition to the places listed below, **Dantica Cloud Forest Lodge ★** ((*C*) **2740-1067;** www.dantica.com) is a small collection of lovely, private bungalows in a beautiful forested setting near the town of San Gerardo de Dota.

MODERATE

Savegre Hotel ★ Also known as Finca Chacón, this place is owned by the local Chacón family, who were pioneers in converting this remote rural farming

---

Rest Your Weary Muscles Here

If you're tired and sore from so much hiking, be sure to check out the small **Aguas Termales Gevi** ((*C*) 2742-5016), located off the road between San Gerardo de Rivas and Herradura. The entrance to these humble hot springs is 1km (1/2 mile) beyond San Gerardo de Rivas. There are two small pools here, as well as showers and changing rooms. The entrance fee is C3,500.

area into a mecca for bird watchers and ecotourists. This small resort is spread around a working apple and pear farm. These fruit trees, as well as the surrounding cloud and rain forests, attract more than 180 species of birds, including the prized Resplendent Quetzal. The rooms are clean and spacious, with tile floors and wood paneling on the walls. Each comes with a little space heater or fireplace, which is often necessary. The lodge is 9km (5½ miles) down a rugged dirt road off the Interamerican Highway. Four-wheel-drive is recommended, although not absolutely necessary

Carretera Interamericana Sur Km 80, San Gerardo de Dota. ✆ **2740-1028.** www.savegre.com. 50 units. $120–$141 double. Rates include breakfast, entrance to their reserve, and taxes. Rates slightly lower in the off season. **Amenities:** Restaurant; bar; spa; free Wi-Fi.

Trogon Lodge ★   This is a pretty little lodge in a beautiful setting. The rooms are in individual and duplex buildings scattered over rolling hillsides and well-tended gardens. The rooms are simple and rustic, and could use a little more light, but they do have gas heaters and plenty of room, and most have a very pleasant little porch or veranda. Trout ponds and a zip-line canopy tour are on site here. Even if you don't fish for the trout yourself—which you can do—you'll often find it on the menu here. This is a sister lodge to Mawamba Lodge (p. 460) in Tortuguero.

Carretera Interamericana Sur Km 80, San Gerardo de Dota. ✆ **2293-8181** in San José, or 2740-1051 at the lodge. www.grupomawamba.com. 23 units. $94 double; $150 junior suite with Jacuzzi. Rates include breakfast. A full meal package runs $30–$39 per person. **Amenities:** Restaurant; bar; lounge.

INEXPENSIVE

Albergue Mirador de Quetzales   This is one of the simpler and more rustic of the quetzal viewing lodges in this area. It's also the closest to the main highway. Also, known as Finca Eddie Serrano, it is run by the friendly local Serrano family. Choose from a series of small wooden cabins and Λ-frame cabins, as well as a few dormitory rooms in the main lodge building. Meals are served family style and both breakfast and dinner are included in the rates, as is a two-hour guided tour of trails through the lodge's private reserve. The quetzal viewing at this place is as good as it gets, especially between December and May, although they can often be spotted year round.

Carretera Interamericana Sur Km 70, about 1km (½ mile) down a dirt road from the hwy. ✆ **8381-8456** or 2200-4185. www.elmiradordequetzales.com. 15 units. $60 per person. Rate includes breakfast and dinner, a 2-hr. tour, and taxes. **Amenities:** Restaurant.

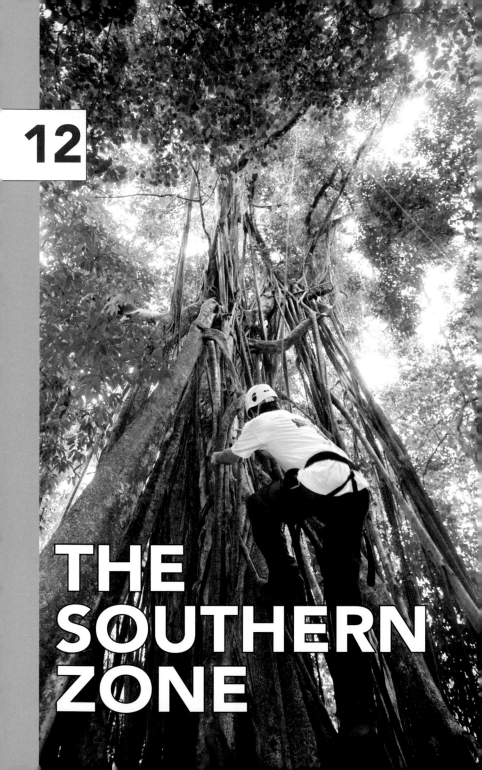

12

THE
SOUTHERN
ZONE

Costa Rica's southern zone is an area of jaw-dropping beauty, with vast expanses of virgin lowland rainforest, loads of wildlife, tons of adventure opportunities, and few cities, towns, or settlements. Lushly forested mountains tumble into the sea, streams still run clear and clean, scarlet macaws squawk raucously in the treetops, and dolphins frolic in the Golfo Dulce. The Osa Peninsula is the most popular attraction in this region and one of the premier ecotourism destinations in the world. It's home to **Corcovado National Park ★★★**, the largest single expanse of lowland tropical rainforest in Central America, and its sister, **Piedras Blancas National Park ★★**. Scattered around the edges of these national parks and along the shores of the Golfo Dulce are some of the country's finest nature lodges. These lodges, in general, offer comfortable to nearly luxurious accommodations, attentive service, knowledgeable guides, and a wide range of activities and tours, all close to the area's many natural wonders.

But this beauty doesn't come easy. You must have plenty of time (or plenty of money—or, preferably, both) and a desire for adventure. It's a long way from San José, and many of the most fascinating spots can be reached only by small plane or boat—although hiking and four-wheeling will get you into some memorable surroundings as well. In many ways, this is Costa Rica's final frontier, and the cities of Golfito and Puerto Jiménez are nearly as wild as the jungles that surround them. Tourism is still underdeveloped here, with no large resorts in this neck of the woods. Moreover, the heat and humidity are more than some people can stand. It's best to put some forethought into planning a vacation down here, and wise to book your rooms and transportation in advance.

THE BEST SOUTHERN ZONE TRAVEL EXPERIENCES

o **Hiking in Corcovado National Park:** The Neotropic's largest single tract of lowland rainforest provides fabulous hiking opportunities, with beautiful forest trails, isolated jungle waterfalls, and a bounty of wildlife spotting opportunities. See p. 423.

o **Paddling a Kayak on the Golfo Dulce:** The calm, protected waters of the "Sweet Gulf" are perfect for kayaking. Gorgeous sunsets and dolphin or whale sightings are additional perks that sometimes come with the territory. See p. 422.

PREVIOUS PAGE: **Climbing a strangler fig on the Psycho Tour.**

- **Landing a Billfish:** The waters of southern Costa Rica are some of the country's richest fishing grounds, with a long list of world record catches. Hook a blue marlin or sailfish for some serious deep sea adventure. See p. 422.

- **Scuba Diving or Snorkeling at Caño Island:** The clear waters around this isolated Pacific island consistently offer up Costa Rica's best snorkeling and scuba diving. You're almost guaranteed to see white tip reef sharks. See p. 415.

The Southern Zone's Top Sustainable Hotels

Bosque del Cabo Rainforest Lodge (p. 429)
Casa Corcovado Jungle Lodge (p. 417)
El Remanso (p. 429)
Golfo Dulce Lodge (p. 436)
Iguana Lodge (p. 428)
La Paloma Lodge (p. 417)
Lapa Ríos (p. 429)
Luna Lodge (p. 430)
Playa Nicuesa Rainforest Lodge (p. 437)
Tiskita Jungle Lodge (p. 445)

- **Riding a Seemingly Endless Wave in Pavones:** This legendary left is well known and probably best left to serious surfers. However, even if this is beyond your ken, a host of other point breaks around the southern zone are perfect for more intermediate surfers, and even rank beginners. See p. 442.

DRAKE BAY ★★

145km (90 miles) S of San José; 32km (20 miles) SW of Palmar

While Drake Bay remains one of the more isolated spots in Costa Rica, the small town located at the mouth of the **Río Agujitas** has boomed a bit over the years. Most of that is due to the year-round operation of the small airstrip here, and the

Dolphin-watching tour in Drake Bay.

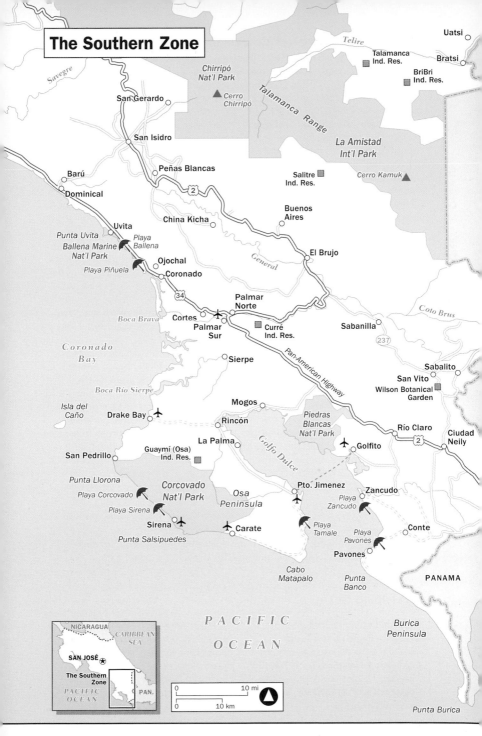

The Southern Zone

Uatsi

Telire

Talamanca
Ind. Res.

Bratsi

BriBri
Ind. Res.

Savegre

Chirripó
Nat'l Park

Talamanca Range

▲ Cerro
Chirripó

San Gerardo

La Amistad
Int'l Park

San Isidro

Cerro Kamuk ▲

Peñas Blancas

Salitre
Ind. Res.

Barú

2

Dominical

Buenos
Aires

China Kicha

Uvita

El Brujo

Punta Uvita

Playa
Ballena

Ballena Marine
Nat'l Park

General

Ojochal

Playa Piñuela

Coronado

Coto Brus

34

Palmar
Norte

Boca Brava

Cortes

Sabanilla

Palmar
Sur

Curré
Ind. Res.

Coronado
Bay

237

Sierpe

Pan-American Highway

Sabalito

Boca Río Sierpe

San Vito

Mogos

Wilson Botanical
Garden

Isla del
Caño

Drake Bay

Piedras
Blancas
Nat'l Park

Río Claro

Rincón

Ciudad
Neily

La Palma

Golfito

2

San Pedrillo

Guaymí (Osa)
Ind. Res.

Golfo Dulce

Punta Llorona

Corcovado
Nat'l Park

Osa
Peninsula

Pto. Jimenez

Zancudo

Playa Corcovado

Playa
Zancudo

Playa Sirena

Sirena

Carate

Playa
Tamale

Conte

Punta Salsipuedes

Playa
Pavones

Pavones

Cabo
Matapalo

Punta
Banco

PANAMA

PACIFIC

Burica
Peninsula

OCEAN

NICARAGUA

CARIBBEAN
SEA

SAN JOSÉ ✪

The Southern
Zone

PACIFIC
OCEAN

PAN.

0   10 mi
0   10 km

Punta Burica

sometimes passable condition of the rough dirt road connecting Drake Bay to the coastal highway—just a decade or so ago there was no road, and the nearest regularly functioning airstrip was in Palmar Sur. That said, the village of Drake Bay is still tiny, and the lodges listed here remain quiet and remote getaways catering to naturalists, anglers, and scuba divers. Tucked away on the northern edge of the Osa Peninsula, Drake Bay is a great place to get away from it all.

The bay is named after Sir Francis Drake, who is believed to have anchored here in 1579. Emptying into a broad bay, the tiny Río Agujitas acts as a protected harbor for small boats and is a great place to do a bit of canoeing or swimming. Many of the local lodges dock their boats and many **dolphin- and whale-watching tours** leave from here. Stretching south from Drake Bay are miles of deserted beaches and dense primary tropical rainforest. Adventurous explorers will find tide pools, spring-fed rivers, waterfalls, forest trails, and some of the best bird-watching in all of Costa Rica. If a paradise such as this appeals to you, Drake Bay makes a good base for exploring the peninsula.

South of Drake Bay are the wilds of the **Osa Peninsula,** including **Corcovado National Park.** This is one of Costa Rica's most beautiful regions, yet it's also one of its least accessible. Corcovado National Park covers about half of the peninsula and contains the largest single expanse of virgin lowland rainforest in Central America. For this reason, Corcovado is well known among naturalists and researchers studying rainforest ecology. If you come here, you'll learn firsthand why they call them rainforests: Some parts of the peninsula receive more than 635cm (250 in.) of rain per year.

Puerto Jiménez (p. 418) is the best base if you want to spend a lot of time hiking in and camping inside Corcovado National Park. Drake Bay is primarily a collection of mostly high-end hotels, very isolated and mostly accessible only by boat. Travelers using these hotels can have great day hikes and guided tours into Corcovado Park, but Puerto Jiménez is the place if you want to have more time in the park or to explore independently. (It has budget hotels, the parks office, and "taxi/bus" service to Carate and Los Patos, from which visitors can hike into the various stations.) From the Drake Bay side, you're much more dependent on a boat ride/organized tour from one of the lodges to explore the park; these lodges offer many other guided outings in addition to visits to the park.

Essentials

Because Drake Bay is so remote, I recommend that you have a room reservation and transportation arrangements (usually arranged with your hotel) before you arrive. Most of the lodges listed here are scattered along several kilometers of coastline, and it is not easy to go from one to another looking for a room.

Helping Out

If you want to help local efforts in protecting the fragile rainforests and wild areas of the Osa Peninsula, contact the **Corcovado Foundation** (✆ **2297-3013;** www.corcovadofoundation.org) or **Osa Conservation** (✆ **2735-5756;** www. osaconservation.org).

Moreover, if you're looking to really lend a hand, both of the aforementioned groups have volunteer programs ranging from trail maintenance to environmental and English-language education to sea-turtle-nesting protection programs.

HOTELS

Aguila de Osa Inn **2**
Casa Corcovado Jungle Lodge **8**
Copa del Arbol **6**
Drake Bay Wilderness Resort **3**
Finca Maresia **5**
Guaria de Osa **7**
Hotel Jinetes de Osa **1**
La Paloma Lodge **4**

Tip: A flashlight and rain gear are always useful to have on hand in Costa Rica; they're absolutely essential in Drake Bay.

GETTING THERE   By Plane: Most people fly directly into the little airstrip at Drake Bay (no phone; airport code: DRK), although some tourists still fly to Palmar Sur (p. 411). All lodges will either arrange transportation for you, or include it in their packages. Both **Nature Air** (© **800/235-9272** in the U.S. and Canada, or 2299-6000 in Costa Rica; www.natureair.com) and **Sansa** (© **877/767-2672** in the U.S. and Canada, or 2290-4100 in Costa Rica; www.flysansa.com) fly directly to Drake Bay twice from San José's Juan Santamaría International Airport. Flights also depart San José daily from the same airport for Palmar Sur. If you're connecting Drake Bay to Manuel Antonio, you are best off using the Palmar Sur connection, as there are direct flights between Quepos and Palmar Sur, but not between Quepos and Drake Bay. Fares range from $120 to $160 each way.

If your travels take you to Drake Bay via Palmar Sur, you must then take a 15-minute bus or taxi ride over dirt roads to the small town of **Sierpe.** This bumpy route runs through several **banana plantations** and quickly past some important archaeological sites. In Sierpe, you board a small boat for a 40km (25-mile) ride to Drake Bay; see "By Taxi & Boat from Sierpe," below. The first half of this trip snakes through a maze of mangrove canals and rivers before heading out to sea for the final leg to the bay. ***Warning:*** Entering and exiting the Sierpe River mouth is often treacherous; I've had several very white-knuckle moments here.

By Bus: Tracopa buses (🕿 **2221-4214** or 2258-8939; www.tracopacr.com) leave San José daily for the southern zone throughout the day, between 5am and 6:30pm from Calle 5, between avenidas 18 and 20. Almost all stop in Palmar Norte, but make sure to ask. The ride takes around 6 hours; the fare is C5,500.

Once in Palmar Norte, ask when the next bus goes out to Sierpe. If it doesn't leave for a while (buses aren't frequent), consider taking a taxi (see below).

By Taxi & Boat from Sierpe: When you arrive at either the Palmar Norte bus station or the Palmar Sur airstrip (airport code: PMZ), you'll most likely first need to take a taxi to the village of Sierpe. The fare should be around $15. If you're booked into one of the main lodges, chances are your transportation is

A flowering banana plant.

included. Even if you're not booked into one of the lodges, a host of taxi and minibus drivers offer the trip. When you get to Sierpe, head to the dock and try to find space on a boat. This should run you another $20 to $40. If you don't arrive early enough, you might have to hire an entire boat, which usually runs around $100 to $150 for a boat that can carry up to six passengers. Make sure that you feel confident about the boat and skipper, and, if possible, try to find a spot on a boat from one of the established lodges in Drake Bay.

By Car: I don't recommend driving to Drake Bay. But if you insist, take the San José–Caldera Highway (CR27) to the first exit past the Pozón toll booth, where you will pick up the Southern Highway, or Costanera Sur (CR34). Take this south through Jacó, Quepos, and Dominical to Palmar Norte, where you'll meet up with the Interamerican Highway (CR2). Take this south to the turnoff for La Palma, Rincón, and Puerto Jiménez (at the town of Chacarita; it's clearly marked). Then at Rincón, turn onto the rough road leading into Drake Bay. This road fords some 10 rivers and is often not passable during the rainy season. Moreover, it only reaches into the small heart of the village of Drake Bay, though almost all of the hotels I list below are farther out along the peninsula, where only boats reach. The only hotels that you can actually drive up to are very basic cabins in town. For the rest, you'd have to find someplace secure to leave your car and either haul your bags quite a way or get picked up in a boat.

DEPARTING If you're not flying directly out of Drake Bay, have your lodge arrange a boat trip back to Sierpe for you. Be sure that the lodge also arranges for a taxi to meet you in Sierpe for the trip to Palmar Sur or Palmar Norte. (If you're on a budget, you can ask around to see whether a late-morning public bus is still running from Sierpe to Palmar Norte.) In the two Palmars, you can make onward plane and bus connections. At the Palmar Norte bus terminal, almost any bus heading north will take you to San José, and almost any bus heading south will take you to Golfito.

Exploring Drake Bay

Beaches, forests, wildlife, and solitude are the main attractions of Drake Bay. Although Corcovado National Park (see "Puerto Jiménez: Gateway to Corcovado National Park," below) is the area's star attraction, plenty of other attractions are in and around Drake Bay. The Osa Peninsula is home to an unbelievable variety of plants and animals: more than 140 species of mammals, some 400 species of birds, and 130 species of amphibians and reptiles. You aren't likely to see anywhere near all of these animals, but you can expect to see quite a few, including several types of monkeys, coatimundis, scarlet macaws, parrots, and hummingbirds. Other park inhabitants include jaguars, tapirs, sloths, and crocodiles. If you're lucky, you might even see one of the region's namesake *osas,* or giant anteaters.

Around Drake Bay and within the national park are many miles of trails through rainforests and swamps, down beaches, and around rock headlands. All of the lodges listed below offer guided excursions into the park. It's also possible to begin a hike around the peninsula from Drake Bay.

All lodges in the area have their own in-house tour operations and offer a host of half- and full-day tours and activities, including hikes in Corcovado National Park, trips to Caño Island, horseback rides, and sportfishing. In some cases, tours are included in your room rate or package; in others, they must be bought a la carte. Other options include mountain biking and sea kayaking. Most

A Baird's tapir.

THOSE MYSTERIOUS stone spheres

Although Costa Rica lacks the great cities, giant temples, and bas-relief carvings of the Maya, Aztec, and Olmec civilizations of northern Mesoamerica, its pre-Columbian residents did leave a unique legacy that continues to cause archaeologists and anthropologists to scratch their heads and wonder. Over a period of several centuries, hundreds of painstakingly carved and carefully positioned granite spheres were left by the peoples who lived throughout the Diquís Delta, which flanks the Terraba River in southern Costa Rica. The orbs, which range from grapefruit size to more than 2m (6½ ft.) in diameter, can weigh up to 15 tons, and many reach near-spherical perfection.

Archaeologists believe that the spheres were created during two defined cultural periods. The first, called the Aguas Buenas period, dates from around a.d. 100 to 500. Few spheres survive from this time. The second phase, during which spheres were created in apparently greater numbers, is called the Chiriquí period and lasted from approximately a.d. 800 to 1500. The "balls" believed to have been carved during this time frame are widely dispersed along the entire length of the lower section of the Terraba River. To date, only one known quarry for the spheres has been discovered, in the mountains above the Diquís Delta, which points to a difficult and lengthy transportation process.

Some archaeologists believe that the spheres were hand-carved in a very time-consuming process, using stone tools, perhaps aided by some sort of firing process. However, another theory holds that granite blocks were placed at the bases of powerful waterfalls, and the hydraulic beating of the water eventually turned and carved the rock into these near-perfect spheres. And more than a few proponents have credited extraterrestrial intervention for the creation of the stone balls.

Most of the stone balls have been found at the archaeological remains of defined settlements and are associated with either central plazas or known burial sites. Their size and placement have been interpreted to have both social and celestial importance, although their exact significance remains a mystery. Unfortunately, many of the stone balls have been plundered and are currently used as lawn ornaments in the fancier neighborhoods of San José. Some have even been shipped out of the country. The **Museo Nacional de Costa Rica** (p. 121) has a nice collection, including one massive sphere in its center courtyard. It's a never-fail photo op. You can also see the stone balls near the small **airports in Palmar Sur** and **Drake Bay,** and on **Isla del Caño** (which is 19km/12 miles off the Pacific coast near Drake Bay).

Snorkelers at Caño Island Biological Reserve.

of these tours run between $60 and $120, depending on the activity, with scuba diving ($100–$140 for a two-tank dive) and sportfishing ($450–$1,500, depending on the size of the boat and other amenities) costing a bit more.

CANOPY TOUR   If you want to try a zip-line canopy adventure, the **Drake Bay Canopy Tour** (✆ **8314-5454;** www.canopytourdrakebay.com) has six cable runs, several "Tarzan swings," and a hanging bridge, all set in lush forests just outside of Drake Bay. The 2-hour tour costs $39.

ISLA DEL CAÑO   One of the most popular excursions from Drake Bay is a trip out to **Isla del Caño** and the **Caño Island Biological Reserve ★★** for a bit of exploring and snorkeling or scuba diving. The island is about 19km (12 miles) offshore from Drake Bay and was once home to a pre-Columbian culture about which little is known. A trip to the island might include a visit to an ancient cemetery, and you'll also be able to see some of the stone spheres believed to have been carved by this area's ancient inhabitants (see "Those Mysterious Stone Spheres," p. 414). Few animals or birds live on the island, but the coral reefs just offshore teem with life and are the main reason most people come here. This is one of Costa Rica's prime **scuba diving sites ★★**. Visibility is often quite good, and the beach has easily accessible snorkeling. All of the lodges listed below offer trips to Isla del Caño. As of 2014, the Costa Rican National Park service has been severely restricting access to the island, and visiting groups are no longer allowed to picnic on the island. Typically, tours arrive in the morning, conduct their snorkel and scuba excursions, and then head back to the mainland for a picnic lunch and some beach time.

NIGHT TOUR   One of the most interesting tour options in Drake Bay is a 2-hour **night tour ★★★** (✆ **8701-7356;** www.thenighttour.com; $35 per person) offered by Tracie Stice, who is affectionately known as the "Bug Lady," and her partner Gianfranco Gómez. Equipped with flashlights, participants get a bug's-eye view of the forest at night. You might see reflections of some larger forest dwellers, but most of the tour is a fascinating exploration of the nocturnal insect and arachnid world, with the occasional discovery of some frogs, toads, or snakes. Consider yourself lucky if she finds the burrow of a trap-door spider or large tarantula. Any hotel in Drake Bay can book the tour for you. However, the travel distance makes it impossible for those staying at hotels outside of walking distance of the town.

WHALE-WATCHING Drake Bay is one of the best places to go **whale-watching** in Costa Rica; humpback whales are commonly spotted in the area between late July and November and December through March. There are currently no dedicated whale-watching operators in the area, but all the hotels listed below can arrange whale-watching, as well as dolphin-spotting, trips.

Drake Bay Beach.

Two resident marine biologists, Shawn Larkin and Roy Sancho, are often hired by the better hotels, but depending on demand and availability, the hotels may send you out with one of their own guides and/or captains.

If you want more information on the local whale-watching scene, or to contact Shawn Larkin directly, head to the website **www.costacetacea.com**. These folks also offer deep-water free diving and snorkel tours aimed at providing the chance to swim in close proximity to the large pelagic fish, mammals, and reptiles found in the area.

Where to Stay & Dine

Given the remote location and logistics of reaching Drake Bay, as well as the individual isolation of each hotel, nearly all the hotels listed below deal almost exclusively in package trips that include transportation, meals, tours, and taxes. I

Where's the Beach?

While the beach at Drake Bay itself is acceptable and calm for swimming, it's far from spectacular. The most popular swimming beach is a pretty small patch of sand, known locally as Cocalito beach, about a 7-minute hike down from La Paloma Lodge. The nicest beaches around involve taking a day trip to either Isla del Caño or San Josesito. The latter is a stunning beach farther south on the peninsula with excellent snorkeling possibilities.

list the most common packages, although all the lodges will work with you to accommodate longer or shorter stays. Nightly room rates are listed only where they're available and practical, generally at the more moderately priced hotels.

In addition to the places listed below, **Guaria de Osa** ★ (© 510/235-4313 in the U.S.; www.guariadeosa.com) is a beautiful lodge near the Río Claro that specializes in yoga, spiritual, and educational retreats.

VERY EXPENSIVE

In addition to the places listed below, **Copa del Arbol** ★★ (© 831/246-4265 in the U.S., or 8935-1212 in Costa Rica; www.copadearbol.com) is another intimate jungle lodge located on the water's edge about midway between the village of Drake Bay and the San Pedrillo ranger station at the entrance to Corcovado National Park.

Aguila de Osa Inn ★   I prefer the location of most of the other lodges listed in this section, as well as the fact that most also have swimming pools. But that said, this is a wonderfully run jungle lodge, with large, airy rooms, great vistas, fabulous food, and attentive, personalized service. Much of the credit goes to owner Bradd Johnson, who is very much a hands-on proprietor and usually at the lodge. The hotel is set on a steep hillside that borders the Agujitas river right near the point where it empties out into Drake Bay. Most rooms have brightly varnished wood floors, and large walls of windows set to take in beautiful views. The rooms are located at the highest point of the property, and can be a bit of a hike for those not in reasonably good condition. The lodge has especially good scuba diving and sport fishing operations, with their own modern boats, top-notch equipment, and knowledgeable skippers and dive masters. This lodge also provides easy access to the nearby tiny village of Drake Bay.

Drake Bay. © **866/924-8452** in the U.S. and Canada, 2296-2190 in San José, or 8840-2929 at the lodge. www.aguiladeosainn.com. 13 units. $440–$660 for 3 days/2 nights; $617 and up for 4 days/3 nights. Rates are per person based on double occupancy and include round-trip transportation from Palmar Sur, and all meals. Closed Oct. **Amenities:** Restaurant; bar; watersports rentals; free Wi-Fi.

Casa Corcovado Jungle Lodge ★   Set right on the border of Corcovado National Park, this lodge has a collection of individual and duplex bungalows built on the site of a former cacao plantation. Most of the former farmland has been reclaimed and the whole operation is surrounded by dense primary forest. Large and well-appointed, the bungalows here don't have any ocean view, though the property has two swimming pools and a semi-private beach. Every afternoon, guests gather at "Margarita Sunset Point" for cocktails and snacks. This is a gorgeous grassy bluff on a high point overlooking the Pacific Ocean, providing a perfect sunset perch. Owner Stephen Lill, is a dedicated environmentalist and involved in numerous local conservation and sustainable development projects.

Osa Peninsula. © **2256-3181.** www.casacorcovado.com. 14 units. $955–$1,215 per person for 3 days/2 nights; $1,160–$1,320 for 4 days/3 nights. Rates are based on double occupancy and include round-trip transportation from San José, all meals, daily tours, park fees, and taxes. Closed Sept 1–Nov 14. **Amenities:** Restaurant; 2 bars; 2 outdoor pools.

La Paloma Lodge ★★★   This has long been one of my favorite nature lodges in Costa Rica, and for good reason. The views are to die for, the setting is sublime, and the wildlife viewing and adventure opportunities are as good as it gets in Costa Rica. The best rooms here are the large private ranchos, but even the slightly more humble standard rooms are large, lush, inviting, and were totally remodeled in 2014. The food and service are top notch as well. A small pool is set on the edge of a jungle-clad hillside, with great views of the ocean and Caño Island in the distance. The lodge takes conservation and sustainable development seriously, and is actively involved in protecting the region. Cocolito Beach is a short hike down a winding trail through the rainforest.

Drake Bay. ✆ **2293-7502.** www.lapalomalodge.com. 11 units. $1,220–$1,550 per person for 4 days/3 nights with 2 tours; $1,475–$1,865 per person for 5 days/4 nights with 2 tours. Rates are based on double occupancy and include all meals, park fees, and indicated tours. Rates slightly lower in off season. Closed Sept 15–Nov 1. **Amenities:** Restaurant; bar; small pool w/spectacular view; free Wi-Fi.

MODERATE

In addition to the spot listed below, you might check out **Finca Maresia** ★ (✆ **2775-0279;** www.fincamaresia.com), a pretty boutique property located between Drake Bay and the national park.

Drake Bay Wilderness Resort ★★   This is one of the first and best located of the lodges in Drake Bay. The resort sits on a large chunk of land with the Agujitas River on one side and the area's namesake Drake Bay on the other. Rooms here are simple, but clean and well maintained. A couple of budget rooms use shared bathroom and shower facilities, while a more plush honeymoon suite is good for those looking to splurge. The owner Marlene's chocolate-chip cookies are regionally renowned.

Drake Bay. ✆ **2725-1715.** www.drakebay.com. 25 units. $650–$900 per person for 4 days/3 nights with 2 tours, including all meals and taxes. **Amenities:** Restaurant; bar; small saltwater pool; free use of canoes and kayaks; free Wi-Fi.

INEXPENSIVE

Hotel Jinetes de Osa   Just off the water at the far southern end of the footpath that runs along the Drake Bay shore, this has long been my best true budget option in the area. The superior rooms here are located higher up on the property and come with wonderful views of the bay. These folks specialize in dive trips and offer full-service PADI certification courses.

Drake Bay. ✆ **866/553-7073** in the U.S. and Canada, or 2231-5806 in Costa Rica. www.jinetesdeosa.com. 9 units. $65–$140 double. Rates include breakfast. **Amenities:** Restaurant; bar; free Wi-Fi.

PUERTO JIMÉNEZ: GATEWAY TO CORCOVADO NATIONAL PARK

35km (22 miles) W of Golfito by water (90km/56 miles by road); 85km (53 miles) S of Palmar Norte

Don't let its small size and languid pace fool you. **Puerto Jiménez ★** is a bustling little burg, where rough jungle gold-panners mix with wealthy ecotourists, budget backpackers, serious surfers, and a smattering of celebrities seeking a small dose of anonymity and escape. Located on the southeastern tip of the Osa Peninsula, the town itself is just a couple of streets wide in any direction, with a ubiquitous soccer field, a handful of general stores, some inexpensive *sodas* (diners), and several bars. Scarlet macaws fly overhead, and mealy parrots provide wake-up calls.

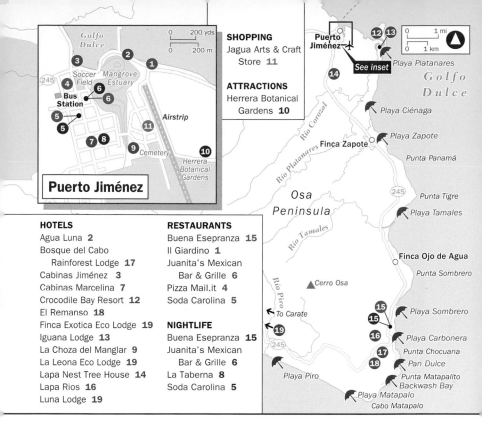

SHOPPING

Jagua Arts & Craft
Store **11**

ATTRACTIONS

Herrera Botanical
Gardens **10**

Puerto Jiménez

HOTELS

Agua Luna **2**
Bosque del Cabo
    Rainforest Lodge **17**
Cabinas Jiménez **3**
Cabinas Marcelina **7**
Crocodile Bay Resort **12**
El Remanso **17**
Finca Exotica Eco Lodge **19**
Iguana Lodge **13**
La Choza del Manglar **9**
La Leona Eco Lodge **19**
Lapa Nest Tree House **14**
Lapa Rios **16**
Luna Lodge **19**

RESTAURANTS

Buena Esepranza **15**
Il Giardino **1**
Juanita's Mexican
    Bar & Grille **6**
Pizza Mail.it **4**
Soda Carolina **5**

NIGHTLIFE

Buena Esepranza **15**
Juanita's Mexican
    Bar & Grille **6**
La Taberna **8**
Soda Carolina **5**

Corcovado National Park has its headquarters here, and this town makes an excellent base for exploring this vast wilderness area. Signs in English on walls around town advertise a variety of tours, including a host of activities outside of the park. If the in-town accommodations are too budget-oriented, you'll find several far more luxurious places farther south on the Osa Peninsula.

This is also a prime surf spot. **Cabo Matapalo** (the southern tip of the Osa Peninsula) is home to several very dependable right point breaks. When it's working, the waves at Pan Dulce and Backwash actually connect, and can provide rides almost as long and tiring as those to be had in more famous Pavones (see "Playa Pavones: A Surfer's Mecca," later in this chapter).

Essentials

GETTING THERE & DEPARTING   By Plane: Both **Nature Air** (℡ **800/235-9272** in the U.S. and Canada, or 2299-6000 in Costa Rica; www.natureair.com) and **Sansa** (℡ **877/767-2672** in the U.S. and Canada, or 2290-4100 in Costa Rica; www.flysansa.com) have daily direct flights to Puerto Jiménez from San José. The flight duration is around 55 minutes, although this flight often includes brief stops in Quepos, Golfito, or Drake Bay. Fares range from $120 to $160, one-way.

Due to the remoteness of this area and the unpredictable flux of traffic, both Sansa and Nature Air frequently improvise on scheduling. Sometimes this means

Hiking in Corcovado National Park.

an unscheduled stop in Quepos, Drake Bay, or Golfito, either on the way to or from San José, which can add some time to your flight. Less frequently, it might mean a change in departure time, so it's always best to confirm.

Taxis are generally waiting to meet all incoming flights. A ride into downtown Puerto Jiménez should cost around C1,500. If you're staying at a hotel outside of downtown, it's best to have them arrange for a taxi to meet you. Otherwise you can hire one at the airstrip. Depending upon how far out on the peninsula you are staying, it could cost up to $80 for a rugged four-wheel-drive vehicle that can carry up to four people.

By Car: Take the San José–Caldera Highway (CR27) to the first exit past the Pozón toll booth, where you will pick up the Southern Highway, or Costanera Sur (CR34). Take this south through Jacó, Quepos, and Dominical to Palmar Norte, where you'll meet up with the Interamerican Highway (CR2). Take this south to the turnoff for La Palma, Rincón, and Puerto Jiménez.

By Bus: Transportes Blanco-Lobo express buses (© **2257-4121** in San José, or 2771-4744 in Puerto Jiménez) leave San José daily at 8am and noon from Calle 12, between avenidas 7 and 9. The trip takes 7 to 8 hours; the fare is C7,000. Buses depart Puerto Jiménez for San José daily at 5am and 9am.

By Boat: Several speedboats work as boat taxis between Puerto Jiménez and Golfito. The fare is C3,000, and the ride takes a little under 30 minutes. These boats leave five or six times throughout the day, or whenever they fill up, beginning at around 5am and finishing up at around 5pm. Ask around town, or at the docks for current schedules.

There is also a daily passenger launch. This slower boat takes 1½ hours and is C1,500. The ferry leaves the public dock in Golfito at 11:30am for Puerto Jiménez. The return trip to Golfito leaves Puerto Jiménez's municipal dock at 4pm. It's possible to charter a water taxi in Golfito for the trip across to Puerto

Jiménez as well. You'll have to pay around $100 for an entire launch, some of which can carry up to 12 people.

VISITOR INFORMATION   Puerto Jiménez is a dirt-lane town on the southern coast of the Osa Peninsula. The public dock is over a bridge past the north end of the soccer field; the bus stop is 2 blocks east of the center of town. You'll find a couple of Internet cafes in town; the best of these is **Cafe Net El Sol** (© **8632-8150;** www.soldeosa.com), which is a great place to book tours and get information, and is also a Wi-Fi hot spot.

CITY LAYOUT   Puerto Jiménez is a dirt-lane town on the southern coast of the Osa Peninsula. The public dock is over a bridge past the north end of the soccer field; the bus stop is 2 blocks east of the center of town.

FAST FACTS   Four-wheel-drive taxis are actually fairly plentiful in Puerto Jiménez. You can usually find them cruising or parked along the main street in town. Alternatively, have your hotel or restaurant call one for you. You can even rent a car down here from **Solid Car Rental** (© **2735-5777;** www.solidcarrental.com).

Exploring Puerto Jiménez

While Puerto Jiménez has typically been a staging ground for adventures much farther out toward Carate and the park, quite a few activities and tours can be undertaken closer to town.

If you're looking to spend some time on the beach, head just east of town for a long, pretty stretch of sand called **Playa Plantanares.** The waves are generally

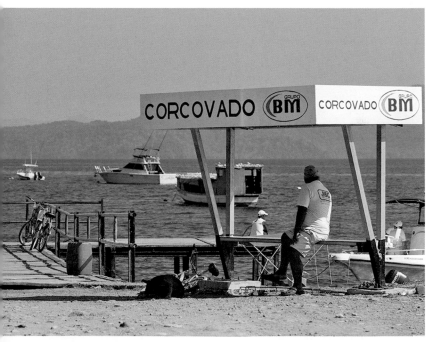

The Puerto Jiménez dock.

fairly gentle, and quite a few hotels have begun to pop up here. If you head farther out on the peninsula, you'll come to the beaches of **Pan Dulce, Backwash,** and **Matapalo,** all major surf spots with consistently well-formed right point breaks. When the waves aren't too big, these are excellent places to learn how to surf.

Osa Aventura (© **2735-5758** or 8372-6135; www.osaaventura.com) and **Osa Corcovado Tour & Travel** (© **8632-8150;** www.soldeosa.com) are local tour companies that offer a host of guided tours and wildlife-watching expeditions around the Osa Peninsula and into Corcovado National Park. Rates run between $80 and $300 per person, depending upon group size and the tour.

AN APTLY NAMED ADVENTURE TOUR   For a real adventure, check in with **Psycho Tours ★★★** (© **8353-8619;** www.psychotours.com). These folks, who also call themselves Everyday Adventures, run a variety of adventure tours, but their signature combo trip features a free climb (with a safety rope attached) up the roots and trunks of a 60m-tall (200-ft.) strangler fig. You can climb as high as your ability allows, but most try to reach a natural platform at around 18m (60 ft.), where you take a leap of faith into space and are belayed down by your guide. This is preceded by an informative hike through primary rainforest, often wading through a small river, and followed by a couple of rappels down jungle waterfalls, the highest of which is around 30m (100 ft.). You can do either one of the above adventures separately, but I recommend the 5- to 6-hour combo tour, which costs $120.

BOTANICAL GARDENS   **Herrera Botanical Gardens ★** (© **2735-5267**) are located on the outskirts of Puerto Jiménez, and the entrance is across from Crocodile Bay. The whole project encompasses over 101 hectares (260 acres) of botanical gardens, working permaculture gardens, and secondary forest. A few platforms built high in the trees are reached by climbing a ladder. A 2¹/₂-hour guided tour of the gardens costs $20, although you can wander the gardens yourself, with a self-guiding map, for $5. If you can't raise them on the phone or set up a visit in advance, head to the **Jagua Arts & Craft Store** (p. 430), which is run by the same folks.

CHOCOLATE TOUR   One unique option is the chocolate tour at **Finca Kobo ★** (© **8398-7604;** www.fincakobo.com), near La Palma, 17km (11 miles) northwest of Puerto Jiménez. These folks offer an informative tour through their organic cacao plantation. You'll learn about and see all the various stages involved in the process of growing cacao and transforming these precious beans into chocolate. At the end of the tour, you'll get to sample some of their handiwork, dipping some local fruit into fresh chocolate fondue. The tour costs $32; children 8 and under are half-price.

KAYAKING   Kayaking trips around the estuary, up into the mangroves and out into the gulf are very popular. **Aventuras Tropicales** (© **2735-5195;** www.aventurastropicales.com), which is set up in front of the soccer field, offers daily paddles through the mangroves, as well as sunset trips where you can sometimes see dolphins. More adventurous multiday kayak and camping trips are also available, in price and comfort ranges from budget to luxury (staying at various lodges around the Golfo Dulce and Matapalo).

SPORTFISHING   If you're interested in doing some **bill-fishing** or **deep-sea fishing,** you'll probably want to stay at or fish with **Crocodile Bay Resort** (© **800/733-1115** in the U.S. and Canada, or 2735-5631 in Costa Rica; www.crocodilebay.com). This upscale fishing lodge is close to the Puerto Jiménez airstrip (airport code: PJM). Alternatively, you can ask at your hotel, or contact **Southern Costa Rica Sportfishing** (© **2735-5298;** www.costaricasportsman. com). Rates can run between $800 and $2,200 for a full day, or between $500 and $900 for a half-day, depending on the boat, tackle, number of anglers, and fishing grounds.

For a truly unique fishing adventure, try fishing for local game from the tenuous perch aboard a single, sit-atop kayak. **Costa Rica Kayak Fishing & Ecotours** (© **2735-5629;** www.costaricakayakfishing.net) offers guided outings. Half-day tours, including fruit, water, snacks, gear, and tackle run between $100 and $150.

SURF LESSONS If you want to learn to surf, contact **Pollo's Surf School ★** (© **8366-6559;** www.pollosurfschool.com), near some excellent learning waves on Pan Dulce beach. A 2-hour lesson runs $55 per person.

Exploring Corcovado National Park ★★★

Exploring Corcovado National Park is not something to be undertaken lightly, but neither is it the expedition that some people make it out to be. The weather is the biggest obstacle to overnight backpacking trips through the park. Within a couple of hours of Puerto Jiménez (by 4WD vehicle) are several entrances to the park; however, the park has no roads, so once you reach any of the entrances, you'll have to start hiking. The heat and humidity are often quite extreme, and frequent rainstorms can make trails fairly muddy. If you choose the alternative—hiking on the beach—you'll have to plan your hiking around the tides when often there is no beach at all and some rivers are impassable.

A mangrove kayak tour near Puerto Jiménez.

Corcovado National Park is amazingly rich in biodiversity. It is one of the only places in Costa Rica that is home to all four of the country's monkey species—howler, white-faced, squirrel, and spider. Its large size makes it an ideal habitat for wildcat species, including the endangered jaguar, as well as other large mammals, like the Baird's tapir. Apart from the jaguar, other cat species found here include the ocelot, margay, jaguarundi, and puma. More than 390 species of birds have been recorded inside the park. Scarlet macaws are commonly sighted here. Other common bird species include any number of antbirds, manakins, toucans, tanagers, hummingbirds, and puffbirds. Once thought extinct in Costa Rica, the harpy eagle has been spotted here as well. Most rivers in Corcovado are home to **crocodiles;** moreover, at high tide, they are frequented by **bull sharks.** For this reason, river crossings must be coordinated with low tides.

Because of its size and remoteness, Corcovado National Park is best explored over several days; however, it is possible to enter and hike a bit of it on day trips. The best way to do this is to book a tour with your lodge on the Osa Peninsula, from a tour company in Puerto Jiménez, or through a lodge in Drake Bay (see "Where to Stay & Dine," above).

GETTING THERE & ENTRY POINTS   The park has four primary entrances, which are really just ranger stations reached by rough dirt roads. When you've reached them, you'll have to strap on a back-pack and hike. Perhaps the easiest one to reach from Puerto Jiménez is **La Leona ranger station,** accessible by car, bus, or taxi.

If you choose to drive, take the dirt road from Puerto Jiménez to Carate (Carate is at the end of the road). From Carate, it's a 3km (1.75-mile) hike to La Leona. To travel there by "public transportation," pick up one of the collective buses (actually, a 4WD pickup truck with a tarpaulin cover and slat seats in the back) that leave Puerto Jiménez for Carate daily at 6am and 1:30pm, returning at 8am and 4pm. Remember, these "buses" are very informal and change their sched-

A hummingbird, one of the many birds you might spot in Corcovado National Park.

ules regularly to meet demand or avoid bad weather, so always ask in town. The one-way fare is around $9. A small fleet of these pickups leaves just south of the bus terminal, and will stop to pick up anyone who flags them down along the way. Your other option is to hire a taxi to suit your schedule, which will charge between $60 and $100 (depending on road conditions) to or from Carate.

En route to Carate, you will pass several campgrounds and small lodges as you approach the park. If you are unable to get a spot at one of the campsites in the park, you can stay at one of these and hike the park during the day.

You can also travel to **El Tigre,** about 14km (8¾ miles) by dirt road from Puerto Jiménez, site of another ranger station. But note that trails from El Tigre go only a short distance into the park.

The third entrance is in **Los Patos,** which is reached from the town of La Palma, northwest of Puerto Jiménez. From here, a 19km (12-mile) trail runs through the center of the park to **Sirena,** a ranger station and research facility

Corcovado National Park

(see "Beach Treks & Rainforest Hikes," below). Sirena has a landing strip used by charter flights.

The northern entrance to the park is **San Pedrillo,** which you can reach by hiking from Sirena or by taking a boat from Drake Bay or Sierpe (see "Beach Treks & Rainforest Hikes," below). It's 14km (8¾ miles) from Drake Bay.

If you're not into hiking in the heat, you can charter a plane in Puerto Jiménez to take you to Carate or Sirena. A five-passenger plane costs between $200 to $450 one-way, depending on your destination. Contact **Alfa Romeo Air Charters** (✆ **2735-5353** or 2735-5112; www.alfaromeoair.com) for details.

FEES & REGULATIONS Park admission is $10 per person per day. Only the Sirena station is equipped with dormitory-style lodgings and a simple soda; the others have basic campsites and toilet facilities. All must be reserved in advance by contacting the **ACOSA** (Area de Conservacion de Osa) in Puerto Jiménez (✆ **2735-5036;** pncorcovado@gmail.com). For a good overview of the park and logistics, check out **www.corcovado.org**. Its offices are adjacent to the airstrip. Only a

Trail Distances in Corcovado National Park

It's 14km (8.7 miles) from La Leona to Sirena. From Sirena to San Pedrillo, it's 23km (14 miles) along the beach. From San Pedrillo, it's 20km (13 miles) to Drake Bay. It's 19km (12 miles) between Sirena and Los Patos.

limited number of people are allowed to camp at each ranger station, so make your reservations well in advance.

BEACH TREKS & RAINFOREST HIKES　The park has quite a few good hiking trails. Two of the better-known ones are the beach routes, starting at either La Leona or San Pedrillo ranger stations. Between any two ranger stations, the hiking is arduous and takes all or most of a day, so it's best to rest for a day or so between hikes if possible. Remember, this is quite a wild area. Never hike alone, and take all the standard precautions for hiking in a rainforest. In addition, be especially careful about crossing or swimming in any isolated rivers or river mouths. Most rivers in Corcovado are home to crocodiles; moreover, at high tide, some are frequented by bull sharks. For this reason, river crossings must be coor-

dinated with low tides. During the wet months (July–Nov), parts of the park may be closed. One of the longest and most popular hikes, between San Pedrillo and La Sirena, can be undertaken only during the dry season.

　　Sirena is a fascinating destination. As a research facility and ranger station, it's frequented primarily by scientists studying the rainforest. The network of trails here can easily keep you busy for several days. Just north of the station lies the mouth of the Río Sirena. Most days at high tide, bull sharks swarm and feed in this river mouth. Large crocodiles also inhabit these waters, so swimming is seriously discouraged. Still, it's quite a spectacle. The **Claro Trail** will bring you to the mouth of the Río Claro. A bit smaller, this river is also home to a healthy crocodile population, although allegedly fewer bull sharks. However, if you follow the Claro Trail upstream a bit, you can find several safe and appropriate swimming spots.

A trail through Corcovado National Park.

WHERE TO STAY & DINE IN THE PARK: CAMPSITES, CABINS & CANTINAS Reservations are essential at the various ranger stations if you plan to eat or sleep inside the park (see "Fees & Regulations," above). **Sirena** has a modern research facility with dormitory-style accommodations for 28 people, as well as a campground, *soda*, and landing strip for charter flights. Camping is available at **La Leona, Los Patos,** and **San Pedrillo** ranger stations. Every ranger station has potable water, but it's advisable to pack in your own; whatever you do, don't drink stream water. Campsites in the park are $4 per person per night. A dorm bed at the Sirena station will run you $8—you must bring your own sheets, and a mosquito net is highly recommended—and meals here are $10 for breakfast, $15 for lunch, and $15 for dinner. Everything must be reserved in advance.

Where to Stay in Puerto Jiménez
VERY EXPENSIVE

Crocodile Bay Resort ★ This high-end sportfishing resort features a fleet of top-notch boats, quality gear and excellent captains. Set on a large piece of land on the outskirts of town, the resort has its own 900-foot long pier jutting out into the Golfo Dulce. Rooms are large, contemporary and comfortable, although I find the decor a bit bland. Service here is very attentive, and in addition to the fishing, a wide range of adventure tours and activities are also offered. And, there's a well-equipped spa, as well.

Puerto Jiménez. ✆ **800/733-1115** in the U.S. and Canada, or 2735-5631 in Costa Rica. www.crocodilebay.com. 40 units. $250–$500 per person based on double occupancy. Rates include breakfast, lunch, and dinner and non-alcoholic beverages. A wide range of fishing and adventure tour packages are available. **Amenities:** Restaurant; bar; Jacuzzi; outdoor pool; large modern spa; watersports equipment rental; free Wi-Fi.

INEXPENSIVE

In addition to the places listed below, **Cabinas Marcelina** (✆ **2735-5007**) is a clean, dependable budget option right in the heart of town. **Agua Luna** (✆ **2735-5393**) is conveniently located, with rooms right at the foot of the town's public dock and close to a mangrove forest.

Cabinas Jiménez ★★ You really can't do better right in town than this waterfront hotel. A perennial budget favorite, this place has a leg up on other budget options around these parts. The large, wood-and-bamboo rancho has a commanding view of the Puerto Jiménez harbor. The owner has a couple of boats and offers excellent tours of the Golfo Dulce and into the nearby mangroves.

Downtown, 50m (165 ft.) north of the soccer field, Puerto Jiménez, Puntarenas. ✆ **2735-5090.** www.cabinasjimenez.com. 11 units. $50–$120 double. **Amenities:** Small outdoor pool; free Wi-Fi.

La Choza del Manglar With expansive gardens and land, this place is nonetheless still virtually next door to the Puerto Jimenez airstrip and cemetery. The large restaurant and lounge area is a popular local gathering place. The rooms come in a wide range of shapes and sizes, but are all a good value. The town and waterfront are each about 3 or 4 blocks away, in opposite directions.

125m (410 ft.) west of the airstrip, Puerto Jiménez. ✆ **888/467-3181** in the U.S. and Canada, or 2735-5605 in Costa Rica. www.manglares.com. 11 units. $30–$70 double. Rates include taxes. **Amenities:** Restaurant; bar; free Wi-Fi.

Costa Rican Family Robinson

For a truly unique family vacation, think about renting the **Lapa's Nest Tree House** ★★ (© 508/714-0622 in the U.S., or 8372-3529 in Costa Rica; www. treehouseincostarica.com), an impressive lodge built up and around a giant Guanacaste tree in the midst of thick forest. This gorgeous home, just 13km (8 miles) north of Puerto Jiménez, is chock-full of creative design touches. Spread over six levels, it features three bedrooms, two bathrooms, and a full kitchen. The price for all of this ranges from $1,500 to $2,900 per week, depending on the season.

Where to Stay in Playa Plantanares

EXPENSIVE

Iguana Lodge ★★   Located on the outskirts of Puerto Jiménez, this beachfront miniresort is friendly and convivial. You'll find rooms in a wide range of prices here. I prefer the second-floor units of the two-story casitas, although the "club rooms" are an excellent value. With a large, open-air, wood-floor studio, yoga is a big attraction here, and there are often classes, or a visiting group conducting a retreat. The gardens are lush and overflowing, with plenty of open-air covered areas to chill, and the gentle Playa Plantanares beach just steps away.

Playa Plantanares. © **800/259-9123** in the U.S. and Canada, or 8848-0752 in Costa Rica. www. iguanalodge.com. 19 units. $150 double club room; $372 casita double; $599 3-bedroom villa. Rates for club room include breakfast. Rates for the casita include dinner, while rates for the villa do not include any meals. **Amenities:** 2 restaurants; bar; Jacuzzi; outdoor lap pool; spa; watersports equipment rental.

Where to Stay & Dine around the Osa Peninsula

As with most of the lodges in Drake Bay, the accommodations listed in this section include three meals a day in their rates and do a large share of their bookings in package trips. Per-night rates are listed, but the price categories have been adjusted to take into account the fact that all meals are included. Ask about package rates if you plan to take several tours and stay awhile: They could save you money.

In addition to the lodges listed below, several other options range from small B&Bs to fully equipped home rentals. Surfers, in particular, might want to inquire into one of the several rental houses located close to the beach at Matapalo. Your best bet for alternative accommodations is to contact Isabelle at **Jiménez Hotels** (© **2735-5702;** www.jimenezhotels.com), which also handles a host of house rentals around the area.

Finally, Carate has several lodges. In addition to the lodges listed below, you can look into **Finca Exótica Eco-Lodge** ★ (© 8828-0817; www.fincaexotica. com), a delightful oceanview lodge, and **La Leona Eco-Lodge** ★ (© 2735-5705; www.laleonaecolodge.com), a tent-camp option on the outskirts of the national park.

This is a very isolated area, with just one rough dirt road connecting all the lodges, nature reserves, and parks. Almost all visitors here take all their meals at their hotel or lodge. If you want to venture away for some good fresh food and simple home cooking, head to Martina's **Buena Esperanza** (no phone), right there on the main road, near Matapalo.

The following lodges are some of the best ecolodges Costa Rica has to offer, and most are pretty pricey. However, keep in mind that despite paying top dollar, the rooms have no TVs, no telephones, no air-conditioning, and the town has no discos, very limited shopping, and no paved roads. Consequently, there are also no crowds and very few modern distractions. All of the lodges listed below are between 40 minutes to a little over an hour outside of Puerto Jimenez, along a rough dirt road, with several river crossings.

VERY EXPENSIVE

Bosque del Cabo Rainforest Lodge ★★★   There's a reason this place is so popular. Actually, there are many reasons, but primarily it's all about the views, attention to detail, great food and service, and rich primary rainforest all around. The best rooms here are the private cabins overlooking the forest and Pacific Ocean below. The wildlife viewing here is simply world-class. Families might want to grab one of the fully equipped houses, while those on a bit more of a budget can opt for one of the garden rooms. Great hiking can be had right from the lodge grounds, and you can climb into a bird- and wildlife-viewing platform high up in a tall Manu tree. These folks have a huge private reserve and have earned "4 Leaves" in the CST Sustainable Tourism program. Owners Phil & Kim Spier are often on hand, and really make sure things run smoothly.

Osa Peninsula. ✆ **2735-5206** or 8389-2846. www.bosquedelcabo.com. 17 units. $175–$350 per person. Rates include 3 meals daily and taxes. $30 per person, round-trip transportation from Puerto Jiménez. **Amenities:** Restaurant; bar; midsize outdoor pool; surfboard rental.

El Remanso ★★   This wonderful collection of rooms, private cabins, and duplexes in thick rainforest is just up the road from Bosque del Cabo. A few of the units have ocean views. Everything is very well done and the service is excellent. Families or groups will want to look at Casa Osa, which sleeps up to eight. For a real treat, be sure to have breakfast atop the tree platform at least one time here. This place uses only renewable energy, has a serious program for sustainable energy and food and waste, and has earned "5 Leaves" in the CST Sustainable Tourism program.

Osa Peninsula. ✆ **2735-5569** or 8814-5775. www.elremanso.com. 14 units. $160–$240 per person. Rates include 3 meals daily and all taxes. **Amenities:** Restaurant; bar; small outdoor pool.

Lapa Ríos ★★   This trailblazing lodge was one of the first to put ecotourism in the Osa Peninsula on the map. The rooms are all very large, with open screen walls, high-peaked thatch roofs, and large private decks overlooking the rainforest and Pacific Ocean in the distance. The rooms are housed in a series of duplex units stretching in a straight line down the edge of a mountain ridge. If you get one of the lower units, be prepared for a bit of a hike to and from the main lodge, restaurant, and pool area. Lapa Ríos sits on a 400-hectare (988-acre) private rainforest reserve, with a well-maintained trail system and abundance of flora and fauna.

Osa Peninsula. ✆ **2735-5130.** www.laparios.com. 16 units. $560–$1,220 double. Rates include 3 meals daily, 2 guided tours per stay, and round-trip transportation btw. the lodge and Puerto Jiménez. Discounts for children 10 and under. **Amenities:** Restaurant; bar; small outdoor pool; all rooms smoke-free.

Luna Lodge ★   In an area renowned for its remote ecolodges, this is one of the most remote. It is literally beyond the "end of the road." Luna Lodge is located up a rugged dirt track high above the tiny village of Carate, where roads end and Corcovado National Park begins. Budget travelers can opt for one of the large, heavy platform tents, while those seeking more privacy and luxury should choose the private bungalows. This lodge is spread over a steep hillside, and some hiking is involved to and from some of the units. The large yoga platform has great views, and the lodge frequently hosts yoga retreats, or offers morning classes.

Carate, Osa Peninsula. ℂ **888/760-0760** in the U.S. and Canada, or 2206-5859 in Costa Rica. www.lunalodge.com. 12 units. $105–$115 per person in tent; $135–$150 per person, room; $165–$195 per person, private cabin. Rates are double occupancy, and include 3 meals daily and taxes. A range of package tours, including round-trip transportation btw. the lodge and Puerto Jiménez, tours, and yoga classes are also available. **Amenities:** Restaurant; bar; small spa; small outdoor pool; all rooms smoke-free; limited free Wi-Fi.

Where to Dine in Puerto Jiménez

You can also get good pizzas and pastas at **Pizza Mail.it** (ℂ **2735-5483**), next to the post office.

Il Giardino ★★ ITALIAN/INTERNATIONAL/SEAFOOD   For years this has been the best restaurant in Puerto Jiménez, and now they've got a waterfront location that matches their fine cooking. The pastas and ravioli are all homemade and delicious, and the seafood is freshly caught and perfectly prepared. It's an odd combination, but these folks also frequently do sushi nights, and are even open for breakfast. Everything is made fresh to order, so the kitchen can be a bit slow at times. When the weather permits, grab one of the open-air tables close to the water, although beware that these tables are as close to the road as they are to the water.

On the beachfront, just down from the public pier, Puerto Jiménez. ℂ **2735-5129.** www.il giardinoitalianrestaurant.com. Main courses C4,000–C13,500. No credit cards. Tues–Sun 7am–11pm.

Juanita's Mexican Bar & Grille TEX-MEX/BAR FOOD   This is the place to come if you're looking for a friendly, casual hangout offering Tex-Mex staples and cold margaritas. They also serve up hearty burgers, onion rings, and a so-so pizza. If you want something even more substantial they also have steaks, sea-food, and chicken dishes. Given the proximity to the sea, I'd recommend the catch of the day.

Downtown, Puerto Jiménez. ℂ **2735-5056.** www.juanitasmexican.com. Reservations not accepted. Main courses C3,500–C8,500. No credit cards. Daily 6:30am–11pm.

Soda Carolina ★ COSTA RICAN   This simple Costa Rican restaurant is the social and tourist hub of Puerto Jiménez. Bright rainforest scenes and animals are painted on the interior walls, while the open-air front walls open up to the city's main street. You can get filling *casados* (plates of the day), fresh grilled fish, and a number of other typical local dishes.

On the main street. ℂ **2735-5185.** Main courses C3,500–C7,000. Daily 6am–10pm.

Shopping

Jagua Arts & Craft Store ★★ (ℂ **2735-5267**) is near the airstrip, and is defi-nitely worth a visit. Owner Karen Herrera has found excellent local and regional art and craft works, including some fine jewelry and blown glass. *Tip:* Many folks head to this store while waiting for their departing flight out of Puerto Jiménez. Be sure to give yourself enough time, as the store has a relatively extensive collection.

Entertainment & Nightlife

If you're looking for any after-tours action in Puerto Jiménez, I recommend you start off at either **Juanita's Mexican Bar & Grille** (p. 430), or **Soda Carolina** (p. 430), both of which are popular with locals, guides, and tourists. For a much more local scene, stop in for an Imperial at **La Taberna** (© **2735-9533**).

If you're staying in the Matapalo area farther out on the Osa and want to hang with some locals, head to **Buena Esperanza** (no phone). This place can actually get pretty lively on a Friday or Saturday night. It's the only game in town, but they've got good game.

GOLFITO: GATEWAY TO THE GOLFO DULCE

87km (54 miles) S of Palmar Norte; 337km (209 miles) S of San José

Despite being the largest and most important city in Costa Rica's southern zone, Golfito, in and of itself, is neither a popular nor a particularly inviting tourist destination. In its prime, this was a major banana port, but following years of rising taxes, falling prices, and labor disputes, United Fruit pulled out in 1985. Things may change in the future, as rumors perennially abound about the potential

The Golfito shoreline.

construction of an international airport nearby, major marina right on the bay, or large-scale tuna farm just offshore. But for the moment, none of these megaprojects have gotten off the drawing board.

That said, Golfito is still a major sportfishing center and a popular gateway to a slew of nature lodges spread along the quiet waters, isolated bays, and lush rainforests of the Golfo Dulce, or "Sweet Gulf." In 1998, much of the rainforest bordering the Golfo Dulce was officially declared the **Piedras Blancas National Park ★★**, which includes 12,000 hectares (29,640 acres) of primary forests, as well as protected secondary forests and pasturelands.

Golfito is set on the north side of the Golfo Dulce, at the foot of lush green mountains. The setting alone gives Golfito the potential to be one of the most attractive cities in the country. However, the areas around the municipal park and public dock are somewhat seedy and the "downtown" section is quite run-down. Still, if you go a bit farther along the bay, you come to the old United Fruit Company housing. Here you'll find well-maintained wooden houses painted bright colors and surrounded by neatly manicured gardens. Toucans are commonly sighted. It's all very lush and green and clean—an altogether different picture from that painted by most port towns in this country. When a duty-free zone was opened here, these old homes experienced a minor renaissance and several were converted into small hotels. Ticos come here in droves on weekends and throughout December to take advantage of cheap prices on name-brand goods and clothing at the duty-free zone; sometimes all these shoppers make finding a room difficult.

Essentials

GETTING THERE & DEPARTING   **By Plane:** Both **Nature Air** (✆ 800/235-9272 in the U.S. and Canada, or 2299-6000 in Costa Rica; www.natureair.com) and **Sansa** (✆ 877/767-2672 in the U.S. and Canada, or 2290-4100 in Costa Rica; www.flysansa.com) have direct flights to the Golfito airstrip (no phone; airport code: GLF). The trip duration is around 1 hour; the fares run $100-$145 each way. Sansa flights return to San José daily at 6:45am.

By Car: Take the San José–Caldera Highway (CR27) to the first exit past the Pozón toll booth, where you will pick up the Southern Highway, or Costanera Sur (CR34). Take this south through Jacó, Quepos, and Dominical to Palmar Norte, where you'll meet up with the Interamerican Highway (CR2). Take this south. When you get to Río Claro, you'll notice a couple of gas stations and quite a bit of activity. Turn right here and follow the signs to Golfito. If you end up at the Panama border, you've missed the turnoff by about 32km (20 miles). The complete drive takes about 6 hours.

By Bus: Direct express buses run by **Tracopa** buses (✆ **2221-4214** in San José or 2775-0365 in Golfito; www.tracopacr.com) leave San José daily at 7am and 3:30pm from the Plaza Viquez at Calle 5 between avenidas 18 and 20. The trip takes 7 hours; the fare is C7,000. Buses depart

A sportfishing vessel in Golfito.

Golfito & the Golfo Dulce

PIEDRAS BLANCAS NATIONAL PARK

Playa San Josecito

Punta Encanto

Playa Gallardo

Bajo Mansito

Punta Agua Fria

Playa Mono

Punta Gallardo

Golfo Dulce

Golfito National Wildlife Reserve

Playa Cacao

Golfito Airport

Golfito

San Francisco

Golfito

To Puerto Jiménez

NICARAGUA

CARIBBEAN SEA

SAN JOSÉ

PACIFIC OCEAN

Golfito

PAN.

0   1 mi
0   1 km

ATTRACTIONS
Casa Orquídeas **3**
Cataratas y Senderos Avellán **4**
Golfito National Wildlife Reserve **5**
Wilson Botanical Gardens **12**

RESTAURANTS
Banana Bay Marina Bar & Grill **10**
Mar y Luna **8**
Samoa del Sur **9**

HOTELS
Banana Bay Marina **10**
Casa Roland Marina Resort **7**
Centro Turístico Samoa del Sur **9**
Fish Hook Marina **11**
Golfo Dulce Lodge **2**
Hotel Sierra **6**
Morphose Mountain Retreat **12**
Playa Nicuesa Rainforest Lodge **1**

Golfito for San José daily at 5am and 1:30pm from the bus station near the municipal dock.

By Boat: Several speedboats work as boat taxis between Golfito and Puerto Jiménez. The fare is C3,000, and the ride takes a little under 30 minutes. These boats leave five or six times throughout the day, or whenever they fill up, beginning at around 5am and finishing up at around 5pm. Ask at the *muellecito* (public dock) for current schedules.

There is also a daily passenger launch. This slower boat takes 1½ hours and is C1,500. The ferry leaves the public dock in Golfito at 11:30am for Puerto Jiménez. The return trip to Golfito leaves Puerto Jiménez's municipal dock at 4pm.

It's also possible to charter a water taxi in Golfito for the trip across to Puerto Jiménez. You'll have to pay around $100 for an entire launch, some of which can carry up to 12 people.

GETTING AROUND   Taxis are plentiful in Golfito, and are constantly cruising the main road all the way from the entrance of town to the duty-free port. A taxi ride anywhere in town should cost around C500. Local buses also ply this loop. The fare for the bus is C120.

If you drive down here and head out to one of the remote lodges on the gulf, you can leave your car at Samoa del Sur (see "Where to Stay," below) for around $12 per day.

If you need to rent a car in Golfito, check in with **Solid Car Rental** (☎ **2775-3333;** www.solidcarrental.com).

If you can't get to your next destination by boat, bus, commuter airline, or car, **Alfa Romeo Air Charters** (☎ **2735-5353** or 2735-5112; www.alfaromeo air.com) runs charters to most of the nearby destinations, including Carate, Drake Bay, Sirena, and Puerto Jiménez. A five-passenger plane should cost around $200 to $450 one-way, depending on your destination.

Exploring Golfito & Surroundings

You won't find any really good swimming beaches right in Golfito. The closest spot is **Playa Cacao,** a short boat ride away, although this is not one of my favorite beaches in Costa Rica. You should be able to get a ride here for around ₡3,000 per person from one of the boat taxis down at the public docks. However, you might have to negotiate hard because these boatmen like to gouge tourists whenever possible. If you really want some beach time, I recommend staying at one of the hotels in the Golfo Dulce (see "Where to Stay," below) or heading over to **Playa Zancudo** (see "Playa Zancudo," later in this chapter).

BOTANICAL GARDENS   About 30 minutes by boat out of Golfito, you'll find **Casa Orquídeas ★★** (☎ **8829-1247**), a private botanical garden lovingly built and maintained by Ron and Trudy MacAllister, who settled this remote piece of land in the 1970s. Most hotels in the area offer trips here, including transportation and a 2-hour tour of the gardens. During the tour, you'll sample a load of fresh fruits picked right off the trees. If your hotel can't, you can book a trip out of Golfito with **Land Sea Tours** (☎ **2775-1614**). If you decide to do it yourself,

the entrance and guided tour is $10 per person, but it will cost you between $80 and $100 to hire a boat for the round-trip ride; the gardens are open daily from 8am to 4pm, and are closed on Fridays. Regularly scheduled tours are on Thursdays and Sundays at 8:30am (three-person minimum).

If you have a serious interest in botanical gardens or bird-watching, consider an excursion to **Wilson Botanical Gardens ★★★** at the **Las Cruces Biological Station** (☎ **2524-0607** in San José or 2773-4004 at the gardens; www. threepaths.co.cr), just outside the town of San Vito, about 65km (40 miles) to the northeast. The gardens are owned and maintained by the Organization for Tropical Studies and include more than 7,000 species of tropical plants from around the world. Among the plants grown here are many endangered species, which make the gardens of interest to botanical researchers. Despite the scientific aspects of the gardens, with so many beautiful and unusual flowers amid the manicured grounds, even a neophyte can't help but be

Wilson Botanical Gardens.

astounded. All this luscious flora has attracted at least 360 species of birds. A 4-hour guided walk costs $38; a shorter, 2-hour hike will run you $28. If you'd like to stay the night here, 12 well-appointed rooms are available. Rates include one guided walk, three meals, and taxes, and run $77 to $98 per person. Reservations are essential if you want to spend the night, and it's usually a good idea to make a reservation for a simple day visit and hike. The gardens are about 6km (3³/₄ miles) before San Vito. To get here from Golfito, drive out to the Interamerican Highway and continue south toward Panama. In Ciudad Neily, turn north. A taxi from Golfito should cost around $40 to $50 each way.

HIKING With a trail head located just on the outskirts of town, the **Golfito National Wildlife Reserve ★** is the closest place to Golfito for a hike in one of the area's typical local lowland rainforests. This reserve is home to much of the same wildlife and flora you'll find in other, more famous national parks. A well-marked trail begins near the ranger station, just beyond the city's airstrip. You can hike it yourself or go as part of an organized tour with **Land Sea Tours** (✆ 2775-1614). Admission is $10, and the refuge is open daily from 8am to 4pm.

About a 20-minute drive over a rough dirt road from Golfito will bring you to the **Cataratas y Senderos Avellán** (Avellán Waterfall & Trails; ✆ 8633-4768; www.avellancr.com). Admission to the site costs C2,500 and includes a 2-hour guided hike through the forests and a visit to a beautiful forest waterfall, with several refreshing pools perfect for swimming. A taxi should cost around $25 one-way. Horseback riding (C12,500) is available, and they even have a zip-line canopy tour (C20,000). Camping is allowed, and meals are served by the friendly owners of the land, the local Gamba family. However, for most folks, the best way to visit this site is to go as part of an organized trip with Land Sea Tours (see above).

SPORTFISHING The waters off Golfito also offer some of the best **sportfishing** in Costa Rica. Most game fish species can be caught here year-round, including blue and black marlin, sailfish, and roosterfish. November through May is the peak period for sailfish and blue marlin. If you'd like to try hooking into a possible world record marlin or sailfish, contact **Banana Bay Marina** (✆ 2775-0838; www.bananabaymarinagolfito.com) or **Fish Hook Marina** (✆ 800/353-0678 in the U.S. and Canada, or 2775-1624 in Costa Rica; http://fish-hook-marina.com). Both of these operations boast a full-service marina, a few waterside rooms for guests, and a fleet of sportfishing boats and captains. A full-day fishing trip costs between $950 and $1,800. You can also try the **Zancudo Lodge** (✆ 800/854-8791 in the U.S. and Canada, or 2776-0008 in Costa Rica; www.thezancudolodge.com), which is based out of the Zancudo Beach Resort (p. 441) in nearby Playa Zancudo. The lodge can arrange pickup in Golfito, and I greatly prefer the Zancudo lodgings and scenery to what you'll find in Golfito.

Where to Stay

In addition to the places mentioned below, sportfishers might check out the rooms offered at either **Banana Bay Marina** (✆ 2775-0838; www.bananabay marinagolfito.com) or **Fish Hook Marina** (✆ 800/353-0678 in the U.S. and Canada, or 2775-1624 in Costa Rica; http://fish-hook-marina.com).

IN GOLFITO
Moderate
Casa Roland Marina Resort ★ This is easily the most modern and luxurious option available in Golfito, although that's not such a high bar to clear. The

hotel is located in the old United Fruit Company compound near the popular duty-free zone, and not on the water. Rooms are comfortable, cool, and kept very clean. The best rooms and suites are on the main floor, as those on the lower level can have much less natural light. There are ample and inviting common areas, and main restaurant and bar area feature some beautiful stained glass works. A lovely, large free-form pool is in a separate recreation area across the street from the main hotel.

Old American zone, near the duty-free zone, Golfito. ☎ **888/398-6435** in the U.S. and Canada, or 2775-3406 in Costa Rica. www.casarolandgolfito.com 53 units. $110–$130 double; $250–$280 suite. Rates include breakfast. **Amenities:** Restaurant; bar; midsize free-form outdoor pool; room service; spa; free Wi-Fi.

Hotel Sierra   Set right between the airstrip and duty-free zone, and within easy walking distance of each, this large resort-style hotel is one of the more popular options for Tico shoppers coming to Golfito to bargain hunt. The rooms are spacious and feature clean tile floors and large windows letting in lots of ambient light. The large outdoor pool is ringed with chaise lounges and shade umbrellas, and features a popular swim-up bar. There's also a small children's pool.

Golfito. ☎ **2775-0666.** www.hotelsierra.com. 72 units. $$60–$90 double. Rates include breakfast. **Amenities:** Restaurant; bar; large outdoor pool; free Wi-Fi.

Inexpensive

Centro Turístico Samoa del Sur   This longstanding waterfront hotel is a safe option and your best bet if you want to be right on the water. The rooms are comfortable, if a bit worn, with red tile floors, hardwood furniture and a long shared veranda. The hotel features a popular restaurant, small marina, pool, and playground, which are open to the public for a fee. The bar and restaurant are popular and can be a bit noisy on weekends. These folks run one of the more dependable and convenient parking lots for travelers with rental cars heading by boat to one of the more remote nature lodges of the Golfo Dulce.

100m (328 ft.) north of the public dock, Golfito. ☎ **2775-0233.** www.samoadelsur.com. 14 units. $60–$80 double. **Amenities:** Restaurant; bar; midsize outdoor pool; room service; kayak rentals.

ALONG THE SHORES OF THE GOLFO DULCE

The lodges listed here are on the shores of the Golfo Dulce. This area has no roads, so you must get to the lodges by boat. I recommend that you have firm reservations when visiting this area, so your transportation should be arranged. If worse comes to worst, you can hire a boat taxi at the *muellecito* (little dock), on the water just beyond the gas station, or La Bomba, in Golfito, for between $50 and $100, depending on your lodging destination.

Golfo Dulce Lodge ★   This longstanding, Swiss-owned nature lodge is set just off a pretty beach and cove deep inside the Golfo Dulce. You must arrive by boat from Golfito as the area has no roads or cars. The lodge has a handful of individual cabins with hardwood floors and private verandas. Each cabin features a hand-carved wooden door and is named after the local animal carved into this door. Three more economical and more basic rooms are in the main lodge building. The only neighbors the lodge has are Ron and Trudy from Casa Orquídeas (p. 434), a lovely homestead and botanical gardens located a few hundred yards away, along the beach. Golfo Dulce Lodge has been awarded "4 Leaves" by the

CST Sustainable Tourism program and is a member of the International Ecotourism Society.

Golfo Dulce. ℂ **8821-5398.** www.golfodulcelodge.com. 8 units. $90–$120 per person double occupancy. Rates include 3 meals daily and taxes. Add $30 per person for transportation to and from Golfito. Minimum 3 night stay. Closed May 1–June 30 and Oct. No credit cards. **Amenities:** Restaurant; bar; small outdoor pool.

Playa Nicuesa Rainforest Lodge ★★★   This is one of the more remote ecolodges in the Southern zone, accessible only by boat, a 30-minute or so ride from Golfito deep inside the Golfo Dulce. The lodge and its various rooms and private cabins are rich in varnished local hardwoods. Try to get one close to the water or set apart in the thick rainforest. Communal meals are served in the large main lodge building. The wildlife and nature viewing here is fabulous. Playa Nicuesa offers fabulous hikes through primary forest on its own 66-hectare (163-acre) private reserve adjoining the much larger Piedras Blancas National Park. Great kayaking and snorkel tours are also on offer on the Golfo Dulce. Finally, the lodge has a yoga deck, some lovely lounge areas facing the gulf, and a small stream.

Golfo Dulce. ℂ **866/504-8116** in the U.S., or 2258-8250 in Costa Rica. www.nicuesalodge.com. 11 units. $215–$360 per person per day, double occupancy. $125 children 6–12. Rates include all meals, taxes, and transfers to and from either Golfito or Puerto Jiménez. A 2-night minimum stay is required during low season, and a 4-night minimum stay is required during high season. Closed Oct 1–Nov 15. **Amenities:** Restaurant; bar; watersports equipment.

EN ROUTE TO WILSON BOTANICAL GARDENS

While the Wilson Botanical Gardens offer the best accommodations in or around the tiny town of San Vito, the place below is a rare exception. Its French-owned and -inspired restaurant is a great place for lunch or dinner on your way to or from the gardens, although call in advance, since the hours are extremely limited.

Morphose Mountain Retreat ★★   This beautiful two-room boutique hotel is an anomaly in the area. Run by the husband-wife team of Kate and Patrick Desvanian, this place is a welcome retreat for bird watchers and folks keen on visiting Wilson Botanical Gardens, while enjoying a bit of luxury and fine dining. The rooms are large and cozy, with a Balinese design theme, and large picture windows taking in fabulous views. The place has the vibe and feel of an intimate family-run B&B, but they also serve lunch and dinner. Patrick is an excellent French-born and trained chef, and the food here is wonderful.

9km (5½ miles) outside of Ciudad Neily, on the road to San Vito. ℂ **8843-8626** or 8704-5346. www.morphosecr.com. 2 units. $75–$95 double; $250 suite. Rates include full breakfast. **Amenities:** Restaurant; bar; outdoor pool.

Where to Dine

Banana Bay Marina Bar & Grill ★ INTERNATIONAL/SEAFOOD   This is Golfito's best bet. Set overlooking the marina and bay, this simple, open-air joint serves up fresh seafood, Continental standards, and typical bar food. Main dishes include a couple of pasta plates, chicken or steak fajitas, shrimp scampi, and Hawaiian chicken. The Bildge burger is large a well-prepared hamburger that comes with your choice of Swiss, Cheddar or Blue cheese, but I usually opt for the fresh mahi-mahi burger, which comes either fried or grilled.

At the Banana Bay Marina, on the waterfront in downtown Golfito. © **2775-080383.** Main courses $6–$18. Daily 7am–9pm.

Mar y Luna COSTA RICAN/SEAFOOD   This friendly bayfront restaurant serves up Tico fare, fresh seafood, and a mix of international dishes. The whole fried fish is the house specialty, but you can also get everything from pepper steak to chicken cordon bleu and a range of pastas and bar food. The sunsets are lovely, and I like to enjoy them with some fresh ceviche and a cool drink on the main dining deck facing the water, under a plain zinc roof held up by roughhewn tree trunks. This place sometimes features live music.

Km 3, on the waterfront, by INVU building. © **2775-0192.** Main courses C3,500–C9,000. Daily 7am–9pm.

Entertainment & Nightlife

Golfito is a rough-and-tumble port town, and it pays to be careful here after dark. Most folks stick pretty close to their hotel bar and restaurant. Of these, the bar/restaurants at **Samoa del Sur, Mar y Luna,** and the **Banana Bay Marina Bar & Grill** ★ are, by far, the liveliest. If you're feeling lucky, you can head to the **casino** at the **Hotel Sierra** (see above). Another popular, if somewhat oddly located, spot is **La Pista** (© **2775-9015**) bar, near the airstrip.

PLAYA ZANCUDO ★

19km (12 miles) S of Golfito by boat; 35km (22 miles) S of Golfito by road

Playa Zancudo is one of Costa Rica's most isolated and undeveloped beach destinations. If you're looking for a remote and low-key beach getaway, it's hard to beat Zancudo. It's pretty far from just about everything, and with relatively few places to stay, it's virtually never crowded. However, the small number of hotel rooms to be had means that the better ones, such as those listed here, can fill up fast in the high season. The beach itself is long and flat, and because it's protected from the full force of Pacific waves, it's one of the calmest beaches on this coast and relatively good for swimming, especially toward the northern end. The beach has a splendid view across the Golfo Dulce, and the sunsets are hard to beat.

> ### Park It
>
> If you drive down to Golfito, you can leave your car at Samoa del Sur (p. 436) and take one of the waterborne routes mentioned above. They charge around $10 per day, and the lot is very secure.

Essentials

GETTING THERE   **By Plane:** The nearest airport is in Golfito. See "Golfito: Gateway to the Golfo Dulce," earlier in this chapter, for details. To get from the airport to Playa Zancudo, your best bets are by boat or taxi.

   By Boat: Water taxis can be hired in Golfito to make the trip out to Playa Zancudo; however, trips depend on the tides and weather conditions. When the tide is high, the boats take a route through the mangroves. This is by far the calmest and most scenic way to get to Zancudo. When the tide is low, they must stay out in the gulf, which can get choppy at times. It costs around $15 to $20 per

Playa Zancudo & Pavones

person for a water taxi, with a minimum charge of $40. If you can round up any sort of group, be sure to negotiate. The ride takes about 30 minutes.

Also, a passenger launch from the *muellecito* (little dock) in Golfito normally leaves daily at noon. Because the schedule sometimes changes, be sure to ask in town about current departure times. The trip lasts 40 minutes; the fare is C6,000. The *muellecito* is next to the town's principal gas station, La Bomba.

If you plan ahead, you can call **Zancudo Boat Tours** (© **2776-0012;** www.loscocos.com) and arrange for pickup in Golfito or Puerto Jiménez. The trip costs $20 per person each way from Golfito or Puerto Jiménez, with a $60 minimum. Zancudo Boat Tours also includes land transportation to your hotel in Playa Zancudo—a very nice perk because the town has so few taxis.

By Car: If you've got a four-wheel-drive vehicle, you can make it out to Zancudo even in the rainy season. To get here, follow the directions for driving to Golfito, but don't go all the way into town. The turnoff for playas Zancudo and Pavones is at El Rodeo, about 4km (2½ miles) outside of Golfito, on the road in from the Interamerican Highway. It's mostly rough, gravel and dirt roads. Follow the few signs and the flow of traffic (if there is any) or stick to the most worn route when in doubt.

An alternative route from Paso Canoas (at the border) is via the towns of La Cuesta and Laurel. This route meets the route mentioned above at the small village of Conte.

A fishing vessel off Playa Zancudo.

A four-wheel-drive **taxi** costs around $75 from Golfito. It takes about 1 hour when the road is in good condition, and about 2 hours when it's not.

By Bus: It's possible to get to Zancudo by bus, but I highly recommend coming by boat from Golfito, or your own car. If you insist, there's one daily bus leaving Golfito for Zancudo at 3pm. Alternately, you can catch one of the Pavones buses and get off in the village of Conte. In theory, a Zancudo–bound bus should be waiting. However, this is not always the case, and you may have to wait, hitchhike, or spring for a cab, if any can be found. The entire trip takes about 3 hours; the fare is around $3.50.

DEPARTING   The public launch to Golfito leaves daily at 7am from the dock near the school, in the center of Zancudo. You can also arrange a water taxi back to Golfito, but it's best to work with your hotel owner and make a reservation at least a day in advance. **Zancudo Boat Tours** will take you for $20 per person, with a $60 minimum. Zancudo will also take you to the **Osa Peninsula** for the same $20 per person, with a $60 minimum. The bus to Golfito leaves Zancudo each morning at 5:30am. You can catch the bus anywhere along the main road.

ORIENTATION   Zancudo is a long, narrow peninsula (sometimes only 90m/295 ft. or so wide) at the mouth of the Río Colorado. On one side is the beach; on the other is a mangrove swamp. One road runs the length of the beach, and along this road, spread out over several kilometers of long, flat beach, you'll find the hotels I mention in this section. It's about a 20-minute walk from the public dock near the school to the popular Cabinas Sol y Mar.

Exploring Playa Zancudo

The main activity at Zancudo is relaxing, and people take it seriously. Every lodge has hammocks, and if you bring a few good books, you can spend quite a number of hours swinging slowly in the tropical breezes. The beach along Zancudo is great for swimming. It's generally a little calmer on the northern end and gets rougher (good for bodysurfing) as you head south. There are a couple of bars and even a disco, but visitors are most likely to spend their time just hanging out at their hotel or in restaurants meeting like-minded folks, reading a good book, or playing board games. If you want to take a horseback ride on the beach, ask at your hotel; they should be able to arrange it for you.

Susan and Andrew England, who run Cabinas Los Cocos, also operate **Zancudo Boat Tours** (© **2776-0012;** www.loscocos.com), which offers snorkeling trips, kayaking tours, trips to the Casa Orquídeas Botanical Garden, hikes on the Osa Peninsula, a trip up the Río Coto to watch birds and wildlife, and more. A boat trip through the Río Coto mangroves will turn up a remarkable number of sea and shore birds, as well as the chance to see a crocodile resting on a riverbank, or a white-faced monkey leaping overhead. Tour prices are $50 to $75 per person per tour, with discounts available for larger groups.

For fishing, ask at your hotel, or contact the **Zancudo Beach Resort** (see below). A full day of fishing with lunch and beer should cost between $500 and $1,800 per boat.

Because a mangrove swamp is directly behind the beach, mosquitoes and sand flies can be a problem when the winds die down, so be sure to bring insect repellent.

Where to Stay

Quite a few fully equipped beach houses are for rent here for long stays. Once again, Susan and Andrew at **Los Cocos** (© **2776-0012;** www.loscocos.com) are your best bet for lining up one of these houses.

VERY EXPENSIVE

Zancudo Beach Resort ★★ This specialized fishing lodge offers up the only upscale lodging to be found in Playa Zancudo. Located towards the far northern end of the mini-Zancudo peninsula, this place has air-conditioned rooms with flat screen televisions and contemporary furnishings and decor. The expansive beachfront compound here offers up beautiful ocean views, and features a refreshing swimming pool surrounded by palm trees, a few of which are strung with hammocks. The restaurant serves up excellent and innovative cuisine, usually featuring at least some part of the daily catch, as well as onsite organically grown greenhouse vegetables. On the lagoon side of the peninsula the lodge maintains a little marina, with a fleet of well-equipped fishing boats.

Playa Zancudo.© **800/854-8791** in the U.S. or Canada, or 2776-0008 in Costa Rica. www.thezancudolodge.com. 16 units. $225 double; $295–$450 bungalow or suite. Rates higher during peak periods. **Amenities:** Restaurant; bar; outdoor pool; free Wi-Fi.

MODERATE

Cabinas Los Cocos ★ Andrew and Susan Robertson have homesteaded this lovely collection of four simple, private cabins, set under tall trees and thick foliage, just steps from the beach. Two of the houses are reclaimed homes from the former United Fruit Company plantation in nearby Golfito. All feature thatch roofs and a private veranda, and offer a kitchen or kitchenette, encouraging longer stays. The Robertsons also run Zancudo Boat Tours, a wonderful operation providing waterborne transportation and tour activities around the region.

Playa Zancudo. © **2776-0012.** www.loscocos.com. 4 units. $70 double. Weekly discounts available. No credit cards.

INEXPENSIVE

Cabinas Sol y Mar ★   These simple rooms and private cabins offer up great value at a friendly little compound that also features Zancudo's best restaurant (see below) and most popular bar. Rooms are simple, but cozy and functional, and they also allow camping for real budget travelers. Rick and Lori will make you feel like part of the family here. Tall palm trees and lush gardens keep the grounds relatively cool during the day, and the beach is right out front.

Playa Zancudo. ℃ **2776-0014.** www.zancudo.com. 6 units. $28–$50 double. **Amenities:** Restaurant; bar; free Wi-Fi.

Where to Dine

In addition to the place listed below, you might try the tasty Italian meals at **Restaurante Macondo** (℃ **2776-0157**) or **Alberto's Puerta Negra** ★ (℃ **2776-0181**). If you want basic Tico fare and some local company, head to **Bar Sussy** (℃ **2776-0107**) or **Soda Katherine** (℃ **2776-0124**).

Finally, for a good breakfast, lunch, or dinner, or perhaps just a midday ice-cream treat, check out the open-air restaurant at **Oceanos Cabinas** ★ (℃ **2776-0921;** www.oceanocabinas.com). These folks serve up excellent freshly caught seafood and are locally famous for their *ceviche.*

Sol y Mar ★★ INTERNATIONAL/SEAFOOD   Most folks visiting Playa Zancudo end up here. Some never leave. This friendly restaurant and bar is undeniably the social (and culinary) center of this tiny beach town. The menu is long and varied, ranging from the fresh daily catch in a Thai coconut curry sauce to dry-rubbed beef served with basil butter. There's also plenty of bar food staples, as well as twice weekly barbeque nights. If there's live music in town, it's likely to be here, and the Sunday horseshoe tournament is a local tradition. These folks serve food all day long, and their breakfasts are my favorite.

At Cabinas Sol y Mar. ℃ **2776-0014.** Main courses C2,500–C9,000. Daily 7am–9pm.

PLAYA PAVONES: A SURFER'S MECCA ★

40km (25 miles) S of Golfito

Hailed as the world's longest rideable left point break, Pavones is a legendary destination for surfing. It takes around 1.8m (6 ft.) of swell to get this wave cranking, but when the surf's up, you're in for a long, long ride—so long, in fact, that it's much easier to walk back through town to where the wave is breaking than to paddle back. The swells are most consistent during the rainy season, but you're likely to find surfers here year-round. Locals tend to be pretty possessive of their turf, so don't be surprised if you receive a cool welcome.

Other than surfing, nothing much goes on here; however, the surrounding rainforests are quite nice, and the beaches feature some rocky coves and points that give Pavones a bit more visual appeal than Zancudo. If you're feeling energetic, you can go for a horseback ride or hike into the rainforests that back up this beach town, or stroll south on the beaches that stretch toward Punta Banco and beyond, all the way to the Panamanian border. This is a forgotten and isolated destination catering almost exclusively to backpackers. Be prepared—Pavones is a tiny village with few amenities, and most of the accommodations are quite basic.

The legendary left at Pavones.

Essentials

GETTING THERE & DEPARTING **By Plane:** The nearest airport with regularly scheduled flights is in Golfito (p. 432). Tiskita Jungle Lodge (see below) has a private airstrip. Depending on space, you might be able to arrange transportation to Pavones on one of its charter flights even if you are not staying there.

By Car: If you've got a four-wheel-drive vehicle, you can make it out to Pavones even in the rainy season. To get here, follow the directions for driving to Golfito (p. 432), but don't go all the way into town. The turnoff for playas Zancudo and Pavones is at El Rodeo, about 4km (2½ miles) outside of Golfito, on the road in from the Interamerican Highway. It's mostly rough, gravel and dirt roads. Follow the few signs and the flow of traffic (if there is any) or stick to the most worn route when in doubt.

An alternative route from Paso Canoas (at the border) goes via the towns of La Cuesta and Laurel. This route meets the route mentioned above at the small village of Conte.

Be sure to pick up your tank in Golfito, Rio Claro or the small town of Laurel, as Pavones has no gas station.

By Bus: Two daily buses (no phone) go to Pavones from Golfito at 10am and 3pm. Trip duration is 2½ hours; the fare is C1050. Buses to Golfito depart Pavones daily at 5:30am and 12:30pm. This is a very remote destination, and the bus schedule is subject to change, so it always pays to check in advance.

Exploring Pavones

Surfing is the big draw in Pavones. For board rentals, head to **Sea Kings Surf Shop** (© **2776-2015;** www.surfpavones.com). If there are no waves, or you want some other form of exercise, check in with the folks at **Shooting Star Yoga** (© **2776-2107;** www.yogapavones.com).

A WILD ride

Surfers first discovered the amazing wave off Pavones in the late 1970s. When conditions are right, this wave peels off in one continuous ribbon for over 2km (1.25 miles). Your skills better be up to snuff, and your legs better be in good shape, if you want to ride this wave.

Pavones got some good press in Allan Weisbecker's 2001 novel "In Search of Captain Zero: A Surfer's Road Trip Beyond The End of the Road." The word was out and surfers began flocking to Pavones from all over. On any given day—when the wave is working—you are likely to find surfers from the United States, Brazil, Argentina, Israel, Australia, Peru, and any other number of countries.

However, the town and wave are not without controversy. Aside from the typical territorial spats that erupt over most popular waves, Pavones has been the site of a series of prominent squabbles and controversies that include land disputes, drug busts, fist fights, and even murders. For a unique and in-depth account of the town, its wave, and some of these controversies, check out Weisbecker's "Can't You Get Along with Anyone?: A Writer's Memoir and a Tale of a Lost Surfer's Paradise."

If you're interested in a guided tour, call **Pavones Tours** (℃ 2776-2119; www.pavonestours.com). They offer a wide range of adventure outings, including horseback rides on the beach and whale- and dolphin-watching cruises in small boats, as well as sportfishing, scuba diving, and kayak trips.

Alternately, you can do a day tour and guided hike at **Tiskita Lodge** (see below), for $25 per person, with advance reservation.

Where to Stay & Dine

In addition to the remote nature lodge listed below, **Riviera Riverside Villas** (℃ 2776-2396; www.pavonesriviera.com) offers modern, plush individual cabins, as well as several fully equipped house rentals, a block or so inland from the water, right alongside the Río Claro (Clear River). **Cabinas La Ponderosa** ★ (℃ 2776-2076; www.laponderosapavones.com) is a small, beachfront collection of cabins and private, rustic villas, a bit outside of town, on the way to Punta Banco.

Right in Pavones, several very basic lodges cater to itinerant surfers by renting rooms for between $10 and $20 per night for a double room; most take walk-in reservations since they don't have phones. That said, for in-town budget lodgings, I recommend **Mira Olas** (℃ 2776-2006; www.miraolas.com), about 2 blocks uphill from the soccer field.

For dining, I recommend **Café de la Suerte** ★ (℃ 2776-2388; www. cafedelasuerte.com), a lively little joint fronting the village soccer field that serves breakfasts and lunches and specializes in vegetarian items, freshly baked goods, and fresh-fruit smoothies. These folks also serve dinner during the high season, and rent out cute, cozy A/C-equipped rooms.

VERY EXPENSIVE

Tiskita Jungle Lodge ★★　This homey and remote ecolodge is the intense and loving handiwork of Peter and Lisbeth Aspinall. Carved into a rainforest covered hillside with stunning views to the Pacific Ocean, the lodge features nine bungalows for a total of 17 rooms. The bungalows feature hardwood floors and large covered balconies strung with hammocks. Trails on the private reserve lead through thick rainforest to jungle waterfalls and idyllic swimming holes. The beach is a relatively short hike downhill, but a good workout on the way back. Below the lodge lies a private airstrip and some reclaimed farm and pasture land. Peter is a pioneer in conservation and ecotourism in Costa Rica. He is also an avid farmer with an impressive and extensive collection of tropical fauna, including a wide range of exotic fruits, vegetables and nuts. The lodge is only open for group travel in the off season.

6km (3³/₄ miles) southeast, down the road from Pavones. ℂ **2296-8125** reservation office in San José, or 2776-2194 at the lodge. www.tiskita.com. 17 units. $570 per person for 3 nights. Additional nights $175 per person. Rates include all meals, 2 daily guided hikes, and taxes. Rates are based on double occupancy. Three night minimum required. Discounts available for children under 12. Packages with transportation to and from Golfito or Puerto Jiménez are available. **Amenities:** Restaurant; bar; small outdoor pool; limited watersports equipment.

THE CARIBBEAN COAST

osta Rica's Caribbean coast is a world apart from the rest of the country. The pace is slower, the food is spicier, the tropical heat is more palpable, and the rhythmic lilt of patois and reggae music fills the air. This remains one of Costa Rica's least discovered and explored regions. More than half of the coastline here is still inaccessible except by boat or small plane. This inaccessibility has helped preserve large tracts of virgin lowland rainforest, which are now set aside as **Tortuguero National Park** ★★ and **Barra del Colorado National Wildlife Refuge** ★. These two parks, on the coast's northern reaches, are among Costa Rica's most popular destinations for adventurers and ecotravelers. Of particular interest are the sea turtles that nest here. Farther south, **Cahuita National Park** ★★ is another popular national park, located just off its namesake beach village. It was set up to preserve 200 hectares (494 acres) of coral reef, but its palm tree–lined white-sand beaches and gentle trails are stunning.

So remote was the Caribbean coast from Costa Rica's population centers in the Central Valley that it developed a culture all its own. The original inhabitants of the area included people of the Bribri, Cabécar, and Kéköldi tribes, and these groups maintain their cultures on indigenous reserves in the Talamanca Mountains. In fact, until the 1870s, this area had few non-Indians. However, when Minor Keith (p. 23) built the railroad to San José and began planting bananas, he brought in black laborers from Jamaica and other Caribbean islands to lay the track and work the plantations. These workers and their descendants established fishing and farming communities up and down the coast. Today dreadlocked Rastafarians, reggae music, Creole cooking, and the English-based patois of this Afro-Caribbean culture give this region a quasi-Jamaican flavor, a striking contrast with the Spanish–derived Costa Rican culture.

The Caribbean coast has only one major city, **Limón,** a major commercial port and popular cruise ship port of call. However, the city itself is of little

To Go, or Not to Go? The Weather Is Nobler

The Caribbean coast has a very unique weather pattern. Whereas you'll almost never get even a drop of rain in Guanacaste during Costa Rica's typical dry season (mid-Nov to Apr), on the Caribbean coast it can rain, at least a bit, almost any day of the year. However, the months of September and October, when torrential rains pound most of the rest of the country, most of the time, are oddly two of the drier and more dependably sunny days along the Caribbean coast.

FACING PAGE: **A green turtle in Tortuguero.**

interest to most visitors, who quickly head south to the coast's spectacular beaches, or north to the jungle canals of Tortuguero.

Over the years, the Caribbean coast has garnered a reputation as being a dangerous, drug-infested zone, rife with crime. This is somewhat deserved because of several high-profile crimes in the area; petty theft is a major problem. Still, overall this reputation is exaggerated. The same crime and drug problems found here exist in San José and most of the more popular beach destinations on the Pacific coast. Use common sense and take normal precautions and you should have no problems on the Caribbean coast.

THE BEST CARIBBEAN COAST TRAVEL EXPERIENCES

o **Landing a Tarpon off Barra del Colorado:** Reaching lengths of between 1.8 to 2.8m (6–8 ft.), and often weighing in at well over 200 pounds, tarpon are a hard-fighting and high-jumping game fish. Barra del Colorado is a prime fishing ground for these fierce fish. See p. 450.

o **Cruising the Rainforest Canals of Tortuguero:** Lined by thick tropical rainforest and rich in wildlife, the canals surrounding Tortuguero are home to manatees, caimans, green macaws, and several monkey species. See p. 456.

o **Tasting Chocolate at the Source:** Taking you "from bean to bar," **Caribeans Chocolate Tour** starts with a walk through an organic cacao farm and ends with a tasting of freshly made, local organic chocolate. See p. 488.

The Caribbean Coast's Top Sustainable Hotels

Almonds & Corals Hotel (p. 490)
Casa Marbella (p. 461)
Casa Verde Lodge (p. 483)
Punta Mona Center for Sustainable Living & Education (p. 488)
Selva Bananito Lodge (p. 464)
Tortuga Lodge (p. 459)
Tree House Lodge (p. 491)

o **Watching Surfers Challenge Salsa Brava:** Sometimes called "Little Pipeline," Puerto Viejo's Salsa Brava is a fast and steep wave that breaks over sharp, shallow coral. The wave is also pretty close to shore, which makes this a good place to watch some world-class surfing. See p. 481.

o **Snorkeling Off Manzanillo:** One of Costa Rica's most bountiful and beautiful coral reefs lies just off the coast of the small village of Manzanillo. In addition to coral, sponges, and reef fish, if you're lucky, you may also catch a glimpse of a dolphin or sea turtle. See p. 487.

BARRA DEL COLORADO ★

115km (71 miles) NE of San José

Most visitors to Barra del Colorado come for the fishing. Tarpon and snook fishing are world-class, or you can head farther offshore for some deep-sea action. Barra del Colorado is part of the same ecosystem as Tortuguero National Park (p. 456); as in Tortuguero, an abundance of wildlife and rainforest fauna lives in the rivers and canals.

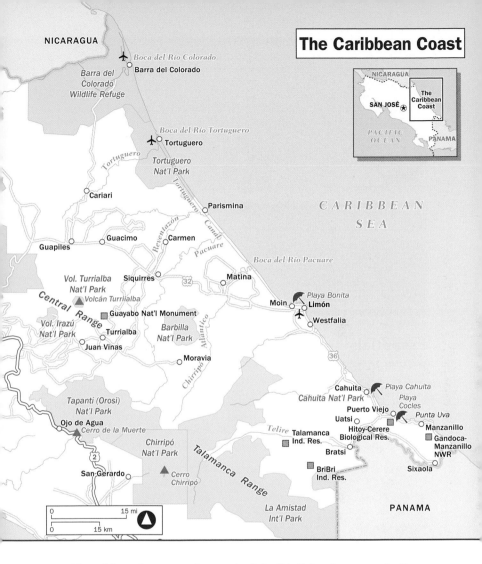

The Caribbean Coast

Named for its location at the mouth of the Río Colorado up near the Costa Rica–Nicaragua border, Barra del Colorado can be reached only by boat or small plane. No roads go in or out of Barra del Colorado. The town itself is a small, ramshackle collection of raised stilt houses, and it supports a diverse population of Afro-Caribbean and Miskito Indian residents, Nicaraguan emigrants, and transient commercial fishermen.

It's hot and humid here most of the year, and it rains a lot, so although some of the lodges have at times risked offering a "tarpon guarantee," they're generally hesitant to promise anything in terms of the weather.

An angler pulling in a tarpon in Barra del Colorado.

Essentials

GETTING THERE & DEPARTING   By Plane: Most folks come here on multiday fishing packages, and most of the area's lodges either include charter flights as part of their package trips or will book you a flight.

By Boat: It is also possible to travel to Barra del Colorado by boat from **Puerto Viejo de Sarapiquí** (see chapter 10). Expect to pay $400 to $600 each way for a boat that holds up to 10 people. Check at the public dock in Puerto Viejo de Sarapiquí or call **Oasis Nature Tours** (© **2766-6108;** www.oasisnature tours.com).

Río Colorado Lodge (© **800/243-9777** in the U.S. and Canada, or 2232-4063/2232-8610; www.riocoloradolodge.com) runs its own launch between Barra del Colorado and San José. If you're staying at the Río Colorado Lodge, be sure to ask about this option (for at least one leg of your trip) when booking.

TOWN LAYOUT   The Río Colorado neatly divides the town of Barra del Colorado. The airstrip is in the southern half of town, as are most of the lodgings. The lodges that are farther up the canals will meet you at the airstrip with a small boat.

Fishing, Fishing & More Fishing

Almost all the lodges here specialize in fishing packages. If you don't fish, you may wonder just what in the world you're doing here. Even though the area offers excellent opportunities for bird-watching and touring jungle waterways, most lodges here still merely pay lip service to ecotourists and would rather see you with a rod and reel.

Fishing takes place year-round. You can fish in the rivers and canals, in the very active river mouth, or offshore. Most anglers come in search of the tarpon, or silver king. **Tarpon** can be caught year-round, both in the river mouth and, to a lesser extent, in the canals; however, they are much harder to land in July and August—the two rainiest months—probably because the river runs so high and is so full of runoff and debris. **Snook,** an aggressive river fish, peak in April, May, October, and November; fat snook, or *calba,* run heavy from November through January. Depending on how far out to sea you venture, you might hook up with **barracuda, jack, mackerel** (Spanish and king), **wahoo, tuna, dorado, marlin,** or **sailfish.** In the rivers and canals, fishermen regularly bring in *mojarra, machaca,* and *guapote* (rainbow bass).

Following current trends in sportfishing, more and more anglers have been using fly rods, in addition to traditional rod-and-reel setups, to land just about all the fish mentioned above. To fish here, you'll need a fishing license ($30), which covers both salt and fresh water, and is good for one year. The lodges in the area either include these in their packages or can readily provide the licenses for you.

Nonfishers should see whether their lodge has a good naturalist guide or canoes or kayaks for rent or use.

Where to Stay & Dine

Almost all of the hotels here specialize in package tours, including all your meals, fishing and tackle, taxes, and usually your transportation and liquor too, so rates are high. With no dependable budget hotels, Barra remains a remote and difficult destination for independent and budget travelers.

Río Colorado Lodge   Founded in 1972 by the legendary fisherman and conservation activist Archie Fields, this fishing lodge can be a little rough around the edges, but nevertheless has been catering to discerning fishermen and women for over four decades. Built up slowly over the years, this rambling complex of wooden structures is connected by a network of raised walkways. Rooms are simple but comfortable, with somewhat dated linens and basic furnishings. The lodge has distinct bar, lounge and dining areas, where folks gather to tell their big fish tales. My favorite feature is the large riverfront deck; my least favorite is their small zoo.

Barra del Colorado. ☎ **800/243-9777** in the U.S. and Canada, or 2232-4063 or 2232-8610 in Costa Rica. www.riocoloradotarponfishing.com. 18 units. $2,673–$3,371 per person double occupancy for 7 days/6 nights with 4 full days of fishing, including 2 nights lodging in San José, all meals and drinks at the lodge, boat, guide, fuel, licenses, and taxes. Nonfishing guests $175–$225 per person per day. **Amenities:** Restaurant; bar; Jacuzzi; Wi-Fi.

Silver King Lodge ★★   If you're looking for a bit of comfort and pampering while stalking some massive tarpon, this dedicated fishing lodge should be your first choice. As at Rio Colorado Lodge (above), the large complex of rooms and common areas is built on pilings above the river and flood levels, and connected by a network of covered wooden walkways. The whole place is awash in varnished hardwoods. The food and service are miles above anything else in the area. The lodge has a lovely outdoor pool and covered Jacuzzi, perfect for unwinding after a hard morning and hot afternoon fishing.

Barra del Colorado. ☎ **877/335-0755** in the U.S.. www.silverkinglodge.net. 10 units. $2,750–$3,960 per person double occupancy for 3 full days of fishing, round-trip air transportation btw. San José and the lodge, all meals at the lodge, liquor, and taxes; $400–$450 per person per extra day, including all fishing, meals, liquor, and taxes. Closed June–Aug and Nov–Dec. **Amenities:** Restaurant; bar; Jacuzzi; small outdoor pool; small spa; free Wi-Fi.

TORTUGUERO NATIONAL PARK ★★

250km (155 miles) NE of San José; 79km (49 miles) N of Limón

Tortuguero is a tiny fishing village connected to the rest of mainland Costa Rica by a series of rivers and canals. This aquatic highway is lined with a mix of farmland and dense tropical rainforest that is home to howler and spider monkeys, three-toed sloths, toucans, and great green macaws. A trip through the canals surrounding Tortuguero is a lot like cruising the Amazon basin—on a much smaller scale.

"Tortuguero" comes from the Spanish name for the giant sea turtles (*tortugas*) that nest on the beaches of this region every year from early March to mid-October (prime season is July–Oct, and peak months are Aug–Sept). The chance to see this nesting attracts many people to this remote region, but just as many come to explore the intricate network of jungle canals that serve as the region's main transportation arteries.

Very important: More than 508cm (200 in.) of rain fall here annually, so you can expect a downpour at any time of the year. Most of the lodges will provide you with rain gear (including ponchos and rubber boots), but it can't hurt to carry your own.

Independent travel is not the norm here, although it's possible. Most travelers rely on their lodge for boat transportation through the canals and into town. At most of the lodges around Tortuguero, almost everything (bus rides to and from, boat trips through the canals, and even family-style meals) is done in groups.

Essentials

GETTING THERE & DEPARTING   By Plane: Nature Air (✆ **800/235-9272** in the U.S. and Canada, or 2299-6000 in Costa Rica; www.natureair.com) has one

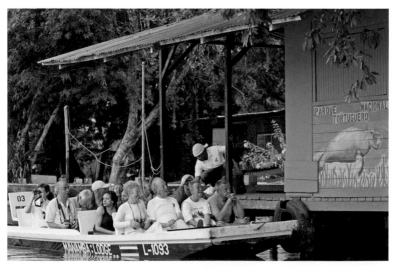

A Tortuguero National Park boat tour.

Caño Palma 1
Biological Station

Cerro de
Tortuguero

BARRA DEL COLORADO
NAT'L WILDLIFE REFUGE

Caño Penitencia

Caño Palacio

NICARAGUA

CARIBBEAN
SEA

Tortuguero

SAN JOSÉ

PACIFIC
OCEAN

PANAMA

Isla
Chica

TORTUGUERO
PROTECTED
AREA

Tortuguero
Airport

CARIBBEAN
SEA

Lagunas del Tortuguero

Laguna Penitencia

Playa
Tortuguero

Tortuguero
Village

Cuatro Esquinas
Ranger Station

I. Cuatro
Esquinas

TORTUGUERO
NATIONAL PARK

HOTELS
Cabinas La Casona **7**
Cabinas Miss Junie **7**
Cabinas Miss Miriam **7**
Cabinas Tortuguero **7**
Casa Marbella **7**
Hotel el Icaco **7**
Laguna Lodge **4**
Manatus Hotel **3**
Mawamba Lodge **5**
Tortuga Lodge **2**
Turtle Beach Lodge **1**

RESTAURANTS
Budda Café **7**
La Casona **7**
Miss Junie's Restaurant **7**
Wild Ginger **7**

ATTRACTIONS
Sea Turtle Conservancy Visitor's
    Center and Museum **6**
Tortugero National Park **8**

flight that departs daily at 6am for **Tortuguero** airstrip (no phone) from Juan Santamaría International Airport in San José. The flight takes approximately 30 minutes; the fare is $95 to $116 each way. The return flight leaves Tortuguero daily at 6:35am for San José.

Additional flights are often added during the high season, and departure times can vary according to weather conditions. In addition, many local lodges operate charter flights as part of their package trips.

Nature Air also offers a morning direct flight from the Tortuguero airstrip to La Fortuna/Arenal departing at 6:35am. Frequency of this flight varies seasonally and fares are between $100 and $135 per person, one-way.

Be sure to arrange with your hotel to pick you up at the airstrip. Otherwise you'll have to plead with one of the other hotels' boat captains to give you a lift, which they will usually do, either for free or for a few dollars.

By Car: It's not possible to drive to Tortuguero. If you have a car, your best bet is either to leave it in San José and take an organized tour, or drive it to Limón or Moín, find a secure hotel or public parking lot, and then follow the directions for arriving by boat below. La Pavona has a secure parking lot useful for those meeting the boats plying the Cariari and La Pavona route outlined below.

By Boat: Flying to Tortuguero is convenient if you don't have much time, but a boat trip through the canals and rivers of this region is often the highlight of any visit. However, be forewarned: Although this trip can be stunning and exciting, it can also be long, tiring, and uncomfortable. You'll first have to ride by bus or minivan from San José to Moín, Caño Blanco, or one of the other embarkation points; then it's 2 to 3 hours on a boat, usually with hard wooden benches or plastic seats. All of the more expensive lodges listed offer their own bus and boat transportation packages, which include the boat ride through the canals. However, if you're coming here on the cheap and plan to stay at one of the less expensive lodges or at a budget cabina in Tortuguero, you will have to arrange your own transportation. In this case, you have a few options.

The most traditional option is to get yourself first to Limón and then to the public docks in **Moín,** just north of Limón, and try to find a boat on your own. You can reach Limón easily by public bus from San José (see "Getting There & Departing," p. 462). If you're coming by car, make sure you drive all the way to Limón or Moín, unless you have prior arrangements out of Cariari or Caño Blanco Marina.

If you arrive in Limón by bus, you might be able to catch one of the periodic local buses to Moín (C300) at the main bus terminal. Otherwise, you can take a taxi for around C7,000 to C8,000, for up to four people. At the docks, you should be able to negotiate a fare of between $50 and $80 per person round-trip with one of the boats docked here. These boats tend to depart between 8 and 10am every morning. You can stay as many days as you like in Tortuguero, but be sure to arrange with the captain to be there to pick you up when you're ready to leave. The trip from Moín to Tortuguero takes between 3 and 4 hours.

It is possible to get to Tortuguero by bus and boat from Cariari. For backpackers and budget travelers, this is the cheapest and most reliable means of reaching Tortuguero from San José. To take this route, begin by catching the 9 or 10:30am direct bus to Cariari from the **Gran Terminal del Caribe,** on Calle Central, Avenida 13 (© **2222-0610**). The fare is C1,450. This bus will actually drop you off at the main bus terminal in Cariari, from which you'll have to walk 4 blocks east to a separate bus station, known locally as *"la estación vieja,"* or the old station. Look for a booth marked **COOPETRACA** or **Clic Clic.** At these booths you can buy your bus ticket for La Pavona. The bus fare is around C1,300. Buy a ticket for the 11:30am bus (a later bus leaves at 3pm).

A boat or two will be waiting to meet the bus at the dock at the edge of the river at around 2:30pm (and again at 4pm). Check out the boats heading to Tortuguero, and pick the one that looks most comfortable and safe, then pay on board. The boat fare to Tortuguero is not regulated, and the price sometimes varies for foreigners. It can be as low as C2,500 each way, which is what locals pay. However, the boat captains often try to gouge tourists. Stand firm; you should not have to pay more than C4,000. Return boats leave Tortuguero for La Pavona every morning at 6 and 11:30am, and 3pm, making return bus connections to Cariari.

Warning: Be careful if you decide to take this route. I've received reports of unscrupulous operators providing misinformation to tourists. Folks from a company called **Bananera** have offices at the Gran Terminal del Caribe and in Cariari, offering to sell you "packaged transportation" to Tortuguero. However, all they are doing is charging you extra to buy the individual tickets described above. Be especially careful if the folks selling you boat transportation aggressively steer you to a specific hotel option, claim that your first choice is full, or insist that you must buy a package with them that includes the transportation, lodging, and guide services. If you have doubts or want to check on the current state of this

A stilt house in Tortuguero.

route, check out the site **www.tortuguerovillage.com**, which has detailed directions about how to get to Tortuguero by a variety of routes.

Finally, it's also possible, albeit expensive, to travel to Tortuguero by boat from **Puerto Viejo de Sarapiquí** (see chapter 10). Expect to pay $500 to $700 each way for a boat that holds up to 10 people. Check at the public dock in Puerto Viejo de Sarapiquí if you're interested. The ride usually takes about 3 to 4 hours, and the boats tend to leave in the morning.

VILLAGE LAYOUT   Tortuguero is one of the most remote locations in Costa Rica. With no roads into this area and no cars in the village, all transportation is by boat or foot. Most of the lodges are spread out over several kilometers to the north of Tortuguero Village on either side of the main canal; the small airstrip is at the north end of the beachside spit of land. At the far northern end of the main canal, you'll see the **Cerro de Tortuguero (Turtle Hill),** which, at some 119m (390 ft.), towers over the area. The hike to the top of this hill is a popular half-day tour and offers some good views of the Tortuguero canal and village, as well as the Caribbean Sea.

Tortuguero Village is a small collection of houses connected by footpaths. The village is spread out on a thin spit of land, bordered on one side by the Caribbean Sea and on the other by the main canal. At most points, it's less than 300m (984 ft.) wide. In the center of the village, you'll find a small children's playground, the town's health clinic, and a soccer field.

If you stay at a hotel on the ocean side of the canal, you'll be able to walk into and explore the village at your leisure; if you're across the canal, you'll be dependent on the lodge's boat transportation. However, some of the lodges across the canal have their own network of jungle trails that might appeal to naturalists.

FAST FACTS   Tortuguero has no banks, ATMs, or currency-exchange houses, so be sure to bring sufficient cash in colones to cover any expenses and incidental charges. The local hotels and shops generally charge a commission to exchange dollars. An Internet cafe (no phone) is right across from the main dock in town, although I prefer the one found at **La Casona** (✆ **2709-8092**), a small restaurant and budget hotel in the heart of the village.

Exploring the National Park

According to existing records, sea turtles have frequented Tortuguero National Park since at least 1592, largely due to its extreme isolation. Over the years, turtles were captured and their eggs were harvested by local settlers; by the 1950s, this practice became so widespread that turtles faced extinction. Regulations controlling this mini-industry were passed in 1963, and in 1970 Tortuguero National Park was established.

Today, four different species of sea turtles nest here: the green turtle, the hawksbill, the loggerhead, and the giant leatherback. The park's beaches are excellent places to watch sea turtles nest, especially at night. As appealingly long and deserted as they are, however, the beaches are not appropriate for swimming. The surf is usually very rough, and the river mouths attract sharks that feed on the turtle hatchlings and many fish that live here.

Green turtles are the most common turtle found in Tortuguero, so you're more likely to see one of them than any other species if you visit during the prime nesting season from **July to mid-October** (Aug–Sept are peak months). **Loggerheads** are very rare, so don't be disappointed if you don't see one. The **giant leatherback** is perhaps the most spectacular sea turtle to watch laying eggs. The largest of all turtle species, the leatherback can grow to 2m (6½ ft.) long and weigh well over 1,000 pounds. It nests from late February to June, predominantly in the southern part of the park. See the "In Search of Turtles" box on p. 105 for more information.

You can explore the park's rainforest, either by foot or by boat, and look for some of the incredible varieties of wildlife that live here: jaguars, anteaters, howler monkeys, collared and

A turtle hatchling heading to sea.

white-lipped peccaries, some 350 species of birds, and countless butterflies, among others. Some of the more colorful and common bird species you might see in this area include the rufescent and tiger herons, keel-billed toucan, northern jacana, red lored parrot, and ringed kingfisher. Boat tours are far and away the most popular way to visit this park, although one frequently very muddy trail starts at the park entrance and runs for about 2km (1.25 miles) through the coastal rainforest and along the beach.

Turtle Tips

- Visitors to the beach at night must be accompanied by a licensed guide. Tours generally last between 2 and 4 hours.

- Sometimes you must walk quite a bit to encounter a nesting turtle. Wear sneakers or walking shoes rather than sandals. The beach is very dark at night, and it's easy to trip or step on driftwood or other detritus.

- Wear dark clothes. White T-shirts are not permitted.

- Flashlights, flash cameras, and lighted video cameras are prohibited on turtle tours.

- Smoking is prohibited on the beach at night.

Although it's a perfect habitat, West Indian manatees (*Trichechus manatus*) are rare and threatened in the canals, rivers, and lagoons of Costa Rica's Caribbean coast. Hunting and propeller injuries are the prime culprits. Your chances of seeing one of these gentle aquatic mammals is extremely remote.

ENTRY POINT, FEES & REGULATIONS   The Tortuguero National Park entrance and ranger station are at the south end of Tortuguero Village. The ranger station is inside a landlocked old patrol boat, and a small, informative open-air kiosk explains a bit about the park and its environs. Admission to the park is $10. However, most people visit Tortuguero as part of a package tour. Be sure to confirm whether the park entrance is included in the price. Moreover, only certain canals and trails leaving from the park station are actually within the park. Many hotels and private guides take their tours to a series of canals that border the park and are very similar in terms of flora and fauna but don't require a park entrance. When the turtles are nesting, arrange a night tour in advance with either your hotel or one of the private guides working in town. These guided tours generally run between $10 and $20. Flashlights and flash cameras are not permitted on the beach at night because the lights discourage the turtles from nesting.

ORGANIZED TOURS   Most visitors come to Tortuguero on an organized tour. All of the lodges listed below, with the exception of the most inexpensive accommodations in Tortuguero Village, offer package tours that include various hikes and river tours; this is generally the best way to visit the area.

In addition, several San José–based tour companies offer budget 2-day/ 1-night excursions to Tortuguero, including transportation, all meals, and limited tours around the region. Prices for these trips range between $150 and $300 per person, and—depending on the price—guests are lodged either in one of the basic hotels in Tortuguero Village or one of the nicer lodges listed below. Reputable companies offering these excursions include **Exploradores Outdoors ★** (© **646/205-0828** in the U.S. and Canada, or 2222-6262 in Costa Rica; www. exploradoresoutdoors.com), **Jungle Tom Safaris** (© **2221-7878;** www.jungle tomsafaris.com), and **Iguana Verde Tours** (© **2231-6803;** www.iguanaverde tours.com). Some operators offer 1-day trips in which tourists spend almost all their time coming and going but that do allow for a quick tour of the canals and lunch in Tortuguero. These trips are good for travelers who like to be able to say, "Been there, done that;" they generally run between $90 and $120 per person.

However, if you really want to experience Tortuguero, I recommend staying for at least two nights.

Alternatively, you could go with **Fran and Modesto Watson ★ (𝒞 2226-0986;** www.tortuguerocanals.com), who are pioneering guides in this region and operate their own boat. The couple offers a range of overnight and multiday packages to Tortuguero, with lodging options at most of the major lodges here.

BOAT CANAL TOURS   Aside from watching turtles nest, the unique thing to do in Tortuguero is tour the canals by boat, keeping your eye out for tropical birds and native wildlife. Most lodges can arrange a canal tour for you, but you can also arrange a tour through one of the operators in Tortuguero Village. I recommend **Daryl Loth (𝒞 8833-0827;** http://casamarbella.tripod.com;), who runs the Casa Marbella (see below) in the center of the village. I also recommend **Ernesto Castillo (𝒞 2709-8070).** If neither of these guides is available, ask for a recommendation at the **Sea Turtle Conservancy Visitors' Center and Museum** (𝒞 **2709-8091**). Most guides charge between $15 to $25 per person for a tour of the canals. If you travel through the park, you'll also have to pay the park entrance fee of $10 per person.

Exploring Tortuguero Village

The most popular attraction in town is the small **Sea Turtle Conservancy Visitors' Center and Museum ★ (𝒞 2709-8091;** www.conserveturtles.org). The museum has information and exhibits on a whole range of native flora and fauna, but its primary focus is on the life and natural history of the sea turtles. Most visits to the museum include a short, informative video on the turtles. All the

Tortuguero Village.

proceeds from the small gift shop go toward conservation and turtle protection. The museum is open daily from 10am to noon and 2 to 5pm. Admission is $1, but more generous donations are encouraged.

In the village, you can also rent dugout canoes, known in Costa Rica as *cayucos* or *pangas.* Be careful before renting and taking off in one of these; they tend to be heavy, slow, and hard to maneuver, and you might be getting more than you bargained for. **Miss Junie** (℃ **2709-8102**) rents lighter and more modern fiberglass canoes for around $5 for 3 hours.

You'll find a handful of souvenir shops spread around the center of the village. The **Paraíso Tropical Gift Shop** has the largest selection of gifts and souvenirs. But I prefer the **Jungle Shop,** which has a higher-end selection of wares and donates 10% of its profits to local schools.

Where to Stay

Although the room rates below may appear high, keep in mind that they usually include round-trip transportation from San José (which amounts to approx. $100 per person), plus all meals, taxes, and usually some tours. When broken down into nightly room rates, most of the lodges are really charging only between $60 and $150 for a double room. *Note:* When I list package rates below, I have always listed the least expensive travel option, which is a bus and boat combination both in and out. All of the lodges also offer packages with the option of a plane flight either one or both ways.

VERY EXPENSIVE

Manatus Hotel ★★   Tortuguero doesn't really have any true luxury lodgings. This is the only option offering up rooms with air-conditioning and televisions, so if that's what you're looking for or need, this is definitely the place for you. The cozy rooms feature varnished wood floors and four-poster beds with white muslin mosquito netting, which is actually mostly for show, as it is entirely open at the top. However, they aren't necessary, as these rooms are well-sealed off from the critters and kept immaculate. The small free-form pool is set close to the main Tortuguero canal, as is a two-story covered deck area perfect for reading a book or watching the boat and crocodile traffic pass by. The hotel also has a small, well-run little spa, as well as an exercise room and art gallery featuring local and regional artists and craftsman. Service is extremely attentive and personal.

Tortuguero. www.manatushotel.com. ℃ **2239-4854** reservations in San José, or 2709-8197 at the hotel. 12 units. $270 per person for 2 days/1 night; $383 per person for 3 days/2 nights. Rates are double occupancy, and include 3 meals daily, taxes, and daily tours. No children under 3 years of age allowed. **Amenities:** Restaurant; bar; outdoor pool; small spa and exercise room; free Wi-Fi.

Tortuga Lodge ★★★   This is my top choice in Tortuguero: The accommodations, service, guides, and food are all a notch above the rest. That said, the rooms do not feature air-conditioning or televisions—this is still a remote ecolodge, after all. The two-story lodging buildings feature standard rooms, junior suites, and one large Penthouse room that is great for families. I think it's worth the slight splurge for the second-floor balcony rooms, but all are well done. The large, canal-front deck is built on several levels stepping up from the water and joining with the large, main dining room and bar, and serves as the social hub for the lodge. The lodge has a delightful stone-lined pool and several trails on site. Costa Rica Expeditions, a leader in sustainable ecotourism in Costa Rica, owns and runs this property.

Tortuguero. ✆ **2257-0766** for reservations in San José, or 2709-8034 at the lodge. www.tortuga lodge.com. 29 units. Starting at $548 per person for 3 days/2 nights. Rates are double occupancy, and include round-trip transportation from San José, 3 meals daily, taxes, and some tours. **Amenities:** Restaurant; bar; small outdoor pool; free Wi-Fi.

EXPENSIVE

Laguna Lodge ★★ This well-run lodge sits on the ocean side of the main canal, about a 20- to 30-minute walk north of Tortuguero Village. Rooms are housed in a series of one-story-buildings—most of them raised off the ground, with wood walls and floors and simple furnishings. All enjoy a shared veranda overlooking the gardens or pool area. There are, in fact, two separate pools, as well as open-air butterfly and frog gardens on site, and the beach is just a couple hundred yards away. Meals are served buffet-style in a large, covered, open-air dining room overlooking canal.

Tortuguero. ✆ **888/259-5615** in the U.S. and Canada, or 2272-4943 in Costa Rica for reservations. www.lagunatortuguero.com. 106 units. $236 per person for 2 days/1 night; $299 per person for 3 days/2 nights. Rates are double occupancy and include round-trip transportation from San José, tours, taxes, and 3 meals daily. Children 5–11 pay half-price. Children 4 and under free. **Amenities:** Restaurant; 2 bars; 2 outdoor pools; free Wi-Fi.

Mawamba Lodge ★ Much like Laguna Lodge (see above) this lodge is a collection of raised wooden buildings set amidst lush gardens on the ocean side of the main canal. This is the closest of the main nature lodges to the town, which is convenient for those looking to spend a bit more time shopping or picking up on the village's local flavor. The rooms are simple and tidy, with walls and floors of dark varnished hardwoods. All come with some sort of shared or private veranda, and most of these are equipped with hammocks or rocking chairs for some serious downtime. The four "superior" rooms are individual bungalows, featuring more space, king beds, large bathrooms with a deep tub and river views. The lodge has several bar and restaurant venues, including one of the main restaurants built on an old barge and moored just off the lodge's river bank. Butterfly, frog and iguana breeding projects insure great wildlife viewing opportunities.

Tortuguero. ✆ **2293-8181.** www.grupomawamba.com. 58 units. $205–$307 per person for 2 days/1 night; $285–$423 per person for 3 days/2 nights. Rates are double occupancy, and include round-trip transportation from San José, 3 meals daily, taxes, and some tours. Discounts for children 5–11. Children 4 and under free. **Amenities:** Restaurant; bar; free-form outdoor pool; free Wi-Fi.

Turtle Beach Lodge ★ Tucked away down a narrow canal on a thin strip of sand and jungle fronting the sea, this is the most isolated of the main Tortuguero nature lodges. The lodge sits on 175 acres of private reserve with miles of private trails and deserted beachfront making this a good place for those looking to get away from it all. The rooms are rustic affairs set on simple concrete foundations, with thin walls that are mostly fine mesh screening. Located some 8km (5 miles) north of the Tortuguero Village (and all of the other lodges), this is also a great lodge for the nighttime turtle tours, as guests here tend to have this section of beach all to themselves during nesting season.

Caño Palma, Tortuguero. ✆ **2248-0707** in San José, or 8837-6969 at the lodge. www.turtlebeach lodge.com. 55 units. $218 per person for 2 days/1 night; $299 per person for 3 days/2 nights. Rates double occupancy, and include round-trip transportation from San José, 3 meals daily, taxes, and tours. **Amenities:** Restaurant; bar; lounge w/satellite TV; Internet; outdoor pool.

INEXPENSIVE

Several basic cabinas in the village of Tortuguero offer budget lodgings for between $25 and $55 per person. **Cabinas Miss Junie** (℡ **2709-8102**) and **Cabinas Miss Miriam** (℡ **2709-8002**) are the traditional favorites, although in my opinion, the best of the batch are the **Hotel El Icaco** (℡ **2709-8044**), **Cabinas La Casona** (℡ **2709-8092**), and **Cabinas Tortuguero** (℡ **2709-8114**).

Casa Marbella ★   This is the best bet in Tortuguero for budget-minded, independent travelers. Co-owned by Daryl Loth, one of the most respected local guides around, this simple B&B occupies a converted home right on the canal in the heart of the village. All rooms are simple, but well kept. The best rooms have views of the water, and, of these, the second-floor superior is the best in class. Daryl either conducts or helps arrange a wide variety of tours and activities in the area.

Tortuguero, Limón. ℡ **2709-8011** or 8833-0827. http://casamarbella.tripod.com. 11 units. $40–$45 double; $55–$65 superior. Rates include breakfast. No credit cards. **Amenities:** Free Wi-Fi.

Where to Dine

Most visitors take all their meals as part of a package at their hotel. The town has a couple of simple sodas (diners) and restaurants. The best of these are **La Casona** (℡ **2709-8092**) and **Miss Junie's** (℡ **2709-8102**).

Budda Café ★ INTERNATIONAL   This is the most popular independent restaurant in Tortuguero—an important distinction because a vast majority of visitors stay at lodges where all their meals are included. Tables and chairs are spread around several open-air spaces, and the best seats are those on a deck jutting out over the water. Pizzas, pastas, stuffed crepes, and a range of main dishes are offered. Start things off with some fresh ceviche, and save room for the excellent desserts. The whole operation has a laid-back, lounge-like atmosphere and the canal-front setting is delightful.

On the main canal, next to the ICE building, Tortuguero Village. ℡ **2709-8084.** www.budda cafe.com. Main courses C4,500–C13,000. Daily 11:30am–8:30pm.

Wild Ginger ★ INTERNATIONAL   Located on the ocean side of the village, this small spot has boldly sought to make a mark on the local dining scene. Their culinary philosophy is defined as "California meets Costa Rica." The menu features everything from seasonal lobster and mango ceviche to a beef tenderloin in a coffee rub. I especially like the ginger-marinated chicken with a passion fruit sauce. For dessert, be sure to try their molten chocolate-espresso cake.

On the ocean-side path, north end of Tortuguero Village. ℡ **2709-8240.** www.wildgingercr.com. Main courses C4,500–C13,000. Tues–Sun 6pm–9pm.

LIMÓN: GATEWAY TO TORTU-GUERO NATIONAL PARK & SOUTHERN COASTAL BEACHES

160km (99 miles) E of San José; 55km (34 miles) N of Puerto Viejo

It was just offshore from present-day Limón, in the lee of Isla Uvita, that Christopher Columbus is said to have anchored in 1502, on his fourth and final voyage to the New World. Believing that this was potentially a very rich land, he

A Fall Festival

Limón's biggest yearly event, and one of the liveliest festivals in Costa Rica, is **Carnaval**, around Columbus Day (Oct 12). For a week, languid Limón shifts into high gear for a nonstop bacchanal orchestrated to the beat of reggae, soca, and calypso music. During the revelries, residents don costumes and take to the streets in a dazzling parade of color. Festivities include marching bands, dancers, and parade floats. If you want to experience Carnaval, make your reservations early because hotels fill up fast. (This advice goes for the entire coast.)

christened it Costa Rica ("Rich Coast"). While never supplying the Spanish crown with much in the way of gold or jewels, the spot where he anchored has proved over the centuries to be the best port on Costa Rica's Caribbean coast—so his judgment wasn't all bad. Today Limón is a rough-around-the-edges port city that ships millions of pounds of bananas northward every year. It also receives a fair share of the country's ocean-borne imports and a modest number of cruise ship callings. On days when a cruise ship is in port, you'll find the city bustling far beyond the norm.

Limón is not generally considered a tourist destination, and few tourists take the time to tour the city, except those stopping here on cruise ships. Very few choose to stay here, and I don't recommend it except during Carnaval—and even then you're better off in Cahuita or Puerto Viejo.

If you want to get in some beach time while you're in Limón, hop in a taxi or a local bus and head north a few kilometers to **Playa Bonita,** a small public beach. Although the water isn't very clean and is usually too rough for swimming, the setting is much more attractive than downtown. This beach is popular with surfers.

Essentials

GETTING THERE & DEPARTING   By Car: The Guápiles Highway (CR32) heads north out of San José on Calle 3 before turning east and passing close to Barva Volcano and through the rainforests of Braulio Carrillo National Park en route to Limón. The drive takes about 2¹/₂ hours and is spectacularly beautiful, especially when it's not raining or misty. Alternately, you can take the old highway, which is also scenic but much slower. This highway heads east out of San José on Avenida Central and passes through San Pedro and then Curridabat before reaching Cartago. From Cartago on, the narrow and winding road passes through Paraíso and Turrialba before descending out of the mountains to Siquirres, where the old highway meets the new. This route takes around 4 hours, more or less, to get to Limón.

By Bus: Transportes Caribeños buses (© **2222-0610** in San José, or 2758-2575 in Limón) leave San José every hour daily between 5am and 7pm from the Caribbean bus terminal (Gran Terminal del Caribe) on Calle Central, Avenida 13. Friday and Sunday, the last bus leaves an hour later at 8pm. The trip duration is around 3 hours. The buses are either direct or local (*corriente*), and they don't alternate in any particularly predictable fashion. The local buses are generally older and less comfortable and stop en route to pick up passengers from the roadside. I highly recommend taking a direct bus, if possible. The fare is C3,155 one-way.

Buses leave Limón for San José every hour between 5am and 7pm, and similarly alternate between local and direct, with the last bus leaving 1 hour later on Sundays. The Limón bus terminal is on the main road into town, several blocks west of the downtown area and Parque Vargas. Buses (© **2758-1572** for the terminal) to **Cahuita** and **Puerto Viejo** leave from here roughly every hour from 5:30am to 7pm daily. Buses to **Punta Uva** and **Manzanillo,** both of which are south of Puerto Viejo, leave Limón daily at 5:30 6:30, 8:30, 10:30am, and 12:30, 3:30, 5:30, and 6:30pm from the same station.

CITY LAYOUT   Nearly all addresses in Limón are measured from the central market, which is aptly located smack-dab in the center of town, or from Parque Vargas, which is at the east end of town fronting the sea. The cruise ship dock is just south of Parque Vargas. A pedestrian mall runs from Parque Vargas to the west for several blocks.

FAST FACTS   A host of private and national banks are in the small downtown area. You can reach the **local police** at © **2758-0365** and the **Red Cross** at © **2758-0125.** The **Tony Facio Hospital** (© **2758-0580**) is just outside of downtown on the road to Playa Bonita.

Exploring Limón

Limón has little for tourists to do or see. The closest true attraction, **Veragua Rainforest Park** (see below), is about a 40-minute drive.

If you end up spending any time in Limón, be sure to take a seat in **Parque Vargas** along the seawall and watch the city's citizens go about their business. Occupying 1 city block on the waterfront, this is a lush and quiet oasis in the heart of downtown. You may even spot some sloths living in the trees here. If you want to shop for souvenirs, head to the **cruise ship terminal** whenever a ship is in port, and you'll find more than your fair share of vendors. Finally, if you're interested in architecture, take a walk around town. When banana shipments built this port, local merchants erected elaborately decorated buildings, several of which have survived the city's many earthquakes, humid weather, and salty sea air. There's a certain charm in the town's fallen grace, drooping balconies, rotting woodwork, and chipped paint. One of the city's most famous buildings is known locally as the **Black Star Line** (© **2798-1948**), located on Avenida 5 and Calle 6. Also called Liberty Hall, this building was built in 1922, as the headquarters for Marcus Garvey's United Negro Improvement Association. Restored several years ago, it serves today as the city's social and cultural meeting place. Check here for traveling art exhibits, and the occasional live music, dance, or theater performance.

Just be careful: Limón is a rough and impoverished port town. Street crime and violence are problems. Tourists should stick to the very well-worn city center, and spots mentioned here. In addition, I don't recommend walking anywhere at night. Even in the daytime, it's probably best to travel in small groups.

Along the Way

If you're driving to the Caribbean coast, you should consider combining the trip with a stop at the Rain Forest Aerial Tram (p. 150), or the Puerto Viejo de Sarapiquí area (p. 341).

Veragua Rainforest Park.

A ONE-STOP SHOP RAINFOREST TOURISM SPOT

Located outside of Limón in a patch of thick rainforest south of the banana town of Liverpool, **Veragua Rainforest Park** ★ (© **2296-5056;** www.veraguarain forest.com) is primarily a destination for cruise ship excursions. However, this extensive complex is a worthy stop for anyone visiting the area. Attractions include a serpentarium, butterfly garden and breeding exhibit, hummingbird garden, extensive insect exhibit, free-range rainforest frog room, zip-line canopy tour, and a short tram ride that takes you to their rainforest trail system. Along the trails, you'll find a beautiful little waterfall. A half-day tour runs $66 per adult and $45 per child, and a full-day tour runs $99 per adult and $75 per child; these tour prices don't include transportation or lunch. The park is open Tuesday through Sunday from 8am to 3pm.

En Route South

Staying at the place listed below is a great way to combine some quiet beach time on the Caribbean coast with a more active ecolodge and bird-watching experience into one compact itinerary.

Selva Bananito Lodge ★★   This remote ecolodge is set high on the slopes of rainforest-covered mountains. The simple, yet spacious, wood cabins feature solar hot-water showers and large wraparound verandas or balconies. All have stunning views of the surrounding forests. On site are great opportunities for hiking and horseback riding, as well as tree-climbing, waterfall rappelling, and zip-line tours. Meals are served family-style in the large open-air main lodge building. The owners are dedicated conservationists; the property was awarded "5 Leaves" in the CST Sustainable Tourism program.

Bananito. © **2253-8118.** www.selvabananito.com. 11 units. $320–$360 double. Rates include 3 meals daily, 1 tour daily, and all taxes. **Amenities:** Restaurant. You'll need a four-wheel-drive vehicle to reach the lodge itself, although most leave their rental cars in Bananito and let the lodge drive them the final bit. You can also arrange to be picked up in San José.

Where to Stay

Hotel Playa Westfalia ★   This beachfront hotel is not in Limón proper. Instead, it's about 5 miles south, just beyond the city's tiny airport. I think the distance and beachfront setting more than compensate for any lack of easy access to Limón's limited urban attractions. The two-story hotel features clean, spacious rooms with red terracotta tile floors, simple decor, and a strong air-conditioning unit. All feature either a balcony, patio or shared veranda. The oceanfront second floor suite is a worthy splurge with good views from its large private balcony. A mid-size pool is between the hotel and the beach, which is a large, long and almost always deserted stretch of dark sand running uninterrupted for miles in each direction.

Just south of Limón, just beyond the airstrip. ℂ **2756-1300** or 2756-1300. www.hotelplaya westfalia.com. 8 units. $90–$105 double; $105–$120 suite. Rates include full breakfast and taxes. **Amenities:** Restaurant; Jacuzzi; outdoor pool; smoke-free rooms; free Wi-Fi.

Park Hotel ★   If you really must overnight in Limón then this should be your first choice. The longstanding Park Hotel sits facing the water in the heart of downtown. A breakwall and pedestrian promenade front the hotel. It's worth the upgrade for one of the ocean facing rooms versus the interior facing ones. The third-floor balcony rooms are the best in the house, with great ocean views. The popular restaurant here serves a mix of local Caribbean fare, traditional Tico standards and some Chinese dishes, perfectly reflecting the cultural mix of Limón.

Limón, Av. 3, btw. calles 1 and 3. ℂ **2798-0555.** www.parkhotellimon.com. 32 units. $72–$98 double. Rates include taxes. **Amenities:** Restaurant; free Wi-Fi.

Where to Dine

Dining options are pretty limited in Limón. In addition to the place listed below, the restaurant at the **Park Hotel** (see above) is a good bet. Try to sample the local staple *paty,* a fried dough concoction that is stuffed with a slightly spicy ground meat filling. You'll find *paty* vendors all over downtown Limón.

If you're looking for a panoramic view head to **Bar & Restaurante El Faro** (ℂ **2758-4020**) or the **Red Snapper** (ℂ **2758-7613;** www.redsnappercr. com), which are located near each other up on El Resplandon, the highest point in town, near all the city's cellphone towers. Both serve up traditional local fare and fresh seafood, and occasionally offer up live music on weekend nights.

Brisas del Caribe SEAFOOD/COSTA RICAN   Located on the north edge of the downtown Parque Vargas, just a half-block from the seawall and ocean, this local favorite is a good choice when you find yourself wandering around Limón. The restaurant serves up local favorites including the ubiquitous rice and beans (which is made with coconut milk). You can get eggs for breakfast with rice and beans, or a plate of fresh fish or stewed chicken with rice and beans for lunch or dinner. When it's not raining, they usually put a few tables out on the sidewalk fronting the local city park.

North side of Parque Vargas, Limón. ℂ **2758-0138.** Main courses C2,500–C8,000. Daily 7:30am–9pm.

CAHUITA ★

200km (124 miles) E of San José; 42km (26 miles) S of Limón; 13km (8 miles) N of Puerto Viejo

Cahuita is a small beach village and the first "major" tourist destination heading south out of Limón. Nevertheless, the boom going on in Puerto Viejo and the beaches south of Puerto Viejo have in many ways passed Cahuita by. Depending on your point of view, that can be a reason to stay or to decide to head farther south. Any way you slice it, Cahuita is one of the more laid-back villages in Costa Rica. The few dirt and gravel streets here are host to a languid parade of pedestrian traffic, parted occasionally by a bicycle, car, or bus. After a short time, you'll find yourself slipping into the heat-induced torpor that affects anyone who ends up here.

The village traces its roots to Afro-Caribbean fishermen and laborers who settled in this region in the mid-1800s, and today the population is still primarily English-speaking blacks whose culture and language set them apart from other Costa Ricans.

People come to Cahuita for its miles of pristine beaches, which stretch both north and south from town. The southern beaches, the forest behind them, and the coral reef offshore (one of just a handful in Costa Rica) are all part of **Cahuita National Park ★★**. Silt and pesticides washing down from nearby banana plantations have taken a heavy toll on the coral reefs, so don't expect the snorkeling to be world-class. But on a calm day, it can be pretty good, and the beaches

A red-eyed tree frog in Cahuita.

are idyllic every day. It can rain almost any time of year here, but the most dependably dry months are September and October.

Essentials

GETTING THERE & DEPARTING   By Car: Follow the directions above for getting to Limón. As you enter Limón, about 5 blocks before the busiest section of downtown, watch for a paved road to the right, just before the railroad tracks. Take this road (CR36) south to Cahuita, passing the airstrip and the beach on your left as you leave Limón. Alternatively, a turnoff with signs for Sixaola and La Bomba is several miles before Limón. This winding shortcut skirts the city and puts you on the coastal road (CR36) several miles south of Limón.

By Bus: Mepe express buses (© **2257-8129;** www.mepecr.com) leave San José daily at 6 and 10am, noon, and 2 and 4pm from the Caribbean bus terminal (Gran Terminal del Caribe) on Calle Central, Avenida 13. The trip's duration is 4 hours; the fare is C4,670. During peak periods, extra buses are often added. However, it's wise to check because this bus line (Mepe) is one of the most fickle.

Alternatively, you can catch a bus to **Limón** (see above) and then transfer to a Cahuita- or Puerto Viejo–bound bus (© **2758-1572**) in Limón. These latter

Cahuita

------ Reef

HOTELS
Alby Lodge **19**
Cabinas Arrecife **14**
Cabinas Spencer **15**
Casa de las Flores **9**
Coral Hill Bungalows **6**
El Encanto Bed and
    Breakfast **11**
Magellan Inn **2**
Playa Negra
    Guesthouse **7**

RESTAURANTS
Choco Latte **17**
Coral Reef **10**
El Girasol **8**
Restaurant Edith **13**
Sobre Las Olas **12**

NIGHTLIFE
Coco's Bar **10**
National Park Restaurant **18**
Reggae Bar **16**

ATTRACTIONS
Aviarios Sloth Sanctuary
    of Costa Rica **3**
Brigitte's Horses **5**
Cahuita National Park **20**
Mariposario Cahuita **4**
Tree of Life Wildlife Rescue
    Center and Botanical
    Gardens **1**

buses leave roughly every two hours between 7:30am and 4:30pm from the main Terminal Talamanca in Limón. Buses from Limón to Manzanillo also stop in Cahuita and leave from the same spot leave roughly every two hours between 6:30am and 6:30pm. The trip takes 1 hour; the fare is C1,190.

Interbus (© **2283-5573;** www.interbusonline.com) has a daily bus that leaves San José for Cahuita at 7:45am. The fare is $47. Interbus buses leave Cahuita daily at both 6:30am and 2pm. Interbus will pick you up at most area hotels in both San José and Cahuita, and offers connections to various other destinations around Costa Rica.

Buses departing **Puerto Viejo** and Sixaola (on the Panama border) stop in Cahuita roughly every two hours between 7am and 7pm en route to San José. However, the schedule is far from precise, so it's always best to check with your hotel. Moreover, these buses are often full, particularly on weekends and throughout the high season. To avoid standing in the aisle all the way to San José, it is sometimes better to take a bus first to Limón and then catch one of the frequent Limón–San José buses. Buses to Limón pass through Cahuita regularly throughout the day. Another tactic I've used is to take a morning bus to Puerto Viejo, spend the day down there, and board a direct bus to San José at its point of origin, thereby snagging a seat.

VILLAGE LAYOUT Cahuita only has about eight dirt streets. The highway runs parallel to the coast, with three main access roads running perpendicular. The

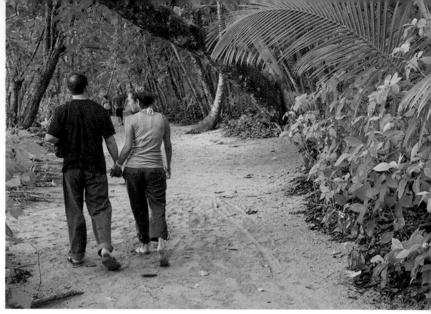

A trail through Cahuita National Park.

northernmost of these access roads bypasses town and brings you to the northern end of Playa Negra. It's marked with signs for the Magellan Inn and other hotels up on this end. The second road in brings you to the southern end of Playa Negra, about 1km (a half-mile) closer to town. The third road is the principal entrance into town. The village's main street in town, which runs parallel to the highway, dead-ends at the national park entrance (a footbridge over a small stream).

Buses drop their passengers off at a bus terminal at the back of a small strip mall on the main entrance road into town. Cabs will be waiting to take you to the lodges on Playa Negra. Alternately, you can head out walking north on the street that runs between Coco's Bar and the small park. This road curves to the left and continues 1.6km (1 mile) or so out to Playa Negra.

FAST FACTS The police station (© **2755-0217**) is located where the road from Playa Negra turns into town. You'll find the post office (© **2755-0096**), as well as a well-equipped pharmacy, **Farmacia Cahuita** (© **2755-0505**), and a branch of the Banco de Costa Rica with an ATM in the small Arena Blancas strip mall in front of the bus station. Several Internet cafes are around the central

---

You *Can* Bring It with You

I recommend packing a picnic lunch, plenty of water, and some snorkel gear and hiking out along the inland rainforest trail, all the way out to Punta Cahuita. Once there, you can spread out a blanket or some towels, snorkel on the reef, and swim in the tide pools, before enjoying your lunch. You can walk along the beach for most of the return trip to town, and stop for a cooling dip or two if the mood strikes.

downtown area of the village. If you can't find a cab in town, ask your hotel to call you one, or try **Alejandro** (© 8875-3209) or **Dino** (© 2755-0012 or 8340-2354).

Exploring Cahuita National Park ★★

This little gem of a national park sits at the southern edge of Cahuita town. Although the pristine white-sand beach, with its picture-perfect line of coconut palms and lush coastal forest backing it, is the main draw here, the park was actually created to preserve the 240-hectare (787-acre) **coral reef** that lies just offshore. The reef contains 35 species of coral and provides a haven for hundreds of brightly colored tropical fish. You can walk on the beach itself or follow the trail that runs through the forest just behind the beach to check out the reef.

One of the best places to swim is just before or beyond the **Río Perezoso (Lazy River),** several hundred meters inside Cahuita National Park. The trail behind the beach is great for bird-watching, and if you're lucky, you might see some monkeys or a sloth. The loud grunting sounds you'll hear off in the distance are the calls of howler monkeys, which can be heard from more than a kilometer away. Nearer at hand, you're likely to hear crabs scuttling amidst the dry leaves on the forest floor—a half-dozen or so species of land crabs live in this region—my favorites are the bright orange-and-purple ones.

The trail behind the beach stretches a little more than 9km (5.6 miles) to the southern end of the park at **Puerto Vargas** (© 2755-0302), where you'll find a beautiful white-sand beach. The best section of reef is off the point at

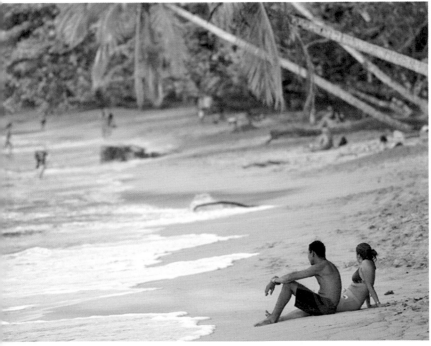

The beach in Cahuita National Park.

Damaged & Endangered

While patches of living, vibrant reef survive off Costa Rica's Caribbean coast, much of it has been killed off, or is severely threatened by over-fishing, pollution, rain, and mud runoff during the rainy season. Much of the damage can be traced to the massive banana plantations that line this coastline, which have had a direct role in increasing the amount of muddy runoff and have dumped tons of plastic and pesticides into the fragile, inshore reef systems.

Punta Cahuita, and you can snorkel here. If you don't dawdle, the 3.8km (2.35-mile) hike to Punta Cahuita should take a little over an hour each way—although I'd allow plenty of extra time to marvel at the flora and fauna, and take a dip or two in the sea. Bring plenty of mosquito repellent because this area can be buggy.

Although you can snorkel from the shore at Punta Cahuita, it's best to have a boat take you out to the nicest coral heads just offshore. A 3-hour **snorkel trip** costs between $20 and $30 per person, with equipment. You can arrange one with any of the local tour companies listed below. *Note:* These trips are best taken when the seas are calm—for safety's sake, visibility, and comfort.

ENTRY POINTS, FEES & REGULATIONS The **in-town park entrance** is just over a footbridge at the end of the village's main street. It has restroom facilities, changing rooms, and storage lockers. This is the best place to enter if you just want to spend the day on the beach and maybe take a little hike in the bordering forest.

The alternate park entrance is at the southern end of the park in **Puerto Vargas.** This is where you should come if you don't feel up to hiking a couple of hours to reach the good snorkeling spots. The road to Puerto Vargas is approximately 5km (3 miles) south of Cahuita on the left.

Officially, **admission** is $10 per person per day, but this is collected only at the Puerto Vargas entrance. You can enter the park from the town of Cahuita for free or with a voluntary contribution. The park is open from dawn to dusk for day visitors.

GETTING THERE **By Car:** The turnoff for the Puerto Vargas entrance is clearly marked 5km (3 miles) south of Cahuita.

By Bus: Your best bet is to get off a Puerto Viejo- or Sixaola-bound bus at the turnoff for the Puerto Vargas entrance (well marked, but tell the bus driver in advance). The guard station/entrance is only about 500m (1,640 ft.) down this road. However, the beach and trails are several kilometers farther.

Beaches & Activities Outside the Park

Outside the park, the best place for swimming is **Playa Negra.** The stretch right in front of the Playa Negra Guesthouse (p. 473) is my favorite spot. The waves here are often good for bodysurfing, boogie-boarding, or surfing. If you want to rent a board or try a surf lesson, check in with Rennie at **Willie's Tours** (see below) or **Brigitte** (see below).

Cahuita has plenty of options for organized adventure trips or tours. I recommend **Cahuita Tours** (© 2755-0101; www.cahuitatours.com), **Willie's Tours** (© 2755-1024 or 8917-6982; www.williestourscostarica.com), and **Roberto Tours** (© 2755-0117). All are located along Cahuita's main road, and offer a wide range of tours ranging from snorkel outings, to rainforest hikes, to visits to nearby indigenous reserves. Most also offer multiday trips to Tortuguero, as well as to Bocas del Toro, Panama.

BUTTERFLY GARDEN   On the main highway, just north of the main entrance to Cahuita, is the **Mariposario Cahuita** (*C* **2755-0361**), a large, informative butterfly-farm attraction that charges $10 and is open Monday to Friday from 9am to 4pm, and weekends by appointment. It's best to come in the early morning on a sunny day, when the butterflies are most active.

HORSEBACK RIDING   Brigitte (*C* **2755-0053**; www.brigittecahuita.com;) offers guided horseback tours for $35 to $75. She also rents mountain bikes and surfboards, and even has a few rooms available.

WILDLIFE VIEWING   Bird-watchers and sloth lovers should head north 11km (7 miles) to **Aviarios Sloth Sanctuary of Costa Rica** ★★ (*C* **2750-0775**; http://www.slothsanctuary.com). Their signature tour features an informative visit to their sloth rehabilitation project and learning center, as well as a 1-hour canoe tour through the surrounding estuary and river system. More than 330 species of birds have been spotted here. You'll get an up-close look at a range of rescued wild sloths, both adults and babies, as well as several bred in captivity. After, you can hike their trail system and look for sloths in the wild. Tours begin at 8am, with the last tour of the day leaving at 2pm. It's best to make reservations in advance. They are closed on Mondays. These folks also offer up a few cozy and quaint rooms right on site if you want to spend more time exploring the bird-watching and wildlife options, as well as sloth rescue project.

Toward the northern end of the dirt road leading out beyond Playa Negra is the **Tree of Life Wildlife Rescue Center and Botanical Gardens** (*C* **2755-0014**; www.treeoflifecostarica.com). Stroll through extensive, well-maintained gardens, where a series of large cages house a range of rescued and recovering local fauna, including toucans, monkeys, coatimundi, deer, wild pigs, or peccaries.

A sloth at the Aviarios Sloth Sanctuary of Costa Rica.

This place is typically open Tuesday through Sunday from 9am to 3pm, however they often close for weeks or even months at a time. Admission is $12.

Where to Stay

In addition to the places listed below, **Coral Hill Bungalows** ★ (☏ **2755-0479;** www.coralhillbungalows.com) has three individual bungalows and a separate two-story house, in a lush garden setting, about a block or so inland from the beach at Playa Negra.

MODERATE

El Encanto Bed & Breakfast ★★   This is a great little hotel on the outskirts of the small village. In fact, El Encanto sits about half-way between the village and Playa Negra, either one a 5 minute or so walk away. Rooms feature varnished wood or red terra cotta floors, and lively regional artworks and textiles to round out the decor. The three-bedroom house with a fully equipped kitchen is perfect for families or those seeking longer stays. The lush gardens, small kidney shaped pool and shady gazebo spread around the grounds create an oasis-like sensation for those staying here. The service here is extremely friendly and accommodating.

Cahuita (just outside of town on the road to Playa Negra). ☏ **2755-0113.** www.elencanto cahuita.com. 8 units. $85 double; $135 suite; $230 house. Rates include full breakfast. Rates slightly lower in off season; higher during peak weeks. **Amenities:** Small outdoor pool; Wi-Fi.

INEXPENSIVE

In addition to the places listed below, **Cabinas Spencer** (☏ **2755-0027**) and its somewhat funky collection of budget rooms is worth considering; its rooms are set just a few feet from the water in the heart of town. Another option is **Casa de las Flores** (☏ **2755-0326;** http://lacasadelasfloreshotel.com), which has neat and cheery rooms set near the main road, right in the center of town, near the heart of the action, yet still close to the national park entrance.

Alby Lodge ★   While relatively close to the town and national park entrance, this place feels quite removed, located on an expansive property at the end of a winding dirt road. The lodge consists of four individual thatch-roofed cabins spread across the grounds and gardens. The cabins themselves are relatively small and simple, but each comes with a small balcony strung with a cozy and inviting hammock. Guests have access to a communal kitchen in the main lodge building, and home of owners Thomas and Yvonne.

Cahuita. ☏ **2755-0031.** www.albylodge.com. 4 units. $60 double. $5 for extra person. No credit cards. **Amenities:** Free Wi-Fi.

Cabinas Arrecife   A seafront location and small pool give this very inexpensive backpacker favorite a leg up over the competition in this town. Set facing the sea, this simple place features a row of rooms in a low concrete building. The rooms themselves are kept neat and come with one twin and one double bed, as well as a table or floor fan. You'll find Cabinas Arrecife on the waterfront, next door to Restaurant Edith (see below).

Cahuita (about 100m/328 ft. east of the Police station. ☏ **2755-0081.** www.cabinasarrecife.com. 12 units. $30 double. Rates include taxes. **Amenities:** Outdoor pool; free Wi-Fi.

Magellan Inn ★   Terry Newton is the second-generation owner/manager of this quaint and cozy bed-and-breakfast. Rooms are simple, and most are on the small size, but the lush gardens, ample covered veranda complete with a Persian rug, attentive service, and lovely pool built into the local coral make this a wonderful choice. This hotel is located a few hundred yards north and inland from Playa Negra.

At the far end of Playa Negra (about 2km/1¼ miles north of Cahuita), Cahuita. ✆ **2755-0035.** www.magellaninn.com. 6 units. $65–$110 double; $105–$130 deluxe. Rates include full breakfast. **Amenities:** Bar; lounge; small outdoor pool; free Wi-Fi.

Playa Negra Guesthouse ★★★ This is the best beachfront hotel in Cahuita. Set just across a dirt and sand lane from the waves, the hotel has well-tended, exuberant gardens, an inviting pool, and beautiful, well-kept rooms and individual cottages. A couple of these cottages come with full kitchens and are good for families or those planning on an extended stay. No meals are served here, but several restaurants are within easy walking distance, and the center of Cahuita is about 1.6km (1 mile) away by foot, bicycle, or taxi.

On Playa Negra (about 1.5km/1 mile north of town), Cahuita. ✆ **2755-0127.** www.playanegra. cr. 6 units. $75–$85 double room; $95 cottage; $160 2-bedroom cottage. **Amenities:** Small outdoor pool; free Wi-Fi.

Where to Dine

Coconut meat and milk figure into a lot of the regional cuisine here. Most nights, local women cook up pots of various local specialties and sell them from the front porches of the two discos or from streetside stands around town; a full meal will cost you around $2 to $5.

In addition to the places listed below, **Coral Reef** (✆ **2755-0133,** at the main crossroads in town) is a good local restaurant, with a cozy open-air second-floor dining space that's great for people-watching. For good, fresh Italian fare, try **El Girasol** (✆ **2755-1164**), a small, elegant family-run joint on the main road into town.

Choco Latte ★ COFFEEHOUSE/CREOLE Located right on the main street near the center of the village, this friendly place is the perfect spot for breakfast, lunch or a coffee break. Eggs to order, omelets, pancakes, and waffles compliment a range of fresh baked breads and pastries when this place opens early. For lunch you can get burritos, sandwiches, burgers, and a few local favorites. They offer up a range of fresh fruit juices, smoothies and coffee drinks, including espresso, cappuccino, latte and their namesake chocolate latte, both hot and iced.

On the main road in town, ½ block south of Coco's Bar. ✆ **2755-0010.** Main courses C3,000–C5,000. No credit cards. Daily 6:30am–2pm.

Cahuita's Calypso Legend

Walter "Gavitt" Ferguson, who turned 95 in 2014, is a living legend. For decades, Ferguson labored and sang in obscurity. Occasionally he would record a personalized cassette tape of original tunes for an interested tourist willing to part with $5. Finally, in 2002, Ferguson was recorded by the local label Papaya Music (www.papayamusic.com). Today, he has two CDs of original songs, "Babylon" and "Dr. Bombodee." Ask around town and you should be able to find a copy. If you're lucky, you might even bump into Gavitt himself.

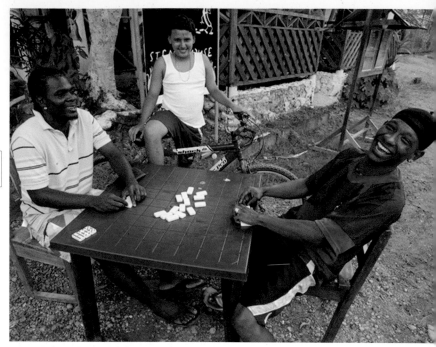

Cahuita locals playing a friendly game of dominoes.

Restaurant Edith ★ CREOLE/COSTA RICAN Miss Edith is a local legend and has been serving up traditional local cooking for decades out of this humble, open-air restaurant. Today she is helped by her daughters and other family members. I recommend ordering the spicy *rondon* (see "That Run-Down Feeling," p. 483) in advance, although everything on the menu is good. These folks even have a range of vegetarian and vegan options. Be forewarned, however, that service can be very slow at times. Ask about cooking classes.

By the police station, Cahuita. ✆ **2755-0248.** Main courses C3,500–C13,000. No credit cards. Daily 7am–10pm.

Sobre Las Olas ★★★ SEAFOOD/ITALIAN This small, oceanfront restaurant not only has the best setting in the region, but it certainly has one of the best settings of any restaurant in Costa Rica. The sea is just steps away, and there's a stunning view down the coastline. The Italian owners specialize in preparing the freshest local seafood in a variety of ways, touching on their home-country heritage and the Caribbean seasonings in equal measure. Start things off with some ceviche or a carpaccio of fresh snapper. On pretty days and nights, you'll definitely want to grab one of the few outdoor tables closest to the water.

Just north of town on the road to Playa Negra. ✆ **2755-0109.** Main courses C5,000–C10,000. Wed–Mon noon–10pm.

Shopping

For a wide selection of beachwear, local crafts, cheesy souvenirs, and batik clothing, try **Boutique Bambata,** which is on the main road near the entrance to the park. This is also a good place to have your hair wrapped in colorful threads and strung with beads. Heading north out of town, similar wares are offered at the **Cahuita Tours** gift shop. For something less organized, local and itinerant artisans in makeshift stands near the park entrance sell handmade jewelry and crafts.

If you're interested in the region, pick up a copy of Paula Palmer's "What Happen: A Folk-History of Costa Rica's Talamanca Coast." The book is a history of Costa Rica's Caribbean coast based on interviews with many of the area's oldest residents. Much of it is in the traditional Creole language, from which the title is taken. It makes for a fun and interesting read, and you just might meet someone mentioned in the book.

Entertainment & Nightlife

Coco's Bar ★, a classic Caribbean watering hole at the main crossroads in town, has traditionally been the place to spend your nights (or days, for that matter) if you like cold beer and very loud reggae and soca music. Toward the park entrance, the **National Park Restaurant** has a popular bar, with loud music and dancing on most nights during the high season and on weekends during the off season, while out toward Playa Negra, the **Reggae Bar** ★ has a convivial vibe, with thumping tropical tunes blasting most nights.

PUERTO VIEJO ★★

200km (124 miles) E of San José; 55km (34 miles) S of Limón

Puerto Viejo is the Caribbean coast's top destination. Even though Puerto Viejo is farther down the road from Cahuita, it's much, much more popular, with a distinctly livelier vibe and many more hotels and restaurants to choose from. Much of this is due to the scores of surfers who come to ride the town's famous and fearsome Salsa Brava wave, and only slightly mellower Playa Cocles (p. 486) beach break. Nonsurfers can enjoy other excellent swimming beaches, plenty of active adventure options, nearby rainforest trails, and a collection of great local and international restaurants.

This area gets plenty of rain, just like the rest of the coast (Feb–Mar and Sept–Oct are your best bets for sun, although it's not guaranteed).

Essentials

GETTING THERE & DEPARTING **By Car:** To reach Puerto Viejo, continue south from Cahuita on CR36 for another 16km (10 miles). Watch for a prominent and well-marked fork in the highway. The right-hand fork continues on to Bribri,

---

Closures along the Caribbean Coast

Costa Rica's maritime land law has only sporadically been enforced along the Caribbean coast. In early 2012, the government issued eviction notices for several coastal businesses in Cahuita and Puerto Viejo, with threats to demolish any constructions. Several of the

businesses are longstanding operations and listed in this book, including Sobre Las Olas (p. 474), Koki Beach (p. 485), and the Lazy Mon (p. 485). While the possibility of the government following through is real, I personally expect things to get tied up in the courts for years.

Sixaola, and the Panamanian border. The left-hand fork (it actually appears to be a straight shot) takes you into Puerto Viejo on 5km (3 miles) of sporadically paved road.

By Bus: Mepe express buses (© **2257-8129** in San José, or 2750-0023 in Puerto Viejo; www.mepecr.com) to Puerto Viejo leave San José daily at 6 and 10am, noon, and 2 and 4pm from the Caribbean terminal (Gran Terminal del Caribe) on Calle Central, Avenida 13. The trip's duration is $4^1/_2$ to 5 hours; the fare is C5,450. During peak periods, extra buses are sometimes added. Always ask if the bus is continuing on to **Manzanillo** (especially helpful if you're staying in a hotel south of town).

Interbus (© **2283-5573**; www.interbusonline.com) has a daily bus that leaves San José for Puerto Viejo at 7:45am. The fare is $47. Interbus buses leave Puerto Viejo daily at 6:30am and 2pm. Interbus will pick you up at most hotels in both San José and Puerto Viejo, and offers connections to various other destinations around Costa Rica.

Alternatively, you can catch a bus to **Limón** (p. 461) and then transfer to a Puerto Viejo–bound bus in Limón. These latter buses (© **2758-1572**) leave roughly every hour between 7am and 4:30pm from the main terminal in Limón. Buses from Limón to Manzanillo also stop in Puerto Viejo and leave daily roughly every two hours between 6:30am and 6:30pm. The trip takes $1^1/_2$ hours; the fare is C1,800 to Puerto Viejo, and C2,420 to Manzanillo.

If you arrive in Puerto Viejo by bus, be leery of hucksters and touts offering you hotel rooms. In most cases, they work on a small commission from whatever hotel or cabina is hiring, and, in some cases, they'll steer you away from one of my recommended hotels or falsely claim that it is full.

A beached barge by Puerto Viejo.

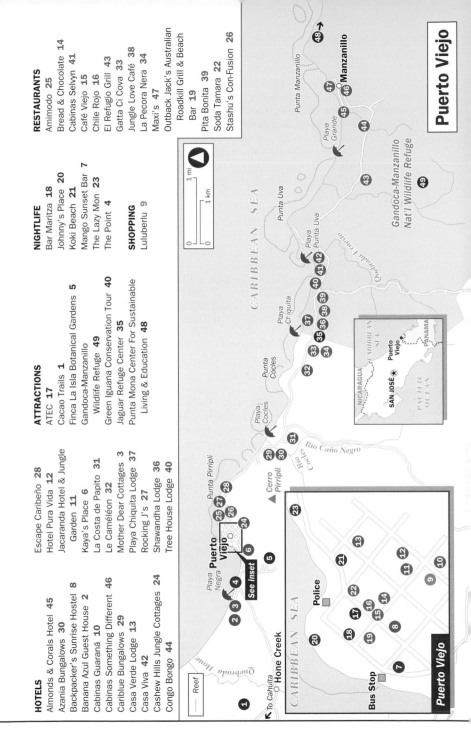

HOTELS

Almonds & Corals Hotel **45**
Azania Bungalows **30**
Backpacker's Sunrise Hostel **8**
Banana Azul Guest House **2**
Cabinas Guaraná **10**
Cabinas Something Different **46**
Cariblue Bungalows **29**
Casa Verde Lodge **13**
Casa Viva **42**
Cashew Hills Jungle Cottages **24**
Congo Bongo **44**

Escape Caribeño **28**
Hotel Pura Vida **12**
Jacaranda Hotel & Jungle
  Garden **11**
Kaya's Place **6**
La Costa de Papito **31**
Le Caméléon **32**
Mother Dear Cottages **3**
Playa Chiquita Lodge **37**
Rocking J's **27**
Shawandha Lodge **36**
Tree House Lodge **40**

ATTRACTIONS

ATEC **17**
Cacao Trails **1**
Finca La Isla Botanical Gardens **5**
Gandoca-Manzanillo
  Wildlife Refuge **49**
Green Iguana Conservation Tour **40**
Jaguar Refuge Center **35**
Punta Mona Center For Sustainable
  Living & Education **48**

NIGHTLIFE

Bar Maritza **18**
Johnny's Place **20**
Koki Beach **21**
Mango Sunset Bar **23**
The Lazy Mon **23**
The Point **4**

SHOPPING

Luluberlu **9**

RESTAURANTS

Amimodo **25**
Bread & Chocolate **14**
Cabinas Selvyn **41**
Café Viejo **15**
Chile Rojo **16**
El Refugio Grill **43**
Gatta Ci Cova **33**
Jungle Love Café **38**
La Pecora Nera **34**
Maxi's **47**
Outback Jack's Australian
  Roadkill Grill & Beach
  Bar **19**
Pita Bonita **39**
Soda Tamara **22**
Stashu's Con-Fusion **26**

Puerto Viejo

Express buses leave Puerto Viejo for San José daily at 9 and 11am and 4pm. Buses for Limón leave daily roughly every two hours between 9:30am and 6:30pm. However, this schedule is subject to change, so it's always best to check with your hotel. Buses to **Punta Uva** and **Manzanillo** leave Puerto Viejo about a half-dozen times throughout the day.

GETTING AROUND   Taxis are fairly easy to come by around Puerto Viejo. You'll either find them hanging around the *parquecito* (little park), or you can try calling **Taxi Jireh** (② **2750-2073**). You can rent scooters and bicycles from a handful of roadside operators around town.

TOWN LAYOUT   The road in from the highway runs parallel to Playa Negra, or Black Sand Beach (not the beach in Cahuita), for a couple of hundred meters before entering the village of Puerto Viejo, which has all of about 10 dirt streets. The sea is on your left and forested hills on your right as you come into town. It's another 15km (9 1/3 miles) south to Manzanillo. This road is paved all the way to Manzanillo, although many sections are nonetheless in fairly rough shape.

FAST FACTS   You'll find a couple of banks and ATMs, as well as the **post office** (② **2750-0404**), near the entrance to town. A **Guardia Rural police office** (② **2750-0230**) is on the beach, near Johnny's Place (see later in this chapter). Several little Internet cafes are around town. There are also a couple of self- and full-service laundromats—the one at **Café Rico** (② **2750-0510**) will give you a free cup of coffee, cappuccino, or espresso while you wait.

Exploring Puerto Viejo

CULTURAL & ADVENTURE TOURS   The **Asociación Talamanqueña de Eco-turismo y Conservación** ★★ (**ATEC;** Talamancan Association of Ecotourism and Conservation; ② **2750-0398;** www.ateccr.org), across the street from the Soda Tamara, is a local organization concerned with preserving the environment and cultural heritage of this area and promoting ecologically sound development. (If you plan to stay in Puerto Viejo for an extended period of time and would like to contribute to the community, ask about volunteering.) In addition to functioning as the local information center, Internet cafe, and traveler's hub, ATEC runs a little shop that sells T-shirts, maps, posters, and books.

ATEC also offers quite a few tours, including **half-day walks** that focus on nature and either the local Afro-Caribbean culture or the indigenous Bribri culture. These walks pass through farms and forests, and along the way you'll learn about local history, customs, medicinal plants, and Indian mythology, and have an opportunity to see sloths, monkeys, iguanas, keel-billed toucans, and other wildlife. A range of different walks lead through the nearby **Bribri Indians' Kéköldi Reserve,** as well as more strenuous hikes through the primary rainforest. **Bird walks** and **night walks** will help you spot more of the area wildlife; there are even overnight treks. The local guides have a wealth of information and make a hike through the forest a truly educational experience. ATEC can arrange snorkeling trips to the nearby coral reefs, as well as snorkeling and fishing trips in dugout canoes, and everything from surf lessons to dance classes. ATEC can also help you arrange overnight and multiday **camping trips** into the Talamanca Mountains and through neighboring indigenous reserves, as well as trips to Tortuguero and even a 7- to 10-day transcontinental trek to the Pacific coast. Half-day tours (and night walks) are $25 to $60, and full-day tours run between $75 and $120. Some tours require minimum groups of 5 or 10 people and several days' advance notice. The ATEC office is open daily from 8am to 9pm.

Local tour operators **Exploradores Outdoors** ★★ (© **2750-2020;** www.exploradoresoutdoors.com) and **Terraventuras** ★ (© **2750-0750;** www.terraventuras.com) both offer a host of half- and full-day adventure tours into the jungle or sea for between $35 and $300 per person. One especially popular tour is Terraventuras' zip-line canopy tour, which features 22 treetop platforms, a large harnessed swing, and a rappel.

HORSEBACK RIDING   For horseback riding, check in with **Seahorse Stables** (© **8859-6435;** www.horsebackridingincostarica.com). A range of guided tours are offered, with rides along the beach, as well as into the rainforest. They even do multiday treks down to Punta Mona (see below).

SCUBA DIVING   Scuba divers can check in with **Reef Runners Dive Shop** (© **2750-0480;** www.reefrunnerdivers.com). These folks frequent a variety of dive sites between Punta Uva and Manzanillo, and if you're lucky the seas will be calm and visibility good—although throughout most of the year, it can be a bit rough and murky here. Reef Runners has an office in downtown Puerto Viejo. Rates run between $80 and $110 for a two-tank boat dive.

A LITTLE MIND & BODY REVITALIZATION   If you're looking for some day-spa pampering, check out **Indulgence Spa** ★★ (© **2750-0536;** http://www.indulgencespa-salon.com). Located at La Costa de Papito (p. 492), these folks have a wide range of massage and treatment options at reasonable rates. They make many of their own oils, masks, wraps, and exfoliants. They also have an in-house salon.

Bliss Massage Center ★ (© **2756-8224**) offers up a similar menu of treatment options in the mini-mall in the center of downtown.

Better suited to a longer stay or organized retreat, **Samasati** (© **800/563-9643** in the U.S., or 2224-1870 in Costa Rica; www.samasati.com) is a lovely jungle yoga retreat and spa, with spectacular hillside views of the Caribbean Sea and surrounding forests. Rates run between $115 and $215 per person per day, depending on occupancy and room type, and include three vegetarian meals per day and taxes. A wide range of tour, massage, and yoga packages are available. If you're staying elsewhere in

A spa treatment at Pure Jungle Spa.

Puerto Viejo or Cahuita, you can come up for yoga classes ($15), meditation ($5), or private massages ($110–$200) with advance notice. Samasati is located a couple of kilometers before Puerto Viejo (near the turnoff for Bribri) and roughly 1.6km (1 mile) up into the jungle.

NOT YOUR EVERYDAY GARDENS　One of the nicest ways to spend a day in Puerto Viejo is to visit the **Finca La Isla Botanical Gardens ★★** (© **8886-8530**), a couple of hundred meters inland from the Black Sand Beach on a side road just north of El Pizote lodge. Peter Kring and his late wife Lindy poured time and love into the creation of this meandering collection of native and imported tropical flora. The trails and experience are a bit rough around the edges, but you'll see medicinal, commercial, and just plain wild flowering plants, fruits, herbs, trees, and bushes. Visitors get to gorge on whatever is ripe at the moment. A rigorous rainforest loop trail leaves from the grounds. The gardens are generally open Friday through Monday from 10am to 4pm, but visits at other times can sometimes be arranged in advance. Entrance to the garden is $5 per person for a self-guided tour of the trails (you can buy their trail map for an extra $1), or $10 for a 2¹/₂-hour guided tour (minimum of three people).

　Cacao Trails ★ (www.cacaotrails.com; © **2756-8186**) is a one-stop attraction featuring botanical gardens, an open-air museum demonstrating cacao cultivation and processing, and a series of trails, a large open-air restaurant, and a swimming pool. You can take canoe rides on the bordering Carbon River, and even watch leatherback sea turtles lay their eggs during the nesting season (p. 456). Admission is $25, including a guided tour. A full-day tour, including lunch and a canoe trip, as well as the guided tour, costs $50. During turtle nesting season, they do night tours to watch sea turtles lay their eggs.

Cacao fruit.

Cacao beans drying in the sun.

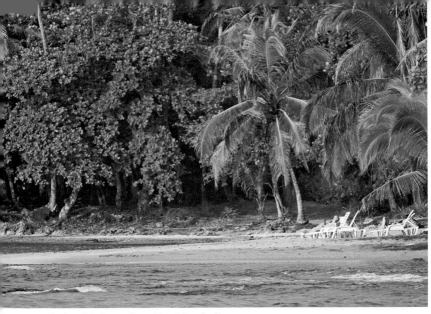
The beach in front of Lazy Mon @ Stanford's.

SUNNING & SURFING **Surfing** has historically been the main draw here, but increasing numbers of folks are coming for the miles of beautiful and uncrowded **beaches** ★★, acres of lush rainforests, and laid-back atmosphere. If you aren't a surfer, the same activities that prevail in any quiet beach town are the norm here—sunbathing, going for a walk on the beach, reading a book, or taking a nap. If you have more energy, choose from a host of tours and hiking options, or you can rent a bicycle or a horse. For swimming and sunbathing, locals like to hang out on the small patches of sand in front of the Lazy Mon @ Stanford's and Johnny's Place. Small, protected tide pools are in front of each of these bars for cooling off. The Lazy Mon has several hammocks and you're likely to stumble upon a pickup beach volleyball match or soccer game here.

If you want a more open patch of sand and sea, head north out to **Playa Negra,** along the road into town, or, better yet, to the beaches south of town around Punta Uva and all the way down to Manzanillo, where the coral reefs keep the surf much more manageable (see "Manzanillo & the Gandoca–Manzanillo Wildlife Refuge," below).

Just offshore from the tiny village park is a shallow reef where powerful storm-generated waves sometimes reach 6m (20 ft.). **Salsa Brava** ★★★, as it's known, is the prime surf break on the Caribbean coast. Even when the waves are small, this spot is recommended only for very experienced surfers because of the danger of the reef. Other popular beach breaks are south of town on Playa Cocles.

Several operators and makeshift roadside stands offer bicycles, scooters, boogie boards, surfboards, and snorkel gear for rent. Shop around to compare prices and the quality of the equipment before settling on any one.

ANOTHER WAY TO GET WET & WILD **Exploradores Outdoors** ★★ (www. exploradoresoutdoors.com; ☏ **646/205-0828** in the U.S., 2222-6262 in San

José, or 2750-2020 in Puerto Viejo) runs daily white-water rafting trips on the Pacuare and Reventazón rivers. The full-day trip, including transportation, breakfast, and lunch, is $99. If you want to combine white-water rafting with your transportation to or from the Caribbean coast, they can pick you up at your hotel in San José or La Fortuna with all your luggage, take you for a day of white-water rafting, and drop you off at day's end at your hotel anywhere on the Caribbean coast from Cahuita to Manzanillo. You can choose to use the option in the other direction, getting dropped off at the hotel of your choosing either in San José or the La Fortuna/Arenal Volcano area. These folks also offer a combination kayaking and hiking tour to Punta Uva, as well as overnight tours to Tortuguero.

Where to Stay

For a longer stay, close to town, you might want to check out **Cashew Hill Jungle Cottages** (✆ 2750-0001; www.cashewhilllodge.co.cr). On a hill just on the outskirts of town, these are simple but immaculate individual one- and two-bedroom bungalows, with kitchenettes.

In addition to the places listed below, **Mother Dear Cottages** ★★ (www.motherdearcr.com) offers two fully equipped, raised stilt cottages right on the beach in Playa Negra.

MODERATE

In addition to the hotels listed below, **Escape Caribeño** (✆ 2750-0103; www.escapecaribeno.com) is another good option in this price range, located on the outskirts of town, just south of Salsa Brava.

Banana Azul Guest House ★★   This boutique, adults-only hotel is located on the far northern end of Playa Negra, and sits just steps from the sand; a welcoming vibe pervades this little place. A vast stretch of undeveloped beach backed by thick forest stretches north from here all the way to Cahuita National Park. The simple rooms and suites are heavy on varnished wood and creative mosaic tile accents; suites feature more space and usually a tub or Jacuzzi. The owners and staff are especially helpful.

Playa Negra Puerto Viejo, Limón. ✆ **877/284-5116** in the U.S. and Canada, or 2750-2035 in Costa Rica. www.bananaazul.com. 14 units. $104–$155 double; $164–$207 suite or apt. Rates include full breakfast. No children 15 and under allowed. **Amenities:** Restaurant; bar; bike rental; Jacuzzi; outdoor pool; free Wi-Fi.

INEXPENSIVE

True budget hounds will find an abundance of basic hotels and cabinas in downtown Puerto Viejo in addition to those listed below. Of these, **Hotel Pura Vida** (✆ 2750-0002; www.hotel-puravida.com) and **Backpackers Sunrise Hostel** (✆ 2750-0028; www.sunrisepuertoviejo.com are both good bets, while **Kaya's Place** (✆ 2750-0690; www.kayasplace.com) is a budget traveler's favorite just on the northern outskirts of town across from Playa Negra.

Cabinas Guaraná   Bold primary colors and assorted artistic touches abound at this friendly downtown hotel. The hotel is set a block inland from the main street through town, and features at least one tall old tree at the center of the complex giving it a quieter feel than you'd expect for such a centrally located lodging. It's worth requesting a room with a private terrace or balcony. Most of these come with a rocking chair or hammock, or both.

1½ blocks inland from Café Viejo, Puerto Viejo, Limón. © **2750-0244.** www.hotelguarana.com. 12 units. $43 double. Rates include tax. Rates slightly lower in off season; higher during peak weeks. **Amenities:** Lounge; communal kitchen; free Wi-Fi.

Casa Verde Lodge ★★ You can't beat Casa Verde right in Puerto Viejo. It has grown from a simple, hostel-like option in the heart of the village to a beautiful mini-resort, with spa services and a lovely, landscaped pool area. The gardens are beautiful and the rooms and grounds are immaculately maintained. The owners, a charming Swiss-Tica couple, are committed to local environmental and educational causes.

Puerto Viejo, Limón. © **2750-0015.** www.cabinascasaverde.com. 17 units, 9 with private bathroom. $40–$50 double with shared bathroom; $62–$75 double with private bathroom. Rates include taxes. Discounts offered for cash payments. **Amenities:** Outdoor pool; massage hut; free Wi-Fi.

Jacaranda Hotel & Jungle Garden This place features a delightful collection of rooms and individual cabins spread around lush gardens and under tall shade trees. Painted murals and artistic mosaic tile walkways add spice to the simple wooden constructions. All beds come with mosquito netting, and the friendly owner is a wealth of local knowledge.

1½ blocks inland from Café Viejo, Puerto Viejo, Limón. © **2750-0069.** www.cabinasjacaranda. net. 14 units with private bathroom. $32–$60 double. **Amenities:** Wi-Fi.

Rocking J's ★ This backpacker favorite is aptly named for its rocking scene. Lodging options range from an open-air thatch-roofed communal hammock area to a second-floor covered camping area where you can pop up your own tent or rent one of theirs. There are also private rooms, and a much coveted treehouse suite. The large compound here features trails to the nearby beach, as well as a host of common areas where guests from all over the world meet to converse and play. A popular restaurant and bar that sometimes features live music are right on site.

Just south of downtown, Puerto Viejo, Limón. © **2750-0665** or 2750-0657. www.rockingjs.com. 35 units, 3 with private bathroom. $7–$12 per person in a tent or hammock; $11–$15 dorm room; $26–$35 double with shared bathroom; $70–$80 double with private bathroom. **Amenities:** Restaurant; bar; free Wi-Fi.

Where to Dine

To really sample the local cuisine, you need to look up a few local women. Ask around for **Miss Dolly, Miss Sam, Miss Isma,** and **Miss Irma,** who all dish out sit-down meals in their modest little *sodas.* In addition to locally seasoned fish and chicken served with rice and beans, these joints are usually a great place to find some *pan bon* (a local sweet, dark bread), ginger cakes, *paty* (meat-filled turnovers), and *rondon* (see below). Just ask around for these women, and someone will direct you to them.

Puerto Viejo has a glut of excellent Italian restaurants; in addition to the places listed below, **Amimodo ★** (© **2750-0257**) serves an excellent lobster ravioli, as well as a carpaccio of home-smoked shark.

That Run-Down Feeling

Rondon soup is a spicy coconut milk–based soup or stew made with anything the cook can "run down"—it usually includes a mix of local tubers (potato, sweet potato, or yuca), other vegetables (carrots or corn), and often some seafood. Be sure to try this authentic taste of the Caribbean.

EXPENSIVE

Café Viejo Lounge Restaurant ITALIAN   Opened more than 15 years ago by three brothers from Rimini, this local hot spot sits right on the main drag in the center of town. It's easy to spot, with white muslin drapes hanging from wooden posts and separating the open-air dining room from the busy streets beyond the veils. Wood-oven pizzas and a wide range of homemade pastas form the backbone of the extensive menu here. You can also order up fresh whole fish, and an assortment of chicken and beef main dishes emphasizing the cuisine of Northern Italy, but with other regional and local influences. The locally sourced fresh lobster ravioli are a house specialty. After the kitchen closes, this place transforms nightly into a hip, electronic European-style club. These folks have a good wine list, and actually take care to properly store their stock and protect it from the often oppressive Caribbean heat.

On the main road. © **2750-0817.** Main courses C5,000–C25,000. Wed–Mon 6–11:30pm.

MODERATE

Stashu's Con-Fusion ★★★ INTERNATIONAL   Stashu is a local legend, and his cooking and restaurant have been a Puerto Viejo mainstay for years, albeit with a couple of different locations and names. This current incarnation serves up his classic mix of world fusion cuisines, with fresh fish, seafood, and vegetarian entrees served up in spicy curries or with Thai- or Mexican-tinged sauces. One of his more popular recent specials is a macadamia-crusted fish filet with a white-wine-and-white-chocolate sauce. The open-air restaurant features a mix of creative artwork and sculptures.

On the main road just south of downtown, about 1 block beyond Stanford's. © **2750-0530.** Main courses C4,000–C18,000. Thurs–Tues 5–10pm.

INEXPENSIVE

Bread & Chocolate ★★ BREAKFAST/AMERICAN   This is a great spot for breakfast, lunch, coffee break—or chocolate fix. You can get a range of typical breakfast plates, as well as sandwiches, salads, and baked goods. As the restaurant's name might suggest, the bread (biscuits, bagels, and such) is baked fresh. And the chocolate is served up as a drink, in a range of truffles, and in several fabulous brownies, including my favorite, the mint-chocolate brownie.

$^{1}/_{2}$ block south of Café Viejo. Downtown Puerto Viejo © **2750-0723.** Main courses C3,000–C3,700. No credit cards. Tues–Sat 6:30am–6:30pm; Sun 6:30am–2:30pm.

Chile Rojo ★ PAN-ASIAN/MEDITERRANEAN   This lively spot has a friendly ambience and sense of camaraderie. Walk up the flight of steps to this lively spot and browse the broad menu featuring pad Thai and other Thai curries, sushi rolls, Indian Tikka-spiced fish, and a range of typical Middle Eastern classics like hummus, falafel and tabouli. Vegetarians have many options to choose from. Monday nights feature a sushi buffet, and weekends often include live music or a DJ.

2nd floor of shopping mall downtown. © **2750-0025.** www.bestchilerojo.com. Main courses C5,500–C7,400. Daily 10am–11pm.

Outback Jack's Australian Roadkill Grill & Beach Bar ★ INTERNATIONAL   This place gets around. Having set up shop first in Brasilito and later in Tárcoles, this lively Australian-themed beach bar and grill has found a happy home in downtown Puerto Viejo. The ramshackle and colorful decor is exuberant, gaudy and whimsical—as is the overall vibe here. The menu features typical bar food appetizers, barbeque ribs, spicy chicken wings and "shrimp on the Bar-bie." You can get whole fried red snapper, and a wide range of grilled meats, including a large, juicy T-bone steak. The mixed grill platter is great for sharing amongst friends.

¾ block south of the bus stop. ℂ **8471-2622.** www.outbackjacks.org. Main courses C3,500–C16,000. Tues–Sun 11am–11pm.

Soda Tamara ★ COSTA RICAN/CARIBBEAN A handful of humble little restaurants around town serve local food made fresh by their namesake owner and chef. None is as popular or longstanding as Soda Tamara. Occupying a prized spot near the water yet still on the town's main road, this open-air spot specializes in rice and beans (made with coconut milk) served with Caribbean-style chicken fish or meat dishes. The low, wooden picket fence that separates this place from the street is painted in the bold red, green, yellow and black colors emblematic of the strong Jamaican influence and heritage of this coastline.

On the main road. ℂ **2750-0148.** Main courses C3,800–C33,000. Daily 11:30am–10pm.

Shopping

Puerto Viejo attracts a lot of local and international bohemians, who seem to survive solely on the sale of handmade jewelry, painted ceramic trinkets (mainly pipes and cigarette-lighter holders), and imported Indonesian textiles. You'll find them at makeshift stands set up by the town's *parquecito* (little park), which comprises a few wooden benches in front of the sea between Soda Tamara and Stanford's.

In addition to the makeshift outdoor stands, a host of well-stocked gift and crafts shops are spread around town. **Luluberlu** ★ (ℂ **2750-0394**), located inland across from Cabinas Guaraná, features locally produced craftwork, including shell mobiles and mirrors with mosaic-inlaid frames, as well as imports from Thailand and India.

Tip: My favorite purchase here is locally produced chocolate, which is made by several local outfits, and can be found for sale at many gift shops and restaurants around town.

Nightlife & Entertainment

For a large party scene and dancing, **Johnny's Place** ★★ (no phone) near the Rural Guard station, is the place to be. The action spills out from the small dance floor and onto the beach most nights, where you'll find candle-lit tables set near the water's edge. Another good waterfront spot is the **Lazy Mon @ Stanford's** ★★ (ℂ **2750-2116;** www.thelazymon.com), with a bit more of a sports bar vibe to it. They've got a pool table, dartboard, and Xbox for you to use. The bar can get rocking at night, and features regular live bands or DJs.

Another option is the **Mango Sunset Bar** ★★ (ℂ **8691-0756**), near the water, beside the bus station, and features either live music or a DJ most nights. For a more sophisticated ambience, try the oceanfront **Koki Beach** ★ (ℂ **2275-0902;** www.kokibeach.com).

For a beachfront sports bar, you can't beat **The Point** ★★ (ℂ **2756-8491**), which is located right at the first point where the road in to Puerto Viejo hits Playa Negra. This convivial, open-air joint features six television screens, and offers up three different Costa Rican microbrews on tap. The menu is a mix of typical American bar food and local fare served at tables that spill out on to the sand. These folks often also feature live music.

An open-air bar on the second floor of **Soda Tamara** (p. 485) is a casual and quiet place to gather after dark. **Rocking J's** (p. 483) sometimes features live music. Finally, for a more local scene, check out **Bar Maritza's** (© **2750-0003**), in the center of town, right across from the basketball court, which seems especially popular on Sunday nights.

PLAYAS COCLES, CHIQUITA, MANZANILLO & SOUTH OF PUERTO VIEJO ★★★

200km (124 miles) E of San José; 55km (34 miles) S of Limón

As you continue south on the coastal road from Puerto Viejo, you'll come to several of Costa Rica's best beaches. Soft white sands are fronted by the Caribbean Sea and backed by thick rainforest. **Playa Cocles** is a popular surf spot, with a powerful and dependable beach break. South of here, the isolated **Playa Chiquita** is characterized by small pocket coves, and calm pools formed by dead coral reefs raised slightly above sea level by the 1991 earthquake. Beyond this lies **Punta Uva,** a long curving swath of beach punctuated by its namesake point (or *punta*), a rainforest-clad mound of land that looks vaguely like a bunch of grapes from the distance. If you come here, be sure to hike the short loop trail up and around the point. From Punta Uva the coastline stretches to **Manzanillo.** Along the way, the white sands are fronted by a living coral reef, which breaks up the waves and keeps the swimming here generally calm and protected. When it's calm (Aug–Oct), the waters down here are some of the clearest anywhere in the country, with good snorkeling among the nearby coral reefs. The tiny village of Manzanillo is literally the end of the road. The shoreline heading south from Manzanillo, located inside the **Gandoca–Manzanillo Wildlife Refuge,** is especially beautiful, with a series of pocket coves and small beaches, featuring small islands and rocky outcroppings offshore, and backed by thick rainforest. This park stretches all the way to the Panamanian border.

Essentials

GETTING THERE & DEPARTING   By Car: A single two-lane road runs south out of Puerto Viejo and ends in Manzanillo. A few dirt roads lead off this paved, but rutted road, both toward the beach and into the mountains.

   By Bus: Follow the directions above for getting to Puerto Viejo. Local buses to Punta Uva and Manzanillo leave Puerto Viejo about a half-dozen times throughout the day.

GETTING AROUND   A taxi from Puerto Viejo should run you around $8 to Punta Uva or $12 to Manzanillo. Alternatively, it's about $1^{1}/_{2}$ hours each way by bicycle, with only two relatively small hills to contend with. Although the road is ostensibly paved all the way to Manzanillo, between the near-constant potholes and washed-out sections, it's almost like riding an off-road trail. Most of the hotels in this area either offer free bicycles, or will help arrange a rental.

   It's also possible to walk along the beach all the way from Puerto Viejo to Manzanillo, with just a couple of short and well-worn detours inland around rocky points. However, I recommend you catch a ride down to Manzanillo and save your walking energies for the trails and beaches inside the refuge.

The Punta Uva shoreline.

AREA LAYOUT As you drive south, the first beach you will hit is **Playa Cocles** ★, which is 2km (1¼ miles) from Puerto Viejo. A little farther, you'll find **Playa Chiquita** ★, which is 5km (3 miles) from Puerto Viejo, followed by **Punta Uva** ★★ at 8.4km (5¼ miles) away, and **Manzanillo** ★★, some 13km (8 miles) away.

FAST FACTS There are no true towns, and no major services to be found along this stretch of coast. However, you can find a few scattered Internet cafes and small markets mixed in with the sporadic string of hotels, private homes, and restaurants that line the main road.

Exploring Playas Cocles, Chiquita, Manzanillo & South of Puerto Viejo

For all intents and purposes, this string of beaches is an extension of Puerto Viejo, and all of the tours, activities, and attractions mentioned above can be enjoyed by those staying here. For organized scuba diving, snorkeling, sportfishing excursions, or dolphin-sighting tours around Manzanillo and the beaches south of Puerto Viejo, check in with the **Asociación de Guías Autóctonos Naturalistas de Manzanillo-Talamanca** (Association of Naturalist Guides; ℂ **2759-9064**) or look for either **Abel Bustamante** (ℂ **2759-9043;** www. manzanillo-caribe.com) or **Omar Cook** (ℂ **2759-9143;** www.costa-rica-manzanillo.com).

MANZANILLO & THE GANDOCA–MANZANILLO WILDLIFE REFUGE ★★

13km (8 miles) south of Puerto Viejo

The **Gandoca–Manzanillo Wildlife Refuge** ★★ encompasses the small village and extends all the way to the Panamanian border. Manatees, crocodiles, and more than 350 species of birds live within the boundaries of the reserve. The reserve also includes the coral reef offshore—when the seas are calm, this is the best **snorkeling** and **diving** spot on this entire coast. Four species of **sea turtles** nest on one 8.9km (5¹/₂-mile) stretch of beach within the reserve between March and July. Three species of dolphins also inhabit and frolic in the waters just off Manzanillo. The waters here are home to Atlantic spotted, bottlenose, and the rare tucuxi. This latter species favors the brackish estuary waters, but has actually been observed in mixed species mating with local bottlenose dolphins. Many local tour guides and operators offer boat trips out to spot them.

If you want to explore the refuge, you can easily find the single, well-maintained trail by walking along the beach just south of town until you have to wade across a small river. On the other side, you'll pick up the trail head. Still, this is a wild and remote area, and I recommend doing the hike with one of the guides mentioned above.

SWEET STUFF ★★   Another great educational tour is the 2-hour **Caribeans Chocolate Tour** (ⓒ **8836-8930** or 8341-2034; www.caribeanschocolate.com) through a working organic cacao plantation and chocolate production facility. The tour shows you the whole process of growing, harvesting, and processing cacao, and of course there's a tasting at the end. The tour runs every Monday at 10am, and Friday and Saturday at 2pm. It costs $26 per person. Tours can be arranged at other times by reservation. When you get around to the tasting, organic wine pairings are also available.

(ORGANIC) PEAS & LOVE ★   Inside the Gandoca–Manzanillo refuge is the **Punta Mona Center For Sustainable Living & Education ★** (no phone;

Wild and unspoiled coastline in Gandoca–Manzanillo Wildlife Refuge.

You'll spot many iguanas on the Green Iguana Conservation Tour.

www.puntamona.org). With organic permaculture gardens and a distinctly alternative vibe, this place is open for day visits, overnight stays, and work-exchange and educational programs.

ESPECIALLY FOR KIDS

Several wildlife rescue centers and animal preservation centers operate in the area. The **Jaguar Refuge Center ★★** (*C* **2750-0710;** www.jaguarrescue. com) is the most extensive of the batch. This small center is located in Playa Chiquita and features a broad assortment of local fauna, including monkeys, sloths, snakes, caimans, turtles, birds, and more. These folks do great educational and rehabilitative work. I have mixed feelings about the human-monkey interactions, but most guests are quite thrilled with the opportunity to enter an enclosure and have direct contact. Note that, despite the name, this place has never housed a jaguar. Guided tours are offered Monday through Saturday at 9:30 and 11:30am. The cost is $15 per person, children under 11 are free. Private tours can be arranged with advance notice.

Also down in Playa Chiquita, at the Tree House Lodge (see above), is the **Green Iguana Conservation Tour** (*C* **2750-0706;** www.iguanaverde.com). This educational tour focuses on the life cycle, habits, and current

On to Panama

Costa Rica's southern zone, particularly Puerto Viejo, is a popular jumping-off point for trips into Panama. The nearest and most popular destination is the island retreat of Bocas del Toro. Most tour agencies and hotel desks in the area can arrange tours to Panama. The most reliable and easiest way to get to Bocas del Toro is to take the daily **Caribe Shuttle** (*C* **2750-0626;** www.caribe shuttle.com), which will take you via land and boat for $32 each way; check the website or call for departure times.

situation of this endangered reptile. The tour features a walk around a massive natural enclosure, as well as a video presentation. The cost is $15. Regular tours are offered Tuesday and Thursday at 10am. Additional tours may be arranged by appointment.

Where to Stay Between Puerto Viejo & Manzanillo

I recommend that you rent a car if you plan to stay at one of these hotels because public transportation is sporadic and taxis aren't always available. If you arrive by bus, however, a rented bicycle or scooter might be all you need to get around once you are settled.

VERY EXPENSIVE

Almonds & Corals Hotel ★ This is Costa Rica's best place for jungle glamping. The individual units here aren't exactly tents, but they do give you the feel of being very close to and in touch with the surrounding nature. Each "room" is a very spacious structure built on raised stilts, with varnished hardwood floors and simple screen walls under soaring roofs. Four-poster wooden beds have shiny white mosquito netting, and a comfortable hammock is strung up in the screened-in balcony. A couple of the larger suites have private Jacuzzi tubs. The lodge is set in a patch of dense forest on the northern end of Playa Manzanillo. A maze of low wooden slat walkways connects the rooms to the main dining area and beach, although an onsite zip-line canopy tour is another popular way to reach the sand.

Manzanillo's beach.

This place has been awarded the maximum "5 Leaves" from the CST Sustainable Tourism program.

Manzanillo, Limón. © **888/373-9042** in the U.S. and Canada, or 2271-3000 reservations in San José, or 2759-9056 at the hotel. www.almondsandcorals.com. 24 units. $250–$350 double. Rates do not include taxes. Children 6–9 $40–$50; free for children 5 and under. **Amenities:** Restaurant; bar; bicycle rental; Jacuzzi; small spa; all rooms smoke-free; watersports equipment rental.

Le Caméléon ★   This boutique hotel is attempting to stake out ground as the only true luxury option along Costa Rica's Caribbean coast. This is the only place around where you'll find rooms with crisp air-conditioning units and flat screen televisions. The hotel has a hip, European vibe and design. The minimalist and stark all-white rooms serve as blank palettes for regularly changing decor and lighting accents. Still, I find the design and decor a bit too divorced from the local culture and environment. Perhaps the best feature of this hotel, is their plush beach club with attentive waiter service and cozy beachfront lounging options. Since opening, the Le Cameleon has had some serious management issues, and poor service has been an issue. Upon my last visit, this seems to have been remedied, but only time will tell.

Playa Cocles, Puerto Viejo, Limón. © **2750-0501.** www.lecameleonhotel.com. 23 units. $300 double; $350–$400 suite. **Amenities:** Restaurant; bar; beach club; Jacuzzi; small outdoor pool; free Wi-Fi.

Tree House Lodge ★★★   These unique houses are easily the best accommodations to be had on the Caribbean coast. Although somewhat rustic and open, the numerous artistic touches and architectural feats make each unit memorable. The namesake Tree House is built on high stilts and reached via a suspension bridge, while the three-bedroom Beach Suite features a massive, domed bathroom lit by fanciful portholes and skylights of multicolored glass. Each of the four units has a full kitchen, but only two are air-conditioned. These folks also run an iguana conservation project (p. 489) and have been awarded "4 Leaves" in the CST Sustainable Tourism program.

Punta Uva, Puerto Viejo, Limón. © **2750-0706.** www.costaricatreehouse.com. 4 units. $200–$390 double. Rates include breakfast and taxes. No credit cards. **Amenities:** Jacuzzi.

MODERATE

In addition to the places listed below, **Casa Viva** (© **2750-0089;** www.puntauva.net) offers beautiful, fully equipped one- and two-bedroom houses just steps from the sand on Punta Uva.

Azania Bungalows ★   This Argentine-owned lodge is comprised of 10 identical individual wooden cabins with high roofs, lots of space and a mix of one Queen-size and two twin beds. One of these twin beds is actually located in a small loft area accessed by a steep and rustic wooden ladder—definitely an option only for limber young ones. Each cabin comes with a private front porch hung with an cozy hammock. The grounds are lush and well-tended and the small pool is quite pretty, with its sculpted rock waterfall. The restaurant serves up a mix of local fare, fresh seafood and Argentine specialties.

Playa Cocles, Puerto Viejo, Limón. © **2750-0540.** www.azania-costarica.com. 10 bungalows. $80–$95 double. Rates include full breakfast. **Amenities:** Restaurant; bar; bike rental; outdoor pool; free Wi-Fi.

The Tree House Lodge.

Cariblue Bungalows ★★ This is a lovely, well-run small resort with expansive grounds, overflowing gardens, cozy rooms, and a good Italian restaurant (Cariblue's owners are Italian). You'll find a range of room options, from budget rooms with no air-conditioning to deluxe rooms, individual bungalows, and large suites. I favor the Superior Bungalows, which are individual wooden cabins raised off the ground a bit, and featuring a nice private balcony. In 2014, Cariblue bought and took over the neighboring beachfront Totem Hotel, giving them a few ocean-view rooms, and even better beach access. This place is located directly in front of Playa Cocles, about 1.6km (1 mile) south of Puerto Viejo.

Playa Cocles, Puerto Viejo, Limón. ✆ **2750-0035.** www.cariblue.com. 29 units. $95–$125 double; $170–$270 suite. Rates include breakfast buffet. Rates slightly lower in off season. **Amenities:** Two restaurants; bar/lounge; bike rental; Jacuzzi; two outdoor pools; free Wi-Fi.

La Costa de Papito ★ Just a short ways down the road from Cariblue (see above) this place is the loving work of New York–transplant Eddie Ryan. The individual and duplex wooden bungalows feature artistically tiled bathrooms and cool, shady verandas. There's no pool here, but the beach is just across the street. The hotel's **Qué Rico Papito** restaurant is excellent, and sometimes features live music.

Playa Cocles, Puerto Viejo, Limón. ✆ **2750-0704.** www.lacostadepapito.com. 13 units. $88–$95 double. Rates include breakfast. **Amenities:** Restaurant; bar; bike rental; small spa; free Wi-Fi.

Shawandha Lodge ★ Set in a patch of thick forest on the inland side of the road near Playa Chiquita, this was one of the first boutique lodges in the area. The individual wooden bungalows are simple, yet beautiful, and spread out amongst the trees and gardens, giving each a good sense of privacy and seclusion. The all feature high-pitched thatch roofs, a comfortable private veranda and beautiful mosaic tile creations in the bathrooms and showers. The French owners have made a definite imprint on the restaurant, which offers up local produce and seafood, with a mix of Caribbean and French-fusion influences.

Puerto Viejo, Limón. © **2750-0018.** www.shawandhalodge.com. 13 units. $110–$145 double. Rates include full breakfast. **Amenities:** Restaurant; outdoor pool; free Wi-Fi.

INEXPENSIVE

Down in Manzanillo, the simple **Cabinas Something Different** (© 2759-9014) is a good option, while **Congo Bongo** (© 2759-9016; www.congo-bongo.com) offers fully equipped houses in a lush forest setting.

Playa Chiquita Lodge ★   These simple rooms are painted lively colors and housed in a series of wooden buildings that run in a line through thick gardens, connected by a raised wooden walkway. A short trail through the rainforest lets you out onto **Playa Chiquita,** a lovely and underdeveloped stretch of beach, broken up by several tide pools and coral outcroppings, and backed by thick forest.

Playa Chiquita, Puerto Viejo, Limón. © **2750-0062.** www.playachiquitalodge.com. 12 units. $70–$80 double. Rates include breakfast. **Amenities:** Restaurant; free Wi-Fi.

Where to Dine Between Puerto Viejo & Manzanillo

In addition to the restaurants listed below, **Cabinas Selvyn** (© 2750-0664) at Punta Uva is an excellent option for local cuisine and fresh seafood, while **Pita Bonita** (© 2756-8173) serves up wonderful Middle Eastern cuisine at an open-air spot between Playa Chiquita and Punta Uva. I've also been hearing great things about the intimate **El Refugio Grill ★★** (© 2759-9007), an Argentine-owned restaurant that offers grilled steaks, sausages, and seafood in a romantic rainforest setting.

Jungle Love Café ★★ INTERNATIONAL   This intimate, family-run restaurant serves up excellent wood-oven pizzas, creative pasta dishes, healthy salads, and a mix of nightly specials. The owner's signature dish is a family pasta recipe with carrots, leeks, and a spicy brandy-cream sauce, served here with fresh shrimp. The Tokyo Tuna adds a local twist to the traditional, Asian-style seared tuna, by adding fresh tamarind juice to the marinade. Save room for the desserts, which are whipped up daily. This place fills up fast, and reservations are definitely recommended.

Playa Chiquita. © **2750-0162.** www.junglelovecafe.com. Main courses C5,500–C8,000. No credit cards. Tues–Sun 5–9:30pm.

La Pecora Nera ★★★ ITALIAN   Whenever I'm asked to name my favorite restaurant in Costa Rica, I always answer, "La Pecora Nera." This place is that good. Chef/owner Ilario Gionnoni is a master and a marvel of perpetual motion. He is constantly innovating, raises his own chickens and pigs, and grows as much of his own fresh fruits, vegetables, and herbs as he can. The menu is long and varied, but I always just ask Ilario what he recommends, or what the special is for that day. The large, multilevel, open-air dining room is dimly lit and romantic. For less elaborate and less expensive fare, Ilario also has **Gatta Ci Cova,** a simpler pasta-and-pizza joint right on the main road, at the entrance to La Pecora Nera.

50m (164 ft.) inland from a well-marked turnoff on the main road south just beyond the soccer field in Cocles. © **2750-0490.** Reservations recommended. Main courses C6,000–C17,500. Tues–Sun 5:30–10pm.

Maxi's ★ COSTA RICAN/CARIBBEAN   This ramshackle beachfront restaurant and bar is a local classic. Large portions of rice and beans are served with freshly caught seafood and large, fried plantain chips, or *patacones*. Ricky, the original owner, has moved to the Central Valley and opened up a branch there, but this place remains open and in the hands of his family here. You'll have to arrive early to get a window seat, but it's worth it.

On the beach, Manzanillo. ✆ **2759-9086.** Main courses C3,500–C10,000; lobster C11,000–C25,000. Daily noon–10pm.

14

PLANNING YOUR TRIP TO COSTA RICA

C osta Rica is no longer the next new thing. Neither is it old hat. As Costa Rica has matured as a tourist destination, things have gotten easier and easier for international travelers. That said, most travelers—even experienced travelers and repeat visitors—will want to do some serious pre-trip planning. This chapter provides a variety of planning tools, including information on how to get there; tips on accommodations; and quick, on-the-ground resources.

GETTING THERE
By Plane

It takes between 3 and 7 hours to fly to Costa Rica from most U.S. cities, the origin of most direct and connecting flights. Most international flights still land in San José's **Juan Santamaría International Airport Juan Santamaría International Airport** (© **2437-2626** for 24-hr. airport information; http://fly2sanjose.com; airport code SJO). However, more and more direct international flights are touching down in Liberia's **Daniel Oduber International Airport** (© **2668-1010;** airport code LIR).

Liberia is the gateway to the beaches of the Guanacaste region and the Nicoya Peninsula, and a direct flight here eliminates the need for a separate commuter flight in a small aircraft or roughly 5 hours in a car or bus. If you are planning to spend all, or most, of your vacation time in the Guanacaste region, you'll want to fly in and out of Liberia. However, San José is a much more convenient gateway if you are planning to head to Manuel Antonio, the Central Pacific coast, the Caribbean coast, or the Southern zone.

Numerous airlines fly into Costa Rica. Be warned that the smaller Latin American carriers tend to make several stops (sometimes unscheduled) en route to San José, thus increasing flying time.

From North America, **Air Canada, American Airlines, Avianca, Copa, Delta, Frontier, Grupo Taca, JetBlue, Interjet, Spirit Air, United,** and **US Airways** all have regular direct flights to Costa Rica.

From Europe, **Iberia** is the only airline with regular routes to San José, some direct and others with one connection. Alternately, you can fly to any major U.S. hub city and make connections to one of the airlines mentioned above.

By Bus

Bus service runs regularly from Panama City, Panama, and Managua, Nicaragua. If at all possible, it's worth the splurge for a deluxe or express bus. In terms of travel time and convenience, it's always better to get a direct bus rather than one that stops along the way—and you've got a better chance of getting a working restroom in a direct/express or deluxe bus. Some even have television sets showing movies.

PREVIOUS PAGE: **A Costa Rican oxcart.**

Several bus lines with regular daily departures connect the major capital cities of Central America. Call **King Quality** (✆ **2258-8834**), **Transnica** (✆ **2223-4242;** http://transnica.com), or **Tica Bus Company** (✆ **2221-0006;** www.ticabus.com) for further information. All of these lines service Costa Rica directly from Managua, with connections to the other principal cities of Central America. Tica Bus also has service between Costa Rica and Panama. None of them will reserve a seat by telephone, and schedules change frequently according to season and demand, so buy your ticket in advance—several days in advance, if you plan to travel on weekends or holidays. From Managua, it's 11 hours and 450km (279 miles) to San José, and the one-way fare is around $30 to $50. From Panama City, it's a 20-hour, 900km (558-mile) trip. The one-way fare is around $35 to $55.

Whenever you're traveling by bus through Central America, try to keep a watchful eye on your belongings, especially at rest and border stops, whether they're in an overhead bin or stored below decks in a luggage compartment.

By Car

It's possible to travel to Costa Rica from North America by car, but it can be difficult. After leaving Mexico, the Interamerican Highway (Carretera Interamericana, also known as the Pan-American Hwy.) passes through Guatemala, El Salvador, Honduras, and Nicaragua before reaching Costa Rica. This highway then travels the length of Costa Rica before entering Panama. All of these countries can be problematic for travelers for a variety of reasons, including internal violence, crime, corrupt border crossings, and visa formalities. If you do decide to undertake this adventure, take the **Gulf Coast route** from the border crossing at Brownsville, Texas, because it involves traveling the fewest miles through Mexico. Those planning to travel this route should purchase a copy of "You Can Drive to Costa Rica in 8 Days!" by Dawn Rae Lessler, which is available from major online bookstores. You might also try to find a copy of "Driving the Pan-Am Highway to Mexico and Central America," by Audrey and Raymond Pritchard, which is harder to find. A wealth of information is also online at **www.sanborns insurance.com** and **www.drivemeloco.com**.

CAR DOCUMENTS You will need a current driver's license, as well as your vehicle's registration and the original title (no photocopies), to enter the country.

CENTRAL AMERICAN AUTO INSURANCE Contact **Sanborn's Insurance Company** (✆ **800/222-0158;** www.sanbornsinsurance.com), which has agents at various border towns in the United States. These folks have been servicing this niche for more than 50 years. They can supply you with trip insurance for Mexico and Central America (you won't be able to buy insurance after you've left the U.S.), driving tips, and an itinerary.

CAR SAFETY Be sure your car is in excellent working order. It's advisable not to drive at night because of the danger of being robbed by bandits, especially in Mexico, Guatemala, El Salvador, and Honduras.

For information on car rentals and gasoline (petrol) in Costa Rica, see "Getting Around: By Car," later in this section.

By Boat

Some 350 cruise ships stop each year in Costa Rica, calling at Limón on the Caribbean coast, and at Puerto Caldera and Puntarenas on the Pacific coast.

The Best Websites About Costa Rica

○ **The Tico Times** (www.ticotimes.net): The English-language "Tico Times" makes it easy for norteamericanos (and other English speakers) to see what's happening in Costa Rica. It features the top story from its weekly print edition, as well as a daily update of news briefs, a business article, regional news, a fishing column, and travel reviews. There's also a link to current currency exchange rates.

○ **Latin American Network Information Center** (http://lanic.utexas.edu/la/ca/cr): This site houses a vast collection of information about Costa Rica, and is hands-down the best one-stop shop for browsing, with helpful links to a diverse range of tourism and general information sites.

○ **Costa Rica Maps** (www.mapcr.com): In addition to selling a wonderful waterproof map of the country, this site features several excellent downloadable nationwide, regional, and city maps, and a host of other useful information.

○ **The U.S. Embassy in Costa Rica** (www.usembassy.or.cr): The official site of the U.S. Embassy in Costa Rica has a good base of information and regular updates of concern to U.S. citizens abroad, as well as about Costa Rica in general.

○ **CostaRicaLiving E-Board** (www.crl-eboard.info): This is an information clearinghouse site put together by the folks at Costa Rica Living newsgroup. The site is chock-full of useful information, suggestions, reviews, and tips. If you want more information, feel free to join the newsgroup. The active newsgroup deals with a wide range of issues, and its membership includes many longtime residents and bona fide experts.

○ **La Nación Digital** (www.nacion.com): If you can read Spanish, this is an excellent site to read regularly or simply browse. The entire content of the country's paper of record is placed online daily, and there's also an extensive searchable archive. It does maintain a small summary of major news items in English, although this section tends to run about a week behind current events.

Many are part of routes that cruise through the Panama Canal. Cruise lines that offer stops in Costa Rica include **Crystal Cruises** (© 888/722-0021; www.crystalcruises.com), **Celebrity Cruises** (© 800/647-2251 www.celebritycruises.com), **Holland America** (© 877/932-4259; www.hollandamerica.com), **Norwegian Cruise Line** (© 866/234-7350; www.ncl.com), **Royal Caribbean** (© 866/562-7625; www.rccl.com), **Regent Seven Seas Cruises** (© 844/473-4368; www.rssc.com), **Silver Sea Cruises** (© 954/787-9067; www.silversea.com), and **Windstar Cruises** (© 800/258-7245; www.windstarcruises.com).

It might pay off to book through a travel agency that specializes in cruises; these companies buy in bulk and stay on top of the latest specials and promotions. Try the **Cruise Company** (© 800/289-5505; www.thecruisecompany.com) or **World Wide Cruises** (© 800/692-7847; www.worldwidecruises.com).

GETTING AROUND
By Plane

Flying is one of the best ways to get around Costa Rica. Because the country is quite small, flights are short and not too expensive. Sansa and Nature Air are the country's domestic airlines. In the high season (late Nov to late Apr), be sure to book reservations well in advance. Both companies have online booking systems (see websites, below).

Sansa (✆ **877/767-2672** in the U.S. and Canada, or 2290-4100 in Costa Rica; www.flysansa.com) operates from a private terminal at San José's **Juan Santamaría International Airport** (see above).

Nature Air (✆ **800/235-9272** in the U.S. and Canada, or 2299-6000 in Costa Rica; www.natureair.com) operates from the main terminal at San José's **Juan Santamaría International Airport** (see above).

By Car

Renting a car in Costa Rica is no idle proposition. The roads are riddled with potholes, most rural intersections are unmarked, and, for some reason, sitting behind the wheel of a car seems to turn peaceful Ticos into homicidal maniacs. But unless you want to see the country from the window of a bus or pay exorbitant amounts for private transfers, renting a car might be your best option for independent exploring. (That said, if you don't want to put up with any stress on your vacation, it might be worthwhile springing for a driver.)

Be forewarned, however: Although rental cars no longer bear special license plates, they are still readily identifiable to thieves and are frequently targeted. (Nothing is ever safe in a car in Costa Rica, although parking in guarded parking lots helps.) Transit Police also seem to target tourists; never pay money directly to a police officer who stops you for any traffic violation.

Before driving off with a rental car, be sure that you inspect the exterior and point out to the rental company representative every tiny scratch, dent, tear, or any other damage. It's a common practice with many Costa Rican car rental companies to claim that you owe payment for minor dings and dents that the company finds when you return the car. Also, if you get into an accident, be sure that the rental company doesn't try to bill you for a higher amount than the deductible on your rental contract.

These caveats aren't meant to scare you off from driving in Costa Rica. Thousands of tourists rent cars here every year, and the large majority of them encounter no problems. Just keep your wits about you and guard against car theft and you'll do fine. Also, keep in mind that four-wheel-drives are particularly useful in the rainy season (May to mid-Nov) and for navigating the bumpy, poorly paved roads year-round.

Among the major international agencies operating in Costa Rica are **Alamo, Avis, Budget, Hertz, National, Payless,** and **Thrifty.** For a complete list of car rental agencies and their contact information, see the "Getting Around" sections of major tourist destinations in this book.

GASOLINE (PETROL) Gasoline is sold as "regular" and "super." Both are unleaded; super is just higher octane. Diesel is available at almost every gas station as well. Most rental cars run on super, but always ask your rental agent what type of gas your car takes. When going off to remote places, try to leave with a full tank of gas because gas stations can be hard to find. If you need to gas up in a small town, you can sometimes get gasoline from enterprising families who sell it by the liter from their houses. Look for hand-lettered signs that say gasolina. At press time, a liter of super cost C760, or roughly $1.38 per liter, and $5.30 per gallon.

ROAD CONDITIONS   The awful road conditions throughout Costa Rica are legendary, and deservedly so. Despite constant promises to fix the problem and sporadic repair attempts, the hot sun, hard rain, and rampant corruption outpace any progress made toward improving the condition of roads. Even paved roads are often badly potholed, so stay alert. Road conditions get especially tricky during the rainy season, when heavy rains and runoff can destroy a stretch of pavement in the blink of an eye.

Note: Estimated driving times are listed throughout this book, but bear in mind that it might take longer than estimated to reach your destination during the rainy season or if roads have deteriorated.

Route numbers are somewhat sporadically and arbitrarily used. You'll also find frequent signs listing the number of kilometers to various towns or cities. Still, your best bets for on-road directions are billboards and advertisements for hotels. It's always a good idea to know the names of a few hotels at your destination, just in case your specific hotel hasn't put up any billboards or signs.

Most car rental agencies now offer the opportunity to rent out GPS units along with your car rental. Rates run between $10 and $15 per day. If you have your own GPS unit, several maps to Costa Rica are available. While you still can't simply enter a street address, most commercial GPS maps of Costa Rica feature hundreds of prominent points of interest (POI), and you should be able to plug in a POI close to your destination.

RENTER'S INSURANCE   Even if you hold **your own car-insurance policy** at home, coverage doesn't always extend abroad. Be sure to find out whether you'll be covered in Costa Rica, whether your policy extends to all persons who will be driving the rental car, how much liability is covered in case an outside party is injured in an accident, and whether the *type* of vehicle you are renting is included under your contract.

DRIVING RULES   A current foreign driver's license is valid for the first 3 months you are in Costa Rica. Seat belts are required for the driver and front-seat passengers. Motorcyclists must wear helmets. Highway police use radar, so keep to the speed limit (usually 60–90kmph/37–56 mph) if you don't want to be pulled over. Speeding tickets can be charged to your credit card for up to a year after you leave the country if they are not paid before departure.

To reduce congestion and fuel consumption, a rotating ban on rush-hour traffic takes place in the central core of San José Monday through Friday from 7 to 8:30am and from 4 to 5:30pm. The ban affects cars with licenses ending in the digits 1 or 2 on Monday; 3 or 4 on Tuesday; 5 or 6 on Wednesday; 7 or 8 on Thursday; and 9 or 0 on Friday. If you are caught driving a car with the banned license plate during these hours on a specified day, you will be ticketed.

BREAKDOWNS   Be warned that emergency services, both vehicular and medical, are extremely limited outside San José, and their availability is directly related to the remoteness of your location at the time of breakdown. You'll find service stations spread over the entire length of the Interamerican Highway, and most of these have tow trucks and mechanics. The major towns of Puntarenas, Liberia, Quepos, San Isidro, Palmar, and Golfito all have hospitals, and most other moderately sized cities and tourist destinations have some sort of clinic or health-services provider.

If you're involved in an accident, contact **National Insurance Institute (INS)** at © **800/800-8000.** You should probably also call the **Transit Police** (© **2222-9330** or 2222-9245); if they have a unit close by, they'll send one. An official transit police report will greatly facilitate any insurance claim. If you can't get help from any of these, try to get written statements from any witnesses. Finally, you can also call © **911,** and they should be able to redirect your call to the appropriate agency.

If the police do show up, you've got a 50-50 chance of finding them helpful or downright antagonistic. Many officers are unsympathetic to the problems of what they perceive to be rich tourists running around in fancy cars with lots of expensive toys and trinkets. Success and happy endings run about equal with horror stories.

If you don't speak Spanish, expect added difficulty in any emergency or stressful situation. Don't expect that rural (or urban) police officers, hospital personnel, service station personnel, or mechanics will speak English.

If your car breaks down and you're unable to get well off the road, check your trunk for reflecting triangles. If you find some, place them as a warning for approaching traffic, arranged in a wedge that starts at the shoulder about 30m (98 ft.) back and nudges gradually toward your car. If your car has no triangles, try to create a similar warning marker using a pile of leaves or branches.

Finally, although not endemic, there have been reports of folks being robbed by seemingly friendly Ticos who stop to give assistance. To add insult to injury, there have even been reports of organized gangs who puncture tires of rental cars at rest stops or busy intersections, only to follow them, offer assistance, and make off with belongings and valuables. If you find yourself with a flat tire, try to ride it to the nearest gas station. If that's not possible, try to pull over into a well-lit public spot. Keep the doors of the car locked and an eye on your belongings while changing the tire, by yourself.

By Bus

This is by far the most economical way to get around Costa Rica. Buses are inexpensive and relatively well maintained, and they go nearly everywhere. The two types are: **Local buses,** the cheapest and slowest, which stop frequently and are generally a bit dilapidated. **Express buses** run between San José and most beach towns and major cities; these tend to be newer units and more comfortable, although very few are so new or modern as to have restroom facilities, and they sometimes operate only on weekends and holidays.

Two companies run regular, fixed-schedule departures in passenger vans and small buses to most of the major tourist destinations in the country. **Gray Line** (© **800/719-3105** in the U.S. and Canada, or 2220-2126 in Costa Rica; www.graylinecostarica.com) has about 10 departures leaving San José each morning and heading or connecting to Jacó, Manuel Antonio, Liberia, Playa Hermosa, La Fortuna, Tamarindo, and playas Conchal and Flamingo. Return trips to San José are daily from these destinations and a variety of interconnecting routes. A similar service, **Interbus** (© **4100-0888;** www.interbusonline.com) has a similar route map and connections. Fares run between $40 and $95, depending upon the destination. Gray Line offers an unlimited weekly pass for all of its shuttle routes for $180.

Beware: Both of these companies offer pickup and drop-off at a wide range of hotels. This means that if you are the first picked up or last dropped off, you might have to sit through a long period of subsequent stops before finally hitting the road or reaching your destination. Moreover, I've heard some horror stories about both lines, concerning missed or severely delayed connections and rude drivers. For details on how to get to various destinations from San José, see the "Getting There" sections in the preceding chapters.

By Taxi

Taxis are readily available in San José and most popular tourist towns and destinations. In San José, your best bet is usually just to hail one down in the street. However, during rush hours and rain storms, and in more remote destinations, it is probably best to call a cab. Throughout the book, I list numbers for local taxi companies in the "Getting Around" sections. If no number is listed, ask at your hotel, or, if you're out and about, at the nearest restaurant or shop; someone will be more than happy to call you a cab.

All city taxis, and even some rural cabs, have meters (*marías*), although drivers sometimes refuse to use them, particularly with foreigners. If this is the case, be sure to negotiate the price up front. Always try to get drivers to use the meter first (say "*ponga la maría, por favor*"). The official rate at press time is C590 per kilometer (1/2 mile). If you have a rough idea of how far it is to your destination, you can estimate how much it should cost from these figures, or you can ask at your hotel how much a specific ride should cost. After 10pm, taxis are legally allowed to add a 20% surcharge. Some of the meters are programmed to include the extra charge automatically, but be careful: Some drivers will use the evening setting during the daytime or (at night) to charge an extra 20% on top of the higher meter setting.

By Thumb

Although buses serve most towns in Costa Rica, service can be infrequent in the remote regions, so local people often hitchhike to get to their destinations sooner. If you're driving a car, people will frequently ask you for a ride. In remote rural areas, a hitchhiker carrying a machete is not necessarily a great danger; use your judgment. Hitchhiking is not recommended on major roadways or in urban areas. In rural areas, it's usually pretty safe. (However, women should be extremely cautious about hitchhiking anywhere in Costa Rica.) If you choose to hitchhike, keep in mind that if a bus doesn't go to your destination, there probably aren't too many cars going there, either. Good luck.

TIPS ON WHERE TO STAY

When the Costa Rican tourist boom began in the late 1980s, hotels popped up like mushrooms after a heavy rain. By the 1990s, the country's first true megaresorts opened, and then more followed, and now still more are under construction or in the planning phase. Except during the few busiest weeks of the year, there's a relative glut of rooms in Costa Rica. That said, most hotels are small to midsize, and the best ones fill up fast throughout much of the year. You'll generally have to reserve well in advance if you want to land a room at any of the more popular or highly rated hotels. Still, in broader terms, the glut of rooms is good news for travelers and bargain hunters. Less popular hotels that want to survive are being forced to reduce their rates and provide better service.

Your best bet in Costa Rica is to negotiate directly with the hotels themselves, especially the smaller ones. Almost every hotel in Costa Rica has e-mail, if not its own website, and you'll find the contact information in this book. However, be aware that response times might be slower than you'd like, and many of the smaller hotels might have some trouble communicating back and forth in English.

Throughout this book, I separate hotel listings into several broad categories: Very Expensive, $250 and up; Expensive, $150 to $250; Moderate, $80 to $150; and Inexpensive, under $80 for a double. Rates given in this book do not include the 13% room taxes, unless otherwise specified. These taxes will add considerably to the cost of your room.

Throughout Costa Rica, rates generally fluctuate somewhat according to season and demand, with a majority of hotels offering lower rates in the off season and charging higher rates during peak periods.

Hotel Options

Costa Rica has hotels to suit every budget and travel style. In addition to the Four Seasons and JW Marriott, the host of amazing boutique hotels around the country will satisfy the high-end and luxury traveler.

Still, the country's strong suit is its **moderately priced hotels.** In the $80-to-$150 price range, you'll find comfortable and sometimes outstanding accommodations almost anywhere in the country. However, room size and quality vary quite a bit within this price range, so don't expect the kind of uniformity that you may find at home.

If you're even more budget- or bohemian-minded, you can find quite a few good deals for less than $80 for a double. But beware: Budget-oriented lodgings often feature shared bathrooms and either cold-water showers or showers heated by electrical heat-coil units mounted at the shower head, affectionately known as "suicide showers." If your hotel has one, do not adjust it while the water is running. Unless specifically noted, all rooms listed in this guide have private bathrooms.

Note: Air-conditioning is not necessarily a given in many midrange hotels and even in some upscale joints. In general, this is not a problem. Cooler nights and well-placed ceiling fans are often more than enough to keep things pleasant, unless I mention otherwise in the hotel reviews.

Bed-and-breakfasts are also abundant. Although the majority are in the San José area, you'll also find B&Bs (often gringo-owned and -operated) throughout the country. Another welcome hotel trend in the San José area is the renovation and conversion of old homes into small hotels. Most are in the Barrio Amón district of downtown San José, which means that you'll sometimes have to put up with noise and exhaust fumes, but these establishments have more character

14

Tips on Where to Stay

than any other hotels in the country. You'll find similar hotels in the Paseo Colón and Los Yoses districts.

Costa Rica has many small nature-oriented **ecolodges.** These lodges offer opportunities to see wildlife (including sloths, monkeys, and hundreds of species of birds) and learn about tropical forests. They range from spartan facilities catering primarily to scientific researchers to luxury accommodations among the finest in the country. Keep in mind that although the nightly room rates at these lodges are often quite moderate, prices start to climb when you throw in transportation (often on chartered planes), guided excursions, and meals. Also, just because you can book a reservation at most of these lodges doesn't mean that they're not remote. Be sure to find out how to get to and from the ecolodge and which tours and services are included in your stay. Then think long and hard about whether you really want to put up with hot, humid weather (cool and wet in the cloud forests), biting insects, rugged transportation, and strenuous hikes to see wildlife.

A couple of uniquely Costa Rican accommodations types that you might encounter are the **apartotel** and the **cabina.** An apartotel is just what it sounds like: an apartment hotel where you'll get a full kitchen and one or two bedrooms, along with daily maid service. Cabinas are Costa Rica's version of cheap vacation lodging. They're very inexpensive and very basic—often just cinder-block buildings divided into small rooms. Occasionally, you'll find a cabina in which the units are actually cabins, but these are a rarity. Cabinas often have clothes-washing sinks (pilas), and some come with kitchenettes; they cater primarily to Tico families on vacation.

STAYING HEALTHY

Staying healthy on a trip to Costa Rica is predominantly a matter of being a little cautious about what you eat and drink, and using common sense. Know your physical limits, and don't overexert yourself in the ocean, on hikes, or during athletic activities. Respect the tropical sun and protect yourself from it. As you climb above 3,000m (10,000 ft.), you may feel the effects of altitude sickness. Be sure to drink plenty of water and not overexert yourself. Limit your exposure to the sun, especially during the first few days of your trip and, thereafter, from 11am to 2pm. Use sunscreen with a high protection factor, and apply it liberally. Remember that children need more protection than adults. I recommend buying and drinking bottled water or soft drinks, but the water in San José and in most of the country's heavily visited spots is safe to drink.

General Availability of Healthcare

In general, Costa Rica has a high level of medical care and services for a developing nation. The better private hospitals and doctors in San José are very good. In fact, given the relatively budget nature of care and treatment, a sizable number of Americans come to Costa Rica each year for elective surgery and other care.

Pharmacies are widely available, and generally well stocked. In most cases, you will not need a doctor's script to fill or refill a prescription.

I list **additional emergency numbers** in the various destination chapters, as well as in "Fast Facts: Costa Rica," below.

If You Get Sick

Your hotel front desk should be your best source of information and assistance if you get sick while in Costa Rica. In addition, your local consulate in Costa Rica

red TIDES

Also known as harmful algal blooms (HAB), red tides are a natural phenomenon occurring in oceans worldwide. Red tides can arise from natural, as well as man-made causes. Some are seasonal; while others may be provoked by pollution or chemical waste. Some are toxic, while others are benign. Harmful algal blooms are often accompanied by dead fish and sea life. Rising sea temperatures have been cited as a cause of an increase in HAB occurrences, although they have been recorded in frigid arctic waters. Some can turn ocean waters a deep red, while color changes from deep green to murky brown have also been documented. Some, in fact, do not affect the water color at all. Tidal changes have no causal link to red tides, so the name is more than a bit of a misnomer.

All red tides are characterized by rapid and massive reproduction of algae or phytoplankton. Anecdotally, Costa Rica may be experiencing an increase in long lasting red tides. Pacific coast beaches have been hardest hit, especially those along the Nicoya Peninsula. Still, red tides have been recorded all along both of the country's coastlines. In Costa Rica, red tides tend to be more common near the start of the rainy season. Most only last a day or so, although some have lasted as long as a couple of weeks. It's extremely hard to tell for certain if a red tide is a dangerous algal bloom or not. If you notice a deep red or unnatural brown tint to the water, it is best to refrain from swimming. Due to dark sands and benign river runoff, many of Costa Rica's beaches often appear to have brownish water that is perfectly safe for swimming. Ask around locally to find out the current water conditions.

can provide a list of area doctors who speak English. I list the best hospitals in San José in "Fast Facts: San José," in chapter 6; these have the most modern facilities in the country. Most state-run hospitals and walk-in clinics around the country have emergency rooms that can treat most conditions, although I highly recommend the private hospitals in San José if your condition is not life threatening and can wait for treatment until you reach one of them.

Regional Health Concerns

TROPICAL ILLNESSES   Your chance of contracting any serious tropical disease in Costa Rica is slim, especially if you stick to the beaches or traditional spots for visitors. However, malaria, dengue fever, and leptospirosis all exist in Costa Rica, so it's a good idea to know what they are.

Malaria is found in the lowlands on both coasts and in the northern zone. Although it's rarely found in urban areas, it's still a problem in remote wooded regions and along the Caribbean coast. Malaria prophylaxes are available, but several have side effects, and others are of questionable effectiveness. Consult your doctor regarding what is currently considered the best preventive treatment for malaria. Be sure to ask whether a recommended drug will cause you to be hypersensitive to the sun; it would be a shame to come down here for the beaches and then have to hide under an umbrella the whole time. Because malaria-carrying mosquitoes usually come out at night, you should do as much as possible to avoid being bitten after dark. If you are in a malaria-prone area, wear long pants and long sleeves, use insect repellent, and either sleep under a mosquito net or burn mosquito coils (similar to incense, but with a pesticide).

Of greater concern is **dengue fever,** which has had periodic outbreaks in Latin America since the mid-1990s. Dengue fever is similar to malaria and is spread by an aggressive daytime mosquito. This mosquito seems to be most common in lowland urban areas, and Puntarenas, Liberia, and Limón have been the worst-hit cities in Costa Rica. Dengue is also known as "bone-break fever" because it is usually accompanied by severe body aches. The first infection with dengue fever will make you very sick but should cause no serious damage. However, a second infection with a different strain of the dengue virus can lead to internal hemorrhaging and could be life threatening.

Many people are convinced that taking B-complex vitamins daily will help prevent mosquitoes from biting you. I don't think the American Medical Association has endorsed this idea yet, but I've run across it in enough places to think that there might be something to it.

One final tropical fever that I think you should know about (because I got it myself) is **leptospirosis.** There are more than 200 strains of leptospires, which are animal-borne bacteria transmitted to humans via contact with drinking, swimming, or bathing water. This bacterial infection is easily treated with antibiotics; however, it can quickly cause very high fever and chills, and should be treated promptly.

If you develop a high fever accompanied by severe body aches, nausea, diarrhea, or vomiting during or shortly after a visit to Costa Rica, consult a physician as soon as possible.

Costa Rica has historically had very few outbreaks of cholera. This is largely due to an extensive public-awareness campaign that has promoted good hygiene and increased sanitation. Your chances of contracting cholera while you're here are very slight.

DIETARY RED FLAGS   Even though the water in San José and most popular destinations in Costa Rica is generally safe, and even if you're careful to buy bottled water, order *frescos en leche* (fruit shakes made with milk rather than water), and drink your soft drink without ice cubes, you still might encounter some intestinal difficulties. Most of this is just due to tender stomachs coming into contact with slightly more aggressive Latin American intestinal flora. In extreme cases of diarrhea or intestinal discomfort, it's worth taking a stool sample to a lab for analysis. The results will usually pinpoint the amoebic or parasitic culprit, which can then be readily treated with available over-the-counter medicines.

Except in the most established and hygienic of restaurants, it's also advisable to avoid *ceviche,* a raw seafood salad, especially if it has any shellfish in it. It could be home to any number of bacterial critters.

BUGS, BITES & OTHER WILDLIFE CONCERNS   Although Costa Rica has Africanized bees (the notorious "killer bees" of fact and fable) and several species of venomous snakes, your chances of being bitten are minimal, especially if you refrain from sticking your hands into hives or under rocks in the forest. If you know that you're allergic to bee stings, consult your doctor before traveling.

At the beaches, you'll probably be bitten by *pirujas* (sand fleas). These nearly invisible insects leave an irritating welt. Try not to scratch because this can lead to open sores and infections. *Pirujas* are most active at sunrise and sunset, so you might want to cover up or avoid the beaches at these times.

Snake sightings, much less snakebites, are very rare. Moreover, the majority of snakes in Costa Rica are nonpoisonous. If you do encounter a snake, stay calm, don't make any sudden movements, and do not try to touch the snake. Avoid sticking your hands under rocks, branches, and fallen trees.

Scorpions, black widow spiders, tarantulas, bullet ants, and biting insects of many types can all be found in Costa Rica. In general, they are not nearly the danger or nuisance most visitors fear. Watch where you stick your hands; in addition, you might want to shake out your clothes and shoes before putting them on to avoid any unpleasant and painful surprises.

TROPICAL SUN   Limit your exposure to the sun, especially during the first few days of your trip and, thereafter, from 11am to 2pm. Use a sunscreen with a high protection factor, and apply it liberally. Remember that children need more protection than adults.

RIPTIDES   Many of Costa Rica's beaches have riptides: strong currents that can drag swimmers out to sea. A riptide occurs when water that has been dumped on the shore by strong waves forms a channel back out to open water. These channels have strong currents. If you get caught in a riptide, you can't escape the current by swimming toward shore; it's like trying to swim upstream in a river. To break free of the current, swim parallel to shore and use the energy of the waves to help you get back to the beach.

[FastFACTS] COSTA RICA

Area Codes   Costa Rica doesn't have area codes. All phone numbers are eight-digit numbers.

Business Hours   Banks are usually open Monday through Friday from 9am to 4pm, although many have begun to offer extended hours. Post offices are generally open Monday through Friday from 8am to 5:30pm, and Saturday from 7:30am to noon. (In small towns, post offices often close on Sat.) Stores are generally open Monday through Saturday from 9am to 6pm (many close for 1 hr. at lunch), but stores in modern malls generally stay open until 8 or 9pm and don't close for lunch. Most bars are open until 1 or 2am, although some go later.

Cellphones   See "Mobile Phones," later in this section.

Crime   See "Safety," later in this section.

Customs   Visitors to Costa Rica are permitted to bring in all manner of items for personal use, including cameras, video cameras and accessories, tape recorders, personal computers, and music players. Customs officials in Costa Rica seldom check tourists' luggage.

Doctors   Your hotel front desk will be your best source of information on what to do if you get sick and where to go for treatment. Most have the number of a trusted doctor on hand. In addition, your local consulate in Costa Rica can provide a list of area doctors who speak English. Also see "Staying Healthy," earlier in this chapter.

Drinking Laws   Alcoholic beverages are sold every day of the week throughout the year, with the exception of the 2 days before Easter and the 2 days before and after a presidential election. The legal drinking age is 18, although it's only sporadically enforced. Liquor—everything from beer to hard spirits—is sold in specific liquor stores, as well as at most supermarkets and even convenience stores.

Driving Rules   See "Getting Around," earlier in this chapter.

Electricity
The standard in Costa Rica is the same as in the United States and Canada: 110 volts AC (60 cycles). However, three-pronged outlets can be scarce, so it's helpful to bring along an adapter.

Embassies & Consulates
The following are located in San José: **United States Embassy,** Calle 120 and Avenida 0, Pavas (② **2519-2000;** http://costarica.usembassy.gov); **Canadian Embassy,** Oficentro Ejecutivo La Sabana, Edificio 5 (② **2242-4400;** http://costarica.gc.ca); and **British Embassy,** Edificio Colón, 11th Floor, Paseo Colón between calles 38 and 40 (② **2258-2025;** www.gov.uk/government/world/costa-rica). San José does not have an Australian, Irish, or New Zealand embassy.

Emergencies
In case of any emergency, dial ② **911** (which should have an English-speaking operator); for an ambulance, call ② **1028;** and to report a fire, call ② **1118.** If 911 doesn't work, you can contact the police at ② **2222-1365** or 2221-5337, and hopefully they can find someone who speaks English.

Family Travel
Hotels in Costa Rica often give discounts for children, and allow children to stay for free in a parent's room. Still, discounts for children and the cutoff ages vary according to the hotel; in general, don't assume that your kids can stay in your room for free.

Some hotels, villas, and cabinas come equipped with kitchenettes or full kitchen facilities. These can be a real money-saver for those traveling with children, and I list many of these accommodations in the destination chapters in this book.

Hotels offering regular, dependable babysitting service are few and far between. If you will need babysitting, make sure that your hotel offers it, and be sure to ask whether the babysitters are bilingual. In many cases, they are not. This is usually not a problem with infants and toddlers, but it can cause problems with older children.

Gasoline
Please see "Getting Around: By Car," earlier in this chapter.

Insurance
For information on traveler's insurance, trip-cancellation insurance, and medical insurance while traveling, please visit http://www.frommers.com/planning.

Internet & Wi-Fi
Cybercafes can be found all over Costa Rica, especially in the more popular tourist destinations. Moreover, an ever-increasing number of hotels, restaurants, cafes, and retailers around Costa Rica are offering high-speed Wi-Fi access, either free or for a small fee. Throughout the book, I list which hotels provide Wi-Fi free, or for a fee.

Language
Spanish is the official language of Costa Rica. However, in most tourist areas, you'll be surprised by how well Costa Ricans speak English. See chapter 15 for some key Spanish terms and phrases.

Legal Aid
If you need legal help, your best bet is to first contact your local embassy or consulate. See "Embassies & Consulates," above, for contact details.

LGBT Travelers
Costa Rica is a Catholic, conservative, macho country where public displays of same-sex affection are rare and considered somewhat shocking. Public figures, politicians, and religious leaders periodically denounce homosexuality. However, gay and lesbian tourism to Costa Rica is quite robust, and gay and lesbian travelers are generally treated with respect and should not experience any harassment.

If you speak Spanish, you'll want to connect with the **Comunidad Arco Iris (CARI;** www.caricr.com), which serves as a meeting place and information clearinghouse for the entire LGBT community.

Mail
At press time, it cost C365 to mail a letter to the United States, and C435 to Europe. You can get stamps at post offices and at some gift shops in large hotels. Given the Costa Rican postal service's track record, I recommend paying an extra C550 to have anything of any value certified. Better yet, use an international courier service or wait until you get home to post it. **DHL,** on Paseo Colón between calles 30 and 32 (② **2209-6000;**

www.dhl.com); **EMS Courier,** with desks at most post offices nationwide (📞 **2223-9766;** www.correos.go.cr); **FedEx,** which is based in Heredia but will arrange pickup anywhere in the metropolitan area (📞 **2239-0576;** www.fedex.com); and **United Parcel Service,** in Pavas (📞 **2290-2828;** www.ups.com), all operate in Costa Rica.

If you're sending mail to Costa Rica, it generally takes between 10 and 14 days to reach San José, although it can take as much as a month to get to the more remote corners of the country. Plan ahead. Also note that many hotels and ecolodges have mailing addresses in the United States. Always use these addresses when writing from North America or Europe. Never send cash, checks, or valuables through the Costa Rican mail system.

Medical Requirements   No shots or inoculations are required to enter Costa Rica. The exception to this is for those who have recently been traveling in a country or region known to have yellow fever. In this case, proof of a yellow fever vaccination is required. Also see "Staying Healthy," earlier in this chapter.

Mobile Phones   Costa Rica uses **GSM** (Global System for Mobile Communications) networks. If your cellphone is on a GSM system, and you have a world-capable multiband phone, you should be able to make and receive calls in Costa Rica. Just call your wireless operator and ask for "international roaming" to be activated on your account. Per-minute charges can be high, though—up to $5 in Costa Rica, depending upon your plan.

Costa Rica has three main cellphone companies and a couple of smaller outfits. The main providers are the government-run ICE/Kolbi and the international giants Claro and Movistar. All offer a range of prepaid and traditional phone plans. Pricing and coverage are competitive, and I don't recommend one over the other.

You can purchase a **prepaid SIM card for an unlocked GSM phone** at the airport and at shops all around the country. A prepaid SIM card costs around $2 to $4. Cards usually come loaded with some minutes, and you can buy additional minutes separately either online or at cellphone stores and ICE offices around the country.

If you don't have your own unlocked GSM phone, you might consider buying one here. Shops around the country offer basic, functional phones with a local line, for prices beginning at around $35.

In addition, most of the major car rental agencies offer cellphone rentals. Rates run around $5 to $7 per day or $25 to $50 per week for the rental, with charges of 50¢ to $1.50 per minute for local calls and $1 to $3 per minute for international calls.

Money & Costs   The unit of currency in Costa Rica is the **colón.** In this book, prices are listed in the currency you are most likely to see quoted. Hence, nearly all hotel prices and most tour and transportation prices are listed in dollars, since the hotels, airlines, tour agencies, and transport companies quote their prices in dollars. Many restaurants do, as well. Still, a good many restaurants, as well as taxis and other local goods and services, are advertised and quoted in colones. In those cases, prices listed are in colones (C).

THE VALUE OF THE COLÓN VS. OTHER POPULAR CURRENCIES

Colones	Aus$	Can$	Euro (€)	NZ$	UK £	US$
550	A$1.07	C1.10	€.73	NZ$1.16	60p	$1.00

The colón is divided into 100 **céntimos.** You'll find gold-hued 5-, 10-, 25-, 50-, 100-, and 500-colón coins.

WHAT THINGS COST IN COSTA RICA	US$	COSTA RICAN COLONES
Taxi from the airport to downtown San José	20.00–40.00	C11,00-C22,00
Double room, moderate	90.00	C49,500
Double room, inexpensive	50.00	C27,500
Three-course dinner for one without wine, moderate	20.00–30.00	C11,000–C16,500
Bottle of beer	1.50–3.00	C825–C1,650
Cup of coffee	1.00–1.50	C550–C825
1 gallon/1 liter of premium gas	5.30 per gallon;	2,915 per gallon; 760 per liter
Admission to most museums	2.00–5.00	C1,100–C2,750
Admission to most national parks	10.00	C5,500

14

Paper notes come in denominations of 1,000, 2,000, 5,000, 10,000 and 20,000 colones. You might hear people refer to a "rojo" or "tucán," which are slang terms for the 1,000- and 5,000-colón bills, respectively. One-hundred-colón denominations are called "tejas," so "cinco tejas" is 500 colones. I've yet to encounter a slang equivalent for the 2,000, 10,000, and 20,000 bills.

Forged bills are not entirely uncommon. When receiving change in colones, it's a good idea to check the larger-denomination bills, which should have protective bands or hidden images that appear when held up to the light.

You can change money at all banks in Costa Rica. Since banks handle money exchanges, Costa Rica has very few exchange houses. One major exception to this is the **Global Exchange** (✆ 2431-0686; www.globalexchange.co.cr) offices at the international airports. However, be forewarned they exchange at more than 10% below the official exchange rate. Airport taxis accept U.S. dollars, so there isn't necessarily any great need to exchange money the moment you arrive.

Hotels will often exchange money and cash traveler's checks, as well; there usually isn't much of a line, but they might shave a few colones off the exchange rate.

If you plan on carrying around dollars to pay for goods and services, be aware that most Costa Rican businesses, be they restaurants, convenience stores, or gas stations, will give a very unfavorable exchange rate.

Your best bet for getting colones is usually by direct withdrawal from your home account via a bank card or debit card, although check in advance if you will be assessed any fees or charges by your home bank. In general, ATMs in Costa Rica still don't add on service fees. Paying with a credit card will also get you the going bank exchange rate. But again, try to get a credit card with no foreign transaction fees.

Be very careful about exchanging money on the streets; it's extremely risky. In addition to forged bills and short counts, street money-changers frequently work in teams that can leave you holding neither colones nor dollars. Also be very careful when leaving a bank. Criminals are often looking for foreigners who have just withdrawn or exchanged cash.

The currency conversions provided in the "Value of the Colón vs. Other Popular Currencies" box were correct at press time. However, rates fluctuate, so before departing, consult a currency exchange website such as **www.oanda.com/currency/converter** to check up-to-the-minute rates.

MasterCard and **Visa** are the most widely accepted credit cards in Costa Rica, followed by American Express. Most hotels and restaurants accept all of these, especially in tourist destination areas. Discover and Diners Club are far less commonly accepted.

Beware of hidden credit card fees while traveling. Check with your credit or debit card issuer to see what fees, if any, will be charged for overseas transactions. Recent reform legislation in the U.S., for example, has curbed some exploitative lending practices. But many banks have responded by increasing fees in other areas, including fees for customers who use credit and debit cards while out of the country—even if those charges were made in U.S. dollars. Fees can amount to 3% or more of the purchase price. Check with your bank before departing to avoid any surprise charges on your statement.

Costa Rica has a modern and widespread network of ATMs. You should find ATMs in all but the most remote tourist destinations and isolated nature lodges. In response to several "express kidnappings" in San José, in which folks were taken at gunpoint to an ATM to clean out their bank accounts, both Banco Nacional and Banco de Costa Rica stopped ATM service between the hours of 10pm and 5am. Other networks still dispense money 24 hours a day.

It's probably a good idea to change your PIN to a four-digit PIN. While many ATMs in Costa Rica will accept five- and six-digit PINs, some will only accept four-digit PINs.

Newspapers & Magazines   Costa Rica has a half-dozen or so Spanish-language dailies, and you can get "Time" magazine and several U.S. newspapers at some hotel gift shops and a few of the bookstores in San José. If you read Spanish, "La Nación" is the paper you'll want. Its "Viva" and "Tiempo Libre" sections list what's going on in the world of music, theater, dance, and more.

Packing   Everyone should be sure to pack the essentials: sunscreen, insect repellent, camera, bathing suit, a wide-brimmed hat, all prescription medications, and so forth. You'll want good hiking shoes and/or beach footwear, depending upon your itinerary. I also like to have a waterproof headlamp or flashlight and refillable water bottle. Lightweight, long-sleeved shirts and long pants are good protection from both the sun and insects. Surfers use "rash guards," quick-drying lycra or polyester shirts, which provide great protection from the sun while swimming.

If you're just heading to Guanacaste between December and March, you won't need anything for the rain. Otherwise, I recommend an umbrella, some rain gear, or both. Most high-end hotels provide umbrellas. If you plan to do any wildlife-viewing, bringing your own binoculars is a good idea, as is a field guide (p. 28).

Passports   Citizens of the United States, Canada, Great Britain, and most European nations may visit Costa Rica for a maximum of 90 days. No visa is necessary, but you must have a valid passport, which you should carry with you at all times while you're in Costa Rica. Citizens of Australia, Ireland, and New Zealand can enter the country without a visa and stay for 30 days, although once in the country, visitors can apply for an extension.

It is advised to always have at least one or two consecutive blank pages in your passport to allow space for visas and stamps that need to appear together. It is also important to note when your passport expires. Many countries require your passport to have at least 6 months left before its expiration in order to allow you into the destination.

See "Embassies & Consulates," above, for whom to contact if you lose your passport while traveling. For other information, contact the following agencies:

Australia   Australian Passport Information Service (✆ **131-232;** www.passports.
gov.au).

Canada   Passport Office, Dept. of Foreign Affairs and International Trade, Ottawa,
ON K1A 0G3 (✆ **800/567-6868;** www.ppt.gc.ca).

Ireland   Passport Office, Setanta Centre, Molesworth Street, Dublin 2 (✆ **01/671-
1633;** www.foreignaffairs.gov.ie).

New Zealand   Passports Office, Dept. of Internal Affairs, 47 Boulcott St., Wellington,
6011 (✆ **0800/225-050** or 04/474-8100; www.passports.govt.nz).

United Kingdom   Visit your nearest passport office, major post office, or travel
agency or contact the Identity and Passport Service (IPS), 89 Eccleston Square, London,
SW1V 1PN (✆ **0300/222-0000;** www.ips.gov.uk).

United States   To find your regional passport office, check the U.S. State Department
website (travel.state.gov/passport) or call the National Passport Information Center
(✆ **877/487-2778**) for automated information.

Petrol   Please see "Getting Around: By Car," earlier in this chapter.

Police   In most cases, dial ✆ **911** for the police, and you should be able to get someone who speaks English on the line. Other numbers for the **Judicial Police** are ✆ **2222-
1365** and 2221-5337. The numbers for the **Traffic Police (Policía de Tránsito)** are
✆ **800/8726-7486** toll-free nationwide, or 2222-9330.

Safety   Although most of Costa Rica is safe, petty crime and robberies committed
against tourists are endemic. San José, in particular, is known for its pickpockets, so never
carry a wallet in your back pocket. A woman should keep a tight grip on her purse (keep it
tucked under your arm). Thieves also target gold chains, cameras and video cameras,
prominent jewelry, and nice sunglasses. Be sure not to leave valuables unsecured in your
hotel room, or unattended—even for a moment—on the beach. Given the high rate of
stolen passports in Costa Rica, mostly as collateral damage in a typical pickpocketing or
room robbery, it is recommended that, whenever possible, you leave your passport in a
hotel safe, and travel with a photocopy of the pertinent pages. Don't park a car on the
street in Costa Rica, especially in San José; plenty of public parking lots are around the
city.

Rental cars generally stick out and are easily spotted by thieves. Don't leave anything
of value in a car parked on the street, not even for a moment. Be wary of solicitous strangers who stop to help you change a tire or take you to a service station. Although most are
truly good Samaritans, there have been reports of thieves preying on roadside breakdowns. See "Getting Around: By Car," above, for more info.

Inter-city buses are also frequent targets of stealthy thieves. Try not to check your bags
into the hold of a bus if they will fit in the rack above your seat. If it can't be avoided, keep
your eye on what leaves the hold. If you put your bags in an overhead rack, be sure you
can see the bags at all times. Try not to fall asleep.

Single women should use common sense and take precaution, especially after dark. I
don't recommend that single women walk alone anywhere at night, especially on seemingly deserted beaches or dark, uncrowded streets.

Senior Travelers   Be sure to mention that you're a senior when you make your travel
reservations. Although it's not common policy in Costa Rica to offer senior discounts, don't
be shy about asking for one anyway. You never know. Always carry some kind of identification, such as a driver's license, that shows your date of birth, especially if you've kept your
youthful glow.

Many reliable agencies and organizations target the 50-plus market. **Road Scholar,**
formerly known as Elderhostel (✆ **800/454-5768** in the U.S. and Canada; www.road

scholar.org), arranges Costa Rica study programs for those ages 55 and older, as well as intergenerational trips good for families. **ElderTreks** (☎ **800/741-7956** in the U.S. and Canada; 0808-234-1714 in the U.K.; www.eldertreks.com) offers small-group tours to Costa Rica, restricted to travelers 50 and older.

Smoking   Many Costa Ricans smoke, but in March 2012, Costa Rica's legislature passed a strict anti-smoking law. Under this law, smoking is prohibited in all public spaces, including restaurants, bars, offices, and such outdoor areas as public parks and bus stops. The law also raises taxes on cigarettes and places restrictions and controls on advertising.

Most higher-end hotels are either entirely nonsmoking, or have at least some nonsmoking rooms. However, many midrange hotels and most budget options are pretty laissez-faire when it comes to smoking. Whenever possible, the presence of nonsmoking rooms is noted in hotel listing description information.

Student Travelers   Although you won't find any discounts at the national parks, most museums and other attractions around Costa Rica do offer discounts for students. It always pays to ask.

Taxes   The national 13% value added tax (often written as IVA in Costa Rica) is added to all goods and services. This includes hotel and restaurant bills. Restaurants also add on a 10% service charge, for a total of 23% more on your bill.

The airport departure tax is $29, and must be purchased prior to check-in. Desks where you can pay this tax are in the main terminal of all international airports. Some local travel agencies and hotels offer to purchase the departure tax in advance, as a convenience for tourists. You must give them authorization, as well as your passport number, and pay a small service fee.

Although you can pay the airport exit tax with a credit card, it is charged as a cash advance. Most credit card companies hit this kind of transaction with a fee and begin charging interest on it immediately. It is best to pay the airport tax in cash, either dollars or colones.

Telephones   Costa Rica has an excellent and widespread phone system. A phone call within the country costs around C10 per minute. Pay phones are relatively scarce. If you do find one, it might take a calling card or 5-, 10-, or 20-colón coins. Calling cards are much more practical. You can purchase calling cards in a host of gift shops and pharmacies. However, there are several competing calling-card companies, and certain cards work only with certain phones. **CHIP** calling cards work with a computer chip and just slide into specific phones, although these phones aren't widely available. Better bets are the **197** and **199** calling cards, which are sold in varying denominations. These have a scratch-off PIN and can be used from any phone in the country. Generally, the 197 cards are sold in smaller denominations and are used for local calling, while the 199 cards are deemed international and are easier to find in larger denominations. Either card can be used to make any call, however, provided that the card can cover the costs. Another perk of the 199 cards is the fact that you can get the instructions in English. For local calls, it is often easiest to call from your hotel, although you may be charged around C150 to C300 per call.

You might also see about getting yourself a local mobile phone; for information on this, see "Mobile Phones" (p. 509).

To call Costa Rica from abroad:

1. Dial the international access code: 011 from the U.S. and Canada; 00 from the U.K., Ireland, or New Zealand; or 0011 from Australia.
2. Dial the country code 506.
3. Dial the eight-digit number.

To make international calls: First dial 00 and then the country code (U.S. or Canada 1, U.K. 44, Ireland 353, Australia 61, New Zealand 64). Next dial the area code and number. For example, if you want to call the British Embassy in Washington, D.C., you would dial 00-1-202-588-7800.

For directory assistance: Dial 1113 if you're looking for a number inside Costa Rica, and dial 1024 for numbers to all other countries.

For operator assistance: If you need operator assistance in making a call, dial 1116 if you're trying to make an international call, and 0 if you want to call a number in Costa Rica.

Toll-free numbers: Numbers beginning with 0800 or 800 within Costa Rica are toll-free, but calling a 1-800 number in the States from Costa Rica is not toll-free. In fact, it costs the same as an overseas call.

Time   Costa Rica is on Central Standard Time (same as Chicago and St. Louis), 6 hours behind Greenwich Mean Time. Costa Rica does not use daylight saving time, so the time difference is an additional hour from early March through early November.

Tipping   Tipping is not necessary in restaurants, where a 10% service charge is always added to your bill (along with a 13% tax). If service was particularly good, you can leave a little at your own discretion, but it's not mandatory. Porters and bellhops get around C500 to C1,000 per bag. You don't need to tip a taxi driver unless the service has been superior; a tip is not usually expected.

Toilets   These are known as "sanitarios," "servicios sanitarios," or "baños." They are marked damas (women) and hombres or caballeros (men). Public restrooms are hard to come by. You will almost never find a public restroom in a city park or downtown area. Public restrooms are usually at most national park entrances, and much less frequently inside the national park. In towns and cities, it gets much trickier. One must count on the generosity of some hotel or restaurant. The same goes for most beaches. However, most restaurants, and, to a lesser degree, hotels, will let you use their facilities, especially if you buy a soft drink or something else. Bus and gas stations often have restrooms, but many of these are pretty grim. In some restrooms around the country, especially more remote and natural areas, it's common practice not to flush any foreign matter, aside from your business, down the toilet. This includes toilet paper, sanitary napkins, cigarette butts, and so forth. You will usually find a little sign advising you of this practice in the restroom.

Travelers with Disabilities   Although Costa Rica does have a law mandating Equality of Opportunities for People with Disabilities, and some facilities have been adapted, in general, there are relatively few buildings, bathrooms, public buses or taxis specifically designed for travelers with disabilities in the country. In San José, sidewalks are particularly crowded and uneven, and they are nonexistent in most of the rest of the country. Few hotels offer wheelchair-accessible accommodations. In short, it can be difficult for a person with disabilities to get around San José and Costa Rica.

Many travel agencies offer customized tours and itineraries for travelers with disabilities. Among them are **Eco Adventure International** (✆ **888/710-9453** in the U.S. and Canada; www.eaiadventure.com); **Flying Wheels Travel** (✆ **507/451-5005;** www.flying wheelstravel.com); and **Accessible Journeys** (✆ **800/846-4537** or 610/521-0339; www.disabilitytravel.com).

Access-Able Travel Source (✆ **303/232-2979;** www.access-able.com) has a comprehensive database of travel agents around the world with experience in accessible travel; destination-specific access information; and links to such resources as service animals, equipment rentals, and access guides.

Another great organization that offers a vast range of resources and assistance to travelers with disabilities is **SATH** (Society for Accessible Travel & Hospitality; ✆ **212/447-7284;** www.sath.org).

VAT   See "Taxes," earlier in this section.

Visitor Information   In the United States or Canada, you can get basic information on Costa Rica by contacting the **Costa Rican Tourist Board** (**ICT,** or Instituto Costarricense de Turismo; ✆ **866/267-8274** in the U.S. and Canada, or 2299-5827 in Costa Rica; www.visitcostarica.com). Travelers from the United Kingdom, Australia, and New Zealand will have to rely primarily on this website, or call direct to Costa Rica, because the ICT does not have toll-free access in these countries.

In addition to this official site, you'll be able to find a wealth of Web-based information on Costa Rica with a few clicks of your mouse. In fact, you'll be better off surfing, as the ICT site is rather limited and clunky. See "The Best Websites about Costa Rica," on p. 498, for some helpful suggestions about where to begin your online search.

You can pick up a map at the ICT's information desk at the airport when you arrive, or at their downtown San José offices (although the destination maps that come with this book are sufficient for most purposes). Perhaps the best map to have is the waterproof country map of Costa Rica put out by **Toucan Maps** (www.mapcr.com), which can be ordered directly from their website or any major online bookseller, like Amazon.com.

Water   Although the water in San José is generally safe to drink, water quality varies outside the city. Because many travelers have tender digestive tracts, I recommend playing it safe and sticking to bottled drinks as much as possible. Also avoid ice.

Wi-Fi   See "Internet & Wi-Fi," earlier in this section.

Women Travelers   For lack of better phrasing, Costa Rica is a typically "macho" Latin American nation. Single women can expect catcalls, hisses, whistles, and car horns, especially in San José. In most cases, while annoying, this is harmless and intended by Tico men as a compliment. Nonetheless, women should be careful walking alone at night throughout the country. Also, see "Safety," earlier in this section.

SPANISH TERMS & PHRASES

15

C osta Rican Spanish is neither the easiest nor the most difficult dialect to understand. Ticos speak at a relatively relaxed speed and enunciate clearly, without dropping too many final consonants. The *y* and *ll* sounds are subtly, almost inaudibly, pronounced. Perhaps the most defining idiosyncrasy of Costa Rican Spanish is the way Ticos overemphasize, and almost chew, their *r*'s.

BASIC WORDS & PHRASES

English	Spanish	Pronunciation
Hello	Buenos días	*bweh-nohss dee-ahss*
How are you?	¿Cómo está usted?	*koh-moh ehss-tah oo-stehd*
Very well	Muy bien	*mwee byehn*
Thank you	Gracias	*grah-syahss*
Goodbye	Adiós	*ad-dyohss*
Please	Por favor	*pohr fah-vohr*
Yes	Sí	*see*
No	No	*noh*

English	Spanish	Pronunciation
Excuse me (to get by someone)	Perdóneme	**pehr-*doh*-neh-meh**
Excuse me (to begin a question)	Discúlpeme	**dees-*kool*-peh-meh**
Give me	Deme	***deh*-meh**
Where is . . . ?	¿Dónde está . . . ?	***dohn*-deh ehss-*tah***
the station	la estación	**la ehss-*tah*-syohn**
the bus stop	la parada	**la pah-*rah*-dah**
a hotel	un hotel	**oon oh-*tehl***
a restaurant	un restaurante	**oon res-tow-*rahn*-teh**
the toilet	el servicio	**el ser-*vee*-syoh**
To the right	A la derecha	**ah lah deh-*reh*-chah**
To the left	A la izquierda	**ah lah ees-*kyehr*-dah**
Straight ahead	Adelante	**ah-deh-*lahn*-teh**
I would like . . .	Quiero . . .	***kyeh*-roh**
to eat	comer	**ko-*mehr***
a room	una habitación	**oo-nah ah-bee-tah-*syohn***
How much is it?	¿Cuánto?	***kwahn*-toh**
When?	¿Cuándo?	***kwan*-doh**
What?	¿Qué?	**keh**
Yesterday	Ayer	**ah-*yehr***
Today	Hoy	**oy**
Tomorrow	Mañana	**mah-*nyah*-nah**
Breakfast	Desayuno	**deh-sah-*yoo*-noh**
Lunch	Almuerzo	**ahl-*mwehr*-soh**
Dinner	Cena	***seh*-nah**
Do you speak English?	¿Habla usted inglés?	**ah-blah oo-*stehd* een-*glehss***
I don't understand Spanish very well.	No entiendo muy bien el español.	**noh ehn-*tyehn*-do mwee byehn el ehss-pah-*nyohl***

NUMBERS

English	Spanish	Pronunciation
zero	cero	***ser*-oh**
one	uno	***oo*-noh**
two	dos	**dohss**

English	Spanish	Pronunciation
three	tres	**trehss**
four	cuatro	**kwah-troh**
five	cinco	**seen-koh**
six	seis	**sayss**
seven	siete	**syeh-teh**
eight	ocho	**oh-choh**
nine	nueve	**nweh-beh**
ten	diez	**dyehss**
eleven	once	**ohn-seh**
twelve	doce	**doh-seh**
thirteen	trece	**treh-seh**
fourteen	catorce	**kah-tohr-seh**
fifteen	quince	**keen-seh**
sixteen	dieciséis	**dyeh-see-sayss**
seventeen	diecisiete	**dyeh-see-syeh-teh**
eighteen	dieciocho	**dyeh-see-oh-choh**
nineteen	diecinueve	**dyeh-see-nweh-beh**
twenty	veinte	**bayn-teh**
thirty	treinta	**trayn-tah**
forty	cuarenta	**kwah-rehn-tah**
fifty	cincuenta	**seen-kwehn-tah**
sixty	sesenta	**seh-sehn-tah**
seventy	setenta	**seh-tehn-tah**
eighty	ochenta	**oh-chehn-tah**
ninety	noventa	**noh-behn-tah**
one hundred	cien	**syehn**
one thousand	mil	**meel**

DAYS OF THE WEEK

English	Spanish	Pronunciation
Monday	lunes	**loo-nehss**
Tuesday	martes	**mahr-tehss**
Wednesday	miércoles	**myehr-koh-lehs**
Thursday	jueves	**wheh-behss**
Friday	viernes	**byehr-nehss**
Saturday	sábado	**sah-bah-doh**
Sunday	domingo	**doh-meen-goh**

SOME TYPICAL TICO WORDS & PHRASES

Birra   Slang for beer.

Boca   Literally means "mouth," but also a term to describe a small appetizer served alongside a drink at many bars.

Bomba   Translates literally as "pump," but is used in Costa Rica for "gas station."

Brete   Work, or job.

Buena nota   To be good, or have a good vibe.

Casado   Literally means "married," but is the local term for a popular restaurant offering that features a main dish and various side dishes.

Chapa   Derogatory way to call someone stupid or clumsy.

Chepe   Slang term for the capital city, San José.

Choza   Slang for house or home. Also called *chante*.

Chunche   Knickknack; thing, as in "whatchamacallit."

Con mucho gusto   With pleasure.

De hoy en ocho   In 1 week's time.

Diay   An untranslatable but common linguistic punctuation, often used to begin a sentence.

Estar de chicha   To be angry.

Fria   Literally "cold," but used to mean a cold beer—*una fria, por favor.*

Fut   Short for *fútbol,* or soccer.

Goma   Hangover.

Harina   Literally "flour," but used to mean money.

La sele   Short for *la selección,* the Costa Rican national soccer team.

Limpio   Literally means "clean," but is the local term for being broke, or having no money.

Macha or **machita**   A blond woman.

Mae   Translates like "man"; used by many Costa Ricans, particularly teenagers, as frequent verbal punctuation.

Maje   A lot like *mae,* above, but with a slightly derogatory connotation.

Mala nota   Bad vibe, or bad situation.

Mala pata   Bad luck.

Mejenga   An informal, or pickup, soccer game.

Pachanga or **pelón**   Both terms are used to signify a big party or gathering.

Ponga la maría, por favor   This is how you ask taxi drivers to turn on the meter.

Pulpería   The Costa Rican version of the "corner store" or small market.

Pura paja   Pure nonsense or BS.

Pura vida   Literally, "pure life"; translates as "everything's great."

Qué torta   What a mess; what a screw-up.

Si Dios quiere   God willing; you'll hear Ticos say this all the time.

Soda   A casual diner-style restaurant serving cheap Tico meals.

Tico   Costa Rican.

Tiquicia   Costa Rica.

Tuanis   Similar in usage and meaning to *pura vida,* above.

Una teja   100 colones.

Un rojo   1,000 colones.

Un tucán   5,000 colones.

Upe!   Common shout to find out if anyone is home; used frequently since doorbells are so scarce.

Zarpe   Last drink of the night, or "one more for the road."

MENU TERMS
FISH

Almejas Clams	**Langosta** Lobster
Atún Tuna	**Lenguado** Sole
Bacalao Cod	**Mejillones** Mussels
Calamares Squid	**Ostras** Oysters
Camarones Shrimp	**Pargo** Snapper
Cangrejo Crab	**Pulpo** Octopus
Ceviche Marinated seafood salad	**Trucha** Trout
Dorado Dolphin or mahimahi	

MEATS

Albóndigas Meatballs	**Jamón** Ham
Bistec Beefsteak	**Lengua** Tongue
Cerdo Pork	**Lomo** Sirloin
Chicharrones Fried pork rinds	**Lomito** Tenderloin
Chorizo Sausage	**Pato** Duck
Chuleta Literally chop, usually pork chop	**Pavo** Turkey
Cordero Lamb	**Pollo** Chicken
Costillas Ribs	**Salchichas** Hot dogs, but sometimes refers to any sausage
Delmonico Rib-eye	

VEGETABLES

Aceitunas Olives	**Lechuga** Lettuce
Alcachofa Artichoke	**Maíz** Corn
Berenjena Eggplant	**Palmito** Heart of palm
Cebolla Onion	**Papa** Potato
Elote Corn on the cob	**Pepino** Cucumber
Ensalada Salad	**Tomate** Tomato
Espinacas Spinach	**Yuca** Yucca, cassava, or manioc
Frijoles Beans	**Zanahoria** Carrot

FRUITS

Aguacate Avocado
Banano Banana
Carambola Star fruit
Cereza Cherry
Ciruela Plum
Durazno Peach
Frambuesa Raspberry
Fresa Strawberry
Granadilla Sweet passion fruit
Limón Lemon or lime
Mango Mango

Manzana Apple
Maracuya Tart passion fruit
Melón Melon
Mora Blackberry
Naranja Orange
Papaya Papaya
Piña Pineapple
Plátano Plantain
Sandía Watermelon
Toronja Grapefruit

BASICS

Aceite Oil
Ajo Garlic
Arreglado Small meat sandwich
Azúcar Sugar
Casado Plate of the day
Gallo Corn tortilla topped with meat or chicken
Gallo pinto Rice and beans
Hielo Ice
Mantequilla Butter
Miel Honey
Mostaza Mustard

Natilla Sour cream
Olla de carne Meat and vegetable soup
Pan Bread
Patacones Fried plantain chips
Picadillo Chopped vegetable side dish
Pimienta Pepper
Queso Cheese
Sal Salt
Tamal Filled cornmeal pastry
Tortilla Flat corn pancake

DRINKS

Agua purificada Purified water
Agua con gas Sparkling water
Agua sin gas Plain water
Bebida Drink
Café Coffee
Café con leche Coffee with milk
Cerveza Beer
Chocolate caliente Hot chocolate

Jugo Juice
Leche Milk
Natural Fruit juice
Natural con leche Milkshake
Refresco Soft drink
Ron Rum
Té Tea
Trago Alcoholic drink

OTHER RESTAURANT TERMS

Al grill Grilled
Al horno Oven-baked
Al vapor Steamed
Asado Roasted
Caliente Hot

Cambio or **vuelto** Change
Cocido Cooked
Comida Food
Congelado Frozen
Crudo Raw

15

SPANISH TERMS & PHRASES

Menu Terms

El baño Toilet
Frío Cold
Frito Fried
Grande Big or large
La cuenta The check
Medio Medium

Medio rojo Medium rare
Muy cocido Well-done
Pequeño Small
Poco cocido or **rojo** Rare
Tres cuartos Medium-well-done

OTHER USEFUL TERMS

HOTEL TERMS

Aire acondicionado Air-conditioning
Almohada Pillow
Baño Bathroom
Baño privado Private bathroom
Caja de seguridad Safe
Calefacción Heating
Cama Bed
Cobija Blanket
Colchón Mattress
Cuarto or **Habitación** Room
Escritorio Desk

Habitación simple/sencilla Single room
Habitación doble Double room
Habitación triple Triple room
Llave Key
Mosquitero Mosquito net
Sábanas Sheets
Seguro de puerta Door lock
Silla Chair
Telecable Cable TV
Ventilador Fan

TRAVEL TERMS

Aduana Customs
Aeropuerto Airport
Avenida Avenue
Avión Airplane
Aviso Warning
Bus Bus
Cajero ATM, also called *cajero automatico*
Calle Street
Cheques viajeros Traveler's checks
Correo Mail, or post office
Cuadra City block
Dinero or **plata** Money
Embajada Embassy
Embarque Boarding
Entrada Entrance

Equipaje Luggage
Este East
Frontera Border
Lancha or **bote** Boat
Norte North
Occidente West
Oeste West
Oriente East
Pasaporte Passport
Puerta de salida or **puerta de embarque** Boarding gate
Salida Exit
Sur South
Tarjeta de embarque Boarding pass
Vuelo Flight

Other Useful Terms

SPANISH TERMS & PHRASES

EMERGENCY TERMS

¡Auxilio! Help!

Ambulancia Ambulance

Bomberos Fire brigade

Clínica Clinic or hospital

Doctor or **médico** Doctor

Emergencia Emergency

Enfermo/enferma Sick

Enfermera Nurse

Farmacia Pharmacy

Fuego or **incendio** Fire

Hospital Hospital

Ladrón Thief

Peligroso Dangerous

Policía Police

¡Váyase! Go away!

15

SPANISH TERMS & PHRASES

Other Useful Terms

Index

A

Abercrombie & Kent, 93
Accommodations, 502–504
best, 8–9
ACTUAR, 74, 92
ADR Adventure Park (Manuel Antonio), 379
Adventure Education Center (AEC) Spanish Institute, 106, 393
Adventures Under the Sun, 107
Adventure trips, 91–93
Africa Mia (near Liberia), 196–197
Aggressor Fleet Limited, 100, 259
Agua Rica Diving Center (Tamarindo), 243
Aguas Azules (Playa Espadilla), 378
Aguas Termales Gevi (San Gerardo de Rivas), 404
Air travel, 74–75, 496, 499
San José, 111–112
Alajuela, 164–170
All Souls' Day, 39
Alma Ata Archaeological Park (Puerto Viejo de Sarapiquí), 343
American crocodile, 83
Amigos del Río, 375
Amphibians, 81–82
Annexation of Guanacaste Day (Liberia), 39
APREFLOFAS, 107
Aqua Sport (Playa Hermosa), 213
Architecture, 26–27
Arenal Hanging Bridges, 303
Arenal National Park, 16, 69, 302
Arenal Volcano, 47, 296, 301–302
accommodations near, 310–313
Ark Herb Farm (Heredia), 171
Art, 25–26, 37
Asociación de Voluntarios para el Servicio en las Areas Protegidas (ASVO), 107–108
Asociación Talamanqueña de Ecoturismo y Conservación (Puerto Viejo), 478
Athica Canopy (near La Fortuna), 304
ATV and four-wheeling tours, 14–15
Jacó, 360
La Fortuna, 303
Manuel Antonio, 377
Playa Nosara, 289
Tamarindo, 242
Auditorio Nacional (San José), 144
Avenida Central (San José), 138

Aventuras del Sarapiquí, 343
Aventuras Naturales, 104, 152
Aviarios Sloth Sanctuary of Costa Rica (near Cahuita), 17, 471

B

Bahía Culebra, 209
Bahía Salinas, 204, 205, 207
Baird's tapir, 76
Bajo del Tigre Trail, 331
Baldi Hot Springs (near La Fortuna), 308
Ballena Marine National Park, 389–390, 396
Ballooning, 102
Bamboo Yoga Play & Danyasa Eco-Retreat (Dominical), 392
Banana plantations, 411
Barra del Colorado, 448–451
Barra Honda National Park, 51, 69, 283
Basílica de Nuestra Señora de los Angeles (Cartago), 180
Basilisk, 83
Bat Jungle (Monteverde), 333–334
Beaches, 44, 51–52
best, 12–14
Bed-and-breakfasts, 503
Beverages, 34–35
Biesanz, Barry, 141–142
Biesanz Woodworks (Escazú), 163–164
Bike Arenal, 95, 306
Biking and mountain biking, 95
La Fortuna area, 306
Manuel Antonio, 377
Tamarindo, 241
Billfish, 15
Birds and bird-watching, 77–81, 96–97
best, 16–17
Cahuita, 471
Caño Negro National Wildlife Refuge, 307
Liberia, 196
Puerto Viejo, 478
Puerto Viejo (Caribbean coast), 478
quetzals, 3, 17, 78, 328, 330, 331, 400, 404
San José, 126
Santa Elena Cloud Forest Reserve, 330
Zoo Ave (Alajuela), 167
Bliss Massage Center (Puerto Viejo), 479
The Blue Flag, 74
Blue Lake, 200, 201
Blue morpho, 86
Boa constrictor, 83
Boat-billed heron, 80
Boat tours and charters, 497–498
Lake Arenal, 300
Manuel Antonio, 375–376
Playa del Coco, 221

Playa Flamingo, 232–233
Playa Hermosa, Playa Panamá and Papagayo, 213
Puerto Viejo de Sarapiquí, 342
Puntarenas, 258–260
near San José, 151–152
Tamarindo, 242–243
Tortuga Island, 151
Tortuguero, 458
Bolas Locas Mini Golf (Tamarindo), 244
Books, 27–28
Bosque Eterno de Los Niños, 331
Botanical gardens
Cahuita area, 471
Else Kientzler Botanical Garden (Sarchí), 176
Golfito, 434
Lankester Gardens (Cartago), 182
Puerto Jiménez, 422
Puerto Viejo (Caribbean coast), 480
Villa Vanilla (near Quepos), 379
Bottle-nosed dolphin, 85
Boutique Annemarie (San José), 142
Brain coral, 85
Braulio Carrillo National Park, 6
Brisas del Nara (Manuel Antonio), 378
Bugs and bug bites, 72, 506–507
Bullfighting, San José, 126–127
Bungee jumping, 150
Business hours, 507
Bus travel, 496–497, 501–502
Butterflies
Arenal area, 302
Cahuita, 471
Manuel Antonio, 377
Monteverde Butterfly Garden, 333
Montezuma, 267–268
Spirogyra Butterfly Garden (San José), 124

C

Cabo Blanco Absolute Nature Reserve, 268–269
Cabo Matapalo, 419
Cabuya, 268
Cacao Trails (Puerto Viejo), 480
Café Britt, 140
Café Britt Farm (near Heredia), 171–172
Café de Playa Beach & Dining Club (Playa del Coco), 220
Cahuita, 466–475
Cahuita National Park, 16, 71, 466, 469–470
Calendar of events, 38–40
Calle Real (Liberia), 195
Calypso Tours, 151–152, 258
Camping, 97
Corcovado National Park, 427
Playa Junquillal, 252

Cañas Church, 194
Canoa Aventura (La Fortuna), 307
Canoe Costa Rica, 104
Canoeing, La Fortuna, 307
Caño Island Biological Reserve, 415
Caño Negro National Wildlife Refuge, 17, 69, 307
Canopy tours (ziplining), 4, 98
  Drake Bay, 415
  Jacó, 360
  La Fortuna area, 303–304
  Malpaís and Santa Teresa, 275–276
  Manuel Antonio, 377–378
  Monteverde, 331–332
  Montezuma, 268
  Papagayo, 213
  Playa del Coco, 220
  Playa Herradura, 354
  Playa Sámara, 282
  Puerto Viejo de Sarapiquí, 342–344
  near San José, 150–151
  Tamarindo, 241–242
Canyoning, 15, 100
  La Fortuna area, 304
  Monteverde, 332
  Turrialba, 187
Capuchin monkey, 99
Carara National Park, 17, 70, 354, 355
Caribbean coast, 43, 46, 447–494
  best experiences, 448
  national parks, 71
  weather pattern, 447
Caribbean Conservation Corporation, 108
Caribeans Chocolate Tour (Gandoca-Manzanillo Wildlife Refuge), 488
Carnaval, Limón, 462
Carrera Campo Traviesa Al Cerro Chirripó, 403
Carrera de San Juan, 39
Cartago, 178–182
Car travel and rentals, 497, 499–501
  San José, 117–118
Casa de Arte (Monteverde), 340
Casa Delagua (between Nuevo Arenal and Tilarán), 319
Casa Orquídeas (near Golfito), 434
CASEM COOP (Monteverde), 340
Casinos
  Jacó, 367
  San José, 149
  Tamarindo, 248
Castro's (San José), 145
Catedral de Alajuela, 165
Catedral de la Inmaculada Concepción (Heredia), 171
Catedral Metropolitano (San José), 120

Catleya (Jacó), 362
Cattle egret, 80
Cecropia, 88
Ceiba tree, 87
Cellphones, 509
Center for Agronomy Research and Development (CATIE; Turrialba), 187
Central American spider monkey, 77
Central Pacific coast, 45–46, 349–405
  best experiences, 349–350
  national parks, 70
Central Valley, 44, 155–188
  national parks, 67–68
Centro Ecuestre del Sol (Santa Ana), 158
Centro Nacional de Arte y Cultura (San José), 121
Centro Panamericano de Idiomas (CPI), 106
Cerro Chato, 305
Cerro de la Muerte, 17, 404
Cerro de Tortuguero, 455
Certificate of Sustainable Tourism Program (CST), 74
Charlie's Adventures, 213
Chaverri Oxcart Factory (Sarchí), 176
Chiclets Tree Tour (Playa Hermosa), 360
Chietón Morén (San José), 142
Children, families with, 508
  best destinations for, 11–12
  La Fortuna, 302
  Liberia, 196
  Manuel Antonio, 378
  Playa Chiquita, 489
  San José, 125
  Tamarindo, 244
Children's Museum (San José), 125
Chirripó National Park, 70, 400–402
Chocolate tours
  Gandoca-Manzanillo Wildlife Refuge, 488
  Monteverde, 335
  Puerto Jiménez, 422
Churchill, 261
Clay-colored robin, 81
Climate, 37–38
Cloud forests, 65–66, 323–324
Club Rio (La Fortuna), 302
Coast to Coast Adventures, 92, 95, 97
Coatimundi, 77
Coconuts (pipas), 33
Cocos Island, 259
CocoZuma Traveller, 266, 268
Coffee, 166
  shopping for, 140
Coffee plantations and tours, 5
  Heredia area, 171–172
  Monteverde area, 334, 335
  Turrialba, 187
Collared peccary, 77

Consulates, 508
Cooking classes, La Fortuna, 302
Copa del Café (San José), 38
Corcovado Foundation, 410
Corcovado National Park, 6, 16, 70–71, 410, 419, 423–427
Corobicí River, 57
Costa Rica Custom Trips, 92
Costa Rica Expeditions, 74, 92, 96, 153, 459
Costa Rica Experts, 93
Costa Rican Art Museum (San José), 123–124
Costa Rican Bird Route, 96
Costa Rican Language Academy (San José), 106
Costa Rica Outdoors, 101
Costa Rica Rainforest Outward Bound School, 107
Costa Rica Spanish Institute (Manuel Antonio), 378
Costa Rica Sun Tours, 74, 92, 96, 153
Courier services, 508–509
Credit cards, 510–511
Crocodiles, 283, 307, 354, 424
Culture, 27–31
Curicancha Reserve, 330
Curú Wildlife Refuge (Playa Tambor), 263–264

D
Damas Island estuary, 375
Del Río (San José), 143
Dental tourism, 108
Desafío Expeditions (near La Fortuna), 304–306, 326
Día de la Pólvora, 39
Día de la Raza (Limón), 39
Día del Boyero (San Antonio de Escazú), 39
Día de los Muertos, 39
Día de San Ramón, 39
Diamante Waterfalls, 392
Disabilities, travelers with, 514
Diving, 100
  Dominical, 391
  Drake Bay, 415
  Isla de Coco, 15, 259
  Jacó, 362
  Manuel Antonio, 376
  Playa del Coco and Playa Ocotal, 221
  Playa Flamingo, 232
  Playa Hermosa, Playa Panamá and Papagayo, 212–213
  Playa Herradura, 355
  Puerto Viejo (Caribbean coast), 479
  Tamarindo, 243
Diving Safaris de Costa Rica, 100, 212
Doctors and hospitals, 507
Doka Estate (Alajuela), 166
Dolphins, 376, 410, 416, 444, 487, 488

Dominical, 387–398
  accommodations in or near,
    392–394, 396–397
  beaches, 389–390
  getting around, 389
  getting there and departing,
    388–389
  layout, 389
  nightlife, 395
  outdoor and wellness activities,
    390–392
  restaurants in or near, 394–395,
    397–398
Dominicalito, 389
Don Juan Coffee Tour, 334
Drake Bay, 408–418
Dry season, 38

E

Eating and drinking, 31–35
Ecocentro Danaus (near La
  Fortuna), 302
Ecoglide (near La Fortuna), 304
Eco Jungle Cruises (near Playa
  Herradura), 354
Ecolodges, 504
Ecolodges and wilderness
  resorts, best, 7
Ecological Sanctuary (near
  Monteverde), 331
Ecosystems, 64–67
Eco Teach, 107
Eco Termales (near La Fortuna),
  309
El Bochinche (San José), 149
El Chorro, 267
El Coconut Beach Club (Playa
  Potrero), 231–232
El Cuartel de la Boca del Monte
  (San José), 146–147
El Día del Boyero (San Antonio
  de Escazú), 160
Electricity, 508
El Fortin (Heredia), 171
El Lobo Estepario (San José),
  147
El Mirador (Arenal National
  Park), 302
El Observatorio (San José), 147
Else Kientzler Botanical Garden
  (Sarchí), 176
El Silencio Mirador y Senderos,
  305
El Sótono (San José), 147
El Steinvorth (San José), 147
El Templo de la Musica
  (Heredia), 171
El Tope and Carnival (San José),
  40
El Trapiche Tour (Monteverde),
  335
El 13 (San José), 146
El Viejo Wildlife Refuge &
  Wetlands, 58, 229
Embassies, 508
Emergencies, 508
Envision Festival (Dominical),
  389
Escazú, 156–164

Escuela D'Amore (Manuel
  Antonio), 106, 378
Etiquette and customs, 30
Exploradores Outdoors, 105,
  152, 457, 479, 481
Explornatura (Turrialba), 187

F

Families with children, 508
  best destinations for, 11–12
  La Fortuna, 302
  Liberia, 196
  Manuel Antonio, 378
  Playa Chiquita, 489
  San José, 125
  Tamarindo, 244
Fer-de-lance, 82
Ferguson, Walter "Gavitt," 473
Ferruginous pygmy owl, 81
Festejos Populares (San José),
  40
Festival Internacional de las
  Artes (San José), 144
Field Guides, 96
Fiesta del Maíz (Upala), 39
Fiesta de los Negritos (Boruca),
  39
Fiesta del Virgen del Mar
  (Puntarenas), 256
Fiesta of the Diablitos (Rey
  Curré), 38–39, 399
Fiesta of the Virgin of Los
  Angeles (Cartago), 39
Fiesta of the Virgin of the Sea
  (Puntarenas), 39
Fiestas of Palmares, 38
Fiestas of Santa Cruz, 38
Figueres, Cecilia "Pefi," 141,
  142
Films, 29
Finca La Isla Botanical Gardens
  (Puerto Viejo), 480
Finca Modelo Canyoning Tour,
  332
Finca Rosa Blanca Coffee
  Plantation Tour (Heredia),
  172
Fincas Naturales/Nature Farm
  Reserve (Manuel Antonio),
  377
Finca Valmy (Manuel Antonio),
  378
Fishing, 101
  Barra del Colorado, 450–451
  Dominical, 391
  Golfito, 435
  Jacó, 362
  Lake Arenal, 304, 319
  Playa del Coco and Playa
    Ocotal, 221–222
  Playa Flamingo, 232–233
  Playa Hermosa, Playa Panamá
    and Papagayo, 213
  Playa Herradura, 355
  Playa Nosara, 289
  Playa Sámara, 282
  Puerto Jiménez, 422–423
  Quepos, 376
  Tamarindo, 243

Flightseeing, Dominical, 391
Flora, 87–89
Flying Crocodile (Playa Buena
  Vista), 283
Football (soccer), 4, 56
  San José, 127–128
Four-wheeling and ATV tours,
  14–15
  Jacó, 360
  La Fortuna, 303
  Manuel Antonio, 377
  Playa Nosara, 289
  Tamarindo, 242
Frog Pond of Monteverde, 333

G

Galería Jacobo Karpio (San
  José), 139
Galería Kandinsky (San José),
  139
Galería Namu (San José), 142
Galería 11-12 (Escazú), 164
Galería Valanti (San José), 140
Gandoca-Manzanillo Wildlife
  Refuge, 486–488
Gays and lesbians, 508
  San José, 149
Global Volunteers, 108
Golden Bean Coffee Tour
  (Turrialba), 187
Golden silk orb-weaver, 86
Golf, 101–102
  Central Valley, 158
  Jacó, 360
  Papagayo Peninsula, 213
  Playa Conchal, 228
  Playa del Coco, 220
  Playa Herradura, 354
  Tamarindo, 242
Golfito, 431–438
Golfito National Wildlife
  Reserve, 435
Grandpa Ninja's B&B, 102
Gray Line Tours, 361
Grecia, 174–175
Green and black poison dart
  frog, 82
Green iguana, 83
Green Iguana Conservation Tour
  (Playa Chiquita), 489–490
Green turtles, 84, 456. See also
  Sea turtles
Guaitíl, 248
Guanacaste and the Nicoya
  Peninsula, 190–252
  best experiences, 191
  in brief, 44
  national parks, 68–69
Guanacaste tree, 87, 196
Guaria morada, 88
Guayabo National Monument,
  67, 187
Gumbo limbo, 88

H

Habitat for Humanity
  International, 108
Hacienda Barú (Dominical),
  391–392

Hacienda Guachipelín (Rincón de la Vieja), 58, 201
Hacienda Pozo Azul (Puerto Viejo de Sarapiquí), 342
Handicrafts
  Guaitíl, 248
  Lake Arenal, 319
  Puerto Jiménez, 430–431
  Puerto Viejo (Caribbean coast), 485
  San José, 141–143
Hang Glide Costa Rica, 102
Hang gliding, 102
Health concerns, 504–507
in the wild, 71–72
Heliconia, 89
Heredia, 170–174
Herrera Botanical Gardens (Puerto Jiménez), 422
Hidden Garden Art Gallery (near Liberia), 199
Hikes and nature walks
  Arenal National Park, 302, 304–305
  best day hikes and nature walks, 16
  Carara National Park, 355
  Chirripó National Park, 400–401
  Corcovado National Park, 426
  Dominical, 391–392
  Golfito, 435
  La Fortuna area, 304–305
  Manuel Antonio, 374–375
  Monteverde, 328–331
  Mount Chirripó, 15–16
  Playa Nosara, 289
  Puerto Viejo (Caribbean coast), 478
  Puerto Viejo de Sarapiquí, 343
  Rincón de la Vieja, 200–201
  Santa Elena Cloud Forest Reserve, 330
  Santa Rosa National Park, 205–206
  Tortuguero, 455
History of Costa Rica, 21–25
Hitchhiking, 502
Holidays, 38
Holis Spa (Manuel Antonio), 379
Holy Week, 39
Horizontes, 74
Horizontes Tours, 92, 153
Horseback riding, 102
  Cahuita, 471
  Dominical, 391
  Jacó, 360–361
  La Fortuna area, 304–306
  Lake Arenal, 300, 319
  Manuel Antonio, 378
  Monteverde, 332
  Montezuma, 268
  Playa del Coco, 221
  Playa Flamingo, 232
  Playa Junquillal (abolitionist movement and), 251
  Playa Nosara, 289
  Puerto Viejo (Caribbean coast), 479
  near San José, 158

Tamarindo, 242
Tambor, 263
Hotlips, 89
Hot springs, 3
  Aguas Termales Gevi (San Gerardo de Rivas), 404
  La Fortuna area, 303, 308–309
  Rincón de la Vieja, 201–202
Howler monkeys, 76, 99
Humpback whale, 85

I
Iglesia de Cañas (Cañas), 194
Iglesia de la Inmaculada Concepción (Liberia), 195
Iglesia La Ermita de la Agonía (Liberia), 195
Iguana Expeditions, 288, 289
Iguana Tours, 375, 376
Imaginative Traveller, 93
INBio Park (Heredia), 172
Independence Day, 39
India Point, 289
Indio Desnudo trail, 205–206
Indulgence Spa (Puerto Viejo), 479
Institute for Central American Development Studies, 107
International Beach Clean-Up Day, 39
Invertebrates, 85–86
Irazú Volcano, 181–182
Irazú Volcano National Park, 67–68
Isla del Caño, 376, 391, 414, 415
Isla del Coco, 259
Itineraries, suggested, 46–62
  adventures, 54–56
  best of San José and the Central Valley, 58–62
  for families, 56–58
  highlights, 46–49
  undiscovered Costa Rica, 50–53

J
Jabiru stork, 78
Jacó, 358–369
  accommodations, 362–364
  exploring, 360–362
  getting around, 359–360
  getting there and departing, 358
  layout, 359
  nightlife, 366–367
  restaurants, 364–366
  side trips from, 367–369
Jade Museum (San José), 122–123
Jaguar, 75–76
Jaguar Refuge Center (Playa Chiquita), 489
Jardín de Serpientes (Puerto Viejo de Sarapiquí), 343–344
Jazz Café (San José), 148
Jazz Café Escazú (San José), 148
Jogging, San José, 127

Journey Latin America, 93
Juan Santamaría Day (Alajuela), 39
Juan Santamaría Museum of Cultural History (Alajuela), 165

K
Kayaking. See also White-water rafting, kayaking and canoeing
  Jacó, 361
  Playa Nosara, 289
  Puerto Jiménez, 422
Keel-billed toucan, 78
Key Largo (San José), 147
Kids Saving The Rainforest, 375
Kiosco (San José), 143
Kiteboarding, 106
Kitesurfing, 15

L
La Avispa (San José), 149
La Cangrejo Waterfall, 200
La Caraña Riding Academy (Santa Ana), 158
La Casa de la Cultura (Puntarenas), 258
La Casa del Soñador (near Cachí), 183–184
La Cascada (Playa Sámara), 283–284
La Casona (San José), 142–143
La Casona (Santa Rosa), 205
La Cruz, 204–205, 207–208
La Fortuna, 296–317
  accommodations, 307–313
  farther afield, 314–317
  exploring, 301–307
  Fiestas Cívicas, 301
  getting around, 300–301
  getting there and departing, 297–299
  layout, 299–300
  nightlife, 314
  restaurants, 313
  shopping, 313–314
  visitor information, 300
La Fortuna Falls, 305–306
La Gran Nicoya (Liberia), 198
Lake Arenal, 15
  along the shores of, 317–323
  windsurfing, 106
Lake Coter, 320
La Negrita (Cartago), 180, 181
Lankester Gardens, 16
Lankester Gardens (Cartago), 182
La Paz Waterfall Gardens, 11, 166
Las Corridas a la Tica (San José), 126–127
Las Cruces Biological Station (near San Vito), 434–435
La Selva Biological Station, 16, 17
Las Pailas, 201
Las Posadas, 39–40
Las Ruinas (Cartago), 180

INDEX

Laughing falcon, 80
Lava Tours, 95
La Ventana (Monteverde), 329
Leafcutter ants, 86
Leatherback sea turtles, 84, 456. *See also* Sea turtles
  Playa Grande, 235–236
LGBT travelers, 508
Liberia, 191–199
  accommodations, 197–198
  outdoor adventures near, 195–197
  restaurants, 198
Librería Internacional (San José), 141
Librería Topsy (Montezuma), 267
Limón, 454, 461–465
Limón Carnival, 39
Litter skink, 83
Llanos del Cortés Waterfall (near Liberia), 195
Loggerheads, 456
Los Altos de Eros (near Tamarindo), 244
Lucky Bug Gallery (Lake Arenal), 319

M

Magnificent frigate bird, 79
Mahogany Park, 151
Mail, 508
Malpaís, 13, 273–279
Mangroves and wetlands, 66
Manta ray, 85
Mantled howler monkey, 76
Manuel Antonio Expeditions, 373, 376
Manuel Antonio National Park, 6, 12, 13–14, 49, 70, 369–387
  accommodations, 379–384
  beaches, 374–375
  exploring the national park, 373–375
  getting around, 372–373
  getting there and departing, 370–372
  for kids, 378
  layout, 373
  nightlife, 386–387
  restaurants, 384–386
  shopping, 386
Manzanillo, 14, 486, 487, 490, 491, 493
Marine toad, 81
Mariposario Cahuita, 471
Mariposario Montezuma Gardens, 267–268
Más x Menos (San José), 143
Meals and dining customs, 32–34
Mealy parrot, 80
Medical and dental tourism, 108
Mercado Central (San José), 143
Metropolitan Cathedral (San José), 120
Miravalles Volcano, 203

Mobile phones, 509
Moín, 454
Money and costs, 509–511
Monkeys, 3, 99, 375, 424
Monteverde, 12, 323–340
  accommodations, 335–337
  exploring, 328–335
  getting around, 327
  getting there and departing, 324, 326–327
  layout, 327
  nightlife, 340
  restaurants, 338
  shopping, 340
  weather, 324
Monteverde Butterfly Garden, 333
Monteverde Cheese Factory, 340
Monteverde Cloud Forest Biological Reserve, 6, 16, 55–56, 69, 328–329
  gift shop, 340
Monteverde Coffee Tour, 335
Monteverde Conservation League, 331
Monteverde Institute, 107
Monteverde Serpentarium, 333
Montezuma, 52, 265–272
Montezuma's oropendola, 79
Montezuma waterfall, 267
Moray eel, 85
Mot Mot Jungle (Arenal), 302
MotoAdventures, 103
Motorcycling, 102–103
Mountain biking, 14
Mount Chirripó, 15–16, 400–402
Mouthless crab, 86
Multispa (San José), 127
Mundo Aventura, 103
Mundoloco El Chante (San José), 148
Museo de Arte Costarricense (San José), 123–124
Museo de Cultura Popular (Heredia), 171
Museo de Guanacaste (Liberia), 195
Museo de Jade Marco Fidel Tristán (San José), 122–123
Museo de Los Niños (San José), 125
Museo Histórico (Puntarenas), 258
Museo Historico Cultural Juan Santamaría (Alajuela), 165
Museo Municipal de Cartago, 180
Museo Nacional de Costa Rica (San José), 121
Museos del Banco Central de Costa Rica (San José), 121
Music, 29–31
Mussurana, 82

N

National Orchid Show (San José), 39
National parks and bioreserves, 67–71

National Stadium (San José), 127
National Symphony Orchestra (San José), 144
National University (Heredia), 170
Natural world, 64–89. *See also* Birds and bird-watching; Whale-watching; wildlife-viewing
  cloud forests, 65–66
  ecosystems, 64–67
  flora, 87–89
  health, safety and etiquette, 71–73
  mangroves and wetlands, 66
  national parks and bioreserves, 67–71
  páramos, 66
  rainforests, 64–65
  responsible tourism, 73–75
  tropical dry forests, 65
  volcanoes, 66–67
  wildlife, 75–86
Nature Air, 74–75
Nature Expeditions International, 93
Nauyaca Waterfalls, 392
Newspapers and magazines, 511
Nicaragua, 205
Nicoya Peninsula, 45, 69, 254
Northern tamandua, 77
Northern zone, 45, 295–347
  best experiences, 295–296
  national parks and bioreserves, 69
Nosara, 288
Nosara Biological Reserve, 289

O

Oasis Nature Tours, 342, 450
Ocelot, 76
Olive ridley sea turtles, 84–85. *See also* Sea turtles
  Playa Hermosa de Jacó, 367
Ollie's Point, 222
Orchid Garden (Santa Elena), 334
Organization for Tropical Studies, 107
Original Canopy Tour, 151, 332
Original Grand Gallery (La Fortuna), 314
Ornamental red ginger, 89
Orosi Church & Religious Art Museum, 184
Orosi Valley, 183–185
Osa Conservation, 410
Osa Peninsula, 6, 410
Osprey, 79
Ostional National Wildlife Refuge, 289
Outdoor activities, 94–106
Overseas Adventure Travel, 93

P

Paca, 77
Pacific coast, 42

Palm plantations, 372
Palo Verde National Park, 68, 196
Panama, 489
Papagayo Peninsula, 209, 211, 212
Paragliding, 102
Páramos, 66
Parasailing, Manuel Antonio, 378
Parque Central (Cartago), 178
Parque del Este (San José), 126, 127
Parque La Sabana (San José), 125–127
Parque Marino del Pacífico (Puntarenas), 258
Parque Nacional Volcán Tenorio, 202–203
Parque Reptilandia (near Dominical), 391
Parque Valle del Sol, 158
Parque Vargas (Limón), 463
Paseo de los Turistas (Puntarenas), 257
Passports, 511–512
Peñas Blancas River, 205, 306, 307
Piedras Blancas National Park, 432
Playa Avellanas, 13, 248–250
Playa Barrigona, 13, 282
Playa Bejuco, 360, 367, 369
Playa Blanca (Guanacaste), 206, 207
Playa Blanca (near Playa Herradura), 352, 360
Playa Bonita, 462
Playa Brasilito, 225, 226
Playa Buena Vista, 282
Playa Cacao, 434
Playa Carrillo, 13, 282
Playa Chiquita, 486, 487, 489
Playa Cocles, 486, 487
Playa Conchal, 225–230
Playa de Jacó, 12, 358–369
Playa del Coco, 217–225
Playa Doña Aña, 258
Playa Escondida, 362
Playa Espadilla, 375
Playa Espadilla Sur, 374
Playa Esterillos, 360, 367, 368–369
Playa Flamingo, 230–235
Playa Garza, 287
Playa Grande, 235–237
Playa Guiones, 287, 288
Playa Hermosa (Guanacaste), 11, 208–213
Playa Hermosa (near Dominical), 389
Playa Hermosa de Jacó, 360, 362, 367–368
Playa Herradura, 350–358
Playa Junquillal, 207, 250–252
Playa La Penca, 226
Playa Manta, 352, 360
Playa Manuel Antonio, 374

Playa Matapalo, 387
Playa Montezuma, 13, 265–272
Playa Nacascolo, 13, 209
Playa Nancite, 206
Playa Naranjo, 206
Playa Negra (Caribbean coast), 470, 481
Playa Negra (Guanacaste), 248–250
Playa Nosara, 254, 287–292
Playa Ocotal, 218, 220
Playa Ostional, 287, 289, 292
Playa Panamá, 209
Playa Pan de Azúcar, 226
Playa Pavones, 442–445
Playa Pelada, 287, 288–289
Playa Plantanares, 421–422
Playa Potrero, 230, 231
Playa Sámara, 13, 254, 279–286
Playa Tamarindo, 11, 237–250. See also Tamarindo
Playa Tambor, 261–264
Playa Tivives, 258
Playa Tulin, 362, 367
Playa Uvita, 390
Playa Zancudo, 53, 438–442
Plaza de la Democracia (San José), 138
Poás Volcano, 166–167
Poás Volcano National Park, 68
Police, 512
Poor man's umbrella, 89
Popular culture, 27–31
Psycho Tours, 422
Pucho's Bar (San José), 149
Puerto Escondido, 374
Puerto Jiménez, 410, 418–431
Puerto Vargas, 469
Puerto Viejo (Caribbean coast), 475–486
Puerto Viejo de Sarapiquí, 341–347
Punta Catedral (Manuel Antonio), 375
Punta Coral, 152, 258
Punta Leona, 352
Punta Mona Center For Sustainable Living & Education (Gandoca-Manzanillo Wildlife Refuge), 488–489
Puntarenas, 45, 254–261
  getting there and departing, 256
Punta Serrucho (Manuel Antonio), 375
Punta Uva, 14
Pura Vida Gardens and Waterfalls, 354–355
Pure Trek Canyoning (near La Fortuna), 300, 304

Q
Quepos, 370, 376
Quetzals, 3, 17, 78, 328, 330, 331, 400, 404

R
Rafting trips, 14. See also White-water rafting, kayaking and canoeing
  Liberia, 196
  Manuel Antonio, 375
Raindrop Spa (Manuel Antonio), 379
Rain Forest Aerial Tram (near Puerto Viejo de Sarapiquí), 344
Rain Forest Aerial Tram Atlantic, 150
Rain Forest Aerial Tram Pacific, 360
Rainforests, 64–65
Rainmaker Park (near Quepos), 378
Rainy season, 38
Rancho Humo (Playa Sámara), 283
Rattlesnake, tropical, 83
Rayuela (San José), 147
Red-backed squirrel monkey, 77
Red-eyed tree frog, 81–82
Red tides, 505
Refugio Herpetologico, 158
Regions in brief, 42–46
Rent A Moto CR-LTD, 103
Reptiles, 82–83
Resplendent quetzal, 3, 17, 78, 328, 330, 331, 400, 404
Responsible tourism, 73–75
Restaurants, 31–32
  best, 9–11
  meals and dining customs, 32–34
  prices, 31–32
  sodas, 5
Rey Curré, 399
Rey de Nosara Language School, 290
Rincón de la Vieja National Park, 16, 50, 69, 199–204
Río Celeste, 202–203
Río Fortuna Waterfall, 305
Río Locos, 105
Río Negro Hot Springs (Cañas Dulces), 202
Rio Perdido, 203
Río Perezoso, 469
Río Sarapiquí Region, 6
Río Shanti (Monteverde), 335
Ríos Tropicales, 105, 152, 196
Río Tempisque Basin, 196
Riptides, 507
Rock climbing, 103
Roman Catholicism, 20
Roseate spoonbill, 80
Ruta de los Conquistadores, 95

S
Safety, 512
  in the wild, 71–72
Sailing. See Boat tours and charters
Sally lightfoot crab, 86
Salsa Brava, 481

Salsa 54 (San José), 145
Salsa Lizano, 4
Samasati (Puerto Viejo), 479
San Isidro de El General,
398–405
San José, 110–153
  accommodations, 128–133
  apartotels, 133
  addresses, 114
  arriving in, 111–113
  best experiences, 110–111
  in brief, 43–44
  day trips from, 149–153
  doctors and hospitals, 118, 119
  entertainment and nightlife,
    143–149
  exploring, 120–128
  getting around, 116–118
  layout, 113–114
  maps, 119
  neighborhoods in brief,
    114–115
  outdoor activities and spectator
    sports, 125–128
  restaurants, 133–138
  safety, 119
  shopping, 138–143
  in suggested itineraries, 46, 54,
    58–60
  visitor information, 113
San Lucas Beach Club
  (Puntarenas), 258
San Pedro (San José), 147–148
Santa Ana, 156, 158
Santa Elena, 327
Santa Elena Cloud Forest
  Reserve, 330
Santa Juana Mountain Tour &
  Canopy Safari, 378
Santa María, 201
Santa Rosa National Park, 5, 12,
  69, 205–206
Santa Teresa, 13, 273–275
Santo Cristo Waterfalls, 392
Saprissa (San José), 127
SarapiquíS Rainforest Lodge,
  343
Sarchí, 175–176
Savegre River, 375
Scarlet macaw, 78
Scarlet macaws, 355
Scarlet rumped tanager, 79
Scuba diving, 100
  Dominical, 391
  Drake Bay, 415
  Isla del Coco, 15, 259
  Jacó, 362
  Manuel Antonio, 376
  Playa del Coco and Playa
    Ocotal, 221
  Playa Flamingo, 232
  Playa Hermosa, Playa Panamá
    and Papagayo, 212–213
  Playa Herradura, 355
  Puerto Viejo (Caribbean coast),
    479
  Tamarindo, 243
Sea life, 84–85
Seasons, 37

Sea Turtle Conservancy, 108
Sea Turtle Conservancy Visitors'
  Center and Museum
  (Tortuguero), 458–459
Sea turtles, 105
  Playa Grande, 235–236
  Playa Hermosa de Jacó, 367
  Playa Nosara, 289
  Playa Ostional, 292
  Tortuguero National Park, 456,
    457–458
Selvatura Park (Monteverde),
  331–332
Sendero Bosque Nuboso
  (Monteverde), 329
Sendero Camino (Monteverde),
  329
Sendero Coladas (Arenal
  National Park), 302
Sendero El Río (Monteverde),
  329
Sendero Tosi (Monteverde), 329
Senior travelers, 512–513
Serendipity Adventures, 95,
  102
Shopping, 35–37
Sibu Chocolate (San José), 141
Sibu Chocolates (Heredia), 171
Sierra Club, 93
Sirena, 424–427
Sky Adventures, 332
Sky Tram, 303–304
Sky Trek, 331, 332
Sky Walk, 330–332
Slender anole, 83
Smithsonian Institute, 93
Smoking, 513
Snakes, 158
  Dominical, 391
  Monteverde Serpentarium, 333
  Puerto Viejo de Sarapiquí,
    343–344
Snorkeling, 100
  Manuel Antonio, 376
  Punta Cahuita, 470
Soccer (fútbol), 4, 56
  San José, 127–128
Southern Explorations, 93
Southern zone, 46, 407–445
  best experiences, 407–408
  national park, 70–71
Spa Aguas de Hermosa, 213
Spanish-language classes, 106
  Manuel Antonio, 378
  Monteverde, 335
  Playa Flamingo, 232
  Playa Nosara, 290
  Playa Sámara, 283
  Tamarindo, 240
Spas and wellness centers, 103.
  See also Yoga classes and
  retreats
  Ama Tierra Retreat & Wellness
    Center (near Jacó), 352
  Jacó, 362
  Malpaís and Santa Teresa, 275
  Manuel Antonio, 379
  Puerto Viejo (Caribbean coast),
    479

San José, 127
Tamarindo, 244
Spa Uno (Manuel Antonio), 379
Spider monkeys, 77, 99
Spirogyra Butterfly Garden (San
  José), 124
Sportfishing, 101
  Barra del Colorado, 450–451
  Dominical, 391
  Golfito, 435
  Jacó, 362
  Lake Arenal, 304, 319
  Playa del Coco and Playa
    Ocotal, 221–222
  Playa Flamingo, 232–233
  Playa Hermosa, Playa Panamá
    and Papagayo, 213
  Playa Herradura, 355
  Playa Nosara, 289
  Playa Sámara, 282
  Puerto Jiménez, 422–423
  Quepos, 376
  Tamarindo, 243
Squirrel monkey, 77, 99
Stand up paddling, 222, 232,
  306
Stone spheres, 414
Strangler fig, 87–88
Student travelers, 513
Studio Metallo (San José), 143
Study and volunteer programs,
  106–108
Sun exposure, 507
Surfing, 14–15, 58, 104
  Dominical, 390
  Jacó, 362
  Malpaís and Santa Teresa, 275
  Playa del Coco, 222
  Playa Espadilla, 375
  Playa Hermosa, Playa Panamá
    and Papagayo, 213
  Playa Nosara, 289–290
  Playa Pavones, 443–444
  Playa Sámara, 282–283
  Puerto Jiménez, 423
  Puerto Viejo (Caribbean coast),
    481
  Tamarindo, 244
Swimming
  Cahuita National Park, 469
  Lake Coter, 320
  San José, 128
Swiss Travel Service, 74, 153,
  196, 213

T
Tabacón Grand Spa Thermal
  Resort (near La Fortuna),
  308
Talamanca Mountains, 110, 478
Tamarindo, 237–250
  accommodations, 244–246
  exploring, 240–244
  getting around, 240
  getting there and departing,
    238, 240
  layout, 240
  nightlife, 248

restaurants, 246–248
shopping, 248
Tapantí National Park, 183
Tauck, 93
Taxes, 513
Taxis, 502
Tayra, 77
Teatro Melico Salazar (San José), 144
Teatro Nacional (San José), 144
Telephones, 513–514
Tennis, Tamarindo, 243
Tenorio National Park, 202–203
TEORetica (San José), 140
Terciopelo Cave, 283
Termales Los Laureles, 309
Terra U (San José), 149
Three-toed sloth, 76
Tico Travel, 104
Tipping, 514
Tirimbina Rainforest Center (Puerto Viejo de Sarapiquí), 343
Titi Conservation Alliance, 375
Toilets, 514
Tortuga Island, 258
Tortuguero National Park, 6–7, 71, 452–461
Tour agencies, 91–93
Tree of Life Wildlife Rescue Center and Botanical Gardens (Cahuita), 471
Trees, 87–88
Tropical Birding, 96
Tropical Bungee, 103, 150, 175
Tropical dry forests, 65
Tropical rattlesnake, 83
Turrialba, 186–188
Turrialba Volcano National Park, 187
Turtles, 105
  Playa Grande, 235–236
  Playa Hermosa de Jacó, 367
  Playa Nosara, 289
  Playa Ostional, 292
  Tortuguero National Park, 456, 457–458

U
Ultralight flying, 102, 283, 391
Undersea Hunter, 100, 259
Uvita Tourist Information Center, 396

V
Vandara Hotsprings, 202
Venado Caverns, 307
Veragua Rainforest Park, 464
Vértigo (San José), 145–146
Victor Emanuel Nature Tours, 96
Vida, 108
Villa Lapas, 354
Villa Vanilla (near Quepos), 379
Violet sabrewing, 79–80
Visitor information, 515
Vista Los Sueños Canopy Tour (Playa Herradura), 354
Volcanoes, 66–67

Volcano visits, near San José, 152–153
Volunteer programs, 107
Vuelta al Lago (Lake Arenal), 306

W
Wakeboarding, Lake Arenal, 320
Water, drinking, 35, 515
Waterfalls, 55
  Dominical, 392
  El Chorro (near Montezuma), 267
  La Cangrejo Waterfall, 200–201
  La Cascada (Playa Sámara), 283
  La Fortuna Falls, 305–306
  La Paz Waterfall Gardens, 166
  Llanos del Cortés Waterfall (near Liberia), 195
  Playa Montezuma, 265, 267
  Waterfall Canopy Tour (Montezuma), 268
Water Ridge, 400
Watersports and equipment rental. See also specific sports
  Montezuma, 268
  Playa Conchal, 228
  Playa Flamingo, 232
  Tamarindo, 243–244
Wave Expeditions, 306
Wayra Instituto de Español (Tamarindo), 107, 240
Weather, 37–38
Websites about Costa Rica, 498
Weddings, 94
Whale shark, 84
Whale-watching, Drake Bay, 410, 416
White-faced monkey, 77
White-water rafting, kayaking and canoeing, 104–105
  La Fortuna area, 306–307
  Puerto Viejo de Sarapiquí, 343
  near San José, 152
White-water tubing, 196
Wildlife-viewing, 75–86
  best places for, 5–7
  Cahuita, 471
  El Viejo Wildlife Refuge & Wetlands, 229
  Gandoca-Manzanillo Wildlife Refuge, 487–488
  near Liberia, 196–197
  Monteverde Cloud Forest Biological Reserve, 328
  Osa Peninsula, 413
  Playa Chiquita, 489–490
  Playa Nosara, 289
  Playa Sámara, 283
  searching for wildlife, 72–73
  Zoo Ave (Alajuela), 167
Wild Riders, 103
Wilson Botanical Gardens (near San Vito), 17, 434–435, 437
Windsurfing and kiteboarding, 15, 106
  Lake Arenal, 320
  Santa Rosa National Park, 207

WINGS, 97
Witch's Rock Canopy Tour, 213
Women travelers, 515

Y
Yoga classes and retreats. See also Spas and wellness centers
  Dominical, 392
  Monteverde, 335
  Playa Nosara, 290
  Puerto Viejo (Caribbean coast), 479–480
  Tamarindo, 244

Z
Zarcero, 177–178
Ziplining (canopy tours), 4, 98
  Drake Bay, 415
  Jacó, 360
  La Fortuna area, 303–304
  Malpaís and Santa Teresa, 275–276
  Manuel Antonio, 377–378
  Monteverde, 331–332
  Montezuma, 268
  Papagayo, 213
  Playa del Coco, 220
  Playa Herradura, 354
  Playa Sámara, 282
  Puerto Viejo de Sarapiquí, 342–344
  near San José, 150–151
  Tamarindo, 241–242
Zoo Ave (Alajuela), 167

Accommodations & Wilderness Lodges

Aguila de Osa Inn (Drake Bay), 417
Albergue Mirador de Quetzales, 405
Alby Lodge (Cahuita), 472
Aldea Hostal (San José), 132
Allegro Papagayo Resort, 215
Alma del Pacifico Hotel (Playa Esterillos), 369
Almonds & Corals Hotel (Manzanillo), 490–491
Alta Hotel (between Escazú and Santa Ana), 160
Ama Tierra Retreat & Wellness Center (near Jacó), 352
Amor de Mar (Montezuma), 8, 270
Anamaya Resort (Montezuma), 269
Apartotel Alamar (Puntarenas), 260
Apartotel Girasol (Jacó), 363
Arco Iris Lodge (Santa Elena), 9, 337
Arenal Backpackers Resort (La Fortuna), 309
Arenal Kioro (near La Fortuna), 310

ACCOMMODATIONS & WILDERNESS LODGES

Arenal Kokoro (near La Fortuna), 312

Arenal Observatory Lodge (near La Fortuna), 7, 312

Arenas del Mar (Manuel Antonio), 9, 380

Aurola Holiday Inn (San José), 129

Azania Bungalows (Playa Cocles), 491

The Backyard (Playa Hermosa de Jacó), 368

Bahía del Sol Beachfront & Boutique Hotel (Playa Potrero), 233–234

Banana Azul Guest House (Playa Negra), 482

Barceló Playa Tambor Beach Resort, 264

Beacon Escazú, 160

Best Western Jacó Beach Resort, 362

Best Western Kamuk Hotel (Manuel Antonio), 383

Bosque del Cabo Rainforest Lodge (Osa Peninsula), 7, 429

Buena Vista Villas and Casas (Manuel Antonio), 379

Byblos Resort (Manuel Antonio), 382

Cabinas Arrecife (Cahuita), 472

Cabinas Guaraná (Puerto Viejo, Limón), 482–483

Cabinas Jiménez (Puerto Jiménez), 427

Cabinas La Casona (Tortuguero), 461

Cabinas Las Olas (Playa Avellanas), 249

Cabinas Las Olas (Playa Hermosa), 368

Cabinas Los Cocos (Playa Zancudo), 441

Cabinas Los Guayabos (near La Fortuna), 313

Cabinas Marielos (Playa Langosta), 246

Cabinas Mar y Cielo (Montezuma), 270

Cabinas Miss Junie (Tortuguero), 461

Cabinas Miss Miriam (Tortuguero), 461

Cabinas San Clemente (Dominical), 394

Cabinas Sol y Mar (Playa Zancudo), 442

Cabinas Something Different (Manzanillo), 493

Cabinas Tortuguero, 461

Cala Luna Boutique Hotel & Villas (Playa Langosta), 244

Camping Antorchas (Dominical), 394

Camping Los Malinches (Playa Junquillal), 252

Canciones del Mar (Jacó), 363

Caño Negro Natural Lodge, 316

Cariblue Bungalows (Playa Cocles), 9, 492

Casa Chameleon (Malpaís), 276

Casa Corcovado Jungle Lodge (Osa Peninsula), 417

Casa de las Tías (San Rafael de Escazú), 160

Casa del Mar (Playa Sámara), 285

Casa Marbella (Tortuguero), 461

Casa Mariposa (San Gerardo), 403

Casa Roland Marina Resort (Golfito), 435–436

Casa Turire (Turrialba), 188

Casa Verde Lodge (Puerto Viejo, Limón), 483

Cascadas Farallas Waterfall Villas (Dominical), 393

Cashew Hill Jungle Cottages (Puerto Viejo), 482

Chachagua Rainforest Hotel & Hacienda, 315

Chalet Nicholas (near Nuevo Arenal), 321–322

Club del Mar Condominiums & Resort (Jacó), 362–363

Coco Beach Hotel & Casino (Playa del Coco), 222–223

Coconut Grove (Dominicalito), 396

Conchal Hotel, 229

Copa del Arbol (Drake Bay), 417

Coral Hill Bungalows (Playa Negra), 472

Costanera Bed & Breakfast (Playa Hermosa), 368

Costa Paraiso Lodge (Dominicalito), 396

Costa Rica Backpackers (San José), 129

Courtyard San José (Escazú), 160

Cristal Azul, 279

Crocodile Bay Resort (Puerto Jiménez), 427

Crowne Plaza Corobicí (San José), 131

Cuna del Angel (near Dominical), 396–397

Domilocos (Dominical), 394

Doubletree Cariari By Hilton, 168

Double Tree Resort by Hilton Puntarenas, 260

Drake Bay Wilderness Resort, 418

Ecoplaya Beach Resort (Salinas Bay), 207–208

El Descanso (San Gerardo), 403

El Diriá (Tamarindo), 245

El Encanto Bed & Breakfast (Cahuita), 472

El Establo Mountain Hotel (Monteverde), 335–336

El Jardín (Montezuma), 270

El Mono Azul Hotel (Manuel Antonio), 383

El Ocotal Beach Resort (Playa del Coco), 222

El Pargo Feliz (Montezuma), 270

El Pelicano (San Gerardo), 403

El Punto Bed & Breakfast (Liberia), 197–198

El Remanso (Osa Peninsula), 429

El Sano Banano (Montezuma), 270

El Silencio Lodge & Spa (Alajuela), 177

El Silencio Lodge & Spa (Bajos del Toro), 315–316

El Velero Hotel (Playa Hermosa, Guanacaste), 216

Escape Caribeño (Playa Negra), 482

Fenix Hotel (Playa Sámara), 284

15 Love Bed & Breakfast (Tamarindo), 245

Finca Rosa Blanca Coffee Plantation & Inn (Heredia), 8, 173

Flamingo Beach Resort, 234

Flamingo Marina Resort Hotel and Club, 234

Florblanca Resort (Santa Teresa), 8, 276

Four Seasons Resort Costa Rica (Papagayo Peninsula), 213–214

Gaia Hotel & Reserve (Manuel Antonio), 380

Gavilán Sarapiquí River Lodge (Puerto Viejo de Sarapiquí), 347

The Gilded Iguana (Playa Guiones), 291

Gran Hotel Costa Rica (San José), 129–130

Hacienda Guachipelín (Rincón de la Vieja), 204

Harbor Reef Surf Resort (Playa Guiones), 291

The Harmony Hotel & Spa (Playa Guiones), 290

Hidden Canopy Treehouses (near Monteverde), 9, 336

The Hideaway Hotel (Playa Sámara), 284

Hilton Garden Inn Liberia Airport, 197

Hilton Papagayo Resort, 214–215

Holiday Inn Express (Escazú), 160

Hostel Pangea (San José), 129

Hotel Aranjuez (San José), 130

Hotel Arco Iris (Playa Langosta), 246

Hotel Belvedere (Playa Sámara), 285

Hotel Borinquen Mountain Resort (Cañas Dulces), 203–204

Hotel Bougainvillea (Heredia), 173

Hotel Brasilito, 229–230
Hotel Cacts (San José), 132
Hotel Capitán Suizo
(Tamarindo), 8, 244–245
Hotel Catalina (Jacó), 363
Hotel Colonial (San José), 128
Hotel Costa Verde (Manuel
Antonio), 383
Hotel Diuwak (Dominical), 393
Hotel Doña Inés (San José), 128
Hotel Don Carlos (San José),
129
Hotel El Icaco (Tortuguero), 461
Hotel Fonda Vela (Monteverde),
337
Hotel Grano de Oro (San José),
8, 131–132
Hotel Guanamar (Puerto
Carrillo), 284
Hotel Hacienda Sueño Azul (Las
Horquetas), 345
Hotel Heliconia (Monteverde),
337
Hotel Hibiscus (Playa Junquillal),
252
Hotel Jinetes de Osa (Drake
Bay), 418
Hotel La Aurora (Montezuma),
270
Hotel La Fortuna, 307–308
Hotel La Punta (Puntarenas),
260
Hotel Las Brisas (Puntarenas),
260
Hotel Las Colinas (La Fortuna),
309–310
Hotel Las Tortugas (Playa
Grande), 236
Hôtel Le Bergerac (San José),
132
Hotel Liberia, 198
Hotel Los Crestones (San Isidro),
403
Hotel Lucy (Montezuma), 271
Hotel Magic Mountain (La
Fortuna), 308–309
Hotel Mar de Luz (Jacó), 364
Hotel Milvia (San José), 132–
133
Hotel Moana (Malpaís), 277
Hotel Nine (Jacó), 363–364
Hotel Parador (Manuel
Antonio), 380
Hotel Pasatiempo (Playa
Langosta), 246
Hotel Perico Azul (Jacó), 364
Hotel Playa Bejuco, 369
Hotel Playa Hermosa Bosque
del Mar, 215
Hotel Playa Negra (Guanacaste),
249–250
Hotel Playa Westfalia (near
Limón), 465
Hotel Poco a Poco (Santa
Elena), 336
Hotel Poseidon (Jacó), 363
Hotel Presidente (San José),
129

Hotel Pueblo Dorado
(Tamarindo), 245
Hotel Punta Islita (Playa Islita),
285–286
Hotel Rincón de San José, 128
Hotel Roca Verde (Dominical),
393
Hotel Royal Corin (near La
Fortuna), 310
Hotel Santo Tomás (San José),
130
Hotel Sí Como No (Manuel
Antonio), 380, 382
Hotel Silencio del Campo (near
La Fortuna), 311–312
Hotel Sugar Beach (Playa Pan
de Azúcar), 224
Hotel Verde Mar (Manuel
Antonio), 383
Hotel Villa Casa Blanca (Playa
Ocotal), 223
Hotel Villas Gaia (Playa
Tortuga), 397
Hotel Zully Mar (Playa
Langosta), 246
Iguana Lodge (Playa
Plantanares), 428
Iguanazul Hotel (Playa
Junquillal), 252
Jacaranda Hotel & Jungle
Garden (Puerto Viejo,
Limón), 483
JW Marriott Guanacaste Resort
& Spa (Hacienda Pinilla),
249
Kap's Place (San José), 129
Kura Design Villas, 396
La Choza del Manglar (Puerto
Jiménez), 427
La Colina Lodge (Monteverde),
337
La Costa de Papito (Playa
Cocles), 492
L'Acqua Viva (Playa Guiones),
290
La Cusinga Lodge (Bahía
Ballena), 397
Lagarta Lodge (Playa Nosara),
291
Laguna Lodge (Tortuguero), 460
Lake Arenal Hotel (between
Tilarán and Nuevo Arenal),
322
La Laguna del Lagarto Lodge
(near Boca Tapada), 317
La Mansion Inn Arenal, 320
La Paloma Lodge (Drake Bay),
7, 417–418
La Parcela (Dominicalito), 396
Lapa Ríos (Osa Peninsula), 429
Lapa's Nest Tree House (near
Puerto Jiménez), 428
La Posada Private Jungle
Bungalows (Manuel
Antonio), 383
La Quinta de Sarapiquí Country
Inn (Chilamate), 346

La Selva Biological Station
(Puerto Viejo de Sarapiquí),
345–346
La Sirena Hotel (Manuel
Antonio), 383
Latitude 10 (Playa Santa Teresa),
276
Leaves & Lizards (near El
Muelle), 314
Le Caméléon (Playa Cocles), 491
Los Altos de Eros (near
Tamarindo), 249
Los Sueños Marriott Ocean &
Golf Resort (Playa
Herradura), 356
Lucky Bug Bed & Breakfast
(Nuevo Arenal), 320
Luna Lodge (Osa Peninsula),
430
Magellan Inn (Playa Negra),
472–473
Makanda by the Sea (Manuel
Antonio), 382
Malpaís Surf Camp & Resort,
278
Manatus Hotel (Tortuguero),
459
Manquenque Ecolodge,
316–317
Marriott Costa Rica Hotel (San
Antonio de Belén), 168–169
Mawamba Lodge (Tortuguero),
460
Mono Congo Lodge (Playa
Negra), 249
Montanas de Agua (Dominical),
394
Monte Azul (Rivas), 403–404
Monteverde Cloud Forest
Biological Reserve, 337
Monteverde Lodge & Gardens,
7, 336
Morphose Mountain Retreat
(near Ciudad Neily), 437
Mother Dear Cottages (Playa
Negra), 482
Mystica (between Tilarán and
Nuevo Arenal), 320–321
Nature Lodge Finca Los
Caballos (Montezuma),
269–270
Nayara Hotel, Spa & Gardens
(near La Fortuna), 310–311
Nosara Beach House, 290
Occidental Grand Papagayo,
215
Pacific Edge (Dominical), 397
Pacuare Lodge (Turrialba), 188
Park Hotel (near Limón), 465
Peace Lodge (near Varablanca),
168
Pelican Hotel (Playa Esterillos),
368
Pensión de la Cuesta (San José),
130
Pensión Santa Elena
(Monteverde), 337
Piramys (Dominical), 394

Playa Chiquita Lodge, 493
Playa Negra Guesthouse (Cahuita), 9, 473
Playa Nicuesa Rainforest Lodge (Golfo Dulce), 7, 437
Pochote Grande (Jacó), 364
Posada Andrea Cristina (Puerto Viejo de Sarapiquí), 347
Posada Nena (Santa Ana), 161
Pranamar Villas & Yoga Retreat (Santa Teresa), 276–277
Pumilio Mountain & Ocean Hotel (between Playa Herradura and Jacó), 357
Pura Vida Hotel (Alajuela), 170
Rara Avis (near Las Horquetas), 346–347
Real InterContinental San José (Escazú), 158, 160
Recreo (Salinas Bay), 208
Residence Inn San José Escazú, 160
Río Chirripó Retreat (San Gerardo), 403
Río Colorado Lodge (Barra del Colorado), 451
Rip Jack Inn (Playa Grande), 236
RIU Guanacaste (Playa Matapalo), 224
Roca Dura (San Gerardo), 403
Rocking J's (Puerto Viejo, Limón), 483
Sámara Tree House Inn, 284
Sandpiper Inn (Playa Hermosa), 368
Savegre Hotel (San Gerardo), 404–405
Selva Bananito Lodge (south of Limón), 7, 464–465

Selva Verde Lodge (Chilamate), 345
Shawandha Lodge (Puerto Viejo, Limón), 492–493
Silver King Lodge (Barra del Colorado), 451
Sleep Inn (San José), 128
The Springs Resort & Spa (near La Fortuna), 311
Studio Hotel (Santa Ana), 161
Sueño del Mar (Playa Langosta), 245
The Suites at Café de Playa (Playa del Coco), 223
Surf Inn Hermosa, 367–368
Tabacón Grand Spa Thermal Resort (near La Fortuna), 311
Talari Mountain Lodge (Rivas), 404
Tambor Tropical, 264
Tango Mar Resort (Playa Tambor), 264
Termales del Bosque (Ciudad Quesada), 314–315
Tico Adventure Lodge (Playa Sámara), 284
Tilajari Resort Hotel (San Carlos), 315
Tirimbina Rainforest Center (Puerto Viejo de Sarapiquí), 345
Tiskita Jungle Lodge (near Playa Pavones), 445
Tortilla Flats (Dominical), 394
Tortuga Lodge (Tortuguero), 7, 459–460
Tranquilo Backpackers (near Santa Teresa), 278

Tree House Lodge (Punta Uva), 491
Trogon Lodge (San Gerardo), 405
Trópico Latino Lodge (Santa Teresa), 277–278
Tryp Sabana by Windham (San José), 131
Turrialtico (Turrialba), 187–188
Turtle Beach Lodge (Tortuguero), 460
Villa Alegre (Playa Langosta), 245
Villa Blanca Cloud Forest & Spa (San Ramón), 316
Villa Caletas (near Playa Herradura), 357
Villa Decary (Nuevo Arenal), 321
Villa Deevena (Playa Negra), 249
Villa del Sueño Hotel (Playa Hermosa, Guanacaste), 216
Villa Lapas (Tárcoles), 357
Villas Nicolás (Manuel Antonio), 383–384
Vista del Valle Plantation Inn (Alajuela), 169–170
Volcano Lodge and Springs (near La Fortuna), 312
Westin Playa Conchal Resort & Spa, 228
Xandari Resort & Spa (Alajuela), 168
Ylang Ylang Beach Resort (Montezuma), 269
Zancudo Beach Resort, 441

PHOTO CREDITS